ACCOUNTING
FOR UNITED STATES
ECONOMIC GROWTH
1929–1969

EDWARD F. DENISON

ACCOUNTING FOR UNITED STATES ECONOMIC GROWTH 1929-1969

THE BROOKINGS INSTITUTION

WASHINGTON, D.C.

Library of Congress Cataloging in Publication Data:

Denison, Edward Fulton, 1915–
    Accounting for United States economic growth,
1929–1969.

    Includes bibliographical references.
    1. United States—Economic conditions—1918–1945.
    2. United States—Economic conditions—1945–
I. Brookings Institution, Washington, D.C.   II. Title.
HC106.3.D3667   330.9′73′09   74-1137
ISBN 0-8157-1804-7
ISBN 0-8157-1803-9 (pbk.)

9 8 7 6 5 4 3 2 1

THE BROOKINGS INSTITUTION is an independent organization devoted to nonpartisan research, education, and publication in economics, government, foreign policy, and the social sciences generally. Its principal purposes are to aid in the development of sound public policies and to promote public understanding of issues of national importance.

The Institution was founded on December 8, 1927, to merge the activities of the Institute for Government Research, founded in 1916, the Institute of Economics, founded in 1922, and the Robert Brookings Graduate School of Economics and Government, founded in 1924.

The Board of Trustees is responsible for the general administration of the Institution, while the immediate direction of the policies, program, and staff is vested in the President, assisted by an advisory committee of the officers and staff. The by-laws of the Institution state, "It is the function of the Trustees to make possible the conduct of scientific research, and publication, under the most favorable conditions, and to safeguard the independence of the research staff in the pursuit of their studies and in the publication of the results of such studies. It is not a part of their function to determine, control, or influence the conduct of particular investigations or the conclusions reached."

The President bears final responsibility for the decision to publish a manuscript as a Brookings book or staff paper. In reaching his judgment on the competence, accuracy, and objectivity of each study, the President is advised by the director of the appropriate research program and weighs the views of a panel of expert outside readers who report to him in confidence on the quality of the work. Publication of a work signifies that it is deemed to be a competent treatment worthy of public consideration; such publication does not imply endorsement of conclusions or recommendations contained in the study.

The Institution maintains its position of neutrality on issues of public policy in order to safeguard the intellectual freedom of the staff. Hence interpretations or conclusions in Brookings publications should be understood to be solely those of the author or authors and should not be attributed to the Institution, to its trustees, officers, or other staff members, or to the organizations that support its research.

Foreword

Steadily rising national income has been a distinctive economic characteristic of the modern world. Modern economic growth began in England late in the eighteenth century, spread to most of Europe and North America in the nineteenth century, and in the twentieth is at least incipient almost everywhere. But income levels and rates of growth vary greatly for reasons that are often obscure.

A nation's aggregate income changes between two dates only if determinants of its output change. Identification of these determinants, measurement of changes in them, and estimation of the effect on output of changes in each is a prerequisite for understanding economic growth. Edward F. Denison has pioneered in developing methods to arrive at such measures and estimates. In previous studies he has used them to analyze the sources of growth in a number of countries and the reasons why growth rates and income levels differ from place to place and from time to time. In this book he further refines techniques of growth analysis and applies them to the United States, whose economy is the world's largest, over a forty-year period.

Denison finds that changes in seven categories were chiefly responsible for long-term growth and for variations in the growth rate: the number of employed persons and their demographic composition; working hours, including the proportion of part-time workers; the education of employed persons; the size of the capital stock; the state of knowledge; the proportion of labor allocated to inefficient uses; the size of markets; and the strength and pattern of short-term demand pressures. Advances in knowledge were the biggest single source of growth. As in Denison's previous studies, lengthier education of the labor force also appears as a major source of growth in the United States, especially in the growth of output per worker.

This book introduces an innovation in national accounting by which potential output is estimated from actual output by the detailed adjustment of determinants of output to allow for differences between actual and potential conditions. The technique yields a potential output series considerably different from those previously available. In one summary analysis Denison divides the forty-year span into five shorter periods. He finds that the growth rates in these periods of potential national income, measured in constant prices, were: 1929–41, 2.6 percent per year; 1941–48, 3.0 percent; 1948–53, 5.0 percent; 1953–64, 3.2 percent; and 1964–69, 4.9 percent. From the sources of growth tables for potential national income it is evident that much larger increases in potential employment and in the capital stock were primarily responsible for growth rates in 1948–53 and 1964–69 so far exceeding those of 1953–64. The most important reasons that explain why the 1929–41 rate fell below postwar rates were the absence of net capital formation and a lower contribution from advances in knowledge than appeared in later years. Denison finds that in the late 1950s and early 1960s actual output fell short of potential output by much smaller amounts than most previous estimates have suggested.

Growth rates of actual output differ from those of potential output because of fluctuations in the proportion of available labor that is in use and fluctuations in the intensity with which resources are employed. The growth rate of actual output was 4.5 percent per year in both 1948–53 and 1964–69, below the growth rate of potential output in those periods but far above the 1953–64 rate.

The author wishes to acknowledge the major contributions to the study made by the other members of the staff engaged upon this project: Erna Tracy, senior secretary, and Barbara L. Wiget, research assistant. He expresses his deep appreciation to both. Barbara P. Haskins edited the volume and Genevieve B. Wimsatt checked it for accuracy. The care and perception required by these duties for so large and integrated a volume were amply forthcoming. The figures are by Fred Powell, the index by Florence Robinson. The project was carried out as part of the Brookings Economic Studies program, which is directed by Joseph A. Pechman.

The cooperation and assistance of the Bureau of Labor Statistics of the U.S. Department of Labor and the Bureau of Economic Analysis of the U.S. Department of Commerce are gratefully acknowledged. The staffs of these agencies cheerfully answered inquiries, provided unpublished data, and in some instances prepared special estimates for this investigation. The author particularly notes the contributions of Robert C. Wasson to the measures of the stock of structures and equipment, Shirley Loftus to those of inventories, Robert Stein to earnings differentials, and Martin Ziegler to the estimates of hours worked. Useful advice was generously provided by Jack Alterman, John A. Gorman, Lawrence Grose, George Jaszi, Denis F. Johnston, Jerome A. Mark, Sophia Travis, Allan H. Young, and many others. The Bureau of Labor Statistics and Bureau of Economic Analysis provided financial as well as intellectual support to portions of this investigation. For this reason the series for labor and capital input and estimates of the sources of growth may be freely reproduced, with credit to this book as the source.

The author benefited greatly from comments on drafts of the manuscript that were provided by Moses Abramovitz, Jack Alterman, Paul A. David, Solomon Fabricant, and Robert Aaron Gordon. George Jaszi, Walter W. McMahon, Arthur M. Okun, George Perry, Jean-Pierre Poullier, and Charles L. Schultze provided helpful suggestions on particular sections.

The views expressed in this book are those of the author and should not be ascribed to other staff members, officers, or trustees of the Brookings Institution, to agencies providing financial support for the project, or to the persons whose assistance is acknowledged.

KERMIT GORDON
President

April 1974
Washington, D.C.

Contents

Appendixes

Text Tables

Appendix Tables

Figures

ACCOUNTING
FOR UNITED STATES
ECONOMIC GROWTH
1929–1969

CHAPTER ONE

-»»><«<-

Introduction

-»»><«<-

In 1929 production of goods and services in the United States exceeded that in any country during any previous year of world history, yet it was only one-fourth as large as United States production today. Thus three-quarters of the entire increase in the annual output of this land area since its first habitation has been achieved in the brief period since 1929. This book examines the changes which created the economic growth of the United States from 1929 to 1969. The postwar period, during which output more than doubled, is considered most intensively.

The size of any nation's output is governed by many determinants, and changes in these determinants cause output to change. Any first-year student of economics can call the more important of them quickly to mind, and any reader of Adam Smith could have done so almost two centuries ago. They include the number, composition, and skills of workers engaged in production, the capital and land with which they work, the existing state of knowledge on producing at low cost, the size of markets served, and the efficiency with which resources are allocated among uses. The list is easily extended.

But which output determinants have actually changed and how much? What is the size of the contribution that changes in each have made to the economic growth of the United States since 1929, since 1948, or over shorter time spans within these periods? Answers can be obtained only by assembling and analyzing a great variety of quantitative data. Estimation of this type is called sources of growth analysis, and that is what this book is about. Its purpose is to allocate the growth rate of output among the determinants that produced growth. It is useful, as well as customary, to group determinants in two broad

categories: under total factor input or under output per unit of input. But there is no general agreement as to which determinants should be classified in each category. I retain this distinction by category but place the main emphasis on individual growth sources.

In this introduction I shall not list the output determinants for which measurement is attempted nor summarize the findings; the reader seeking a summary is referred to Chapters 8 and 9, the last two in the book. Instead, this introduction describes what this study contains that is new, expresses my hope that the statistical series introduced here can be kept up to date, and explains the organization of the book.

What's New?

This is the third time I have published estimates of the sources of economic growth in the United States. The two previous studies were not, to be sure, devoted exclusively to this topic. *The Sources of Economic Growth in the United States and the Alternatives Before Us* gives equal attention to the amount by which the growth rate could be altered by changing each of the determinants of output, and provides a "menu of choices available to increase the growth rate."[1] *Why Growth Rates Differ: Postwar Experience in Nine Western Countries* provides estimates not only for the United States but also for eight countries of Western Europe.[2] It focuses upon the reasons that levels of output and postwar growth rates of output differed among these countries. But both books were much concerned with historical analysis of the sources of U.S. growth. *The Sources of Economic Growth* covered the period from 1909 to 1957, and *Why Growth Rates Differ* from 1950 to 1962. The reader may reasonably ask why I find it necessary to offer another book on this topic, and what he will find that is new or different.

Time Span

One new element is the extension of the time span covered. After 1962, the end of the period covered in *Why Growth Rates Differ*, output rose much faster than hitherto, and one reason for undertaking the present study was to ask why.

---

1. Edward F. Denison, *The Sources of Economic Growth in the United States and the Alternatives Before Us*, Supplementary Paper 13 (Committee for Economic Development, 1962 [reprinted 1973]); hereinafter referred to as *The Sources of Economic Growth.*
2. Edward F. Denison, assisted by Jean-Pierre Poullier, *Why Growth Rates Differ: Postwar Experience in Nine Western Countries* (Brookings Institution, 1967); hereinafter referred to as *Why Growth Rates Differ.*

How much of the change was cyclical and how much, if any, reflected more fundamental factors? The pattern that emerged was unexpected, and it is sufficiently simple to permit some of the main points to be summarized in a few sentences without great loss of accuracy.

Through 1964 the acceleration merely reflected cyclical expansion; in response to strengthening demand more of the nation's available labor was being put to work and employed resources were being used with increasing intensity. The ratio of actual to potential output continued to move up until 1966, then moved down until 1969, when this study ends. Meanwhile, more important changes occurred: in 1965 the growth rate of potential output itself jumped abruptly and sharply, largely as the direct consequence of accelerated growth of labor and capital input. The higher rate was maintained through the rest of the decade. The change in the growth rate of potential output is quantified, and its sources detailed, in Chapters 7, 8, and 9.

Annual Data

This study differs from its predecessors in the greater frequency of detailed data. Estimates of output and all output determinants are offered for every year from 1947 through 1969, thus providing continuous series for the postwar period. Annual series for many of the individual determinants are useful in themselves. The purpose of providing a full set of annual series, however, is not to encourage detailed analysis of the sources of growth on a year-to-year basis, which would be absurd, but to permit complete flexibility in the choice of time periods for detailed analysis. To permit analysis and comparisons over longer time spans, estimates are provided for the years 1929, 1940, and 1941 as well. Tables showing detailed allocations of growth rates among growth sources are provided for the eight time spans which examination of the data indicated to be of greatest interest. Similar tables for other periods can be easily constructed from the indexes presented.

Improved Estimating Procedures

My general approach to the measurement of the contributions of the various sources to the growth rate has remained unchanged from that adopted in my first estimates in *The Sources of Economic Growth,* but statistical implementation of this approach has been greatly improved. Some of these improvements were instituted in *Why*

Growth Rates Differ. Many others are new in this study. All series have been completely reworked.

SEPARATION OF BUSINESS EMPLOYMENT. One improvement, which affects the estimates for almost all components of labor input, eliminates an assumption that was required in the previous studies.

Both my previous and present labor input estimates take into account the age, sex, education, and working hours of employed persons because groups of individuals who differ with respect to these characteristics also differ with respect to the average value of their contributions to output. But output of governments, households, and institutions is measured by a conventional procedure which prevents changes in the composition of persons employed (as measured by these characteristics) from affecting measured output as they do in the business sector. Except for military personnel, this characteristic of output measurement was accommodated indirectly in earlier studies. I first measured changes in the composition of all employed civilians and then reduced the amounts that would otherwise have been calculated as their effects on output in proportion to the percentage of employed civilians who worked outside the business sector. This procedure assumed that the characteristics of civilians employed in business changed in the same way as those of all employed civilians.

The present study handles the problem directly. General government, households, and institutions are isolated as a separate sector, and the persons this sector employs are separated from those employed in business. The two sectors are then separately analyzed (as are the services of dwellings and property income from abroad, which had already been treated separately in *Why Growth Rates Differ*). This has required the development of series for hours, age-sex composition, and education that refer specifically to persons employed in business. It has been a tedious task to develop separate data for this portion of employed persons, but it proved possible to do so. Such an approach has also required that the weights applied to work performed by persons with different characteristics, which were previously based on earnings of all employed persons, be replaced with weights based only on earnings of persons employed in the business sector. This has the incidental advantage of eliminating from the data used to obtain earnings differentials the groups— employees of government, churches, and educational institutions, in particular—whose wages are most influenced by considerations that may impair the proportionality of wages and marginal products which the procedure assumes.

The separation of the two sectors also permitted incidental improvements in the estimates for a number of growth sources other than labor input components, including economies of scale.

BUSINESS FLUCTUATIONS. Much greater pains have been taken in this study to ensure that the labor input measures faithfully reflect short-term cyclical changes in the distribution of employment and hours worked among age-sex and education groups. This is more necessary than before because of the introduction of annual series.

Isolation of the effect of short-term fluctuations in the pressure of demand upon output per unit of input is among the most difficult problems in growth analysis. It is well known that there is a pronounced cyclical movement in productivity, but its magnitude and timing are not easy to identify and it cannot be assumed that the size of the effect of demand intensity on productivity is the same in similar phases of different business cycles. In *The Sources of Economic Growth* the problem was avoided by comparing only years that I then thought to be sufficiently comparable in cyclical position, and sufficiently far apart, to allow the effect of changes in this determinant on the intervening growth rate to be ignored. This expedient was not available in *Why Growth Rates Differ*. I was forced to attempt explicit estimates, but was not at all satisfied with the method by which the estimates were derived. For the present study I have devised and adopted a wholly new procedure—described in Chapter 6 and Appendix Q—which I regard as far more satisfactory, and which yields different results from my previous studies in most time periods.

CURTAILMENT OF ASSUMPTIONS. My previous analyses of growth sources have required the introduction of some assumptions that were founded on little more than judgment. Such assumptions have not been wholly eliminated but they have been whittled down. In earlier studies I called particular attention to three:

1. Weights for Education Groups. In order to construct a comprehensive labor input series, weights must be assigned to workers with different amounts of education. These weights should be based upon earnings differentials among workers who differ in education but who are similar in other characteristics that affect earnings. The prob-

lem is that individuals with different amounts of education also differ in other characteristics. I previously assumed that, among male workers of the same age, three-fifths of the difference between the average earnings of those with eight years of education and the average earnings of those with other amounts of education was due to the difference in education itself while the remaining two-fifths reflected other characteristics that happened to be associated with both education and earnings. This assumption is discarded in the present study. As explained in Appendix I, Part 1, the effects of most of the other characteristics upon earnings differentials were eliminated by standardization, and direct estimates were made of the effects of those which could not be eliminated in this way.

2. Effect of Weekly Hours on Input. A reduction in weekly hours of work usually does not curtail output proportionally, partly because of reduced fatigue. The size of the partially offsetting change in output per hour was assumed in the previous studies. This is still the case, but refinements in procedures have reduced the sensitivity of the results to any error in the assumption. Also, changes in working hours since 1940 have been such that errors in the assumption would introduce far less error into the estimates than was the case in earlier periods.

3. The Contribution of Economies of Scale. The estimated size of the contribution of economies of scale to growth was previously obtained by use of an assumption which was based only on judgment. In the present study gains from economies of scale are derived, instead, by a formal statistical procedure, and the results qualify as estimates in the same sense that the term is ordinarily used in modern economic literature. But the procedure still is less satisfactory than the methods used for most other growth sources.

CONSISTENCY OF DATA. Growth analysis requires consistency between measures of output and input, and consistency over time in all series used. Although this ideal is never wholly attainable, great efforts to achieve it have been made in this study and I believe it has been approached more closely than hitherto. Adjustments in the data to improve both types of consistency were introduced whenever necessary and feasible—and this was frequent.

CHANGES IN PREVIOUS ESTIMATES. The estimated contributions of most determinants to output growth from 1950 to 1962 are close to those obtained in *Why Growth Rates Differ,* but for three growth sources the estimates vary by 0.1 percentage points or more. Revisions of the 1929–57 estimates that were provided much earlier in *The Sources of Economic Growth* are more pervasive. Detailed comparisons with both of the earlier studies are provided in Appendix S.[3]

Supplementary Data

This study required the preparation of estimates for many types of data in accordance with classifications for which no estimates were previously available. Nearly all the estimates entering into my analysis—both adjustments of old series and series not previously available—are published here, mainly in the appendixes. Most of them can contribute to research on a variety of topics other than growth, and I hope that they will not be overlooked by scholars who could make use of them.

Separate Estimates for Nonresidential Business

This study is concerned with all parts of the economy covered by the national income and product series, but for many types of analysis, including almost any that focus upon productivity change, it is also desirable to examine a more homogeneous universe. Government, households, and institutions are motivated by different considerations than business firms, their output is measured in a different way, and the determinants of their measured output are not the same. The output of dwellings, most of which are owner-occupied, and net earnings from investment abroad also have quite special characteristics. It is useful to be able to eliminate all these special entities and to examine growth in the relatively homogeneous domestic nonresidential business sector. Procedural changes introduced in this study have made it possible to do this. Chapters 4 through 8 (except for part of Chapter 7) are devoted entirely to domestic nonresidential business. Chapter 8 provides an analysis of the sources of growth of nonresidential business output which is as complete as that presented in Chapter 9 for the economy as a whole.

Within nonresidential business, estimates are not provided by industry. Data needed to estimate components of total factor input, defined on the comprehensive basis adopted in this study, are largely lacking, and even an attempt to use the fragmentary data available would be an enormous undertaking. For components of output per unit of input both information and a clear conceptual basis for a feasible allocation by industry are absent. The problem may be illustrated by advances in knowledge which improve intermediate products provided by one industry to another—raw materials, supplies, containers, or capital goods—and result in more final products for sale to final consumers without an increase in labor and capital. A concept for industrial classification of this output gain is elusive. In what industry should the impact of the introduction and improvement of the computer be measured, and why? Should a paint that can be applied in less time be considered to raise productivity in paint manufacturing, in the industries applying paint, in the industries on whose walls it appears, or perhaps in some other industry where this type of paint was developed? What about a paint that lasts longer? Whatever principle one might adopt to answer such questions, information to implement it consistently is largely absent.[4]

---

3. I am aware of no other publications that furnish estimated contributions of growth sources for the United States in anything approaching the detail I provide. However, some studies provide estimates that allow comparisons on a different basis, or for certain groupings of determinants. The estimates of the U.S. Bureau of Labor Statistics for manhours and output per man-hour and those of John W. Kendrick for total factor input and output per unit of input are discussed in note 4. John Gorman has estimated total factor input and output per unit of input for nonfinancial corporations (John A. Gorman, "Nonfinancial Corporations: New Measures of Output and Input," *Survey of Current Business,* Vol. 52 [March 1972], pp. 21–28). His series are conceptually similar to those of Kendrick. Statistically, they are reasonably comparable to mine when appropriate adjustments are made for differences in definition and scope. Estimates of total input and output per unit of input by Jorgenson and Griliches (as first published and after revisions which bring their estimates closer to mine) are presented and compared with those in *Why Growth Rates Differ,* and differences between us discussed in Edward F. Denison, Zvi Griliches, and Dale W. Jorgenson, "The Measurement of Productivity," Special issue of the *Survey of Current Business,* Vol. 52 (May 1972), Pt. 2 (Brookings Reprint 244). The voluminous literature on production functions bears some relationship to my estimates, and there are many publications which relate to individual determinants.

4. This discussion is not intended to disparage existing estimates of changes in output by industry. They have certainly proved useful for a variety of purposes despite conceptual objections. Three main sets of data for output and/or selected inputs are available by industry. They can be compared with my series at an aggregate level and appear sufficiently consistent with them to allow their joint use.

The U.S. Bureau of Economic Analysis (BEA, formerly the Office of Business Economics) regularly provides gross national product in constant prices, by industry. The data differ in definition from my output series, which is national income, but are closely comparable statistically with my

Estimates for Potential Output

An innovation in this study which is particularly exciting to the author is the extension of sources of growth analysis to provide a tool for evaluation of the current position of the economy and of relatively short-run changes in output.

The difference between the actual value of each output determinant and its "potential" value—its level if the pressure of demand upon available resources had been at a standardized level—has been calculated for each year. The results are combined to secure the difference between total actual output and total potential output.[5] An estimate of the "gap" between actual and potential output provides important information. It is indispensable in policy formulation for economic

---

estimates because I rely upon BEA data. A reconciliation of the two output series is provided in Appendix A.

The U.S. Bureau of Labor Statistics (BLS) provides estimates of total labor hours and output (GNP) per manhour for many industries (and for nonfinancial corporations) as well as for the whole economy and its main sectors. At the aggregate level statistical differences between the BLS estimates and mine, though present, are minor, partly because I rely upon BLS data for average hours. Comparisons are provided in Appendixes E and M.

Kendrick's important new book provides estimates by industry for the postwar period 1948–66 that are closer to mine in concept (John W. Kendrick, assisted by Maude R. Pech, *Postwar Productivity Trends in the United States, 1948–1969* [Columbia University Press for the National Bureau of Economic Research, 1973]). Earlier years are covered in John W. Kendrick, assisted by Maude R. Pech, *Productivity Trends in the United States* (Princeton University Press for the National Bureau of Economic Research, 1961).

Kendrick measures output not only by gross national product but also by net national product, which moves very much like national income, which I use. He provides estimates, by industry, of man-hours worked, gross and net capital stock, total factor input with labor input measured by hours, and output per unit of input. If dwellings were removed from Kendrick's business sector so that it would correspond to my nonresidential business sector, his estimates of total factor input would be conceptually close to those which my study would yield for that sector if labor input were measured by man-hours rather than by the more comprehensive measure I adopt. (My series for man-hours and labor input are shown in Table 4-1, columns 3 and 8.) To adjust sources of growth tables for nonresidential business in Chapter 8 of this study to Kendrick's basis, the contribution of all components of labor input except "employment" and "average hours" should be transferred from "total factor input" to "output per unit of input." We use such similar sources and procedures that large statistical differences in any period are unlikely. Industry breakdowns of input components omitted by Kendrick do not seem feasible, and there would be little point in my duplicating his work. I regard his studies and mine as useful complements to one another. (Comparisons cannot be made between Kendrick's series for output per unit of total weighted input and any of my series; see *The Sources of Economic Growth*, p. 227, note 6, for comment.)

5. Potential output is fully defined in Chapter 7.

stabilization and demand management. The President's Council of Economic Advisers, of course, has made such estimates routinely, but I believe sources of growth analysis can provide estimates of the gap that are statistically more accurate and conceptually more appropriate for the uses to which they are put. In some periods, such as 1964–65 and again in 1969, my estimates differ substantially from those of the Council of Economic Advisers. The estimates based on sources of growth analysis also permit the gap between actual and potential output to be divided among the determinants that contribute to it.

Addition to actual output of the gap between actual and potential output provides an estimate of potential output each year. The resulting series displays a pattern of potential output growth during the postwar years that is quite different from that shown by series previously available. Periods of very fast growth of potential output in the early postwar years and again from 1964 to 1969 emerge, with the longer intervening period from 1953 through 1964 appearing as one of much slower growth. The growth of potential output is found to be low from 1929 to 1941. From 1941 to 1948 it is moderately below the rate from 1953 to 1964.

Any series for potential output allows one to divide the change in actual output from one date to another between the change in potential output and the change in the gap between actual and potential output. But if the series for potential output is derived from actual output by adjustment of separate output determinants, as in this study, it is possible to add a new dimension to growth analysis.

Estimates of the sources of growth of actual output over a stated time span can then be matched with corresponding estimates of the sources of growth of potential output. The estimates on a "potential" basis are more appropriate for analysis of long-term growth sources than the estimates on an "actual" basis and thus are of great interest in themselves. In addition, they permit one to analyze the growth of actual output in either of two ways. One still can look directly at actual changes in the determinants of output and their contributions to growth. But now one can also examine sources of growth estimates on a potential basis and the amount by which the contribution of each separate source to the actual growth rate differs from its contribution to the potential growth rate.

For eight time periods allocations by source are provided for the growth rates of total actual national income and total potential national income, and of actual national income per person employed and potential national income per person potentially employed as well. All of these estimates are provided both for the economy as a whole and for the nonresidential business sector.

Sources of growth analysis provides a useful framework for projections of future output. It makes it possible to incorporate information about the future that does not fit into other classifications. The broadening of the scope of the estimates to include data on a potential basis increases the suitability of the historical record which they provide for use in projections. But no projection is attempted in this book.[6]

The Need to Keep Estimates Current

My past analyses of the sources of growth have sometimes been referred to as growth accounting. With the many statistical improvements incorporated in the present study, the introduction of annual series based on consistent formal methods for all components, and the expansion of the analysis to cover potential as well as actual national income and the relationships between them, this description may no longer be overly pretentious. At any rate, I have ventured to incorporate the term "accounting for growth" in the title of this book.

The reception accorded my earlier studies has encouraged me to believe that sources of growth analysis has contributed significantly to the understanding of economic growth. Numerous requests for updating of my previous estimates have led me to conclude that it would be highly desirable to keep the new series presented here up to date. The contribution that I believe estimates like those newly introduced in the present book can make to evaluation both of the current position of the economy at any time and of relatively short-run economic changes can be realized *only* if the series are kept current. This is not a task for an individual research worker. His proper role in relation to new statistical series is at the experi-

mental and developmental stage. Certainly, further testing and improvement are required, but I think growth accounting has now reached the stage when it ought to be institutionalized. If the data are to be kept up to date (a task which includes the frequent revision of series as government data upon which they are based are revised), growth accounting must become the responsibility of an organization.

Growth accounting is closely related to the national income and product accounts, estimates of persons engaged in production, and capital stock series which are the responsibility of the Bureau of Economic Analysis. It is also closely related to the series for employment, hours, and other labor characteristics which are the responsibility of the Bureau of Labor Statistics, as well as to the BLS series for output per man-hour. Most of the data used in growth accounting originate in these two agencies, and both have contributed importantly to the present study by helping the Brookings Institution to finance portions of the research for this project and by providing special estimates and unpublished details of their published estimates. If they conclude, as I have, that regular extension of the estimates, accompanied by continuing research into their improvement, would contribute to understanding of the American economy, it would be reasonable for them to undertake the job.

Organization of the Book

This book, like most studies which provide new estimates, has the double function of presenting substantive results and describing the data upon which they are based. To proffer the results without the evidence would be pointless. Every reader should wish to know the exact meaning of each series and how it was derived before deciding how much credence to place in the findings. But the dual function poses a difficult organizational problem when the subject is very broad, all the series analyzed are new, and a detailed description of the derivation of all estimates is necessary.

Scientific progress requires that an investigator describe his procedures in such detail that they can be duplicated by others. If this is not done, results cannot be verified or refuted, nor even appraised. Neither can any investigator build upon the work of his predecessors. In the field of economics, full documentation has been most strongly advocated and most consistently practiced by the

---

6. An illustrative projection to 1980 is described in a paper delivered at the December 1972 meeting of the International Economic Association in Moscow, and which is scheduled for publication by the association. Edward F. Denison, "Sources of Growth Accounting as the Basis for Long-Term Projection" (1972; processed).

National Bureau of Economic Research. Its importance was first brought home to me in the early 1940s when I was a member of the Department of Commerce national income staff. We were able to build upon the pioneering studies conducted at the National Bureau by Simon S. Kuznets, William H. Shaw, Harold G. Barger, and others only because these authors had admirably documented their work. It may be a practical impossibility to describe estimates in such detail that another investigator can reproduce every single number to the last decimal point, but I have tried to approach this ideal closely. The incentive to do so was strengthened by the hope that others may undertake continuation of the series as well as their improvement.

Complete description, however, requires more words and supporting tables than the average reader is likely to have time to study. I have tried to meet this problem by assigning detailed descriptions of sources and procedures, and a great deal of other material as well, to appendixes. Appraisals of the estimates, comparisons with related series, tests of the reasonableness of estimates, reasons for choosing one procedure over others, a great deal of supplementary data, and even some substantive results not central to this inquiry are in the appendixes. I have tried to write for the reader who has an interest in the subject as a whole and an intense interest in certain of the many individual topics covered. Such a reader can meet his needs by reading the chapters and those appendixes which are on topics of greatest interest to him. The chapters provide a careful description of the meaning of each series or component and a brief description of its derivation. The descriptions usually suffice to give an impression concerning reliability but any detailed appraisal requires reference to the appendixes.[7]

I have no desire to burden the reader of my previous writings on growth with unnecessary repetition. When I have nothing new to say about a subject I have condensed the discussion as much as possible, often confining myself to a brief mention and some citations.

This study is organized as follows. Chapter 2 introduces the measures of actual output that will be analyzed. Chapter 3 divides this output among the four sectors in which it originates, and an-alyzes the sources of output growth in the three smaller sectors. Chapters 4, 5, and 6 introduce series for determinants of actual output in the nonresidential business sector. Chapter 7 introduces series for potential output in both the whole economy and nonresidential business. Chapter 8 organizes the data referring to nonresidential business in the form of sources of growth tables. Chapter 9 combines the data for the four sectors and provides sources of growth tables for the whole economy. The table of contents amplifies this thumbnail sketch of the book's organization.

Current Status of Data Utilized

The Office of Business Economics and the Bureau of Labor Statistics are the primary sources of most of the data that I have used in this study, especially for postwar years.[8] These agencies periodically revise their series in order to incorporate new data. This is desirable, but such revisions create a problem in any investigation that requires an extended period of time for its completion.

I originally used series from these agencies as they stood in June 1971. Data for 1929 through 1967 have not subsequently been changed, and for these years all data used are the same as those currently published (as of March 1974). BLS data for 1968 and 1969 used in the analysis have also remained unchanged, but the July 1971 issue of the *Survey of Current Business* presented revisions of OBE's national accounts data for the years 1968 and 1969. These changes were incorporated in the present study wherever they could appreciably affect the results. Revisions affecting national income and product in current and constant prices and the division of national income by sector were incorporated into all the tables and analyses in the chapters of this book and in Appendix A, Table A-1, the summary supporting table for the output measures. However, some of the details of estimation were bypassed, and 1968 and 1969 are omitted from certain detailed supporting tables of Appendix A. The 1971 OBE revisions also changed national income by type of income, slightly in 1968 but a great deal in 1969. Data for the nonlabor share of corporate national

---

7. The descriptions in the chapters are largely confined to the postwar estimates. Sources for 1929, 1940, and 1941 are sometimes quite different.

8. The name of the Office of Business Economics was changed to Bureau of Economic Analysis in January 1972, but almost all publications of that agency utilized in this study carry the name of the Office of Business Economics. Henceforth, I shall refer to the agency as the Office of Business Economics, or OBE.

income shown in Table O-3 and used to estimate the effects of fluctuations in the intensity of demand upon output per unit of input are based upon the revised data. The revisions have been incorporated in the tables of Appendix J, in which income by type is used to derive weights to combine inputs in the nonresidential business sector, to the same extent as in Appendix A. The year 1969 is omitted from Table J-1, the main income share table, because 1969 data were not used in deriving the weights. The July 1971 revisions of the 1968 and 1969 OBE employment estimates were trivial. They were disregarded and are not incorporated in any of the tables.

In summary, all of the July 1971 revisions of the 1968 and 1969 data that could possibly affect my analysis were incorporated, while those which could not were generally ignored. The OBE revisions of estimates for 1968 and 1969 in the July 1972 *Survey of Current Business* were trivial and have not been incorporated; OBE made no additional revisions in the July 1973 issue.

CHAPTER TWO

━━━━━≫≫≪≪━━━━━

Output
and
Income

━━━━━≫≫≪≪━━━━━

National income, which is also known as net national product valued at factor cost, is used to measure the value of the nation's output in this study. National income in current prices is the value of the net output of goods and services produced by the nation's economy when each component of output is valued by the factor cost of producing it. National income may alternatively be described as the aggregate earnings of labor and property accruing from the current production of goods and services in the nation's economy.[1] The nation's economy in this context refers to the labor and property supplied by U.S. residents.

The series I use to measure changes in output is national income in constant prices: the value of the net output of goods and services produced by the nation's economy when each component of final output is valued at its factor cost in 1958, the base year selected by the U.S. Office of Business Economics (OBE) for its constant-price series. The factor cost of a product—the earnings of labor and property derived from its production—differs from its market price in two ways: indirect business taxes incorporated in its market price are eliminated whereas subsidies (which are not part of its market price) are included.

Factor cost valuation is, in principle, a little more convenient than market price valuation for analysis of productivity changes. If the earnings of resources are the same in all activities, a mere shift in the allocation of resources from a lightly taxed to a heavily taxed commodity (or from a subsidized to an unsubsidized one) raises the real product at market prices whereas such a shift leaves product at factor cost unchanged. Analysis of a market price measure of net output would necessitate adding a purely statistical "source" of growth to represent the effect upon the market price series of shifts in the composition of output between lightly and heavily taxed or subsidized commodities. The contribution of these shifts, which may be positive or negative, would be the difference between the growth rates of the two measures. In fact, this difference is slight and the choice between use of a market price and a factor cost measure of net output is trivial.[2]

Gross national product (GNP) valued at market price differs from national income for the additional reason that capital consumption is not deducted from business purchases of durable capital goods. Consequently, gross national product, as its name implies, is a partially duplicated measure of production, which therefore is not suitable for growth analysis. Insofar as a large output is a proper goal of society and objective of policy, it is net output that measures the degree of success in achieving this goal. There is no more reason to wish to maximize capital consumption incurred in the production of, say, television sets than there is to maximize the metal used in their production, and no more reason to include it in the output measure to be adopted for growth analysis. Because growth rates of gross and net product are only moderately different, the choice between these measures might not appear to be very important, but this is not the case in a study of the *sources* of growth. An increase in depreciation must be regarded as a contribution to GNP growth that is entirely ascribable to capital. Capital will therefore always be responsible for a larger fraction of the growth rate of gross product than of net product if capital consumption increases at all.

Estimates of National Income

The method by which my national income series is estimated will now be summarized. It is described fully in Appendix A.

---

1. When I use the word "production" I refer to all activities involved in delivering a product to its final buyer.

2. Appendix A provides a detailed description of the derivation of my series for national income in current and constant prices. Tables A-1 and A-10 compare national income with net national product and gross national product.

To measure national income in *current* prices I make only one adjustment to the national income series contained in the official OBE national income accounts (NIA).[3] The NIA series for capital consumption has two remediable defects. First, depreciation is not valued at the prices prevailing in the current year but instead at a mixture of prices prevailing in the current and past years. Second, the method of computing depreciation has changed from time to time with changes in tax laws and regulations and accounting practice. To OBE's national income series I have therefore added capital consumption allowances, which enter into the computation of national income, as measured in the national income accounts and subtracted a substitute series that is free from these two defects. In the series substituted, all capital consumption is valued each year in prices of that year, and a uniform procedure is followed throughout the period. The series selected is based on one of several depreciation series prepared by the Office of Business Economics as part of its capital stock study. It is computed by use of the straight-line depreciation formula, average service lives based on Bulletin F, the Winfrey distribution of retirements around the average service life, and use of the "current cost 2" price series for nonresidential structures.[4]

National income in *constant* (1958) prices is the sum of the values of final products when each is valued at its 1958 factor cost. The Office of Business Economics does not provide this series. It was obtained by deducting capital consumption valued at 1958 prices from the OBE series for GNP in 1958 prices, replacing 1958 market price weights by 1958 factor cost weights, and adjusting

the data to conform statistically to the current-price estimates.[5]

Conventions paralleling those adopted for the current-price estimates are used to measure capital consumption valued at 1958 market prices: straight-line depreciation, Bulletin F service lives, the Winfrey distribution, and the "constant cost 2" price series for nonresidential structures. These data are also from OBE. Deduction of capital consumption from gross national product in 1958 prices provided net national product at 1958 market prices. The components of net national product were then reweighted by 1958 factor cost weights to obtain national income in 1958 prices. Reweighting could be undertaken with only limited detail, but the major differences in weights were taken into account. The value of the statistical discrepancy in the national accounts (shown in Table A-2), deflated by the implicit GNP deflator for the business sector, was deducted from the aggregate so obtained in order to maintain statistical consistency with the current-dollar national income figures and with the employment series used. Thus my output measure is that which is derived, statistically, from the income side of the national accounts. The index of real national income is in practice very similar to that of real net national product at market prices minus the statistical discrepancy.

Total national income in current and constant (1958) prices is shown in Table 2-1 for the years 1947–69 and also for 1929, 1940, and 1941. This table also shows estimates of total population, total employment, and total hours worked.

The population series, prepared by the U.S. Bureau of the Census, includes the armed forces overseas.

Employment is defined as the average number of persons employed during the year, full time or part time, in the United States economy. The employment series was specially developed for the present study; it is described in Appendix C. For maximum statistical consistency between the national income and employment series, the *movement* of the employment series is based mainly on estimates compiled by OBE as part of its national accounting program. The OBE series I use measures the "average number of full-time and part-

3. National income accounts data for 1929–63 are published in U.S. Department of Commerce, Office of Business Economics, *The National Income and Product Accounts of the United States, 1929–1965: Statistical Tables,* A Supplement to the *Survey of Current Business* (1966). Data for 1964 are published in the July 1968 issue of the *Survey of Current Business,* for 1965 in the July 1969 issue, and for 1966–69 in the July 1970 issue. Revisions for 1968–69 published in the July 1971 issue are incorporated where changes are significant (see Chap. 1, pp. 7–8). Unpublished detail for all years was provided by the Office of Business Economics. (These sources will hereinafter be referred to as "national income accounts.") The capital stock study estimates used are unpublished series provided by the Office of Business Economics, some of which were specially prepared for this investigation.

4. See Lawrence Grose, Irving Rottenberg, and Robert C. Wasson, "New Estimates of Fixed Business Capital in the United States, 1925–65," *Survey of Current Business,* Vol. 46 (December 1966), pp. 34–40.

5. In addition, the OBE series for expenditure for private nonresidential construction, which is a component of GNP, was changed by use of the series 2 price deflator. See Appendix A for explanation.

Table 2-1. Total National Income in Current and Constant Prices, Population, Employment, and Hours Worked, 1929, 1940–41, and 1947–69

| Year | Total national income (billions of dollars) | | Population, July 1 (thousands) (3) | Employment, average for the year (thousands) (4) | Total hours worked weekly (millions) (5) |
	Current prices (1)	Constant prices (1958) (2)			
	Excluding Alaska and Hawaii				
1929	84.7	161.4	121,875	47,535	2,332
1940	79.3	181.5	132,122	51,080	2,196
1940 excluding work relief	77.7	178.0	...	48,250	2,126
1941	102.1	215.8	133,402	55,583	2,413
1941 excluding work relief	100.9	213.1	...	53,374	2,359
1947	194.1	255.2	144,126	59,361	2,516
1948	218.5	270.1	146,631	60,333	2,535
1949	212.3	265.8	149,188	59,047	2,447
1950	235.3	290.8	151,684	60,756	2,519
1951	271.6	312.9	154,287	64,617	2,675
1952	284.9	323.5	156,954	65,869	2,714
1953	299.3	337.3	159,565	66,721	2,736
1954	299.3	331.3	162,391	64,995	2,637
1955	328.2	358.8	165,275	66,470	2,704
1956	347.0	367.8	168,221	67,940	2,743
1957	362.0	371.1	171,274	68,107	2,710
1958	363.6	363.6	174,141	66,393	2,616
1959	396.3	391.1	177,073	67,793	2,684
1960	409.7	399.4	179,893	68,434	2,695
	Including Alaska and Hawaii				
1960	411.2	400.8	180,671	68,721	2,706
1961	424.4	408.1	183,691	68,693	2,686
1962	457.6	435.3	186,538	70,220	2,750
1963	482.4	453.6	189,242	70,951	2,772
1964	519.3	480.1	191,889	72,379	2,819
1965	566.1	513.0	194,303	74,619	2,911
1966	622.0	545.2	196,560	77,937	3,017
1967	654.5	557.6	198,712	79,479	3,041
1968	712.3	585.1	200,706	81,492	3,101
1969	763.9	599.6	202,677	83,614	3,169

Sources: Columns 1 and 2, Table A-1; column 3, population with armed forces included, U.S. Bureau of the Census, *Current Population Reports*, Series P-25, No. 481, "Estimates of the Population of the United States and Components of Change: 1940 to 1972" (1972), Table 2, p. 11, except for 1929 figure, which is reported in *Economic Report of the President Together with the Annual Report of the Council of Economic Advisers, February 1971*, p. 215; column 4, Tables C-1 and C-7; column 5, Table E-2.

time employees" (covering wage and salary workers) and the number of active proprietors of unincorporated businesses; estimates of unpaid family workers are then added. A series so constructed for the most part measures jobs rather than people. However, the level of the series presented here has been adjusted to correspond to a count of employed persons rather than a count of jobs by use of the average ratio of the count of employed persons reported in the Current Population Survey (CPS) to the series based on OBE estimates. This procedure was preferred to direct use of CPS estimates because (as explained in Appendix C) it yields estimates of the number of employed persons that are almost certainly more

consistent with the output data, and probably more accurate, than the annual CPS estimates.

The estimates of total hours worked, which were also specially developed for this study, are described in Appendix E. Estimates of average hours worked in postwar years are almost entirely derived from Bureau of Labor Statistics (BLS) data.

Table 2-2 shows in index form national income in constant (1958) prices, together with indexes of income per capita, per person employed, and per hour worked, and those of the population, employment, and hours series from which they were computed. I have used 1958 as a base year only to conform with the base year for price deflation. Indexes are shown to two decimal points to avoid rounding errors in subsequent analysis of short-term changes; no implication as to accuracy is intended.

To construct the indexes in Table 2-2, the basic data in Table 2-1 were used. They consist of two sets of overlapping series. One, running from 1929 through 1960, refers to the coterminous United States. The second, running from 1960 through 1969, also includes Alaska and Hawaii.[6] In Table 2-2, data for the two series were linked at 1960.

Growth rates between any two years shown can be readily computed from these indexes. They are simply the "interest rates" which, when compounded annually, would bring the initial value of a series to its final value over the elapsed time span.[7] Starting from 1929, 1941, 1950, and 1960, for example, growth rates of the income series in constant prices over the time span until 1969 were as follows:[8]

	Total	Per capita	Per person employed	Per hour worked
1929–69	3.33	2.03	1.89	2.55
1941–69	3.70	2.18	2.12	2.68
1950–69	3.86	2.31	2.15	2.64
1960–69	4.58	3.25	2.32	2.76

The main purpose of this study is to investigate and explain growth rates of total real national income and national income per person employed. The index of national income per capita diverges from that of national income per person employed only because of changes in the ratio of employed persons to total population. The index shown for national income per hour worked in the whole economy provides background information; it will not be separately analyzed.

Work relief employees of the federal government and state and local governments represented 5.5 percent of total employment in 1940 and 4.0 percent in 1941 (see Table C-4). The value of

their output in current prices was measured by their compensation in the construction of national income and product aggregates. To obtain a value in 1958 prices, OBE necessarily used a linking procedure, since there was no such category of employment and output in 1958. This category of workers is unique in that they were employed for the sake of employment rather than for their output, which was incidental. They can be regarded as outside the normal economy that is being investigated. In Table 2-2 indexes are shown including and excluding persons on work relief. It is apparent that their presence considerably depressed output per worker.

Course of National Income

Analyses in this book are based upon series covering 1929, 1940, 1941, and each individual year from 1947 through 1969. Data for the years between 1929 and 1947 or 1948 are difficult to use in growth analysis because of the effects of the depression and World War II. The major effort needed to prepare annual series for that period seemed unwarranted. However, estimates were made for the least abnormal years in this period, 1940 and 1941, in order to avoid a gap of nearly two decades. Estimates end with 1969 because of the unavoidable time lag required for preparation and publication.

To place the years to be analyzed in perspective. Figure 2-1 shows the index of total national income in constant prices in all years from 1925 through 1971. Years covered in this study are shown with asterisks.[9] The series is plotted on a logarithmic scale so that equal vertical distances on the chart represent equal percentage differences in national income rather than differences that are equal in absolute amount. This practice is followed in all subsequent charts on which indexes are plotted.

The year 1929, with which the analysis begins, terminated the generally prosperous 1920s. Output was at a record high, 6.6 percent above 1928, the previous record year. Because of the ensuing depression, during which production fell far below the economy's capacity to produce, 1929 remained the peak until 1937, eight years later. Even in 1939 national income exceeded its 1929 value by only 2.5 percent.

6. The difference between the two 1960 national income figures measures the amount added to national income when the geographic coverage of the series was changed. It understates national income originating in Alaska and Hawaii. Some persons physically located in these states were already considered to be within the nation's economy when it referred geographically to the coterminous United States. Also, most property income earned by residents of these states was inadvertently or unavoidably included.

7. See Chapter 3, pages 21–23 for a fuller explanation of the terminal years method which is used in computing the growth rates.

8. The 1941–69 growth rates for per person employed and per hour worked are based on 1941 data excluding work relief.

9. See Appendix B for data on years not covered by this study.

Table 2-2. Indexes of National Income in Constant Prices, Population, Employment, and Hours Worked, 1929, 1940–41, and 1947–69[a]
1958 = 100

| | National income | | | | | | |
Year	Total (1)	Per capita (2)	Per person employed (3)	Per hour worked (4)	Population (5)	Employment (6)	Man-hours worked (7)
1929	44.39	63.42	62.00	49.79	69.99	71.60	89.15
1940	49.92	65.80	64.88	59.47	75.87	76.94	83.94
1940 excluding work relief	48.95	. . .	67.36	60.24	. . .	72.67	81.26
1941	59.35	77.47	70.89	64.36	76.61	83.72	92.22
1941 excluding work relief	58.61	. . .	72.91	64.99	. . .	80.39	90.18
1947	70.18	84.80	78.49	72.99	82.76	89.41	96.15
1948	74.28	88.22	81.74	76.65	84.20	90.87	96.91
1949	73.09	85.32	82.18	78.15	85.67	88.94	93.53
1950	79.97	91.81	87.39	83.04	87.10	91.51	96.30
1951	86.05	97.12	88.42	84.17	88.60	97.32	102.23
1952	88.96	98.70	89.67	85.74	90.13	99.21	103.75
1953	92.75	101.22	92.30	88.70	91.63	100.49	104.57
1954	91.10	97.69	93.06	90.37	93.25	97.89	100.81
1955	98.67	103.96	98.55	95.48	94.91	100.12	103.34
1956	101.15	104.71	98.85	96.49	96.60	102.33	104.83
1957	102.04	103.75	99.47	98.50	98.35	102.58	103.59
1958	100.00	100.00	100.00	100.00	100.00	100.00	100.00
1959	107.54	105.76	105.32	104.81	101.68	102.11	102.60
1960	109.83	106.32	106.56	106.63	103.30	103.07	103.00
1961	111.83	106.47	108.54	109.37	105.03	103.03	102.25
1962	119.28	111.83	113.25	113.97	106.66	105.32	104.66
1963	124.28	114.86	116.78	117.78	108.20	106.42	105.52
1964	131.56	119.91	121.19	122.60	109.72	108.56	107.31
1965	140.57	126.53	125.60	126.85	111.10	111.92	110.82
1966	149.40	132.93	127.80	130.09	112.39	116.90	114.84
1967	152.78	134.47	128.16	132.00	113.62	119.21	115.74
1968	160.32	139.70	131.16	135.83	114.76	122.23	118.03
1969	164.30	141.77	131.01	136.20	115.89	125.41	120.63

Source: Computed from data underlying Table 2-1.
a. Series excluding and including Alaska and Hawaii were linked at 1960.

In 1940, the second year covered in my analysis, unemployment and emergency work relief employment remained massive but the economy was vigorously expanding. National income, including the output of emergency workers, stood 12.5 percent above 1929. From 1940 to 1941, national income rose an additional 18.9 percent. This is the largest year-to-year percentage gain ever recorded in the period, beginning with 1891, for which annual estimates are available. It raised national income in 1941 to a point 33.7 percent above the 1929 predepression peak.

From 1941 my indexes skip to 1947. In the interim, national income had jumped to a wartime high in 1944, then receded until 1947. At its peak in 1944, national income was 41 percent above 1941, an output level made possible by employment of an extraordinarily large percentage of the population (counting the armed forces, whose services are included in national income), by long working hours, by very intensive utilization of employed labor and capital, and doubtless by other special wartime conditions as well. In 1947, when my analysis resumes, national income was 18.2 percent above 1941, but 16.2 percent below 1944. The 1944 peak was not regained until 1951, seven years later.

From 1947 through 1969, the period for which annual data are provided, national income rose by 134 percent. The increase was irregular. Percentage changes varied widely from year to year as well as over longer periods, the result both of changes in the rate at which potential output was growing and of fluctuations of actual output around the potential level. (The two causes are disentangled in Chapter 7.) Actual declines in the

Figure 2-1. Index of Total National Income, 1925–71
Based on data in 1958 dollars

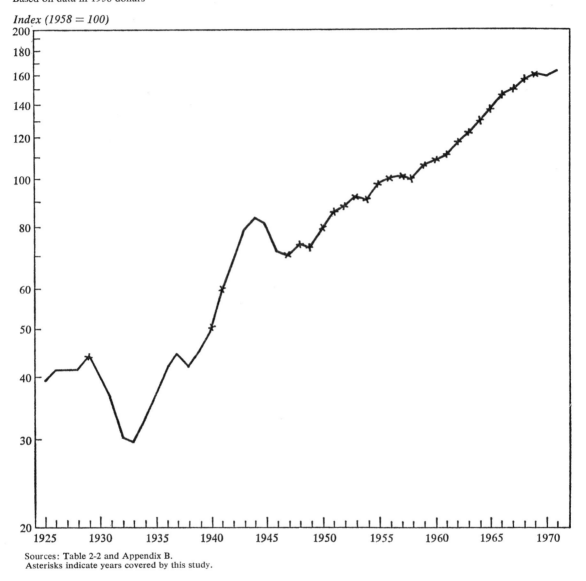

Index (1958 = 100)

Sources: Table 2-2 and Appendix B.
Asterisks indicate years covered by this study.

calendar year series were experienced only in 1949, 1954, and 1958; quarterly data show an additional decline between the first quarters of 1960 and 1961. These interruptions in the steady climb were in no way comparable in size or duration to the catastrophic decline from 1929 to 1933, nor to the 1944–47 fallback from the wartime peak.

After the period covered by this study, another interruption to the rise in national income oc-

curred from 1969 to 1970. But after the drop in 1970 national income surpassed the 1969 level in 1971. It continued its upward movement in 1972 and 1973.

The course of national income per person employed is shown in Figure 2-2. Two figures are shown for 1940 and 1941; one includes and the other excludes work relief employment.

Output per person employed rose in every year or period shown except 1969, but the *size of in-*

Figure 2-2. Index of National Income per Person Employed, 1929, 1940–41, and 1947–69
Based on data in 1958 dollars

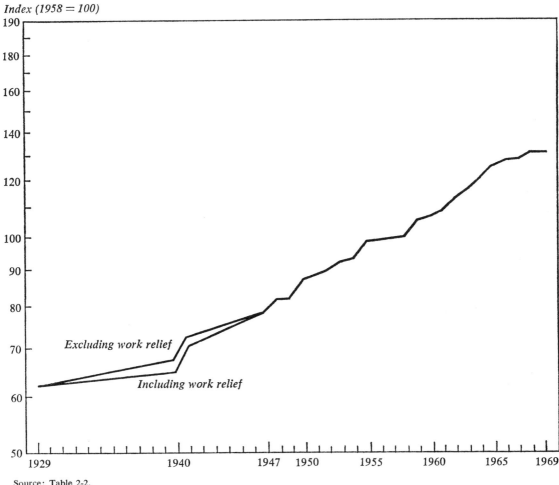

Index (1958 = 100)

Source: Table 2-2.
Note. The years 1930–39 and 1942–46 are not plotted.

creases was irregular not only from year to year but also over longer periods. The gain was slight from 1955 to 1958 and only moderate from 1965 to 1969.

Growth Rates for Selected Periods

Data for twenty-six individual years are provided in this study, so it is possible to analyze the change in any determinant of output between any two of twenty-six years. To summarize the findings, however, it will be necessary to choose a limited number of time spans. I have used eight.

For long-term analysis, I present data for the entire forty-year period from 1929 to 1969, and for the 1929–48 and 1948–69 periods within it.

For shorter-term analysis, I have divided the forty years into five periods which range from five to twelve years in length. The first, 1929–41, spans the Great Depression. The second, 1941–48, covers World War II and the immediate reconversion to peacetime production. The data allow the postwar period to be subdivided in any way one chooses. My choice of the 1948–53, 1953–64, and 1964–69 periods is based upon the path of "potential" national income, a series to be discussed in Chapter 7. The years 1953 and 1964 separate periods of fast and slower growth of potential output. Use of the same periods for actual national income, which moves erratically, will facilitate comparisons between the series. For other purposes, different periods may be preferred. In examining individual determinants of actual output no special attention will be paid to these periods, but many of these determinants did change course at about these dates.

Over the whole period from 1929 to 1969, average annual rates of growth were 3.33 percent for national income, 1.41 for employment, and 1.89 for national income per person employed.[10] Table 2-3 provides similar rates for all the periods distinguished. They are based on data excluding emergency workers in 1941.

It is apparent from Table 2-3 that rates of change in all three series differed widely in the various time spans. There is an interesting contrast among the postwar periods. Total national income grew much less from 1953 to 1964 than in the five-year periods preceding and following those years, whereas national income per person employed grew the most during that 1953–64 period. The growth rate of total national income was two-fifths higher in 1964–69 than in 1953–

10. Growth rates of the components of a series do not quite add to the growth rate of the series, but they nearly do so unless the growth rate is very high. The present case, in which they fall short by an "interaction factor" of 0.03 percentage points, is typical. The exact relationship is: $1.0141 \times 1.0189 = 1.0333$.

64, while the growth rate of national income per person employed was about two-fifths lower. The rate of employment expansion from 1964 to 1969 was more than four times that experienced from 1953 to 1964.

Chapter 9 gives a breakdown by source of each of the growth rates for total national income and national income per person employed shown in Table 2-3. The intervening chapters discuss separate determinants of output and provide the data for a comprehensive exploration of the reasons that the rates differ so much among periods.

Table 2-3. Growth Rates of Total National Income and Employment, and National Income per Person Employed, Eight Selected Periods, 1929–69

Period	Total national income	Employment	National income per person employed
Long periods			
1929–69	3.33	1.41	1.89
1929–48	2.75	1.26	1.47
1948–69	3.85	1.55	2.27
Shorter periods			
1929–41[a]	2.34	0.97	1.36
1941–48[a]	3.44	1.77	1.65
1948–53	4.54	2.03	2.46
1953–64	3.23	0.70	2.51
1964–69	4.54	2.93	1.57

Source: Computed from data underlying Table 2-2.
a. Based on data excluding work relief employees.

CHAPTER THREE

➤➤❰❰❰

Nonprofit Activities, Dwellings, and International Assets

➤➤❰❰❰

Growth analysis is facilitated and its accuracy enhanced if the economy is divided into four parts: general government, households, institutions, and foreign governments; services of dwellings; international assets; and nonresidential business. The first three, which together account for less than one-fifth of national income in constant prices, are examined in this chapter. The fourth, which consists of all business (including farming) except the services of dwellings, will require much more extended analysis.

Each of the three sectors considered here has the special characteristics that all of the national income originating in it accrues to a single factor of production, the value of output in current prices is the earnings of that factor, and changes in real output are ascribable to that factor.

National Income by Sector

Tables 3-1 and 3-2 divide national income in current and constant prices by sector of origin. Sources of the data are provided in Appendix D. Figure 3-1 shows an index (1958 = 100) of constant-price national income for each of the four sectors.

General Government, Households, Institutions, and Foreign Governments

The largest of the three sectors examined in this chapter consists of the value of labor services purchased directly by groups regarded in the national accounts as the final purchasers of the nation's output. Four types of entity, all of them outside the profit-making business sectors of the economy, are included. The largest is general government (all government except government enterprises such as the Post Office and municipally owned utilities). Nonprofit organizations providing services to individuals are the second type. Private households are included because they employ domestic servants. The fourth, of trivial importance, is foreign governments and international organizations, insofar as they employ U.S. citizens within the United States.[1] The value of production taking place in the sector is simply the value assigned to the work of the individuals it employs.

In 1969, general government, households, and institutions accounted for 17.3 percent of national income measured in current dollars and 12.9 percent measured in 1958 dollars. Twenty-five percent of all persons employed in the United States worked in this sector (Table C-1). This percentage had been 13 in 1929 and 16 in 1947. All other employment occurs in nonresidential business.

In current prices, national income originating in this sector represents both the earnings of labor employed in the sector and the value of production, as measured by the Office of Business Economics (OBE), that takes place in the sector. To obtain the value of output in constant (1958) prices, OBE extrapolates, by components, the 1958 value of output in current prices by its estimates of the quantity of labor used. (A more detailed description is provided later in this chapter.) Thus it can be stated unequivocally that changes in output in this sector, as measured, are due exclusively to changes in the quantity of labor it uses. From 1960 to 1969, for example, the change in the amount of labor employed by general government, households, and institutions contributed $21.3 billion of the total increase of $198.8 billion in the value of real national income (Table 3-2).

The output originating in this sector has sometimes risen more than that originating in nonresidential business, but most of the time—and rather persistently since the late 1950s—it has risen less (see Figure 3-1). In contrast, increases in employ-

1. For brevity, foreign governments and international organizations will usually be ignored in labeling this sector.

Table 3-1. National Income in Current Prices, by Sector, 1929, 1940–41, and 1947–69
Billions of dollars

Year	Total national income (1)	Work relief (2)	Total national income, excluding work relief (3)	National income originating in: General government,[a] households, and institutions (4)	Services of dwellings[b] (5)	International assets (6)	Nonresidential business[b] (7)
			Excluding Alaska and Hawaii				
1929	84.7	0.0	84.7	7.2	5.0	0.8	71.7
1940	79.3	1.6	77.7	8.6	2.7	0.4	66.0
1941	102.1	1.2	100.9	10.7	3.0	0.4	86.8
1947	194.1	0.0	194.1	21.9	3.8	0.8	167.6
1948	218.5	0.0	218.5	23.1	4.1	1.0	190.4
1949	212.3	0.0	212.3	25.4	5.4	1.0	180.6
1950	235.3	0.0	235.3	27.3	5.9	1.1	200.9
1951	271.6	0.0	271.6	34.3	6.8	1.3	229.2
1952	284.9	0.0	284.9	38.4	8.1	1.3	237.1
1953	299.3	0.0	299.3	39.7	9.8	1.3	248.5
1954	299.3	0.0	299.3	40.6	11.5	1.6	245.6
1955	328.2	0.0	328.2	43.3	12.2	1.8	270.9
1956	347.0	0.0	347.0	46.4	12.6	2.1	285.9
1957	362.0	0.0	362.0	49.7	13.5	2.2	296.7
1958	363.6	0.0	363.6	53.6	14.8	2.0	293.2
1959	396.3	0.0	396.3	56.6	15.1	2.1	322.4
1960	409.7	0.0	409.7	60.4	16.9	2.3	330.0
			Including Alaska and Hawaii				
1960	411.2	0.0	411.2	60.7	16.9	2.3	331.2
1961	424.4	0.0	424.4	64.9	17.8	2.9	338.7
1962	457.6	0.0	457.6	69.7	19.4	3.2	365.3
1963	482.4	0.0	482.4	74.2	21.2	3.3	383.7
1964	519.3	0.0	519.3	80.3	23.2	3.9	411.8
1965	566.1	0.0	566.1	86.3	25.7	4.1	449.9
1966	622.0	0.0	622.0	96.9	27.5	4.1	493.6
1967	654.5	0.0	654.5	107.9	29.3	4.5	512.7
1968	712.3	0.0	712.3	120.5	30.4	4.7	556.7
1969	763.9	0.0	763.9	132.4	32.5	4.3	594.7

Sources: Columns 1 to 3, Table 2-1; other columns, see Appendix D for derivation. Detail may not add to totals because of rounding.
a. Excludes work relief; includes foreign governments.
b. The small amount of labor income in the dwellings sector is classified with "Nonresidential business."

ment in general government, households, and institutions have generally exceeded those in nonresidential business. Employment series are compared in Figure 3-2.

Services of Dwellings Industry

Residential structures constitute a very large portion of total capital stock. In 1968, their net value was 82 percent as large as that of all fixed capital and inventories owned by the remainder of the business sector. Similarly, residential sites comprise a very large portion of the total value of land in the business sector.

The earnings in current dollars of dwellings and their sites have been isolated and are shown in Table 3-1, column 5. I do not subdivide these earnings between capital and land.

The "services of dwellings" *industry* may be defined as the provision of housing services. The establishments in this industry are owner-occupied and tenant-occupied nonfarm and farm dwellings. By definition, all residential structures and residential land in the country are used in this industry.[2] Factor input in this industry consists only of residential structures and land.[3]

The net value in constant prices placed on the output of this industry can be isolated, and it is shown in Table 3-2, column 5. It is evident from Figure 3-1 that, since 1941, national income has

2. In the OBE industry classification system, the nonfarm portion of the services of dwellings industry is included in "real estate" and the farm portion in "farms."
3. Except for a small amount of labor employed in apartment houses, which is classified in nonresidential business. For discussion, see Appendix D.

Table 3-2. National Income in Constant Prices, by Sector, 1929, 1940–41, and 1947–69
Billions of 1958 dollars

Year	Total national income (1)	Work relief (2)	Total national income, excluding work relief (3)	National income originating in:			
				General government,[a] households, and institutions (4)	Services of dwellings[b] (5)	International assets (6)	Nonresidential business[b] (7)
			Excluding Alaska and Hawaii				
1929	161.4	0.0	161.4	20.1	3.2	1.4	136.7
1940	181.5	3.5	178.0	25.7	3.2	1.0	148.1
1941	215.8	2.7	213.1	32.0	3.6	0.9	176.6
1947	255.2	0.0	255.2	36.1	6.1	1.1	212.0
1948	270.1	0.0	270.1	36.6	6.5	1.2	225.9
1949	265.8	0.0	265.8	38.3	7.4	1.2	218.9
1950	290.8	0.0	290.8	39.8	8.0	1.3	241.8
1951	312.9	0.0	312.9	47.7	8.9	1.2	255.2
1952	323.5	0.0	323.5	50.7	9.8	1.2	261.9
1953	337.3	0.0	337.3	50.8	10.7	1.3	274.5
1954	331.3	0.0	331.3	50.1	11.6	1.6	268.0
1955	358.8	0.0	358.8	50.9	12.4	1.8	293.7
1956	367.8	0.0	367.8	51.9	13.1	2.0	300.9
1957	371.1	0.0	371.1	52.9	13.9	2.1	302.2
1958	363.6	0.0	363.6	53.6	14.8	2.0	293.2
1959	391.1	0.0	391.1	54.3	15.3	2.2	319.3
1960	399.4	0.0	399.4	55.6	16.8	2.3	324.7
			Including Alaska and Hawaii				
1960	400.8	0.0	400.8	55.9	16.8	2.3	325.8
1961	408.1	0.0	408.1	57.3	17.7	2.9	330.3
1962	435.3	0.0	435.3	59.8	19.0	3.4	353.3
1963	453.6	0.0	453.6	61.1	20.5	3.4	368.8
1964	480.1	0.0	480.1	62.8	22.3	3.9	391.2
1965	513.0	0.0	513.0	64.8	24.3	4.1	419.8
1966	545.2	0.0	545.2	69.3	25.7	3.9	446.4
1967	557.6	0.0	557.6	73.1	27.4	4.3	452.8
1968	585.1	0.0	585.1	75.7	28.7	4.5	476.2
1969	599.6	0.0	599.6	77.2	30.3	4.0	488.1

Sources: Columns 1 to 3, Table 2-1; other columns, see Appendix D for derivation. Detail may not add to totals because of rounding.
a. Excludes work relief; includes foreign governments.
b. The small amount of labor output in the dwellings sector is classified with "Nonresidential business."

risen at a far higher rate in the dwellings industry than in nonresidential business.

Because the output of residential capital and land in the whole economy is the same as the output of the dwellings industry, the contribution of residential capital and land to the increase in total national income can be computed directly from Table 3-2. Of the increase of $198.8 billion in real national income from 1960 to 1969, for example, $13.5 billion are from this source.

Increases in the real output of dwellings shown for periods since 1940 are so large that the estimates may be questionable (see Appendix D, page 179). Whether or not the dwellings estimates are correct, securing the contribution of dwellings to the increase in total output directly

from the details of the national income series ensures consistency between estimates of the contribution and of total output. Any error in the estimate of total output growth attributable to estimated output of dwellings cannot affect the estimated contributions of other growth sources.

International Assets

National income originating in the business sector of the economy represents the value of business production occurring within the geographic boundaries of the United States whether resources are owned by residents or foreigners. The excess of property income received by U.S. residents from abroad over property income paid by the United States to foreign residents must be added

Figure 3-1. National Income by Sector, 1929, 1940–41, and 1947–69[a]

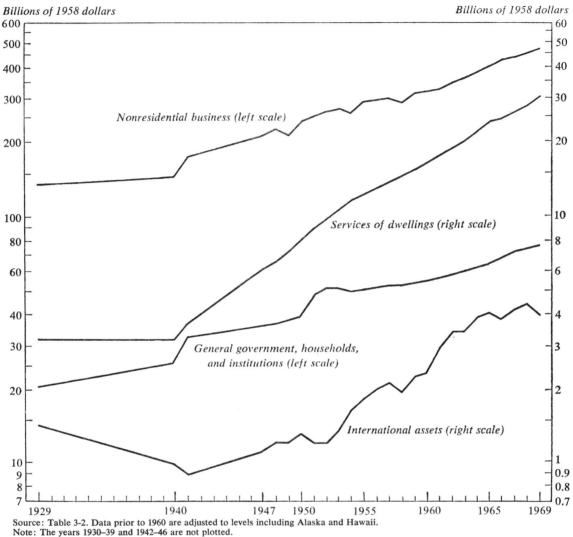

Billions of 1958 dollars   *Billions of 1958 dollars*

Source: Table 3-2. Data prior to 1960 are adjusted to levels including Alaska and Hawaii.
Note: The years 1930–39 and 1942–46 are not plotted.
a. Excludes work relief.

to secure the earnings of labor and property supplied by residents of the nation.[4] When national income is viewed as an output measure, the adjustment is required to include the value of foreign output attributable to U.S. capital and to exclude the value of U.S. output attributable to foreign capital. The actual statistical series for net property income from abroad does not conform

4. No adjustment for labor earnings is required. Earnings of American residents employed abroad by U.S. employers are already included in the other sectors. The biggest item is the compensation of the U.S. residents employed abroad by the United States government. Similarly, the compensation of foreigners employed in the United States (chiefly by foreign governments and international organizations) is omitted.

to the definition very well because only earnings actually remitted between countries are counted (except in the case of branch profits). Consequently, the series is affected not only by earnings but also by decisions as to the amount of earnings that are to be remitted.

Changes in the net flow of property income from abroad in constant prices do, nevertheless, indicate the contribution of internationally owned assets to changes in national income as measured. Thus, of the $198.8 billion increase in national income in constant prices from 1960 to 1969, $1.7 billion represents the increase in net property income from abroad and hence the contribution of international assets (Table 3-2, column 6).

Figure 3-2. Employment by Sector, 1929, 1940–41, and 1947–69[a]

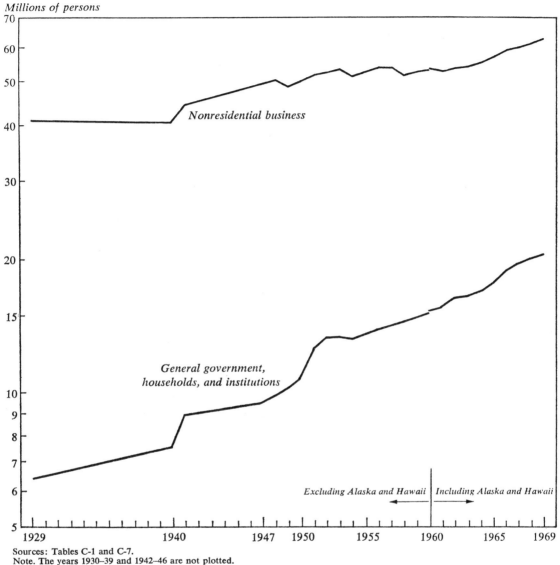

Millions of persons

Nonresidential business

*General government,
households, and institutions*

Excluding Alaska and Hawaii | *Including Alaska and Hawaii*

Sources: Tables C-1 and C-7.
Note. The years 1930–39 and 1942–46 are not plotted.
a. Excludes work relief.

Nonresidential Business

Nonresidential business covers the entire domestic business sector of the economy, as defined by the Office of Business Economics, except for the services of dwellings. It includes corporations, partnerships, sole proprietorships, mutual financial institutions, government enterprises, cooperatives, and other miscellaneous forms of business, as well as organizations such as trade associations or chambers of commerce that primarily serve business. The distinguishing feature of the sector as a whole is that it sells its products for a price.

Output in this sector is, with minor exceptions, measured directly. It is not inferred from the behavior of labor, capital, or land input.

Contributions of the Sectors to Growth

Table 3-2 isolates the contributions made to real national income each year by the four sectors; the contribution made to the change in total national income from any one date to any other by each sector can therefore be readily calculated. From 1948 to 1969, for example, the increase in national income was divided among sectors as follows (in millions of dollars) : [5]

	Increase in national income in 1958 prices, 1948–69
Total	327,334
Sector:	
General government, households, and institutions	40,181
Services of dwellings	23,849
International assets	2,828
Nonresidential business	260,476

If the growth of output in each sector can subsequently be allocated among the sources (or determinants) of its own growth, this information will permit the sectors to be combined in order to divide the growth of total national income among its sources.

I express my final estimates of the sources of growth as contributions to the growth rate of national income rather than as dollar amounts. The procedure followed to secure the contributions of the sectors requires explanation.

From any one year to the following year, the contribution of each sector to the percentage change in real national income is simply the dollar change in national income originating in that sector expressed as a percentage of national income in the earlier year; the sum of these percentages equals the percentage change in national income. But the averaging of such annual data to secure the growth rate and contributions to the growth rate over longer periods would not provide the most useful measures. This procedure would require one to define the "growth rate" as the average (arithmetic mean) of the annual percentage changes in national income. Although the contribution of each source would accurately depict the contribution to that "growth rate," the rate itself would not be satisfactory because the figure depends on the value of national income not only in the years compared but also in the intervening years. It is much more satisfactory to use the compound interest rate between the terminal years of the period. [6]

The 1948–69 growth rate that is obtained by use of the terminal years method is 3.85. The con-

tributions of the four sectors computed in a comparable way need to be determined. The contribution of each sector is the amount that its average contribution to annual percentage changes in national income would have represented if the output of each sector and total output had changed each year by a percentage equal to its growth rate over the period as a whole. To make the calculation in practice, one need only compute percentage distributions of national income among the four sectors for the terminal years of the period; interpolate these percentages to obtain a synthetic interpolated percentage for the next-to-last year; average the distributions for the first and next-to-last year; [7] and multiply the resulting percentage for each sector by the growth rate of national income in the sector, computed by the terminal years method.

Table 3-3 summarizes the calculations, and provides the results, for all of the eight selected time periods. [8] The growth rates of national income measured in constant prices in the whole economy and of national income originating in each of the four sectors are shown first. Below is the average of the percentage distributions of national income in the first year of the period and the interpolated percentage for the next-to-last year. The percentages have been changed in the table to ratio form and labeled as the weights to be applied to the growth rates in each sector. Finally, the contributions of each sector to the growth rates of total national income, obtained as the product of the sector's growth rate and its weight, are given.

---

5. Data are in millions of dollars to avoid discrepancies from rounding, and adjustments are introduced to eliminate the effect of adding Alaska and Hawaii to the series in 1960.

6. Suppose, for example, that national income is 100 in one year and 110 two years later. If the percentage change

were the same, 4.88, each year so that national income in the intervening year were 104.88, the average change over the two years would also be 4.88. But if the intervening year were 90, the growth rate so calculated would be 6.11. If it were 101, the growth rate would be 4.96; if 109, then 4.55. These differences and corresponding differences in the contributions would appear even though the first and third years, and hence all differences between them, were identical in all respects in each case. The method using terminal years yields a growth rate of 4.88 over the two years regardless of the intervening year.

7. This is equivalent to averaging percentages for the first year and interpolated percentages for all other years except the last year. The distribution in the last year enters the calculation for the next period.

8. In all time periods spanning 1960, national income in the later year was multiplied by the 1960 ratio of national income excluding Alaska and Hawaii to national income including those states before the calculations were made. Calculations were based on data for national income in millions of dollars and weights carried to more decimal places than those shown.

Table 3-3. Growth Rates of National Income by Sector and Contributions of the Sectors to the Growth Rate of Total National Income, Eight Selected Periods, 1929–69[a]

Based on data in 1958 dollars

Period	Whole economy (1)	General government, households, and institutions (2)	Services of dwellings (3)	International assets (4)	Nonresidential business (5)
Growth rate of sector national income					
Long periods					
1929–69	3.33	3.41	5.76	2.66	3.22
1929–48	2.75	3.22	3.72	−0.93	2.68
1948–69	3.85	3.59	7.64	6.02	3.72
Shorter periods					
1929–41	2.34	3.98	0.95	−3.76	2.16
1941–48	3.44	1.92	8.64	4.11	3.58
1948–53	4.54	6.78	10.62	1.65	3.98
1953–64	3.23	1.89	6.90	10.67	3.24
1964–69	4.54	4.23	6.35	0.62	4.52
Weight for calculation of contributions					
Long periods					
1929–69	1.00	0.1263	0.0350	0.0077	0.8310
1929–48	1.00	0.1296	0.0218	0.0066	0.8420
1948–69	1.00	0.1322	0.0367	0.0055	0.8257
Shorter periods					
1929–41	1.00	0.1362	0.0186	0.0066	0.8386
1941–48	1.00	0.1439	0.0199	0.0042	0.8319
1948–53	1.00	0.1415	0.0270	0.0041	0.8273
1953–64	1.00	0.1415	0.0384	0.0057	0.8144
1964–69	1.00	0.1299	0.0480	0.0075	0.8145
Contribution to growth rate of whole economy					
Long periods					
1929–69	3.33	0.43	0.20	0.02	2.68
1929–48	2.75	0.42	0.08	−0.01	2.26
1948–69	3.85	0.47	0.28	0.03	3.07
Shorter periods					
1929–41	2.34	0.54	0.02	−0.03	1.81
1941–48	3.44	0.27	0.17	0.02	2.98
1948–53	4.54	0.96	0.28	0.01	3.29
1953–64	3.23	0.27	0.26	0.06	2.64
1964–69	4.54	0.55	0.30	0.01	3.68

Source: Derived from Table 3-2. See text for explanation of computation of growth rates and sector contributions. Occasional discrepancies between the sum of the sector contributions and the growth rate of total national income, which occur because of rounding, have been eliminated.

a. Based on data excluding work relief employees. In all time periods spanning 1960, national income in the later year was multiplied by the 1960 ratio of national income excluding Alaska and Hawaii to national income including those states before the calculations were made. Calculations were based on data for national income in millions of dollars and weights carried to more decimal places than those shown.

For the postwar period from 1948 to 1969, for example, of the growth rate of national income of 3.85 percent a year, 0.47 percentage points resulted from the increase in labor used in general government, households, and institutions; 0.28 points from the increase in the services provided by the stock of dwellings; and 0.03 percentage points from the increase in the remitted earnings of international assets. To give these figures a more concrete meaning, if a growth rate equal to any sector's contribution were applied to total 1948 national income, the dollar increase from 1948 to 1969 obtained for total national income would just equal the dollar increase in the output

of the sector. The contribution of each sector is the amount by which the growth rate of total national income would have been lowered if there had been no change in that sector while the other sectors changed as they did.

The contributions of the three smaller sectors are of interest without additional detail because each can be identified with a single input, although for two of the three it is useful to dig deeper into the data, and this will be done in the remainder of this chapter. In contrast, the growth of national income in nonresidential business is due to changes in a great many determinants, and the finding that it contributed 3.07 points to the

3.85 percent growth rate of national income from 1948 to 1969 is useful chiefly as the starting point for further analysis in later chapters.

Labor Input in the General Government, Households, and Institutions Sector

The *total* contribution made to growth of the national income measure by changes in labor input in government, households, and institutions has already been calculated. In this section, series needed to divide this contribution among the various characteristics of labor are developed. This will permit estimates for this sector to be combined with those for business to provide estimates for the whole economy.

When considering the nonresidential business sector in Chapter 4, I measure labor input by examining employment, hours worked and efficiency offsets to changes in average hours, the age-sex composition of man-hours worked, and the level of education. My estimate of total labor input in that sector and its contribution to growth of output takes account of all these characteristics of labor, but I also present estimates for each characteristic separately.

As previously noted, OBE measures changes in real output in government, households, and institutions by changes in labor input. But it measures labor input in a very different way than I do in the business sector.[9] For consistency with the output measure, the OBE measure of labor input in this sector must be accepted. To see what is implied, the OBE procedures must be examined.

OBE obtains the value of output in 1958 prices in components of general government by extrapolating the 1958 value of output in current prices by its estimate of the number of full-time equivalent employees. The procedure followed in households and institutions has the same effect: current-dollar employee compensation is deflated by an index of average compensation per full-time equivalent employee. The calculation in constant prices is made separately for a limited group of industries. Within general government, the output of

civilian employees (except work relief) is calculated separately for federal employees, state and local school employees, and other state and local employees. The calculation for military employees is made separately for branches of the services, and in the major branches separately for officers and enlisted personnel. (This is the only point at which an occupational classification is used.) Within households and institutions, the calculation is made separately for each two-digit industry.

The procedure implies that output (hence, labor input) per full-time equivalent employee does not change in any separately treated segment of the nonbusiness sector but may change in the sector as a whole if the distribution of full-time equivalent employment among segments changes.

In 1958, the value of output (in billions of dollars) was distributed among broad components as follows:[10]

	Value of output
General government	42.1
Federal, military	10.5
Federal, civilian	10.1
State and local, school	10.5
State and local, nonschool	11.0
Private households	3.5
Nonprofit institutions	7.9
Nonprofit member-ship organizations	3.3
Other	4.6
Foreign governments	0.0

Labor input in this sector is shown in index form in Table 3-4, column 6. I now turn to the problem of dividing this series among components.

Employment

Table 3-4, column 1, provides an index of full-time and part-time employment in general government (except work relief), households, and institutions. In the absence of changes in employment composition or working hours, the index of labor input in the sector (column 6) would have been the same. In fact, there is an appreciable difference in some time periods.

Hours

OBE's use of full-time equivalent employment to extrapolate output introduces an allowance for changes in the proportions of full-time and part-

9. I have suggested elsewhere that use of a labor input series constructed by techniques similar to those I use in the business sector would improve OBE's measure of output. It would also permit the artificial techniques of growth analysis necessarily adopted in this section for consistency with the OBE output series to be avoided. See Edward F. Denison, "U.S. National Income and Product Estimates: Evaluation and Some Specific Suggestions for Improvement," *Survey of Current Business*, Vol. 51 (July 1971), Pt. 2, pp. 43–44.

10. Data are from the OBE national income accounts, Tables 1.7 and 6.1, and unpublished estimates. The value for foreign governments is $22 million, which rounds to $0.0 billion in the table.

Table 3-4. General Government (Excluding Work Relief), Households, and Institutions: Indexes of Sector Labor Inputs, 1929, 1940–41, and 1947–69[a]

1958 = 100

Year	Employment (1)	Effect of changes in hours on a year's work				Composition of labor (except effect of hours) (5)	Total labor input (6)
		Total (2)	Average hours (3)	Implied efficiency offset (4)			
1929	44.2	107.1	127.8	83.8		79.1	37.4
1940	52.1	105.6	114.9	91.9		87.1	47.9
1941	61.7	106.5	113.0	94.2		91.0	59.8
1947	65.6	101.8	106.9	95.2		101.0	67.4
1948	67.6	101.7	105.3	96.6		99.3	68.3
1949	70.6	101.9	103.7	98.3		99.3	71.4
1950	74.1	101.8	103.6	98.2		98.5	74.3
1951	87.0	101.7	104.5	97.3		100.6	89.0
1952	91.6	101.4	104.6	96.9		101.9	94.6
1953	92.1	101.3	104.3	97.1		101.7	94.8
1954	91.3	100.9	103.4	97.6		101.6	93.5
1955	93.5	100.5	102.9	97.7		101.0	94.9
1956	96.1	100.2	101.9	98.3		100.6	96.9
1957	98.0	100.2	100.9	99.3		100.6	98.7
1958	100.0	100.0	100.0	100.0		100.0	100.0
1959	101.5	99.9	99.5	100.4		100.0	101.3
1960	103.6	99.8	99.5	100.3		100.5	103.8
1961	106.8	99.6	98.8	100.9		100.0	106.3
1962	111.6	99.0	98.3	100.7		100.5	111.0
1963	113.5	99.1	98.5	100.6		100.8	113.4
1964	116.5	99.1	97.4	101.8		100.9	116.5
1965	120.0	99.0	97.7	101.3		101.3	120.3
1966	128.8	97.9	97.6	100.3		101.9	128.5
1967	134.4	98.1	97.8	100.3		102.9	135.6
1968	138.7	98.2	97.1	101.1		103.2	140.6
1969	140.9	98.0	97.4	100.6		103.8	143.3

Sources: Column 1, derived from Table C-7, columns 3 and 9; column 2, see text for derivation; column 3, an index of total hours (total hours equal hours in the whole economy excluding work relief from Table E-2, column 1, and note c, minus hours in the business sector from Table E-1, column 4) ÷ column 1; column 4, column 2 ÷ column 3; column 5, column 6 ÷ columns 1 and 2, see text for explanation; column 6, derived from Table 3-2, column 4.

a. Series excluding and including Alaska and Hawaii are linked at 1960.

time employees and in the average hours of part-time employees. How large is this allowance? The fact that OBE's series for full-time equivalent employment differ from its series for full-time and part-time employment in only four segments of the sector that are of any importance facilitates its measurement.[11] The series for real output in the sector that OBE would have obtained if the 1958 value of output in these four segments had been extrapolated by full-time and part-time employment instead of full-time equivalent employment was computed. The ratio of this series to the real output series used by OBE was computed for

11. They are: public education; state and local non-school employment, except work relief; private households; and the "nonprofit membership organizations" industry. Full-time equivalent employment and full-time and part-time employment in each of these segments are published in the OBE national income accounts, Tables 6.3 and 6.4.

each year. The ratios measure the effect of changes in hours on labor input and output in this sector. They are shown, multiplied by 100 to convert them to index form, in Table 3-4, column 2. The long-term decline in this index results from an increasing proportion of part-time workers.

The OBE deflation procedure makes no allowance for changes in the average hours of full-time workers. In this sector changes in full-time hours therefore do not change labor input or output as measured. Consequently, any reduction in full-time hours implies a fully offsetting increase in output per hour. Table 3-4, column 3, shows an index of the average hours of all workers (full-time and part-time combined) in this sector.[12] If

12. Appendix E describes how these hours were estimated. For the armed forces a conventional figure of forty hours a week is used at all dates.

output per person employed were proportional to hours worked, it would have declined as average hours fell at a rate corresponding to this index. Division of column 2 by column 3 in Table 3-4 therefore yields an index, shown in column 4 as the "efficiency offset" which measures the implied effect upon output per *hour* in this sector of changes in the average hours of full-time workers.[13] When labor input in the business sector is analyzed in the following chapter, I, too, allow for the fact that a reduction in full-time hours affects labor input (and output) per hour favorably. However, I estimate this efficiency offset to be much smaller for wage and salary workers employed in the business sector than the OBE procedure implies for those employed in government, households, and institutions.

Other Aspects of Labor Composition

OBE makes no specific allowance for changes in the composition of employment or man-hours worked with respect to age-sex composition, education, or other aspects of labor quality, nor (apart from changes in hours) is there any way that changes in the average quality of labor within any separately deflated segment can affect OBE's estimates.

However, because each segment is treated separately, shifts in the composition of employment between low-wage and high-wage segments do affect the labor input index. The implication of the OBE procedure is that the quality of labor in each segment does not change, but that a shift from low-wage to high-wage segments implies an increase in the average value or quality of the labor provided in this part of the economy as a whole, and a contrary shift a decrease. Average base-year earnings are lower in military employment, and much lower in private households and in some of the nonprofit organization segments, than they are in the civilian government segments. The effects of shifting composition can be measured by dividing (1) the index, previously computed, of the real output measure that would have been secured if, in all segments, OBE extrapolations had been based on full-time and part-time employment rather than on full-time equivalent

employment by (2) the index of full-time and part-time employment in the sector as a whole. The resulting index, shown in Table 3-4, column 5, measures the allowance for changes in the composition of labor in the nonbusiness sector (other than through changes in hours) that is implicit in the OBE series for real output.

The biggest change in this index is a sharp increase prior to 1947, due to the declining weight of domestic service. There is also appreciable variation in its rate of change during the postwar period.

Contributions to Growth

The index of total labor input, shown in Table 3-4, column 6, which is the same as the index of national income in this sector, is equal to the product of the component indexes. The growth rates of national income and the components of labor input in this sector are given in the upper half of Table 3-5. The rate for each component also measures its contribution to the growth rate of real national income originating in this sector.[14] The contribution of each component within this sector to the growth rate of total national income in the whole economy is shown in the lower half of Table 3-5. This contribution equals the product of the contribution to the sector growth rate and the weight of the sector as given in Table 3-3; equivalently, the contribution of the sector from Table 3-3 can be allocated in proportion to the contributions to the sector growth rate.

The meaning of the figures can be illustrated by the 1929–69 estimates for employment. If the number of persons employed in this sector had not changed from 1929 to 1969 while all other determinants of national income (including average hours and other characteristics of labor in this sector) had nevertheless changed as they did, the growth rate of national income would have been lower than it was by 2.94 percentage points in this sector alone and by 0.37 percentage points in the economy as a whole. Similarly, if there had been no reduction in hours per worker in this sector, the 1929–69 growth rates of sector and total national income would have been raised by 0.21 and 0.03 percentage points, respectively.

---

13. The statistical procedure is slightly defective in that, while Table 3-4, column 2, holds the weights of industry components constant, column 3 does not. Also, OBE's division of employment between full-time and part-time workers may differ from that implied by the average hours index. Consequently, the breakdown of column 2 between columns 3 and 4 is inexact.

14. Because of interaction terms previously described, the sum of the growth rates of the separate indexes falls short of the growth rate of national income, but the difference is so trivial that it often does not appear when growth rates are rounded to two decimal points. The component growth rates have been adjusted when necessary to avoid a discrepancy.

**Table 3-5. General Government (Excluding Work Relief), Households, and Institutions:
Contributions of Sources to Growth Rates of Sector and Total National Income, Eight Selected Periods, 1929–69**
Based on data in 1958 dollars

| Period | National income (1) | Employment (2) | Effect of changes in hours | | | Other labor characteristics (6) |
			Total (3)	Average hours (4)	Implied efficiency offset (5)	
			Contributions to sector growth rate			
Long periods						
1929–69	3.41	2.94	−0.21	−0.67	0.46	0.68
1929–48	3.22	2.27	−0.26	−1.01	0.75	1.21
1948–69	3.59	3.56	−0.18	−0.37	0.19	0.21
Shorter periods						
1929–41	3.98	2.84	−0.04	−1.02	0.98	1.18
1941–48	1.92	1.31	−0.64	−1.00	0.36	1.25
1948–53	6.78	6.39	−0.09	−0.19	0.10	0.48
1953–64	1.89	2.16	−0.20	−0.63	0.43	−0.07
1964–69	4.23	3.90	−0.24	0.00	−0.24	0.57
			Contributions to growth rate of whole economy			
Long periods						
1929–69	0.43	0.37	−0.03	−0.09	0.06	0.09
1929–48	0.42	0.29	−0.03	−0.13	0.10	0.16
1948–69	0.47	0.47	−0.03	−0.05	0.02	0.03
Shorter periods						
1929–41	0.54	0.39	−0.01	−0.14	0.13	0.16
1941–48	0.27	0.18	−0.09	−0.14	0.05	0.18
1948–53	0.96	0.91	−0.02	−0.03	0.01	0.07
1953–64	0.27	0.31	−0.03	−0.09	0.06	−0.01
1964–69	0.55	0.51	−0.03	0.00	−0.03	0.07

Sources: Column 1, Table 3-3; columns 2–6, contributions to sector growth rate, computed from Table 3-4; and contributions to growth rate of whole economy, obtained by allocating column 1 in proportion to values of contributions to sector growth rate.

The figure for the whole economy would have been 0.09 in the absence of an efficiency offset to the effects of shorter hours in the sector, but the estimates imply that greater output per hour by full-time workers resulting from their shortened hours offset 0.06 points of this amount. In this sector, as already stressed, the estimate is no more than an implication of the method by which output is measured.[15]

The category shown as "other labor characteristics," which results from compositional shifts among segments in which base-year earnings differ, is too broad to be combined with components isolated in the business sector, and in any case has a different meaning. However, it is not wholly unrelated to changes in the "age-sex" composition of hours worked, and in the composition of workers by level of education, because these characteristics of workers are partly responsible for the differences among segments in base-year average

earnings. An investigation of the reasons for base-year earnings differences among the segments separately deflated by OBE and detailed tracing of the effects of shifting weights would be required to permit the contribution of "other labor characteristics" to be further allocated. However, the large rise in the index for this component before 1948 is known to reflect mainly the declining weight of employment in private households and in certain types of nonprofit organization in which average earnings are low; low earnings in these segments are associated with a labor force that both has a low level of education and is largely female. Prior to 1948 it would not be unreasonable to divide the contribution of "other labor characteristics" equally between changes in age-sex composition and education.

The index for "other labor characteristics" moves upward moderately over the 1948–69 period as a whole.[16] There was an extraordinary increase in employment in components in which the level of education of employed persons is par-

15. In one period, 1964–69, the estimate yields a small negative efficiency offset when there is no change in average hours. This is not an inconsistency because it results from a change in the implied mix of workers among full-time and part-time jobs.

16. Between 1953 and 1964, however, the movement is downward.

ticularly high (a characteristic that raises base-year average earnings).[17] In this sense the rise in education of persons employed in the sector raised even measured output per worker in the sector. Among other shifts in the composition of employment were irregular changes in military employment and a persistent rise in the female share of civilian employment.

Services of Dwellings Sector

National income in the housing sector depends not only upon the supply of dwellings and the costs associated with their maintenance and operation but also upon the division of the housing stock between units that are occupied and those that are vacant.[18] It is interesting and possible to separate the two determinants.

OBE worksheets provide series needed to obtain the space rental value of vacant nonfarm dwellings as well as that of occupied units (which is included in national product).[19] The space rental value of all nonfarm units can therefore be obtained in current prices and, because the price deflator is the same as for occupied units, in 1958 prices as well. (Vacant farm units are omitted entirely.) Among the years covered by this study the ratio of the space rent of occupied nonfarm dwellings to that of all nonfarm dwellings was lowest in 1929, which followed a building boom of excessive proportions, and highest in 1947, when the housing shortage was at its peak. The subsequent decline was abrupt until 1952.

Vacancies affect national income originating in the dwellings sector by about the same absolute (dollar) amount as they affect space rent because the deductions from rent—depreciation, maintenance costs, and taxes—continue when units are vacant and hence are little affected by vacancies. Consequently, it is possible to compute what

national income in constant prices in the sector would have been if all nonfarm units were occupied, or if the ratio of space rent on occupied nonfarm dwellings to space rent on all nonfarm dwellings had been at any specified level.

Table 3-6, column 1, shows in index form nonlabor national income originating in the sector, valued in 1958 prices. Column 2 shows what this index would have been if the ratio of the space rent of occupied nonfarm dwellings to the space rent of all nonfarm dwellings had been the same as it was in the base year 1958. It is clear that the huge rise in housing stock was the dominant influence on the postwar rise in dwellings national income. Column 3 shows the effects of variations from 1958 in the occupancy ratio upon nonlabor national income originating in the sector. This series rises from 92.5 in 1929 to 108.0 in 1947,

Table 3-6. Services of Dwellings: Indexes of Sector Output and Its Determinants, 1929, 1940–41, and 1947–69
1958 = 100

Year	Sector national income (1)	Sector national income at constant (1958) occupancy ratio (2)	Effect of changes in occupancy ratio (3)
1929	21.7	23.5	92.5
1940	21.8	23.3	93.6
1941	24.3	25.2	96.5
1947	40.8	37.8	108.0
1948	43.5	40.7	107.0
1949	50.0	47.6	105.1
1950	53.7	50.8	105.6
1951	59.8	58.4	102.4
1952	65.9	64.6	102.0
1953	72.0	70.8	101.7
1954	78.2	77.0	101.6
1955	83.8	82.8	101.2
1956	88.0	87.3	100.8
1957	93.8	93.5	100.3
1958	100.0	100.0	100.0
1959	103.3	103.5	99.9
1960	113.5	113.9	99.6
1961	119.2	119.5	99.7
1962	128.0	128.5	99.6
1963	138.0	138.7	99.5
1964	150.2	151.4	99.2
1965	163.6	165.5	98.9
1966	173.5	175.1	99.1
1967	184.9	185.7	99.6
1968	193.3	193.5	99.9
1969	204.0	203.9	100.0

Sources: Column 1, computed from data underlying Table 3-2, column 5; columns 2 and 3, see text for derivation.

17. These components are the provision of public and nonprofit education (elementary, secondary, and college). Data in Chapter 4 and Appendix I show, in fact, that much of the postwar increase in the number of college-educated adult workers in the economy as a whole has been directed toward the teaching of young people.

18. Units, such as seasonal dwellings, that are reserved for the use of their owners or tenants are treated as if occupied in the national accounts, and their rental value is included in personal consumption expenditures. I define them as "occupied" in the present discussion.

19. The ratio of "space rental value" to "contract rental value" (which includes costs of facilities and utilities) is assumed to be the same for vacant as for occupied nonfarm dwellings in this calculation.

then falls back to 102.0 by 1952.[20] Changes are then slightly downward until 1965 and slightly upward thereafter.

The upper portion of Table 3-7 divides the growth rate of national income in the dwellings sector itself between the effects of changes in the supply of dwellings and the effects of changes in the occupancy rate. The lower portion provides a similar division of the contribution of the dwellings sector to the growth of total national income.[21]

Housing has been a very fast-growing sector of the economy ever since 1941. It has contributed far more to the growth of national income than to its level. Table 3-7 makes it clear that the growth of the housing supply itself has been by far the dominant element in this development. Changes in the occupancy ratio, which may be regarded as a component of the change in output per unit of input in the economy as a whole (see tables in Chapter 9), had a relatively minor effect but did contribute appreciably to differences between certain periods.

20. It fluctuates more than a similar series for space rental value because national income in the sector runs at a much lower level while the effects on the two series of changes in the occupancy ratio are the same in dollar amount.

21. The procedures were the same as those used to secure sources of growth estimates for general government, households, and institutions.

Table 3-7. Services of Dwellings: Contributions of Sources to Growth Rates of Sector and Total National Income, Eight Selected Periods, 1929–69
Based on data in 1958 dollars

Period	National income (1)	Quantity of housing (2)	Effect of changes in occupancy ratio (3)
Contributions to sector growth rate			
Long periods			
1929–69	5.76	5.56	0.20
1929–48	3.72	2.95	0.77
1948–69	7.64	7.96	−0.32
Shorter periods			
1929–41	0.95	0.59	0.36
1941–48	8.64	7.14	1.50
1948–53	10.62	11.63	−1.01
1953–64	6.90	7.13	−0.23
1964–69	6.35	6.19	0.16
Contributions to growth rate of whole economy			
Long periods			
1929–69	0.20	0.19	0.01
1929–48	0.08	0.06	0.02
1948–69	0.28	0.29	−0.01
Shorter periods			
1929–41	0.02	0.01	0.01
1941–48	0.17	0.14	0.03
1948–53	0.28	0.31	−0.03
1953–64	0.26	0.27	−0.01
1964–69	0.30	0.29	0.01

Sources: Column 1, Table 3-3, column 3; columns 2 and 3, contributions to sector growth rates, computed from Table 3-6, columns 2 and 3, and contributions to growth rate of the whole economy, obtained by allocating column 1 in proportion to values of sector growth rates.

CHAPTER FOUR

❯❯❯✕❮❮❮

Labor Input in Nonresidential Business

❯❯❯✕❮❮❮

More than four-fifths of all production takes place in the nonresidential business sector. This chapter begins the analysis of the sources of growth of the national income created in this part of the economy. The determinants of growth in nonresidential business itself are of separate interest because the sector is much more homogeneous than the whole economy with respect both to measurement of output and to the motivations and behavior of producing units.

Sources of growth in this sector will be divided into two broad groups: changes in inputs and changes in output per unit of total input. The analysis of inputs rests on the general proposition that enterprises seek to minimize costs of production and hence to use inputs of different types in proportions that minimize their costs. If they succeed in doing so, or if errors by individual enterprises are offsetting, the earnings of different types of inputs will be proportional to their marginal products. The presumption of this study is that, on the average for all enterprises in the sector, the tendency toward proportionality of factor prices and marginal products under conditions of reasonably high employment is sufficiently strong for relative earnings to provide an adequate measure of the relative marginal products of different inputs, and hence of the weights appropriate for combining them.[1] Relative earnings are used as

1. See *Why Growth Rates Differ,* Chapter 4, for a fuller discussion of the topic of this paragraph. The presumption is strengthened in the present study by elimination of government, private households, and institutions from the universe within which it is applied. (For full citation of *Why Growth Rates Differ,* see Chap. 1, note 2, of this book.)

weights not only to combine total inputs of labor, capital, and land to arrive at a measure of total input, but also to weight different types of input within these broad categories to arrive at a comprehensive index for each of the three. This chapter is concerned only with labor input. Chapter 5 measures other inputs and total input, after which changes in output per unit of input are examined.

Labor input is the same in nonresidential business as it is in the whole business sector because the services of dwellings sector, as defined, does not use labor. Only persons employed in general government, households, and institutions are excluded. Consequently, the data in this chapter are usually described as referring to "business" employment.

My measure of labor input does not treat employed persons or the total hours they work as a homogeneous mass. Its construction recognizes that hours worked by different groups contribute different average amounts to the value of output; relative earnings are used as weights to combine components. Thus labor input takes into account not only the number of persons employed in business and the hours they work, but also the personal characteristics of workers that affect their contribution to production, if they are characteristics whose distribution among the employed population changes.

I measure employment, hours worked (including a distinction between full-time and part-time workers, and an allowance for the effect of differences in hours of work upon output per hour), and the distribution of total hours worked among persons classified by age and sex and by level of education. I make the specific assumption that the distribution of the population by innate ability and academic aptitude has not changed. I introduce the convention that differences in the average hours worked by full-time workers of the same sex who are employed in farming, as nonfarm self-employed or unpaid family workers, or as nonfarm wage and salary workers, are not to be construed as an indication that labor input per worker differs among these three groups. Some characteristics of workers that may affect output that I do not attempt to measure are discussed briefly at the end of this chapter.

In principle, one could measure labor input by: (1) subdividing workers employed in business among a vast number of groups that are homogeneous with respect to hours worked and all their measurable personal characteristics that affect output; (2) constructing an index of the number in each group each year; and (3) weighting the various indexes by the value of labor, as measured by earnings, of workers in each group. But this is not feasible. Instead, I consider employment and the various characteristics of employed persons in sequence.[2] The various measures refer to labor employed in the business sector.[3]

Readers who may prefer a less comprehensive definition of labor input than the one adopted here can nevertheless take advantage of the statistical findings. Because a separate index is shown for each characteristic included, one or more can be omitted without difficulty. The effect of changes in average working hours is shown in three parts; a reader who prefers a different classification of growth sources or different assumptions as to the effect of hours changes can omit any or all components.[4]

The labor input measure presented is designed for use in measuring the effect of changes in the quantity and composition of work upon *output*. The series does not measure the *disutility* or welfare cost of work performed. An attempt to measure disutility would require a completely different approach.

Employment

The starting point for labor input measurement is employment. Derivation of the employment series for the business sector is described in full detail in Appendix C.[5] Employment is defined as the number of *persons* employed. The movement of the series nevertheless is based largely on data from the U.S. Office of Business Economics (OBE) that measure jobs rather than persons. The Current Population Survey (CPS), the only direct source of estimates of persons employed, was used solely to establish the average employment level. As explained in Appendix C, the series constructed provides estimates of the number of

persons employed that are statistically more consistent with the measurement of output, and judged also to be more accurate, than the CPS estimates. Table 4-1, column 1, shows the employment series in index form. Series including and excluding Alaska and Hawaii are linked at 1960.

Employment in the business sector is affected not only by influences that determine total employment—the size of the population and its distribution by sex and age, labor force participation rates, and the percentage of the labor force employed—but also by the proportion of total employment that is absorbed by general government, households, and institutions. The business share of total employment was 86.5 percent in 1929 and 84.0 percent in 1947 but only 76.7 percent in 1963 and 75.4 percent in 1969. Because of these sharp changes, the course of business employment has been very different from that of total employment.

Business employment increased by 8.7 million, or 21.2 percent, from 1929 to 1947, and by 13.0 million, or 26.0 percent, from 1947 to 1969.[6] The annual growth rate of business employment was almost the same in the two periods as a whole: 1.07 from 1929 to 1947 and 1.06 from 1947 to 1969. However, during a long span of years in the middle of the postwar period business employment showed no increase; the 1956 level was not exceeded until 1963. Most of the entire postwar expansion occurred after that date. From 1947 to 1963 business employment increased by only 4.3 million, or 8.7 percent, whereas the increase in the six years from 1963 to 1969 was 8.7 million, or 15.9 percent. The annual growth rate was 0.52 percent from 1947 to 1963 and 2.49 percent from 1963 to 1969. About one-half of the difference of approximately two percentage points between these rates appears to reflect cyclical influences and the other half changes in labor force growth and in the importance of employment elsewhere in the economy.[7]

Average and Total Hours of Work

An index of the average weekly hours worked by persons employed in the business sector is shown in Table 4-1, column 2. Column 3 provides an

---

2. The order in which characteristics are considered only trivially affects the measurement of labor input. As explained at the end of this chapter, it has more effect on the measurement of its individual aspects. This is particularly true of the point in the analysis at which weighting by sex is introduced.

3. Some of the measures developed do not refer *exactly* to persons employed in the business sector, but in all cases the universe analyzed differs so little from the business sector that appreciable errors from lack of exact correspondence are unlikely.

4. Appendix R (pp. 340–43) discusses these possibilities.

5. Employment in the business sector is equal to the sum of columns 2, 3, and 5 of Table C-1. Totals are given in Table D-2.

6. These figures are adjusted to eliminate the increase due to addition of Alaska and Hawaii to the employment series.

7. According to estimates in Table 7-3, column 5, the growth rate of potential employment in the sector was 0.76 percent in 1947–63 and 1.76 percent in 1963–69.

Table 4-1. Nonresidential Business: Indexes of Sector Labor Input, 1929, 1940–41, and 1947–69[a]

1958 = 100

					Efficiency of an hour's work as affected by changes in hours due to:			
Year	Employment (1)	Average weekly hours (2)	Total weekly hours (3)	Age-sex composition of total hours (4)	Intragroup changes (5)	Specified intergroup shifts (6)	Amount of education (7)	Labor input (8)
1929	79.26	122.82	97.34	99.60	92.71	96.67	83.71	72.74
1940	78.42	110.47	86.62	101.06	98.58	96.66	90.42	75.42
1941	85.62	111.31	95.32	100.22	98.23	97.46	90.73	82.98
1947	96.08	106.87	102.69	100.00	99.02	98.74	93.30	93.68
1948	97.39	106.15	103.38	99.80	99.00	98.80	93.85	94.71
1949	94.07	104.86	98.63	99.76	99.37	98.51	94.67	91.18
1950	96.38	104.99	101.19	99.72	99.26	98.74	95.20	94.15
1951	100.21	104.84	105.06	99.93	99.14	99.25	95.54	98.70
1952	101.35	104.37	105.76	100.14	99.72	99.40	96.08	100.86
1953	102.85	103.77	106.72	100.33	99.87	99.64	96.60	102.93
1954	99.75	102.68	102.43	100.67	99.62	99.47	97.39	99.51
1955	101.97	103.10	105.13	100.34	99.84	99.74	97.80	102.73
1956	104.07	102.38	106.55	99.88	99.64	99.98	98.31	104.23
1957	103.87	100.87	104.77	99.78	100.07	100.12	98.95	103.64
1958	100.00	100.00	100.00	100.00	100.00	100.00	100.00	100.00
1959	102.27	100.72	103.00	99.74	99.91	100.24	100.58	103.48
1960	102.94	100.05	102.99	99.41	99.91	100.32	101.29	103.94
1961	101.99	99.48	101.45	99.49	100.08	100.30	102.11	103.45
1962	103.56	99.83	103.39	99.28	99.66	100.50	102.59	105.47
1963	104.45	99.55	103.97	99.35	99.56	100.74	103.04	106.75
1964	106.35	99.45	105.78	98.91	99.49	100.87	103.51	108.68
1965	109.66	99.60	109.21	98.23	99.30	101.07	104.14	112.12
1966	113.56	98.71	112.11	97.60	99.70	101.35	104.71	115.77
1967	114.96	97.25	111.80	97.58	100.06	101.51	105.44	116.84
1968	117.61	96.80	113.85	97.34	100.17	101.58	106.12	119.67
1969	121.08	96.18	116.45	96.62	100.25	101.69	106.71	122.40

Sources: Indexes are computed from data contained in the following tables: Column 1, Table C-1, columns 2, 3, and 5; column 2, Table E-1, column 8; column 3, Table E-1, column 4; column 4, Tables F-2 and F-5; columns 5 and 6, see text for derivation; column 7, Table I-21, column 5; column 8, computed as the product of columns 3 through 7. See text for further explanation.

a. Series excluding and including Alaska and Hawaii were linked at 1960.

index of total weekly hours, which is equal to the product of the employment index and the average hours index. Appendix E provides a full description of procedures followed to obtain the estimates.

My estimates of average hours worked in the 1947–69 period are derived by use of U.S. Bureau of Labor Statistics (BLS) estimates. BLS developed its estimates in the course of compiling its series for total hours in the private economy that is based mainly on establishment reports. My estimates of total hours in the business economy are the sum of estimates for three groups of workers. They are: (1) all farm workers, (2) nonfarm self-employed and unpaid family workers, and (3) nonfarm wage and salary workers employed in the business sector. Average hours for each group, derived from BLS data, were multiplied

by my employment estimates, given in Table C-1. Published BLS data for nonfarm wage and salary workers measure average hours *paid for* per *job;* they were adjusted with the aid of unpublished BLS estimates to measure average hours *worked* per *person* employed. Total weekly hours worked in the business sector were divided by my estimates of employment in the business sector to obtain average hours. The data for total and average hours from which the indexes are computed are presented in Table E-1 of Appendix E.

Average weekly hours worked per person employed in the business sector declined 13.0 percent from 1929 to 1947 and 10.0 percent from 1947 to 1969. In the postwar period, the decline was much sharper before the late 1950s and after 1965 than in the interim years. Average hours are moderately sensitive to fluctuations in business activity, and they rose in the year following each of the recession years 1949, 1954, 1958, and 1961. The persistence of the postwar downtrend is indicated by the fact that average hours failed to decline in only one other postwar year, 1965. The average annual rate of decline from 1947 to 1969 was 0.48 percent. This decline was nearly half as large as the 1.06 percent annual rate of increase in employment, and total hours worked increased at an average rate of only 0.57 percent. The postwar increase in total hours worked in the business sector was even more concentrated in years after 1963 than the employment increase. Their growth rate was 0.08 percent from 1947 to 1963 and 1.91 percent from 1963 to 1969.

The index of average hours in the business sector provides no indication of changes that occurred in the average hours worked by homogeneous groups of workers. Neither does a series for average hours in itself provide any indication of the effect of changing hours upon labor input or output. I shall consider these subjects as soon as the effects of age and sex on labor input have been measured.

The Age-Sex Composition of Hours Worked

The proportions of total hours worked by males and females, and within each sex by individuals of different ages, change over time. An average hour worked has a different value in each demographic group. It is necessary to develop an index to allow for the effect of changes in these proportions.

The calculation of such an index rests on the assumption that average earnings in the ten age-sex groups distinguished are proportional to the marginal products of labor, per hour worked, of these groups. If this assumption is correct, it is necessary and legitimate to consider an average hour worked by a demographic group whose average hourly earnings are twice as high as those of another group to represent twice as much labor input.

Estimated differentials in hourly earnings in the business sector are indicated in Table 4-2, column 1. They are expressed as percentages of average earnings for all hours worked in the business sector. However, this method of presentation does not affect my results; *relative* earnings of the ten groups are what matter. In only two groups,

Table 4-2. Nonresidential Business: Average Hourly Earnings (1966) and Percentage Distributions of Total Hours and Earnings (1968), by Sex and Age

Sex and age group	Hourly earnings as percentage of average for all groups, 1966 (1)	Percentage of total hours worked, 1968 (2)	Percentage of total earnings, 1968 (3)
Male			
14–19	36	3.97	1.44
20–24	77	6.99	5.42
25–34	114	16.22	18.61
35–64	128	41.62	53.62
65 and over	88	2.49	2.21
Female			
14–19	49	2.25	1.11
20–24	59	4.34	2.58
25–34	68	5.11	3.50
35–64	68	16.23	11.11
65 and over	54	0.78	0.42
Total	100	100.00	100.00

Sources: Table F-2, column 1, and Table F-5. Percentages are rounded and may not add to 100.00.

males in the 25–34 and 35–64 age brackets, are earnings above the average for all workers.

My assumption implies that an average hour's work by males 35 to 64 years of age, for example, is 2.17 times as valuable as an average hour's work by females 20 to 24 years of age (128 ÷ 59). The assumption is valid insofar as earnings differentials among age-sex groups reflect differences in the value of the work that is actually performed. It does not matter whether these differences result from differences in the value of the work the groups are able and willing to do (because of variations in skill, training, experience, and strength; in attitudes; in home, marital, and school responsibilities that inhibit the assumption of responsibility on the job or working at inconvenient hours; in continuity of labor force participation; and the like) or from failure to use abilities that are present. Such failure may occur because abilities are not recognized or because of discrimination in employment practices with respect to hiring, training, promotion, or dismissal so that one group or another cannot reach its full work capability. Potential abilities that are unused do not affect output; a newsboy might make a competent publisher but his unused potentiality has no more effect than if it did not exist.[8] An

8. An improvement *over time* in the allocation of workers (classified by age and sex or by other characteristics) among jobs could raise the average productivity of all workers and hence total output. If such a change occurred I would not wish to classify the gain as a contribution of labor input but instead as a contribution of output per unit of input (specifically, of improved resource allocation).

error is introduced into the calculation by discrimination only insofar as relative earnings are affected by differences in pay for identical work. My use of earnings weights implies a judgment that this type of discrimination, failure to provide "equal pay for equal work" when all costs are taken into account, does not greatly affect differentials in earnings among age-sex groups.[9]

The derivation of the earnings differentials is described in detail in Appendix F, Part 1. The differentials, which refer primarily to 1966 although some 1967 data entered the procedure, were used throughout the period of my estimates because there seemed to be no substantial change in them. At least, I was unable to derive differentials for other dates that could confidently be regarded as diverging from those of 1966–67 because of a real change in differentials as distinguished from estimating errors.[10] The earnings data on which the differentials in Table 4-2, column 1, are based refer to civilians employed in private industries, excluding government enterprises, rather than to persons employed in the business sector; there is little reason to suppose that this affects the differentials appreciably. The hourly earnings differentials used as weights to combine groups are estimates. Possible errors in the weights—both in the data for 1966–67 and in the assumption that differentials were stable over time—are greatest for the 14–19 age group of each sex. Fortunately, no plausible change in the weights for these groups would change appreciably the labor input index I shall calculate because this age group obtains a very small share of total earnings. The most important differentials, those between males and females in the middle age ranges, are securely founded.

Columns 2 and 3 of Table 4-2 indicate the importance of the various age-sex groups in the business sector in a recent year. They show percentage shares of the groups in total hours and in total earnings. It may be observed that males 25 to 64 years of age represent a higher proportion of total hours and earnings in the business sector than in the civilian economy as a whole. Both civilian general government and private households employ much higher proportions of females than business.

Percentage distributions of total hours worked, by sex and age, are shown in Table F-5 for each year covered by the analysis. Their derivation is fully described in Appendix F, Part 2. The distributions are based on data from the Current Population Survey because establishment reports do not provide detail of this type on a comprehensive basis.[11]

An index measuring the effect of changes in the age-sex composition of man-hours worked upon labor input was obtained by weighing each age-sex group's percentage of hours worked by its average hourly earnings. (See Appendix F, Part 3.) The index is shown in Table 4-1, column 4. It is equivalent to an index of the average hourly earnings in the business sector that would have resulted if there had been no change in average hourly earnings within each age-sex group. The index increased 0.40 percent from 1929 to 1947 and declined 3.38 percent from 1947 to 1969, equivalent to growth rates of 0.02 and −0.15, respectively. Most of the postwar reduction occurred after 1963: the 1963–69 growth rate was −0.47, indicating a large reduction in the proportion of total business hours worked by males in the prime working ages.

Multiplication of the age-sex composition index by the index of total weekly hours worked (Table 4-1, column 3) would yield an index (not shown) of labor input that reflects the aspects considered thus far. This index is precisely the same as the index that would be obtained by measuring the total hours worked by each age-sex group and weighting the total hours of each group by average hourly earnings.[12]

The index exhibits a fairly distinct cyclical pattern: it tends to rise in recession years because recession curtails most strongly hours worked by young people. Aside from cyclical fluctuations, the index has changed course twice during the

---

9. See *Why Growth Rates Differ*, pp. 70–108, for additional discussion, and for evidence of the similarity of differentials in various countries.

10. If differentials changed substantially over time I would change weights periodically, and link fixed-weight indexes, as I do in combining labor and capital input.

11. The distributions of hours worked by age and sex in Table F-5 actually represent hours worked by civilians other than nonfarm wage and salary workers employed by government and private households, rather than hours worked in the business sector. Thus hours worked by persons employed by nonprofit institutions are inappropriately included and hours worked by persons employed in government enterprises excluded. The numbers in these groups are small proportions of the totals.

An effort was made to eliminate discontinuities that changes in procedures introduce into CPS data. However, changes in the distributions from 1952 to 1953 and from 1966 to 1967 may still be affected.

12. Statistical implementation of this procedure would require allocation of the total weekly hours shown in Table E-1, column 4, by the percentages shown in Table F-5.

postwar period. It declined each year from 1947 to 1950, rose each year from 1950 to 1954, and thereafter declined until 1969. The 1954–69 decline was interrupted only in the recession years 1958 and 1961, and in 1963 (which was also a year in which unemployment increased). Cyclical fluctuations magnified the amplitude of the longer swings but probably did not alter the turning points.

Over the whole period since 1929, the dominant influence on the age-sex composition index has been the rising proportion of hours worked by females, which has tended to depress the index. The biggest and most consistent change has been among females in the 35–64 age bracket. Their percentage of the total increased from 10.4 percent in 1947 to 16.4 percent in 1969 and rose in every individual year except 1968.[13] From time to time, and notably from 1929 to 1940, the influence of the rise in hours worked by adult females has been more than offset by a reduction in the percentage of hours worked by teenagers.

The percentage of hours worked by males in the 35–64 bracket, the group that is largest and has the highest hourly earnings, dominates the movement of the index, and has moved rather closely with it. The percentage for this group was 43.3 in 1947, 42.8 in 1950, 44.5 in 1954, and 40.5 in 1969. Percentages for the only other group with above-average earnings, males 25–34, followed a generally similar course but with a low in 1951 and a high in 1953 (rather than in 1950 and 1954) and a renewed upturn after 1966. The decline from 1953 to 1966 was large: from 19.2 to 15.7 percent. The percentage for females 25–34 increased from 1947 to 1952, then declined until 1964, and since that date has risen sharply.

The shares of total hours worked by the remaining groups distinguished are much smaller. The postwar course of the percentage for males 65 and over was downward until 1966 and that for females 65 and over was upward until 1961. After these dates both trends were reversed for a time but were resumed in 1968 (in the case of females) and 1969 (in the case of males). The percentages worked by the young age groups, which embrace small age spans, are quite sensitive to changes in the age distribution of the population as well as to changes in school attendance

and, in the case of males, to the draft. Nevertheless, it can be observed that the shares of males and females 14–19 and 20–24 years of age all declined from 1947 or 1948 to a date in the middle or late 1950s, and then increased.

The Pattern of Changes in Hours

The average number of hours worked in a year by persons employed in the business sector has been measured, but it is more difficult to calculate the effect of changes in average hours upon the amount of work performed. Two types of question are involved. The first is essentially factual, although the facts are hard to obtain: What effect does a change in the average hours worked by a homogeneous group of workers have upon the amount of work they perform in an hour? The second is as much a matter of convenient classification as of fact and interpretation of data: If full-time workers shift from activities in which hours are long to activities in which they are shorter (perhaps because shorter hours are more efficient in the latter activities), do we wish to say that their input of labor declines?

Before turning to these questions, I indicate the general pattern of working hours and changes in them. I begin by dividing persons employed in the business sector among twelve groups. The first division is among three categories whose hours differ greatly: (1) nonfarm wage and salary workers, (2) nonfarm proprietors and unpaid family workers, and (3) persons employed on farms. Each of these groups is then divided by sex. Because the previous index introduced into the labor input measure a lower value for an average hour worked by females than by males, it will be necessary, for consistency, to treat the two sexes separately in all subsequent measures; the effect of any change upon the labor input content of an average hour worked by females must receive less weight than a similar percentage change for males. Also, average hours of the two sexes differ so much that division by sex is required merely to trace developments accurately. Finally, each of the resulting six groups is further divided between full-time workers and part-time workers, making twelve groups in all.[14] Appendix G de-

---

13. Data cited in this discussion are based on Table F-5. That table provides two series that overlap in 1966. Percentages cited for years prior to 1966 have been adjusted by the small difference between the two 1966 figures.

14. The age-sex index introduced different weights for each age group as well as for each sex, so that ideally average hours would be calculated separately for each age group within each of these twelve groups or, at least, within the two groups of full-time nonfarm wage and salary workers,

scribes the derivation of the annual estimates of employment, total weekly hours, and average weekly hours for each of the twelve groups distinguished, presented in Tables G-1, G-2, and G-3. In general, total employment and hours in the three major groups, which had been derived largely from establishment reports, were allocated among subgroups by use of CPS data.

The division between full-time and part-time workers, though difficult, is essential for any useful analysis of working hours. Average hours may change either because the hours of full-time workers change or because the proportions of full-time workers and part-time workers change. The implications for the efficiency of an hour's work are very different in the two cases. One major purpose of the division therefore is to derive a series that measures the average hours of full-time workers in each category.

My definition of full-time employment corresponds to that adopted by the Bureau of Labor Statistics in 1969 for members of the "full-time labor force employed on full-time schedules."[15] Full-time workers in any specific week consist of employed persons who actually worked thirty-five hours or more and those who usually do so but did not in that week because of "noneconomic reasons." Persons in the latter category may have worked one to thirty-four hours, or they may not have worked at all (in which case they appear in labor force statistics as "employed, with a job but not at work"). Noneconomic reasons for not working thirty-five hours or more include vacations, holidays, illness, and a miscellany of personal reasons, as well as bad weather and industrial disputes.

Part-time workers in any week include employed persons who usually work one to thirty-

four hours (whether they work part time by choice or because they could not find full-time jobs) and did so in that particular week; persons who usually work one to thirty-four hours but did not work at all for noneconomic reasons; and persons who usually work thirty-five hours or more but worked one to thirty-four hours for economic reasons. "Economic reasons" include slack work (the largest category), material shortages, and repairs to plant or equipment. Persons who work less than thirty-five hours because they start or end a job during the week are also in this category and are counted as part-time workers. Full-time workers plus part-time workers equal total employment. (Persons working no hours for economic reasons are not counted as employed, but as unemployed.)

Based on these definitions, the average hours of full-time workers decline if there is a reduction in the hours they work in a full week or if they take more time off from work for vacations, holidays, personal reasons, illness, or other noneconomic reasons. In the analysis to follow, I assume that changes in average hours of full-time workers affect efficiency in the same way whether they result from changes in full-week hours or in time off for noneconomic reasons.[16]

The numbers of persons in the six categories of full-time workers in a recent year, 1968, are shown in Table 4-3, column 1, and the average weekly hours they worked in column 2. The data show great differences among the categories in average hours worked, and also indicate that hours in most categories are rather long even after reduction for time not worked because of vacations, holidays, sickness, personal, and other reasons.[17] That reduction is substantial. Column 3 shows the estimated average weekly hours of persons at work thirty-five hours or more; they indicate the average hours that full-time workers

---

which are of most importance. Each age group would then be separately weighted. It is not possible to develop continuous time series in this detail. However, the omission cannot appreciably impair the further analysis because, *within* the categories of full-time workers distinguished, average hours do not vary much by age; this is shown by information available for certain dates. The hours of full-time teenagers are moderately below average, but few full-time workers are teenagers so they scarcely affect the full-time averages by sex. Observed changes in age distribution are too small to influence changes in average full-time hours (within each category for each sex) in the absence of big differences among age groups in average hours of full-time workers.

15. BLS, however, does not provide a corresponding series for average hours per person employed. The data for average hours of "workers on full-time schedules" published in the CPS reports refer to average hours of persons at work, which are longer.

16. It seems reasonable enough to assume that an increase in time off for vacations, holidays, and various personal reasons, and for illness if due to a rising proclivity to stay at home when ill or to feign illness, will affect efficiency in a way similar to a reduction in full-week hours. At least, I do not know how to improve upon this assumption. These are the chief factors governing the trend of time lost from work. The average hours series is also affected by changes in the actual incidence of illness, and in time lost because of industrial disputes and bad weather. Time lost for these reasons, for which the case for an efficiency offset is less clear, tends to be erratic in the short run. However, it does not appear to affect significantly annual data for large aggregates.

17. Hours of nonfarm wage and salary workers were even longer in all other years covered by this study except 1958 than they were in 1968.

Table 4-3. Nonresidential Business: Average Hours of Full-Time Workers and Persons at Work Thirty-Five Hours or More per Week, 1968

| | | Final estimates | | Estimates based on CPS, average weekly hours of: | |
| | | | Average weekly hours of: | | |
Type of worker and sex	Number of full-time workers (thousands) (1)	Persons employed full-time (2)	Persons at work 35 hours or more (3)	Persons employed full time (4)	Persons at work 35 hours or more (5)
Nonfarm wage and salary workers					
Male	30,153	42.4	45.7	42.1	45.4
Female	13,603	37.9	41.2	37.6	40.9
Nonfarm self-employed and unpaid family workers					
Male	4,111	53.5	57.6	50.2	54.3
Female	1,200	52.3	55.3	49.1	52.1
Farm workers					
Male	2,385	55.5	61.2	53.8	59.5
Female	326	47.7	49.9	46.3	48.5

Sources: Columns 1 and 2, Tables G-1, G-2, and G-3; column 3, figures are approximations, obtained by adding columns 2 and 5, and subtracting column 4; column 4, data for persons 16 years of age and over were calculated from CPS data, described on page 198; column 5, calculated from CPS data in the same way as column 4.

Note. The stubs to the table rows describe the classification followed in the final estimates. The estimates based on CPS follow a slightly different classification. The first two rows of figures refer to wage and salary workers in nonagricultural industries except government and private household workers. The last two rows include persons employed in agricultural service industries as well as on farms.

worked in a typical (as distinguished from an "average") week in 1968. Persons in all categories, except female nonfarm wage and salary workers, averaged more than forty-five hours in such a week. These data are consistent with my estimates of persons employed and total hours, which were derived from establishment data. The last two columns of Table 4-3 show alternative estimates of average hours derived directly from CPS household survey data. They do not differ from my adjusted estimates enough for the choice between them to alter the general picture either of the length of hours in the business sector or of the size of differentials among groups.

Changes in average hours are summarized in Table 4-4. Column 1 reproduces the index of average hours of all persons employed in the business sector that was presented in Table 4-1, column 2; it dropped 10.0 percent from 1947 to 1969. An index of the average hours of persons employed full time, presented in column 2, declines only two-thirds as much in this period because the depressing effect of the increase in part-time employment is eliminated. The decline in this index, too, is in large measure the result of shifts in employment composition. Indexes for none of the six component groups (shown in columns 3 to 8) decline as much as the general average. The index for male nonfarm wage and salary workers, by far the largest group, declined only 2.3 percent

from 1947 to 1969; indeed, there was little change in the hours of any of the male groups.

Columns 9 and 10 show indexes of the average hours of all workers, and of all full-time workers, computed with fixed employment weights.[18] They indicate the effect of changes in hours *within* the groups (twelve groups for all workers, six for full-time workers) as distinguished from the effect of changes in the relative size of groups. From 1947 to 1969 the index for all workers drops 3.4 percent, that for full-time workers 2.9 percent. Thus most of the 10.0 percent drop observed in average hours during the postwar period is a reflection of changes in employment composition rather than of changes in hours within more homogeneous groups. Shifts in composition have been from full-time to part-time employment, from male to female employment, and from farm employment and nonfarm self-employment to nonfarm wage and salary employment; all had the effect of shortening average hours in the business sector as a whole.

The pattern of change from 1929 to 1947, which spans years in which really major changes in hours occurred, had been quite different. Aver-

18. The average of 1950 and 1966 employment weights are used for this calculation. For full-time workers, the groups distinguished are those shown in Table 4-4, columns 3 to 8. The calculation for all workers also distinguishes the six corresponding groups of part-time workers.

Table 4-4. Nonresidential Business: Indexes of Average Weekly Hours Worked by Employed Persons, by Type of Worker and Sex, 1929, 1940–41, and 1947–69[a]

1958 = 100

			Full-time workers							
			Nonfarm wage and salary workers		Nonfarm self-employed and unpaid family workers		Farm workers		Standardized indexes	
Year	All workers (1)	All (2)	Male (3)	Female (4)	Male (5)	Female (6)	Male (7)	Female (8)	All workers (9)	All full-time workers (10)
1929	122.82	118.09	116.64	115.15	111.30	115.62	106.79	108.74	112.76	114.82
1940	110.47	107.56	104.36	103.03	99.59	103.48	102.92	104.83	102.93	103.48
1941	111.31	107.33	105.33	103.97	100.51	104.43	102.92	104.85	103.67	104.34
1947	106.87	103.79	102.61	101.26	97.89	101.71	104.29	106.23	101.70	102.05
1948	106.15	103.77	102.58	101.32	98.05	101.77	104.41	106.34	102.19	102.06
1949	104.86	103.43	102.16	101.06	98.20	102.00	102.51	105.63	102.34	101.62
1950	104.99	103.68	103.08	101.97	98.11	101.85	102.07	104.49	102.87	102.27
1951	104.84	103.09	102.94	101.34	98.22	102.04	103.03	105.26	102.41	102.15
1952	104.37	101.72	101.71	100.71	98.13	102.02	100.91	102.63	101.15	101.11
1953	103.77	100.86	100.59	99.82	98.07	101.88	101.98	103.99	100.46	100.37
1954	102.68	101.63	101.21	100.68	98.99	104.24	101.38	104.10	100.65	101.00
1955	103.10	101.27	101.61	101.14	98.19	102.02	100.82	95.21	100.43	101.06
1956	102.38	101.02	101.18	100.63	99.63	104.41	100.87	103.15	100.66	100.98
1957	100.87	99.82	100.17	99.29	100.43	101.50	99.33	95.43	99.84	99.91
1958	100.00	100.00	100.00	100.00	100.00	100.00	100.00	100.00	100.00	100.00
1959	100.72	100.32	101.26	100.20	99.49	99.16	99.15	102.01	100.03	100.62
1960	100.05	99.89	100.90	98.56	100.06	101.67	99.84	104.14	99.65	100.25
1961	99.48	99.82	101.18	98.63	99.48	100.27	98.57	102.69	99.70	100.21
1962	99.83	100.14	101.73	98.53	100.02	98.95	101.46	99.51	99.66	100.75
1963	99.55	99.98	102.01	99.28	100.49	95.20	101.53	104.05	99.76	100.84
1964	99.45	99.89	102.46	97.02	100.22	97.57	102.07	103.34	99.64	100.88
1965	99.60	99.95	102.44	97.82	101.07	99.44	102.91	101.17	99.99	101.23
1966	98.71	98.80	101.66	97.27	100.21	97.03	101.89	102.50	99.44	100.45
1967	97.25	97.56	100.57	96.03	98.30	97.98	102.04	102.35	98.49	99.41
1968	96.80	97.22	100.22	95.67	98.68	99.79	101.49	102.38	98.20	99.17
1969	96.18	96.97	100.29	95.82	98.00	97.14	101.57	104.63	98.23	99.14

Sources: Computed from data underlying Tables G-1, G-2, and G-3.
a. Series excluding and including Alaska and Hawaii are linked at 1960.

age hours of all workers in the business sector fell by 13.0 percent. Even after standardization, those of all workers fell by 9.8 percent and those of full-time workers by 11.1 percent. Most of these large reductions had occurred by 1941.

Effect of Changes in Hours within Labor Force Groups

The general shape of a curve relating hours to output for any given category of workers can be described with some assurance. If working hours are very long, the adverse effects of fatigue upon productivity are so great that output per worker increases if hours are shortened (and output per hour increases much more). The effects of fatigue are reinforced by a tendency for absenteeism,

which is costly, to be excessive when hours are long, and by important institutional factors. If hours are shortened further, a point is reached below which output per worker declines while output per hour continues to increase. At this stage, increases in output per hour only partially offset the reduction in hours worked. Finally, if hours become very short, the proportion of time spent in starting and stopping work may become so great that even output per hour declines as hours are shortened.

The difficulty in deriving such a curve empirically is that the evidence as to the location of the critical points is inadequate. Nevertheless, it is impossible to measure labor input at all, or to analyze sources of growth, without introducing assumptions about such curves. I have discussed available evidence and expert opinion elsewhere.[19] Here, I shall merely describe the assumptions and procedures I follow to estimate the effect of changes in working hours upon the work done in an hour. They yield an index of the efficiency offset to changes in average hours occurring *within* the groups of workers distinguished; this is the index shown in Table 4-1, column 5.

Some Assumptions and Their Implications

To secure the estimates, the following assumptions have been made for each labor force group: PART-TIME WORKERS. In 1969 there were 10.2 million part-time workers in the business sector, and they worked an average of 17.8 hours a week. Part-time workers accounted for 16.1 percent of business employment but only 7.4 percent of total hours worked. In earlier years their shares of total employment and hours were smaller.

Part-time workers are a heterogeneous group. They include both regular part-time workers (the bulk of the total) and those on part time for "economic reasons." The hours of regular part-time workers are rarely the same as those an establishment operates. Hours worked are too short for a reduction to be likely to affect efficiency by reducing fatigue or similar factors. On the other hand, because of the special role many play in meeting peak daily, hourly, or seasonal labor needs, it is unlikely that if hours drop efficiency drops because of time spent in starting and stopping work. I assume that (insofar as changes in hours are concerned) changes in total labor input of part-time workers of each sex are proportional to changes in the total hours they work. An index of labor input per person employed is therefore the same as an index of average hours, and labor input per hour does not change.

Calculations to implement this assumption are simplified by combining part-time workers of each sex in the three labor force groups. This was permissible because, for this calculation, an hour's work by a part-time worker in any of the groups isolated is considered to be the same amount of labor input.

FULL-TIME NONFARM WAGE AND SALARY WORKERS. Full-time wage and salary workers employed in nonfarm industries are much the largest of the groups distinguished; in 1969 they represented 71.2 percent of business employment and 75.3 percent of total hours.

19. *Why Growth Rates Differ*, pp. 59–64.

I judge that, throughout the period covered in this study, hours for this group have been within the range in which the effect of changes in hours upon the work done in a year is partially offset by a change in output per hour *resulting from the change in hours*. I also judge that the size of the offset declines as hours are shortened. In the absence of solid comprehensive data, one can only guess at the size of the offsets corresponding to different hours levels. I shall assume, for males and females separately, that at the levels of average weekly hours (including vacations and holiday weeks) worked in 1960, a small change in average hours worked per week by a representative group of workers has a 30 percent offset in output per man-hour. These levels, according to my estimates, were 42.7 for males and 39.0 for females.[20] (These levels correspond to about 46.0 and 42.2, respectively, for full workweeks.) I further assume that if weekly hours were ten hours longer (52.7 for males and 49.0 for females) a small change in average hours worked would be fully offset in output per man-hour. Intermediate points are set by proportional interpolation, which yields a change in the offset percentage of 0.7 percentage points for each change of 0.1 hours. This same relationship is extrapolated to shorter hours. Introduction of these assumptions permits curves for males and females to be constructed that relate hours to indexes measuring the work done in an hour.[21] The curves for males imply that output per hour is a maximum at 38.4 hours a week and output per worker is a maximum at 52.7 hours. The corresponding points for females are 34.7 and 49.0, respectively.

However, one need use only a tiny part of this range during the postwar period. Indeed, postwar changes in average hours have been so small that the index of labor input and the analysis of the sources of growth would not be altered much by even a substantial change in the assumption as to the size of the productivity offset when hours of workers in this category change. From 1947

20. In this discussion (and also in the calculations), average hours for males shown in Table G-1 for years prior to 1966 have been adjusted for comparability with later data by use of the difference (0.1 hours) between the two 1966 averages shown in that table.

21. In some cases a change in hours of full-time workers tends to be accompanied by a change in the hours that capital goods are used. The assumption here, and also for other groups, is intended to allow for the effect of any such related changes in capital hours upon output so that no adjustment to measures of capital input is introduced on this account.

through 1969 male hours ranged only from a low of 42.3 in 1958 to a high of 43.6 in 1950. My assumption implies that these points correspond to 42.4 and 43.3 hours, respectively, when measured in 1960 efficiency units. The range of female hours was greater, from a low of 37.9 in 1968 to a high of 40.3 in 1950; my assumption implies that these points correspond to 38.2 and 39.8 hours, respectively, when measured in 1960 efficiency units. This range is still too small to permit errors in the assumption concerning the efficiency offset to have much effect on the postwar labor input measure because, in this category, the weight of females is less than one-fifth of the total weight.

In contrast to the postwar period, changes in weekly hours of full-time nonfarm wage and salary workers from 1929 to 1940 were large. Therefore, the change in the index of labor input for workers in this category over any time span including this period is sensitive to the particular assumption that is introduced concerning the size of the productivity offset. For example, average weekly hours of males were reduced from 49.3 in 1929 to 43.4 in 1947, or by 12.0 percent. My curve yields an estimate that this reduction cut their input by 5.6 percent. The percentages for females are similar: a 12.1 percent reduction in their hours is estimated to have cut their input by 5.5 percent. Table H-1 shows the portions of the curves required for the estimates.

It will be noted that no productivity offset to a change in hours is introduced, for this or for other groups, when a change in the proportions of males and females alters average hours for the two sexes combined.

FULL-TIME FARM WORKERS. Full-time workers employed in farming work long hours. Their hours may be assumed to lie within the range where the productivity offset to a change in hours is very large. (Indeed, the average hours of males, who receive about 95 percent of the weight in this category, have been well above the level at which I assume the productivity offset for nonfarm wage and salary workers to be complete, while average hours of the small female group of full-time farm workers have been approximately at that level.) I make the specific assumption, separately for each sex, that changes in average weekly hours worked on farms have not affected the amount of work done in a week; the productivity offset is presumed to be complete. Consequently, changes in average hours of male or female full-time farm

workers do not affect my measure of labor input when the indexes for average hours and the efficiency offset are combined; the index for the efficiency of an hour's work is the reciprocal of the index for average hours. This is fortunate because hours of farm workers are difficult to define and to measure. Indeed, this limitation upon the data was a supplementary reason for making the above assumption.[22] Again, the postwar change in average hours has been small, especially since 1950, so the assumption chosen does not greatly affect the measure of labor input. For males, the reduction was from 57.0 in 1947 and 55.8 in 1950 to 55.5 in 1969. For females, who receive very little weight in the farm category, the change was from 49.4 in 1947 and 48.6 in 1950 to 48.8 in 1969.[23] Even changes from 1929 to 1947 were not great.

FULL-TIME NONFARM PROPRIETORS AND UNPAID FAMILY WORKERS. The conceptual and statistical reasons for ignoring hours changes in measuring the labor input of full-time workers in farming, thus assuming a complete efficiency offset to hours changes, also apply to full-time nonfarm proprietors and unpaid family workers. For both males and females, hours are very long—well above the level at which I assumed the productivity offset for nonfarm wage and salary workers to be complete. There is the additional consideration that hours of this group in large degree reflect local custom with respect to the time establishments are open and, for this reason alone, changes have a large efficiency offset. I adopt the same assumption and procedures as in farming.

In practice, postwar changes in the hours of this group have been so small that between 1947 and 1969 it scarcely matters what assumption is made. Hours of males were 0.1 hours, or 0.2 percent, longer in 1969 than in 1947. The lightly weighted hours of females were 2.3 hours, or 4.3 percent, shorter. For both sexes the reductions from 1929 to 1940 are estimated to have been large, but because of inadequate data for 1929 little reliance can be placed upon the estimated changes. By the procedure adopted, my measure

22. My series for average hours of the small and very lightly weighted female farm group shows occasional erratic changes, including pronounced dips in 1955 and 1957. The procedure adopted prevents these erratic movements from affecting my series for labor input.

23. Average hours shown in Table G-3 for years prior to 1966 have been adjusted here for comparability with later data by use of the difference between the two 1966 averages shown in that table.

of total labor input is unaffected by these hours estimates.

Calculation of the Index

To secure the index shown in Table 4-1, column 5, which implements these assumptions, separate indexes for males and females were first constructed for each pair of adjacent years.[24] The indexes were combined by using total earnings of males and females in the second of the paired years as weights. The weights are those implied by my age-sex composition calculations; for each sex they are equal to the sum of the products for the age groups of total hours worked and the average hourly earnings weight. The weight of females ranges from 10.9 percent of the total weight in 1929–40 and 14.1 percent at the beginning of the postwar period to 19.4 percent in 1968–69. The annual indexes for both sexes combined were linked to secure the continuous index on a 1958 base. I call this index the "efficiency of an hour's work as affected by changes in hours due to intragroup changes."

The index for each sex in each year, with the preceding year equal to 100, was computed as follows:

1. Employment and total hours worked by each sex in the preceding year and in the current year were divided among the four labor force groups (three full-time groups and all part-time workers combined) that have been enumerated. (Tables G-1, G-2, and G-3 provide the data.)

2. Labor input *per worker* in the current year, expressed as the "efficiency equivalent" of the average number of hours worked in the preceding year, was calculated for each labor force group by use of the assumption for that group just described.[25] These efficiency equivalents to average hours worked in the preceding year were multiplied by employment in the current year to secure labor input in the current year expressed as the efficiency equivalent of total hours worked in the preceding year. The products were added to secure a total for the business sector.

3. Labor input in the current year, so calculated, was divided by total actual hours in the current year to secure the desired index. This index represents the estimated change from the preceding year in the efficiency of an hour's work that resulted from changes in average hours worked *within* the labor force groups distinguished.[26]

Changes in the Index

From 1929 to 1947 changes in the working hours of the labor force groups distinguished raised the efficiency of an hour's work an estimated 6.8 percent, equivalent to an annual rate of 0.37 percent. In contrast, the index rose only 1.2 percent from 1947 to 1969, an average of 0.06 percent a year. The reason that the postwar change was small, of course, is that over this period changes in the average hours of full-time workers were small in all groups, especially in the heavily weighted male groups. There were, however, short-term movements of appreciable size in the index. Four year-to-year changes were as large as 0.4 percent, and over the most recent four-year period, 1965–69, the index rose by 1.0 percent. Irregularities in the annual changes in this index cancel the effect on total labor input of fluctuations in the average hours worked by male and female full-time workers in agriculture and in nonfarm self-employment, and partially offset fluctuations in the hours of full-time nonfarm wage and salary workers.

Changes in Average Hours Resulting from Changing Employment Composition

The percentages of full-time male and female workers in nonresidential business who are nonfarm wage and salary workers have increased while the percentages who are farm workers and nonfarm self-employed and unpaid family workers have declined. The percentage of full-time males who are in the latter two groups fell from 29.6 in 1947 to 17.3 in 1969, and the corresponding percentage of females fell from 15.0 to 9.8. The major decline was in the farm category (Table 4-5). Because average weekly hours worked by full-time nonfarm wage and salary workers are much shorter than those worked by the other groups, these shifts reduced the average hours worked by all full-time workers of each sex. If the effect of this reduction in hours upon my measure of labor

24. Calculations for 1929–40 and 1941–47 were made as if all changes between the terminal dates had been at a steady rate.

25. References to labor input here refer only to the effects of changes in working hours within the labor force groups distinguished.

26. Current-year weights are used for both actual hours and hours expressed in terms of efficiency units, so changes in the composition of hours worked do not affect this index.

input were not offset, the movement of full-time workers from farming or nonfarm self-employment would reduce labor input. This procedure would count farm and self-employed workers as far more labor input than nonfarm wage and salary workers because their hours are much longer.

I believe this result is not convenient or desirable. The index I shall shortly describe, shown in Table 4-1, column 6, prevents such shifts from reducing labor input. It introduces into my labor input measure the convention that a year of full-time employment (when performed by the same individual or individuals with similar characteristics) represents the same amount of labor input in any of these three groups in place of the convention that an hour of work in each type of employment is equivalent. For example, if full-time workers shift from one group to another, and if they work the average hours of their old group before moving and of their new group after moving, my index of labor input is unchanged. My preference for this convention rests on three considerations.

First, the matter may be viewed from the standpoint of labor input measurement. Suppose a typical group of male or female full-time farm workers shifts to nonfarm wage and salary employment. Without my index, labor input would be unchanged if the hours of the workers who move were as long in their new nonfarm wage-salary jobs as those of farm workers but would drop sharply if they worked the hours of other nonfarm wage-salary workers. This would conflict with my estimates of the effect of changing the hours of nonfarm wage and salary workers. My assumption about the relationship between hours and output in nonfarm wage and salary employment implies, I believe correctly, that the difference between output per man when nonfarm hours are at their actual level and at the very long farm level is much smaller than the difference between man-hours at the two levels of hours. A similar statement is implied for a shift from nonfarm self-employment to nonfarm paid employment.

Second, my decision to eliminate from my labor input measure the effect of such shifts on average hours rests also on doubt that reported hours for the farm and nonfarm self-employed really are comparable to those for nonfarm wage and salary workers. If they are not, the statistical reduction in average hours that appears when a shift occurs is overstated. Whether the differences between hours in the three labor force groups are "real" or due to a different conception of what hours "worked" mean in these activities, it is notable that when, in the early stages of industrialization, attempts were made to transfer farm hours to factories they were quickly found to be unsuitable.[27]

There is a third and quite different consideration behind my choice of the convention that a year rather than an hour of full-time work in the three types of employment is to be counted as equivalent labor input. The effect of this choice upon the amount of the growth rate that I ascribe to changes in labor input is offset mainly in my estimates of the contribution made to growth by improvement in resource allocation as labor shifts from farming and self-employment to nonfarm wage and salary employment. With the classification of growth sources that results from my method of measuring labor input, the net gains in output per person employed that result from reallocation appear in a single series. This is convenient because my findings are presented in

Table 4-5. Nonresidential Business: Percentage Distributions of Full-Time Employment, by Type of Worker and Sex, 1947 and 1969

Sex and year	Total (1)	Nonfarm wage and salary workers (2)	Nonfarm self-employed and unpaid family workers (3)	Farm workers (4)
Males				
1947	100.0	70.4	12.2	17.4
1969	100.0	82.7	11.2	6.1
Females				
1947	100.0	85.0	9.1	5.9
1969	100.0	90.2	7.7	2.0

Sources: Computed from Tables G-1, G-2, and G-3. Data for 1947 were adjusted for comparability with 1969 to take account of differences in 1966 percentages computed from data classified on the old and new bases. Percentages are rounded and may not add to 100.0.

27. "The custom of working from 'sunup to sundown' was introduced into the factory at its organization. This schedule was popular in agriculture, and it was assumed that it could be followed in industry. However, it was soon discovered that a system practicable in one setting was not by nature satisfactory in another. Several factors made the long working day more onerous in industry than on the farm. Labor is subjected to greater and more persistent pressure in industry than in agriculture. Respite from toil and slackening of pace [are] easier in the latter than in the former. Nor is it necessary for a farm laborer to travel an hour or two from his home to the job. Consequently, dissatisfaction with the long working day arose soon after the Industrial Revolution." (Philip Taft, *Economics and Problems of Labor* [3rd ed., Stackpole Company, 1955], p. 311).

terms of the sources of increase in output per person employed rather than in output per man-hour. Because, total employment being given, such employment shifts actually raise total output *and* reduce average hours as actually measured, they contribute more to the rise in output per man-hour in the business sector than to the rise in output per person employed. If I did not eliminate the impact of the hours reduction from my measure of labor input, I would show a larger contribution to growth from resource reallocation and a smaller contribution from labor input than I do. To examine the full effects of employment shifts on output per person employed in that framework, one would have to consider both the negative effect of employment shifts on labor input via the change in average hours and the positive contribution to output per man-hour. This would be not only inconvenient but also unrealistic because the reduction in average hours is a necessary concomitant of the employment shifts.

Procedures

I call the measure that eliminates the effect of these shifts the index of the "efficiency of an hour's work as affected by changes in hours due to specified intergroup shifts." The mechanics of its construction are as follows:

STEP ONE. An index for each year was first constructed for each sex, with the preceding year equal to 100, using the following procedure:

a. For each of the three categories of full-time workers, average hours in the current year were multiplied by employment in the preceding year. The products for the three categories were added. Their total was divided by employment in the preceding year to obtain the average hours of full-time workers that would have prevailed in the current year, given the hours actually worked by each group, if the distribution of full-time employment in the current year had been the same as in the preceding year. This standardized figure was then divided by actual average hours of full-time workers in the current year to obtain the desired index for full-time workers. The index measures the effect upon the current year's average hours of the difference between the distribution of full-time employment in the current year and in the preceding year.

b. The corresponding index for part-time workers was taken as 100 each year because an hour's work by part-time workers was regarded as the same amount of labor input in each of the three labor force groups.

c. The indexes for full-time workers and part-time workers were combined by use as weights of total hours worked by each group in the current year. This yielded the annual index for each sex.

STEP TWO. The annual indexes for the two sexes were combined by use as weights of the total earnings of the two sexes in the current year, a procedure similar to that followed in constructing the series for the effect of "intragroup" changes.

STEP THREE. The annual indexes were linked to secure a continuous index with 1958 equal to 100.

Changes in the Index

The index (Table 4-1, column 6) rose by 2.1 percent from 1929 to 1947, an average of 0.12 percent a year, and by 3.0 percent from 1947 to 1969, an average of 0.13 percent a year. The postwar rise was interrupted only in recession years. These interruptions were due to absolute declines in the number of full-time nonfarm wage and salary workers, not to increases in the numbers of farm and nonfarm self-employed workers.

Education of Workers

Educational background decisively conditions both the types of work an individual is able to perform and his proficiency in any particular occupation. It would be wholly unsatisfactory to count the average high school graduate and the average worker with, say, four years of primary education as contributing the same amount of labor input.

A sharp upward shift in the educational background of the American labor force has upgraded the skills and versatility of labor and contributed to the rise in national income. It has enhanced the skills of individuals within what is conventionally termed an occupation, often with considerable changes in the work actually performed; it has also permitted a shift in occupational composition from occupations in which workers typically have little education and low earnings toward those in which education and earnings are higher. Education also heightens an individual's awareness of job opportunities, and thereby the chances that he is employed where his marginal product is greatest. A more educated work force—from top management down—also is better able to learn about and use the most efficient production practices.[28]

---

28. For a more extended discussion of the effects of education upon labor input, see *Why Growth Rates Differ*, Chap. 8.

Construction of the Education Index

An index that measures changes in labor input resulting from changes in education can be constructed if two types of information are available. One is the relative values, or marginal products, of work performed by persons who have different levels of education (and, because of length of education, different amounts of work experience at a given age) but who are similar in other characteristics; such information can be inferred from data on earnings. The second type is the distribution of work done at various dates among persons with different levels of education. An index, designed for use with the labor input series already introduced, has been constructed for the business sector and is shown in Table 4-1, column 7. The weights and distributions used in its construction refer to full-time equivalent employment rather than to total hours worked, but there is no reason to suspect that this difference perceptibly alters the index. The derivation and characteristics of the index are described fully in Appendix I, and a brief summary is given below.

STEP ONE. The first step was to establish differentials between the average earnings of *otherwise similar* individuals who had completed nine different levels of schooling. These earnings, expressed as percentages of the average earnings of those with eight years of education, are shown in Table 4-6, column 1. They provide the weights required for construction of an index.

The basic data used in their derivation are

1959 earnings of males who, as reported in the 1960 Census of Population, were in the experienced civilian labor force on April 1, 1960. They represent a 5 percent sample of the entire population. Because an approximation to differentials in the business sector is the objective, men in occupations largely outside the business sector (such as the teaching profession, clergy, and police force) were eliminated. To exclude the effects on earnings differentials among education groups of most earnings determinants, other than education, that happen to be correlated with education, the data were then standardized by age, region, race, and attachment to farm or nonfarm occupations.[29] Separate differentials were established for each of thirty-two groups based on a cross-classification of men by the above four characteristics. The thirty-two sets of differentials were then weighted by total earnings of men in each group. Because age is one of the determinants distinguished, the differentials are appropriate for use with the age-sex composition indexes already derived.[30] Specific adjustments were made to eliminate the effects upon earnings differentials among persons

29. Farm and nonfarm workers were treated separately to eliminate the effects on earnings of correlation between education (which is low in farming) and misallocation of labor (which depresses farm earnings). Standardization by industry or occupation is not, in general, desired (see p. 227).
30. Four ten-year age brackets in the 25–64 age range were used. Differentials in the 25–34 age bracket were imputed to younger age groups, and in the 55–64 age bracket to older age groups.

Table 4-6. Nonresidential Business: Percentage Distributions of Male and Female Workers, by Highest School Grade Completed, October 1948 and March 1970

| Highest school grade completed | Weight[a] (1) | Percentage distribution of full-time equivalent employment | | | |
| | | October 1948 | | March 1970 | |
		Males (2)	Females (3)	Males (4)	Females (5)
None	75	1.49[b]	0.90[b]	0.42	0.21
Elementary, 1–4	89	7.27[b]	3.47[b]	2.46	1.00
Elementary, 5–7	97	14.64	9.88	7.07	4.19
Elementary, 8	100	21.04	18.15	10.82	8.14
High school, 1–3	111	20.17	18.77	17.91	18.16
High school, 4	124	23.10	37.33	36.77	50.60
College, 1–3	147	6.58	7.51	12.67	12.70
College, 4	189	3.52[b]	2.99[b]	7.27	3.49
College, 5 or more	219	2.19[b]	0.99[b]	4.62	1.52
Total	. . .	100.00	100.00	100.00	100.00

Sources: Column 1, Table I-13, column 9; columns 2 to 5, Table I-15. Percentages are rounded and may not add to 100.00.
a. Expressed as a percentage of the weight of persons having completed 8 years of education.
b. Broader education groups were divided between the detailed groups shown here by use of 1959 proportions.

with different amounts of education of differences in academic aptitude and in the socioeconomic status of parents. The resulting differentials refer to education at each level of the average quality and quantity (as indicated by days of school attended at each level) that persons employed in the business sector in 1959 had actually received.

Earnings are adjusted to a full-time equivalent basis, so that the earnings differentials among education groups are not affected by differences among education groups in labor force participation rates or in the prevalence of unemployment or part-time employment. Because of this feature and of the separate treatment of thirty-two labor force groups among which hours and education may differ, the differentials in full-time equivalent earnings, as standardized and adjusted, are probably quite close to differentials in hourly earnings, similarly standardized and adjusted. Only insofar as hours of full-time workers vary with level of education *within* the thirty-two labor force groups distinguished in the standardization process does any effect on earnings of hours differences among education groups remain in the differentials. The 1959 weights were used for all periods in the absence of information indicating that they should be changed. The ratio of female to male earnings is estimated to be the same at all education levels, and the weights derived for males were therefore also used for females. Weights derived in this study are compared with those previously used in Table I-14.[31]

STEP TWO. The second step was to develop, separately for each sex, percentage distributions of full-time equivalent business employment by level of education for the twelve postwar dates from 1948 to 1970 for which CPS surveys of levels of education are available. The distributions at the first and last of these dates are shown in Table 4-6, columns 2 to 5, and at all twelve dates in Table I-15. In 1948, 44 percent of males employed in business had eight years of education or less; in 1970, only 21 percent. The percentage who finished high school (with or without attending college) jumped from 35 to 61. The percentages with five years or more, four years, and one to three years of college all doubled.

The original CPS data report the level of education of all employed civilians 18 years of age

and over. Estimated distributions confined to persons employed in business were derived by eliminating the principal groups of government, household, and institutional workers. This meant using data by occupation from these surveys supplemented by cross-classifications by occupation and industry from the decennial population censuses. The distributions for persons of each sex employed in the business sector were then divided into three parts covering, respectively, full-time farm workers, full-time nonfarm workers, and all part-time workers. Percentage distributions by level of education were computed for each part. These distributions were then so weighted as to maintain consistency with the labor input series, already described, that measure the effects of changes in hours of work. The distributions for full-time farm and nonfarm business workers were weighted by the number of full-time workers in each category to obtain a combined distribution for all full-time workers of each sex in the business sector.[32] The distributions for all full-time workers and all part-time workers of each sex were combined by use as weights of total hours worked by each group.

It is of some interest that smaller percentages of persons employed in the business sector appear at the extremes of the education distributions than is the case for all employed persons. Differences are especially pronounced among females. Women with the least education are heavily concentrated in private household employment, while a large proportion of female college graduates are engaged in teaching.

STEP THREE. The distributions of each sex by level of education were multiplied by the earnings weights to obtain indexes (shown in Table I-17) for all survey dates, expressed with the weight of persons with eight years of education equal to 100. At this stage, persons who had completed the same school grade were counted as having received an equivalent education at all dates.

STEP FOUR. Annual indexes similar to those just described were developed from the data for survey dates. (They are shown in Table I-18.) To obtain the annual estimates an interpolation procedure was introduced that takes account of the positive relationship between the education

31. The previous weights were based on earnings data for all civilians. At the top of the educational distribution, earnings differentials are wider in nonresidential business than in the civilian economy as a whole.

32. Full consistency with the hours series would have required that separate distributions for full-time nonfarm wage and salary workers and for full-time nonfarm proprietors and unpaid family workers be similarly combined by employment weights. This could not be done, but the possible error is trivial.

index and the level of unemployment. Because unemployment is concentrated among the less educated, the distribution of employed persons by level of education shifts upward when unemployment rises. Annual indexes were also prepared for 1929, 1940, and 1941.

STEP FIVE. An adjustment to these indexes was introduced because the "highest school grade completed" does not provide an unchanging measure of the amount of education received by persons leaving school at the elementary and secondary levels. The facts, in brief, are as follows. The length of the school term in large cities has scarcely changed over the period, which runs well back into the last century, during which persons employed at dates covered in this study (1929–69) were educated. The length of the school term in smaller places was originally much shorter than in big cities but it has gradually attained big-city standards. The number of days during the school term that pupils are absent from school has been greatly reduced. The adjustment is based on the propositions that: (1) only for persons who *regularly* attended big-city schools does the highest school grade completed provide a constant measure of the amount of education obtained; and (2) at any given date, the number of days of school attended provides an appropriate ratio to convert the education received by other students to equivalence with that received by students regularly attending big-city schools at the same grade level, or of the same age. (Grade level and age are roughly interchangeable.) The statistical implementation of this proposition is an approximation.

No such adjustment was made for persons with no education nor for those completing one or more years of college. Persons completing the same level of higher education are counted as having the same amount of education whenever they attended school.

STEP SIX. The adjusted indexes for each sex were converted to time series indexes (shown in Table I-21). They were weighted by total earnings to obtain the final index for both sexes combined. The procedure used to combine the indexes for males and females was the same as the one used to construct the index for the efficiency of an hour's work as affected by "intragroup" changes in hours.[33]

33. Ideally, the index for each sex would have been obtained by computing a separate index for each age group and combining these indexes by use of total earnings as weights,

The index takes account only of the quantitative aspects of formal education. It is assumed that persons who reached any given educational level had studied a curriculum equally appropriate for their subsequent participation in economic life regardless of the date at which they were educated. If any changes occurred in the "quality" of education, other than by extension of the school year and improved attendance, this is not reflected.

Above all, it should be noted that the index is intended only as a component of labor input, not as an indication of all the economic effects of education. In particular, the effect, if any, of an increase in the level of education on the rate at which knowledge of how to produce at low cost advances is not captured by the index. Nor should it be.

Movement of the Education Index

The distributions in Table 4-6 indicate the large shift during the postwar years in the distribution of full-time equivalent business employment by highest school grade completed. The upward trend has, of course, been under way for a much longer period. From 1947 to 1969 the index (Table 4-1, column 7), which also takes account of the change in school days, rose 14.4 percent, or at an annual rate of 0.61 percent. The rate from 1929 to 1947 had been almost the same, 0.60 percent.

Of the total postwar growth rate of the index, 0.46 points resulted from the shift in the distribution by highest school grade completed and 0.15 points from the increase in days of school attendance per year by persons reaching elementary and secondary levels. The latter factor had been more important in the 1929–47 period, accounting for 0.26 points of the growth rate of the index. The index for males rose much more during the postwar period than that for females: the growth rates were 0.65 and 0.42, respectively.

The postwar increase in amount of education

in the same way as the indexes for the two sexes. This was not possible; the actual indexes imply use of full-time equivalent employment of persons, 18 and over, as weights to combine age groups. Omission from the distributions of persons under 18, whose weight in total earnings is trivial, helps to minimize the difference in weights, but persons aged 18 to about 30 and those over 65 are overweighted. This matters only if indexes for these age groups would differ appreciably from those for other age groups. The fact that the education index has been rising at an almost constant rate for many years strongly suggests that this is not the case.

was smaller in the business sector than in the civilian economy as a whole. Indexes, based on use of the same weights as for full-time equivalent business employment, are available for the entire civilian labor force and for all civilian employment (Table I-18, columns 1 and 3). These indexes have not been adjusted for changes in school attendance per year of school, but the adjustment would differ little from that estimated for full-time equivalent (FTE) business employment. Without this adjustment, 1947–69 growth rates of indexes for various groups compare as follows:

	Males	*Females*
Civilian labor force	0.56	0.38
Civilian employment	0.55	0.38
FTE business employment	0.49	0.27

The most important single reason that the indexes for business employment rose less than those for all employment was the absorption of large numbers of college graduates into teaching (including college teaching). This was especially important among females, and hence is partially responsible for the difference between the growth rates for males and females in the business sector. The main reason for this difference, however, is that the rise in education of the whole female labor force has been much smaller than that of the male labor force. The fact that the female labor force was becoming older contributed a little to this difference, but the main cause was a smaller rise in the education of the female than of the male population.[34]

The education index, as already indicated, has a definite countercyclical pattern. Absorption of the unemployed into employment dampened the rise in the index during the 1960s. In the absence of changes in unemployment, the growth rate of the index would have been fairly constant throughout the postwar period—indeed, since 1929.

Labor Input

A comprehensive index of labor input in the business sector can now be constructed by multiplication of the separate indexes already derived. This

comprehensive index is shown in Table 4-1, column 8.

Changes in Labor Input

Labor input in the business sector has followed a highly irregular course, not only from year to year but also over longer periods. Growth rates of the index over certain periods compare as follows:

1929–48	1.40
1929–41	1.10
1941–48	1.91
1948–69	1.23
1948–53	1.68
1953–64	0.49
1964–69	2.41

The increase from 1964 to 1969—12.6 percent in only five years—was quite extraordinary. Even before 1964 the growth rate had begun to accelerate. Nearly all of the 1953–64 increase occurred after 1961.

Figure 4-1 compares the index of labor input with the indexes of employment and hours worked. The divergence between the labor input and employment indexes is, on the whole, surprisingly small in most periods; the biggest differences appear before 1940 and at the beginning and end of the postwar period. From 1940 to 1969 labor input rose by 62.3 percent and employment by 54.4 percent. Rising educational qualifications were only moderately more than sufficient to offset the depressing effects of a sharp rise in the female component of employment, of a large increase in the number of women and students working part time, and of hours reductions for full-time nonfarm wage and salary workers.[35] Labor input has risen much more than the total number of hours worked.

The order in which its various components were introduced does not affect the index for labor input.[36] The order does, however, affect the individual indexes. Most important is the point at which weighting by sex is introduced. This was done after calculation of the indexes for employment and average hours but before calculation of

34. Application of the same weights to distributions of the whole population, 18 years of age and over, in October 1952 and March 1969 yields a rise over that period of 8.1 percent for males and 5.3 percent for females. Comparable changes for the civilian labor force were 9.7 percent for males and 6.3 percent for females (see Table I-17). These calculations do not include allowance for changes in school attendance per year of school.

35. The percentage of part-time workers in the business economy each year is shown in Table G-4. It was 16.1 percent in 1969. If a discontinuity in 1966 is bridged by use of overlapping estimates, the comparable 1947 percentage was about 10.3.

36. Except perhaps trivially, as a result of my inability to handle with precision certain unimportant relationships, already cited, among the various changes that were occurring.

Figure 4-1. Nonresidential Business: Indexes of Labor Input, Employment, and Hours Worked, 1929, 1940–41, and 1947–69

Index (1958 = 100)

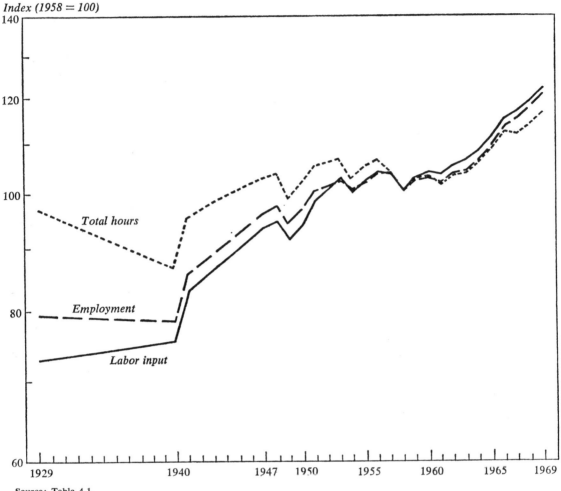

Source: Table 4-1.
Note. The years 1930–39 and 1942–46 are not plotted.

the other indexes. Over the postwar period as a whole, female employment rose far more than male employment and average hours worked by females fell more, so that introduction of weighting by sex at the *beginning* of the procedure would have yielded a smaller increase in employment, and a smaller decline in average hours. The increase in total hours would be less than I show. Over the postwar period the female index for the efficiency offset to "intragroup" changes in hours rose more than that for males while the female indexes for "specified intergroup shifts" and for education both rose less than the corresponding indexes for males. Consequently, if weighting by

sex had been introduced at the *end* of the procedure, the first of these indexes would have risen more and the other two less than those I show. The employment index and, of course, the age-sex index itself are more sensitive to the point in the analysis at which weighting by sex is introduced than the other series.

Unmeasured Characteristics

The measure of labor input is as comprehensive as I can make it, but it does not cover all of the characteristics of workers that are related to output, that may change over time, and hence that may contribute to increases or decreases in production.[37]

Changes in the work effort per hour worked that is exerted by workers of a given age and sex, and with a given level of education are captured by the index only if they result from changes in the length of working hours. Quite possibly no other changes have occurred, so inclusion of their effects would not alter the index. But it is conceivable that the omission is important, or may become so in the future.

Time lost because of sickness is appropriately omitted from labor input, but the health of workers while they are at work, which may affect their output, is not measured. I do not believe that changes during the period covered by this study have been sufficient to affect total labor input perceptibly.[38]

Changes in experience are measured, because of the weighting by age, unless there is a change in the amount of experience held by persons of the same age and sex.[39] When the experience of age-sex groups declines as a result of the extension of formal education, this change is also reflected in the labor input index. Because the education weights are based on a comparison of earnings of persons of the same age, they measure the difference between the addition to earnings as a result of more education and the loss of earnings as a result of less experience. Consequently, the education index measures only the excess of the gain in labor input from additional education over the loss from the associated reduction in work experience. The experience of women of a given age may have changed because of a change in the work habits of married women, particularly those with children, but the direction of any change is unclear.[40] A perceptible error in the labor input index from this source is scarcely conceivable in view of the small weight of female workers in the total index. I know no other reasons to suspect a significant change in the relationship between age and experience for workers of a given sex.[41]

The education index measures only the effects of changes in formal education, beginning with the first grade, that is received in regular schools or institutions of higher education, and equivalent programs. The effects of changes in the average amount of other types of education or training (which must be distinguished from "experience") received by persons of the same age and sex, and with the same amount of formal education, are omitted.[42] These include kindergarten and nursery school, courses taken from commercial and trade schools, adult self-education programs including correspondence school courses, the new manpower training programs, apprenticeship programs, and short-term courses and seminars provided by employers that are not a normal accompaniment of a worker's job. Within formal education, possible changes in the quality of education received at each level, or in the relationship between curriculum and participation in economic life, are not taken into account.

Color is not among the characteristics of workers that were considered in the construction of the labor input index and it is not clear that it should be, but in any case it appears that the effect of including color would be negligible. The percentages of nonwhite racial groups in the entire civilian labor force 14 years of age and over, and in six age-sex groups among which average earnings vary widely, are shown for 1954 and 1969 in the following table. Although 1954 is the

37. A much fuller discussion of most unmeasured characteristics will be found in *Why Growth Rates Differ*, especially Chapters 8 and 9 and Appendixes F and G. The discussion of experience in that volume is not wholly applicable to the present estimates because a more detailed age break is used in the present study.

38. In *Why Growth Rates Differ*, p. 114 and Appendix G, I discussed estimates by Hector Correa of the relationship between changes in nutrition and economic growth. Correa and Cummins have subsequently concluded that changes in calorie intake had no effect on U.S. postwar economic growth, the position I had taken earlier. Hector Correa and Gaylord Cummins, "Contribution of Nutrition to Economic Growth," *American Journal of Clinical Nutrition*, Vol. 23 (May 1970), p. 564.

39. Among persons of each sex, with or without standardization by years of school completed, not only total work experience but also experience in the job currently held rises systematically with age. See Edward J. O'Boyle, "Job Tenure, January 1968: How It Relates to Race and Age," Reprint 2637, with notes and detailed statistics added, from *Monthly Labor Review*, Vol. 92 (September 1969), Special Labor Force Report 132, pp. 16–23, esp. Tables A and I.

40. Single women typically have more experience than married women of the same age, and their proportion of all women workers has been declining rapidly. On the other hand, the experience of older married women presumably has risen because of earlier entry or reentry into the labor force after children are born. The rise in part-time work further clouds the picture.

41. Except that in 1940 and 1941 many workers had less experience than would normally be the case because of the heavy unemployment of the 1930s.

42. There appears to be a pronounced tendency at any point in time for the amount of other types of education to rise with amount of formal education among persons of the same age and sex. The education index automatically captures the effect of changes in the average amount of other types of education that is merely an accompaniment of the rise in formal education.

first year for which these data are available, labor force participation rates dating back to 1948 show that 1954 percentages are in line with other years.[43] The table also shows the shares of the age-sex groups in total earnings in nonresidential business.

	Percentage of civilian labor force that is nonwhite			Percentage of total labor earnings in nonresidential business, 1969
	1954	1969	Change	
Total	10.78	11.05	+0.27	100.0
Males				
25–64	9.18	9.61	+0.43	71.4
14–15	13.81	9.84	−3.97	0.2
Other ages	11.28	11.48	+0.20	9.0
Females				
25–64	13.86	13.22	−0.64	15.0
14–15	18.58	6.81	−11.77	0.1
Other ages	11.61	11.89	+0.28	4.3

43. Data are from *Manpower Report of the President, 1971*, Tables A-3 and A-4. The percentages of 1969 earnings in each demographic group for the business sector are based on my age-sex composition calculations, except that percentages for the 14- and 15-year-olds are rough approximations.

Suppose that within each age-sex group the percentage of nonwhites changed by the same number of points in business employment as it did in the civilian labor force, and further suppose that, in each age-sex group, average annual earnings of nonwhites (computed on a full-year, but not a full-time equivalent employment, basis) were as much as 40 percent lower than the average for all workers in the group. Under these conditions, weighting employment in each demographic group by color, and combining the groups by use of total earnings weights, would lower total labor input in 1969 by only 0.09 percent, relative to 1954, in comparison with the results obtained without weighting by color. This is less than 0.01 percent per year. The purpose of this calculation is simply to illustrate that weighting by color could scarcely change the results; it is not intended as an estimate.[44]

44. To appropriately introduce color into the weighting scheme would require not only a breakdown of *business* employment by color but also, because color is so correlated with other characteristics that *are* introduced, a cross-classification of each of these characteristics with color.

CHAPTER FIVE

Capital, Land, and Total Input in Nonresidential Business

An index of the total labor, capital, and land used to produce goods and services in the nonresidential business sector is developed in this chapter. In addition to the labor input series already presented, its construction requires measures of the input of nonresidential land and two types of business capital: inventories, and nonresidential structures and equipment. The index of total factor input is a weighted average of the indexes of these four broad categories of inputs. I shall first describe the weights and procedures used to combine the four indexes, and then the series that are used to measure capital and land inputs.

The Weighting Structure

To combine the four inputs, the weight used for each input is its estimated share of their combined earnings. The reason that earnings are used as weights can be stated briefly. At current prices, national income originating in the sector consists of the earnings of the labor, capital, and land used in the sector, together with some amount of "pure" profit. The total earnings of each factor can be viewed as equal to the number of units of the factor and its price, or earnings, per unit. The marginal product of each factor is the extra output that would be added by one additional unit of that factor when the quantities of the other factors are held constant. If enterprises combine the four factors in such a way as to minimize costs,

they will use them in such proportions that the marginal products per unit of the several factors are proportional to their prices, or earnings, per unit. Unless this condition is satisfied, enterprises could reduce costs by substituting one factor for another. Departures from this situation are assumed to be small or offsetting so that total earnings of the four inputs are proportional to the number of units of each times its marginal product.[1]

It follows that if a small percentage increase in the number of units of all of the factors would increase output of the sector by x percent, then a percentage increase of the same amount in the number of units of only one factor would increase output by x times the share of that factor in total earnings in the sector.

I shall measure total input *as if* a given percentage increase in all inputs would increase output by that same percentage even though I do not believe this to be the case. The business sector actually operates under increasing returns to scale so that an increase of, say, 1 percent in every input would raise output by more than 1 percent, but this extra gain is classified as a change in output per unit of input rather than as an increase in total input (see Chapter 6). Weights summing to 100 percent are therefore used so that if each input were to increase by 1 percent, total input would also increase by 1 percent.

Appendix J describes the detailed procedures followed to secure the weights. The statistical problems encountered, and the extent to which the earnings weights are sensitive to choices among alternative estimating procedures are also discussed. Table J-2 shows the actual weights used in each period. I provide here only a capsule summary of the procedures.

Annual estimates of the earnings of each factor were first prepared. (They are shown in Table J-3.) Labor earnings are equal to employee compensation in nonresidential business plus a portion of the income of unincorporated enterprises. Nonlabor earnings, obtained by deducting labor earnings from national income originating in nonresidential business, were first divided among nonfarm corporations, farms, and nonfarm noncorporate business property (Table J-3). Within each of these subsectors nonlabor earnings were allocated among nonresidential structures and equipment, inventories, and land in proportion to their values, measured in current prices (Table J-4). The underlying assumption is that *within* each subsector

---

1. There is no need to specify the scale of a "unit."

Table 5-1. Nonresidential Business: Weights Used to Combine Inputs, Selected Periods, 1929–69

Input	1929–40	1968–69	Highest	Lowest	Average 1929–69
Labor	79.15	80.00	81.88	77.95	79.54
Nonresidential structures and equipment	11.29	12.04	12.22	11.08	11.54
Inventories	4.62	3.90	5.54	3.75	4.58
Land	4.94	4.06	4.95	3.27	4.35
Total	100.00	100.00	...	...	100.00

Source: Table J-2, which also provides the weights for other periods.

the ratio of earnings to asset values is the same for the three types of assets. Total earnings of each of the three nonlabor inputs were obtained by adding the estimates for the subsectors.

Nonlabor earnings average about one-fifth of total earnings. As measured, they include an ingredient of "pure" profit (presumably positive in most postwar years) which could not be eliminated from the earnings of capital and land. If there are no offsetting biases (some possibilities are noted in Appendix J), shares of capital and land are overstated relative to the share of labor in an average year, but no correction for this was attempted. The annual series for the shares were smoothed in 1948–69, however, in order to eliminate the effects of pronounced *fluctuations* in profits that occurred in the course of postwar business cycles—fluctuations which do not reflect changes in the relative marginal products of labor, capital, and land at standardized utilization rates.[2] More importantly, data for the depressed 1930s, World War II, and the immediate postwar conversion years have been replaced by shares interpolated between 1929 and 1948. These adjustments prevent changes in the movement of the total input index over a period of years from being sensitive to the particular date at which the various inputs (especially capital inputs) were added. The 1929–40 estimates are affected the most. If the nonlabor share were not adjusted, the capital weight would be severely understated in that period.

The index of total factor input in the postwar period is a chain index of annual percentage changes. The percentage change between each year and the next is a weighted average of the percentage changes in the four input indexes. The weights are the averages of the adjusted earnings shares in the two years compared and consequently correspond to average marginal products (at the average postwar level of utilization) dur-

ing the period in which changes were taking place. In the 1929–40 and 1941–47 periods, annual growth rates of the input indexes between the terminal dates were substituted for annual percentage changes and average weights over the period were used.

The weights for every period are shown in Table J-2. Table 5-1 shows the weights in the earliest and latest periods, the highest and lowest weights for each input during the entire period, and the average weight over the whole 1929–69 period. Two characteristics stand out. First, labor accounts for about four-fifths of total input at all dates. Second, there is little trend in the weights and fluctuations throughout the period are moderate.

Certain assumptions required to derive the shares are detailed in Appendix J. Use of shares as weights rests on the proposition that, under demand conditions such as might have been foreseen by producers (approximated here by use of the postwar average), departures from the least-cost combination of factors are either small or random and offsetting so that relative earnings at any date correspond to the relative marginal products of employed resources at that date.[3]

Capital Input

To measure the two types of capital input in the nonresidential business sector (inventories, and nonresidential structures and equipment), I make use of the values in constant 1958 prices of the

---

2. The average postwar levels of the shares were retained.

3. This proposition directly justifies use of my procedure to obtain an estimate of the effect of a change in any input upon the sector's output only when output in constant prices is measured by use of *current-period* relative product prices to weight output components. It is necessary to assume that output measured by use as product weights of 1958 relative prices would rise by the same percentage. But this is a minor qualification.

No such assumption is needed when I combine the four sectors analyzed because data used for this purpose are in 1958 prices. This is an important advantage because the other sectors are essentially one-factor sectors, and relative prices of the total outputs of the sectors both change considerably and correspond to changes in relative input prices.

stock of privately owned capital of each type that is used in the sector. This is, in general, the capital that contributes to the earnings of capital in, and the value of the output of, the sector. However, there are some borderline difficulties in the distinction between government and private capital, and also in the valuation of used assets passing from government to business. These matters are discussed in Appendix K; they affect mainly the measurement of structures and equipment within the 1940–50 period. All data used were provided by the Office of Business Economics (OBE), but I am solely responsible for the choice of series for structures and equipment from among alternatives available in OBE's capital stock study.

Measurement of Inventory Input

The values of inventories in 1958 prices and an index of these values are shown in Table 5-2, columns 1 and 2. The series is the one from which OBE measures the "change in business inventories" in 1958 prices, a component of its constant-dollar GNP series. To measure inventory input each year, values at the beginning and end of the year were averaged. The OBE series covers private business comprehensively. Raw materials, work in process, finished goods, supplies, spare parts, crops (but not growing crops), and livestock are all included.

Derivation of Structures and Equipment Series

Two series are shown in Table 5-2 for the value of the stock of nonresidential structures and equipment: gross stock and net stock. Both are drawn from the array of series available from the OBE capital stock study.[4]

These series were estimated by the perpetual inventory method. The procedure, in brief, was as follows.

1. Each year gross private investment in nonresidential structures and producers' durable equipment, valued in current prices, was divided among a large number of types of structures and equipment.

2. Annual gross private investment in each category was next converted to 1958 prices by deflation of the current-dollar expenditure estimates.

The price series for the equipment components are those used to deflate these components of GNP. However, the GNP deflators for nonresidential construction are believed to have an upward bias because to a large extent they are based on prices paid for inputs into construction rather than the price of completed structures. The GNP deflators thus do not allow for changes in productivity in on-site construction work. In the estimates for Table 5-2, columns 3–7, these deflators were replaced by OBE's nonresidential construction "price series 2," which attempts to eliminate this bias and yields OBE's capital stock estimates in "constant price 2."[5]

3. An average service life was assigned to each type of equipment or structure. These service lives were based on the Bureau of Internal Revenue's Bulletin F, supplemented by OBE estimates when necessary to fill gaps. Bulletin F service lives are, in general, longer than those permitted in 1973 by the Internal Revenue Service. Service lives used for each very detailed category are constant throughout the period.[6] (Nonfarm trucks and various types of equipment used on farms, for which information on changes in lives was irregularly available, are exceptions.)

4. Each year's investment in any category enters the gross stock when it is purchased and remains in it until it is estimated to be discarded. It is not assumed that all of the investment in a category made in a particular year disappears

4. A general description of the study appears in Lawrence Grose, Irving Rottenberg, and Robert C. Wasson, "New Estimates of Fixed Business Capital in the United States, 1925–65," *Survey of Current Business,* Vol. 46 (December 1966), pp. 34–40. The particular series I have selected are from computer printouts and unpublished tables provided by OBE.

5. Price indexes for capital goods are hard to construct and are not highly accurate. The chief problems stem from frequent changes in products and, for components built to buyer specifications, absence of uniformity. Whether the price series can be shown to have a persistent upward bias even when "price series 2" is used for nonresidential construction is a matter of controversy. See, for example, Robert J. Gordon, "Measurement Bias in Price Indexes for Capital Goods," *Review of Income and Wealth,* Series 17, No. 2 (June 1971), pp. 121–74; and Joel Popkin and Robert Gillingham, "Comments on 'Recent Developments in the Measurement of Price Indexes for Fixed Capital Goods,'" *Review of Income and Wealth,* Series 17, No. 3 (September 1971), pp. 307–09. See also Edward F. Denison, Zvi Griliches, and Dale W. Jorgenson, "The Measurement of Productivity," Special issue of the *Survey of Current Business,* Vol. 52 (May 1972), Pt. 2, pp. 15–18, 52, 70–72, 96–97 (Brookings Reprint 244).

6. Indexes of the total business capital stock would not change much if service lives that are uniformly shorter or longer by even quite large percentages were to be substituted for Bulletin F lives. An assumption that service lives for particular categories of capital goods have, on balance, been *changing* as time passed would affect the indexes by larger amounts. The increase in structures and equipment is overstated if, as some believe, the intensity of use of equipment has increased so that it wears out more rapidly than in the past and service lives have therefore been declining. If that is so the increase in net output is also overstated because the rise in depreciation is too small.

Table 5-2. Nonresidential Business: Capital Stock Values in Constant Prices and Indexes, 1929, 1940–41, and 1947–69
Values in billions of 1958 dollars; indexes, 1958 = 100[a]

| | Inventories | | Nonresidential structures and equipment | | | | |
| | | | Values | | Indexes | | |
Year	Value (1)	Index (2)	Gross stock (3)	Net stock (4)	Gross stock (5)	Net stock (6)	Weighted average (7)
1929	74.3	58.54	419.5	230.9	65.94	65.92	65.94
1940	72.1	56.86	416.7	198.8	65.50	56.76	63.31
1941	79.4	62.61	420.6	201.7	66.11	57.58	63.98
1947	93.2	73.46	432.8	212.9	68.04	60.77	66.22
1948	95.4	75.19	452.1	229.5	71.07	65.52	69.68
1949	95.7	75.44	470.1	243.3	73.90	69.47	72.79
1950	97.8	77.12	486.7	255.0	76.51	72.79	75.58
1951	107.4	84.67	504.7	267.4	79.33	76.35	78.59
1952	114.6	90.29	522.3	279.0	82.10	79.65	81.49
1953	116.7	91.95	539.6	290.1	84.82	82.82	84.32
1954	116.1	91.53	556.4	300.7	87.47	85.86	87.06
1955	118.3	93.27	574.4	312.0	90.29	89.06	89.98
1956	123.9	97.67	595.6	325.8	93.62	93.01	93.47
1957	127.0	100.09	617.7	340.0	97.10	97.05	97.08
1958	126.9	100.00	636.1	350.3	100.00	100.00	100.00
1959	128.5	101.30	652.1	358.4	102.51	102.31	102.46
1960	132.6	104.55	670.1	368.5	105.35	105.19	105.31
1961	135.4	106.73	688.2	378.3	108.18	108.01	108.14
1962	139.4	109.88	706.7	388.4	111.09	110.89	111.04
1963	145.3	114.49	727.4	400.4	114.35	114.31	114.34
1964	151.0	119.05	751.0	415.0	118.05	118.47	118.16
1965	158.4	124.88	780.4	435.0	122.69	124.18	123.06
1966	169.9	133.90	817.2	460.8	128.46	131.55	129.23
1967	180.7	142.41	856.2	487.6	134.60	139.21	135.75
1968	188.0	148.16	894.7	512.7	140.64	146.38	142.08
1969	195.0	153.72	935.4	538.7	147.04	153.78	148.72

Sources: Columns 1, 3, and 4, Office of Business Economics, data are averages of values at the beginning and end of the years (columns 3 and 4 are based on use of Bulletin F service lives and the Winfrey distribution, column 4 is based on use of straight-line depreciation); columns 2, 5, and 6, computed from columns 1, 3, and 4; column 7, a weighted average of column 5 (weighted 3) and column 6 (weighted 1).

a. Indexes are computed from capital stock data in millions of dollars. The values have been rounded to a tenth of a billion.

from the gross stock simultaneously, after expiration of the average service life. Instead, more realistically, retirements are dispersed around the average service life. The Winfrey S-3 distribution is used to obtain this dispersion. The gross stock at any date consists of the capital goods that have entered the stock in the past and have not yet been retired.

5. The net stock series shown is equal to gross stock less accumulated depreciation with depreciation computed by use of the straight-line formula.

6. Data from the OBE capital stock series, as published or ordinarily made available, include institutional structures used by nonprofit organizations. OBE estimated the amounts included, for use in this study, and they have been eliminated so that the estimates in Table 5-2 are confined to business capital.

7. For use in this study, values of the capital stock at the beginning and end of each year were averaged to approximate the average value during the year.

Measurement of Capital Input

Given the capital stock data, how should capital input be measured?[7] If all capital goods were like the "wonderful one hoss shay," their ability to perform services would not change during their service lives. In that case the gross stock, which places an unchanging value on each item throughout its useful service life, would provide the correct capital stock series for capital input measure-

7. This subject is discussed in more detail in Edward F. Denison, "Final Comments" (conclusion of interchange between Denison and Jorgenson–Griliches on major issues in productivity measurement), in "The Measurement of Productivity," pp. 101–04.

ment. Use of this assumption probably would lead to no great error but it is extreme. The performance of at least some types of capital goods deteriorates unless maintenance and repair costs (which are deducted to obtain net output) are increased as a good ages; it may deteriorate in any case. Also, newer capital goods are more likely to be in the place and use where they are most advantageous to production.

To introduce an allowance for rising maintenance expense and deterioration of capital services with the passage of time, I have adopted the following expedient. To measure input of structures and equipment I have used a weighted average of indexes of the gross stock and net stock based on straight-line depreciation, with the gross stock weighted three and the net stock one. This series is shown in Table 5-2, column 7. The procedure implies that, on the average, a capital good with one-half of its useful service life exhausted can contribute seven-eighths as much to net output (when net output itself is measured by use of straight-line depreciation and after deduction of maintenance costs) as an otherwise identical good that is unused, and three-fourths as much shortly before its retirement.[8] The difference between the gross stock index (Table 5-2, column 5) and the weighted average index (column 7) measures the change that would be introduced into my capital input index if I had made no allowance for deterioration with age. Doubling my allowance (by weighting gross stock three and net stock two) would change the capital input index by a smaller amount. Differences in movement between the gross stock and capital input series are usually small and in most periods trivial, so the capital input series is not very sensitive to the exact amount of deterioration assumed. However, there are certain short periods in which the difference between the growth rates of gross stock and net stock is appreciable.

Improvements in Design Not Measured

One important characteristic of the capital input indexes must be clearly understood to interpret them properly. Improvements in the design of capital goods that raise their net contribution to output are not regarded as representing an increase in capital input (except insofar as they change the cost of a capital good).

At any point in time the business capital stock consists of items acquired by business at a wide range of dates—in the terminology of economists, of different "vintages." As time passes, the older vintages are replaced by newer vintages. Some capital goods continue to be produced without significant change for many years and are similar in different vintages, but many others are not. Suppose that capital goods of the types entering into all the different vintages were all to be produced at the same date.[9] It would then be found that the ratio of the productivity of capital goods to their cost of production was higher for goods of the types entering into later vintages than for those of the types entering into earlier vintages.

Constant-price capital stock series combine the assortment of capital goods of different vintages (as well as those of the same vintage) that are in the stock by use as weights of the cost of acquiring them in a base year (1958). If no goods of a particular type were actually acquired in the base year, the weight for that type is the estimated amount that they would have cost in that year if they had been known and produced.[10] One can imagine alternative series that would equate capital goods of different vintages by their marginal products (ability to contribute to net output) in the base year or, if they were not actually in use in that year, by what their marginal products would have been in that year if they had been known and in use. Series of the former type, such as I use, are commonly denoted as "K" by economists and those of the alternate type by "J."[11] It

---

8. When the Winfrey distribution is incorporated into the estimates, the series is quite insensitive to the assumption about deterioration in the last year or so of service life. Because there is some evidence that goods are well maintained until, but only until, a decision is made to discard them, a sharper decline at the very end of service might be warranted even though many capital goods are retired well before they are worn out, because they become obsolete. The Bulletin F service lives, of course, took obsolescence into account; they were estimates of the periods of actual service as shortened by obsolescence. Within the period of actual service, the pattern of deterioration used in capital input measurement should not reflect obsolescence due to the appearance of more modern capital goods.

9. This would, of course, actually be possible only at the most recent date. It never happens in practice because it is unprofitable to produce obsolescent capital goods.

10. This should be construed as only an approximate description of the actual data, which derive from the use of a great variety of price series and procedures.

11. This terminology has become customary since publication of Robert M. Solow's article, "Investment and Technical Progress," in Kenneth J. Arrow, Samuel Karlin, and Patrick Suppes (eds.), *Mathematical Methods in the Social Sciences, 1959,* Stanford Mathematical Studies in the Social Sciences 4 (Stanford University Press, 1960), pp. 89–104. "K" and "J" correspond to what I designated "method 1" and "method 3," respectively, in Edward F. Denison, "Theoretical Aspects of Quality Change, Capital Consump-

is clear that a series of the J type would rise more over any time span than a series of the K type. The reason is that improvements in the design of structures and equipment resulting from advances in knowledge cause the ratio of marginal product in base year prices to cost under base year conditions to increase as successive vintages move into the stock of structures and equipment. There is a parallel in the inventory series because materials and supplies also change over time.

There is no real alternative to use of a series of the K type because the J type is impossible to construct. Fortunately, use of K to measure input in a study such as this is as desirable as it is necessary. It leads to a convenient classification of the sources of growth because it corresponds to basic determinants of output changes. Advances in the state of knowledge and net investment are each important contributors to growth. It is convenient to consider all of the effects of advances in knowledge as a single growth source (rather than to have a portion of these effects classified as a contribution of the increase in capital input) so that the contribution of "advances in knowledge" can be identified with actual accretions to technical and managerial knowledge, and the contribution of capital can be identified with saving and investment. The difference between indexes of J and K (which when multiplied by the capital shares represents the amount at issue) is not a result of investment but of advances in knowledge and it is not altered by changing the rate of investment.[12]

Capital Utilization Not Measured

My index of the input of structures and equipment refers to the fixed capital stock standing ready for use by business. It does not measure variations in the average hours that capital is actually used nor other aspects of intensity of use, such as the speed with which machines are operated.

In the short run, the intensity of capital utilization fluctuates with variations in the pressure of demand, but in this respect capital input is no dif-

ferent from land input or labor input. Labor input contains a substantial overhead element even though changes in working hours are taken into account in its measurement. My input series may be regarded as measures of the labor, capital, and land physically present in business establishments and available for use in production. Changes in the intensity of their use that result from variations in the pressure of demand on these "employed" resources therefore affect my series for output per unit of input. In Chapter 6 I try to isolate this effect for all the factors combined.[13] This is difficult enough, and I shall not attempt the even more difficult task of making separate estimates for the individual factors of production.

The hours that capital is used may also change in the longer run but such changes, if they occur, are merely manifestations of changes in other output determinants that are separately measured so need not be given separate consideration.[14] A possible exception is the prevalence of shift work when industry weights are held constant. My estimate, based on limited data, is that a series for the prevalence of shift work based on use of constant industry weights, were it available, would not change much apart from short-term fluctuations related to demand pressure.[15]

Movement of Capital Input

Both types of capital input have risen much more than labor input in the sector over the whole period covered in this study. Inventories increased by 163 percent from 1929 to 1969 and input of nonresidential structures and equipment by 126

tion, and Net Capital Formation," in Conference on Research in Income and Wealth, *Problems of Capital Formation: Concepts, Measurement, and Controlling Factors,* Studies in Income and Wealth, Vol. 19 (Princeton University Press for the National Bureau of Economic Research, 1957), pp. 215–61, 281–84.

12. Except to the usually trivial extent that it may temporarily affect the lag of actual business practice behind the best known. See pages 82–83.

13. See pages 66 67.
14. This topic is discussed by Edward F. Denison in Denison, Griliches, and Jorgenson, "The Measurement of Productivity," pp. 55–57.
15. For further discussion of shift work in various parts of the economy, see *Why Growth Rates Differ,* pp. 152–54.

Since the completion of that study, Paul Taubman and Peter Gottschalk, using Bureau of Labor Statistics data, have developed a series, covering only capital used by production workers in manufacturing establishments, that measures changes in the average workweek of such capital as a result of (1) changes in the average workweek of manufacturing production workers and (2) changes in the prevalence of shift work in manufacturing as a whole. (Paul Taubman and Peter Gottschalk, "The Average Workweek of Capital in Manufacturing," *Journal of the American Statistical Association,* Vol. 66 [September 1971], pp. 448–55.) Division of their series by the average workweek of production workers yields an approximate series for the prevalence of shift work. The series, which covers 1952–68, does not hold industry weights constant and is, of course, affected by short-term fluctuations in demand pressure. It shows minor fluctuations but no trend from 1952 through 1965, then rises in 1966–68.

percent, changes which compare with a 68 percent increase in labor input. The series for structures and equipment declined from 1929 to 1941 as a consequence of the collapse of investment during the depression, and even by 1947 it was scarcely above its 1929 level. But in the postwar period the input of structures and equipment increased more than input of either labor or inventories. Increases in both components of capital input, like that in labor input, were especially large after about 1963.

These findings result from the data I have used to measure capital stock in nonresidential business and the way I have used them to measure capital input. It is no secret, of course, that the measurement of both capital stock and capital input is controversial. Differences relate, for example, to the classification of growth sources, appraisals of available statistics, and conjectures as to how services of capital goods change with age. The findings here reflect my best judgment on these and other disputed issues.[16]

Land Input

An ideal index of land input would take each parcel of land available in the base period and use an input index for each parcel that would remain 100 unless there was some change in its quality.[17] The indexes for the separate parcels would then be weighted by their base period economic rent. In the absence of a change in land area or in the quality of any parcel, the total land input index necessarily would always remain 100. This would continue to be the case if the weights for the parcels were changed frequently and short-period, fixed-weight indexes were linked to obtain a continuous series.

The total land area of the country has not, in fact, changed. There have been transfers between government, nonprofit, and residential land, on the one hand, and land available for nonresidential business use on the other. However, these switches have been trivial compared to the total area of land available to the nonresidential business sector. The total acreage of private land (within which residential land is a tiny portion of the total area) has changed very little during the period covered (see Table 5-3). Hence, the index could not change much unless *net* transfers were highly concentrated in land with very high economic rent when in nonresidential business use —more concentrated than seems possible.

Some adjustment for changes in the quality of agricultural, mineral, and forest land would be desirable, but I have not found this feasible nor does it seem likely that such changes could affect the index greatly. More than one-half of the total weight (estimated earnings) of nonresidential business land relates to land whose value derives from its location (commercial and industrial sites, railroad properties, and the like). For this dominant component, changes in physical characteristics are of no consequence and questions of quality change hardly arise. Over one-third of the weight

Table 5-3. Area of Private Land, Selected Years, 1920-69

Millions of acres

	Private land	
Year	*Including Indian land* (1)	*Excluding Indian land* (2)
Excluding Alaska and Hawaii		
1920	1,404	n.a.
1930	1,411	1,359
1940	1,404	n.a.
1945	1,395	1,338
1950	1,399	1,342
1954	1,399	1,343
1959	1,376	1,322
Including Alaska and Hawaii		
1959	1,385	1,332
1964	1,378	1,328
1969	1,367	1,317

Sources: 1920 and 1940, U.S. Bureau of the Census, *Historical Statistics of the United States: Colonial Times to 1957* (1960), p. 240; 1930, 1945 1950, and 1954, U.S. Department of Agriculture, Agricultural Research Service, *Major Uses of Land in the United States: Summary for 1954*, Agriculture Information Bulletin 168 (January 1957), pp. 90, 92; 1959, excluding and including Alaska and Hawaii, U.S. Department of Agriculture, Economic Research Service, *Major Uses of Land and Water in the United States, with Special Reference to Agriculture: Summary for 1959*, Agricultural Economic Report 13 (July 1962), p. 17; 1964 and 1969, U.S. Bureau of the Census, *Statistical Abstract of the United States, 1973* (1973), p. 197.

n.a. Not available.

16. Some issues have already been discussed. A view of T. K. Rymes is considered later in Chapter 9. Appendix K, as noted on page 53, examines problems related to government capital. A number of issues are discussed in my interchange already cited with Dale W. Jorgenson and Zvi Griliches in the May 1972 *Survey of Current Business;* and in Daniel Creamer, "Measuring Capital Input for Total Factor Productivity Analysis: Comments by a Sometime Estimator," *Review of Income and Wealth,* Series 18, No. 1 (March 1972), pp. 55–78. The literature on the subject is enormous.

17. See Edward F. Denison, *The Sources of Economic Growth,* pp. 90–94, for my reasons for preferring to measure land *available* for use rather than land actually in use. (For full citation, see Chap. 1, note 1, of this book.)

in an average year refers to agricultural land and something over one-tenth to mineral and forest land.[18]

I shall assume land input in the nonresidential business sector to have been constant throughout the period. Larger errors in this assumption than seem likely would be required to affect my analysis appreciably. Land receives an average weight of only 4.35 percent in the index of total factor input in the sector. It would require an annual change of 0.23 percent in the index of land input to alter my estimate of the annual change in total factor input (or of the contribution of land

to growth of output in the sector) by even 0.01 percentage points.

Total Factor Input

Table 5-4 repeats the indexes for the four major types of input, which are also compared in Figure 5-1. Table 5-4 presents, in addition, the index of total factor input in the sector. The method by which the input indexes were combined to obtain total factor input has already been described.[19] The index shown for input of all reproducible

---

18. The weight of farm land in the total can be calculated from data in Appendix J. The proportion given for mineral and forest land is an order-of-magnitude estimate.

19. Appendix L compares this series with those obtained by some alternative formulas. Use of a Cobb-Douglas production function, with unchanged elasticities equal to average share weights in the whole period, yields an index that is almost indistinguishable from the one I adopt.

Table 5-4. Nonresidential Business: Indexes of Sector Inputs, and Sector National Income per Unit of Total Factor Input, 1929, 1940–41, and 1947–69[a]

1958 = 100

Year	Sector national income in 1958 prices (1)	Indexes of inputs						Sector national income per unit of input (8)
		Labor (2)	Inventories (3)	Non-residential structures and equipment (4)	All reproducible capital (5)	Land (6)	Total factor input (7)	
1929	46.63	72.74	58.54	65.94	63.34	100.00	72.12	64.66
1940	50.51	75.42	56.86	63.31	61.02	100.00	73.79	68.45
1941	60.23	82.98	62.61	63.98	63.30	100.00	80.06	75.23
1947	72.29	93.68	73.46	66.22	68.16	100.00	89.12	81.11
1948	77.04	94.71	75.19	69.68	71.09	100.00	90.54	85.09
1949	74.66	91.18	75.44	72.79	73.33	100.00	88.40	84.45
1950	82.45	94.15	77.12	75.58	75.79	100.00	91.17	90.44
1951	87.02	98.70	84.67	78.59	80.13	100.00	95.52	91.10
1952	89.31	100.86	90.29	81.49	83.82	100.00	97.91	91.22
1953	93.62	102.93	91.95	84.32	86.32	100.00	99.98	93.63
1954	91.40	99.51	91.53	87.06	88.20	100.00	97.67	93.58
1955	100.18	102.73	93.27	89.98	90.81	100.00	100.67	99.51
1956	102.61	104.23	97.67	93.47	94.54	100.00	102.51	100.10
1957	103.06	103.64	100.09	97.08	97.84	100.00	102.59	100.45
1958	100.00	100.00	100.00	100.00	100.00	100.00	100.00	100.00
1959	108.88	103.48	101.30	102.46	102.17	100.00	103.17	105.53
1960	110.73	103.94	104.55	105.31	105.12	100.00	103.99	106.48
1961	112.25	103.45	106.73	108.14	107.78	100.00	103.98	107.95
1962	120.01	105.47	109.88	111.04	110.75	100.00	106.07	113.15
1963	125.28	106.75	114.49	114.34	114.38	100.00	107.64	116.38
1964	132.96	108.68	119.05	118.16	118.38	100.00	109.80	121.09
1965	142.68	112.12	124.88	123.06	123.51	100.00	113.35	125.88
1966	151.69	115.77	133.90	129.23	130.39	100.00	117.31	129.31
1967	153.89	116.84	142.41	135.75	137.41	100.00	119.20	129.10
1968	161.86	119.67	148.16	142.08	143.60	100.00	122.37	132.27
1969	165.89	122.40	153.72	148.72	149.99	100.00	125.48	132.21

Sources: Column 1, computed from data underlying Table 3-2, column 7; column 2, Table 4-1, column 8; columns 3 and 4, Table 5-2, columns 2 and 7; column 6, land estimated to be 100 in all years, see text; columns 5 and 7, see text; column 8, column 1 ÷ column 7.

a. Series excluding and including Alaska and Hawaii are linked at 1960.

capital (inventories, and structures and equipment, combined) was computed by a similar procedure.

Table 5-4 also shows the index of total output (national income measured in 1958 prices) in the sector and a series for output per unit of total factor input obtained by dividing the index of output by the index for total input. Output per unit of input is analyzed in the following chapter.

Labor comprised, on the average, nearly 80 percent of total input between 1929 and 1969. About 16 percent of input consisted of the two types of capital, which in the long run have risen

more than labor, and 4 percent was land, which has not increased at all. Under these circumstances some similarity between the indexes of labor input and of total input is not surprising. The increase in total factor input over the whole forty-year period from 1929 to 1969 was only moderately greater than the increase in labor input alone: 74.0 percent as against 68.3 percent. But from 1948 to 1969 the difference was bigger; increases were 38.6 percent and 29.2 percent, respectively. Both total input and labor input have risen much more than man-hours worked, which

Figure 5-1. Nonresidential Business: Indexes of Labor, Capital, and Land Inputs, 1929, 1940–41, and 1947–69

Index (1958 = 100)

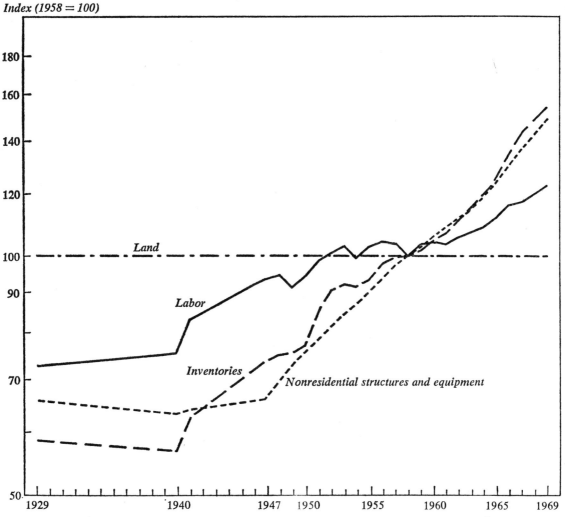

Sources: Tables 4-1 and 5-4.
Note. The years 1930–39 and 1942–46 are not plotted.

Table 5-5. Nonresidential Business: Growth Rates of Factor Inputs and Man-Hours Worked, Eight Selected Periods, 1929–69

| Period | Factor inputs | | | | | Man-hours worked (6) |
	Labor (1)	Inventories (2)	Nonresidential structures and equipment (3)	Land (4)	Total factor input (5)	
1929–69	1.31	2.44	2.05	0.00	1.39	0.45
1929–48	1.40	1.33	0.29	0.00	1.20	0.32
1929–41	1.10	0.56	−0.25	0.00	0.87	−0.17
1941–48	1.91	2.65	1.23	0.00	1.77	1.17
1948–69	1.23	3.46	3.68	0.00	1.57	0.57
1948–53	1.68	4.11	3.89	0.00	2.00	0.64
1953–64	0.49	2.38	3.12	0.00	0.86	−0.08
1964–69	2.41	5.24	4.71	0.00	2.71	1.94

Sources: Columns 1 to 5, computed from Table 5-4; column 6, computed from Table 4-1.

are often used as an alternative indicator of input. This index (shown for the sector in Table 4-1) rose by only 19.6 percent from 1929 to 1969 and by 12.6 percent from 1948 to 1969.

Table 5-5 shows, for selected periods, the growth rate of each of the major inputs and of total factor input in the sector. Growth rates of man-hours worked are also shown for comparison.

CHAPTER SIX

➤➤❯❰❰❰

Output per Unit
of Input
in Nonresidential
Business

➤➤❯❰❰❰

Measures of total factor input and output per unit of input consolidate changes in a great many determinants of output into two broad groups. In the absence of additional detail, this two-way division of the growth of nonresidential business output would provide only limited information.

Total factor input was *obtained* by combining indexes for separate components; these indexes will subsequently be used to secure appropriate detail for the contribution of inputs. But output per unit of input cannot be obtained in the same way because separate indexes for all its individual components cannot be independently derived. This series is measured by dividing the index of national income by the index of total factor input.

The determinants included in output per unit of input have jointly contributed even more to the growth of output in the nonresidential business sector than those whose effects are classified in total input. From 1929 to 1969 the average annual growth rates of output per unit of input and total factor input were 1.80 percent and 1.39 percent, respectively. Although both rates were higher in the postwar period alone, the difference between them was about the same. Productivity increase accounted for less of output growth in the whole economy than it did in this sector alone, but the fraction was still nearly half. Consequently, much of the story of growth would be

left untold if changes in output per unit of input were not assigned to specific output determinants.

Determinants of output per unit of input are numerous. Changes in any of them can alter the national income and thus contribute, positively or negatively, to growth between two dates. In the very long run, two are responsible for most of the productivity increase: advances in knowledge of how to produce at low cost and gains from economies of scale made possible by expansion of the size of markets as the economy grows. Many other determinants describe reasons that productivity falls short of the maximum that would be possible if resources were allocated and used with perfect efficiency, given the state of knowledge and the size of markets. These affect the growth rate only during a transitional period within which the economy moves to a more, or less, efficient position. However, such shifts may take place over quite long time spans. There are also irregular factors that dominate short-term movements of the productivity series and are sometimes important even in comparisons of years which are decades apart.

Changes in output per unit of input are divided among some of its determinants in this chapter. The division cannot be either complete or precise but even partial and approximate estimates are useful if made with care.[1]

The first column of Table 6-1 repeats the series for output per unit of input in the sector that is presented in Table 5-4. Subsequent columns provide indexes of the effects of changes in individual determinants upon the composite index. The indexes for total output per unit of input and its components shown in Table 6-1 are all measured on a scale such that a difference of, say, 1 percent in the value of an index in any year would change total national income in nonresidential business by an estimated 1 percent.[2]

1. Procedures used for most determinants are refinements of those applied in *Why Growth Rates Differ* (for full citation, see Chap. 1, note 2, of this book). Estimates are adapted to take account of the fact that in *Why Growth Rates Differ* they referred to productivity change in the whole economy, whereas in this chapter they refer to productivity change in the nonresidential business sector; estimates relating to the whole economy are discussed in Chapter 9. To secure the effects of changes in the intensity of the pressure of demand, an entirely new, and superior, method has now been adopted.

2. In this respect these indexes are similar to that for total factor input in Table 5-4, column 7, but not, of course, to indexes for the separate inputs as they are presented in Tables 4-1 and 5-4. The percentage change in sector national income that would result from a difference of 1 percent in the index for a single input is the product of 1 percent and the weight of the input. For example, in a period during which labor input represents 80 percent of total input, a

Table 6-1. Nonresidential Business: Indexes of Sector Output per Unit of Input, 1929, 1940–41, and 1947–69

1958 = 100

Year	Output per unit of input (1)	Gains from reallocation of resources from: Farming (2)	Gains from reallocation of resources from: Nonfarm self-employ-ment (3)	Effect of weather on farm output (4)	Changes in intensity of utilization of employed resources resulting from: Work stoppages (5)	Changes in intensity of utilization of employed resources resulting from: Fluctua-tions in intensity of demand (6)	Economies of scale, advances in knowledge, and all other determinants: Total (semi-residual) (7)	Economies of scale (8)	Advances in knowledge and all other (residual) (9)
1929	64.66	91.18	99.45	100.11	100.04	104.76	67.96	89.35	76.07
1940	68.45	92.00	98.96	99.35	100.04	103.11	73.36	91.39	80.28
1941	75.23	93.58	99.79	100.00	99.99	107.95	74.63	91.88	81.23
1947	81.11	96.61	99.84	99.56	99.97	102.45	82.48	94.93	86.88
1948	85.09	96.85	99.81	100.35	99.98	105.51	83.15	95.35	87.21
1949	84.45	96.67	99.46	99.97	99.93	104.26	84.33	95.67	88.15
1950	90.44	97.13	99.59	100.28	99.96	107.30	86.92	96.00	90.55
1951	91.10	98.09	100.00	99.79	100.01	105.36	88.33	96.67	91.37
1952	91.22	98.39	100.06	99.90	99.89	103.21	89.96	97.47	92.30
1953	93.63	98.79	100.24	100.16	99.99	101.86	92.69	98.14	94.45
1954	93.58	98.62	100.00	100.12	100.01	100.75	94.06	98.65	95.35
1955	99.51	99.05	100.20	100.20	99.99	104.39	95.86	98.93	96.90
1956	100.10	99.63	100.27	100.12	99.98	102.98	97.20	99.33	97.85
1957	100.45	99.92	100.28	99.90	100.02	101.45	98.91	99.72	99.18
1958	100.00	100.00	100.00	100.00	100.00	100.00	100.00	100.00	100.00
1959	105.53	100.26	100.25	100.03	99.85	102.70	102.35	100.28	102.07
1960	106.48	100.52	100.27	100.14	100.01	101.32	104.11	100.61	103.48
1961	107.95	100.56	100.13	100.11	100.02	101.35	105.63	101.01	104.58
1962	113.15	100.89	100.33	100.02	100.01	103.19	108.28	101.43	106.76
1963	116.38	101.18	100.55	100.11	100.02	103.40	110.48	101.91	108.41
1964	121.09	101.50	100.58	99.98	100.01	105.61	112.32	102.45	109.64
1965	125.88	101.75	100.88	100.22	100.01	106.76	114.60	103.12	111.13
1966	129.31	102.14	101.26	99.86	100.01	106.96	117.05	103.95	112.60
1967	129.10	102.36	101.38	100.17	99.97	104.71	118.64	104.62	113.40
1968	132.27	102.50	101.45	100.15	99.97	104.01	122.14	105.25	116.05
1969	132.21	102.69	101.52	100.07	99.98	101.71	124.64	105.99	117.60

Sources: Column 1, Table 5-4, column 8; column 2, Table N-2, column 1; column 3, see Appendix N, pages 289-90; column 4, see Appendix O, page 291; column 5, Table O-1, column 2; column 6, Table O-4, column 4; column 7, Table O-4, column 5; column 8, Table P-1, column 4; column 9, column 7 ÷ column 8.

I turn now to a discussion of these component indexes. Only a summary discussion will be provided here. More detailed discussion and full descriptions of the estimates are provided in Appendixes N, O, and P. The order in which determinants are examined is dictated solely by convenience for the process of estimation; it has no other logic.

Reallocation of Resources from Farming and Nonfarm Self-Employment

The more nearly that employed resources are allocated to the uses in which their contributions to the value of output are greatest, the larger is output per unit of input. Mainly because shifting patterns of demand for labor have long been reducing the requirements for farm labor while the actual transfer of labor has lagged, overallocation of labor to farming has been a chronic condition. Indeed, throughout the period covered by this study it was by far the biggest type of misallocation of resources among uses.

1 percent change in the index for labor input or for any of its components, as they are presented in Table 4-1, would change national income in the sector by 0.8 percent. This difference in the form of presentation is taken into account when the indexes are used to calculate estimates of the sources of growth (see p. 103).

As farm employment shrank, the fraction of total business employment thus misallocated declined. Farming used about 22.7 percent of total labor input in the nonresidential business sector in 1929, 14.7 percent in 1947, and 5.1 percent in 1969. Thus, the percentage of *total* business labor misallocated to farming would have been much reduced even if the percentage of *farm* labor that was excessive had not declined—which it has. The labor input figures cited are approximately consistent with those developed for the sector as a whole in Chapter 4: they distinguish between full-time and part-time employment, and they take account of the composition of employment by sex and by level of education. The farm percentage of the sector's national income, measured in 1958 prices, is smaller than its percentage of labor input and has declined less: from 11.4 percent in 1929 to 7.6 percent in 1947 and 4.2 percent in 1969. The drop in the farm percentage of the sector's labor input from 1947 to 1969 (9.6 percentage points) was nearly three times as large as the drop (3.4 points) in the farm percentage of the sector's national income.

The gain in output per unit of input resulting from reduction in the overallocation of labor to farming is calculated from two estimates. First, it is estimated that if labor input in the nonfarm portion of nonresidential business had been larger by 1 percent in any year, nonfarm output in the sector would have been larger by 0.8 percent, approximately the labor share of national income. Second, it is estimated that if labor input in farming had been smaller by 1 percent in any year, farm output (farm national income in 1958 prices) would have been smaller by 0.33 percent. This estimate supposes that the reduction in labor would be concentrated on small farms with little output to about the same extent as was the actual reduction of labor in farming.

These two estimates permit a calculation of the percentage by which national income in the nonresidential business sector as a whole would have been raised each year if labor input in the sector had been divided between farm and nonfarm work in the following year's proportion. This percentage is my estimate of the gain from one year to the next in output per unit of input that resulted from the shift of resources from farming to nonfarm jobs. The annual percentages were linked to obtain a continuous index, shown in Table 6-1, column 2. A full discussion of the series and its construction appears in Appendix N.

No allowance is made for any increase in output resulting from a shift of capital and land from farming because it is not certain that too much capital or land has been allocated to farming. In any case, the farm share of these inputs declined much less than that of labor.

The shift of labor out of agriculture has been nearly continuous. Aside from the deep depression years of the 1930s, which are omitted from the table, the decline in the farm share of labor input in the business sector was interrupted only in 1949 and 1954, years in which nonfarm employment fell more than farm employment. The gain in output per unit of input resulting from the shift was considerable. Over the whole period from 1929 to 1969, the index implies, output per unit of input in the nonresidential business sector was raised by an average of 0.30 percent a year, nearly one-sixth of the growth rate of output per unit of input from all sources. The contribution of the shift from farming was as much as 0.34 percentage points from 1950 to 1960. It declined to 0.24 from 1960 to 1969, but even in the 1965–69 period was still 0.23. In view of the small size of remaining farm employment, it is somewhat remarkable that the contribution had not fallen more than this by 1965–69. An extraordinarily large rise in nonfarm business employment helped to sustain the reduction in the proportion of farm employment that led to the gain in productivity, but the contraction in farm employment itself continued to be substantial in this period. It is fairly evident that in the near future the gain in output per unit of input resulting from the shift out of farming must drop sharply.

My estimate of the gain from the movement of labor out of farming embraces both of what sometimes are counted as two different sources of output growth. The more important (in the United States) is sometimes called the "shift effect": because the value of output per unit of input is greater in nonfarm business than in farm production, a shift in weights away from farming raises the average value in the two combined. The less important source is the favorable effect upon output per unit of input *within* farming of eliminating workers who are underemployed, or very inefficiently employed, on small farms having an almost trivial value of output. In some studies reduction of underemployment or inefficient use is classified as an increase in effective labor input rather than a component of productivity change.

Persons who are underemployed or whose

labor is very wastefully utilized are also present among the nonfarm self-employed and unpaid members of their families. Not very long ago, the numbers of such persons were substantial. These individuals work in enterprises that are not only small but also highly inefficient. Little or no paid labor is hired, which holds down out-of-pocket expenses and enables an enterprise to survive when it could not do so if labor had to be paid in cash. Turnover among such enterprises is high as hopeful newcomers replace their unsuccessful predecessors. But many endure as long as their owners can subsist on the small earnings obtained, and disappear only with owners' disability or death. Members of this "fringe" group among the self-employed contribute little to the value of production, but if hired by larger enterprises they could contribute as much to output as other workers.

Such persons are only a fraction—today, a small fraction—of the total number of self-employed and unpaid family workers engaged in nonfarm activities. However, the *reduction* in the share of nonfarm business employment that is represented by the self-employed and unpaid family workers appears to have occurred among this fringe group, rather than among those who are independent professionals, operate more sizable establishments, do well as craftsmen, repairmen, or the like, or are simply unqualified for paid jobs. The reduction in the percentage of labor input in *nonfarm* nonresidential business that consists of self-employed and unpaid family workers was from 15.15 percent in 1929 to 14.12 percent in 1951 (after a brief postwar upturn), and to 11.46 in 1969 (Table N-4).

Transfer of workers from the fringe group among the self-employed to paid employment contributed to the rise in productivity. The index shown in Table 6-1, column 3, is my estimate of the effect on output per unit of input in the sector. It was calculated on the assumption that, as the importance of self-employment diminished, an increase in wage and salary employment only one-fourth as large as the decline in self-employment was required to obtain production of equal value. This assumption takes into consideration not only that those leaving self-employment had a low value of output per person, but also that the work they formerly did could often be absorbed by those remaining in that status. Appendix N discusses this assumption and fully describes the calculation of the index. No allowance is made for possible savings in capital or land.

It is estimated that the shift from nonfarm self-employment to paid employment raised output per unit of input in the sector by an average of 0.05 percent a year over the whole period from 1929 to 1969. The decline in the importance of self-employment was continuous except in recession years, when wage and salary employment dropped sharply, and immediately after World War II. In the immediate postwar years large numbers of new, small firms were started, many with aid from the GI bill; most survived only until the hopeful entrepreneurs had lost their capital and credit. This episode is manifested in a temporary decline in the index until 1949, followed by an especially large rise in the following years. Some fluctuations in the rate of change in the index from year to year may reflect errors in the estimated numbers of self-employed and, especially, unpaid family workers. Errors of this type largely offset corresponding errors in the labor input index, which was constructed by use of the same employment data.

The series described in this section are designed to measure the effects of shifts from farming and nonfarm self-employment upon output per unit of input as I have measured it, or upon output per employed person. Their construction is consistent with a convention adopted in measuring labor input. Otherwise-similar full-time workers are counted as contributing the same amount of input whether they are engaged in farming, employed as nonfarm wage and salary workers, or employed as nonfarm self-employed and unpaid family workers—even though there are large differences in the average weekly hours reported for these groups.[3] The series therefore do not measure the effect of the shifts upon output per *man-hour worked* in the nonresidential business sector; this effect was much larger because the shift reduced average hours worked by employed persons. Neither do the series measure the effect of the shifts upon *total* national income in the nonresidential business sector, because employment may also have been affected. Historically, according to Durand, the population movement from the farm lowered employment of teenage boys and older men but raised employment of women by a larger amount.[4] Such effects on employment are automatically reflected in the employment series.

---

3. See pages 41–43.
4. John D. Durand, *The Labor Force in the United States, 1890–1960* (Social Science Research Council, 1948), pp. 63–73.

Irregular Fluctuations

Irregular fluctuations in output per unit of input may be due to one-time random events which defy systematic identification and measurement. But they result chiefly from recurrent and identifiable conditions. Four of these conditions appear important enough to require discussion and an attempt at measurement. They are (1) irregular fluctuations in farm output associated chiefly with the weather and other natural conditions, (2) work stoppages resulting from labor disputes, (3) variations in the intensity with which employed resources are used as a result of changes in the pressure of demand, and (4) variations in the number and composition of days in the year. The third is by far the most important.

Estimates of the effects of the first three of these conditions are presented in Table 6-1, columns 4 to 6. They are shown as indexes with 1958 equal to 100, so that an entry for a specific year of 101, for example, means that conditions were sufficiently more favorable that year than they were in 1958 to make output per unit of input in the sector 1 percent higher than it would have been with conditions as they were in 1958; thus the base does not refer to average or typical conditions. The effects of the fourth condition (variation in the calendar) could not be measured, and the inability to do so seriously restricts analysis of very short-term changes in productivity.

The conditions examined in this section are not sources of long-term growth but they do substantially influence the movement of output per unit of input. Their effects are often large enough to affect comparisons even of years that are rather widely separated in time.

Irregular Fluctuations in Farm Output

Variations in weather and such natural conditions as pest infestation introduce irregular fluctuations into farm output. Their effect on productivity in the nonresidential business sector as a whole was approximated by a simple device. Actual national income in the nonresidential business sector each year was compared with a hypothetical figure obtained by substituting for the actual farm output component of that total its five-year average, centered in that year.[5] The ratio of the actual to the hypothetical national income

figure was then calculated each year. The index of these ratios is shown in Table 6-1, column 4.

The average postwar value of the index was 100.05, so a figure higher than this indicates better-than-average conditions. The extreme range of the index is 0.8 percent during the postwar period, and 1.0 percent if all years shown are considered. In Table 6-1, division of column 1 by column 4 would yield an index showing what the movement of output per unit of input in the sector would have been in the absence of irregular fluctuations in farm output.

Work Stoppages Due to Labor Disputes

Work stoppages resulting from labor disputes tend to reduce output per unit of input even though time not worked, whether in industries involved in disputes or in other industries, is excluded from labor input. Capital and land left idle are not eliminated from the input measure, and the productivity of workers remaining at work may be impaired. An index of the effect of work stoppages on output per unit of input in the sector is shown in Table 6-1, column 5. Because it is impossible to take account of the fact that every strike is different, the series is necessarily crude.[6] Appendix O, Part 2, provides a full description of its derivation, of which the following is a summary.

The percentage of total work time in the nonresidential business sector that was lost by workers (not only strikers) employed in establishments involved in disputes was computed by use of Bureau of Labor Statistics (BLS) data. The percentage by which output per unit of input in the sector was impaired by developments within firms involved in disputes was estimated to be three-tenths as large as the percentage of time lost. Of the three-tenths, two-tenths correspond approximately to the weight of nonlabor inputs, and offset the inclusion in total input of idle capital and land ordinarily used by persons on strike or laid off in struck establishments. The remaining one-tenth is a conservative allowance for the continuance of depreciation during disputes (which reduces net output), for the possible impairment of productivity of persons who remain at work for struck firms, and for the possible idling of nonlabor inputs ordinarily used by nonstrikers who are laid off by unstruck establishments of struck firms.

No systematic data are available for time lost by employees of firms that buy from, sell to,

---

5. The moving average was adjusted to smooth out declines which appeared on two occasions. Details of the construction of the index are provided in Appendix O, Part 1.

6. Errors in this index are offset by errors in the following index—for fluctuations in the pressure of demand—because of the method used to estimate the latter series.

transport the products of, or are otherwise connected with firms involved in disputes. However, principal work stoppages were examined to see whether they affected other industries enough to disturb the continuity of the annual series for output per unit of input.[7] The 1952 and 1959 steel strikes seem to have done so. In making the calculation already described, estimated time lost in other industries as a consequence of these strikes was added to time lost in establishments involved in disputes.

The average value of this index in the postwar period, 1947–69, is 99.98 (Table 6-1, column 5). The extreme range of fluctuation is less than 0.2 percent.

Fluctuations in Intensity of Demand

The business cycle strongly influences changes in productivity. As the strength of demand for business products fluctuates up or down, business responds by adjusting production. In most industries, including almost all those engaged in distribution or the provision of services, production adjusts automatically and simultaneously when sales vary; a lag may occur in industries filling orders from inventory. Although business also adjusts total input, neither the magnitude nor the timing of the adjustment is, or can be, the same for input as for output. In consequence, the intensity with which employed resources are used not only fluctuates but does so in a complex and irregular fashion; the irregularity is intensified by the phenomenon of labor hoarding. Such fluctuations in intensity of use greatly affect the movement of output per unit of input.

Table 6-1, column 6, provides my estimate of the effect upon output per unit of input of differences from 1958 in the utilization of employed resources resulting from fluctuations in demand pressure. The average postwar value of the index is 103.53, so index values above this figure indicate years in which this condition was more favorable than average, lower figures years in which it was less favorable.[8] The range within which the index fluctuates is large: more than 7 percent within the postwar period, almost 8 percent if the prewar years shown are included. The range would be even greater if extreme years such as 1933 and 1942 had also been included.

Because fluctuations in demand affect productivity so much, it was essential that a reasonably

satisfactory method of estimating this series be found. Otherwise, it would have been necessary to confine analysis of productivity trends to intervals between years that seem fairly comparable with respect to intensity of utilization and which are far enough apart to minimize the effect of any incomparability upon growth rates; moreover, selection of comparable years would have been difficult. In my opinion, a reasonably satisfactory solution was found. The series, though imperfect, appears adequate to allow calculation of a series for productivity, with the effects of this determinant removed, that can sensibly be analyzed over fairly short time periods.

Appendix O, Part 3, describes in detail the nature of the problem, the reasoning behind the method adopted, and the method itself. It also examines for reasonableness the estimates obtained for individual years. Below is a brief sketch of my approach and procedure.

The problem was to find an independent series whose movement is affected by changes in intensity of utilization in the same way and at the same time as productivity, and which is not greatly affected in the short run by other influences. Reflection suggested that the nonlabor share—specifically, nonlabor earnings in corporations expressed as a percentage of corporate national income—would provide such a series.[9] A preliminary test showed that annual changes in productivity were in fact highly correlated with annual changes in the corporate nonlabor share. Consequently, the nonlabor share is the chief ingredient entering into the estimates, whose derivation I now summarize.

An adjusted productivity series was first constructed by dividing column 1 of Table 6-1 by columns 2, 3, and 4; this eliminated the effects on output per unit of input of all the determinants, except work stoppages, that have been isolated thus far. For the years from 1947 through 1969, the ratio of adjusted productivity to its postwar trend value was then correlated with the deviation (in percentage points) of the corporate nonlabor share from its postwar trend value. As expected, the relationship was close; the value of $\bar{r}^2$ (r^2 corrected for degrees of freedom) was 0.90 (see page 300). Residuals were randomly distributed over time.

The regression equation was then applied to each year's nonlabor share to obtain a "calcu-

---

7. See pages 293–94.
8. Table O-4, column 3, and Table O-5, column 1, show the index as a ratio to the postwar average.

9. As elsewhere in this study, depreciation was computed by a consistent method and valued at current prices to arrive at the nonlabor share.

lated" value for the ratio of output per unit of input to its trend value. Because fluctuations in intensity of utilization are the only factor known or believed to contribute to correlation between productivity and the nonlabor share (wage-price movements were found not to do so), these calculated ratios (when converted to a 1958 base) could be used directly as an index of the effects of fluctuations in the intensity of utilization upon output per unit of input. Because work stoppages affect utilization (and hence productivity and the nonlabor share) in much the same way as do fluctuations in the pressure of demand, the series so obtained measures the combined effects of both; it was therefore divided by the work stoppage index (Table 6-1, column 5) to secure a preliminary series for column 6.

A further adjustment, rather minor in its effect, was introduced to secure the final series shown in column 6. It was recognized that short-run changes in the nonlabor share could result not only from changes in intensity of utilization but also from irregular changes in the relationship between wages and prices; such movements probably are a main reason that the correlation between productivity and the nonlabor share is not even closer than it is. The adjustment introduced was designed to eliminate the effect exerted on the preliminary utilization index by the effects of irregular wage-price movements on the nonlabor share.[10]

Changes in the intensity of utilization of employed resources are responsible for most of the short-term irregularities that remain in the output per unit of input series after account has been taken of resource allocation, the weather, and work stoppages (see Figure O-2). They appreciably affect productivity differences even between years that are quite far removed in time.

Length and Composition of the Year

The fourth recurrent irregular factor differs from the others in that it results from inconsistent and inaccurate data rather than from real developments in the economy. Unfortunately, it proved impossible to prepare even a rough annual index of its effects. These, I am convinced, are often so large, relative to the average annual change in productivity, as to require a major qualification of

comparisons of annual changes in productivity, or of even two-year and perhaps three-year changes. The topic is discussed in Appendix O, Part 4. The problem, in brief, is as follows.

A year may consist of fifty-two weeks and a Sunday, fifty-two weeks and two weekdays, or anything in between. Total factor input and all its components, however, are measured on a weekly average basis or the equivalent. No input series is affected by differences in the length of the year so these can be ignored in considering changes in input series.[11] Output, in contrast, purports to measure total output during a calendar year. If it actually did so, output and therefore output per unit of input would be affected by differences in the calendar. In that case, annual output could be "seasonally adjusted" for differences in the calendar if the relative importance in production of different days of the week were known, much as a "trading day" adjustment is used to seasonally adjust monthly retail sales. Assumed but reasonable weights suggest, for example, that because of variations in the calendar alone true output, and therefore (given the input measure) output per unit of input, should have risen 0.7 percent from 1967 to 1968, and fallen 0.4 percent from 1968 to 1969.[12]

The main problem arises because the series by which output is measured does not correspond to true output; it is affected by the calendar but in a way that cannot be ascertained. The reason is that employee compensation, the largest component of national income, is not reported on an accrual basis but instead corresponds to wages paid each year. Workers are most often paid on a weekly basis. For employers paying every Friday, employee compensation includes fifty-two payroll periods in most years but fifty-three when there is an extra Friday. The frequency with which payroll periods end on each of the days of the week is unknown, as is the frequency of daily, weekly, biweekly, semimonthly, monthly, and other pay periods. Payments surely were appreciably bigger (because of the calendar) in 1948, which had fifty-three Thursdays and Fridays, than in 1967, which had only a fifty-third Sunday (an unlikely payday). The direction of the difference between other years can sometimes be inferred; the calendar probably contributed even more to

---

10. Figure O-1 compares the index before and after the introduction of the adjustment. Available data allowed calculation of the adjustment only from 1948 on. For this and other reasons, I regard the estimate of the index for 1947 as unreliable.

11. The situation is quite different for holidays. The series for labor input (though not the capital and land series) take full account of changes in their frequency and the days of the week on which they fall.

12. See Table O-7 and its description in Appendix O.

the 1967–68 gain in measured output and productivity than to the gain in true output. But even a qualitative statement as to the direction of error is not always possible. Information is wholly inadequate for construction of a continuous time series for calendar effects.

An Intermediate Productivity Series

Before remaining determinants of output in nonresidential business—advances in knowledge, economies of scale, and many others—are considered

separately, their joint effects will be examined. Division of column 1 of Table 6-1 by columns 2 through 6 yields a series for output per unit of total factor input in the nonresidential business sector from which gains from the shifts of resources out of agriculture and nonfarm self-employment have been removed and the effects of three irregular determinants eliminated. For brevity, I shall refer to the resulting series, shown in column 7, as the "semiresidual." It is a much smoother series than that for total output or total output per unit of input. In Figure 6-1 the index

Figure 6-1. **Nonresidential Business: Indexes of Total Output and the Semiresidual, 1929, 1940–41, and 1947–69**

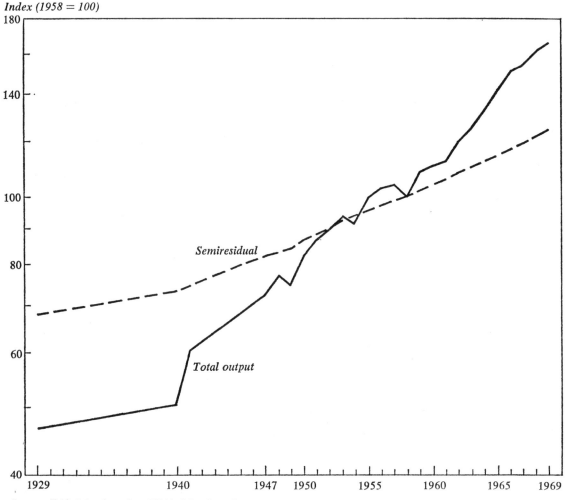

Index (1958 = 100)

Sources: Table 5-4, column 1, and Table 6-1, column 7.
Note. The years 1930–39 and 1942–46 are not plotted.

of the semiresidual is compared with the total output series from which it was derived by elimination of the effects of changes in inputs and, insofar as they could be measured, reallocation of resources and irregular factors. Its major movements will now be examined, but no attempt at explanation will be made in this section.[13]

To facilitate comparisons, a "growth rate triangle" for the semiresidual is presented in Table 6-2. It shows the growth rate of the semiresidual (rounded to one decimal point) from every year for which an estimate is available to every other year, and thus provides all of the information which can be obtained from this series.

The growth rate of the semiresidual over the whole period from 1929 to 1969 (using unrounded data underlying Table 6-2) was 1.53 percent. The period divides naturally into three main subdivisions. The first, 1929 to 1940 or 1941, spans the Great Depression. Measured from 1929 to 1940 the growth rate was 0.70; from 1929 to 1941, 0.78; their average is 0.74. The second subdivision spans World War II and the reconversion years. The growth rate was 1.58 from 1940 to 1948, and about the same, 1.56, from 1941 to 1948.[14] The third subdivision covers the postwar years from 1948 to 1969, in which the growth rate was 1.95 percent. Varying the latter period a little (for example, to 1948–68 or 1949–69) would only slightly change this figure.

Thus the rate from 1929 to 1940/41 was far below the rate thereafter. The rate from 1940/41 to 1948 was much closer to the postwar rate.[15]

13. One reason for devoting extended attention to this intermediate productivity series is that its construction does not require the difficult separation of gains from advances in knowledge from gains resulting from economies of scale which is introduced later in this chapter. This division is frequently cited in economic literature as the classic example of the difficulties encountered in isolating the effects of individual determinants upon time series (or more often, in fitting "production functions" from time series data by use of correlation analysis).

14. I prefer not to use 1947 in dividing broad periods for this series. First, the immediate postwar conversion was still under way. Second, national accountants believe the continuation of World War II price controls into 1947 caused prices in the business sector to be understated, and output therefore to be overstated, relative to other years covered in this study. The effect of the overstatement of output passes through in its entirety to the semiresidual, causing the rise from 1947 to 1948 to be understated. Third, the utilization index for 1947 is unusually subject to error. However, as already noted, use of 1948 suffers from the defect that the calendar was especially favorable.

15. Although I have discarded the 1947 observation, it should perhaps be noted that the rate from 1940 to 1947 was only 0.20 percentage points below that from 1947 to 1969.

The growth rate to 1969 is 1.85 if the calculation is started in 1941 and 1.95 if it is started in 1948. Thus the broad picture that emerges so far is a growth rate of about 0.8 percent from 1929 to 1941 and a much higher rate of about 1.9 from 1941 to 1969.

Were there changes in the growth rate within the 1948–69 period? To consider this question, I disregard all rates covering periods of one or two years because they are too much affected by the calendar and possibly by other erratic factors as well to provide usable evidence. The remaining 190 rates are those shown in italics within the growth rate triangle (Table 6-2). Seventy-six of these 190 rates are 1.9 percent, the same as the rate for the period as a whole, and 148 are 1.8 to 2.0 percent. Of the remainder, fourteen are 1.7 and seven are lower than this; fifteen are 2.1 and six are higher than this. Thus there is a heavy concentration around the whole-period rate. Perusal of the detailed patterns of rates leads to two main conclusions.

First, there has been no sustained tendency for the rate to rise or fall during the postwar period. This is seen most easily by a division of the period into halves, with use of a few alternative time spans as a check. From 1948 or 1949 to 1958 or 1959, the growth rates were 1.9 or 2.0. From 1958 or 1959 to 1968 or 1969, they were 2.0. More detailed examination of the table confirms this conclusion.

Second, growth of the semiresidual was smaller during the middle of the postwar period than at either end. This is best seen by examination of a succession of three-, four-, or five-year growth rates. For example, if the lowest italicized numbers are scanned diagonally downward across the columns, one sees a series of nineteen three-year growth rates running from 1948–51 through 1966–69. The first five such rates are 2.0 to 2.2. The next five range from 1.4 to 1.7. The last nine are 1.8 to 2.1. A similar mid-period dip appears if one follows four-year rates or five-year rates across the table.

Although the appearance of such a dip is fairly clear, I find it impossible, on the basis of this series alone, to specify its magnitude or to date the middle period. If one simply wished to maximize differences, he would date it 1953–58; this yields growth rates of 2.2 for 1948–53, 1.5 for 1953–58, and 2.0 for 1958–69. However, replacement of 1958 by 1961 yields almost as large differences; the rates are: 1948–53, 2.2; 1953–61,

Table 6-2. Nonresidential Business: Growth Rates of the Semiresidual, 1929–69

Base year	Terminal year												
	1940	1941	1947	1948	1949	1950	1951	1952	1953	1954	1955	1956	1957
1929	0.7	0.8	1.1	1.1	1.1	1.2	1.2	1.2	1.3	1.3	1.3	1.3	1.3*
1940	...	1.7	1.7	1.6	1.6	1.7	1.7	1.7	1.8	1.8	1.8	1.8	1.8
1941	...	...	1.7*	1.6	1.5	1.7	1.7	1.7	1.8	1.8	1.8	1.8	1.8
1947	...	...	...	0.8	1.1	1.8	1.7	1.8	2.0	1.9	1.9	1.8	1.8
1948	...	...	...	...	1.4	2.2	2.0	2.0	2.2	2.1	2.1	2.0	1.9
1949	...	...	...	...	...	3.1	2.3	2.2	2.4	2.2	2.2*	2.0	2.0
1950	...	...	...	...	...	...	1.6	1.7	2.2	2.0	2.0	1.9	1.9
1951	...	...	...	...	...	...	...	1.8	2.4	2.1	2.1	1.9	1.9
1952	...	...	...	...	...	...	...	...	3.0	2.3	2.1	2.0	1.9
1953	...	...	...	...	...	...	...	...	...	1.5	1.7	1.6	1.6
1954	...	...	...	...	...	...	...	...	...	...	1.9	1.7	1.7
1955	...	...	...	...	...	...	...	...	...	...	...	1.4	1.6
1956	...	...	...	...	...	...	...	...	...	...	...	...	1.8
1957	...	...	...	...	...	...	...	...	...	...	...	...	...
1958	...	...	...	...	...	...	...	...	...	...	...	...	...
1959	...	...	...	...	...	...	...	...	...	...	...	...	...
1960	...	...	...	...	...	...	...	...	...	...	...	...	...
1961	...	...	...	...	...	...	...	...	...	...	...	...	...
1962	...	...	...	...	...	...	...	...	...	...	...	...	...
1963	...	...	...	...	...	...	...	...	...	...	...	...	...
1964	...	...	...	...	...	...	...	...	...	...	...	...	...
1965	...	...	...	...	...	...	...	...	...	...	...	...	...
1966	...	...	...	...	...	...	...	...	...	...	...	...	...
1967	...	...	...	...	...	...	...	...	...	...	...	...	...
1968	...	...	...	...	...	...	...	...	...	...	...	...	...

Source: Table 6-1, column 7.
* Growth rates between years in which the calendar is identical; see Table O-7, column 2.

1.6; 1961–69, 2.1. Moreover, such an approach is greatly compromised by the aberrantly large 3.0 percent increase from 1952 to 1953. If this erratic rise is regarded as more appropriately grouped with the following than with the preceding years, and 1953 is therefore replaced by 1952 in the calculations, the mid-term dip is greatly reduced. One then obtains: 1948–52, 2.0; 1952–58, 1.8; and 1958–69, 2.0. Or, with 1958 replaced by 1961: 1948–52, 2.0; 1952–61, 1.8; and 1961–69, 2.1. The 1953 increase could perhaps best be divided between the early and middle periods, which would yield an intermediate estimate of the size of the dip. Because even time spans of three years and more are somewhat affected by calendar differences, there is value, as a check, in examining the eleven growth rates between years in which the calendar was identical which lie within the italicized triangle. Such an examination confirms the presence of a mid-period dip, but contributes no clear indication of its duration or magnitude.

At the end of the 1960s and the start of the 1970s, there was speculation that the trend rate of increase in productivity might have declined sharply. This fear was somewhat alleviated when the Bureau of Labor Statistics series for output per man-hour subsequently showed large gains as the economy moved into the phase of strong cyclical expansion, supporting the view that its earlier poor performance had been at least partially cyclical in character. The semiresidual suggests that through 1969, at least, there was no deceleration in productivity advance that is not explained by determinants already explored— mainly, demand-related changes in intensity of utilization. From 1966 to 1969, the growth rate of the semiresidual was 2.1, and the rate from any other year in the 1960s to 1969 is at least 2.0, slightly above the postwar average. The change from 1968 to 1969 was 2.0 percent despite the fact that 1968 had one more weekday than 1969. The particularly poor performance of output per man-hour from 1968 to 1969 was, I believe, due partly to the calendar but chiefly to weakening in demand for products combined with delayed reduction in employment and hours.[16]

16. See pages 306–07.

					Terminal year							Base year
1958	1959	1960	1961	1962	1963	1964	1965	1966	1967	1968	1969	
1.3	1.4	1.4	1.4	1.4	1.4*	1.4	1.5	1.5	1.5	1.5	1.5	1929
1.7	1.8	1.8	1.8	1.8	1.8	1.8	1.8	1.8	1.8	1.8*	1.8	1940
1.7*	1.8	1.8	1.8	1.8	1.8	1.8	1.8	1.8	1.8	1.8	1.8*	1941
1.8*	1.8	1.8	1.8	1.8	1.8	1.8	1.8	1.9	1.8	1.9	1.9*	1947
1.9	1.9	1.9	1.9	1.9	1.9	1.9	1.9	1.9	1.9	1.9	1.9	1948
1.9	2.0	1.9	1.9	1.9	1.9	1.9	1.9	1.9*	1.9	2.0	2.0	1949
1.8	1.8	1.8	1.8*	1.8	1.9	1.8	1.9	1.9	1.8*	1.9	1.9	1950
1.8	1.9	1.8	1.8	1.9*	1.9	1.9	1.9	1.9	1.9	1.9	1.9	1951
1.8	1.9	1.8	1.8	1.9	1.9	1.9	1.9	1.9	1.9	1.9	1.9	1952
1.5	1.7*	1.7	1.6	1.7	1.8	1.8	1.8	1.8	1.8	1.9	1.9	1953
1.5	1.7	1.7	1.7	1.8	1.8	1.8	1.8*	1.8	1.8	1.9	1.9	1954
1.4	1.7	1.7	1.6	1.8	1.8	1.8	1.8	1.8*	1.8	1.9	1.9	1955
1.4	1.7	1.7	1.7	1.8	1.8	1.8	1.8	1.9	1.8	1.9	1.9	1956
1.1	1.7	1.7	1.7	1.8	1.9*	1.8	1.9	1.9	1.8	1.9	1.9	1957
...	2.4	2.0	1.8	2.0	2.0	2.0	2.0	2.0	1.9	2.0	2.0*	1958
...	...	1.7	1.6	1.9	1.9	1.9	1.9	1.9	1.9	2.0	2.0	1959
...	...	...	1.5	2.0	2.0	1.9	1.9	2.0	1.9	2.0	2.0	1960
...	...	...	...	2.5	2.3	2.1	2.1	2.1	2.0*	2.1	2.1	1961
...	...	...	...	...	2.0	1.8	1.9	2.0	1.8	2.0	2.0	1962
...	...	...	...	...	...	1.7	1.8	1.9	1.8	2.0	2.0	1963
...	...	...	...	...	...	...	2.0	2.1	1.8	2.1	2.1	1964
...	...	...	...	...	...	...	...	2.1	1.7	2.1	2.1	1965
...	...	...	...	...	...	...	...	...	1.4	2.2	2.1	1966
...	...	...	...	...	...	...	...	...	...	3.0	2.5	1967
...	...	...	...	...	...	...	...	...	...	...	2.0	1968

The size and movement of components of the semiresidual are next examined.

Economies of Scale

Growth of an economy automatically means growth in the average size of the local, regional, and national markets for end products that business serves. Growth of markets brings opportunities for greater specialization—both among and within industries, firms, and establishments—and opportunities for establishments and firms within the economy to become larger without impairing the competitive pressures on firms that stimulate efficiency. Longer production runs for individual products become possible. So, in almost all industries including wholesale and retail trade, do larger transactions in buying, selling, and shipping. This is important, because the length of runs and the size of the transactions in which business deals are major determinants of unit costs. Larger regional and local markets permit greater geographic specialization and less transporting of products. The opportunities for greater specialization, bigger units, longer runs, and larger transactions provide clear reason to expect increasing returns in the production and distribution of many products, and examples of increasing returns are plentiful.

There are almost no necessary offsets from industries operating under decreasing returns to scale because increasing cost is almost never a necessary concomitant to the growth of demand for a product. Although individual establishments and firms can become too large for efficiency, their number can be multiplied without limit. There is no necessity to carry specialization beyond the point at which it is efficient.[17] When land is counted as an input there is no reason to expect decreasing returns to scale for any product unless some very unusual situation is present.[18]

In my opinion, it is clear from general knowl-

17. Amplification of the general statements in the paragraph above and references to some of the evidence will be found in *Why Growth Rates Differ*, Chap. 17, esp. pp. 226–27.

18. An assumption that an economy operates under constant returns to scale when land is not counted as an input (as in some studies) implies increasing returns to scale when land is counted as an input (as in this study).

edge and many studies that the United States business economy operates under increasing returns to scale, and that the size of the gains is large enough to contribute importantly to the growth of total output. One can go further and quantify this contribution only by arriving at some judgment as to the *size* of the gains from economies of scale realized as the economy grows. When writing *The Sources of Economic Growth* and *Why Growth Rates Differ,*[19] I introduced such a judgment and estimated the size of the gains even though this procedure could yield only what Phyllis Deane described as "notional" estimates of the contributions of this growth source.[20] It seemed to me then, and still seems, useful to present estimates even though they are based only on one's best judgment, or guess, and the estimates are subject to a substantial margin of possible error.

In these previous studies I based the calculation on the assumption that an increase in any other determinant of output that would have sufficed to raise the total national income by 1.0 percent under conditions of constant returns to scale actually increased output by 1.1 percent: that is, that economies of scale amounted to 10 percent. This meant that cost reductions resulting from economies of scale associated with the growth of the national market were credited with being the source of one-eleventh of the growth rate of national income.

This assumption referred to the economy as a whole. In selecting the 10 percent figure, I of course took into account that only in the nonresidential business sector can economies of scale contribute significantly to the increase in measured output.[21] The percentage for this sector alone must be higher than that for the whole economy. The assumption actually implied that economies of scale augment the growth rate in the nonresidential business sector that other determinants would provide under constant returns to scale by about one-eighth, or 12.5 percent, so that one-ninth, or 11.11 percent, of long-term growth in

the sector was due to economies of scale.[22] Whatever the true figure may be—and data developed in this study provide an opportunity to reexamine it—it is better to relate the calculation to the growth of output in the nonresidential business sector alone than to growth in the whole economy, and this is done in the present study.

For analysis of any but very long time periods there is also a problem of developing an appropriate series for output of the sector (the measure of the size of markets) to which such a fraction may be applied. Economies of scale, in the sense used here, are related to the size of markets that business is organized to serve, and ideally one would use an output series that corresponds to these markets.[23] Clearly, one does not wish to use actual output, which fluctuates in response to the pressure of demand and for other reasons. But neither is a measure of potential, or high employment, output appropriate. After an extended period of underutilization, such as the 1930s or the later 1950s and early 1960s, business does not anticipate and is not organized to serve markets as large as those that would prevail at the potential level.

Actually, I wish to conduct two types of analysis: to use data already developed to reappraise the *size* of economies of scale in this sector; and then, using this estimate, to derive a series for the effect of economies of scale on the growth of output in the sector. Both require use of an output series. A minimum adjustment to the index of actual national income originating in the sector, which clearly is appropriate for either purpose, is removal of the effects of irregular fluctuations upon output per unit of input. Fluctuations in the two series relating to utilization arise precisely because actual output diverges from the scale that business anticipates and is organized to serve. Fluctuations in farm output cannot be anticipated or affect the organization of business. Division of the index of national income by the three indexes for the irregular factors provides a series with the effects of the latter eliminated. For the first purpose—analysis of data referring to the postwar

19. For full citations of *The Sources of Economic Growth* and *Why Growth Rates Differ,* see Chapter 1, notes 1 and 2.

20. Phyllis Deane, book review of *Why Growth Rates Differ,* in *American Economic Review,* Vol. 58 (September 1968), pp. 980–82.

21. There may be a trivial effect in the provision of housing services deriving from the increase in the number of houses built.

22. These percentages refer to a situation in which the business sector grows at the same rate as the whole economy and assume the sector contributes 80 percent of total output. The actual percentage varies somewhat.

23. So-called short-run economies of scale are merely a substitute term for most (all except the lagged response of inputs to changes in demand) of what has already been measured in my series for intensity of utilization of employed resources.

period in order to evaluate the size of gains from economies of scale—this adjustment of the actual national income index is probably sufficient, provided very short-term comparisons are not made.

Size of Economies of Scale

By correlating indexes already developed for the nonresidential business sector, it is possible to secure an estimate of the size of gains from economies of scale that can be compared with that previously assumed. If in any period the series for constant-price national income with the effects of measured irregular factors removed is called Y and its growth rate is designated $\dot{Y}$, then

(1) $$\dot{Y} = \dot{M} + \dot{O} + \dot{S},$$

when the last three terms are given the following definitions and a trivial interaction term is ignored.

$\dot{M}$ is the contribution that would have been made to the growth of Y by determinants already measured if constant returns to scale prevailed. Statistically, it is the growth rate of an index constructed as the product of the index of total factor input and the two indexes for gains from resource reallocation.

$\dot{O}$ is the contribution that would have been made to the growth of Y by determinants not yet measured, except economies of scale, if constant returns to scale prevailed. These include advances in knowledge and a variety of presumably much less important determinants. Its value is unknown.

$\dot{S}$ is the additional contribution to the growth of Y that results from increases in $\dot{M}$ and $\dot{O}$ because the economy operates under increasing returns to scale. My approach to economies of scale takes for granted that the size of economies-of-scale effects accompanying changes in other determinants (except irregular factors) is the same for total factor input and for components of output per unit of input. Because a change in a determinant that raises output per unit of input simply reduces the quantity of input required to produce a given quantity of output, and thus releases inputs to produce more output of other or the same products, there is no reason to doubt that this is so. Hence, if the gains from economies of scale associated with $\dot{M}$ and $\dot{O}$ are designated $\dot{S}m$ and $\dot{S}o$, respectively,

(2) $$\dot{S}m/\dot{M} = \dot{S}o/\dot{O}.$$

From the indexes already provided, $\dot{Y}$, $\dot{M}$, and $(\dot{O} + \dot{S})$ can be obtained for any period; the

last term is the growth rate of the semiresidual.[24] I need to separate $\dot{S}$ from $\dot{O}$. I could do so if either $\dot{S}/(\dot{M} + \dot{O})$ or $\dot{S}/\dot{Y}$ were known (each ratio can be readily derived from the other). On a reasonable assumption, it is possible to estimate the value of $\dot{S}/(\dot{M} + \dot{O})$ by correlating $\dot{O} + \dot{S}$ with $\dot{M}$. Under a more stringent assumption, it is also possible to estimate the value of $\dot{S}/\dot{Y}$ by correlating the value of $\dot{O} + \dot{S}$ with $\dot{Y}$.

A simple example, using numbers for two time periods in which all values are assumed to be known, illustrates the method. (With only two periods, correlations are, of course, perfect.) The illustrative numbers are as follows:

	Period 1	Period 2
$\dot{M}$	3.00	5.00
$\dot{O}$	1.00	1.00
$\dot{M} + \dot{O}$	4.00	6.00
$\dot{S}$	0.50	0.75
$\dot{Y} = \dot{M} + \dot{O} + \dot{S}$	4.50	6.75
$\dot{O} + \dot{S}$	1.50	1.75

Values of $\dot{M}$ and $\dot{O}$ in the example are picked at random *except* that the value of $\dot{O}$ is assumed to be the same in both periods. In the example $\dot{S}/(\dot{M} + \dot{O})$ is assumed to be 0.125, the figure implied by the assumption used in my earlier studies; the value $\dot{S}/\dot{Y}$ is therefore 0.11111. Other values in the illustration are derived from these.[25] Two regression lines that require only numbers corresponding to those actually available for the real economy can be calculated from the illustrative figures.

First, $\dot{O} + \dot{S} = 1.125 + 0.125\dot{M}$. The coefficient of $\dot{M}$ is the value of $\dot{S}/(\dot{M} + \dot{O})$, which is to say that it is 1/100 of the percentage, 12.5, by which economies of scale amplify the contribution of $\dot{M}$ and $\dot{O}$ to output growth in the example.

Second, $\dot{O} + \dot{S} = 1 + 0.11111\dot{Y}$. The coefficient of $\dot{Y}$ is the value of $\dot{S}/\dot{Y}$, or 1/100 of the percentage of the growth rate of output that is ascribable to economies of scale in the example.[26]

The purpose of the example is simply to illustrate the meaning of the coefficients of $\dot{M}$ and $\dot{Y}$ that are obtained by similar correlations of real data. The exact reproduction of the values of the

24. The indexes of $\dot{Y}$ and $\dot{M}$ are shown in Table P-1.

25. For simplicity I have obtained $\dot{Y}$ by addition, thus ignoring the trivial interaction term among $\dot{M}$, $\dot{O}$, and $\dot{S}$.

26. The constant term in the first equation is $\dot{O}$ raised by the assumed effect of associated economies of scale, and the constant in the second equation is $\dot{O}$. However, the constant term is not of interest in actual analysis.

economies-of-scale ratios results from the special assumption in the example that the value of $\dot{O}$ is the same in the periods compared. However, the coefficient of $\dot{M}$ in the first equation will continue to measure $\dot{S}/(\dot{M}+\dot{O})$ accurately even if $\dot{O}$ is not constant, so long as $\dot{O}$ is not correlated with $\dot{M}$; absence of correlation between $\dot{O}$ and $\dot{M}$ is a weaker requirement than the necessity for $\dot{O}$ to be the same in each period. This relaxation of the assumption is not possible in the second equation, however; absence of correlation between $\dot{O}$ and $\dot{M}$ is not sufficient to ensure that the value of the coefficient of $\dot{Y}$ in the second equation measures the importance of economies of scale accurately.

Because it requires a weaker assumption, the first equation is preferable in an attempt to derive the importance of economies of scale from correlation of actual data. But I stress that a reasonably accurate estimate is obtained even from the first equation only in the absence of much correlation between $\dot{M}$ and $\dot{O}$. Only then does a systematic relationship between the growth rate of M, total input and measured gains from resource reallocation, and that of $O + S$, the semiresidual, result almost entirely from the inclusion in the semiresidual of gains from economies of scale associated with the growth of inputs and resource reallocation.

I know of no persuasive reason to expect much correlation between $\dot{M}$ and $\dot{O}$ and consequently regard the assumption that it is absent as reasonable, but readily admit the possibility that some line of causation has been overlooked.[27] Hence, the assumption that such correlation is absent is not a comfortable one. I venture an estimate of the size of economies of scale by a procedure that requires this assumption only because I know of no better procedure and because the data used are more suitable than any previously available for the purpose.

Even though the second equation is less reliable than the first because its use requires a more stringent assumption, it provides a useful check in estimating the importance of economies of scale. An assumption that $\dot{O}$, which cannot be

observed directly, does not vary enough during the postwar period to invalidate the results is not implausible, and the degree of consistency between estimates derived from the two equations provides some indication as to whether $\dot{O}$ does depart much from constancy.[28]

Data for 1947–69 were used to estimate both equations. This required selection of time spans over which to compute growth rates. I have already concluded that growth rates of the semiresidual for periods shorter than three years are too dubious for use because of calendar differences, and that even three years may be insufficient. Very short periods are also undesirable because changes in the output measure used may depart from changes in the output level that corresponds to the size of the markets business is organized to serve. On the other hand, lengthening the period reduces the number of observations. Except for these considerations, there was no clear criterion for the length of the period. Calculations were actually made using data for four-, five-, six-, and seven-year periods.[29] To avoid any need to select particular years for the computation of growth rates, all possible periods were used. For the four-year calculations, for example, the correlations were based on nineteen observations representing growth rates from 1947 to 1951, 1948 to 1952, and so on, up to 1965 to 1969. Increasing the time span by one year reduces the number of observations by one. (Hence, sixteen observations were used for the seven-year calculations.) The pertinent results are summarized in Table 6-3. They are discussed in more detail in Appendix P, and full results are shown in Table P-2.

The coefficients of $\dot{M}$ in the first equation, which provide estimates of the amount by which the contributions of other output determinants are augmented by economies of scale, are shown in Table 6-3, column 1. Based on use of four-, five-, six-, or seven-year time spans, they indicate

27. Nothing in the statistical procedures by which M and $O + S$ are derived would tend to introduce correlation between their growth rates, so if such correlation is present it must arise from some economic relationship between some component of M and some component of O. Probably the most plausible possibility is that a sudden burst of inventions might induce a faster growth of capital stock. But any correlation that may arise from this or some similar economic relationship is almost certainly dissipated by leads and lags when $\dot{M}$ and $\dot{O}+\dot{S}$ refer to the same time period.

28. The second equation must and does predict the value of the semiresidual better than the first equation but this difference is meaningless. It is due to the fact that in the second equation, unlike the first, the independent variable (national income with the effects of irregular factors on output per unit of input eliminated) includes the dependent variable (the semiresidual).

29. Results from the use of three-year time spans were also calculated and are shown in Table P-2, but were immediately discarded not only because three years were thought to be too short a period on a priori grounds but also because all measures of significance showed them to yield much less reliable results than those for any of the longer periods.

Table 6-3. Nonresidential Business: Estimates of the Importance of Economies of Scale Based on Correlations of 1947–69 Data

Length o, time span	Value of $\dot{S}/(\dot{M} + \dot{O})$ estimated from first equation (1)	Value of $\dot{S}/\dot{Y}$ Estimated from second equation (2)	Implied by column 1 (3)
Four-year	0.1635	0.1496	0.1405
Five-year	0.1589	0.1459	0.1371
Six-year	0.1331	0.1237	0.1175
Seven-year	0.1450	0.1308	0.1266

Sources: Columns 1 and 2, Table P-2; column 3, computed as column 1 ÷ (1 + column 1).

that economies of scale added 13.3 to 16.4 percent to the contribution of other determinants, a fairly narrow range. All the coefficients are above the percentage of 12.5 implied by the assumption I used in my previous studies, but are well within the range that I regarded as reasonable.[30]

The coefficients of $\dot{Y}$ in the second equation, which provide estimates of the proportion of growth that is provided by economies of scale, are shown in Table 6-3, column 2. All are below the coefficients of $\dot{M}$, as they should be. Their values are a little above those (shown in column 3) which would be consistent with the values based on $\dot{M}$, but the differences are small. This is encouraging because it suggests that among periods of four years or more in length variations in the value of $\dot{O}$ were small.

Use of four-, five-, six-, and seven-year growth rates provides four alternative estimates of the same numbers, and there is no good reason to prefer one to another. Statistical tests (shown in Table P-2) attach the greatest significance to the seven-year rates and the least to the six-year rates in both equations, but differences are not large enough to require that they be taken seriously. I therefore use as my estimate the simple average of the four coefficients of $\dot{M}$ shown in Table 6-3, column 1, which is 0.1501 or, rounded, 15 percent. Thus I estimate that economies of scale add 15 percent to the contribution that would be made to growth in the sector by changes in other determinants (except irregular factors) under constant returns to scale. This implies that 13.04 per-

cent ($100 \times 0.15 \div 1.15$) of long-term growth in the sector (about one-sixth more than I have previously assumed) results from economies of scale.[31] This is the best method of deriving an estimate that I can devise, and I shall use it to replace the assumption made in my previous studies. But no reader should suppose that I imagine it to be highly reliable.

An Index of Gains from Economies of Scale

The estimate just derived must next be used to calculate the contribution made to the growth rate by economies of scale associated with the size of the national market.[32] This requires an appropriate series for the growth of the market. There is no problem for long time spans between reasonably comparable years. For example, after the effects of irregular factors upon output per unit of input are removed, national income in the sector was 3.50 times as large in 1968 as in 1929, a growth rate of 3.26 percent. With changes in actual and "potential" or "high-employment" national income about the same as this, there is no reason to suppose that the organization of business had not adjusted to an expansion in markets of about this size. If 13.04 percent of the growth rate in the sector resulted from economies of scale, then about 0.43 percentage points (13.04 percent of the growth rate of 3.26) were contributed by economies of scale. By use of a compound-interest table this estimate is easily converted to an index of the effects of economies of scale that is similar in form to those shown for other determinants in Table 6-1. The 1968 index is about 118 percent of the 1929 index.

At the other extreme, year-to-year changes in such an index cannot be measured accurately, even if any error in the estimate of the importance of economies of scale is ignored, because short-term changes in the size of the markets business is organized to serve cannot be measured accurately. I was initially tempted to omit an annual index, and to confine to longer time spans the introduction of any division of the semiresidual be-

30. In *Why Growth Rates Differ* I suggested 20 percent for the whole economy as about the highest number that would not be widely regarded as unreasonable (p. 227). This translates to about 24 percent for the nonresidential business sector.

31. The estimate that would be obtained by averaging column 2 of Table 6-3 is 13.75 percent.

32. My procedures ignore the complication, which appears unimportant for the United States, that business also sells in foreign markets. Adoption of one possible expedient to allow for this complication, the addition of exports to business output, could scarcely change my results. The procedure would be questionable because foreign trade is affected by changes in trade barriers as well as by growth of market size.

tween economies of scale and other determinants. This would, however, have restricted analysis to the particular time spans I selected. An annual index based on the best output measure I could derive for this special purpose is therefore provided, but only to permit flexibility in the choice of time periods to be analyzed. The series is shown in Table 6-1, column 8, and described in Appendix P, Part 2. In my opinion the difficulty of measuring changes in the size of the national market appropriately does not seriously impair comparisons of dates that are at least four or five years apart. This is simply an empirical judgment reached by examining the output data during the postwar period.

The estimates assume that the addition made to the contribution of other growth determinants by economies of scale was an unchanging 15 percent throughout the 1929–69 period. If technological and managerial knowledge did not change, the size of this percentage almost surely would diminish as the economy becomes bigger. But as markets and the scale of output grow, knowledge of technology and business organization develops about, and adapts to, the new situation that exists with enlarged markets, and opportunities for scale economies are constantly replenished. This replenishment, to be sure, may not suffice to offset fully the tendency that would otherwise be present for gains to diminish as output rises. If such is the case, I underestimate the gains in the earlier part of the period relative to the latter part. In a previous study I made a token allowance for this possibility which is not retained in the present study. But unless the reduction is much bigger than I thought probable then, or do now, such an allowance would scarcely change the estimates.

In previous studies I also pointed out that the estimates refer to the gains in productivity that growth of markets permits, and that in any particular time span the gains actually achieved are not necessarily the same. This is also true of the present estimates, which are based on the growth of output (as adjusted) in each period rather than on any direct observation of gains achieved. From a classification standpoint this characteristic is not troublesome. Although it would be useful to know whether business became more or less efficient in any time span, measured against some moving frontier of the greatest possible efficiency allowed by the state of knowledge and the size of markets, it is hardly necessary (and certainly is impossible)

to isolate and transfer to economies of scale that part of the change in efficiency brought about by failure to seize opportunities for scale economies, or by making up for a previous failure to seize such opportunities.[33]

Miscellaneous Determinants

Estimates have now been provided for all output determinants that are to be independently measured. In Table 6-1, division of the index of the semiresidual in column 7 by the index of the effects of economies of scale in column 8 yields, in column 9, an index of the residual, labeled "advances in knowledge and all other." It includes the effects on output of all determinants that have not been measured separately.

In a recent article I provided and explained a classification of growth sources that was designed to be both comprehensive and free of duplication.[34] Sources appearing in that classification for which indexes have not already been provided in this book may be divided among three groups.

Two sources, though not shown in tables, were previously estimated not to have affected output and therefore are not classified in the residual. They are the "health" of persons at work (a component of labor input in the classification) and "changes in the extent to which the use of multiple labor shifts permit economizing in the use of capital in particular uses, apart from changes resulting from variations in the pressure of demand."

Advances in knowledge, the main source that is included in the residual, will be the subject of the last section of this chapter. In using "advances in knowledge" broadly, I shall mean not only the source described in the classification as "changes in the state of knowledge—technical, managerial, or organizational—that govern the amount of output that business can obtain by use of a given quantity of resources," but also the sources described as "changes in the amount by which out-

33. In previous studies I showed a separate estimate (put at about 0.05 percentage points) for the contribution made to growth by economies of scale associated with the "independent growth of local markets." This referred to increased concentration of local markets as a consequence of population shifts and the spread of automobile ownership. I omit such an entry in the present study because of the extreme difficulty of estimating it and the possibility that, by the procedures now adopted, its effects may be captured in other series, including the economies of scale series just described.

34. Edward F. Denison, "Classification of Sources of Growth," *Review of Income and Wealth*, Series 18, No. 1 (March 1972), pp. 1–25.

put obtained with the average production technique actually used falls below what it would be if the best technique were used because of changes in the extent to which existing knowledge is available to those in a position to apply it" and because of "changes in the time lag between the dates at which business structures and equipment are installed (incorporating knowledge of design at that date) and the dates at which they are in use."

Composition of Miscellaneous Determinants

The remaining items in the residual comprise the "miscellaneous determinants" covered by the present section. They are grouped among the following six types in the classification.

1. Changes in "other personal characteristics of workers [that is, those not measured], such as effort exerted, experience on present job, training other than formal education."

2. Changes in "the extent to which the allocation of individual workers among individual jobs departs from that which would maximize national income."[35]

3. "Changes in the amount by which output obtained with the average production technique actually used falls below what it would be if the best technique were used, because of . . . changes in obstacles imposed (usually by government or labor union regulation) against efficient utilization of resources in the use to which they are put."

4. "Changes in the cost of 'business services to government,' such as collecting taxes or filing statistical reports, and changes in the adequacy of 'government services to business,' such as provision of law courts or roads for business use."

5. "Changes in aspects of the legal and human environment within which business must operate that affect costs of production by business. One example is the honesty of the public in general and customers or suppliers in particular, which affects business costs of protection against robbery, fraud, etc., and may even govern the determination of whether or not certain types of

business operation, such as self-service, are feasible. Another example, currently important in many countries, is changes in requirements imposed to limit polluting in the process of production."

6. "Changes in productive efficiency that take place independently of changes in any of the other determinants. Economists are sometimes reluctant to admit existence of this determinant because it is inconvenient. I am convinced that efficiency, so defined, differs among countries and surmise that it may vary over time within a country. One plausible explanation is that efficiency actually achieved is affected by the strength of competitive pressures upon firms to minimize costs."

My two earlier books on economic growth contain almost everything I can usefully say about these miscellaneous output determinants.[36] Consequently, the remainder of this section is brief.

Effects on Growth Rate

Most output determinants in this group—unlike employment, education, the capital stock, or the state of knowledge—do not have pronounced long-term trends, but neither are they of the type that simply impose irregular annual movements. Changes in them, if they occur at all, tend to affect growth rates over periods of intermediate length.

Most are of the type that prevent output per unit of input from reaching the level that the state of knowledge and its dispersion, the size of markets, and the age composition of the capital stock would permit; they affect the growth rate only if the percentage by which they do so changes between two dates. For example, suppose that, in the absence of some important impediment to efficient allocation or use of employed resources, national income originating in the nonresidential business sector would have been higher by $3 billion in 1969 (in 1969 prices) than it actually was. This is 0.5 percent of national income in the sector. If the impediment cut national income in the sector by 0.5 percent in 1948 as well, its contribution to the 1948–69 growth rate would be zero. This calculation requires only an estimate that the loss from the impediment was unchanged; it is unnecessary to know that the percentage loss was 0.5 percent. For many output

---

35. The classification also includes changes in "the extent to which the allocation—among industries or products, or among firms categorized by size, degree of risk, or other significant characteristics—of each type of input *in the aggregate* departs from that which would maximize national income" (item 4a, p. 22). Only reallocations of labor from farming and nonfarm self-employment have been separately measured. I believe these to be the chief components of this source in the United States, but note that other changes are in "miscellaneous determinants."

36. *The Sources of Economic Growth*, Chaps. 15 through 20. *Why Growth Rates Differ*, Chaps. 3, 9, 17 (Part 3), 18; parts of Chaps. 12, 20, 21; and Appendixes M, N.

determinants the best estimate is "no change," and hence a zero contribution; if an index were included in Table 6-1 for such a determinant, the index value would be the same in 1948 and 1969. Suppose instead that the obstacle had worsened, and had cut output by only 0.3 percent in 1948, two-fifths less than the 0.5 percent in 1969. The index value in 1969 would then be 99.8 percent of the 1948 value and the contribution of the determinant to the 1948–69 growth rate would be −0.01 percentage points. This calculation requires an estimate of the change in the cost imposed by the determinant (0.2 percent of the sector's national income) but not an estimate of the total cost. For most miscellaneous determinants, one can easily conclude that any change could have had only a trivial effect on the growth rate.

I estimated in previous studies that the contribution of many components of miscellaneous determinants to the growth rate was 0.00. For a few I provided estimates other than zero. Thus, I estimated that the introduction of resale price maintenance ("fair trade") laws, which led to unnecessarily large use of labor in the big retail trade industry, subtracted 0.04 percentage points from the 1929–57 growth rate, and that the rise of other obstacles to the efficient allocation and use of resources (other than those related to farming) subtracted an additional 0.03 points. However, the "fair trade" estimate partially overlaps the series presented in the present study for gains from the reduction of nonfarm self-employment, which were reduced in that period by "fair trade" laws.

One can discern the direction in which some other changes affected productivity. For example, discrimination in job placement against women and against racial and religious minorities prevents the most efficent allocation of individual workers among jobs. Since 1941 discrimination has apparently been declining; at least, many antidiscrimination laws and regulations have been introduced, and the concentration of sex-race groups by type of job has diminished a little. Insofar as the effect was to shift workers among jobs in such a way that the average marginal product per hour of all workers in the sector was raised, the reduction in discrimination raised productivity. But it appears unlikely that the contribution to the growth rate could have exceeded, say, 0.02 percentage points. On the negative side, increased requirements for record keeping and reporting placed upon business by governmental units have

tended to reduce productivity, but this amount, too, appears small in growth rate terms.

I shall not add here to these examples. Let me merely express the judgment—tentatively, and subject to refutation by additional research—that the net effect on the growth rate of changes in the miscellaneous determinants has been slight relative to the growth rate of the residual (which includes the effect of these determinants). The effect was probably negative in the period from 1929 to 1940 or 1941, when massive unemployment was encouraging measures intended to spread or raise employment; since then even the sign of the contribution is doubtful.

Possible Changes

Let me stress that this judgment does not necessarily extend to the period since 1969 or the years immediately ahead. Several changes that do or may affect measured productivity adversely (which is not a criterion by which to assess their desirability) are now taking place, simultaneously and over a brief time span. Most prominent are major and far-reaching controls for environmental protection which require firms to use labor and capital for protection of the environment that could otherwise be used to provide measured output.[37] The cost of the required measures is higher in the short run than it is likely to be in the long run because of the need to develop appropriate new technology and different sources of supply; because of immobility; and because delays in securing approval for new plants threaten to cause shortages of some products, especially fuels and power, that are used by other firms.

Major new legislation to promote employee and consumer safety is a second source of increased costs. A third source has been a rise in the incidence of crime, particularly holdups of business establishments, thefts of their merchandise (including shoplifting), and embezzlement.[38] Wage

37. Costs of environmental protection that are borne directly by governments and individual consumers (that is, that appear in the national accounts as components of government or consumer purchases, rather than as part of the price paid for purchases of other products from business) do not lower measured output per unit of input in the business sector or the economy as a whole.

38. The main adverse effect on productivity comes from the costs of protection incurred for the hiring of guards, installation of protective devices, and adoption of special procedures to thwart crime. In addition, thefts from inventory directly reduce measured output, and in some cases establishments are forced to move from particularly crime-ridden areas that would otherwise be the most efficient locations.

and price controls—introduced in 1971, relaxed in 1972, and subsequently reimposed and again liberalized—are a possible fourth source. If long continued they may raise overhead costs, distort resource allocation, and introduce uneconomic labor turnover.

Much more speculative are two developments that may affect workers' attitudes and hence performance. First is the belief that young workers today are less inclined to work hard and steadily and are less responsive to material rewards than their predecessors. The view that the young "don't work like we did at their age" has been common for generations and I regard the suggestion of a recent sudden change somewhat skeptically, but it is just possible that there may be more to the idea this time than in the past. Second, programs to hire the "hard core" unemployed that do not require them to meet as stringent performance standards as those applied to the ordinary work force pose a possible danger: acceptance of lower standards for a special group in an establishment may reduce performance standards for the rest of the work force in that establishment. On the other hand, such programs may help to remove irrelevant hiring tests or other forms of disguised discrimination.

A new development in 1973 was the interruption of the flow of oil from Arabia, together with sharp price increases. The interruption occurred when supplies were already tight and seemed likely to reduce output per unit of input, at least temporarily. There will be a lasting impairment if, as proposed, higher-cost domestic fuel sources are developed to replace Middle East supplies permanently.

It is not my purpose here to guess at the quantitative effect of such assorted new developments, nor do I imply that favorable changes may not also occur. I wish only to caution that it is not safe to disregard the possible impact on the post-1969 productivity trend of changes in the group of "miscellaneous determinants."

Advances in Knowledge

As knowledge relevant to production advances, the output that can be obtained from a given quantity of resources rises. The advance in knowledge is the biggest and most basic reason for the persistent long-term growth of output per unit of input.

The term "advances in knowledge" must be construed comprehensively. It includes what is usually defined as technological knowledge—knowledge concerning the physical properties of things, and of how to make, combine, or use them in a physical sense. It also includes "managerial knowledge"—knowledge of business organization and of management techniques construed in the broadest sense. Advances in knowledge comprise knowledge originating in this country and abroad, and knowledge obtained in any way: by organized research, by individual research workers and inventors, and by simple observation and experience.

The term must, however, be limited in a study of the sources of growth of any output series to those advances in knowledge that allow the same amount of *measured* output to be obtained with less input. In the business sector, this limitation has to do mainly with "unmeasured quality change." The introduction of new and improved products for final sale from the business sector to consumers and government provides the buyer with a greater range of choice, or enables him to meet his needs better with the same use of resources, but it does not, in general, contribute to growth as measured; it results in "noneconomic" or "unmeasured" quality change. Hence, advances in knowledge that permit business to supply final products different from those previously available are excluded. One other significant exclusion is imposed by the way price indexes are compiled. The development of new forms of business organization in retail trade (self-service stores and supermarkets, for example) or in personal service establishments directly serving the public does not raise measured output or productivity in the United States. With these important exceptions, the definition is comprehensive.[39]

I have found no way to measure changes in the state of knowledge directly. The effect of the adoption of advances in knowledge on output per unit of input in the sector can, however, be approximated indirectly. I have expressed the opinion that the net impact on the residual of the miscellaneous determinants summarized in the preceding section was small. If this judgment is correct, then the residual index shown in Table 6-1, column 9, approximates the effect on output

39. See *Why Growth Rates Differ,* Chap. 3, for a discussion of these points. In the same publication, Chap. 20, and in *The Sources of Economic Growth,* Chap. 21, I discuss the concept of advances in knowledge and various aspects of the topic more extensively than in this study.

per unit of input of the introduction of advances in knowledge into the production process.

Besides possible effects of miscellaneous determinants, the index picks up errors in all of the series entering into its calculation, insofar as these are not offsetting, because it is obtained as a residual rather than directly calculated. There are seventeen such series. They are the measure of output itself; six series entering into labor input (Table 4-1); three series for capital and land input (Table 5-4); the weights used to combine labor, capital, and land (Table J-2); and six components of output per unit of input (Table 6-1). Every effort has been made in this study to assure statistical consistency between the output and input measures in order to avoid the introduction into the residual of errors from use of inconsistent data. I have noted several points in my procedures at which an error in the data used to obtain the series for one separately measured output determinant will be systematically matched by an offsetting error in another, so it is not the case that the "residual" picks up all errors in the series entering into its construction which are not randomly offsetting. But it remains true that many possible types of error will affect the residual unless they offset one another by chance. Hence, interpretation of the series as a measure of the effects of advances in knowledge does require some reliance upon the national accountant's guardian angel: the tendency for errors to be offsetting when estimates are prepared in detail for many components and subcomponents of a series.

A correct series for the effects upon output per unit of input of changes in knowledge has a unique characteristic. Barring calamities like the barbarian overthrow of the Roman Empire, it can move in only one direction: up. It is therefore somewhat reassuring (and, in fact, even rather remarkable) that the index in column 9 of Table 6-1 has this characteristic even on an annual basis, despite the fact that no statistical procedures introduced would assure it—and despite irregular factors, like the calendar, whose effects could not be estimated. The series actually rises substantially between every pair of adjacent years shown: by at least 0.7 percent except from 1947 to 1948, when the increase is 0.4 percent.[40]

40. I have indicated previously (on p. 69, note 14) that 1947 output is probably overstated, which would lead to understatement of this 1947–48 percentage increase. Other difficulties with 1947 have also been noted.

Variations in the rate of increase in the series from year to year or between brief periods obviously cannot be taken as indications of changes in the rate at which knowledge is incorporated into production, let alone the rate at which knowledge advances. Over reasonably long time spans the index does provide an indication of the importance of advances in knowledge to growth, and I know of no method except the residual method by which any indication can be obtained.

The growth rate of the semiresidual has already been examined. For selected periods it is divided in Table 6-4 between the contribution of economies of scale associated with growth of the national market and my final residual, which, although it includes the miscellaneous determinants, I interpret as an approximation to the contribution made by the introduction of advances in knowledge.

Over the postwar period from 1948 to 1969, the estimates credit economies of scale with a contribution of 0.51 percentage points to the growth rate of national income in the sector, and advances in knowledge (together with miscellaneous unmeasured determinants) with 1.43 percentage points. The contribution attributed to advances in knowledge is equal to 38 percent of the growth rate of total national income in the nonresidential business sector and 67 percent of the growth rate of output per unit of input.

The earlier examination of the semiresidual

Table 6-4. Nonresidential Business: Growth Rates of the Semiresidual and Components, Eight Selected Periods, 1929–69

	Growth rates		
Period	Semiresidual total (1)	Economies of scale (2)	Incorporation of advances in knowledge, and miscellaneous determinants (3)
1929–69	1.53	0.43	1.10
1929–48	1.07	0.34	0.72
1929–40/41	0.74	0.22	0.51
1940/41–48	1.57	0.53	1.03
1948–69	1.95	0.51	1.43
1948–52/53	2.10	0.57	1.52
1952/53–61	1.73	0.38	1.34
1961–69	2.09	0.60	1.48

Source: Computed from Table 6-1, columns 7, 8, and 9.

showed that within the postwar period a subperiod of slower growth intervened between subperiods of faster growth. The semiresidual grew much less during the Great Depression than thereafter, and moderately less during the World War II and immediate reconversion period than during the postwar years. Gains from economies of scale contributed strongly to most of these differences.[41] Table 6-4 indicates that they were responsible for half the difference between the early (1948–52/53) and middle (1952/53–61) postwar periods and for three-fifths of the difference between the middle and late (1961–69) postwar periods.[42] They also account for one-fourth of the difference between the depression and postwar rates of growth of the semiresidual.

Contribution in Postwar Years

The contribution of advances in knowledge (together with other unmeasured determinants of output per unit of input) retains some of the semiresidual's dip in the middle of the postwar period, but its basic stability is much more noteworthy. The biggest difference between postwar periods distinguished is less than 0.2 percentage points. One can attach little economic significance to fluctuations as small as this when (aside from the averaging of 1952 and 1953) the whole period deliberately was so divided as to show the biggest differences obtainable. When periods are selected by this criterion, even minor errors in data can be expected to produce some variation. The important observations about the postwar estimates are that the contribution of advances in knowledge to the postwar growth of nonresidential business output was apparently of the order of 1.4 percent a year, and that it had no persistent tendency to rise or fall.

Earlier Periods

The growth rate of the residual (Table 6-4, column 3) from 1940/41 to 1948 is 0.4 percentage points below the postwar rate, but I must note again that changing the dividing year from 1948 to 1947 greatly reduces the difference between the periods. The index provides only weak evidence of a change since 1940 in the rate at which the incorporation of new knowledge into the productive process has been raising output per unit of input.

The prewar estimates demand more extended comment. The growth rate of the residual was only 0.5 over the depression period from 1929 to 1940 or 1941, whereas it was above 1.3 after those dates and 1.4 after 1948. The difference of 0.8 or 0.9 percentage points is substantial. Its appearance in the estimates raises two types of questions. One concerns the reliability of the indication that a substantial change occurred, the other the interpretation of the finding if its reality is accepted.

Does the difference result in part from statistical errors in the underlying basic data? Series for national income, employment, hours, education, and other magnitudes are based on less satisfactory statistical sources from 1929 to 1940/41 than in later periods. New sources appeared during the years 1938 to 1941 that greatly enhanced the accuracy of the series thereafter. These include payroll and employment tabulations from the unemployment insurance and old age insurance programs, major improvements introduced in the enterprise censuses for 1939 and the population census for 1940, tabulations of tax data for proprietorships and partnerships, and the Current Population Survey.[43] Coverage of prices and average working hours has been extended more gradually. The presence of widespread unemployment in 1940 and 1941 introduced special difficulties in the preparation of many estimates for these years, including the basic national income estimates upon which the output measure relies. The fact that data were weaker in the early years is not more likely to result in understatement than in overstatement of the growth rate of the residual series from 1929 to 1940/41, but the

41. The estimated size of the contributions of economies of scale varies mainly as a result of variations in the rate at which labor and capital were being added in the sector.

42. Dividing lines between periods are necessarily rather arbitrary but those used in the table are as reasonable as any for this particular analysis. Use of the average of 1952 and 1953 as a dividing point has the effect of allocating the aberrantly large increase in the semiresidual in 1953 between the preceding and following periods.

43. In addition, changes in census reporting created problems of matching census data for 1939 and 1940 with data from earlier censuses so as to obtain accurate measures of changes. The most difficult was probably the adjustment for comparability of payrolls and employment in manufacturing as reported in the 1937 and the 1939 censuses of manufactures. Because adjustments of employment and payrolls were consistent, most of any error in this adjustment would not be reflected in the residual series now being examined but some part would be, as problems were concentrated in the highest-paid categories of workers.

range of likely error in either direction is appreciably greater than in the postwar period.

Does anything in my analytical procedures contribute to the difference? Three possibilities come to mind.

1. I have followed the Department of Commerce procedure in using a deflated output series which is based on 1958 price weights throughout. This base year is near the middle of the postwar period, and relative prices for the components of the output of the nonresidential business sector may have been fairly close to the average postwar relationships. However, the base year was seventeen years beyond the end of the 1929–41 period, and its appropriateness for that period is questionable. Substitution of 1929 or 1941 price weights for 1958 weights raises the growth rate of nonresidential business national income by an average of 0.2 percentage points, and approximately this difference probably carries over to the residual.[44]

2. My estimate of the strength of the efficiency offset to changes in the hours worked by full-time nonfarm wage and salary workers is not firmly based. Complete omission of the efficiency offset for these workers would lower the growth rate of total input by about 0.22 percentage points from 1929 to 1941, when full-time hours dropped sharply, but by only 0.02 points from 1941 to 1969, and thus would narrow the gap between the growth rates of the residual in these two time spans by 0.2 points. If the strength of the efficiency offset is overestimated, the difference between the depression and subsequent growth rates of the residual index is thereby exaggerated by some fraction of this amount.

3. The estimate of the effects of demand on intensity of utilization strongly affects a comparison of the 1929–41 and 1941–48 growth rates of the residual, but a comparison of the 1929–48 and postwar rates, which also differ greatly, is not very sensitive to possible errors in the demand intensity index. Errors in cyclical adjustment may affect the timing of a rise in the growth rate of the residual but would not produce a rise where it did not exist.

44. An average of 1929 and 1941 weights is preferable to use of an intermediate year, in which the depression may have distorted price relationships considerably. Reweighting in this test was based on substantial detail but less than the records of the Office of Business Economics would permit. Changing the base year in the analysis would affect the resource reallocation indexes so the change in the growth rate of the residual need not be just the same as that in the growth rate of output.

In sum, my best estimate is that there was a difference of 0.8 to 0.9 percentage points between the prewar growth rate of the residual from 1929–40/41 and its growth rate from 1940/41 or 1948 to 1969, so long as 1958 weights are used; but prewar data are weaker than postwar data and this difference may be overstated or understated, possibly substantially, by estimating errors. Use of a prewar base period to measure output for the prewar period would reduce the difference to 0.6 or 0.7 points.

If, as I consider highly probable but not absolutely certain, there is in fact a significant difference between the prewar and postwar periods, two questions of interpretation arise.

1. Is part of the difference due to the "miscellaneous determinants" discussed in the preceding section? Probably it is, because restrictive practices introduced during the depression restrained productivity growth. But I doubt that they account for much over one-tenth of a percentage point of the difference. This would still leave about three-fourths of a point as the estimated amount to be accounted for by the rate of introduction of new knowledge (which could, however, be cut to as little as one-half point by reweighting output).

2. Was the lower rate from 1929 to 1940/41 merely a depression phenomenon, or was the postwar rate also higher than the rate prior to 1929? An attempt to combine results from this study and *The Sources of Economic Growth,* together with examination of other series, suggests that the rate from 1909 to 1929 was substantially below the postwar rate or the rate since 1940/41, though probably above the rate from 1929 to 1940/41. Advances in knowledge probably contributed more to growth during the last three decades than they did over any earlier period of comparable length. But I shall not attempt to quantify these statements.

Advances in Knowledge and the "Lag"

I have been careful to refer to the residual series under discussion as an estimate of the effects of *incorporating* new knowledge into the productive process. The "best" practice possible with the knowledge available at any given time may be distinguished from the average practice actually in use. Translating this distinction into a classification suitable for growth sources, one may distinguish in principle between the contribution of advances in knowledge and the contribution (positive or negative) that may be made by a change in the lag of average practice behind the best known. This is a useful distinction but it is difficult to give it precision. One has to consider first the techniques that would be used each year by the most advanced enterprises or other producing units anywhere in the world if they were free to adopt the techniques they regarded as most efficient, without restrictions imposed from outside or by their own past actions (including investment actions). The increase that would take place in output per unit of input because of advances in knowledge if all firms were in this position corresponds to my conception of the contribution of advances in knowledge as such. The actual technique used on the average by all enterprises in a country will always be behind or below this standard, and average practice may improve more or less rapidly than the best if average practice moves closer to or farther from the best. The difference between the contribution actually made by changes in average practice and the contribution that would be made if all producers could, and always did, use the best practice, I regard as

the contribution of the "change in the lag in application of knowledge." There will be no contribution from this source if the rate at which advances in knowledge are made does not change and the lag or differential between best and average practice does not change.

Although I do not attempt to divide my residual index to distinguish between the contributions of advances in knowledge and the "change in the lag in the application of knowledge," I venture the judgment that the effect of any change in the lag was unlikely to be important after 1950. The rise in the index during the earliest postwar years may have been stimulated a little by delayed introduction of new techniques and machinery, especially in the production of products such as automobiles whose output was wholly or largely discontinued during World War II. Extremely low investment may have delayed introduction of new techniques during the 1930s.

If the contribution made to productivity growth by the incorporation of new knowledge into production rose sometime around 1940, as seems to be the case, the acceleration of the advance in knowledge itself may have started earlier.

—➤➤✕◀◀—

Potential National Income

—➤➤✕◀◀—

This chapter interrupts the analysis of output changes in nonresidential business in order to introduce a series for potential output. The most common use for a potential output series is in the calculation of the gap between the economy's actual and potential output. Proper management of aggregate demand by fiscal and monetary policy requires knowledge of this gap. Closely related to this use is the estimation of the "high-employment" budget of the federal government. But a series for potential output is also useful in analysis of long-term growth. Availability of such a series makes it possible to divide changes in output between what are often called demand-related changes and supply-related changes.

Definition and Approaches to Measurement

The reason for developing a potential output series in this study is to permit the effects on national income of short-term fluctuations in intensity of demand (measured by the difference between actual and potential output) to be distinguished from the effects of other determinants. To secure potential national income, I therefore adjust actual national income only to eliminate the effects of differences among years in the level of, and pattern of short-term change in, aggregate demand; all other conditions present each year are taken as given. The latter conditions include, among many others, the size and composition of the population and the capital stock, the state of

knowledge, the numbers in the armed forces, the weather, and the length of the year.[1]

To secure potential national income in any year, no adjustment to actual national income is made on the grounds that determinants of output other than demand pressure would have been different in that year if past history had been different.[2] I do not seek to construct a series that removes the effects of past history. Neither does the potential series trace the course of any "golden path" of growth, nor of any "equilibrium" rate of growth.

The Trend versus the Direct Approach

Statistical estimates of potential output are of two general types. The difference can be illustrated by the two procedures that the Council of Economic Advisers (CEA) has used to derive alternative series for potential GNP at a 4 percent unemployment rate. One procedure is to estimate a trend growth rate for potential GNP over an extended period; to place the trend line at a level estimated to correspond to a 4 percent unemployment rate in a base period; and then to read the potential GNP estimate for each year from the trend line so placed. By this trend method, potential GNP each year is an estimated trend value obtained without reference to actual GNP that year.

The second approach—the "direct approach"—starts with actual output each year and adjusts it to take direct account of the effects of demand fluctuations. The adjustment must take account of the difference between actual and potential unemployment, labor force, hours of work, and productivity—or their equivalents if, as in my series, a different classification is used. The council has

1. Labor disputes are among the many other conditions that are taken as given and thus treated as independent of the strength of demand. In fact, there is some systematic relationship between demand and strike frequency (Andrew R. Weintraub, "Prosperity versus Strikes: An Empirical Approach," *Industrial and Labor Relations Review*, Vol. 19 [January 1966], pp. 231–38), but this relationship is so overwhelmed by random fluctuations that the influence of demand on time lost as a result of labor disputes cannot be eliminated satisfactorily from annual data.

2. For example, if there had been no depression to lower capital formation and the birth rate during the 1930s, the capital stock in 1948 and the labor force in 1969 clearly would have been bigger than they were. Quite possibly working hours would have been longer at both dates. Many other determinants of output might also have been different from what they were. Even the moderate postwar business fluctuations affected future years. The capital stock in 1969 would have been smaller had the preceding period been one of recession instead of boom. Again, if there had been no wars since 1865 or more wars than there were, or if the various immigration restrictions had been imposed at an earlier or later date than they were, employment and its composition by age and sex would have been different at all dates covered by this study.

tried to do this by applying "Okun's law."[3] By this procedure, called the "unemployment method," potential GNP is estimated to differ from actual GNP each year by a percentage that is equal to 3.2 times the difference between the actual unemployment rate that year and 4 percent.[4] The potential national income series I shall derive is of the second general type, but my method of adjusting actual output to potential is very different from the council's unemployment method and yields substantially different results.

The two approaches have different implications for the meaning of the gap between actual and potential output. By the direct approach, which I adopt, the gap is strictly confined to the estimated effects of the strength of demand. By the trend approach, the gap also includes three types of effects that are not related to demand.

The first results from the fact that the determinants of long-term changes in output (hours of work, to give a single example) need not and do not change at a smooth trend rate, quite apart from the effects of demand intensity. By the trend approach, the effects of changes in the trends of the determinants and of departures of the determinants from trend for reasons unrelated to demand appear in the *difference* between actual and potential output, except insofar as the former are reflected in an occasional change introduced in the trend of potential output itself.[5] This does not happen if the direct approach is used because both actual and potential output series reflect changes in trend and departures from trend that are not related to demand.

Second, the weather, labor disputes, the size of the armed forces, and other factors that do not change smoothly affect output in any year. The trend approach puts these effects in the difference between actual and potential output. By the direct approach, they affect both output series, not the difference between them.

Third, estimates of actual output contain unknown errors of estimate and are affected by the calendar. These errors and calendar effects are contained in the difference between the two output series by the trend method but not by the direct method because they affect both series.

The capital stock is an important output determinant and its treatment in direct and trend-based estimates requires separate comment. Investment and, consequently, changes in the capital stock move with the business cycle. The direct estimates of potential output that I present for each year are based upon the size and age distribution of the capital stock as it actually existed that year, not as it might have existed if investment in preceding years had been different. Trend-based potential output series, in contrast, smooth away the influence of the business cycle upon the size of the capital stock. In this particular respect the council's direct estimates based upon the unemployment rate appear to be similar to the trend-based estimates rather than to my direct estimates, because capital stock does not enter the estimation procedure and the 3.2 multiplier is applied to the unemployment gap whether preceding years have been prosperous or depressed.

CEA Use of Potential GNP Estimates

The Council of Economic Advisers has used potential GNP in short-term analysis to estimate past gaps between actual and potential output that resulted from failures of demand management policies, to forecast the future gap that will need to be corrected by demand management policies, and to calculate the high-employment federal budget for use as an instrument of demand management. For these uses, the gap appropriate for examination clearly is that defined by the direct rather than the trend approach (including use of the actual capital stock). Nevertheless, the council relies chiefly on the gap derived from the trend line, using the direct estimates secured from the application of Okun's law only to help it in estimating the trend line and as a periodic check. Successive councils apparently have concluded that the trend approach yields a superior statistical result each year even though it is less appropriate conceptually. In comparison with the council's own direct estimates, this may well be so. Although

3. Arthur M. Okun, "Potential GNP: Its Measurement and Significance," in American Statistical Association, *Proceedings of the Business and Economic Statistics Section* (1962), pp. 98–104, reprinted in Okun, *The Political Economy of Prosperity* (Brookings Institution, 1970), Appendix.

4. The council has made both series available in mimeographed form and most analyses of potential output and the federal high-employment budget are based upon them. Differences between these two series and actual GNP are shown below in Table 7-4, columns 2 and 3. The trend-based series has been irregularly published in chart form in the council's annual reports, most recently in *Economic Report of the President Together with the Annual Report of the Council of Economic Advisers, February 1970*, p. 85. The federal budget released in January 1973 continued to report the high-employment receipts of the federal government.

5. Because the trend rate actually used by the council is discretely changed at intervals of unequal length, it is hard to be precise as to its intended meaning.

the article in which Okun first presented the "law" contributed significantly to understanding of the reasons for and average magnitude of differences between potential and actual output, use of the relationship to derive annual (and, a fortiori, quarterly) series for potential output has two important weaknesses.

The first is that reference to a 4 percent unemployment rate simply is insufficient specification to permit even an adequate definition of potential output. Use of Okun's law implies that demand-caused fluctuations in productivity are directly and simultaneously related to the level of the unemployment rate. But productivity is more closely linked to changes in demand intensity in product markets than to its level, and—partly because of labor hoarding—unemployment is not in any case a good indicator of demand pressure at any particular time. Consequently, demand can affect productivity very differently in years in which the unemployment rate is the same.[6] At the same unemployment rate, productivity is higher when output is rising at its trend rate than when it is falling, and it is still higher when output is rising sharply. Productivity is likely to be higher when unemployment is 5 percent and output is sharply increasing than when unemployment is 3 percent and output is stagnant or falling.[7] Average working hours, too, are greatly affected by *changes* in demand. A second weakness is that use every year of one unchanging ratio for the entire economy to adjust for the effects of demand on productivity, on employment, on average hours, and on the composition of employment (when classified by age-sex and education groups, and by class of worker) simply is much too crude and summary a procedure to yield good results.

My Definition of Potential National Income

The annual series for potential national income developed and presented here is based upon separate adjustments for inputs and productivity, and the input adjustments are derived in great detail. Attention is also given to the sectors of the economy. The procedure relies upon the estimates and

methodology developed in previous chapters to analyze actual national income.

I *define* potential national income in 1958 prices in any year as the value that national income (in 1958 prices) would have taken if (1) unemployment had been at 4 percent; (2) the intensity of utilization of employed resources had been that which *on the average* would be associated with a 4 percent unemployment rate; and (3) other conditions had been those which actually prevailed in that year. To conform with current labor force definitions, "4 percent" refers to the percentage of the civilian labor force 16 years of age and over that is unemployed. The term "on the average" refers to the average of a hypothetical random sample of years in which unemployment is 4 percent but output is changing by amounts larger than, the same as, or smaller than the trend rate of change. Neither price movements nor the composition of unemployment enters the definition; these points are discussed below on pages 94–97. The meaning of the potential national income series will be made more precise in the process of describing and commenting upon the method of estimation.

I also compute alternative series where 3.5 percent and 4.5 percent are substituted for 4 percent in the definition. However, when I refer to potential output I shall mean the 4 percent variant unless otherwise indicated.

Method of Estimation

Two main adjustments of actual national income are required to obtain potential national income. The first, an adjustment to output per unit of input, allows for the difference between actual output and the output that the labor, capital, and land treated in my estimates as employed would have produced under potential conditions. The second, an adjustment to total input, allows for the effect upon output of the difference between actual and potential labor input when output per unit of input is at the potential level.

Adjustment for Output per Unit of Input

The first adjustment is designed to eliminate the effects of fluctuations in demand upon output per unit of input. The objective is to obtain the output that the resources measured as actually in use would have produced under standardized demand conditions.

---

6. The trend approach, in contrast, implies use of a trend productivity figure; hence, it implies use of different adjustments of actual productivity at any given unemployment rate. This is the reason for its apparent superiority over the Okun's law procedure with respect to estimates of annual changes.

7. See Appendix O, Part 3, especially pages 305–08, including Table O-5.

For the nonresidential business sector an output series with the proper *movement* can be obtained by dividing actual national income in this sector by the index shown in Table 6-1, column 6. This index, already described, measures the effect on output per unit of input of "changes in the intensity of utilization of employed resources resulting from fluctuations in the intensity of demand."[8]

To set the *level* of potential output, the value of this index that corresponds to potential conditions was estimated to be 103.86 when (as in Table 6-1) 1958 is 100. This value corresponds to a 4 percent unemployment rate when a regression line between this index and the unemployment rate is computed for the postwar period. In the nonresidential business sector, the part of my definition of potential national income that refers to the "intensity of utilization that would on the average be associated with a 4 percent unemployment rate" is thus interpreted to mean that this index stands at 103.86 percent of its 1958 level.

It was necessary to set the potential level of the index by this indirect method because to obtain it directly one would require a large sample of years in which demand pressure was becoming more intense, becoming less intense, and remaining stable; and in all of which unemployment was 4 percent. There actually are no years at all in which unemployment averaged exactly 4 percent and there is no wide range of years in which unemployment even approximated 4 percent. Nevertheless, the potential value selected for the index appears to be approximately consistent with that which might be derived from average historical experience with low unemployment.

Among the six postwar years in which unemployment was nearest to 4 percent (in the 3.7 to 4.3 range) the index was higher than 103.86 in three and lower in three. There were nine postwar years altogether in which unemployment was *less* than 4 percent. In four of these years the actual value of the demand intensity index was below and in five above 103.86. In these nine years the unemployment rate averaged 3.5 percent and the average value of the index was 103.98. This is slightly (0.12 percent) above the index value selected for the 4 percent variant of potential output, as would be expected—though slightly (0.13 percent) below the value of 104.12

selected by the same procedure for the 3.5 percent variant of potential output (see pages 332–33).[9]

The adjustment to actual national income in the nonresidential business sector that is required to eliminate the effect upon output per unit of input of the difference between intensity of utilization of employed resources under actual and potential conditions is shown in Table 7-1, column 2.[10] Because intensity of utilization in any particular year is more closely related to changes in demand pressure than to the level of unemployment, the adjustment to actual output for intensity of demand is not necessarily positive when unemployment is above 4 percent nor negative when unemployment is below 4 percent.

No adjustment to allow for the effect of demand intensity upon productivity is made outside the nonresidential business sector. There probably is no such effect in "general government, households, and institutions," but even if there were it would not affect actual output as measured and therefore would not create a difference between actual and potential output. Any reasonable adjustment of net property income from abroad to allow for the effects of fluctuations in intensity of domestic demand would be trivial relative to the size of total national income.

The situation in the housing sector is somewhat different in that national income originating in housing is affected by the proportion of dwellings that are occupied as well as by the size of the housing stock, and this proportion has changed

---

8. The reasonableness of its behavior in individual years is examined in Appendix O, pages 305–08 and 311.

9. To round out the comparisons I note that among the fourteen postwar years in which unemployment exceeded 4 percent, the demand intensity index was above 103.86 in five years and below it in nine. In these fourteen years unemployment averaged 5.35 percent and the index averaged 0.62 percent below the 4 percent potential value. During the whole twenty-three-year postwar period, the unemployment rate was below 4 percent in nine years and the demand intensity index above 103.86 in nine.

Although none of the subgroups of years is nicely balanced with respect to the size and timing of output changes (which is the reason that selection of the potential level of the index was based on a correlation using all years), their examination suggests that it would be hard to support a potential value of the index differing from that selected by much more than, say, 0.1 percent in either direction. Changing the potential value of the index by 0.1 percent would change my estimate of total potential national income in 1958 prices by only $0.5 billion in 1969 and by less in all earlier years.

10. The 1929 calculation will illustrate the procedure. Actual national income in the sector, measured in 1958 prices, was $136.7 billion (Table 3-2), the demand intensity index was 104.76, and the potential value of the index, as in all other years, was 103.86. The adjustment of −$1.2 billion is equal to $\left(136.7 \times \dfrac{103.86}{104.76}\right) - 136.7$.

Table 7-1. Derivation of Potential National Income, 4 Percent Unemployment Variant, 1929, 1940–41, and 1947–69
Billions of 1958 dollars

Year	Actual national income (1)	Plus: Adjustment to output per unit of input (2)	Plus: Adjustments for labor input		Equals: Potential national income (5)	Excess of actual over potential	
			Work relief (3)	Other (4)		Amount (6)	Percent (7)
			Excluding Alaska and Hawaii				
1929	161.4	−1.2	0.0	−2.2	158.0	3.4	2.2
1940	181.5	1.1	−3.5	21.4	200.5	−19.0	−9.5
1941	215.8	−6.7	−2.7	9.3	215.7	0.1	0.0
1947	255.2	2.9	0.0	−0.5	257.6	−2.4	−0.9
1948	270.1	−3.5	0.0	−2.0	264.6	5.5	2.1
1949	265.8	−0.8	0.0	6.5	271.5	−5.7	−2.1
1950	290.8	−7.8	0.0	3.8	286.8	4.0	1.4
1951	312.9	−3.6	0.0	−3.6	305.7	7.2	2.4
1952	323.5	1.6	0.0	−4.7	320.4	3.1	1.0
1953	337.3	5.4	0.0	−5.1	337.6	−0.3	−0.1
1954	331.3	8.3	0.0	7.4	347.0	−15.7	−4.5
1955	358.8	−1.5	0.0	1.0	358.3	0.5	0.1
1956	367.8	2.6	0.0	1.0	371.4	−3.6	−1.0
1957	371.1	7.2	0.0	2.6	380.9	−9.8	−2.6
1958	363.6	11.3	0.0	16.3	391.2	−27.6	−7.1
1959	391.1	3.6	0.0	8.3	403.0	−11.9	−3.0
1960	399.4	8.1	0.0	9.9	417.4	−18.0	−4.3
			Including Alaska and Hawaii				
1960	400.8	8.2	0.0	9.9	418.9	−18.1	−4.3
1961	408.1	8.2	0.0	16.3	432.6	−24.5	−5.7
1962	435.3	2.3	0.0	8.8	446.4	−11.1	−2.5
1963	453.6	1.6	0.0	9.3	464.5	−10.9	−2.3
1964	480.1	−6.5	0.0	5.4	479.0	1.1	0.2
1965	513.0	−11.4	0.0	0.6	502.2	10.8	2.2
1966	545.2	−12.9	0.0	−4.3	528.0	17.2	3.3
1967	557.6	−3.7	0.0	−1.7	552.2	5.4	1.0
1968	585.1	−0.7	0.0	−3.7	580.7	4.4	0.8
1969	599.6	10.3	0.0	−2.9	607.0	−7.4	−1.2

Sources: Columns 1 and 3, Table 3-2, columns 1 and 2; column 2, see text for derivation; column 4, Table Q-6, column 22; column 5, columns (1 + 2 + 3 + 4); column 6, column 1 − column 5; column 7, column 6 ÷ column 5.

over time. But fluctuations are only trivially related to changes in the intensity of aggregate demand. The important changes in the proportion have occurred gradually and stem from the relationship between long swings in the residential building cycle and variations in the number of households. By use of data described and defined in Chapter 3, it is possible to estimate the amount by which actual national income in the dwellings sector differs from what it would have been if the ratio of the space rental value of occupied nonfarm dwellings to that of all nonfarm dwellings had been constant. Table 7-2 provides such estimates; for the constant occupancy ratio, the average ratio from 1956 through 1969 (a period which excludes the years of housing shortage following World War II) was used. Entries in the table are positive when the occupancy ratio was below the 1956–69 average. I do not add these amounts in moving from actual to potential national income in Table 7-1 because they do not result from fluctuations in the pressure of aggregate demand and could not have been eliminated by demand management policy. But anyone who desires to add them may do so by using Table 7-2.

Adjustment of Factor Input

A second adjustment to actual national income is required to obtain potential national income. It is necessary to estimate the amount by which total factor input would have been different if unemployment had been at 4 percent and the intensity of utilization of employed resources at the rate associated on the average with 4 percent unem-

Table 7-2. Services of Dwellings: Sector National Income at Average 1956–69 Occupancy Ratio Less Actual Sector National Income
Billions of 1958 dollars

Year	Amount	Year	Amount
1929	0.3	1957	−0.1
1940	0.2	1958	−0.1
1941	0.1	1959	0.0
1947	−0.5	1960	0.0
1948	−0.4	1961	0.0
1949	−0.4	1962	0.0
1950	−0.4	1963	0.0
1951	−0.2	1964	0.1
1952	−0.2	1965	0.2
1953	−0.2	1966	0.2
1954	−0.2	1967	0.0
1955	−0.2	1968	0.0
1956	−0.1	1969	−0.1

Source: See text for derivation.

ployment; then it is necessary to calculate the effect of such a difference in factor input upon national income. Only the labor component of total input must be changed because my series for the other inputs refer to capital and land available for business use, and the effects of demand-related changes in their actual utilization are already included in Table 7-1, column 2.

One simplifying assumption is introduced in making the calculation for labor. I assume that if the unemployment rate had been at 4 percent rather than at its actual rate, the entire change in employment would have appeared among nonfarm wage and salary workers in the business sector. This simplification is reasonable. Farm employment, employment of nonfarm proprietors and unpaid family workers, employment in general government, and even employment in households and institutions are not much affected by short-term changes in the strength of total demand. A moderate error in the assumption adopted would have little effect on the results for the whole economy, because of offsets. A possible alternative assumption—that employment in each category would have been changed proportionally—is far less realistic. My procedure also implies, reasonably, that in government, households, and institutions the ratio of full-time equivalent employment to full-time and part-time employment is the same under actual and potential conditions.

In 1940 and 1941, one modification of this assumption is made. If unemployment had been at 4 percent there would have been no work relief program. Work relief workers are therefore elimi-

nated from general government employment, and the value of their output is deducted from actual national income (Table 7-1, column 3). Thereafter, these workers are treated as unemployed (except in the estimation of the labor force response to unemployment).

Very detailed procedures were followed to secure the difference between actual and potential labor input in the nonresidential business sector each year and to compute the effect of this difference upon output. They are fully described in Appendix Q, and cannot be appraised without reference to that appendix. Appendix Q also provides components of the adjustment. Here, I shall attempt merely to outline the approach.

STEP ONE. The first step was to estimate, by sex and age, the difference between the total hours worked by persons actually employed as nonfarm wage and salary workers in the business sector and the hours these persons would have worked under potential conditions. Nonfarm business wage and salary workers have been divided among four groups (Table G-1): full-time workers of each sex and part-time workers of each sex. To calculate total potential hours, by sex, the difference between the potential and actual division of employed persons of each sex between full-time and part-time workers and the difference between the potential and actual average hours of each group were estimated. Differences between total actual and total potential hours of employed nonfarm business wage and salary workers of each sex were then distributed by age like actual hours. It should be noted that the potential estimates were made by estimating differences from actual data each year; they are not smooth trend estimates. All other estimates entering into the potential input series were also made in this way.

STEP TWO. The difference between civilian employment and 96 percent of the civilian labor force—the number of persons in the labor force who would have moved between employed and unemployed status if the total civilian unemployment rate had been 4 percent—was calculated. These workers were distributed among age-sex groups. Persons transferred were then assigned the same average potential hours as employed persons in the same age-sex group, as derived from the estimates described in step 1.

STEP THREE. The change that would have occurred in the number of persons in the labor force itself if the unemployment rate had been 4 percent was estimated, separately for each age-sex group. Employment was adjusted by 96 percent of the change in the labor force so as to retain the 4 percent unemployment rate. Persons added or subtracted from employment were assigned the same average potential hours as employed persons in the same age-sex group.

The size of the labor force response to unemployment is not a settled matter. On the contrary, it is much debated.[11] Fortunately, the effect of this uncertainty on the estimates of potential national income is greatly curtailed by the fact that differences between actual and potential labor force are confined to demographic groups whose labor input *per worker* is far below average because of their short average working hours and characteristics that reduce their output per hour.

STEP FOUR. The differences between the total actual and potential hours of each age-sex group that are related to average hours worked by employed workers, transfers of workers between employment and unemployment, and labor force response were next combined (see Table Q-3). Estimates were then made of differences, for nonfarm business wage and salary workers, between actual and potential values of the labor input indexes for education and the efficiency offset to hours changes.[12] From these data the ratio of the potential labor input of nonfarm wage and salary workers in the nonresidential business sector to their actual labor input was then computed. This ratio was multiplied by the total current-dollar earnings of nonfarm wage and salary workers to

obtain the potential earnings of such workers based on actual earnings per unit of labor input.[13]

STEP FIVE. To obtain the percentage difference between the potential and the actual labor contribution to output for all workers in the nonresidential business sector, the difference in current dollars between actual and potential earnings of nonfarm wage and salary workers was divided by total labor earnings in the sector.[14]

STEP SIX. The percentage difference between the potential and the actual labor contribution to output of all workers in the sector was multiplied by the ratio of total labor input to total factor input in the sector. This provided the percentage difference between potential total factor input and actual total factor input in the sector.[15]

STEP SEVEN. Column 2 of Table 7-1 was added to actual national income originating in the nonresidential business sector measured in 1958 dollars (Table 3-2, column 7) in order to obtain the national income in the sector that the actual inputs would have provided if they had been utilized at the potential level of intensity of utilization.[16] This figure was multiplied by the percentage, obtained in step 6, by which potential and actual

11. Labor force response to changes in unemployment (or, more generally, to employment and earnings opportunities) has been a controversial subject for decades. Reviews of the controversy are provided for the period up to 1957 by Clarence D. Long, *The Labor Force under Changing Income and Employment* (Princeton University Press for the National Bureau of Economic Research, 1958), Chaps. 10 and 11; and for the more recent period by William G. Bowen and T. Aldrich Finegan, *The Economics of Labor Force Participation* (Princeton University Press, 1969), Chaps. 15 to 17, and by Jacob Mincer, "Labor-Force Participation and Unemployment: A Review of Recent Evidence," in Robert Aaron Gordon and Margaret S. Gordon, *Prosperity and Unemployment* (John Wiley, 1966), pp. 73–112. The estimates used here are based upon an analysis by George Perry. As explained in Appendix Q, it is particularly appropriate for this study because Perry used my employment series in his analysis. The labor force is estimated to shrink when unemployment rises. The estimated size of the response is in the middle range of available estimates. The estimate reflects current employment opportunities. Employment opportunities in the indefinitely remote past may affect labor force size at any date, but this is irrelevant to measurement of potential output.

12. See Table Q-6, with description of derivation in Appendix Q.

13. Percentage differences between potential and actual labor input of nonfarm wage and salary workers are usually about one-fifth smaller than percentage differences between total potential and total actual hours for this group, but the proportion varies from year to year. Differences between actual and potential hours deriving from the average hours worked by employed persons represent more labor input per hour than differences deriving from the number of employed persons.

14. The last calculation must be based upon labor earnings rather than labor input to avoid consistently overstating potential national income by adding to it the costs of overallocation of labor to farm and self-employment that would be present under potential conditions.

This use of the earnings ratio automatically introduces into the adjustment an estimate of the effect upon output of the difference between actual and potential values of my two resource allocation indexes and of the closely related "intergroup shift" index that enters into labor input. A cyclical decline in employment of nonfarm business wage and salary workers lowers these indexes and also lowers correspondingly the ratio of the total earnings of these workers to total labor earnings in the nonresidential business sector. For this reason it is inappropriate and unnecessary to make separate allowance for resource allocation effects. Although an error can be introduced into the size of the adjustment by differential cyclical changes in the average earnings of nonfarm wage and salary workers and other groups, amounts involved are small and I cannot improve upon the procedure. But see also pages 336–37.

15. "Total factor input" is here used loosely because, as explained in the preceding footnote, the ratio includes the difference between the actual and potential levels of the resource allocation indexes, which are components of output per unit of input.

16. The effect is to include in the adjustment of input the so-called statistical interaction term between the adjustment for productivity and the adjustment of input.

total factor input differ. This calculation yields the difference (in 1958 dollars) between actual and potential national income in the nonresidential business sector that is due to the difference between actual and potential input. The series is shown in Table 7-1, column 4.

Comparison of columns 2 and 4 in Table 7-1 shows the relationship between the two adjustments to be highly erratic. It is impossible to derive a satisfactory series for potential output unless the effects of departures from potential conditions on productivity and on input are estimated separately.

My series for potential national income, obtained by adding the two adjustments to actual national income and deducting work relief output, is shown in Table 7-1, column 5. Columns 6 and 7 show the amounts and the percentages by which actual national income exceeded or fell short of potential national income.[17]

The 3.5 and 4.5 Unemployment Variants

Series for potential national income with 3.5 percent and 4.5 percent substituted for 4 percent in the definition of potential conditions were also calculated. The series are shown and their derivation is described in Appendix Q, Part 2. The 3.5 percent series is about 0.8 or 0.9 percent above the 4 percent variant each year while the 4.5 percent series is about 0.8 or 0.9 percent below it.

Comparison of Potential and Actual National Income

The 4 percent unemployment variant of potential national income is plotted as the solid line on Figure 7-1. Even though its value was estimated

17. If my series is approximately correct, the percentage differences in Table 7-1, column 7, show that one method sometimes used to eliminate the effect of fluctuations in demand from the actual output series is not satisfactory. This method assumes comparability between years that represent business cycle peaks and then, if a continuous series is desired, applies a constant growth rate between those dates. (In *The Sources of Economic Growth*, I myself assumed comparability among peaks from 1929 to 1957.) Table 7-1 indicates that the years usually selected as business cycle peaks are not really comparable to one another with respect to the ratios of actual to potential output. Actual national income exceeded potential national income by 2.2 percent in 1929 and 2.1 percent in 1948; it fell below potential by 0.1 percent in 1953, 2.6 percent in 1957, 4.3 percent in 1960, and 1.2 percent in 1969.

The method also limits the dating of changes in growth rate trends to the peak years. Like all trend-based methods, a series based upon the peak-to-peak method also differs conceptually from my potential output series in ways already noted.

independently each year, the series is fairly smooth during the postwar period. However, it is not wholly free of irregular year-to-year movements. The shaded area spans the range between the 3.5 percent and 4.5 percent unemployment variants. Actual national income is plotted in dashes. To avoid a break when Alaska and Hawaii enter the data, values in earlier years have been raised in this chart by using the 1960 ratios including and excluding these two states. A semilogarithmic scale is used, as usual, so that equal vertical distances on the figure indicate equal percentage differences or changes.

If it could be assumed that economic policy was directed toward keeping actual output at the level of the 4 percent variant of potential national income, the difference between the two lines would measure the amount by which policy was unable or failed to achieve this objective. Table 7-1 provides the actual numbers for these differences.

The 4 percent unemployment variant of potential national income traces a path that lies above actual output most of the time. Most years in which actual national income did equal or exceed potential national income lie within periods during which the United States was engaged in hostilities abroad. The impression that actual output has rarely matched potential output, as defined, except in periods of hostilities would, of course, be strengthened if the depression decade from 1930 to 1939 and the World War II period were plotted on the chart.

The United States appears to have become committed to a goal, or at least a hope, of bringing and keeping actual output to equality with potential output measured at a 4 percent unemployment rate or thereabouts. Realistic evaluation of this goal must recognize that it is not, as is sometimes supposed, a mere description of a condition usually attained in past periods of peace and to which we would like to return. It is a lofty goal—not to be attained without new approaches, and perhaps not without heavy cost.

A study of growth is more concerned with changes in potential national income itself than with departures of actual national income from potential. Four periods can be distinguished within the postwar years. In the first, 1947–49, growth was relatively small (although it may be understated if, as suggested earlier, the price deflator for 1947 is too low). A four-year period of very fast growth of potential output followed from 1949 to 1953; the growth rate was 5.60 percent.

Figure 7-1. Actual and Potential National Income, 1929, 1940–41, and 1947–69[a]

Billions of 1958 dollars

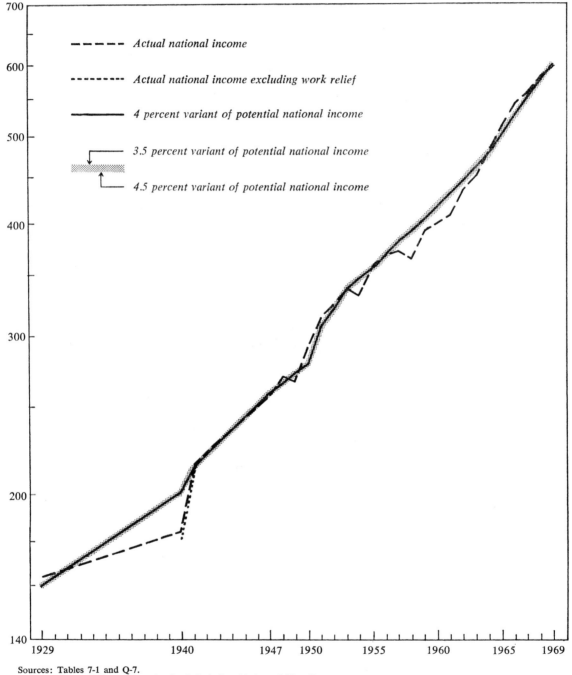

Sources: Tables 7-1 and Q-7.
a. Data prior to 1960 are adjusted to levels including Alaska and Hawaii.
Note. The years 1930–39 and 1942–46 are not plotted.

Over the next eleven years, from 1953 to 1964, the rate was 3.20 percent. From 1964 to 1969, the growth rate of potential output was again high, 4.85 percent. The periods are clearly delimited. The lowest annual percentage change during the periods of fast growth is well above the highest annual percentage change during the periods of slow growth. The figure indicates that 1953 and 1964 are appropriate years at which to divide the postwar period for the purpose of analyzing the sources of growth of potential output. Such an analysis is presented in subsequent chapters.[18] Little will be said here, therefore, about the reasons for the changes in growth rates. I merely note that differences in rates of growth of labor and capital input largely account for the changes in the growth rate of potential output.[19]

Two characteristics of the periods of fast growth are, however, immediately obvious.[20] The two periods of fastest growth correspond both to periods of hostilities, in Korea and Vietnam, and to the periods when the ratio of actual to potential output was high. Data for the latter comparison are shown below. Also shown, because it is an important part of the picture, is the growth rate of prices, specifically, the implicit price deflator for national income. The implicit price deflator is the ratio of national income in current prices to national income in constant prices (see Tables 3-1 and 3-2).[21]

	1947 –49	1949 –53	1953 –64	1964 –69
Growth rate of potential national income	2.66	5.60	3.20	4.85
Average percentage by which actual exceeded potential national income	0.0	1.2	−3.0	1.2
Growth rate of national income deflator	2.47	2.66	1.82	3.33

That the postwar periods of fast growth of potential output coincided with periods in which the ratio of actual to potential output was high is a striking fact. I cannot stress too strongly that this

association does not prove that one was the cause of the other, nor show which was cause and which effect if a causal relationship in fact existed. (I return to this topic in Chapter 9.)

At all times policymakers have had every incentive to prevent actual output from falling below potential output in order to maximize incomes and output and to minimize unemployment. They usually have not distinguished clearly between changes in potential and actual output, but it is safe to assert, at the very least, that when they or their advisers did make such a distinction they did not believe a high ratio of actual to potential output was *adverse* to a high growth rate of potential output. Fear that high employment would impede growth was not a restraint.

That actual output was not more frequently as large as potential output was due to fear of inflation and its economic and political consequences, including consequences for the balance of payments. One may argue that policymakers attached too great importance to inflation and that on occasion they feared inflation when it was not in fact imminent, but the table above is consistent with their belief—and the opinion of most economists—that the rate of price increase was positively related to the ratio of actual to potential output, and that to hold the ratio high was to risk inflation.

If there is more than a random connection between war and high utilization, it is because in periods of hostilities the need to expand defense output and the difficulty of curtailing civilian demand override fears of inflation or, alternatively, bring price controls as a perhaps symbolic substitute for price restraint by the usual mechanisms. High demand and high utilization could as easily have been secured in different periods if they had been the times when the price constraint was disregarded.

The growth rate of potential output was much lower from 1929 to 1948 than from 1948 to 1969: 2.75 percent as compared with 4.02. To obtain accurate rates for subdivisions of the earlier period is difficult because of problems in estimating potential national income in 1940 and 1941.[22]

18. To avoid use of 1947 data or a one-year period, I shall replace the 1947–49 and 1949–53 periods with a 1948–53 period, in which the growth rate of potential national income was 4.99 percent.

19. See pages 138–42.

20. In characterizing such periods one must, of course, omit the initial year from which the growth rate calculation starts.

21. The increase in real output from 1947 to 1949 is likely to be understated and that in prices overstated. Note also that the average percentage by which actual exceeded potential national income excludes the first year of each period.

22. Three conditions make the estimates of potential national income for 1940 and 1941 more uncertain than those for other years. First, the adjustments to actual labor input are large, especially in 1940. Second, these years fell within a period of almost two decades within which there were no peacetime years when unemployment did not greatly exceed 4 percent, so it is hard to establish relationships appropriate for those dates. Third, data useful for adjustments are less ample and accurate than they became in the postwar years.

The estimates obtained show a surprisingly big increase in potential output from 1940 to 1941. This may be correct as the unusual increase is fully explained by directly estimated determinants; the 1940–41 movement of the semiresidual (which is the same on a potential as on an actual basis) is of about average size (see Table 6-1, column 7). However, potential output may be underestimated in 1940 or overestimated in 1941.

The estimates imply the following growth rates of potential national income:

Period	Growth rate	Period	Growth rate
1929–41	2.63	1929–40	2.19
1941–48	2.96	1940–48	3.53
1948–69	4.02	1948–69	4.02

I have greater confidence in the comparisons in which 1941 is used as a dividing point.[23] These estimates do not show the period spanning World War II to have been one of particularly fast growth of potential output.[24] The rate of 2.96 percent is about the same as that which, in the late 1940s and early 1950s, was recognized as the past long-term growth rate. It was not greatly above even the rate spanning the depressed 1930s and it was far below the postwar rate. The 1940–48 rate is higher than the one for 1941–48 but still well below the postwar rate. World War II was, of course, very different from the Korean and Vietnamese periods in that civilian investment and many kinds of civilian production were cut back rather than increased.

Potential Employment and National Income per Person Employed

The procedures used to secure potential national income also provide estimates of potential employment. Hence, it is possible to calculate national income per person employed when both numerator and denominator are measured on a potential basis. These series are shown in the first three columns of Table 7-3.[25]

23. The fact that the size of the required adjustment is far smaller in 1941 than in 1940 is the main consideration in this preference.

24. The war period itself, of course, was a fast growth period.

25. The behavior of the series suggests that potential national income per person employed may be understated and potential employment overstated in some or all of the peak unemployment years of the postwar recessions. Use of these years (1949, 1954, 1958, and 1961) should therefore be avoided in trend analysis. See pages 330–32 for a discussion of this point.

Similar series for the nonresidential business sector are shown in Table 7-3, columns 4 to 6. The entire difference between actual and potential employment or output in the economy as a whole is assigned to this sector. (In addition, work relief employees and their output are transferred to it in 1940 and 1941.) This procedure seems realistic, but I caution that if some of the employment difference were assigned to "general government, households, and institutions," this would alter the series for nonresidential business.

The following chapters analyze the growth of potential and actual national income per person employed, as well as total national income. Here, I merely point out that the sharp acceleration in the growth of potential national income after 1964 was accompanied by acceleration in growth of potential national income per person employed, but it was mainly the growth of potential employment that increased. The increase in the growth rate of potential national income per person employed is nevertheless noteworthy because it contrasts with a drop of over 0.9 percentage points when a similar calculation is made for actual national income per person employed (see Table 2-2). Growth rates for the whole economy and the sector in 1953–64 are compared with those in 1964–69 in the following table.

	Growth rates	
	1953–64	1964–69
Whole economy		
Potential national income	3.20	4.85
Potential employment	1.06	2.41
Potential national income per person employed	2.12	2.39
Nonresidential business		
Potential national income	3.20	4.90
Potential employment	0.75	1.95
Potential national income per person employed	2.43	2.90

Use of a Constant 4 Percent Unemployment Rate

I have followed tradition by defining potential output with reference to an unchanging rate of unemployment. In deriving the series I have consequently measured the difference between actual labor input and the labor input that would be forthcoming if unemployment were 4 percent and intensity of utilization were at the rate that on the average would be associated with 4 percent unemployment. Use of the unemployment rate in

Table 7-3. Potential National Income, Employment, and Potential National Income per Person Potentially Employed: Whole Economy and Nonresidential Business Sector, 1929, 1940–41, and 1947–69
Value data in 1958 dollars

	Whole economy			Nonresidential business		
Year	Potential national income (billions of dollars) (1)	Potential employment (thousands) (2)	Potential national income per person potentially employed (dollars) (3)	Potential national income (billions of dollars) (4)	Potential employment (thousands) (5)	Potential national income per person potentially employed (dollars) (6)
	Excluding Alaska and Hawaii					
1929	158.0	46,796	3,376	133.3	40,380	3,301
1940	200.5	55,732	3,542	170.6	48,165	3,542
1941	215.7	57,095	3,778	179.2	48,144	3,722
1947	257.6	59,117	4,357	214.4	49,601	4,322
1948	264.6	59,972	4,412	220.4	50,164	4,394
1949	271.5	60,894	4,459	224.6	50,649	4,434
1950	286.8	61,959	4,629	237.8	51,205	4,644
1951	305.7	63,724	4,797	248.0	51,097	4,854
1952	320.4	64,636	4,957	258.8	51,348	5,040
1953	337.6	65,320	5,168	274.8	51,960	5,289
1954	347.0	66,355	5,229	283.7	53,112	5,342
1955	358.3	66,684	5,373	293.2	53,115	5,520
1956	371.4	67,905	5,469	304.5	53,960	5,643
1957	380.9	68,223	5,583	312.0	54,006	5,777
1958	391.2	69,250	5,649	320.8	54,738	5,861
1959	403.0	69,246	5,820	331.2	54,513	6,076
1960	417.4	69,981	5,964	342.7	54,952	6,236
	Including Alaska and Hawaii					
1960	418.9	70,274	5,961	343.9	55,167	6,234
1961	432.6	71,557	6,046	354.8	55,983	6,338
1962	446.4	71,827	6,215	364.4	55,547	6,560
1963	464.5	72,724	6,387	379.7	56,174	6,759
1964	479.0	73,632	6,505	390.1	56,644	6,887
1965	502.2	75,101	6,687	409.0	57,598	7,101
1966	528.0	77,486	6,814	429.2	58,698	7,312
1967	552.2	79,251	6,968	447.4	59,647	7,501
1968	580.7	80,915	7,177	471.8	60,680	7,775
1969	607.0	82,926	7,320	495.5	62,374	7,944

Sources: Column 1, Table 7-1, column 5; column 2, Table C-1, column 1, minus Table C-7, column 3, plus Table Q-5, column 10; column 3, column 1 ÷ column 2; column 4, the sum of Table 3-2, column 7, and Table 7-1, columns 2 and 4; column 5, the sum of Table D-2, column 1, an Table Q-5, column 10; column 6, column 4 ÷ column 5.

this way stemmed initially from the belief that it provided an indication of the tightness of the market for labor, as well as from a belief that unemployment above some low percentage was undesirable and that a measure of the output required to prevent unemployment from exceeding that rate was needed.

Tightness of the Labor Market

It is now argued, I believe correctly, that for various reasons the tightness of the labor market when unemployment is at 4 percent has been increasing.

1. Germane to the entire period since 1929 are the facts that few self-employed persons (farm or nonfarm) appear in unemployment counts and that the definition of unemployment excludes even the possibility that unpaid family workers can be counted as unemployed. As these groups have declined in relative importance, a constant unemployment rate for wage and salary workers has implied a rising unemployment rate for the whole labor force.

2. George Perry has pointed out, and my estimates confirm, that the proportion of total available labor input that is unused when the unemployment rate is 4 percent has been declining since 1955 because unemployment has been increasingly concentrated among age-sex groups whose members typically work shorter-than-aver-

age hours and make a below-average contribution per hour, as indicated by below-average hourly earnings. Hence, a constant unemployment percentage has meant a declining labor reserve measured in terms of effective labor input.[26]

3. Perry has also argued, as has the Council of Economic Advisers, that young and female workers not only provide less labor input than males in the prime working ages but also that they (a) are not close substitutes for male workers and (b) normally have a higher unemployment rate than adult males.[27] Consequently, a constant degree of unemployment for adult males, and a constant degree of tightness in the labor market for adult males, has implied a rising total unemployment rate as the proportion of other workers in the labor force has risen.

Although the point is correct, putting it in terms of age-sex groups does not bring out clearly, nor fully measure the effects of, two of the main developments that underlie the change. One is the increase all through the postwar period in the part-time labor force, which has a much higher unemployment rate than the full-time labor force and is highly compartmentalized. There has been an enormous increase during the postwar period in the number of students desiring part-time jobs, but only during hours that do not interfere with school requirements and only at the place where they attend school. The number of such jobs has risen greatly but has not been able to absorb fully the increase in the number of job seekers so that the number unemployed, too, has greatly increased.[28] There has also been a very big increase in the number of nonstudent women in the part-time labor force. The economy has shown remarkable adaptability in providing part-time jobs for women too, but it has been unable to absorb all of the increase in the number wanting part-time jobs. The other development has been the increase in the number of reentries into the labor force by persons who wish to work only intermittently, and who are counted as unemployed during periods after reentry when they are seeking a job. Students—the millions simultaneously seeking vacation jobs each summer and unemployed until they find them, as well as those seeking temporary after-school work—are the clearest example. The situation among women is less simple; although the number of women working has greatly increased, so has the number working regularly.

4. It is argued, plausibly, that unemployment insurance, welfare programs, and other developments have reduced the cost to the individual of unemployment and relieved the pressure upon him to take a job not wholly to his liking.[29]

Potential national income would probably rise less if it were defined in terms of a constant degree of tightness in the labor market instead of a constant unemployment rate. It is plausible that over the forty-year period covered by Figure 7-1 a potential output series so defined might slide gradually downward from somewhere near the upper end of the shaded range to somewhere near the lower end of that range.

Price Movements

When the Committee for Economic Development introduced the high-employment budget as a criterion for fiscal policy in 1947, it was supposed that prices would not rise, or at least would not rise much, if actual output did not exceed high-employment output. It defined high-employment output as the output that would be consistent not only with a constant (low) unemployment rate but also with stable prices.[30]

Price movements do not enter into my definition of potential output. It now appears unlikely that an unemployment rate as low as 4 percent is consistent with price stability. Moreover, it is even doubtful that a potential output series defined as consistent with both (1) *any* constant degree of tightness in the labor market and (2) *any* constant percentage change in prices could be developed. At least, it is now widely believed that the amount

26. George L. Perry, "Changing Labor Markets and Inflation," *Brookings Papers on Economic Activity* (3:1970), pp. 411–48.

27. Ibid., and *Economic Report of the President Together with the Annual Report of the Council of Economic Advisers*, January 1972, pp. 113–16.

28. The size of the changes reported for student labor force participation strains belief, but if changes are overstated it means that the reported unemployment rate has an upward bias over time.

29. Still another point is sometimes alleged—that the extension of minimum wage laws has prevented young workers from taking jobs which would be available and which they would accept in the absence of a minimum wage, and that this has raised the unemployment rate. A detailed investigation by the Bureau of Labor Statistics failed to uncover evidence to substantiate this allegation. (U.S. Bureau of Labor Statistics, *Youth Unemployment and Minimum Wages*, Bulletin 1657 [1970].)

30. For a discussion of the origin of the policy statement by the Committee for Economic Development, *Taxes and the Budget: A Program for Prosperity in a Free Economy* (CED, 1947), see Herbert Stein, *The Fiscal Revolution in America* (University of Chicago Press, 1969), pp. 220–26.

of product price increase that accompanies any given degree of tightness in labor markets has risen. Some date the change only from 1969 or 1970, and among them some think it may turn out to be temporary. Others consider the change has been taking place for a long time and is permanent. If the relationship has changed, one can define an output series which would be consistent with either constant labor force tightness (or, alternatively, a constant unemployment rate) or with a constant rate of price change, but not with both. In presenting a potential output series I express no view as to whether the pressure exerted upon prices at any given ratio of actual to potential output has or has not changed over time.[31]

Comparison with CEA Estimates

My estimates of the gap between actual output and the 4 percent variant of potential output differ markedly from the two similar series prepared by the Council of Economic Advisers to which I have already referred. To make comparison possible, I have adjusted my estimates of the gap, which are valued at factor cost, to the market price concept because the CEA series are valued at market prices.[32] The three series are shown at 1958 market prices in Table 7-4 and Figure 7-2.[33] The two

Table 7-4. Gross National Product: Various Estimates of Actual Less Potential, 1929, 1940–41, and 1947–71
Billions of 1958 dollars

| | | CEA series | | |
Year	Denison series (1)	Based on unemployment rate (2)	Based on trend (3)	Perry series (4)
1929	3.7	n.a.	n.a.	n.a.
1940	−21.2	n.a.	n.a.	n.a.
1941	0.1	n.a.	n.a.	n.a.
1947	−2.7	1.1[a]	n.a.	n.a.
1948	6.3	2.6[a]	n.a.	−12.3
1949	−6.4	−20.0[a]	n.a.	−25.5
1950	4.5	−14.7[a]	n.a.	−9.0
1951	8.0	8.5[a]	n.a.	4.4
1952	3.5	12.3	−0.7	1.9
1953	−0.3	14.4	3.1	4.6
1954	−17.5	−20.2	−17.0	−15.8
1955	0.6	−5.5	−0.8	−1.1
1956	−4.0	−1.9	−8.1	−7.6
1957	−10.9	−3.9	−17.5	−17.4
1958	−30.8	−40.1	−39.1	−37.8
1959	−13.3	−22.4	−27.6	−26.2
1960	−20.2	−23.9	−33.4	−31.9
1961	−27.3	−42.8	−42.1	−40.7
1962	−12.4	−26.1	−28.4	−27.3
1963	−12.1	−29.4	−27.6	−25.5
1964	1.2	−21.9	−19.2	−17.1
1965	12.0	−10.3	−5.0	−3.6
1966	19.1	4.4	11.0	11.5
1967	6.0	3.2	2.2	1.4
1968	4.9	9.5	6.7	5.5
1969	−8.2	11.4	−3.2	−6.3
1970	n.a.	−21.7[a]	−38.4	−41.9
1971	n.a.	−45.9[a]	−51.6	n.a.

Sources: Column 1, product of Table 7-1, column 6, and the ratio of Table A-6, column 4, to the sum of columns 5, 6, and 7 of Table A-7; columns 2 and 3, CEA data (except as noted); column 4, *Brookings Papers on Economic Activity* (3:1971), the current-dollar series on p. 554, divided by the implicit deflator for GNP.

a. Calculated by the author by use of the formula applied in other years.

n.a. Not available.

31. In this, as in other chapters, no comprehensive bibliography is provided, but reference to a few publications not cited elsewhere is appropriate. James W. Knowles popularized the term "potential output" in his pioneer studies, *Potential Economic Growth of the United States during the Next Decade,* Materials prepared for the Joint Committee on the Economic Report by the Committee Staff, 83 Cong. 2 sess. (1954); and *The Potential Economic Growth in the United States,* Study Paper 20, Materials prepared in connection with the Study of Employment, Growth, and Price Levels for consideration by the Joint Economic Committee, 86 Cong. 2 sess. (1960). Michael E. Levy reviewed estimates and approaches up to 1963 in "Potential GNP: Concept and Measurement," in Levy, *Fiscal Policy, Cycles and Growth,* Studies in Business Economics 81 (National Industrial Conference Board, 1963), Chap. 5. Among later estimates not shown here are those by Edwin Kuh ("Measurement of Potential Output," *American Economic Review,* Vol. 56, Pt. 1 [September 1966], pp. 758–76), and Lester C. Thurow and L. D. Taylor ("The Interaction between the Actual and the Potential Rates of Growth," *Review of Economics and Statistics,* Vol. 48 [November 1966], pp. 351–60).

32. The fact that my series refers to net national product and theirs to gross national product does not affect the absolute (dollar) size of the gap.

33. George Perry has also derived a potential GNP series, and although I shall not discuss its behavior I have included his estimates of the "gap" in Table 7-4. Perry deals separately with employment, average hours, output per man-hour, and age-sex composition, although only for the economy as a whole. His procedure combines a direct estimate of the gap between the actual and potential labor force in

CEA series only begin in 1952. However, the CEA series derived from the unemployment rate by use of Okun's law is easily computed, and I have ventured to include estimates for 1947–51 to show the implications of the method for that period. The other CEA series, that obtained by

each age-sex group with estimated trend values for average hours worked and for output per "weighted" man-hour, the weights referring to the age-sex composition of potential hours worked. For a complete description, see George L. Perry, "Labor Force Structure, Potential Output, and Productivity," in *Brookings Papers on Economic Activity* (3:1971), pp. 533–65.

Figure 7-2. Actual Less Potential GNP at 1958 Market Prices: Three Estimates, 1947–69

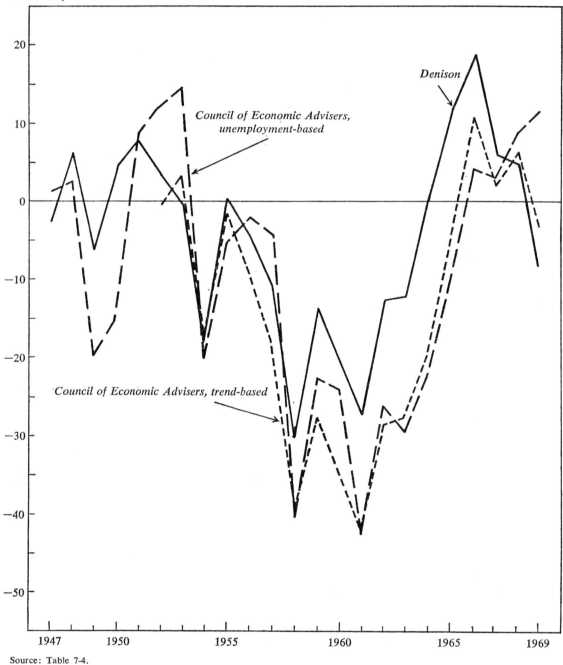

Billions of dollars

Source: Table 7-4.

deducting actual output from an estimated trend value, cannot be carried backwards because the CEA has not specified a trend rate prior to 1952.

Limitations and Differences among Estimates

In one respect the three series are in moderate agreement: in most years they give the same signal as to whether actual output had moved up or down from the previous year relative to potential output. However, there are striking exceptions. For example, my series shows that actual output declined relative to potential output in both 1968 and 1969, the CEA series based on the unemployment rate shows that it increased in both 1968 and 1969, and the CEA series based on use of trend values shows that it increased in 1968 and declined in 1969. The three series also fail to agree on the direction of movement in 1952, 1953, 1956, 1960, and 1963. There are much greater differences among the three series in the size (as distinguished from the direction) of the movement in the gap from year to year, and in the actual amount by which actual and potential output differ.

Perhaps the most interesting difference is one which prevails throughout the period from 1956 through 1966. In all of these years my series shows actual output to have been much higher relative to potential output than the CEA series that is based on trend; from 1958 through 1966, it also indicates a much higher ratio of actual to potential output than the CEA series based on the unemployment rate.[34]

What is responsible for this large difference over so extended a period? Because I believe that my series is the best of the three, I shall restate the question: Why did the council overstate potential output for a whole decade? But I recognize, of course, that final judgment will rest on careful evaluation by other analysts.

The unpublished CEA estimates of the gap based on the unemployment rate assume potential GNP differs from actual GNP by a percentage equal to 3.2 times the difference between the unemployment percentage and 4 percent. Okun ascribed little more than half of the coefficient of 3.2 to the difference between actual and potential man-hours. The remainder he ascribed to cyclical fluctuations in output per man-hour. The procedure implies that in the economy as a whole the percentage difference between actual and potential hours worked and the percentage difference between actual and potential output per man-hour are each a constant multiple of the difference between the unemployment rate and 4 percent. My estimates support neither assumption. The output per man-hour assumption is especially weak, and not only for year-to-year movements. In a period when the unemployment rate is persistently above 4 percent, firms come to anticipate an output level that is below the potential level and have time to adjust actual inputs toward correspondence with their output anticipations. Okun's method increasingly overestimates the average size of the gap between potential and actual output per man-hour in such a period.

The estimate of potential GNP based on trend is the one which CEA published and, apparently, upon which it chiefly relied. It exceeded actual GNP by an average of $21.5 billion (in 1958 prices) from 1956 through 1966. The corresponding figure from my series is only $9.0 billion.[35] The Council of Economic Advisers obtained the value for potential GNP from which it computed the gap by the following procedure. Potential GNP was assumed equal to actual GNP in mid-1955 (the average of the second and third quarters) in order to establish the level of the series. Estimates for other years were made by assuming that the growth rate of potential GNP was 3.5 percent from the first quarter of 1952 through the fourth quarter of 1962, 3.75 percent from the fourth quarter of 1962 through the fourth quarter of 1965, and 4 percent from the fourth quarter of 1965 through the fourth quarter of 1969. (Thereafter, 4.3 percent has been used, but this does not affect the present comparison.)

Only a small part of the 1956–66 difference between the CEA trend series for the gap and my series stems from the CEA's choice of a base level. For 1955 as a whole, the CEA estimates that actual GNP was $0.8 billion below potential (in 1958 prices) while I estimate that it was $0.6 billion above potential. The difference is only $1.4 billion, and the addition of Alaska and Hawaii to actual output with no adjustment of potential GNP by the CEA canceled even this difference from 1960 on.

Almost all of the difference stems from the CEA's choice of growth rates. As stated earlier,

---

34. My series shows a higher ratio than either CEA series in 1967 as well, but the difference was relatively small.

35. At the end of the period potential GNP was below actual GNP in my series, which offset much of the earlier deficiency.

my series suggests that the course of potential output would be traced fairly well by trend rates of 3.20 from 1953 to 1964 and 4.85 from 1964 to 1969.[36] The CEA was putting the growth rate of potential output higher throughout the 1956–64 period: by 0.30 points until 1962 and by 0.55 points thereafter. This overstatement, as I view it, was eventually offset by use of too low a rate after 1964, which in time caused the two estimates of the gap to reverse position. But this did not happen until 1968.

Selection of growth rates must have posed a difficult problem for the council. The trend of potential GNP can no more be calculated without a series from which to compute it than any other trend. The only potential GNP series available to the council was the one it obtained from the unemployment rate. That series was not used directly because of its erratic movements, but it seems fairly evident that in initially selecting trend rates the CEA was trying to develop a potential GNP series that preserved the general movement and average level of the series based on unemployment rates while eliminating irregularities in it. The council seems also to have been reluctant to revise trend rates for past periods as additional experience became available. Although the proximate reason that the CEA's trend-based estimates of the size of the gap in 1956–66 differ markedly from my estimates is that their trend rates differ greatly from those implied by my direct estimates of the gap, the real source of the difference (if I am correct as to the basis for their trend rates) is that my direct estimates differ greatly from the CEA's direct estimates based upon the unemployment rate. Thus the real question for evaluation is which of the direct estimates provides more reliable results; the trend-based series cannot provide independent evidence because there is no independent method of estimating trends.[37]

36. These refer to national income but would be little changed if computed for GNP.
37. Trend-based series could also, of course, be derived from my direct estimates. It is possible, too, in the spirit of George Perry's estimates to which reference has been made on page 97, note 33, to combine trend-based estimates for some components, such as those contained in the semi-residual, with direct estimates for all other components. Such series would differ from the direct estimates only by the smoothing out of minor irregularities if the trend changes I have noted were followed faithfully. See Appendix Q, Part 3, for further discussion, and for an illustrative, partially trend-based, series which makes no use of my direct estimates of demand-related fluctuations in productivity.

Policy Implications of Differences

It is interesting to speculate how the choice between the CEA series and mine would have affected evaluation of the economic situation, and therefore of appropriate policy, if both series had been available at the time. From 1956 until 1963, the choice would not have been crucial. My series shows an increasingly smaller shortfall of actual output than do the CEA series, but one that was nevertheless quite sufficient to warrant support for an expansionary policy. In each of the last two years of that period, 1962 and 1963, my series shows actual GNP $12 billion below potential GNP (in 1958 prices) while the CEA trend-based series shows it $28 billion below.

In the next two years, however, the series were flashing contradictory signals. My estimates show actual GNP about equal to potential GNP as early as 1964 (actually, $1 billion higher, in 1958 prices). In sharp contrast, the CEA estimates show potential above actual GNP by $19 billion, according to its trend-based series, and by $22 billion, according to its direct estimates based on the unemployment rate, indicating a very comfortable cushion against the possibility of inflation. My estimates show that by 1965 actual GNP had risen $12 billion above potential GNP whereas the CEA estimates show actual GNP still below potential by $5 billion according to its trend-based series and by $10 billion according to its direct estimate. These results for years in which the formulation of macroeconomic policy was a crucial matter are so contradictory as to demand further investigation.

The Estimates for 1964 and 1965

If the various estimates of the GNP gap are reduced by one-tenth, to convert them from a market-price to a factor-cost basis, and compared with my estimates of actual national income, they imply that actual national income exceeded or fell short of potential national income by the following percentages:

	1964	1965
Denison	+0.2	+2.2
CEA, based on trend	−3.5	−0.9
CEA, based on unemployment rate	−3.9	−1.8

The civilian unemployment rate was 5.2 percent in 1964 and 4.5 in 1965. My estimates (Table 7-1, columns 4 and 5) imply that the difference between actual and potential labor input would by itself have caused actual national income to fall below potential by 1.1 percent in 1964 and by 0.1 percent in 1965; the 1965 percentage is as small as this because the actual working hours of employed workers were estimated to be well above their potential hours in that year and this largely offset the employment gap.[38]

Although there is room for some difference of opinion as to the size of the shortfall of labor input in 1964 and 1965, its scope is small relative to the big differences among estimates of the output gap. The bulk of the disagreement about the output gap must stem from a difference of view (actual or implied) as to the cyclical position of output per unit of input. A difference between actual and potential output per unit of input can arise only in nonresidential business. If my estimates of the labor input gap and its effect on output were to be accepted, then the various estimates of the output gap would imply the following estimates of the productivity gap in nonresidential business expressed as a percentage of actual national income per unit of input in that sector:

	1964	1965
Denison	+1.7	+2.7
CEA, based on trend	−3.0	−0.9
CEA, based on unemployment rate	−3.7	−2.1

My potential output estimates thus rest on the belief that productivity in 1964 was well above the level it would have taken, on the average, in a sample of years in which unemployment was 4 percent but in which output was changing by random amounts—and that it was far above such a level in 1965. My estimates imply that less than average productivity gains were to be anticipated when output advances receded to a normal rate, even though unemployment were to stabilize or continue to decline. This actually occurred after 1966.

That productivity was below potential in 1964 and 1965—as the council's estimates imply—is, in my opinion, implausible.[39] To support this statement I do not rely solely on my direct estimates that the cyclical position of output per unit of input was higher in 1965 than in any other postwar year except 1950 and 1966 (Table 6-1, column 6). I also point out that output per unit of input was higher in 1965, relative to a postwar trend line based on all postwar years, than it was in any other postwar year except 1950 and 1966. To reach the value implied by even the lower of CEA's potential national income estimates for 1965, output per unit of input would have had to exceed the trend line by almost as large a percentage as it did in 1950, the postwar year in which the deviation was greatest of all.[40] Unless the CEA means to identify the productivity component of potential output with about the highest cyclical position ever reached, its 1964–65 estimates of potential output are much too big.[41]

Importance of Potential Output Series

The difference between actual and potential output is an important economic series. It is required not only for studies of long-term growth but also for current economic analysis. I believe the procedures described in this chapter and Appendix Q provide better and more carefully defined estimates than any available hitherto. At the very least, they are estimates that in the future should be available to analysts and policymakers as alternatives to those obtained by the CEA procedures. This will not be possible unless the entire body of estimates presented in this book is brought up to date annually, and such a task probably can be performed only by government agencies.

Even then, I caution, the method could not directly provide current quarterly series. Given the times at which data become available (particularly the July completion date of detailed national income and product series), it would be near the end of one year before an annual estimate for the preceding year could be completed. Use of some form of the trend method probably would be necessary to extrapolate the most recent estimates of potential output to current quarterly series. But the current quarterly estimates would be tied to direct estimates for the recent past, and the basis for gauging the current trend rate of potential output growth would also be greatly improved.

---

38. See Table Q-3, column 3, and the description of the estimates in Appendix Q, Part 3.

39. I do not believe that one could construct a reasonable estimate of the gap due to factor input that is sufficiently larger than mine to eliminate even the implied productivity shortfall for the trend-based estimate for 1965, the smaller of the two CEA gaps shown above.

40. The series for output per unit of input on which this statement is based excludes (as is highly desirable) the effects of gains from reallocation of resources, the weather in farming, and labor disputes. Annual percentage deviations from trend are shown in Table O-2, column 4.

41. Even if the council really intends to eliminate the business cycle from the capital stock corresponding to potential output (which, as I noted earlier, is in a crude way the effect of its procedures), this could justify raising potential output only slightly. It would, however, impair the series for use in judging appropriate stabilization policy.

-»>×<«-

Sources of Growth of Nonresidential Business Output

-»>×<«-

Estimates required to analyze the sources of growth of national income have now been completed. In this and the following chapter they are brought together in the form of tables showing the sources of growth of four output measures in eight selected time periods.

Data presented in this chapter refer to output of the nonresidential business sector. They are of particular interest because the nonresidential business sector is more homogeneous than the whole economy. Its production is sold on the market, and market transactions establish the value of this output in current prices. Value in constant prices is obtained by dividing current values by price indexes, or by an equivalent procedure. Thus output is measured in a way that is generally uniform and statistically independent of input measures. Only in trivial instances does an assumption that output and input move alike enter the process of estimation. But it is not only in statistical measurement that the sector is more homogeneous than the economy as a whole. Nearly all production is carried on by business enterprises which are organized for profit; use various types of labor, capital, and land in their operations; and must seek to combine these factors in proportions which minimize their costs if they are to achieve their goal of profit maximization.[1]

For analysis of some growth sources, data for nonresidential business are even more informative than data for the economy as a whole, which also

1. The main exceptions are mutual financial intermediaries and government enterprises.

includes the three special sectors examined in Chapter 3. This is especially true of components of output per unit of input and of components of labor input other than employment. Because the contribution made to the growth of measured output in nonresidential business by components of output per unit of input has no counterpart elsewhere in the economy, the behavior and effects of these components can be seen more clearly in a context in which the changing weight of nonresidential business in the economy as a whole does not affect the numbers. Similarly, components of labor input which refer to changes in the composition or quality of labor either do not contribute to changes in output as actually measured in other parts of the economy or do so in a different way than in nonresidential business.

For many purposes, however, it is essential to deal with the economy as a whole. Chapter 9 provides estimates for the whole economy that are similar to those provided in this chapter for nonresidential business alone. In considering the estimates provided in the present chapter, the reader must bear in mind that only a partial picture of the economy is presented.

Meaning and Derivation of Estimates

Output at any date depends on many determinants, and it is changes in these determinants that cause output to change—that is, economic growth. An analysis of the sources of growth over any time span identifies the determinants that have changed and the contribution that changes in each have made to the change in output. The size of the contribution of a determinant depends upon its importance and the amount by which it has changed. If it has not changed at all its contribution is zero.

It is convenient to focus the analysis on growth rates and the contributions to these growth rates that were made by changes in the several output determinants. Use of growth rates, rather than percentage changes, indexes, or absolute changes, permits valid comparisons among time periods of unequal length, and it holds statistical interaction terms to small size. The use of terminal years to compute growth rates prevents ups and downs that may have occurred during the intervening years from distorting the results or rendering them incomparable with each other.

The thirty-two growth rates that will be divided among sources of growth in this chapter are shown in Table 8-1. They refer to growth rates of total actual national income, actual national in-

Table 8-1. Nonresidential Business: Growth Rates, Eight Selected Periods, 1929–69
Percent per annum

Time span	Actual national income		Potential national income	
	Total	Per person employed	Total	Per person potentially employed
Long periods				
1929–69	3.22	2.14	3.33	2.22
1929–48	2.68	1.57	2.68	1.52
1948–69	3.72	2.65	3.92	2.86
Shorter periods				
1929–41	2.16	1.50	2.50	1.01
1941–48	3.58	1.69	3.00	2.40
1948–53	3.98	2.85	4.51	3.78
1953–64	3.24	2.93	3.20	2.43
1964–69	4.52	1.85	4.90	2.90

Sources: Calculated from Table 3-2, column 7, Table D-2, column 3, and Table 7-3, columns 4 and 6.

come per person employed, total potential national income, and total potential national income per person potentially employed. All refer to national income originating in the nonresidential business sector, valued in 1958 prices.

Because it is impossible to present and discuss growth rates between all possible pairs of years, periods of particular interest were selected. One purpose of the analysis is to measure the sources of past long-term growth. To meet this purpose, estimates are presented for the entire forty-year period covered by the study, 1929–69, and for the entire postwar period, 1948–69. To complete the long-term analysis, data for 1929–48 are also provided.

Another purpose is to discover the sources of the pronounced changes in growth rates that are observed from time to time. For this purpose the forty-year span is divided into five periods. The first runs from 1929, the last year before the onset of depression, to 1941, the last and most prosperous subsequent year before United States participation in World War II. The second, 1941–48, spans the World War II period and reconversion to peacetime production. By 1948 reconversion had been completed.[2] The postwar years are divided into 1948–53, 1953–64, and 1964–69 periods. The years 1953 and 1964 were selected as dividing points because, as found in the pre-

2. Also, abolition of World War II price controls had eliminated the distortion that noncompliance with controls remaining in 1946 and 1947 introduced into price, and hence output, measures.

ceding chapter, they rather sharply separate the periods of fast growth of total potential output in the whole economy which occurred at the beginning and end of the postwar years covered by this study from the longer period of slower growth during the middle of the period. They appear to be as appropriate as any for analysis of sector output, and of actual as well as potential output.

Although the dates selected to divide periods appear appropriate for analysis of the output measures they do not, of course, correspond to the dates at which pronounced changes, if any, in the behavior of every determinant of output occurred. These can be ascertained only by examination of the annual indexes for determinants. They have already been presented and discussed.

Total Actual National Income

To secure the estimates of the sources of growth of total actual national income in the nonresidential business sector (shown in Tables 8-2 and 8-5), the following procedure was used in each time period. The growth rate of total output was allocated between total input and total output per unit of input in proportion to the growth rates of the two series. The contribution of output per unit of input was allocated among its components in proportion to the growth rates of the individual indexes. The contribution of total input was allocated among labor, inventories, nonresidential structures and equipment, and land in proportion to the products of the growth rates of the input indexes and their average weights during the period. The contribution of labor input was allocated among its components in proportion to the growth rates of the separate labor input indexes. Finally, discrepancies between totals and the sums of more detailed components that arise because of rounding were eliminated.

The estimate for each component is only slightly different from that which would be obtained without the allocation procedure: that is, by measuring the contribution of total input, total output per unit of input, and each component of output per unit of input as the growth rate of its index, and each component of input as the product of the growth rate of its index and its average weight (using the labor weight for all labor input components). For example, over the whole 1929–69 period the growth rates of total input and total output per unit of input were 1.39 and 1.80, amounts which compare with contributions of 1.40 and 1.82 when the growth rate of output,

3.22, is allocated between them so as to eliminate the discrepancy due to "statistical interaction" between the sum of their growth rates and the growth rate of output.

If the allocation procedure were not used, the contribution of any determinant might be said to measure what the growth rate of output would have been if that determinant had changed as it did but there had been no change in other determinants. With its use, it is preferable to define the contribution of each determinant as the amount by which the growth rate of output would have been reduced (or increased, if the contribution is negative) if that determinant had not changed but all other determinants had changed as they actually did. This description is more accurate not only because of the treatment of the statistical interaction term but also, and more importantly, because each of the indexes and the weights were obtained by taking all of the other conditions affecting output as they actually existed throughout a period, not as they would have been had they remained unchanged for that time span.[3]

Total Potential National Income

Sources of growth of total potential national income in the sector (shown in Tables 8-2 and 8-6) were obtained by a procedure paralleling that used for total actual national income, but with indexes referring to potential conditions where the indexes differ. These indexes, not previously presented in this form, are provided in Table R-1. Because the construction of certain indexes was partially independent of the derivation of the potential national income series itself, in most periods they imply growth rates of potential national income a little different from those actually obtained. The differences, which are shown in Appendix R, were eliminated in the sources of growth tables by adjusting the components to remove this discrepancy along with discrepancies arising from rounding and statistical

interaction.[4] Care was taken to avoid significant distortion of comparisons between time periods or between the estimates for actual and potential output.

Output per Person Employed

Derivation of the sources of growth of actual output per person employed (Tables 8-4 and 8-9) and of potential output per person potentially employed (Tables 8-4 and 8-10) was similar to that for the corresponding estimates for total output, but employment itself disappears from the tables and the growth rates of nonlabor inputs are computed per person employed (or potentially employed).

For many growth sources, contributions to the growth rates of two or more of the four output measures are the same or would be the same were it not for small differences due to rounding, statistical interaction, and the necessity, just discussed, of "forcing" the components of potential output to agree with totals. Table R-6 indicates these cases. They are also noted in the following section.

Classification of Growth Sources

The value of any set of estimates of the sources of growth depends upon the user's understanding of the classification adopted. The classification followed here is based chiefly on my judgment as to what groupings are useful, but availability of information dictated decisions in some borderline cases. Lack of information limits severely the amount of detail that can be provided for some growth sources. The classification has the characteristic, of course, that the sum of the contributions of the sources equals the growth rate. The same change cannot be credited to two determinants. It also has the characteristic that the contribution of each determinant is measured against a no-change situation. If a determinant does not change, its contribution to growth is zero.[5]

Earlier chapters carefully described each determinant and the reader is referred to them for a fuller discussion, but it will be useful to review the classification in the context of sources of

---

3. A rather pedantic definition can be given that is still more exact because it limits all measures to small changes as well as corresponding to the method of estimation. The contribution of each growth determinant in any period is the amount by which the percentage change in output in any one year of the period would have been reduced if the determinant under consideration had not changed in that year, if that determinant had changed in all other years of the period by a percent equal to its growth rate over the period, and if every other determinant had changed in each year of the period by the same percentage as its growth rate over the period.

4. Differences in the long periods were negligible. The largest differences (0.08 and 0.09 percentage points) occurred in the 1929–41 and 1941–48 shorter periods.

5. See Edward F. Denison, "Classification of Sources of Growth," *Review of Income and Wealth*, Series 18, No. 1 (March 1972), pp. 1–25, for further discussion of these and other characteristics of the classification of growth sources.

growth. The necessity, to conserve space, of severely curtailing table stubs makes such a review even more necessary. The following discussion of the classification in this section should be regarded as a unit because it is not possible, without tedious repetition, to make the description of each determinant wholly self-contained. The discussion of economies of scale, in particular, conditions the definitions of almost all the other determinants. The reader may wish to look ahead to Tables 8-2 and 8-4 in following this discussion (see pages 111 and 114).

Growth of output may be obtained by the use of more labor and property resources or by increasing the output obtained from the same quantity of resources. The contributions of *total factor input* and *total output per unit of input* distinguish changes in output that result from increases in the quantity of labor performed by individuals with various characteristics relevant to production, in the quantity of capital, and in the quantity of land from changes that result from raising total output per unit of labor, capital, and land. To give this broad statement precision, the components of each must be described.

Labor

The contribution to growth of the change in *labor* input refers to the increase in output that results from the increase in the amounts of labor of all types that are used in production in the sector. It is obtained as the sum of several components.

EMPLOYMENT. This estimate refers to the contribution that would have been made by the change in the number of persons employed *if* there had been no change in the hours they worked and no change in their composition by age, sex, or amount of education. Employment is not measured on a full-time equivalent basis; full-time and part-time workers are counted equally. (The reduction in labor input per worker resulting from increasing part-time employment is counted in the "hours" component of labor input.)

Other components of labor input allow for the fact that there were changes in hours and composition. All are calculated on a per-person-employed basis, even in the tables for total ouput, so as to measure the change in labor input per person employed. For this reason the entries for all components of labor input except employment are the same (aside from rounding and interaction) in the tables for total national income and in those for national income per person employed. Employment itself does not appear in the tables for output per person employed, and in those tables "total labor input" refers to labor input per person employed. All components of labor input make different contributions to actual and to potential output. Not only do actual and potential employment and actual and potential average hours move differently, but so does the composition of hours worked when classified by the age, sex, or education of workers.

HOURS. The sources of growth tables provide a summary estimate, labeled *hours,* of the net effect of changes in average working hours upon output. This estimate is not based upon a supposition that a given percentage change in the average hours worked by all employed persons, combined, changes labor input proportionately and therefore has the same effect on output as a percentage change of the same size in employment. The results that would be obtained from such an assumption are, however, shown in the tables with the label *average hours.*

I base my *hours* estimates on the belief that the effects of changes in the average hours worked by all persons employed in the sector depend upon the reasons that average hours change. To implement this, I divided persons employed in the sector among eight groups: full-time workers of each sex who are employed as nonfarm wage and salary workers, as nonfarm self-employed and unpaid family workers, and as farm workers, and part-time workers of each sex in all types of activity. The levels of average hours differ greatly among these eight groups so that changes in their weights greatly affect the average hours of all persons employed in nonresidential business, and such changes have had a major influence upon the course of average hours.

It was estimated that a change in average hours in the sector as a whole does indeed mean a proportional change in labor input if it results from a change in the relative numbers of full-time workers and part-time workers, from a change in the average hours of part-time workers, or from a change in the relative numbers of male and female workers. However, if the change in the combined average results from two other types of change it is judged to alter labor input less than proportionally or not at all. The two remaining subcomponents of the "hours" line ("efficiency offset" and "intergroup shift offset") implement these judgments.

A change in sector average hours resulting from a reduction (or increase) in the average hours of full-time nonfarm wage and salary workers of either sex is estimated to result in an increase (or decrease) in work done per hour worked, and hence in a percentage reduction (or increase) in labor input per worker that is smaller than the percentage change in average hours. When a change is reported in the average hours of full-time farm workers or of full-time nonfarm self-employed and unpaid family workers of either sex, the change is assumed to have no effect on labor input but rather to be fully offset in labor input per hour. These procedures are implemented by including in the tables the line labeled *efficiency offset*.[6]

Average hours in the sector may also change because of a shift in the distribution of full-time workers of either sex among the three labor force groups distinguished. Such changes are not considered to change labor input at all; otherwise-similar individuals who are nonfarm wage and salary workers, nonfarm self-employed and unpaid family workers, or farm workers are counted as the same amount of labor input if each works the average full-time hours of persons of his or her own sex in the category in which he or she is employed. The effects of such shifts upon the "average hours" component are offset in the line labeled *intergroup shift offset* in the sources of growth tables.[7]

The contribution of changes in *hours* is obtained as the sum of the three subcomponents.[8] In most periods average hours have declined and all three groups of reasons distinguished have contributed to the decline. Hence, the contribution of hours is ordinarily negative but less so than that of "average hours" because the contributions of both the "efficiency offset" and the "intergroup shift offset" are positive.[9]

6. In Chapter 4 the index from which this line is derived is given the fuller heading, "efficiency of an hour's work as affected by changes in hours due to intragroup changes."
7. In Chapter 4 this component is termed "efficiency of an hour's work as affected by changes in hours due to specified intergroup shifts."
8. The procedure introduces a slight inconsistency in the added figure for "hours" because, as explained in Chapter 4, weighting by sex was not introduced in the calculation of the "average hours" subcomponent but was introduced before calculating the other two subcomponents. No inconsistency is present when the "hours" and "age-sex" components of labor input are combined.
9. Appendix R, section 6, shows how sources of growth estimates that would correspond to some different assumptions as to the effects of hours changes can be derived from the tables.

AGE-SEX COMPOSITION. Hours worked by persons who differ in age and sex are not considered to represent the same amount of labor input. Rather, the relative amounts of labor input embodied in an average hour worked by persons in each of ten age-sex groups are measured as proportional to average hourly earnings. Since the employment and average hours series make no such distinction, it is introduced as a separate entry in the *age-sex composition* line. The contribution of age-sex composition is positive when the proportion of total hours worked by persons in the highly weighted groups—particularly males 35 to 64 years of age—rises, and negative when the proportion worked by persons in the groups that receive low weights rises.

EDUCATION. Full-time equivalent years of work performed by persons with different amounts of education are also regarded as different amounts of labor input. They are weighted in accordance with average earnings differentials among persons employed in the sector who differ only with respect to amount of education. The final component of labor input, the contribution of *education*, measures the amount by which output per worker has been altered by the change in the educational background of employed persons (or potentially employed persons in the case of the tables referring to potential output). The same change in the educational backgrounds of males and females is considered to represent the same percentage change in the labor input of each, but changes for males are weighted more heavily to accord with the age-sex weighting already introduced in the labor input measure. Since the educational distribution of employed persons has been steadily and strongly rising, the contribution of education is positive in all periods and tables.

A few points about the education component must be mentioned, even in a brief summary. First, only regular, formal education is counted (except insofar as other types of education are systematically related to formal education). Second, the estimate is a measure of the contribution to output made by increased skills and versatility of workers as a result of additional education when the state of knowledge in the society is given. Neither the fact that advances in knowledge permit new knowledge to be transmitted in educational institutions nor the possibility that a more educated population may advance the frontiers of knowledge more rapidly is reflected in the education estimate. Both are regarded as parts of the processes by which new knowledge originates, is disseminated, and enters into the process of production. Third, the size of the contribution made by education in any time period depends upon the difference between the education of persons who left employment during the period and those who entered it. It thus reflects not only or mainly changes in the education provided to young people during that period, but also the lagged effects of changes made over many previous decades. Fourth, the education estimates, like all other labor input components except employment, are measured on a per-person basis so that the increase in school attendance required to hold the average education of a growing population constant does not enhance the contribution of education.

Changes in the intensity of work are taken into account in the labor input measure only insofar as they are the consequences of changes in the duration of working hours and measured in the "efficiency offset" line. It is recognized that intensity of utilization of labor, like that of capital and land, varies with fluctuations in the strength of demand pressures, but the effects of such variations upon actual output are measured in the "intensity of demand" component of output per unit of input. (The definition of potential output precludes the possibility of its being affected by such fluctuations.) It is possible that the intensity of an average hour's work may also have changed in the longer run as a consequence of changes in attitudes, incentives, living standards, or other influences. I have no evidence that such a change occurred and regard it as unlikely that, if it did, it was of sufficient size to affect growth rates importantly in the periods examined.

The estimate of the contribution of labor to growth is based upon the number and personal characteristics of workers and the amount of work that they perform. It is not, and is not intended to be, affected by the use to which labor is put nor how it is organized. I regard changes in the products workers produce, the industries in which they are employed, and the occupations in which they are classified as irrelevant to input measurement. If such changes—or changes in the uses to which capital or land are put—alter the total national income in constant prices, this is regarded as a component of output per unit of input.

Capital and Land

The contributions made by changes in the quantities of *inventories, nonresidential structures and equipment,* and *land* to growth require relatively few comments because the categories themselves are self-explanatory.[10] The main point to recall is that capital input is so defined and measured that changes in output which result from improvements in the design of capital goods are classified as contributions of advances in knowledge, not of capital.

Capital and land, like labor, are regarded as in use so long as they remain in establishments and available for service. Unlike labor, they are not laid off or sent home early when work is slack so, by the definition adopted here, there is no difference between actual and potential capital or land input. Consequently, contributions to the growth rates of total potential and total actual national income are the same, aside from interaction and statistical adjustments. The effects on actual output of variations in the intensity of use of capital, land, and labor which accompany fluctuations in demand pressure are measured as a single estimate in the "intensity of demand" line of the tables.[11]

Changes in the amounts of capital and land per person employed differ from those for capital and land per person potentially employed because the denominators are different. For this reason contributions to growth rates of national income per person employed differ from contributions to potential national income per person potentially employed.

Components of Output per Unit of Input

The remaining entries in the tables are components of output per unit of input. Whether examined on an actual or a potential basis the contribution of each to total output and to output per person employed is necessarily the same, except for the effects of rounding, interaction, and the like. With the same qualification, the contributions of most components to actual and to potential national income are the same. Exceptions are "intensity of demand," which disappears when output is measured on a potential basis, and "im-

10. Dwellings are not present in the nonresidential business sector. I use the term "nonresidential structures" here only to avoid confusion when the sectors are combined in the following chapter.

11. Long-run changes in the "average hours" of capital and land, if they occur, cannot be counted as a separate source of growth because they are chiefly manifestations of changes in other determinants (see p. 56).

proved resource allocation" resulting from movement of labor out of "farms" and "nonfarm self-employment." The resource allocation estimates differ because the allocation of labor under actual conditions departs from what it would be under potential conditions.

The contribution of "advances in knowledge and n.e.c." (not elsewhere classified) is measured as a residual but this provides no excuse for lack of clarity as to its content. Indeed, only its careful definition will permit work leading to more detail in the estimates to go forward in a constructive way. Conceptually, it can be divided between "advances in knowledge" and the "miscellaneous determinants" described in Chapter 6 (which correspond to the "n.e.c." portion of the table stubs).

ADVANCES IN KNOWLEDGE AND N.E.C. The contribution of advances in knowledge is a comprehensive measure of the gains in measured output that result from the incorporation in production of new knowledge of any type, regardless of the source of that knowledge, the way it is transmitted to those who can make use of it, or the way it is incorporated into production. The reference to "measured" output is important. What is usually called "unmeasured" or "noneconomic" quality change in end products does not raise measured output so that advances in knowledge which lead to "unmeasured" quality change in end products (including the introduction of wholly new end products) make no contribution to the growth of output as measured.[12]

Advances in knowledge might in principle be divided between new knowledge that makes increases in output possible and changes in the lag of average actual practice behind the best practice possible with the knowledge available at each date. I attempt no such division, but regard changes in the lag as unlikely to have had more than a minor effect over the whole 1929–69 period or the period after about 1950. Very low investment in the 1930s and wartime interruption of the production of some peacetime products during World War II

probably caused the lag to increase from 1929 to 1947 and decline from 1947 to 1950.

The "n.e.c." portion of "advances in knowledge and n.e.c." refers to the effects of a large number of determinants that have not been quantified. These are believed to be individually small and on average as likely to be favorable as unfavorable except in the depression period when they probably were slightly adverse.[13] Because of their inclusion, the estimates provide only an approximation to the contribution made by the incorporation of advances in knowledge.

To the extent that they are not offsetting, some types of error in the estimates for other determinants also affect this estimate. This, of course, is not a matter of classification but of accuracy.

IMPROVED RESOURCE ALLOCATION. These lines refer to the gains in output that have resulted from bringing the allocation of resources within the sector nearer to the optimal allocation. The effects of only two types of change in resource allocation are measured, but I believe them to have been by far the most important changes. The *farm* component refers to the gains from reducing the percentage of all of the labor used in the nonresidential business sector that is overallocated to farming, while the *nonfarm self-employment* component refers to the gains from reducing the percentage that is misallocated to nonfarm self-employment and unpaid family labor. Because it is the *percentage* distribution of labor input that is important here, the size of the gains depends upon the change in nonfarm wage and salary employment in the sector as well as upon the changes in farm employment and nonfarm self-employment themselves. The difference between the actual and potential estimates for these sources reflects the difference between actual and potential nonfarm wage and salary employment. The criterion against which misallocation is appraised is maximum output (which is not necessarily the same as maximum welfare) *per worker* in the sector. This is so in the tables referring to total as well as to per-worker output. In particular, if the shift of population from rural to urban areas has altered labor force participation rates, this is reflected in the contribution of employment, not in the farm component of resource reallocation.

12. The contribution of advances in knowledge is net of the adverse effect upon the change in output per unit of input of an increase in the labor and capital currently devoted to securing new knowledge, but only when costs are borne by business itself. This results from the fact that business labor and capital devoted to research are included in input but are counted as output only when the work is performed on contract for nonbusiness buyers, chiefly the federal government. The effect of this deduction on the size of the contribution of advances in knowledge is minor.

13. This judgment as to their collective unimportance refers only to the estimates presented. It does not imply a belief that the determinants are always and everywhere unimportant or could not change.

ECONOMIES OF SCALE. Gains from *economies of scale* refer to the rise in output per unit of input that is made possible by changes in the size of the markets that business serves. Economies of scale are realized only as production is reorganized or adapted to secure the lower costs that growing markets permit, so the estimate is based upon the size of the economy that business is estimated to have anticipated in organizing production.[14] Economies of scale are not limited to those internal to firms. As explained in Chapter 6, specialization of all sorts is covered by my use of the term.

Growing markets are simply a reflection of a rising national income, so the size of markets business expects to serve is governed by the contributions of all the determinants that precede economies of scale in the tables for total national income. It would therefore be entirely appropriate to eliminate economies of scale as a separate growth determinant and to allocate its contribution among the preceding determinants. As a first approximation, an allocation based upon their contributions to total actual national income would be reasonable, and I shall use this procedure in some supplementary analyses. I have chosen not to do this in the standard tables in order to be able to show the contribution of economies of scale separately, and to keep their entire contribution in output per unit of input (since its wording clearly implies such a classification). I have measured the contributions of all other sources as if the economy were operating under constant returns to scale, so that to the definition of their contributions must be added the stipulation that the size of markets is taken as given.

IRREGULAR FACTORS. Farm output and productivity in any year are affected by the weather and other natural conditions. The effect of differences between the initial and terminal years on the

growth rate over each period analyzed is measured in the line, *weather in farming*. Similarly, the effect of labor disputes upon output per unit of input is measured in the line, *labor disputes*.[15] Because potential national income is defined to differ from actual national income only with respect to demand conditions, these entries appear in potential as well as actual national income tables.[16] I have pointed out that year-to-year changes in output and output per unit of input are much affected by the calendar, but such effects, which are not measured, are probably slight over the periods examined here, all of at least five years' duration.

By far the most important of the irregular factors is the effect of changes in the intensity of utilization of employed resources resulting from fluctuations in intensity of demand, shortened in the tables to *intensity of demand*. The contribution refers to the effect on the growth rate of changes in intensity of utilization of all employed inputs between the initial and terminal years of each period. This determinant disappears from the potential national income tables. In most periods to be analyzed demand-related fluctuations in intensity of utilization are the principal source of difference between the growth rates of actual and potential national income.

Two Important Characteristics

Two features of the classification need stressing. First, my intent is to draw the line between the contributions of capital and of advances in knowledge in such a way that the former measures growth that results from saving and investment (in this chapter, the portion invested in nonresidential business) and the latter measures comprehensively growth that results from advances in knowledge that permit goods and services to be produced with less input. The distinction is basic because completely different causes govern the behavior of the two determinants, and the actions that would be appropriate to influence them differ fundamentally. My measure of capital input is, properly, so measured that capital does not capture the contribution of inventions and other advances in knowledge that are manifested in the

14. The size of markets is, of course, affected by barriers to international trade. Such barriers are artificially imposed by countries or their trading partners and can be changed by their actions. Like other obstacles to the most efficient allocation and use of resources, barriers to international trade are regarded as a separate output determinant, and the contribution to growth made by changes in their restrictiveness as a separate growth source. In analysis of growth in Europe I have shown estimates for the effects of changes in international trade barriers. It is one of many miscellaneous determinants for which my best estimate of the contribution to growth in the United States is approximately zero and which are omitted from the tables.

For classification of "economies of scale related to the independent growth of local markets see p. 76, note 33.

15. In Chapter 6 it is called "changes in intensity of utilization of employed resources resulting from work stoppages."

16. It may be noted that workers idled by labor disputes, as well as those idle in both nonfarm and farm activities because of bad weather, are simply omitted from labor input and do not enter the analysis at all.

form of improved capital goods design, and this is the principal point to be noted. However, there is a sense in which the distinction between capital and advances in knowledge is somewhat compromised by another measurement procedure. I defer its discussion until the following chapter because it refers to dwellings as well as to nonresidential business capital.[17]

Second, my intent is to measure the contribution of each input independently of changes in the efficiency with which it is allocated among uses. Gains or losses in output that result from changes in the degree to which the allocation of each resource approaches the optimum are classified in output per unit of input (preferably in the resource allocation category, otherwise in the n.e.c. portion of "advances in knowledge and n.e.c.").

Sources of Growth over Long Periods

The forty years spanned by this study include the Great Depression and World War II. These periods were of great importance in the nation's economic history but highly abnormal. Some of the abnormalities which developed were reversed in the following decades. It is consequently impossible to be sure whether the whole period since 1929 or the postwar period alone provides a more representative picture of the relative importance of various growth sources in the long run. For examination of long-term growth we shall look at both—with some reference also to the 1929–48 period.

Total National Income

The growth rates of total actual national income in the sector were 3.22 from 1929 to 1969 and 3.72 from 1948 to 1969. The corresponding growth rates of total potential national income in the sector were 3.33 and 3.92. Table 8-2 allocates these rates by source. That growth rates of actual output were below those of potential output in both 1929–69 and 1948–69 is due almost entirely to the happenstance that the final year, 1969, was one of much lower intensity of utilization of employed resources than the initial years, 1929 and 1948. For examination of the sources of long-term growth it is best to eliminate the effects of this determinant, as well as the small effects upon other determinants of fluctuations of demand

about the potential level. These deviations reflect only special characteristics of the terminal years of the periods. For long-term analysis I therefore concentrate on the sources of growth of potential national income.

MAJOR DETERMINANTS OF LONG-PERIOD GROWTH. Changes in the employment, hours, and age-sex composition components of labor input are interrelated, and it is useful to look at their combined contribution to growth of potential output before considering them separately. This contribution was sizable. From 1929 to 1969 it was 0.57 percentage points, or 17 percent of the total growth rate. From 1948 to 1969 it was 0.50 percentage points.

The detailed estimates show that changes in potential employment of the size experienced would have contributed 0.86 percentage points to the growth rate in 1929–69 and 0.83 points in 1948–69 if there had been no change in working hours or in employment composition. The shortening of working hours offset 0.23 percentage points of this amount in 1929–69 and 0.21 in 1948–69.[18] The contribution of labor was further reduced, by 0.06 percentage points in 1929–69 and 0.12 in 1948–69, with the shift in composition of hours worked away from males in the prime working ages. All of this shift occurred after 1948.

Rising educational attainment was a major source of economic growth in the sector. It was responsible for nearly one-half of the entire contribution of labor to the 1929–69 growth rate and just one-half of the labor contribution in 1948–69. Increased education per worker contributed 0.49 percentage points, some 15 percent of the total, to the growth rate in 1929–69 and almost the same amount, 0.50 points, in 1948–69.

The size of the contribution made to long-term growth by the increase in capital, unlike that of labor, depends critically on which of the long periods one examines. Over the forty-year period structures and equipment contributed 0.24 percentage points and inventories 0.11 points to the

---

17. See pages 133–35.

18. I estimate that the adverse effect of hours reduction was only slightly greater in 1948–69 than in 1929–69 as a whole, even though the yearly decline in average hours was much bigger in 1929–48 than in 1948–69, because the reasons for the change in average hours were quite different. Intergroup shifts affected average potential hours similarly in the two periods, but in 1929–48 the remainder of the decline stemmed chiefly from the reduction of full-time hours from a high level which, I estimate, was offset to a considerable extent by greater efficiency per hour. After 1948 rising part-time employment, to which there is no offset in greater efficiency per hour worked, increased in relative importance.

Table 8-2. Nonresidential Business: Sources of Growth of Sector Actual National Income and Sector Potential National Income, Three Long Periods, 1929–69

Contributions to sector growth rate in percentage points

	Total actual national income			Total potential national income		
	1929–69	*1929–48*	*1948–69*	*1929–69*	*1929–48*	*1948–69*
Sector national income	**3.22**	**2.68**	**3.72**	**3.33**	**2.68**	**3.92**
Total factor input	**1.40**	**1.21**	**1.58**	**1.41**	**1.23**	**1.59**
Labor	1.05	1.11	1.00	1.06	1.13	1.00
Employment	0.85	0.86	0.84	0.86	0.89	0.83
Hours	−0.23	−0.24	−0.22	−0.23	−0.23	−0.21
Average hours	−0.49	−0.60	−0.38	−0.48	−0.60	−0.36
Efficiency offset	0.16	0.27	0.05	0.15	0.27	0.04
Intergroup shift offset	0.10	0.09	0.11	0.10	0.10	0.11
Age-sex composition	−0.06	0.01	−0.12	−0.06	0.00	−0.12
Education	0.49	0.48	0.50	0.49	0.47	0.50
Capital	0.35	0.10	0.58	0.35	0.10	0.59
Inventories	0.11	0.07	0.15	0.11	0.07	0.15
Nonresidential structures and equipment	0.24	0.03	0.43	0.24	0.03	0.44
Land	0.00	0.00	0.00	0.00	0.00	0.00
Output per unit of input	**1.82**	**1.47**	**2.14**	**1.92**	**1.45**	**2.33**
Advances in knowledge and n.e.c.[a]	1.11	0.73	1.44	1.12	0.73	1.45
Improved resource allocation	0.35	0.34	0.37	0.36	0.36	0.37
Farm	0.30	0.32	0.29	0.31	0.33	0.29
Nonfarm self-employment	0.05	0.02	0.08	0.05	0.03	0.08
Economies of scale	0.43	0.35	0.51	0.44	0.35	0.52
Irregular factors	−0.07	0.05	−0.18	0.00	0.01	−0.01
Weather in farming	0.00	0.01	−0.01	0.00	0.01	−0.01
Labor disputes	0.00	0.00	0.00	0.00	0.00	0.00
Intensity of demand	−0.07	0.04	−0.17	...	...	...

Sources: Table 8-1; contributions derived from Tables 3-3, 4-1, 5-4, 6-1, 6-4, 7-3, J-2, and R-1. Procedure described in text.
a. n.e.c. Not elsewhere classified.

growth rate of potential national income in the sector, giving a total capital contribution of 0.35 points, or 10.5 percent of the growth rate. This amount is held down by the 1929–48 period in which capital increased but little and its contribution was only 0.10 points. The capital contribution in the postwar period alone was much bigger: 0.59 points, or 15.1 percent of the growth rate in that period. Indeed, two-fifths of the entire difference between the 1929–69 and 1948–69 growth rates of the sector's potential national income is directly attributable to capital, and the figure becomes 45 percent if it is adjusted to count associated gains from economies of scale.

The depression and World War II were responsible for the small size of capital's contribution to 1929–48 growth. But what are we to assume as to the effect of this deficiency on the subsequent 1948–69 period? One common supposition is that investors have in mind a minimum expected rate of return which they are willing to accept, that this rate is constant, and that invest-

ment proceeds until—but only until—the rate of return is driven down to that level. Acceptance of this view would suggest that by 1969 the size of the stock of structures, equipment, and inventories would have been about the same whether or not the depression and World War II had occurred.[19] In that case, the contribution of capital to the growth rate over the whole 1929–69 period could be regarded as representative, and the contribution in the postwar period as abnormally large because investment was swollen by the need to make up the shortage present in 1948. Although the contribution of capital to postwar growth no doubt *was* boosted by the 1948 deficiency, this interpretation seems to me to overstate the effect of the earlier upon the later period. If it were correct, one would expect to find the rate of growth of the capital stock (and its contribution to output growth) biggest early in the

19. There were long periods of slack in the economy, so it is safe to assume that investors were able to invest as much over the postwar period as a whole as they desired.

period and then persistently declining (though with cyclical fluctuations superimposed) as the backlog of capital shortage was eliminated and rates of return fell. The capital stock data show no such pattern. Capital was, in fact, growing most rapidly in the last of the short periods studied (1964–69).[20]

The category "advances in knowledge and n.e.c." was the biggest single source of sector growth, directly responsible for 1.12 percentage points, or 34 percent, of the growth rate of potential output in 1929–69, and 1.45 percentage points, or 37 percent, in 1948–69. It accounts for even a larger part of the difference between 1929–48 and 1948–69 growth rates than does capital. Effects of any favorable or unfavorable changes in a variety of other output determinants are included, but I believe their net effect to be small enough to allow these estimates to approximate the contribution made by the incorporation into the productive process of advances in knowledge.

Advances in knowledge, as I have stressed, encompass knowledge of both the technological and the managerial and organizational types, so long as they permit reduction in unit costs. Their origin is diverse and the estimated contribution covers all advances regardless of origin. Besides contributing to the growth of measured output, advances in knowledge make it possible for consumers to choose among new and improved products and enhance welfare in this additional way.

Advances in knowledge are not only the largest source of long-term growth of total output, accounting for one-third or more of the total; they are also, in a very real sense, the most fundamental source of long-term growth of output per unit of input.

"Economies of scale" have, to be sure, also contributed importantly to growth in the sector: 0.44 percentage points in 1929–69 and 0.52 points in 1948–69. This is a little over 13 percent of the growth rate of potential national income in both periods.[21] Although their contribution to the

growth of output and output per unit of input is about one-third as large as that of advances in knowledge—and they too may be expected to contribute to growth indefinitely—there is a significant difference between the two. Economies of scale are a passive source of growth, derivative from the growth of sector output that is provided by other determinants.

Remaining sources of productivity change—both those I have isolated and those covered by the n.e.c. portion of "advances in knowledge and n.e.c."—refer mainly to changes in the extent to which output falls below what it would be if resources could be allocated and used with perfect efficiency. They can contribute to growth only during a transition period, although this period may be long.

Two such sources have in fact contributed importantly to growth throughout the long periods examined here. The reduction in the proportion of the sector's labor that was underutilized or inefficiently utilized in farming contributed 0.31 percentage points to the growth rate in 1929–69 and 0.29 points in 1948–69. A similar reduction in the much smaller proportion of the sector's labor that fell within the "fringe" category of nonfarm self-employed and unpaid family workers contributed 0.05 points to the growth rate in 1929–69 and 0.08 points in 1948–69.[22] Addition of the two components yields 0.36 percentage points, or almost 11 percent, of the growth rate as the contribution made by improved resource allocation in 1929–69, and 0.37 points as the 1948–69 contribution.

"Irregular factors" did not affect the 1929–69 growth rate of potential national income at all. They subtracted 0.01 points from the 1948–69 rate because 1948 happened to be an especially favorable year for agriculture.[23]

Although the value of sources of growth tables lies chiefly in the estimates of the contributions of individual output determinants it is sometimes useful, as is customary, to summarize them in two categories: changes in inputs and changes in

---

20. This statement is not, to be sure, applicable to capital per person employed; the growth rate of this measure does show some deceleration, but the deceleration is moderate.

21. Aside from a small smoothing adjustment, economies of scale are estimated to have raised by 15 percent the contribution made to actual output of the sector by all determinants except irregular factors. Consequently, their contribution is almost sure to be estimated at about 13 percent of the growth rate of potential national income in all periods as long as those analyzed here.

22. A short-lived bulge in the number of unincorporated enterprises immediately after World War II made the latter figure larger than it would have been otherwise (and the 1929–48 contribution of this determinant smaller).

23. For analysis of long-term growth, growth rates of potential national income could well be adjusted to eliminate the effects of irregular factors. In the present study they are too trivial to warrant introduction of still another output measure.

output per unit of input. By my grouping of determinants, changes in total factor input contributed 1.41 percentage points, or 42 percent, of the sector's potential output growth rate of 3.33 percent per year in 1929–69, while changes in output per unit of input contributed 1.92 points. In 1948–69 changes in total factor input contributed 1.59 points, or 41 percent, of the potential output growth rate of 3.92 percent and output per unit of input 2.33 points.

These figures result from the particular way in which determinants are grouped. Although I prefer this grouping for most uses of the data, there may be uses for which a different grouping would be appropriate. The detail provided permits any reader to approximate the estimates that would be obtained with other groupings by merely moving components from one category to the other. To illustrate, he might wish to classify under output per unit of input the effect of the increase in work done per hour that results from shortening the hours of full-time workers within homogeneous groups, or the increase in output per worker that results from the shift of full-time workers from

activities in which customary full-time hours are long to those in which they are short. He need only place the "efficiency offset" or "intergroup shift offset" components of "hours" under output per unit of input. With both reclassifications, total factor input contributed 1.44 percentage points to the 1948–69 growth rate and output per unit of input 2.48 points.

ECONOMIES OF SCALE ISOLATED AND ALLOCATED. The first two columns of Table 8-3 recapitulate the percentage distributions among sources of the 1929–69 and 1948–69 growth rates of total sector potential national income. A condensation of the classification followed in the preceding table is used. As pointed out earlier, the contribution of each source except economies of scale measures the gains or losses in output that would have resulted from changes in that determinant if the economy had operated under constant returns to scale (or with markets of constant size).

The third and fourth columns of Table 8-3 show distributions based on an alternative classification. Economies of scale are eliminated as a separate growth source and allocated among the

Table 8-3. Nonresidential Business Sector Potential National Income, Total and per Person: Percentage Distributions of Growth Rates among Sources with Economies of Scale Isolated and Allocated among Other Sources, 1929–69 and 1948–69

	Total potential national income, with economies of scale:				Potential national income per person potentially employed, with economies of scale:			
	Isolated		Allocated		Isolated		Allocated	
	1929–69 (1)	1948–69 (2)	1929–69 (3)	1948–69 (4)	1929–69 (5)	1948–69 (6)	1929–69 (7)	1948–69 (8)
Sector national income	100.0	100.0	100.0	100.0	100.0	100.0	100.0	100.0
Total factor input	42.3	40.6	48.9	46.7	14.4	18.9	23.9	27.3
Labor								
Except education	17.1	12.8	19.8	14.8	−13.1	−11.5	−9.0	−8.7
Employment	25.8	21.2	29.7	24.5	...	...	5.9	4.5
Hours	−6.9	−5.4	−7.8	−6.1	−10.4	−7.3	−11.7	−8.4
Age-sex composition	−1.8	−3.1	−2.1	−3.6	−2.7	−4.1	−3.2	−4.9
Education	14.7	12.8	17.1	14.8	22.1	17.5	25.2	20.3
Capital	10.5	15.1	12.1	17.1	7.7	14.3	9.9	17.1
Land	0.0	0.0	0.0	0.0	−2.3	−1.4	−2.3	−1.4
Output per unit of input	57.7	59.4	51.1	53.3	85.6	81.1	76.1	72.7
Advances in knowledge and n.e.c.[a]	33.6	37.0	38.7	42.6	50.0	50.3	57.7	58.0
Improved resource allocation	10.8	9.4	12.3	11.0	16.2	12.9	18.5	15.0
Economies of scale	13.2	13.3	...	...	19.4	18.2	...	...
Irregular factors	0.0	−0.3	0.0	−0.2	0.0	−0.3	0.0	−0.3

Sources: Columns 1–4, derived from Table 8-2; columns 5–8, derived from Tables 8-2 and 8-4.
a. n.e.c. Not elsewhere classified.

other determinants.[24] The contribution of every other source then includes estimated gains (or losses) from economies of scale that result from the expansion of markets as a consequence of the change in that determinant. This raises the contribution of each by about 15 percent. It also transfers that part of the contribution of economies of scale which is related to the growth in inputs from output per unit of input to total factor input, an effect which makes use of the latter terms somewhat misleading.

National Income per Person Employed

Long-period growth rates of actual national income produced in nonresidential business per person employed in the sector are divided among

24. The contribution of economies of scale is distributed among other sources except irregular factors in proportion to their contributions to the growth rates of actual total national income in the sector as shown in Table 8-2. (Use of potential national income would yield almost identical results but is slightly less consistent with the procedures used to measure gains from economies of scale.)

sources of growth in the first three columns of Table 8-4. A similar division of long-period growth rates of potential sector national income per person potentially employed in the sector is provided in the last three columns. Discussion again focuses on the potential estimates. Measured in percentage points, the contribution of each component of output per unit of input to growth is necessarily the same for output per person employed as for total output, except for occasional small differences due to rounding and statistical interaction. The contributions of labor, capital, and land inputs are smaller because they measure the effect of changing the amount of input per person employed, and employment has risen. Increases in inputs required merely to preserve the amount of input per person employed make no contribution to growth of output per worker.

MAJOR DETERMINANTS OF LONG-PERIOD GROWTH. Potential labor input per person contributed 0.20 percentage points to potential output per person

Table 8-4. Nonresidential Business: Sources of Growth of Sector Actual National Income per Person Employed and Potential National Income per Person Potentially Employed, Three Long Periods, 1929–69
Contributions to sector growth rate in percentage points

	Actual national income per person employed			Potential national income per person potentially employed		
	1929–69	1929–48	1948–69	1929–69	1929–48	1948–69
Sector national income	**2.14**	**1.57**	**2.65**	**2.22**	**1.52**	**2.86**
Total factor input	**0.33**	**0.11**	**0.52**	**0.32**	**0.09**	**0.54**
Labor	0.20	0.25	0.16	0.20	0.24	0.17
Hours	−0.23	−0.24	−0.22	−0.23	−0.23	−0.21
Average hours	−0.49	−0.60	−0.38	−0.48	−0.60	−0.36
Efficiency offset	0.16	0.27	0.05	0.15	0.27	0.04
Intergroup shift offset	0.10	0.09	0.11	0.10	0.10	0.11
Age-sex composition	−0.06	0.01	−0.12	−0.06	0.00	−0.12
Education	0.49	0.48	0.50	0.49	0.47	0.50
Capital	0.17	−0.08	0.40	0.17	−0.09	0.41
Inventories	0.06	0.01	0.10	0.06	0.01	0.10
Nonresidential structures and equipment	0.11	−0.09	0.30	0.11	−0.10	0.31
Land	−0.04	−0.06	−0.04	−0.05	−0.06	−0.04
Output per unit of input	**1.81**	**1.46**	**2.13**	**1.90**	**1.43**	**2.32**
Advances in knowledge and n.e.c.[a]	1.10	0.73	1.44	1.11	0.72	1.44
Improved resource allocation	0.35	0.34	0.36	0.36	0.36	0.37
Farm	0.30	0.32	0.28	0.31	0.33	0.29
Nonfarm self-employment	0.05	0.02	0.08	0.05	0.03	0.08
Economies of scale	0.43	0.34	0.51	0.43	0.34	0.52
Irregular factors	−0.07	0.05	−0.18	0.00	0.01	−0.01
Weather in farming	0.00	0.01	−0.01	0.00	0.01	−0.01
Labor disputes	0.00	0.00	0.00	0.00	0.00	0.00
Intensity of demand	−0.07	0.04	−0.17	...	...	...

Sources: Table 8-1; contributions derived from Tables 4-1, 5-4, 6-1, 6-4, 7-3, D-2, J-2, and R-1.
a. n.e.c. Not elsewhere classified.

potentially employed in 1929–69 and 0.17 points in 1948–69. The contribution was positive only because the rise in education was more important than the decline in working hours and the change in age-sex composition, both of which reduced labor input per person employed.[25]

Capital input per person employed contributed 0.17 percentage points to the growth rate of potential national income per person employed in 1929–69, and 0.41 points in 1948–69. The difference between the 1929–48 and 1948–69 periods noted in the discussion of total income is even more striking on a per-person-employed basis. The figure for 1929–48 is actually negative (−0.09 percentage points, and almost the same when actual rather than potential employment is used) because the stock of structures and equipment increased less than did employment.

Because the quantity of land did not change, the amount of land available per person employed declined as employment increased, reducing the growth rate of potential national income per person employed by 0.05 percentage points in 1929–69 and 0.04 in 1948–69.

The proportion of the growth rate of output per worker provided by each determinant is very different from its proportional contribution to the growth rate of total output even if its contribution is the same when expressed in percentage points. Columns 5 and 6 of Table 8-3 provide percentage distributions of the 1929–69 and 1948–69 growth rates of potential national income per person potentially employed in the sector. What stands out is that half of the sector growth rate in both periods resulted from advances in knowledge.[26] The next largest contributor was increased education of the labor force. In 1929–69 this was followed, in order of size, by economies of scale, the reallocation of labor away from farming and from nonfarm self-employment, and capital. In 1948–69 capital contributed more than improved resource allocation.

The last two columns of Table 8-3 provide the

percentage distributions of these growth rates that are obtained by use of the alternative classification. In this classification, the size of markets is no longer regarded as an independent determinant of output but rather as a consequence of the other determinants. Economies of scale are therefore eliminated as a separate growth source, and their contribution is distributed among the other sources.[27]

By this classification the increase in employment itself contributes to the increase in output per person employed. Indeed, it must do so in an economy operating under increasing returns to scale; the size of employment helps to establish the size of an economy and therefore of the markets served by its business enterprises. This positive contribution is larger than the negative contribution made by land, which also results directly from the change in employment when the quantity of land available is fixed.[28] Thus population growth has been slightly favorable to long-term growth of output per worker unless (as is unlikely) the long-term change in some other determinant, such as capital per worker, was adversely affected by a rather considerable amount. This conclusion has, of course, been common ever since economists recognized that a fixed supply of land has been only a small retardant to economic growth in a modern industrial economy.

DETERMINANTS OF GROWTH WITH ECONOMIES OF SCALE ALLOCATED. When economies of scale are isolated, as in the standard classification used in columns 5 and 6 of Table 8-3, the contribution of each source (except economies of scale) measures the contribution that changes in that determinant made to the growth rate when the size of markets is included among the other conditions which are held constant or, alternatively expressed, would have made if the economy operated under constant returns to scale. By the classification used in columns 7 and 8 of Table 8-3, the contribution from each source includes an estimate for the associated gains from changes in the size of markets which the change in that source made possible. The following summary

---

25. Components of labor input other than employment were already measured on a per-person-employed basis in the analysis of total national income so the detail need not be examined again. I reiterate, however, that much of the hours contribution of −0.21 percentage points in 1948–69 represents the increasing proportion of part-time workers. If the calculations were on a full-time equivalent basis, the growth rate of output per person employed would itself be higher and the negative contribution of hours would be smaller.

26. This assumes acceptance of my judgment that the size of the n.e.c. component is small, and more likely slightly negative than positive over the 1929–69 period.

27. The distribution among sources is proportionally the same as for actual national income in the sector.

28. It will be larger so long as the product of the labor share of national income in the sector and the economies-of-scale coefficient for the sector, estimated here at about 0.12 (0.8 × 0.15), exceeds the land share of national income in the sector, estimated here as about 0.04. Exact values depend on the date to which they refer, since income share weights vary.

description of changes from 1929 to 1969 makes use of the percentage distributions in Table 8-3, column 7.[29]

The nonresidential business sector accounts for more than four-fifths of the nation's production. The total value of the net output of nonresidential business in 1969 was 8.26 times its 1929 value when measured in current prices with products combined by use of factor cost weights. Employment in the sector, having increased by 53 percent, was 1.53 times as big in 1969 as in 1929. Therefore the current-dollar value of national income per person employed in the sector was 5.41 times as large in 1969 as in 1929. Prices of final products (measured at factor cost so that indirect business taxes are excluded) had risen in 1969 to 2.32 times their 1929 level. Consequently, the sector's output per worker was 2.33 times as big in amount in 1969 as in 1929, equivalent to a growth rate of 2.14 percent a year. Demand pressure was stronger in 1929 than in 1969, with the consequence that a slightly larger proportion of the nation's potential labor was in use in 1929 and that the labor and capital resources in use were used more intensively. This difference refers only to the particular years compared and has no significance for long-term growth analysis. If demand conditions in 1929 and 1969 had been similar, constant-price national income per person employed would have been 2.41 times as big in 1969 as in 1929 and its growth rate would have been 2.22. The latter figure is the percentage by which potential national income per person potentially employed would have increased in each of the forty years if growth had occurred at a constant rate. (The *absolute* annual increase in output per worker would then have been 2.41 times as large at the end as at the beginning of the period.)

Suppose all the determinants of output had also changed at a steady rate; then in any year the 2.22 percent increase in potential output per worker would have been:

• Reduced by almost 58 percent (to 0.96 percent per annum) if no new knowledge had been incorporated into the process of production.

• Reduced by over 25 percent if the educational background of workers had not risen.

• Reduced by 18.5 percent if the proportion of labor misallocated to farming and to nonfarm

self-employment had not declined (15.9 percent and 2.6 percent, respectively, if only one had not declined).

• Reduced by almost 10 percent if the quantities of structures and equipment and inventories per worker had not increased (6.4 percent and 3.5 percent, respectively, if only one had not increased).

• Raised by nearly 12 percent if hours of work had not fallen, which would (among other things) imply that the massive entry of part-time workers into the labor force had not occurred.

• Reduced by 0.3 percent if there had been no change in employment, in age-sex composition, or (as was actually the case) in the *total* quantity of land available. These determinants are highly interrelated on a per-worker basis, but we can say that the annual percentage change would have been reduced by 5.9 percent, had it been possible to keep employment unchanged without affecting age-sex composition or the amount of land per worker; raised by 3.2 percent, had it been possible for age-sex composition to remain unchanged without affecting employment; and raised by 2.3 percent, had it been possible to increase the total quantity of land so as to leave land per worker unchanged.

Column 8 of Table 8-3 provides estimates for similar statements about the 1948–69 period, in which the growth rate of potential national income per person employed was considerably higher, 2.86 percent per annum. Capital provided a bigger percentage of growth in this period than in 1929–69: 17 percent as against 10 percent. Education and resource allocation provided smaller percentages. Neither made a smaller contribution to the growth rate in the postwar period; their percentage contributions were smaller only because the growth rate itself was bigger.

The enormous extent to which long-term gains in output per worker in nonresidential business have rested upon advances in knowledge, and the great though much smaller extent to which they have depended upon changes in education of the labor force, reduction of the wasteful use of labor in farming and self-employment, and the increase in capital per worker, could scarcely be made more clear.

Sources of Growth in Shorter Periods

What determinants were responsible for the large differences among growth rates in the shorter periods distinguished? In particular, why were

---

29. The next paragraph, which is included to remind the reader of the meaning and derivation of the growth rate itself, draws upon data from earlier chapters. The reader is referred to Tables 3-1, 3-2, and 7-3 in particular.

most growth rates in nonresidential business so much higher in the 1948–53 and 1964–69 periods than they were in the much longer intervening period from 1953 to 1964? Why did growth rates of actual national income per person employed in the sector show exactly the opposite pattern?

Total National Income: Postwar Years

Sources of growth of total actual national income can be examined in two ways. One can look directly at the determinants of actual national income which are shown for the shorter periods in Table 8-5. Or one can look at the determinants of potential national income, shown in Table 8-6, and then at the sources of difference between growth rates of actual and potential output.

Either way, it is useful to have the differences between the actual and potential rates and the reasons for them clearly in mind. Table 8-7 compares the rates and shows the differences between the contributions of the sources to the two sets of rates.

Both the 1948–53 and 1964–69 growth rates exceeded the 1953–64 rate by larger amounts when the comparison is of potential rather than

when it is of actual output. This may come as a surprise, inasmuch as it is usual to think of potential output as the more stable series.[30]

By definition, actual and potential national income differ in any year only because actual demand conditions differ from potential conditions in that year. The effect of differences between terminal years with respect to demand pressure on the growth rates of actual output in the short periods is divided in Table 8-7 between two broad components. One is the change in the proportion of the labor potentially available to the sector that is actually in use, together with related effects on overallocation to farming and self-employment. The other is the effect on output per unit of input of differences in the intensity of utilization of employed labor, capital, and land. (Small differences in "other components" are due only to rounding, interaction, and "forcing.")

The two broad components had opposite effects on the growth rate in all five short periods. This reflects the particular dates used to delimit

30. *Annual* fluctuations in potential national income *are*, of course, smaller than those in actual national income.

Table 8-5. Nonresidential Business: Sources of Growth of Sector Actual National Income, Five Shorter Periods, 1929–69

Contributions to sector growth rate in percentage points

	1929–41	1941–48	1948–53	1953–64	1964–69
Sector national income	**2.16**	**3.58**	**3.98**	**3.24**	**4.52**
Total factor input	**0.88**	**1.79**	**2.03**	**0.86**	**2.73**
Labor	0.88	1.50	1.35	0.40	1.95
Employment	0.52	1.46	0.88	0.25	2.13
Hours	−0.21	−0.29	−0.08	−0.25	−0.29
Average hours	−0.64	−0.54	−0.36	−0.32	−0.54
Efficiency offset	0.38	0.09	0.14	−0.02	0.12
Intergroup shift offset	0.05	0.16	0.14	0.09	0.13
Age-sex composition	0.04	−0.05	0.09	−0.11	−0.38
Education	0.53	0.38	0.46	0.51	0.49
Capital	0.00	0.29	0.68	0.46	0.78
Inventories	0.03	0.14	0.21	0.10	0.22
Nonresidential structures and equipment	−0.03	0.15	0.47	0.36	0.56
Land	0.00	0.00	0.00	0.00	0.00
Output per unit of input	**1.28**	**1.79**	**1.95**	**2.38**	**1.79**
Advances in knowledge and n.e.c.[a]	0.56	1.04	1.62	1.39	1.43
Improved resource allocation	0.25	0.49	0.49	0.28	0.42
Farm	0.22	0.49	0.40	0.25	0.23
Nonfarm self-employment	0.03	0.00	0.09	0.03	0.19
Economies of scale	0.23	0.54	0.58	0.40	0.68
Irregular factors	0.24	−0.28	−0.74	0.31	−0.74
Weather in farming	−0.01	0.05	−0.04	−0.02	0.02
Labor disputes	0.00	0.00	0.00	0.00	−0.01
Intensity of demand	0.25	−0.33	−0.70	0.33	−0.75

Sources: Table 8-1; contributions derived from Tables 4-1, 5-4, 6-1, 6-4, and J-2.
a. n.e.c. Not elsewhere classified.

Table 8-6. Nonresidential Business: Sources of Growth of Sector Potential National Income, Five Shorter Periods, 1929–69
Contributions to sector growth rate in percentage points

	1929–41	1941–48	1948–53	1953–64	1964–69
Sector national income	**2.50**	**3.00**	**4.51**	**3.20**	**4.90**
Total factor input	**1.33**	**1.10**	**1.86**	**1.12**	**2.38**
Labor	1.33	0.81	1.17	0.68	1.60
Employment	1.14	0.49	0.59	0.61	1.59
Hours	−0.25	−0.21	−0.06	−0.25	−0.25
Average hours	−0.73	−0.38	−0.29	−0.35	−0.44
Efficiency offset	0.39	0.07	0.12	−0.01	0.09
Intergroup shift offset	0.09	0.10	0.11	0.11	0.10
Age-sex composition	−0.04	0.08	0.16	−0.17	−0.27
Education	0.48	0.45	0.48	0.49	0.53
Capital	0.00	0.29	0.69	0.44	0.78
Inventories	0.03	0.14	0.22	0.09	0.22
Nonresidential structures and equipment	−0.03	0.15	0.47	0.35	0.56
Land	0.00	0.00	0.00	0.00	0.00
Output per unit of input	**1.17**	**1.90**	**2.65**	**2.08**	**2.52**
Advances in knowledge and n.e.c.[a]	0.54	1.04	1.65	1.37	1.45
Improved resource allocation	0.41	0.27	0.44	0.34	0.37
Farm	0.31	0.36	0.39	0.27	0.22
Nonfarm self-employment	0.10	−0.09	0.05	0.07	0.15
Economies of scale	0.23	0.54	0.60	0.39	0.69
Irregular factors	−0.01	0.05	−0.04	−0.02	0.01
Weather in farming	−0.01	0.05	−0.04	−0.02	0.02
Labor disputes	0.00	0.00	0.00	0.00	−0.01

Sources: Table 8-1; contributions derived from Tables 4-1, 5-4, 6-4, 7-3, J-2, and R-1.
a. n.e.c. Not elsewhere classified.

the periods. It would not necessarily, nor even usually, be the case in other time spans. In the postwar periods it occurred mainly because 1953 and 1969 were years in which productivity was adversely affected by low intensity of utilization of employed resources despite low unemployment, in the prewar periods because 1941 was a year in which productivity was favorably affected by high intensity of utilization of employed resources despite high unemployment.

Changes in intensity of utilization of employed resources were adverse to productivity growth from 1948 to 1953 and from 1964 to 1969 but favorable from 1953 to 1964. On the other hand, actual labor input rose more than potential labor input in 1948–53 and 1964–69, but less in 1953–64. The two effects were about equal in 1953–64 so the growth rates of actual and potential output were close to one another. The effect of changes in intensity of utilization was much the larger of the two in 1948–53 and 1964–69, so the growth rates of actual output fell below those of potential output.

Relationships among the components of labor input and resource allocation are highly systematic. When actual employment rises more than potential employment, the effect is reinforced by a more pronounced decline in the percentage of actual than of potential employment that is allocated to farm employment and nonfarm self-employment. However, in the same circumstance changes in the indexes of average hours, age-sex composition, and education are less favorable for actual than for potential employment because changes in unemployment and the difference between actual and potential labor force, combined, are concentrated among young people, women, and the less educated. The difference in the movement of average hours is usually (always in these time periods) at least partly offset by the "efficiency offset" and intergroup shifts.

I turn now to the differences among the postwar periods. To facilitate this examination, Table 8-8 shows for both actual and potential national income the sources of the differences between the high 1948–53 and 1964–69 growth rates and the lower 1953–64 growth rates.

Consider first column 4, which refers to the

Table 8-7. Nonresidential Business: Sector National Income, Actual Less Potential Growth Rates of Total National Income, by Sources, Five Shorter Periods, 1929–69

Contributions to sector growth rate in percentage points

	1929–41	1941–48	1948–53	1953–64	1964–69
Growth rates					
Actual national income	2.16	3.58	3.98	3.24	4.52
Potential national income	2.50	3.00	4.51	3.20	4.90
Actual less potential	−0.34	0.58	−0.53	0.04	−0.38
Differences in contributions (actual less potential)					
Labor input and resource allocation	−0.61	0.91	0.23	−0.34	0.40
Labor	−0.45	0.69	0.18	−0.28	0.35
Employment	−0.62	0.97	0.29	−0.36	0.54
Hours	0.04	−0.08	−0.02	0.00	−0.04
Average hours	0.09	−0.16	−0.07	0.03	−0.10
Efficiency offset	−0.01	0.02	0.02	−0.01	0.03
Intergroup shift offset	−0.04	0.06	0.03	−0.02	0.03
Age-sex composition	0.08	−0.13	−0.07	0.06	−0.11
Education	0.05	−0.07	−0.02	0.02	−0.04
Improved resource allocation	−0.16	0.22	0.05	−0.06	0.05
Farm	−0.09	0.13	0.01	−0.02	0.01
Nonfarm	−0.07	0.09	0.04	−0.04	0.04
Intensity of use of employed resources due to demand pressures	0.25	−0.33	−0.70	0.33	−0.75
Other components[a]	0.02	0.00	−0.06	0.05	−0.03

Sources: Derived from Tables 8-5 and 8-6.

a. Entries in this line result from rounding, interaction terms, and the "forcing" of the components of potential national income so that they add to the total growth rates.

excess of the growth rate of potential national income in 1964–69 over the 1953–64 growth rate. The much higher growth rate in the late 1960s than in 1953–64 was due overwhelmingly to the faster growth of potential labor and capital input. They account directly for 1.26 percentage points of the difference of 1.70 points between growth rates in the two periods, and indirectly for nearly all of the 0.30 points attributed to economies of scale. Of the 1.26 points, 0.92 are ascribable to faster growth of labor input and 0.34 to capital. Enhancement of the contribution of labor would have been even larger, by 0.10 percentage points, if the contribution of employment had not been partially offset by an accelerated shift in the age-sex composition of hours worked. "Advances in knowledge and n.e.c.," reallocation of resources, and irregular factors were all more favorable in 1964–69 but together accounted for only 0.14 percentage points, or one-twelfth, of the difference between growth rates of potential output in the two periods.

That the 1948–53 growth rate of potential output was higher than that of 1953–64 also was due mainly to the contribution of inputs, as shown in column 3 of Table 8-8. Inputs were directly responsible for 0.74 of the difference of 1.31 points

in growth rates and indirectly responsible for two-thirds of the 0.21 percentage point difference in gains from economies of scale. Of the 0.74 percentage points, labor accounted for 0.49 points and capital 0.25. Labor contributed more to growth in the early than in the middle postwar period not because potential employment in the sector grew more rapidly but because of two other determinants. Hours changes, which were minimal, deducted 0.19 points less from the growth rate in 1948–53 than in 1953–64. Changes in the age-sex composition of hours worked were favorable in 1948–53 and unfavorable in 1953–64, and the difference accounted for 0.33 points of the difference in growth rates. Gains from "advances in knowledge and n.e.c." contributed 0.28 points more in the early than in the middle period.[31] Resource allocation contributed 0.10 points more

31. The difference is exaggerated a little by the forcing of components of potential national income, which was in opposite directions in the two periods. The growth rate of the index for this determinant (Table 6-1, column 9) fell only 0.25 points. The drop may reflect some "catching-up" in the application of knowledge when investment in civilian industries was resumed immediately after the war. However, it should be noted that there would be no fall to explain if 1952 rather than 1953 were used to divide the period, 1948–52 and 1952–64 growth rates of the index are 1.43 and 1.44, respectively.

Table 8-8. Nonresidential Business: Sources of Differences between Postwar Shorter-Period Growth Rates of Sector Actual and Potential National Income

Differences in contributions in percentage points

	Actual national income		Potential national income	
	1948–53 less 1953–64 (1)	1964–69 less 1953–64 (2)	1948–53 less 1953–64 (3)	1964–69 less 1953–64 (4)
Sector national income	0.74	1.28	1.31	1.70
Total factor input	1.17	1.87	0.74	1.26
Labor	0.95	1.55	0.49	0.92
Employment	0.63	1.88	−0.02	0.98
Hours	0.17	−0.04	0.19	0.00
Age-sex composition	0.20	−0.27	0.33	−0.10
Education	−0.05	−0.02	−0.01	0.04
Capital[a]	0.22	0.32	0.25	0.34
Land	0.00	0.00	0.00	0.00
Output per unit of input	−0.43	−0.59	0.57	0.44
Advances in knowledge and n.e.c.[a,b]	0.23	0.04	0.28	0.08
Improved resource allocation	0.21	0.14	0.10	0.03
Economies of scale[a]	0.18	0.28	0.21	0.30
Irregular factors				
Weather, labor disputes	−0.02	0.03	−0.02	0.03
Intensity of demand	−1.03	−1.08	...	...

Sources: Derived from Tables 8-5 and 8-6.
a. Differences between contributions to actual and potential growth rates are not significant for these components.
b. n.e.c. Not elsewhere classified.

Table 8-9. Nonresidential Business: Sources of Growth of Sector Actual National Income per Person Employed, Five Shorter Periods, 1929–69

Contributions to sector growth rate in percentage points

	1929–41	1941–48	1948–53	1953–64	1964–69
Sector national income per person employed	1.50	1.69	2.85	2.93	1.85
Total factor input	0.23	−0.07	0.90	0.55	0.08
Labor	0.36	0.04	0.47	0.15	−0.18
Hours	−0.21	−0.29	−0.08	−0.25	−0.29
Average hours	−0.64	−0.54	−0.36	−0.32	−0.54
Efficiency offset	0.38	0.09	0.14	−0.02	0.12
Intergroup shift offset	0.05	0.16	0.14	0.09	0.13
Age-sex composition	0.04	−0.05	0.09	−0.11	−0.38
Education	0.53	0.38	0.46	0.51	0.49
Capital	−0.10	−0.03	0.48	0.41	0.36
Inventories	0.00	0.04	0.15	0.09	0.11
Nonresidential structures and equipment	−0.10	−0.07	0.33	0.32	0.25
Land	−0.03	−0.08	−0.05	−0.01	−0.10
Output per unit of input	1.27	1.76	1.95	2.38	1.77
Advances in knowledge and n.e.c.[a]	0.55	1.02	1.62	1.39	1.41
Improved resource allocation	0.25	0.49	0.49	0.28	0.42
Farm	0.22	0.49	0.40	0.25	0.23
Nonfarm self-employment	0.03	0.00	0.09	0.03	0.19
Economies of scale	0.23	0.53	0.58	0.40	0.68
Irregular factors	0.24	−0.28	−0.74	0.31	−0.74
Weather in farming	−0.01	0.05	−0.04	−0.02	0.02
Labor disputes	0.00	0.00	0.00	0.00	−0.01
Intensity of demand	0.25	−0.33	−0.70	0.33	−0.75

Sources: Table 8-1; contributions derived from Tables 4-1, 5-4, 6-1, 6-4, 8-5, and J-2.
a. n.e.c. Not elsewhere classified.

because the shift of labor from agriculture was more pronounced than in 1953–64.

Growth rates of total *actual* national income in the sector in 1948–53 and 1964–69 were 0.74 and 1.28 percentage points, respectively, above the rate in 1953–64, as shown in columns 1 and 2 of Table 8-8. The early and late postwar rates would have exceeded the rate in the middle period far more—by 1.77 points and 2.36 points, respectively—if the intensity of utilization of employed resources had not changed. The great bulk of these differences which would have appeared in that circumstance can be ascribed to greater additions to inputs (chiefly to labor input but also to capital) in the fast growth periods. The resource allocation components were of some importance in both periods and "advances in knowledge and n.e.c." in the first period.

Output per Worker: Postwar Years

Tables 8-9 and 8-10 show sources of growth of the sector's actual and potential national income per person employed in the shorter periods. Table 8-11, derived from them, indicates differences between postwar periods on a per-person-employed

basis; it is similar in form to Table 8-8. The focus on output per worker provides a quite different perspective from the similar analysis of total sector output.

It is convenient again to consider the estimates for potential output first. The growth rate of potential output per person employed was much higher in 1948–53 than in 1964–69 and therefore exceeded the mid-period rate by a much larger amount: 1.35 percentage points as against 0.47. The reasons that the early and late postwar rates exceeded the 1953–64 rates were also quite different.

As indicated in column 4 of Table 8-11, capital and economies of scale were mainly responsible for the difference of 0.47 points between the 1953–64 and 1964–69 growth rates of potential output per worker. Capital accounts for 0.16 points and economies of scale for 0.30. But the fast growth of employment in 1964–69 was ultimately responsible for most of the rapid expansion of total output that provided the greater gains from scale economies, as well as for the offsetting change of 0.05 points in the contribution of land. Differences between the two periods in the contributions

Table 8-10. Nonresidential Business: Sources of Growth of Sector Potential National Income per Person Potentially Employed, Five Shorter Periods, 1929–69
Contributions to sector growth rate in percentage points

	1929–41	*1941–48*	*1948–53*	*1953–64*	*1964–69*
Sector national income per person employed	1.01	2.40	3.78	2.43	2.90
Total factor input	−0.15	0.49	1.13	0.35	0.41
Labor	0.18	0.33	0.59	0.06	0.01
Hours	−0.26	−0.20	−0.05	−0.26	−0.25
Average hours	−0.74	−0.37	−0.28	−0.35	−0.44
Efficiency offset	0.39	0.07	0.12	−0.02	0.09
Intergroup shift offset	0.09	0.10	0.11	0.11	0.10
Age-sex composition	−0.04	0.08	0.16	−0.17	−0.27
Education	0.48	0.45	0.48	0.49	0.53
Capital	−0.25	0.19	0.57	0.32	0.48
Inventories	−0.05	0.11	0.18	0.06	0.14
Nonresidential structures and equipment	−0.20	0.08	0.39	0.26	0.34
Land	−0.08	−0.03	−0.03	−0.03	−0.08
Output per unit of input	1.16	1.91	2.65	2.08	2.49
Advances in knowledge and n.e.c.[a]	0.54	1.04	1.64	1.37	1.44
Improved resource allocation	0.40	0.28	0.44	0.34	0.35
Farm	0.31	0.36	0.39	0.27	0.21
Nonfarm self-employment	0.09	−0.08	0.05	0.07	0.14
Economies of scale	0.23	0.54	0.60	0.39	0.69
Irregular factors	−0.01	0.05	−0.03	−0.02	0.01
Weather in farming	−0.01	0.05	−0.03	−0.02	0.02
Labor disputes	0.00	0.00	0.00	0.00	−0.01

Sources: Table 8-1; contributions derived from Tables 4-1, 5-4, 6-4, 7-3, 8-6, J-2, and R-1.
a. n.e.c. Not elsewhere classified.

of other determinants were relatively small and offsetting. Among them the most important was the enlargement in 1964–69 of the size of the negative contribution of the age-sex composition component of labor input.

A variety of output determinants were responsible for the high growth rate of potential national income per person employed in 1948–53. As in 1964–69, both components of capital and scale economies help to explain why the rate in 1948–53 was above that in 1953–64, but so do most other determinants. Labor input per worker contributed 0.53 percentage points more in 1948–53 than in 1953–64; changes in both the hours and age-sex composition components were much more favorable. "Advances in knowledge and n.e.c." and the shift of labor from agriculture also made larger contributions in the earlier period.

When actual national income per person employed is examined, the question raised about the other growth rates is reversed. One must ask, why were growth rates *lower* in 1948–53 and 1964–69 than in 1953–64? The 1948–53 rate was only 0.08 percentage points below the mid-period rate but

the 1964–69 rate was below it by 1.08 points, or nearly two-fifths.

The main answer given by my estimates is clearly indicated in the first two columns of Table 8-11. Fluctuations in the intensity of utilization of employed resources that result from fluctuations in demand pressure greatly curtailed the growth of output per worker from 1948 to 1953 and again from 1964 to 1969, whereas such fluctuations contributed to the increase in output per worker from 1953 to 1964. In the absence of these changes in intensity of utilization of employed resources, the growth rate of national income per worker would have been the same in the 1953–64 and 1964–69 periods (at 2.60) and higher by 0.95 percentage points (at 3.55) in 1948–53.

This answer rests upon my finding that intensity of utilization of employed resources was much higher because of demand conditions and therefore much more favorable to high productivity in 1948 and 1964 than it was in 1953 or 1969, even though unemployment rates were not lower in 1948 and 1964.

That other determinants also contributed, in

Table 8-11. Nonresidential Business: Sources of Differences between Postwar Shorter-Period Growth Rates of Sector Actual and Potential National Income per Person Employed
Differences in contributions in percentage points

	Actual national income per person employed		Potential national income per person potentially employed	
	1948–53 less 1953–64 (1)	1964–69 less 1953–64 (2)	1948–53 less 1953–64 (3)	1964–69 less 1953–64 (4)
Sector national income per person employed	−0.08	−1.08	1.35	0.47
Total factor input	**0.35**	**−0.47**	**0.78**	**0.06**
Labor	0.32	−0.33	0.53	−0.05
Hours	0.17	−0.04	0.21	0.01
Age-sex composition	0.20	−0.27	0.33	−0.10
Education	−0.05	−0.02	−0.01	0.04
Capital	0.07	−0.05	0.25	0.16
Land	−0.04	−0.09	0.00	−0.05
Output per unit of input	**−0.43**	**−0.61**	**0.57**	**0.41**
Advances in knowledge and n.e.c.[a,b]	0.23	0.02	0.27	0.07
Improved resource allocation	0.21	0.14	0.10	0.01
Economies of scale[a]	0.18	0.28	0.21	0.30
Irregular factors				
Weather, labor disputes	−0.02	0.03	−0.01	0.03
Intensity of demand	−1.03	−1.08	...	...

Sources: Derived from Tables 8-9 and 8-10.
a. Differences between entries for actual and potential national income in these lines result from rounding, interaction terms, and the "forcing" of the components of potential national income so that they add to the total growth rates.
b. n.e.c. Not elsewhere classified.

one direction or the other, to changes in the growth rate of actual output per person employed is also evident from the first two columns of Table 8-11. In part these differences reflect changes already reviewed in the context of potential national income, but two additional comments are required.

The ratio of actual employment to potential employment in the sector rose in 1948–53 and, more strongly, in 1964–69, but it fell in 1953–64. As previously noted, an increase in the ratio of actual to potential employment cuts labor input and land input per person employed but raises the gains from resource reallocation, while a decline in the ratio has the opposite effects. The considerable differences between the actual and potential entries for these determinants in Table 8-11 mirror this pattern.

Changes in capital input per person actually employed were more similar in the three periods than changes in capital input per person potentially employed. Consequently, capital contributed much less to interperiod differences in actual growth rates. The increase in the growth rate of total capital input from 1953–64 to 1964–69, though large, was less than the increase in the growth rate of employment, so the capital contribution actually declined.

Prewar Short Periods

The 1941–48 growth rate of total potential national income was 3.00 percent. It is divided by sources in Table 8-6 (page 117). If the effects of irregular factors (in this case, the effect of weather on farm output) are removed, the 1941–48 growth rate was only 0.13 percentage points below that in the middle postwar period from 1953 to 1964, though well below the rate in the whole postwar period. There were, however, some substantial differences between the sources of growth in 1941–48 and 1953–64. Labor input contributed 0.13 percentage points more in 1941–48, a difference which is more than accounted for by a difference of 0.25 points in the age-sex composition component. The shift from farming contributed 0.09 points more and economies of scale 0.15 points more. Contributing substantially less in 1941–48 were capital (0.15 points), "advances in knowledge and n.e.c." (0.33 points), and, because of the burst of new unincorporated firms in the immediate postwar years, reallocation from nonfarm self-employment (0.16 points).

The lowest growth rate of potential national income, 2.50, is observed in the 1929–41 period. If the effects of irregular factors are removed, the 1929–41 rate was 0.44 percentage points below even the 1941–48 rate. This was so even though the contribution of labor was higher by 0.52 points in 1929–41 (because of the employment component) and the contribution of resource reallocation was higher by 0.14 points. Nonresidential structures and equipment, inventories, "advances in knowledge and n.e.c.," and economies of scale all contributed much less in 1929–41 than in 1941–48, or in any other period; they were mainly responsible for the lower growth rate of potential national income over the depression period.

Potential national income per person employed grew almost as much per year from 1941 to 1948 as from 1953 to 1964, and slightly (0.04 percentage points) more if the effects of irregular factors are removed, but in 1929–41 this growth rate was only 1.01 percent per year, far below any other period. As shown in Table 8-10, changes in all determinants except education and reallocation of resources were unfavorable to rapid growth in 1929–41, most of them highly unfavorable in comparison with all other periods.[32] In the cases of capital (which made a *negative* contribution of 0.25 points) and economies of scale, this unfavorable result clearly was a consequence of the long and severe depression. Gains from resource reallocation would have been greater than they were in the absence of the depression. The depression probably also affected adversely the contribution of "advances in knowledge and n.e.c." but is unlikely to have been the main reason that this source contributed much less in 1929–41 than in any later period.[33]

Actual growth rates in 1929–41 and 1941–48, and their distributions among sources, were dominated by cyclical movements in the proportion of potential labor input which was actually used and in the intensity of utilization of employed resources.[34]

32. This statement treats "hours" as a single source.
33. This topic is discussed on pages 81–83.
34. The data are shown in Tables 8-5 and 8-9 but will not be discussed further.

Sources of Growth in the Economy as a Whole

⇶⇶⇶

The total net product of the United States economy, as measured by national income at 1958 prices, was three and three-fourths times as large in 1969 as in 1929. During this forty-year period total output grew at an annual rate of 3.33 percent per year, and output per person employed at an annual rate of 1.89 percent. Potential output rose even more: total potential output at an annual rate of 3.41 percent, and potential output per person potentially employed at a rate of 1.95 percent. All of these rates were higher after 1948. All fluctuated greatly between shorter periods.

What changes in the determinants of output produced this growth and how much did each contribute? What determinants were responsible for the sharp changes in growth rates within this forty-year time span? This chapter presents the summary findings of how growth in output has occurred in the whole economy. Growth rates themselves are of greater interest when they refer to the whole economy rather than to the non-residential business portion of it as in Chapter 8, and the sources of growth of total output are similarly of broader interest. Moreover, because the sectors other than nonresidential business use large and changing fractions of the nation's labor and capital, only data referring to the whole economy can be related to changes in the nation's population, labor force, employment, investment, and saving.

The thirty-two growth rates for the entire economy that will be analyzed by source in this chapter are shown in Table 9-1. They correspond to the rates for the nonresidential business sector that were discussed in Chapter 8.[1] Attention is also called to Appendix S, which provides estimates of sources of growth of actual output for 1950–62 and 1929–57 and compares them with estimates for those periods obtained in my earlier studies.

Derivation and Classification of Contributions by Source

Previous chapters have analyzed growth in the four sectors into which the economy has been divided: general government, households, and institutions; dwellings; international assets; and nonresidential business. The contribution made to the growth rate of total actual national income in the whole economy by each growth source in the first three, special, sectors was calculated in Chapter 3, and Table R-2 provides similarly computed data for the nonresidential business sector. The total contribution of each growth source, shown for long periods in the first three columns of Table 9-4 and for shorter periods in Table 9-9 (see pages 127 and 138), is obtained by simply adding the data for the separate sectors.

1. The organization of this chapter is also generally similar to that of Chapter 8. But the points stressed and some of the questions raised are quite different, and the preliminary discussion can be greatly curtailed because Chapter 8 covered most of the necessary background material.

Table 9-1. Whole Economy: Growth Rates, Eight Selected Periods, 1929–69
Percent per annum

Time span	Actual national income		Potential national income	
	Total	Per person employed	Total	Per person potentially employed
Long periods				
1929–69	3.33	1.89	3.41	1.95
1929–48	2.75	1.47	2.75	1.42
1948–69	3.85	2.27	4.02	2.44
Shorter periods				
1929–41	2.34[a]	1.36[a]	2.63	0.94
1941–48	3.44[a]	1.65[a]	2.96	2.24
1948–53	4.54	2.46	4.99	3.21
1953–64	3.23	2.51	3.20	2.12
1964–69	4.54	1.57	4.85	2.39

Sources: Tables 2-3 and 7-3.
a. Based on data excluding work relief employees.

Most individual growth sources in fact contribute to growth in only one sector. The contribution of such a source to the growth rate of total national income is simply the product of (1) the total contribution made to that growth rate by the sector in which the source appears, and (2) the percentage of the *sector* growth rate which is contributed by that source. Only labor input and some of its components appear in more than one sector—namely, in nonresidential business and in the sector covering general government, households, and institutions.

Contributions to growth rates of total *potential* national income were also obtained by adding data for the four sectors. The sector data are provided in Tables R-4 and R-5.

Contributions to growth rates of national income per person employed and potential national income per person potentially employed were derived from the aggregate data and the series from which they were computed.

The contributions of a source to the growth rates of two or more of the four output measures are often the same by definition except for the effects of statistical interaction, rounding, or adjustments to make the detail of the potential estimates add exactly to the growth rate. Table R-6 and the adjacent discussion indicate these cases.

Most of the detailed output determinants shown in the tables contribute to growth only in nonresidential business. A review of their definitions was provided in Chapter 8 (pages 104–10) and need not be repeated. Measured in percentage points, their contributions to the growth rate of national income in the whole economy are, of course, smaller than their contributions to the growth rate of national income in the nonresidential business sector, and the percentages by which they are smaller change from period to period.

Two entries under capital arise in the special sectors. *Dwellings,* as defined, include residential land, but their contribution to growth can be regarded as almost purely the result of the change in residential capital. *International assets* measure the contribution made by changes in the excess of the earnings of American-owned assets abroad over those of foreign-owned assets in the United States. Under output per unit of input one new entry appears. *Dwellings occupancy ratio* measures the effect on national income of changes in the proportion of dwelling units occupied. All of these entries are fully described in Chapter 3.

Labor input can be subdivided in two ways. In Tables 9-2 and 9-3 the major division is between labor employed in general government, households, and institutions and labor employed in nonresidential business; the detail for the two sectors is kept separate. This classification shows the importance in the long periods of the contribution made to growth by the addition of labor in general government, households, and institutions. It was one-third of the total labor contribution in 1929–69 and even more in 1948–69. The fractions are much bigger than the share of this growing sector in the *level* of labor input even at the end of the period. The proportions of the labor contribution to both actual and potential output that stem from general government, households, and institutions fluctuated widely between the shorter periods.

In subsequent sources of growth tables a different classification is followed. The division of labor input by sector is eliminated and the detailed entries for the sectors are combined. This causes no classification problems for *employment* or for *hours* (and components thereof), but a reminder of the meaning of the hours entries in general government, households, and institutions is needed. The contribution of *average hours* is computed in the same way as in business, but the effect of changes in hours upon output, shown in the *hours* lines, and the size of the *efficiency offset,* merely reflect the implications of the method used by the Office of Business Economics (OBE) to measure output in the sector. In general, changes in average hours in general government, households, and institutions that result from changes in full-time hours do not affect measured output or, therefore, the contribution of "hours." Their effects are canceled in the efficiency offset component. In this sector, only changes in average hours that result from the changing proportion of part-time workers or from changes in average part-time hours affect measured output and thus appear as contributions of hours. Consequently, the effect of changes in hours in the sector is usually small, −0.01 to −0.03, except in 1941–48. There is no entry for *intergroup shifts* because farming and self-employment are absent from the sector.

The *unallocated* line in the tables merely reflects changes in the importance of employee groups that OBE distinguishes within general government, households, and institutions when it measures the sector's output (and among which earnings differed in the base year 1958). OBE

Table 9-2. Contribution of Labor Input to Growth Rates of Total Actual National Income, by Sector and Source, Eight Selected Periods, 1929–69

Contributions to growth rate in percentage points

	1929–69	1929–48	1948–69	1929–41[a]	1941–48[a]	1948–53	1953–64	1964–69
Labor input	**1.31**	**1.36**	**1.30**	**1.29**	**1.52**	**2.07**	**0.60**	**2.15**
General government, households, and institutions	0.43	0.42	0.47	0.54	0.27	0.96	0.27	0.55
Employment	0.37	0.29	0.47	0.39	0.18	0.91	0.31	0.51
Hours	−0.03	−0.03	−0.03	−0.01	−0.09	−0.02	−0.03	−0.03
Average hours	−0.09	−0.13	−0.05	−0.14	−0.14	−0.03	−0.09	0.00
Efficiency offset	0.06	0.10	0.02	0.13	0.05	0.01	0.06	−0.03
Unallocated	0.09	0.16	0.03	0.16	0.18	0.07	−0.01	0.07
Nonresidential business	0.88	0.94	0.83	0.75	1.25	1.11	0.33	1.60
Employment	0.71	0.73	0.70	0.44	1.22	0.72	0.20	1.75
Hours	−0.19	−0.20	−0.18	−0.18	−0.24	−0.06	−0.21	−0.24
Average hours	−0.41	−0.51	−0.32	−0.55	−0.44	−0.29	−0.26	−0.45
Efficiency offset	0.13	0.24	0.04	0.32	0.07	0.12	−0.02	0.10
Intergroup shift offset	0.09	0.07	0.10	0.05	0.13	0.11	0.07	0.11
Age-sex composition	−0.05	0.01	−0.10	0.04	−0.04	0.07	−0.09	−0.31
Education	0.41	0.40	0.41	0.45	0.31	0.38	0.43	0.40

Sources: Tables 3-5 and R-2.
a. Based on data excluding work relief employees.

Table 9-3. Contribution of Labor Input to Growth Rates of Total Potential National Income, by Sector and Source, Eight Selected Periods, 1929–69

Contributions to growth rate in percentage points

	1929–69	1929–48	1948–69	1929–41	1941–48	1948–53	1953–64	1964–69
Labor input	**1.32**	**1.37**	**1.31**	**1.66**	**0.95**	**1.94**	**0.83**	**1.85**
General government, households, and institutions	0.43	0.43	0.48	0.54	0.28	0.97	0.27	0.55
Employment	0.37	0.30	0.47	0.39	0.19	0.91	0.31	0.51
Hours	−0.03	−0.03	−0.02	−0.01	−0.09	−0.01	−0.03	−0.03
Average hours	−0.09	−0.13	−0.05	−0.14	−0.14	−0.03	−0.09	0.00
Efficiency offset	0.06	0.10	0.03	0.13	0.05	0.02	0.06	−0.03
Unallocated	0.09	0.16	0.03	0.16	0.18	0.07	−0.01	0.07
Nonresidential business	0.89	0.94	0.83	1.12	0.67	0.97	0.56	1.30
Employment	0.72	0.75	0.68	0.96	0.41	0.49	0.50	1.30
Hours	−0.19	−0.20	−0.17	−0.21	−0.17	−0.05	−0.21	−0.21
Average hours	−0.40	−0.51	−0.29	−0.62	−0.31	−0.24	−0.29	−0.36
Efficiency offset	0.13	0.23	0.03	0.33	0.06	0.10	−0.01	0.07
Intergroup shift offset	0.08	0.08	0.09	0.08	0.08	0.08	0.09	0.08
Age-sex composition	−0.05	0.00	−0.10	−0.03	0.06	0.13	−0.14	−0.22
Education	0.41	0.39	0.42	0.40	0.37	0.40	0.41	0.43

Sources: Tables R-4 and R-5.

takes no direct account of age, sex, or education in its measurement of labor input, so changes in these characteristics of persons employed in general government, households, and institutions do not affect measured national income except in the sense that they are responsible for the differences in the level of earnings of groups which OBE treats separately.[2] The *age-sex composition* and *education* components of labor input in the sources of growth tables result only from changes that occurred in nonresidential business.

2. Changes in education and age-sex composition *within* such a group do not affect the output estimates at all. See Chapter 3.

Table 9-4. Sources of Growth of Total National Income, Actual and Potential, Three Long Periods, 1929–69
Contributions to growth rate in percentage points

	Total actual national income			Total potential national income		
	1929–69	*1929–48*	*1948–69*	*1929–69*	*1929–48*	*1948–69*
National income	3.33	2.75	3.85	3.41	2.75	4.02
Total factor input	1.81	1.49	2.10	1.82	1.50	2.11
Labor	1.31	1.36	1.30	1.32	1.37	1.31
Employment	1.08	1.02	1.17	1.09	1.05	1.15
Hours	−0.22	−0.23	−0.21	−0.22	−0.23	−0.19
Average hours	−0.50	−0.64	−0.37	−0.49	−0.64	−0.34
Efficiency offset	0.19	0.34	0.06	0.19	0.33	0.06
Intergroup shift offset	0.09	0.07	0.10	0.08	0.08	0.09
Age-sex composition	−0.05	0.01	−0.10	−0.05	0.00	−0.10
Education	0.41	0.40	0.41	0.41	0.39	0.42
Unallocated	0.09	0.16	0.03	0.09	0.16	0.03
Capital	0.50	0.13	0.80	0.50	0.13	0.80
Inventories	0.09	0.05	0.12	0.09	0.05	0.12
Nonresidential structures and equipment	0.20	0.03	0.36	0.20	0.03	0.36
Dwellings	0.19	0.06	0.29	0.19	0.06	0.29
International assets	0.02	−0.01	0.03	0.02	−0.01	0.03
Land	0.00	0.00	0.00	0.00	0.00	0.00
Output per unit of input	1.52	1.26	1.75	1.59	1.25	1.91
Advances in knowledge and n.e.c.[a]	0.92	0.62	1.19	0.92	0.62	1.19
Improved resource allocation	0.29	0.29	0.30	0.30	0.31	0.31
Farm	0.25	0.27	0.23	0.26	0.28	0.24
Nonfarm self-employment	0.04	0.02	0.07	0.04	0.03	0.07
Dwellings occupancy ratio	0.01	0.02	−0.01	0.01	0.02	−0.01
Economies of scale	0.36	0.29	0.42	0.36	0.29	0.43
Irregular factors	−0.06	0.04	−0.15	0.00	0.01	−0.01
Weather in farming	0.00	0.01	−0.01	0.00	0.01	−0.01
Labor disputes	0.00	0.00	0.00	0.00	0.00	0.00
Intensity of demand	−0.06	0.03	−0.14	...	...	...

Sources: Table 9-1; contributions derived from Tables 3-3, 3-5, 3-7, R-2, R-3, R-4, and R-5.
a. n.e.c. Not elsewhere classified.

The tables that refer to national income per person employed detail the determinants that have produced changes in national income per person employed in the economy as a whole. For example, if the national income provided by the stock of dwellings increases more than total employment, this raises national income per person employed (even though there is no employment in the dwellings sector). If the education of persons employed in business advances, this contributes to a rise in output in nonresidential business and hence in the whole economy, but the contribution to the growth of national income per person employed in the whole economy is necessarily smaller than the contribution to the growth of national income per person employed in nonresidential business because the extra output it made possible is divided among more people.

Growth of Total Output over Long Periods

The chief purpose of examining long time spans is to discover the important sources of long-term growth and their relative importance in raising the nation's output. Table 9-4 provides estimates of the sources of growth of both actual and potential output. The growth rate of actual national income differs from that of potential national income in any time span only because the first and last years of the period are not comparable with respect to short-term demand pressures. Even though 1929, 1948, and 1969 are all regarded as high employment years, demand pressure was much weaker in 1969 than in the other years and increases in actual output from 1929 to 1969 and from 1948 to 1969 were less than increases in potential output. The differences were due mainly

Table 9-5. Total Potential National Income: Percentage Distributions of Growth Rates among Sources with Economies of Scale Isolated and Allocated among Other Sources, Three Long Periods, 1929–69

	Estimates with economies of scale isolated			Estimates with economies of scale allocated		
	1929–69 (1)	1929–48 (2)	1948–69 (3)	1929–69 (4)	1929–48 (5)	1948–69 (6)
National income	100.0	100.0	100.0	100.0	100.0	100.0
Total factor input	53.4	54.5	52.5	58.7	60.0	57.5
Labor	38.7	49.8	32.6	42.8	54.9	35.8
Employment	32.0	38.2	28.6	35.2	42.2	31.3
Hours	−6.5	−8.4	−4.7	−7.3	−9.5	−5.5
Average hours	−14.4	−23.3	−8.5	−16.1	−25.8	−9.7
Efficiency offset	5.6	12.0	1.5	6.2	13.1	1.7
Intergroup shift offset	2.3	2.9	2.2	2.6	3.3	2.5
Age-sex composition	−1.5	0.0	−2.5	−1.8	0.0	−2.7
Education	12.0	14.2	10.4	14.1	16.4	11.9
Unallocated	2.6	5.8	0.7	2.6	5.8	0.7
Capital	14.7	4.7	19.9	15.8	5.1	21.6
Inventories	2.6	1.8	3.0	2.9	2.2	3.5
Nonresidential structures and equipment	5.9	1.1	9.0	6.7	1.1	10.2
Dwellings	5.6	2.2	7.2	5.6	2.2	7.2
International assets	0.6	−0.4	0.7	0.6	−0.4	0.7
Land	0.0	0.0	0.0	0.0	0.0	0.0
Output per unit of input	46.6	45.5	47.5	41.3	40.0	42.5
Advances in knowledge and n.e.c.[a]	27.0	22.5	29.6	31.1	26.2	34.1
Improved resource allocation	8.8	11.3	7.7	10.0	12.7	9.0
Farm	7.6	10.2	6.0	8.5	11.6	7.0
Nonfarm self-employment	1.2	1.1	1.7	1.5	1.1	2.0
Dwellings occupancy ratio	0.3	0.7	−0.2	0.3	0.7	−0.2
Economies of scale	10.6	10.5	10.7	...	...	...
Irregular factors	0.0	0.4	−0.2	0.0	0.4	−0.2
Weather in farming	0.0	0.4	−0.2	0.0	0.4	−0.2
Labor disputes	0.0	0.0	0.0	0.0	0.0	0.0

Sources: Derived from Tables 9-4 and R-7.
a. n.e.c. Not elsewhere classified.

to the effects of demand on intensity of utilization of employed resources. The growth rate of actual output fell below that of potential output by 0.08 percentage points in 1929–69 and by 0.17 percentage points in 1948–69. For examination of the sources of long-term growth the estimates of potential national income, which are unaffected by the short-term demand situation in the particular years bounding the time periods chosen, are of greater relevance than those of actual national income.

Estimates on a potential basis are provided by source in the last three columns of Table 9-4 for the whole period from 1929 to 1969, in which the growth rate of potential output was 3.41 percent, and for the 1929–48 and 1948–69 periods, in

which the rates were 2.75 and 4.02 percent, respectively. The data are also summarized in Figure 9-1 (page 129).

Capital and advances in knowledge were primarily responsible for the marked rise in the growth rate of potential output from 1929–48 to 1948–69, which amounted to 1.27 percentage points, or some 47 percent. Capital contributed 0.67 percentage points more in the postwar period than in 1929–48, and all four components of capital contributed to the difference. "Advances in knowledge and n.e.c." contributed 0.57 percentage points more in the later period. The latter change is probably due largely to a more rapid rate of advance in new knowledge relevant to production after the war, but depression-induced re-

Figure 9-1. Sources of Growth of Total Potential National Income, Three Long Periods, 1929–69

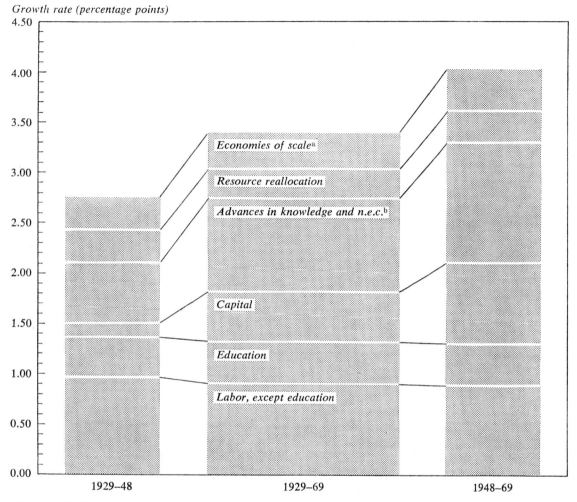

Growth rate (percentage points)

Economies of scale[a]

Resource reallocation

Advances in knowledge and n.e.c.[b]

Capital

Education

Labor, except education

1929–48   1929–69   1948–69

Source: Table 9-4.
a. Includes housing occupancy ratio and irregular factors.
b. n.e.c. Not elsewhere classified.

strictions against efficient practices probably contributed to it. There probably was also some widening of the gap between actual and best practice in 1929–48, followed by a narrowing in the early years of the 1948–69 period.[3] The contribution of economies of scale in 1948–69 was 0.14 percentage points bigger than in 1929–48, a consequence of the faster expansion of markets, but it was the changes in the contributions of capital and advances in knowledge that made this faster expansion possible.

3. It is also possible that the estimate for 1929–48 is understated (see pp. 81–82).

Growth with Economies of Scale as a Separate Source

I turn now to the relative importance of growth sources. The first three columns of Table 9-5 provide percentage distributions among sources of the growth rates of potential national income in the long periods. Chiefly because the contribution of capital was atypically small in 1929–48, I shall confine my discussion to the whole 1929–69 period and the postwar period. The changes from 1929–48 to 1948–69 described above necessarily mean that capital and, to a lesser extent, advances in knowledge played larger relative roles in postwar growth than in growth over the whole forty-year period and that most other sources played correspondingly smaller parts.

Approximately 53 percent of the growth of total potential national income in both 1929–69 and 1948–69 resulted directly from increasing the quantity of labor, capital, and land; and 47 percent from the increase in output per unit of input.[4] The share of total factor input is bigger in the whole economy than in nonresidential business because all of the increase in output in the other sectors is directly attributable to labor and capital input (except for changes in the dwellings occupancy ratio). In the postwar period the contribution of capital was considerably bigger in the whole economy than it was found to be in nonresidential business. It reached 0.80 percentage points, or one-fifth of the growth rate. Some 0.32 percentage points of this contribution came from dwellings and international assets, as against 0.48 points from capital used in nonresidential business. The share of the capital contribution provided by dwellings and international assets was big, but smaller than the share of these assets in the capital stock. As its wording implies, output per unit of input includes all of the gains from economies of scale that were made possible by the growth of markets for business output. Economies of scale were a very important growth source, estimated to account for more than one-tenth of the growth rate of output and 23 percent of the growth rate of output per unit of input in both periods.

Estimates with Economies of Scale Allocated

A classification in which economies of scale are identified as a separate growth source provides information that would otherwise be lost, is convenient for purposes of estimation, and eliminates a possible source of error for most entries. But, as pointed out in Chapter 8, when the contribution of a determinant is described as the amount by which the growth rate would have been reduced if that determinant had not changed while all others changed as they actually did, "all others" must include the size of markets since that is a separate determinant. This is artificial in

the sense that most output determinants necessarily affect the size of the markets that business serves. It is therefore useful, in addition, to estimate contributions for the other determinants which include their effect on the size of business markets and hence on economies of scale. The last three columns of Table 9-5 provide a percentage distribution of growth rates by source which conforms to this practice (data in percentage points are shown in Table R-7).[5]

It will be noted that this classification transfers to total factor input the portion of the economies of scale contribution that was made possible by the increase in inputs. Only insofar as market expansion resulted from changes in the other determinants of output per unit of input does its effect on economies of scale remain in the total contribution of output per unit of input. The remaining amount is, however, substantial because advances in knowledge and reduction in the over-allocation of resources to farming and to nonfarm self-employment are major growth sources. They free labor, capital, or land to produce more of either the same products for which they were previously used or other products; they consequently lead to larger markets and economies of scale in the same way as an equivalent increase in the amount of labor, capital, and land used in the nonresidential business sector.

The following are percentage distributions for the two periods of most interest; they are based on a condensation of the classification in which gains from economies of scale are allocated.

	Percent of growth rate	
	1929–69	*1948–69*
Potential national income	100.0	100.0
Advances in knowledge and n.e.c.	31.1	34.1
More work done, with account taken of the characteristics of workers except education	28.7	23.9
More capital	15.8	21.6
Increased education per worker	14.1	11.9
Improved resource allocation	10.0	9.0
Dwellings occupancy ratio and irregular factors	0.3	−0.5

By these groupings long-term growth in the United States is shown as due almost entirely to five types of change.

---

4. This statement is, of course, based on the grouping of growth sources between "total factor input" and "output per unit of input" that is adopted in the tables. It was pointed out in Chapter 8 that estimates for alternative groupings can be obtained by the simple transfer of components.

5. The allocation, as in the preceding chapter, is proportional to contributions to the growth rate of actual national income in nonresidential business made by determinants other than irregular factors and economies of scale themselves.

1. ADVANCES IN KNOWLEDGE. Most important has been the advance in technological, managerial, and organizational knowledge. This statement expresses my judgment that over these long periods changes in the large number of miscellaneous determinants included in the "n.e.c." portion of "advances in knowledge and n.e.c." have individually been minor and have tended to be offsetting. Hence, I believe, the 31 percent of 1929–69 growth and the 34 percent of 1948–69 growth estimated for the combined grouping can appropriately be used as an approximation to the contribution made by incorporation of advances in knowledge alone.

This estimate is obtained as a residual because there is no way to estimate it directly. The main disadvantage of this procedure for growth analysis is not lack of accuracy (though greater accuracy would be welcome) but the absence of detail—a more serious handicap for advances in knowledge than for other determinants.

A principal reason for the study of growth is to be able to answer questions of the type: If we alter any determinant of the level of output by x amount, how much will output be altered as a result? Historical analysis and comparisons of different time periods and countries are helpful in all cases, but for most determinants it is at least possible to secure such an estimate without actually undertaking a historical analysis. Instead, the same techniques that I have used to measure contributions to past growth made by observed past changes in a determinant can be applied to estimate the effect of an assumed change. For the state of knowledge this avenue is closed; only historical analysis can provide any perspective.

My estimate is that the advance in knowledge, with associated gains from economies of scale included, contributed 1.37 percentage points to the growth rate in the postwar period. Although the rate showed no trend within the postwar period, this postwar figure appears high in a longer historical perspective. Over the whole 1929–69 period the contribution was 1.06 percentage points, and it is not likely that the figure was higher in any earlier period.

The estimates presented permit some inferences. For example, it can be inferred that if the rate at which knowledge relevant to production advanced in the postwar period were to drop by, say, one-tenth, the future growth rate would be 0.14 percentage points lower than if knowledge continued to advance at the postwar rate. On the other hand, the future growth rate would be raised by 0.14 percentage points—above what it would be otherwise—if ways could be found to raise by one-tenth the rate at which knowledge advances. The perspective thus obtained could not be secured without such a historical analysis. But far more information would be provided if it were possible to divide the contribution between advances in technological knowledge and in managerial or organizational knowledge, and between advances originating in this country and those originating abroad. It would be a bigger step forward if each could then be further divided to show the contribution resulting from advances in knowledge obtained in various ways. In the case of technological knowledge, for example, how much results from organized research, how much from invention by individuals, how much from small accretions due to observation and experience in the process of production? Acquisition of such information is needed to formulate an efficient public policy to foster growth by accelerating advances in knowledge, if such a policy is desired. The classification of growth sources I have adopted has deliberately kept the scope of advances in knowledge comprehensive, so that it could accommodate such further detail. Among the greatest challenges to future research on economic growth is to devise techniques which could provide it.

2. AMOUNT OF WORK DONE. By the groupings used in the text table at the left, the second biggest source of growth is that labeled "more work done, with account taken of characteristics of workers except education." Included here are all components of labor input except education. Thus defined, the increase in work done contributed almost 29 percent of 1929–69 growth and 24 percent of postwar growth.

The detailed components of this aggregate, shown in Table 9-5, are not without interest or analytical value, and the total could not have been obtained without giving separate attention to each. But it should be realized that the detailed components are interrelated, and for this reason I have combined them here. For example, a feature of the postwar labor force was the entry of large numbers of women and students who sought and obtained part-time jobs and were not available for full-time jobs. In the absence of this development the contribution of employment would necessarily have been smaller and the contributions of hours and age-sex composition would necessarily have been larger (that is, smaller negative contributions). It is correct to state, as the sixth column of Table 9-5 implies, that the 1948–69 growth rate would have been raised by 5.5 percent if hours had not changed, or by 2.7 percent if age-sex composition had not changed, while all other determinants including employment had changed as they did. But given the development just described, the increase in employment actually observed could not have been achieved without a corresponding reduction in the hours and age-sex composition indexes.

3. CAPITAL. The contributions of the four components of capital input have been combined in the text table on page 130. By the groupings used in that table, the combined four components of capital were the third biggest source of growth. Capital accounted for nearly 16 percent of the growth rate in 1929–69 and nearly 22 percent in the postwar period.

The large contribution of capital in 1948–69 was obtained with a net investment rate that averaged 7.6 percent in these years if both the numerator (net investment in the four types of capital assets) and the denominator (net national product) are measured in 1958 prices.[6]

The detailed estimates show that in 1948–69 the increase in nonresidential structures and equipment alone accounted for 10.2 percent of the growth rate of potential national income, dwellings for 7.2 percent, business inventories for 3.5 percent, and international assets for 0.7 percent. The proportion of the postwar growth rate accounted for by the increase in the services provided by dwellings is noteworthy. It is much bigger than the proportion observed over periods of more than very short duration in other countries or in previous American experience.

4. EDUCATION. The fourth biggest source of long-term growth was the increase in the average amount of education held by workers employed in the business sector. The resulting increase in their skills and versatility was the source of 14 percent of the 1929–69 growth rate and 12 percent of the higher 1948–69 rate.

The increase in the education of persons employed in business has made so sizable a contribution to growth since 1929 because the shift in the distribution of workers by amount of education has been massive. This shift, in turn, has reflected the remarkable increase in the amount of education received by young people which has taken place over a much longer period—nearly a century, in fact, because persons who retired at the beginning of the 1929–69 period were educated forty to sixty years earlier. Similarly, if the education of young people were to remain at the present level, education would continue to contribute importantly to growth for several decades as older persons with less education were replaced by young entrants into the labor force. The contribution of education has been attained, of course, only by a great increase per person in the quantity of labor and property resources consumed in providing education, as well as in the time spent in school by students, some of which would otherwise have been allocated to production of measured output. In the terminology now popular among economists, it was the consequence of greatly increasing investment in human capital.

The average education of persons working in government, households, and institutions has increased even more than that of persons in the business sector, and government has absorbed a disproportionate share of the increase in the college-educated labor force, but no contribution to the increase in the nation's output, as it is now measured, can be ascribed to this increase.[7]

5. IMPROVED RESOURCE ALLOCATION. Improved resource allocation is the fifth and last of the large sources of long-term growth. As shown on page 130, it accounted for 10 percent of the growth rate of potential national income in 1929–69 and 9 percent in 1948–69. The estimate in fact includes only the gains from reducing the over-allocation of labor to farming and to nonfarm self-employment, but I do not believe a fuller accounting would change the figures very much. Of the two measured changes, the reduction of surplus labor in farming was much the more important; it alone accounted for 8.5 percent of the 1929–69 growth rate and 7.0 percent of the 1948–69 rate. Some analysts distinguish between gains

---

6. The ratio is based on the measures of output and depreciation used in this study. Market price values were used in the calculation but factor cost values apparently would yield about the same result, at least for 1958. Deduction of $2,361 million for "transfers to foreigners" from the sum of the figures given in Table A-9 for "net private domestic investment" and "net exports of goods and services" yields net investment rates of 4.30 percent for net national product and 4.34 percent for national income in 1958.

7. As explained earlier in discussing the "unallocated" component of labor input, this sentence is not precise, but the effect of changes in the education of persons employed outside the business sector cannot be extricated and would have no real meaning if it could be.

from reducing underemployment (or disguised unemployment, or labor inefficiently utilized in the activity to which it is put) and gains from moving labor from activities in which returns to fully and efficiently utilized labor are low to those in which they are higher. This estimate includes both.

Its large contribution over a forty-year period surely qualifies improved resource allocation as a significant long-term growth source (although one must consider that in some previous period resource allocation was worsening and reducing the growth rate). The possibility for such a large contribution over a long period required the sustained presence of substantial misallocation of employed labor. This condition arose only because of the unusual combination of a large and continuing change in the most efficient allocation of labor with a set of conditions which were uniquely unfavorable to swift elimination of labor from the activities in which labor requirements declined. These included, above all, the unimportance of paid labor, but also important were the "way of life" aspects of farming and self-employment and, especially in farming, geographic separation of areas of decreasing and rising demand for labor.

Relationships between Capital and Advances in Knowledge

This section interrupts the main discussion to examine a point in classification that has not been previously discussed. My estimates for the contributions of the capital components are designed to correspond to growth that results from adding to capital by saving and investment, and which could have been altered by changing the amount of the nation's saving and investment. The contribution of advances in knowledge is intended to represent the entire contribution of new knowledge, and therefore the amount which could have been altered by changing the rate at which new knowledge appeared and was incorporated into production.

Estimates for the contribution of capital could impinge on those for advances in knowledge in two ways. One, which has previously been discussed, is so handled that the estimates conform unambiguously to the definitions just given. Design improvements leading to "unmeasured" or "noneconomic" quality change in capital goods are not counted as increasing capital input; consequently, capital does not "steal" that part of the contribution of advances in knowledge which

takes the form of improvements in capital goods.[8] The second way, on the other hand, does raise a question as to definitions, desirable classification, and their relationship to my estimates. This question, though not new, has been raised most recently and, in my view, effectively by T. K. Rymes.[9]

As time passes, capital goods can be produced with a diminishing quantity of inputs because advances in knowledge lower their production costs. Given this situation, what should be considered the same amount of saving or investment at different dates? My estimates imply that identical bundles of capital goods (including inventories) acquired at two dates represent the same amount of capital (in constant prices) and hence by implication the same amount of investment, and correspondingly that the amounts of saving needed to provide funds to purchase identical bundles of capital goods represent the same amount of saving. By this definition, my estimates for the contribution of capital correspond to the effects of saving and investment, as is desired.

Rymes believes that counting identical capital goods as the same amount of capital input has implications that are not appropriate for analysis of the sources of long-term growth. He correctly stresses that capital is merely an intermediate product, itself a part of some year's output but one which is not wanted for its own sake but only for the contribution it makes later to the production of final products. He then argues, as have members of the Cambridge school of economists in the past, that the proper way to equate saving and investment made at two dates is by the quantity of consumption goods forgone to release resources for the production of investment goods. Adoption of this definition would reduce my estimates of the contribution of capital and raise my estimates of the contribution of advances in knowledge because the same amount of saving and investment defined as consumption forgone yields increasing quantities of capital goods as time passes. It seems to me that the case for the definitions proposed by Rymes, or something like them, is more persuasive when one focuses on the con-

8. One might like to know how much of the contribution of advances in knowledge is incorporated into production in this way, but there is no satisfactory method by which to estimate it.

9. T. K. Rymes, "The Measurement of Capital and Total Factor Productivity in the Context of the Cambridge Theory of Capital," *Review of Income and Wealth,* Series 18, No. 1 (March 1972), pp. 79–108.

tribution of advances in knowledge rather than capital. Advances in knowledge do raise productivity in the production of capital goods and hence allow the production of more capital goods with the same input. When the additional capital thus provided enters production the contribution made by this extra capital is not counted as a contribution of advances in knowledge, as Rymes would like, but as a contribution of capital.

One way of classifying the contribution of this extra capital whose acquisition was made possible by advances in knowledge is not "right" and the other "wrong"; the Rymes proposal would simply delve further for ultimate reasons for changes in output than does my classification. But an estimate of the amount involved in the choice would be of interest. How much of my estimate of the capital contribution would be transferred to advances in knowledge if I were to adopt the Rymes classification? Since it is interesting to have even a rough idea of the magnitude, I have attempted in Table 9-6 to derive estimates for my long

periods according to the Rymes classification despite formidable difficulties that must greatly qualify the results.

Components of domestic capital stock—inventories, nonresidential structures and equipment, and dwellings—are produced in the nonresidential business sector (unless they are imported). In that sector advances in knowledge (and "n.e.c.") raised output of all types per unit of input at annual rates of 1.10 in 1929–69, 0.72 in 1929–48, and 1.43 in 1948–69.[10] I raise these rates by 15 percent to include associated gains from economies of scale.[11] Line 2a of Table 9-6 shows the growth rates after this adjustment.

The calculation requires similar rates that pertain specifically to the production of each of the three types of capital good. These can be estimated crudely by use of relative prices. Under certain conditions, long-run differences between growth rates of the prices of products are the

10. Based on the index in column 9 of Table 6-1.
11. See page 75.

Table 9-6. Capital Contribution to Be Transferred to Advances in Knowledge If Investment Is Defined as Consumption Forgone: Derivation of Estimates, Three Long Periods, 1929–69

	1929–69	*1929–48*	*1948–69*
1. Growth rates of price indexes			
a. Net output in nonresidential business	2.23	2.57	1.93
b. Stock of inventories	1.81	2.43	1.24
c. Stock of nonresidential structures and equipment	2.86	3.01	2.72
d. Stock of dwellings	3.27	4.04	2.58
2. Growth rates of contribution of advances in knowledge and associated gains from economies of scale			
a. Net output in nonresidential business	1.26	0.83	1.64
b. Stock of inventories (1a − 1b + 2a)	1.68	0.97	2.33
c. Stock of nonresidential structures and equipment (1a − 1c + 2a)	0.63	0.39	0.85
d. Stock of dwellings (1a − 1d + 2a)	0.22	−0.64	0.99
3. Growth rates of inputs			
a. Inventories	2.44	1.33	3.46
b. Nonresidential structures and equipment	2.05	0.29	3.68
c. Dwellings	5.55	2.93	7.98
4. Ratio of growth rates of advances in knowledge and associated gains from economies of scale to growth rates of inputs			
a. Inventories (2b ÷ 3a)	0.689	0.729	0.673
b. Nonresidential structures and equipment (2c ÷ 3b)	0.307	1.345	0.231
c. Dwellings (2d ÷ 3c)	0.040	−0.218	0.124
5. Contribution of capital to growth rate of potential national income			
a. Inventories	0.09	0.05	0.12
b. Nonresidential structures and equipment	0.20	0.03	0.36
c. Dwellings	0.19	0.06	0.29
6. Amount to be transferred to advances in knowledge to conform to alternative classification			
a. Inventories (4a × 5a)	0.06	0.04	0.08
b. Nonresidential structures and equipment (4b × 5b)	0.06	0.04	0.08
c. Dwellings (4c × 5c)	0.01	−0.01	0.04
d. Total (6a + 6b + 6c)	0.13	0.07	0.20

Sources: See text for derivation.

same as differences between the growth rates of total factor productivity in their production.[12] The calculation assumes this to be the case over these time spans and further assumes that incorporation of new knowledge into production is the reason for differences in the rate of change in output per unit of input. Growth rates of price indexes for total nonresidential business output and for each of the three capital components are shown in lines 1a to 1d of Table 9-6.[13] The estimated growth rate of productivity in the production of each type of capital as a result of advances in knowledge (including associated gains from economies of scale) is the rate for all products in the sector minus, or plus, the amount by which the growth rate of prices for the capital component exceeds, or falls short of, that for all products. Rows 2b to 2d show the estimates.

In Table 9-6, rows 3a to 3c show the growth rates of each of the capital inputs as I have measured them, and rows 4a to 4c the ratios to these rates of the growth rates of productivity in their production (due to advances in knowledge, including associated economies of scale). Multiplication of these ratios by my estimates of the contributions of capital to growth of potential national income (shown in rows 5a to 5c) in accordance with my standard classification provides estimates of the amount of that contribution which would be transferred from capital to advances in knowledge if the Rymes classification were adopted.[14] The combined amounts for the capital components are 0.13 percentage points in 1929–69 and 0.20 points in 1948–69, or about one-fourth of the total capital contribution, as I measure it, in each of these periods.[15] The proportion is much higher for inventories and much lower for dwellings.

If these estimates, in turn, are raised 15 percent to include associated gains from economies of scale, we have the amounts required to adjust the last three columns of Table 9-5 to conform to the Rymes definitions. Use of those definitions would reduce the percentage of growth contributed by capital from 15.8 to 11.4 in 1929–69, from 5.1 to 2.2 in 1929–48, and from 21.6 to 15.9 in 1948–69. It would raise the percentage contributed by "advances in knowledge and n.e.c." from 31.1 to 35.5 in 1929–69, from 26.2 to 29.1 in 1929–48, and from 34.1 to 39.8 in 1948–69. I again stress that the calculation is intended only to give a rough notion of the amount by which adoption of the Rymes classification might change the estimates.

Growth of Output per Person Employed over Long Periods

Table 9-7 shows the sources of growth of actual national income per person employed and potential national income per person potentially employed over the three long periods. Differences between the actual and potential growth rates stem almost entirely from the "intensity of demand" component of output per unit of input, although in 1948–69 changes in hours contributed a little to the shortfall of actual below the potential growth rate. As previously explained, the estimates on a potential basis are of greater interest for examination of the sources of long-term growth.

The growth rate of potential national income per person potentially employed was 1.42 in 1929–48, 2.44 in 1948–69, and 1.95 in 1929–69. The contributions of most determinants in 1948–69 differed somewhat from their contributions in 1929–48, but it is clear that capital and "advances in knowledge and n.e.c." were almost exclusively responsible for the sharp rise in the growth rate. The contributions of these two growth sources to the rise were almost identical.

The 1929–48 period, in which the contribution of capital was negative, is clearly abnormal but there is no way to establish the extent to which the abnormally low capital formation in this period caused the postwar contribution of capital

---

12. See *The Sources of Economic Growth*, Chap. 19. (For full citation, see Chap. 1, note 1, of this book.)

13. All are at market prices. The price index for nonresidential business is derived from the detail of my estimates for output at current and constant prices. The price indexes for inventories and nonresidential structures and equipment are implicit deflators for the capital stock. Capital stock data rather than investment data are used in order to secure correct weighting of components. As elsewhere in this study, price deflator 2 is used for nonresidential structures. There is no significant weighting problem for residential construction and the investment deflator is used.

14. These estimates are applicable to actual as well as to potential national income, and to estimates on a per-person-employed basis as well.

15. The increase in the price index for dwellings is likely to be overstated, leading to understatement of the amounts to be transferred. But even if it were assumed that productivity rose as much in residential construction as in non-

residential business as a whole (an extreme assumption), this would raise the amounts to be transferred by only 0.03 points in 1929–69, 0.04 in 1929–48, and 0.02 in 1948–69.

Table 9-7. Sources of Growth of Actual National Income per Person Employed and Potential National Income per Person Potentially Employed, Three Long Periods, 1929–69
Contributions to growth rate in percentage points

	Actual national income per person employed			Potential national income per person potentially employed		
	1929–69	1929–48	1948–69	1929–69	1929–48	1948–69
National income	**1.89**	**1.47**	**2.27**	**1.95**	**1.42**	**2.44**
Total factor input	**0.40**	**0.23**	**0.56**	**0.40**	**0.20**	**0.59**
Labor	0.23	0.34	0.13	0.23	0.32	0.16
Hours	−0.22	−0.23	−0.21	−0.22	−0.23	−0.19
Average hours	−0.50	−0.64	−0.37	−0.49	−0.64	−0.34
Efficiency offset	0.19	0.34	0.06	0.19	0.33	0.06
Intergroup shift offset	0.09	0.07	0.10	0.08	0.08	0.09
Age-sex composition	−0.05	0.01	−0.10	−0.05	0.00	−0.10
Education	0.41	0.40	0.41	0.41	0.39	0.42
Unallocated	0.09	0.16	0.03	0.09	0.16	0.03
Capital	0.22	−0.06	0.48	0.22	−0.07	0.48
Inventories	0.03	0.00	0.06	0.03	0.00	0.06
Nonresidential structures and equipment	0.05	−0.08	0.18	0.05	−0.09	0.18
Dwellings	0.13	0.03	0.22	0.13	0.03	0.22
International assets	0.01	−0.01	0.02	0.01	−0.01	0.02
Land	−0.05	−0.05	−0.05	−0.05	−0.05	−0.05
Output per unit of input	**1.49**	**1.24**	**1.71**	**1.55**	**1.22**	**1.85**
Advances in knowledge and n.e.c.[a]	0.90	0.60	1.16	0.90	0.60	1.16
Improved resource allocation	0.29	0.29	0.30	0.29	0.30	0.30
Farm	0.25	0.27	0.23	0.25	0.27	0.23
Nonfarm self-employment	0.04	0.02	0.07	0.04	0.03	0.07
Dwellings occupancy ratio	0.01	0.02	−0.01	0.01	0.02	−0.01
Economies of scale	0.35	0.29	0.41	0.35	0.29	0.41
Irregular factors	−0.06	0.04	−0.15	0.00	0.01	−0.01
Weather in farming	0.00	0.01	−0.01	0.00	0.01	−0.01
Labor disputes	0.00	0.00	0.00	0.00	0.00	0.00
Intensity of demand	−0.06	0.03	−0.14	...	...	...

Sources: Table 9-1; contributions derived from Tables 2-2, 3-2, 3-4, 3-6, 4-1, 5-4, 6-4, 7-3, J-2, and R-1.
a. n.e.c. Not elsewhere classified.

to be abnormally large, and hence to judge as to the relative "representativeness" of the 1929–69 and 1948–69 periods.

Percentage distributions of the sources of growth of potential national income per person potentially employed are shown in Table 9-8, both with economies of scale classified as a separate source of growth and with them allocated back to the sources responsible for the growth of markets for business output.[16] Following are the percentages, based on a condensed classification, for the two periods of most interest; determinants are listed in the order of their contributions to the 1929–69 growth rate.[17]

16. I shall not give further consideration to the Rymes variant of the classification.
17. Economies of scale and employment itself appear in only one classification and are ranked by their contributions in that classification. As explained in Chapter 8, employment becomes a source of growth of output per worker when economies of scale are allocated among other sources because increases in business employment contribute to market expansion.

	Percent of growth rate:			
	With economies of scale isolated		With economies of scale allocated	
	1929 –69	1948 –69	1929 –69	1948 –69
Potential national income per person potentially employed	100.0	100.0	100.0	100.0
Advances in knowledge and n.e.c.	46.2	47.5	53.3	54.5
Education per worker	21.0	17.2	24.6	19.7
Economies of scale	17.9	16.8	...	...
Improved resource allocation	14.9	12.3	16.9	14.3
Capital per worker	11.3	19.7	13.3	22.5
Employment itself	...	...	5.1	4.0
Dwellings occupancy ratio	0.5	−0.4	0.5	−0.4
Irregular factors	0.0	−0.4	0.0	−0.4
Land per worker	−2.6	−2.0	−2.6	−2.0
Labor input per worker, except education	−9.3	−10.7	−11.3	−12.3

Table 9-8. Potential National Income per Person Potentially Employed: Percentage Distributions of Growth Rates among Sources with Economies of Scale Isolated and Allocated among Other Sources, Three Long Periods, 1929–69

	Estimates with economies of scale isolated			Estimates with economies of scale allocated		
	1929–69 (1)	1929–48 (2)	1948–69 (3)	1929–69 (4)	1929–48 (5)	1948–69 (6)
National income	100.0	100.0	100.0	100.0	100.0	100.0
Total factor input	**20.5**	**14.1**	**24.2**	**29.2**	**24.6**	**32.0**
Labor	11.8	22.5	6.6	18.5	32.4	11.5
Employment	...	...	...	5.1	7.7	4.0
Hours	−11.3	−16.2	−7.8	−12.8	−18.3	−9.0
Average hours	−25.1	−45.1	−13.9	−28.2	−50.0	−16.0
Efficiency offset	9.7	23.2	2.5	10.8	25.4	2.9
Intergroup shift offset	4.1	5.6	3.7	4.6	6.3	4.1
Age-sex composition	−2.6	0.0	−4.1	−3.1	0.0	−4.5
Education	21.0	27.5	17.2	24.6	31.7	19.7
Unallocated	4.6	11.3	1.2	4.6	11.3	1.2
Capital	11.3	−4.9	19.7	13.3	−4.2	22.5
Inventories	1.5	0.0	2.5	2.1	0.7	3.3
Nonresidential structures and equipment	2.6	−6.3	7.4	4.1	−6.3	9.4
Dwellings	6.7	2.1	9.0	6.7	2.1	9.0
International assets	0.5	−0.7	0.8	0.5	−0.7	0.8
Land	−2.6	−3.5	−2.0	−2.6	−3.5	−2.0
Output per unit of input	**79.5**	**85.9**	**75.8**	**70.8**	**75.4**	**68.0**
Advances in knowledge and n.e.c.[a]	46.2	42.3	47.5	53.3	49.3	54.5
Improved resource allocation	14.9	21.1	12.3	16.9	23.9	14.3
Farm	12.8	19.0	9.4	14.4	21.8	11.1
Nonfarm self-employment	2.1	2.1	2.9	2.6	2.1	3.3
Dwellings occupancy ratio	0.5	1.4	−0.4	0.5	1.4	−0.4
Economies of scale	17.9	20.4	16.8	...	...	...
Irregular factors	0.0	0.7	−0.4	0.0	0.7	−0.4
Weather in farming	0.0	0.7	−0.4	0.0	0.7	−0.4
Labor disputes	0.0	0.0	0.0	0.0	0.0	0.0

Source: Derived from Tables 9-7 and R-7.
a. n.e.c. Not elsewhere classified.

Five positive groups of sources and one that is negative are dominant. Economies of scale were the third biggest source over the whole period, and the fourth biggest in the postwar years, when the size of markets is classified as a separate determinant of output. With their contribution allocated, the number of large positive growth sources is reduced to four.

When economies of scale are thus allocated, advances in knowledge are seen to be responsible for more than half of the growth of potential output per worker in both periods. Increased education per worker was the second biggest growth source over the whole period, contributing one-fourth of the total, and the third biggest postwar source, contributing one-fifth of the total. The shift of labor from farming and nonfarm self-employment to nonfarm wage and salary employment and the increase in capital per person employed were the third and fourth largest growth sources over the period as a whole. In the postwar years alone, capital stood second only to advances in knowledge. Much of the capital contribution in both periods represents the increase in the services provided by the stock of dwellings as distinguished from capital used in conjunction with labor to produce output in nonresidential business.

The main negative source was the decline in labor input per worker as a result of reductions in working hours and in the proportion of total hours that were worked by adult males. The increase in part-time employment, which was especially large in the postwar years, contributed to both of these developments.[18]

18. A partial offset was provided by the "unallocated" component which reflects shifts in the composition of employment in general government, households, and institutions.

Growth of Total Output in Shorter Periods

Tables 9-9 and 9-10 provide estimates of the sources of growth of total actual national income and total potential national income, respectively, in the five shorter periods into which the forty-year time span covered by this study is divided. The estimates for potential national income in the three postwar periods are examined first.[19]

Potential National Income

It will be recalled from Chapter 7 that each year's estimate of total potential national income was obtained by adding or subtracting from actual national income a direct estimate of the amount by which the divergence between actual and potential conditions caused actual national income to

19. I shall omit a discussion of the prewar short periods because it would largely duplicate material in Chapter 8.

differ from potential national income in that year. Examination of the resulting series for potential national income showed that it rose much faster in the early and late postwar periods than in the middle postwar period, and that 1953 and 1964 rather clearly were the dividing points. The choice of 1948–53, 1953–64, and 1964–69 periods for analysis was based on this finding. The estimates show that the growth rate of potential national income dropped from 4.99 percent a year in 1948–53 to 3.20 percent in 1953–64, or by more than one-third, and then jumped by one-half, to 4.85 percent a year, in 1964–69. This is not at all the pattern implied by other estimates of potential output, which imply a moderate and gradual rise in the growth rate.

In discussing Table 9-10 I shall, of course, be concerned with isolating the growth sources responsible for these remarkable changes in the growth rate of potential output. But I shall also

Table 9-9. Sources of Growth of Total Actual National Income, Five Shorter Periods, 1929–69
Contributions to growth rate in percentage points

	1929–41[a]	1941–48[a]	1948–53	1953–64	1964–69
National income	2.34	3.44	4.54	3.23	4.54
Total factor input	1.26	1.92	2.95	1.30	3.08
Labor	1.29	1.52	2.07	0.60	2.15
Employment	0.83	1.40	1.63	0.51	2.26
Hours	−0.19	−0.33	−0.08	−0.24	−0.27
Average hours	−0.69	−0.58	−0.32	−0.35	−0.45
Efficiency offset	0.45	0.12	0.13	0.04	0.07
Intergroup shift offset	0.05	0.13	0.11	0.07	0.11
Age-sex composition	0.04	−0.04	0.07	−0.09	−0.31
Education	0.45	0.31	0.38	0.43	0.40
Unallocated	0.16	0.18	0.07	−0.01	0.07
Capital	−0.03	0.40	0.88	0.70	0.93
Inventories	0.02	0.12	0.18	0.08	0.18
Nonresidential structures and equipment	−0.03	0.12	0.38	0.29	0.45
Dwellings	0.01	0.14	0.31	0.27	0.29
International assets	−0.03	0.02	0.01	0.06	0.01
Land	0.00	0.00	0.00	0.00	0.00
Output per unit of input	1.08	1.52	1.59	1.93	1.46
Advances in knowledge and n.e.c.[b]	0.46	0.86	1.34	1.13	1.15
Improved resource allocation	0.22	0.42	0.41	0.24	0.34
Farm	0.19	0.42	0.33	0.21	0.19
Nonfarm self-employment	0.03	0.00	0.08	0.03	0.15
Dwellings occupancy ratio	0.01	0.03	−0.03	−0.01	0.01
Economies of scale	0.19	0.45	0.48	0.32	0.56
Irregular factors	0.20	−0.24	−0.61	0.25	−0.60
Weather in farming	−0.01	0.04	−0.03	−0.02	0.02
Labor disputes	0.00	0.00	0.00	0.00	−0.01
Intensity of demand	0.21	−0.28	−0.58	0.27	−0.61

Sources: Table 9-1; contributions derived from Tables 3-3, 3-5, 3-7, and R-2.
a. Based on data excluding work relief employees.
b. n.e.c. Not elsewhere classified.

show that the sources of growth estimates and the data behind them strongly support the estimated changes in the growth rate itself.

COMPARISON OF 1964–69 AND 1953–64 PERIODS. Table 9-11, column 4, shows, in full detail, the amount by which the contribution of each determinant to growth of potential national income in 1964–69 exceeded its contribution in 1953–64. The estimates tell a remarkably simple story. The growth of potential output was so much greater in 1964–69 because labor and capital input increased much more and therefore contributed much more to the growth rate. Of the total difference of 1.65 percentage points in the growth rate, 1.02 percentage points were directly attributable to labor, and 1.00 points of this amount to employment alone. An addition of 0.25 points was directly attributable to capital. The only other sizable increase, 0.26 points, was in the contribution of economies of scale, and this is a reflection of the

faster expansion of markets made possible by the accelerated growth of labor and capital.

How do these results support the belief that the very sharp rise in the growth rate of potential output that I have estimated to have occurred actually did happen? The following points are germane.

1. Of the rise of 1.65 percentage points in the growth rate, 1.60 points are ascribable to the determinants whose contributions are estimated directly and only 0.05 points to the residual estimate for "advances in knowledge and n.e.c." Hence, the rise in the growth rate of potential output implied by the direct estimates is barely different from that which would be independently obtained by an analysis of changes in output determinants over the period. Put differently, it is almost identical with the rise that could have been projected in 1964 if one had perfectly foreseen the changes in the economy for which information

Table 9-10. Sources of Growth of Total Potential National Income, Five Shorter Periods, 1929–69
Contributions to growth rate in percentage points

	1929–41	1941–48	1948–53	1953–64	1964–69
National income	**2.63**	**2.96**	**4.99**	**3.20**	**4.85**
Total factor input	**1.64**	**1.35**	**2.84**	**1.52**	**2.79**
Labor	1.66	0.95	1.94	0.83	1.85
Employment	1.35	0.60	1.40	0.81	1.81
Hours	−0.22	−0.26	−0.06	−0.24	−0.24
Average hours	−0.76	−0.45	−0.27	−0.38	−0.36
Efficiency offset	0.46	0.11	0.12	0.05	0.04
Intergroup shift offset	0.08	0.08	0.09	0.09	0.08
Age-sex composition	−0.03	0.06	0.13	−0.14	−0.22
Education	0.40	0.37	0.40	0.41	0.43
Unallocated	0.16	0.18	0.07	−0.01	0.07
Capital	−0.02	0.40	0.90	0.69	0.94
Inventories	0.03	0.12	0.18	0.07	0.18
Nonresidential structures and equipment	−0.03	0.12	0.39	0.28	0.46
Dwellings	0.01	0.14	0.32	0.28	0.29
International assets	−0.03	0.02	0.01	0.06	0.01
Land	**0.00**	**0.00**	**0.00**	**0.00**	**0.00**
Output per unit of input	**0.99**	**1.61**	**2.15**	**1.68**	**2.06**
Advances in knowledge and n.e.c.[a]	0.46	0.86	1.36	1.12	1.17
Improved resource allocation	0.34	0.23	0.36	0.28	0.30
Farm	0.26	0.30	0.32	0.22	0.18
Nonfarm self-employment	0.08	−0.07	0.04	0.06	0.12
Dwellings occupancy ratio	0.01	0.03	−0.03	−0.01	0.01
Economies of scale	0.19	0.45	0.49	0.31	0.57
Irregular factors	−0.01	0.04	−0.03	−0.02	0.01
Weather in farming	−0.01	0.04	−0.03	−0.02	0.02
Labor disputes	0.00	0.00	0.00	0.00	−0.01

Sources: Table 9-1; contributions from Tables R-4 and R-5.
a. n.e.c. Not elsewhere classified.

Table 9-11. Sources of Differences between Postwar Shorter-Period Growth Rates of Total Actual and Potential National Income
Differences in contributions in percentage points

	Actual national income		Potential national income	
	1948–53 less 1953–64 (1)	1964–69 less 1953–64 (2)	1948–53 less 1953–64 (3)	1964–69 less 1953–64 (4)
Total national income	1.31	1.31	1.79	1.65
Total factor input	1.65	1.78	1.32	1.27
Labor	1.47	1.55	1.11	1.02
Employment	1.12	1.75	0.59	1.00
Hours	0.16	−0.03	0.18	0.00
Average hours	0.03	−0.10	0.11	0.02
Efficiency offset	0.09	0.03	0.07	−0.01
Intergroup shift offset	0.04	0.04	0.00	−0.01
Age-sex composition	0.16	−0.22	0.27	−0.08
Education	−0.05	−0.03	−0.01	0.02
Unallocated	0.08	0.08	0.08	0.08
Capital	0.18	0.23	0.21	0.25
Inventories	0.10	0.10	0.11	0.11
Nonresidential structures and equipment	0.09	0.16	0.11	0.18
Dwellings	0.04	0.02	0.04	0.01
International assets	−0.05	−0.05	−0.05	−0.05
Land	0.00	0.00	0.00	0.00
Output per unit of input	−0.34	−0.47	0.47	0.38
Advances in knowledge and n.e.c.[a]	0.21	0.02	0.24	0.05
Improved resource allocation	0.17	0.10	0.08	0.02
Farm	0.12	−0.02	0.10	−0.04
Nonfarm self-employment	0.05	0.12	−0.02	0.06
Dwellings occupancy ratio	−0.02	0.02	−0.02	0.02
Economies of scale	0.16	0.24	0.18	0.26
Irregular factors	−0.86	−0.85	−0.01	0.03
Weather in farming	−0.01	0.04	−0.01	0.04
Labor disputes	0.00	−0.01	0.00	−0.01
Intensity of demand	−0.85	−0.88	. . .	. . .

Sources: Derived from Tables 9-9 and 9-10.
a. n.e.c. Not elsewhere classified.

is available in retrospect. The remaining points discuss the changes in labor and capital which were responsible for the change in the growth rate.

2. Employment was the main source of accelerated growth. The estimate that employment contributed one percentage point more to the growth rate of potential output in 1964–69 than in 1953–64 is derived from an estimate that the growth rate of the potential labor force jumped by 1.34 percentage points: from 1.07 in 1953–64 to 2.41 in 1964–69.[20] The finding that there was a great acceleration in growth of the potential labor force is inescapable if one relies on establishment data for employment. Although estima-

tion of the potential labor force requires adjustment of the actual labor force, the years compared were not so different with respect to employment opportunities as to make the adjustment dominate the movement. The growth rate of George Perry's actual labor force aged 16 and over (which is consistent with my data) accelerated by 1.66 points (from 0.90 percent per year in 1953–64 to 2.56 in 1964–69).[21] His reduction of the change to 1.34 points on a potential basis seems

20. In this and following calculations the effect of adding Alaska and Hawaii to labor force data is eliminated by linking.

21. Perry's actual and potential labor force series are discussed in Appendix Q. They appear in "Labor Force Structure, Potential Output, and Productivity," in *Brookings Papers on Economic Activity* (3:1971), p. 563. The growth rate of the Current Population Survey series for the actual labor force (including 14- and 15-year-olds) shows a smaller, though still sizable, rise of 0.99 points. Appendix C explains why I think establishment employment data should be preferred over CPS data for time series analysis, espe-

entirely adequate to allow for labor force response to employment opportunities. About 0.51 points of the 1.34 point rise in the growth rate of the potential labor force could have been expected from population movements alone.[22] The rest reflected changing labor force participation rates. These were in accordance with observed trends. The rise of 1.34 points from 1953–64 to 1964–69 in the growth rate of Perry's potential labor force, which is based on direct adjustment of each year's actual data for labor force response to unemployment, compares with a rise of 1.37 points in his series for the "trend" labor force.

Two points may be noted about other labor input components. Reference to Table 9-3 shows that 0.08 percentage points of the rise in the growth rate stemmed from measured output per worker in general government, households, and institutions. This figure is based directly on the OBE data for actual output, so its accuracy as a component of the change observed in the measured growth rate can hardly be questioned. The net effect of my refinements of employment to measure labor input in nonresidential business was to reduce the jump in the contribution of labor input by 0.06 points; the accelerated decline in the age-sex index more than accounted for this change.

3. The other large change from 1953–64 to 1964–69 was in the contribution of capital. This increased by 0.25 percentage points, about one-fourth as much as the contribution of labor. The contribution of international assets dropped 0.05 points and that of dwellings increased by 0.01 points; both figures are based directly upon the OBE data that enter the output measure. The contribution of capital used in nonresidential business increased by 0.29 points, divided between inventories (0.11) and nonresidential structures and equipment (0.18). The capital potentially available for business use in any year is the capital stock actually present, so it is necessary only to look at estimates of the capital stock to confirm that a sharp acceleration in the growth of the

stock occurred.[23] The OBE data I have used show the following growth rates.

	Inventories	*Nonresidential structures and equipment*	
		Gross stock	*Net stock*
1953–64	2.38	3.09	3.31
1964–69	5.24	4.49	5.36
Increase	2.86	1.40	2.05

All other capital stock estimates of which I am aware also show a sharp acceleration in the rate of accumulation between these periods and the fact of such an acceleration has never, to my knowledge, been questioned. Unless capital is completely disregarded as an output determinant, one must conclude that changes in the capital stock were much more favorable to growth in 1964–69 than in 1953–64.[24]

Since labor and capital both increased much more rapidly in 1964–69 than in 1953–64, total factor input must also have done so, regardless of the selection of weights to combine them.

COMPARISON OF 1948–53 AND 1953–64 PERIODS. The growth rate of potential national income was also high in 1948–53, exceeding the 1953–64 rate by 1.79 percentage points. Differences between these two periods in the contributions of the sources are detailed in the third column of Table 9-11.

Most—1.11 percentage points—of the difference is again in labor input, but only 0.59 points of this amount stemmed from the growth rate of potential employment. The growth rate of the potential labor force was 1.69 in 1948–53 and 1.07 in 1953–64. The difference of 0.62 points

---

cially for use in conjunction with national income or product data.

22. For this calculation the population was divided into eighteen age-sex groups, and the 1957 ratio of potential employment to population for each group was multiplied by population each year. The growth rate of this standardized series was 1.09 in 1953–64 and 1.60 in 1964–69. Age groups used were: 14–15, 16–17, 18–19, 20–24, 25–34, 35–54, 55–64, 65–69, and 70 and over.

23. The question as to whether the capital stock would have changed differently if the ratio of actual to potential output had been different is relevant to a discussion of why potential output changed as it did but not to a discussion of how much it actually changed and what made it change.

24. Capital grew more and contributed more to growth in both the 1948–53 and 1964–69 periods of fast growth than in 1953–64, and the ratio of net investment to net national product, measured in 1958 prices, happened also to be higher. Net investment averaged 9.8 percent of net national product in 1948–52, 6.8 percent in 1953–63, and 7.5 percent in 1964–68. (The last year of each of my periods is omitted in this calculation because investment made during that year has only a limited effect on the year's output.) However, the temporal relationship between the net investment ratio and the growth rate of capital stock is indirect, partial, and tenuous. There is no reason to expect a close relationship between the two magnitudes in short periods. See *Why Growth Rates Differ,* especially pp. 121–22 and 138–39. (For full citation see Chap. 1, note 2, of this book.)

between the periods compares with differences of 0.68 points for Perry's potential labor force aged 16 and over, 0.77 points for his actual labor force, and 0.77 points for his "trend" labor force.[25] The difference between the periods is due to labor force participation rates rather than to population movements.

Table 9-3 shows that, of the remaining difference of 0.52 points between the labor contributions in the two periods, 0.10 percentage points stemmed from the OBE estimates of output per worker in general government, households, and institutions and 0.42 from my estimates of potential labor input per worker in nonresidential business. Of the latter amount 0.27 points resulted from changes in the age-sex composition of hours worked, which were strongly favorable in 1948–53 and unfavorable in 1953–64, and 0.16 points from the hours component, which deducted less in the earlier period than in 1953–64.

Capital contributed 0.21 points more in 1948–53 than in 1953–64. A smaller contribution from international assets was almost offset by a larger contribution from dwellings. The difference arising from nonresidential business capital was 0.22 points. Capital stock in the sector was growing much faster in the earlier period. The growth rate of the stock of inventories was 1.73 points higher in 1948–53 than in 1953–64 while growth rates of the gross and net stock of nonresidential structures and equipment were higher by 0.53 and 1.49 percentage points, respectively.

Though labor and capital accounted for the bulk of the difference between the two periods, especially when their effects on economies of scale are included, Table 9-11 shows that the contributions of various other components also differed between the two periods. However, of the total difference of 1.79 points, the directly estimated components accounted for 1.55 points, or 86 percent. Consequently, the sharp drop from 1948–53 to 1953–64 in the growth rate of potential national income implied by the estimates obtained in Chapter 7 is confirmed (like the rise after 1964) by analysis of the sources of growth. The size of the difference in the residual estimate is only 0.24 points.

In summary, sources of growth analysis over time provides an explanation for the changes in the growth rate of potential national income that were derived in Chapter 7 by direct adjustment of each year's actual national income to potential conditions.

Actual National Income

Actual national income differs from potential national income for two broad reasons. Actual labor input and resource allocation differ, and output per unit of input differs because of intensity of utilization of employed resources. For each postwar year, Figure 9-2 shows the percentage by which actual national income differed from potential national income for each of these reasons. Between any pair of years chosen at random the two reasons are almost as likely to affect the growth rate of actual output in opposite directions as in the same direction. This was the case in all three of the postwar short periods.

Changes in the proportion of potential labor input that was in use together with the related change in the relation of actual to potential resource allocation were favorable to growth of actual national income in both 1948–53 and 1964–69 and unfavorable in 1953–64. However, the pattern of changes in the intensity of utilization of employed labor and capital was just the opposite and these changes were much more important, as the following reconciliation of growth rates shows:[26]

	1948–53	1953–64	1964–69
Actual national income	4.54	3.23	4.54
Potential national income	4.99	3.20	4.85
Difference, by source: Total	−0.44	0.03	−0.31
Input	0.11	−0.22	0.29
Resource allocation	0.05	−0.04	0.04
Intensity of utilization, employed resources	−0.58	0.27	−0.61

For this reason the 1948–53 and 1964–69 growth rates of actual national income exceeded the 1953–64 rate somewhat less than in the case of potential national income. The differences were nevertheless very large, with the growth rate in both 1948–53 and 1964–69 exceeding that in 1953–64 by 1.31 percentage points.

The contributions of the sources to the growth rates of actual national income in all the shorter periods are detailed in Table 9-9 and presented

---

25. The difference of 0.77 points for the actual labor force compares with a difference of only 0.20 points in the growth rate of the CPS labor force series which, as indicated before, should not be used with national income and product data.

26. Detail under "difference, by source" does not equal totals because of the effects of interaction, rounding, and forcing on growth sources not shown.

Figure 9-2. Percentage Divergence of Actual from Potential National Income by Broad Source, 1947–69

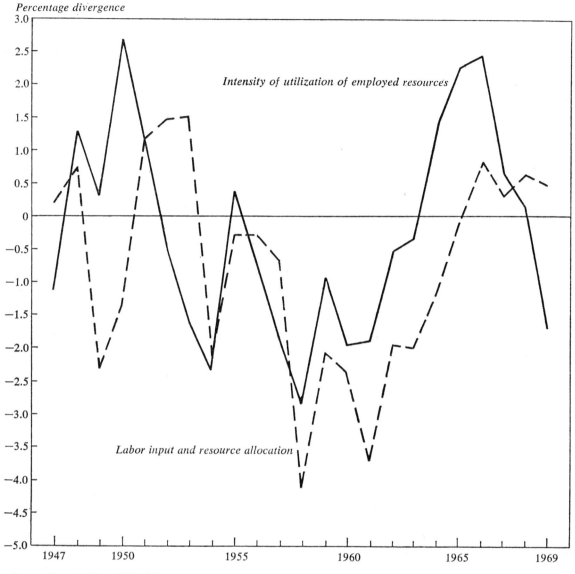

Percentage divergence

Intensity of utilization of employed resources

Labor input and resource allocation

Source: Computed from Table 7-1.

graphically in Figure 9-3. The first two columns of Table 9-11 show differences between the postwar short period growth rates by detailed source.

Growth of Output per Person Employed in Shorter Periods

Sources of growth of actual national income per person employed in shorter periods are shown in

Table 9-12 (page 146) and those of potential national income per person potentially employed in Table 9-13 (page 147). Both reveal interesting patterns.

Comparison of 1964–69 and 1953–64 Periods

The growth rate of potential output per person potentially employed, in contrast to that of total potential output, was only moderately (0.27 per-

Figure 9-3. Contributions to Growth Rates of Total Actual National Income, Five Shorter Periods, 1929–69

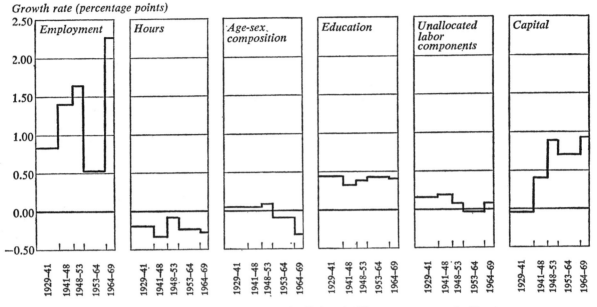

Source: Computed from Table 9-9.   a. n.e.c. Not elsewhere classified.   b. Effect on output per unit of input.

centage points) higher in 1964–69 than in 1953–64 (Table 9-13, page 147).

On a net basis, almost all (0.24 percentage points) of the increase was due to economies of scale resulting from the faster increase in *total* labor and capital input. The growth of neither labor nor capital input per person employed changed much. Among the labor input components, the contributions of hours and education scarcely changed. That of age-sex composition fell by 0.08 points, and that of the "unallocated" component, reflecting compositional shifts in general government, households, and institutions, increased by an offsetting 0.08 points. The total contribution of the capital components actually fell a little, by 0.05 percentage points, despite a modest increase of 0.08 points in the contribution of capital used in the nonresidential business sector. The switch from a sharp increase to a decline in net income from abroad per person employed subtracted 0.07 percentage points, while the contribution of dwellings income per person employed dropped 0.06 points as the increase in employment accelerated. The faster increase in potential wage and salary employment in 1964–69 did, however, yield a gain from reallocation of labor from nonfarm self-employment that was larger by 0.06 points than it was in 1953–64 and restrict

the decline in the contribution of the shift from farming to 0.04 points.

Actual national income per person employed grew much *less* in 1964–69 than in 1953–64 (Table 9-12). The growth rate fell 0.94 percentage points, or 37 percent. The effect of fluctuations in the intensity of demand on output per unit of input—the "cyclical" factor in productivity—was mainly responsible. It added 0.27 points to the 1953–64 growth rate and subtracted 0.60 points in 1964–69. Even if the effect of this determinant were eliminated, however, the growth rate of actual national income per person employed would have dropped a bit (0.07 percentage points) whereas the growth rate of potential national income per person potentially employed rose by 0.27 points. There are two chief reasons for this remaining difference, both consequences of the fact that unemployment and the associated "labor force gap" rose from 1953 to 1964 and fell from 1964 to 1969. First, an increase in the numbers of unemployed and "discouraged" workers raises labor input per person employed while a decrease in their numbers reduces it because these groups, combined, represent less potential labor input per worker (as measured by education, age-sex composition, and hours) than do the employed. Second, the fact that actual employment rose less

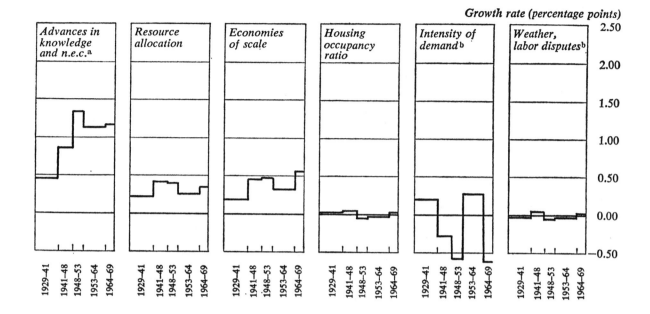

Growth rate (percentage points)

than potential employment from 1953 to 1964 and more from 1964 to 1969 automatically meant that capital and land input per person employed rose more on an actual than a potential basis in the earlier period and less in the later period. A partial offset occurs in the resource allocation components, which are favorably affected by fast growth of nonfarm wage and salary employment. Comparison of Tables 9-12 and 9-13 shows that of the difference of 0.34 percentage points between the changes in actual and potential national income per person employed that were not due to intensity of utilization, 0.22 stemmed from labor, 0.15 from capital and land, and −0.08 from resource reallocation.

Comparison of 1948–53 and 1953–64 Periods

In contrast to 1964–69, the high growth rate of total potential national income in 1948–53 was accompanied by a high growth rate of potential national income per person potentially employed. This is not unexpected since it has already been observed that employment itself was responsible to a much smaller extent for the fast growth of total potential output in 1948–53 than in 1953–64.

At 3.21, the growth rate of potential output per worker in 1948–53 was far above the 1953–64 rate of 2.12. Several determinants contributed sizably to the difference of 1.09 percentage points.

Labor input per worker potentially employed was responsible for 0.52 points, almost half of the total, with hours, age-sex composition, and the "unallocated" component all contributing importantly. Capital per worker potentially employed was responsible for 0.14 points of the difference, "advances in knowledge and n.e.c." for 0.23 points, improved resource allocation for 0.09, and economies of scale for 0.17; other sources provided small offsets.

The growth rate of *actual* national income per person employed was nevertheless slightly (0.05 percentage points) lower in 1948–53 than in 1953–64. This was only because of the decisive effect of changes in intensity of demand upon output per unit of input. In the absence of demand-related changes in productivity, the growth rate of actual national income per person employed would have been 0.78 points higher in 1948–53 than in 1953–64. This was less than the difference observed for potential national income per person potentially employed (1.09 points) for the same reasons that the comparable difference was smaller between 1964–69 and 1953–64.

Prewar Estimates

I shall comment upon the short period estimates prior to 1948 only to the extent of noting how small the growth rate of potential national

Table 9-12. Sources of Growth of Actual National Income per Person Employed, Five Shorter Periods, 1929–69
Contributions to growth rate in percentage points

	1929–41[a]	*1941–48*[a]	*1948–53*	*1953–64*	*1964–69*
National income per person employed	**1.36**	**1.65**	**2.46**	**2.51**	**1.57**
Total factor input	**0.29**	**0.16**	**0.92**	**0.60**	**0.15**
Labor	0.46	0.12	0.44	0.09	−0.11
Hours	−0.19	−0.33	−0.08	−0.24	−0.27
Average hours	−0.69	−0.58	−0.32	−0.35	−0.45
Efficiency offset	0.45	0.12	0.13	0.04	0.07
Intergroup shift offset	0.05	0.13	0.11	0.07	0.11
Age-sex composition	0.04	−0.04	0.07	−0.09	−0.31
Education	0.45	0.31	0.38	0.43	0.40
Unallocated	0.16	0.18	0.07	−0.01	0.07
Capital	−0.14	0.11	0.55	0.53	0.35
Inventories	−0.01	0.04	0.09	0.05	0.07
Nonresidential structures and equipment	−0.09	−0.05	0.19	0.20	0.16
Dwellings	−0.01	0.11	0.27	0.23	0.14
International assets	−0.03	0.01	0.00	0.05	−0.02
Land	−0.03	−0.07	−0.07	−0.02	−0.09
Output per unit of input	**1.07**	**1.49**	**1.54**	**1.91**	**1.42**
Advances in knowledge and n.e.c.[b]	0.46	0.84	1.30	1.12	1.13
Improved resource allocation	0.21	0.41	0.39	0.23	0.33
Farm	0.18	0.41	0.32	0.21	0.18
Nonfarm self-employment	0.03	0.00	0.07	0.02	0.15
Dwellings occupancy ratio	0.01	0.03	−0.03	−0.01	0.01
Economies of scale	0.19	0.44	0.47	0.32	0.54
Irregular factors	0.20	−0.23	−0.59	0.25	−0.59
Weather in farming	−0.01	0.04	−0.03	−0.02	0.02
Labor disputes	0.00	0.00	0.00	0.00	−0.01
Intensity of demand	0.21	−0.27	−0.56	0.27	−0.60

Sources: Table 9-1; contributions are derived from Tables 2-2, 3-2, 3-3, 3-4, 3-6, 5-4, 6-1, 6-4, and J-2.
a. Based on data excluding work relief employees.
b. n.e.c. Not elsewhere classified.

income per person potentially employed was in 1929–41. At 0.94 percent per annum, it was less than half that experienced in any subsequent period—despite relatively large contributions from labor and resource allocation. In comparison with 1953–64, the period with the next lowest growth rate, labor input contributed 0.29 points more and resource allocation 0.08 percentage points more in 1929–41, but capital and land contributed 0.81 points less, "advances in knowledge and n.e.c." 0.65 points less, and economies of scale 0.12 points less.

The Roles of Demand and War

An examination of sources of growth by the use of a classification such as that adopted in this study has often been described as an analysis from the "supply side." This description is, of course, wholly accurate if it means that such a study provides no information as to the reasons that demand for the nation's output is strong in some periods and weak in others. That is quite a different subject from growth analysis. If a study of growth can contribute to it at all, it is only incidentally, by providing information that may be useful or suggestive for such an analysis. This study attempts, however, to contribute to demand management policy in a different way. It shows in Chapter 7 how sources of growth analysis can be used to develop improved estimates of the gap between actual and potential output, so that policymakers are better able to judge the direction in which demand should be influenced and by how much.

A type of question that is pertinent to growth analysis is: How has the strength of demand (regardless of the factors governing it) affected growth? The time period the questioner has in mind must determine the line of inquiry.

This study has attacked short-run demand as-

Table 9-13. Sources of Growth of Potential National Income per Person Potentially Employed, Five Shorter Periods, 1929–69

Contributions to growth rate in percentage points

	1929–41	*1941–48*	*1948–53*	*1953–64*	*1964–69*
National income	**0.94**	**2.24**	**3.21**	**2.12**	**2.39**
Total factor input	**−0.04**	**0.64**	**1.11**	**0.48**	**0.40**
Labor	0.31	0.35	0.54	0.02	0.04
Hours	−0.22	−0.26	−0.06	−0.24	−0.24
Average hours	−0.76	−0.45	−0.27	−0.38	−0.36
Efficiency offset	0.46	0.11	0.12	0.05	0.04
Intergroup shift offset	0.08	0.08	0.09	0.09	0.08
Age-sex composition	−0.03	0.06	0.13	−0.14	−0.22
Education	0.40	0.37	0.40	0.41	0.43
Unallocated	0.16	0.18	0.07	−0.01	0.07
Capital	−0.28	0.31	0.63	0.49	0.44
Inventories	−0.04	0.10	0.11	0.04	0.09
Nonresidential structures and equipment	−0.18	0.06	0.23	0.18	0.21
Dwellings	−0.02	0.13	0.29	0.22	0.16
International assets	−0.04	0.02	0.00	0.05	−0.02
Land	−0.07	−0.02	−0.06	−0.03	−0.08
Output per unit of input	**0.98**	**1.60**	**2.10**	**1.64**	**1.99**
Advances in knowledge and n.e.c.[a]	0.45	0.86	1.33	1.10	1.14
Improved resource allocation	0.34	0.22	0.35	0.26	0.28
Farm	0.26	0.30	0.31	0.21	0.17
Nonfarm self-employment	0.08	−0.08	0.04	0.05	0.11
Dwellings occupancy ratio	0.01	0.03	−0.03	−0.01	0.01
Economies of scale	0.19	0.45	0.48	0.31	0.55
Irregular factors	−0.01	0.04	−0.03	−0.02	0.01
Weather in farming	−0.01	0.04	−0.03	−0.02	0.02
Labor disputes	0.00	0.00	0.00	0.00	−0.01

Sources: Table 9-1; contributions are derived from Tables 3-2, 3-3, 3-4, 3-6, 5-4, 6-1, 6-4, 7-3, J-2, and R-1.
a. n.e.c. Not elsewhere classified.

pects directly and comprehensively. Provision of annual series for both potential and actual output permits the growth rate between any two dates to be divided into the amount that is due to the growth of potential output and the amount that is due to differences between the years compared with respect to the level of, and pattern of short-term changes in, demand pressure. The latter amount can be further divided, by use of Table 7-1, between the effects of demand pressures upon output per unit of input and upon labor input. Finally, in eight time periods, the tables showing sources of growth for actual and potential national income in this and the preceding chapter permit this amount to be divided in much more detail both for the whole economy and for the nonresidential business sector.

One may also inquire as to the effect of demand pressures during periods of intermediate length (such as the five to twelve years covered by my shorter periods) upon the growth rate of potential output itself. Does potential output grow more over such periods if the ratio of actual output to potential output is high or if it is low? In Chapter 7 I noted that periods of fast growth of potential output corresponded to periods in which this ratio was high. The tables in this chapter, particularly Tables 9-10 and 9-11, show that most of the postwar variation in the growth rate of potential output was due to fluctuations in the rate of change of labor input and other determinants which appear to be largely independent of this ratio.[27] Most of the variation in the growth rate of potential output cannot, I therefore conclude, be ascribed to strength or weakness of demand during these periods. But Table 9-10 does show that capital also played a role in these postwar fluctuations in the growth rate of potential output and

27. It has been argued that strong demand for labor attracts marginal workers into the labor force and they remain in the labor force after demand again weakens, so that strong demand has a cumulative and lasting effect on the size of the labor force. There probably is such an effect, but I would not give it much emphasis as an explanation of postwar developments.

capital was, of course, of dominant importance in explaining the very low 1929–41 growth rate. Some of the postwar fluctuation in the capital contribution is presumably associated with changes in the growth rate of potential labor input and other determinants of potential output itself, but an important part is surely due to differences in the strength of demand, whatever their origin. The fact that 1948–53 and 1964–69 were, on the whole, boom periods while 1953–64 was not contributed to the differences in the rate of capital accumulation in these periods. The negative contribution of capital in 1929–41 was even more obviously the direct consequence of the depression.[28] It is largely because of capital that I conclude that, within the range observed, a high ratio of actual to potential output has been favorable to growth of potential national income over intermediate time periods.[29] But I do not regard the amount involved as very large except in disastrous periods like the Great Depression.

Moreover, it should not be supposed that it is obvious that a continuously high rate of utilization is favorable to growth of potential output, because there is at least one well-known chain of causation which operates in a different fashion. The American economy relies upon competition among firms to secure efficient operation. Both the carrot of profit and the stick of loss, which also entails a threat of forced cessation of a firm's operations or replacement of its management, are prime movers of the business economy. Recessions reinforce the stick powerfully, if temporarily, by making profits hard to earn and losses common. To a degree they may substitute for strong interfirm competition. It is a commonplace observation that it is during recessions that firms pay strictest attention to costs and tighten up operations. Improvements and economies instituted then persist into the future recovery. This point, it should be observed, suggests that *fluctuations* in business activity, not a low *average* level of activity, are favorable to growth. It may well be that the demand pattern most conducive to long-term growth is one in which actual output averages close to potential output but fluctuates about it, with occasional periods of short but fairly sharp recession. Such a pattern would have described the actual postwar experience of the United States had it not been for the abortion of the 1959–60 recovery.[30]

This last observation, however, verges on expression of a judgment with respect to a question upon which this study does not pretend to throw much light: What is the effect of demand upon growth in the long run? Its meaning can be illustrated in extreme form by asking another question: If the 1930s had been a period of prosperity rather than depression, would today's total national income, national income per worker, and national income per capita be higher, the same, or lower than they are? But the effect of variations in demand pressure within a range much narrower than would include the 1930s is, of course, of greater practical interest. If historical analysis can illuminate this question at all, it is only by examination and comparison of a number of countries over very long time spans.[31]

In Chapter 7 I observed that postwar periods of high growth of potential output coincided not only with a high ratio of actual to potential output but also with periods of hostilities and rising defense expenditures. I suggested that, if the connection were more than random, it must be because

---

28. The sustained high unemployment of the 1930s presumably had other unfavorable effects on the growth rate of potential output from 1929 to 1941. It encouraged laws and practices to promote employment at the expense of efficiency. It meant loss of experience on the part of employed persons who later returned to employment. The very low level of gross capital formation may have impeded introduction of more efficient methods. I doubt that postwar fluctuations were of sufficient size to have had quantitatively important effects of these types.

29. Associations in the postwar periods suggest that the growth rate of potential output is likely to affect the ratio of actual to potential output just as the latter ratio may affect the potential growth rate. Thus changes in potential employment were the biggest determinant of changes in the growth rate of potential output between postwar periods. Postwar periods of rapid growth of potential employment were periods of even faster growth of actual employment, and fast growth of employment was accompanied by fast growth of capital stock, which reinforced the growth of potential national income. Fast growth of employment is conducive to an accompanying strong demand for capital to equip the extra workers, and a strong demand for capital is favorable to a strong aggregate demand situation.

30. Had it followed the pattern of other postwar recoveries, the 1959–60 recovery would have proceeded until actual output reached or exceeded potential output and it would have been followed by a period of high output. Instead, business turned down in 1960 before output had approached potential, and the next recovery did not bring actual output up to the potential level until 1964.

31. The Social Science Research Council has sponsored such a study, with strong emphasis upon demand. The first two of the analyses for individual countries have appeared in print: Jean-Jacques Carré, Paul Dubois, and Edmond Malinvaud, *La Croissance française: Un essai d'analyse économique causale de l'après-guerre* (Paris: Editions du Seuil, 1972); and Kazushi Ohkawa and Henry Rosovsky, *Japanese Economic Growth: Trend Acceleration in the Twentieth Century* (Stanford University Press and Oxford University Press, 1973).

these were also periods in which fears of inflation were overridden by the greater fear, or the impossibility, of raising taxes quickly enough and sufficiently to offset the expansionary effects of rising defense outlays; the extra expansion of demand then contributed to high capital and labor utilization which in turn stimulated investment.

It is possible that changes in the size of the armed forces may also have played a role. The analytical basis for this suspicion is Clarence Long's finding that in World War II expansion of the armed forces by use of the draft raised the labor force participation rate sharply.[32] Some draftees themselves would not otherwise have been in the labor force, while the departure of others from their families, often with a curtailment of earnings, and sometimes with a reduction in births, caused wives and other dependents to enter the labor force. A reduction in the armed forces presumably had the opposite consequences, reinforced by benefits available to veterans for education which reduced labor force participation. If the same process operated during the postwar period, it would help to explain why the potential labor force rose faster in 1948–53 and 1964–69 than in 1953–64.[33] The strength of the armed forces rose from 1,468,000 in 1948 to 3,545,000 in 1953, fell to 2,720,000 in 1964 (after a low of 2,516,000 in 1960), and rose again to 3,463,000 in 1969 (Table C-7). But this suggestion is only a hypothesis.

Some Concluding Observations

Growth accounting neither rests upon nor provides any grand general model or general theory of the ultimate reasons for modern economic growth and variations in growth. It does try to provide facts concerning changes in determinants of output and their effects upon output to which such a model or general theory must conform, and against which more limited generalizations may also be tested. Studies for various places and times are gradually bringing an accumulation of such information.

This study has found that changes in only a

few of the many determinants of output account for almost all of the growth of the American economy over a forty-year period, and for variations in the growth rate within that time span. They were:

• Employment, with account taken of the age and sex of workers entering and leaving employment and of the conventions adopted to measure output in general government, households, and institutions.

• Working hours, including the effects of changes in the proportions of part-time workers.

• The education of employed persons.

• The capital stock, with account taken of practices actually followed in measuring output of dwellings and international assets.

• The state of knowledge.

• The proportion of labor misallocated (by the criterion of maximum output) to farming and to small and inefficient family enterprises in the nonfarm sector.

• The size of markets.

• The strength of, and pattern of short-term change in, demand pressures.

The same determinants were found to be largely responsible for growth in European countries, and for differences among nine nations in postwar growth rates—except that recovery from wartime distortions was of clear importance in some countries in the early postwar years.

It is reasonable to suppose that the same determinants will dominate future growth, and that among them will be found the main variables that the United States would need to influence if it wished to adopt a policy of influencing the growth rate in the future.

Yet it must not be supposed that they explain all differences in output. Statistical evidence of this is to be found in international comparisons of levels of output. These determinants—and others whose effects have been measured—can explain only a fraction of the wide margin by which output per person in the United States exceeds that in Western Europe. Other factors—perhaps stronger competition to force efficiency, perhaps better management, perhaps a harder-working labor force, perhaps something else entirely—must account for the remainder. Until the cause of the unexplained output gap can be identified and measured, we can only refer to these factors as "residual efficiency," or the "x-factor."

I have not found it possible to deal satisfactorily with quality of management at the statistical

32. Clarence Long, *The Labor Force under Changing Income and Employment* (Princeton University Press for the National Bureau of Economic Research, 1958).

33. As previously noted, population movements do not entirely explain the higher 1964–69 rate and do not explain the 1948–53 rate at all.

level. Strictly speaking, management is merely a type of labor and the quality of management no more requires a separate entry in sources of growth tables than does the quality of any other separate occupational group. But management occupies a peculiarly strategic position in the labor force, and estimates of labor input I am able to construct handle the special qualifications of management very incompletely.

Although I judge that changes in the "miscellaneous" or "n.e.c." components of the classification did not affect growth much in the United States in the time span considered here, this does not mean that they cannot do so or may not do so in the future. Indeed, in Chapter 6 I suggested several determinants that may change adversely and impair future growth. Moreover, most determinants which refer to aspects of misallocation and wasteful or inefficient use of resources fall in this category. In a previous study I examined possibilities for raising the growth rate by improving resource allocation and removing obstacles to efficient production. Although I concluded that the possible additions to future long-term growth that one might hope to secure in this way appear small when measured in percentage points, I also noted that even small gains are worthwhile and

that it is in this area that steps to achieve gains in output can be undertaken at the lowest real cost.

Finally, the determinants of output examined in this study may be influenced by many aspects of the American society and economy—by everything that affects birth rates, by the level and structure of taxation, by attitudes toward work and saving, and by government policies that affect incentives, to suggest only a few. But these background conditions exert their influences by affecting determinants of the type examined here, and their effects can be studied only by attempting to appraise which of these determinants they affected, and in which direction and by what amount they did so. Estimates based on a classification like the one used here are therefore necessary for any serious appraisal of the effects of such background conditions.

And so I conclude with the ready admission that this book, comprehensive though it may appear in comparison with most quantitative studies of growth, makes no pretense of dealing with everything that affects growth. That would require encyclopedic presentation not only of almost everything known about the American people and the American economy but of much that has yet to be learned as well.

Appendixes

APPENDIX A

⇢⇢⟩⟨⟨⟨

Estimates of National Income, Net National Product, and Gross National Product

⇢⇢⟩⟨⟨⟨

This appendix describes the derivation of my series for national income at factor cost (NI) in current and constant prices. Derivation of the NI series requires prior derivation of series for gross national product at market prices (GNP) and net national product at market prices (NNP).

The Series and Their Derivation

All three series are shown in current and constant prices in Table A-1. Although they differ slightly from similar series published by the Office of Business Economics (OBE),[1] all data were provided by OBE; they come either from its national income accounts (NIA) or from its capital stock study (CSS).[2] However, my choices among al-

1. The Office of Business Economics does not publish either NNP or NI in constant prices.
2. National income accounts data for 1929 to 1963 are published in U.S. Department of Commerce, Office of Business Economics, *The National Income and Product Accounts of the United States, 1929–1965: Statistical Tables,* A Supplement to the *Survey of Current Business* (1966). Data for 1964 are published in the July 1968 issue of the *Survey of Current Business,* for 1965 in the July 1969 issue, for 1966–69 in the July 1970 issue. Revisions for 1968–69 published in the July 1971 issue are incorporated

Table A-1. Gross National Product, Net National Product, and National Income in Current and Constant (1958) Prices, 1929, 1940–41, and 1947–69
Billions of dollars

Year	Current prices			Constant prices		
	GNP	NNP	NI	GNP	NNP	NI
	Excluding Alaska and Hawaii					
1929	102.4	92.4	84.7	201.0	176.6	161.4
1940	98.6	89.3	79.3	224.5	200.5	181.5
1941	124.1	113.8	102.1	262.4	237.8	215.8
1947	230.6	213.3	194.1	307.9	282.4	255.2
1948	259.8	239.4	218.5	325.9	298.3	270.1
1949	256.4	234.4	212.3	323.5	294.0	265.8
1950	283.5	259.2	235.3	353.1	321.6	290.8
1951	325.3	297.4	271.6	379.2	345.8	312.9
1952	343.6	313.6	284.9	392.2	357.3	323.5
1953	361.9	330.5	299.3	409.0	372.9	337.3
1954	362.4	330.0	299.3	403.7	366.3	331.3
1955	396.1	361.6	328.2	435.6	396.7	358.8
1956	420.7	382.5	347.0	447.2	406.5	367.8
1957	441.6	400.0	362.0	452.7	410.4	371.1
1958	446.2	402.7	363.6	446.1	402.7	363.6
1959	484.8	439.3	396.3	477.4	432.8	391.1
1960	503.7	456.6	409.7	488.3	442.3	399.4
	Including Alaska and Hawaii					
1960	505.2	458.0	411.2	489.7	443.8	400.8
1961	521.2	472.6	424.4	499.1	451.9	408.1
1962	560.3	509.8	457.6	530.6	481.9	435.3
1963	591.2	538.6	482.4	552.6	502.2	453.6
1964	634.3	578.9	519.3	583.9	531.5	480.1
1965	688.6	630.0	566.1	622.6	567.8	513.0
1966	751.5	688.4	622.0	661.2	603.4	545.2
1967	795.3	726.6	654.5	677.8	617.0	557.6
1968	867.7	793.0	712.3[a]	711.2	647.3	585.1[a]
1969	934.1	851.3	763.9[a]	730.4	663.2	599.6[a]

Sources: Tables A-2, A-4, A-5, and A-7. See text for derivation of 1960 estimates excluding Alaska and Hawaii.
a. See text for derivation.

ternative OBE series and my manipulations of the data are entirely my own responsibility. In general, I have minimized departures from OBE's NIA procedures.

My national income estimates for 1968 and 1969 were initially obtained before OBE's July 1971 revisions of the NIA, and were revised to take account of the NIA revisions by use of approximate procedures because corresponding revisions of unpublished income detail and of the depreciation estimates from the CSS were not immediately available. These years are omitted from Tables A-5, A-6, and A-7.

where changes are significant (see pp. 7–8). Unpublished detail for all years was provided by the OBE. The capital stock study estimates used are unpublished series provided by the Office of Business Economics, some of which were specially prepared for this investigation.

153

Gross National Product

Table A-2 shows the differences between my GNP series and the regularly published series which OBE compiles by summing types of expenditure. Differences arise because adjustments were made to ensure maximum statistical consistency with labor input estimates, to change the valuation of institutional depreciation, and to change the valuation of private nonresidential construction at constant (1958) prices.

TO SECURE MAXIMUM STATISTICAL CONSISTENCY. Aggregate GNP, NNP, and NI in current prices can be measured as the sum either of expenditures (from the "product side" of the accounts) or of charges against expenditures (from the "income side"); the difference is the statistical discrepancy in the NIA. OBE follows the convention of reporting totals for GNP and NNP from the expenditure side, for NI from the income side. In contrast, I have used data from the income side for all three series. Hence, my GNP differs from that of OBE by the amount of the statistical discrepancy in the NIA. For the constant price series, I have deflated the statistical discrepancy by OBE's implicit deflator for business gross product (implying that the discrepancy arises in the business sector).

Use of output data obtained from the income side of the NIA secures maximum statistical consistency between my output series and my labor

Table A-2. Derivation of Gross National Product in Current and Constant (1958) Prices, 1929, 1940–41, and 1947–69[a]
Billions of dollars

	Current prices				Constant prices				
								Plus:	
							Plus:	Adjustment of deflator	
		Less:	Plus:			Less:	Adjustment	for private	
		Statis-	Adjustment			Statis-	of insti-	nonresi-	
	GNP	tical	of insti-	Equals:	GNP	tical	tutional	dential	Equals:
	from	discrep-	tutional	GNP	from	discrep-	depre-	construc-	GNP
Year	NIA	ancy	depre-	(Denison)	NIA	ancy	ciation	tion	(Denison)
	(1)	(2)	ciation (3)	(4)	(5)	(6)	(7)	(8)	(9)
1929	103.1	0.7	0.0	102.4	203.6	1.3	−0.1	−1.1	201.0
1940	99.7	1.0	0.0	98.6	227.2	2.3	−0.1	−0.3	224.5
1941	124.5	0.4	0.0	124.1	263.7	0.8	0.0	−0.5	262.4
1947	231.3	0.9	0.2	230.6	309.9	1.2	0.2	−1.1	307.9
1948	257.6	−2.0	0.2	259.8	323.7	−2.4	0.3	−0.6	325.9
1949	256.5	0.3	0.2	256.4	324.1	0.4	0.3	−0.5	323.5
1950	284.8	1.5	0.2	283.5	355.3	1.8	0.2	−0.6	353.1
1951	328.4	3.3	0.3	325.3	383.4	3.8	0.3	−0.7	379.2
1952	345.5	2.2	0.2	343.6	395.1	2.4	0.3	−0.8	392.2
1953	364.6	3.0	0.3	361.9	412.8	3.3	0.3	−0.8	409.0
1954	364.8	2.7	0.3	362.4	407.0	3.0	0.3	−0.6	403.7
1955	398.0	2.1	0.2	396.1	438.0	2.3	0.3	−0.4	435.6
1956	419.2	−1.1	0.3	420.7	446.1	−1.2	0.4	−0.5	447.2
1957	441.1	0.0	0.4	441.6	452.5	0.0	0.4	−0.3	452.7
1958	447.3	1.6	0.4	446.2	447.3	1.6	0.4	0.0	446.1
1959	483.7	−0.8	0.3	484.8	475.9	−0.8	0.3	0.3	477.4
1960	503.7	−1.0	0.4	505.2	487.7	−1.0	0.4	0.6	489.7
1961	520.1	−0.8	0.4	521.2	497.2	−0.7	0.4	0.8	499.1
1962	560.3	0.5	0.5	560.3	529.8	0.5	0.4	0.8	530.6
1963	590.5	−0.3	0.4	591.2	551.0	−0.3	0.4	0.9	552.6
1964	632.4	−1.3	0.5	634.3	581.1	−1.2	0.5	1.1	583.9
1965	684.9	−3.1	0.6	688.6	617.8	−2.9	0.5	1.4	622.6
1966	749.9	−1.0	0.6	751.5	658.1	−0.9	0.5	1.6	661.2
1967	793.9	−0.7	0.7	795.3	675.2	−0.6	0.6	1.5	677.8
1968	864.2	−2.7	0.8	867.7	706.6	−2.3	0.7	1.6	711.2
1969	929.1	−4.1	1.0	934.1	724.7	−3.3	0.8	1.6	730.4

Sources: Columns 1, 2, and 5, Office of Business Economics, national income accounts; other columns, see text for derivation. Detail may not add to totals because of rounding.

a. Alaska and Hawaii are included beginning with 1960.

input series. The gain stems mainly from the fact that employee compensation, its largest component, and the OBE employment series, upon which I chiefly rely for my index of employment, derive mainly from the same reports and are processed in the same way.

The choice between OBE's income side and product side estimates considerably affects some year-to-year movements of GNP, NNP, and NI in constant prices. It affects long-term growth rates only slightly because OBE has (rightly, in my judgment) relied mainly upon the income estimates when divergencies between the series developed, and adjusted the product estimates to conform. Hence, estimates from the product side do not really provide an alternative measure of long-term output growth.[3]

TO ADJUST INSTITUTIONAL DEPRECIATION. OBE's GNP in current prices includes as a component institutional depreciation measured at historical cost.[4] I have substituted institutional depreciation figures at "current cost 2." In the constant price series I have used estimates at "constant cost 2." (The terms are explained below.) The differences between the series are shown as adjustments in Table A-2, columns 3 and 7.[5]

These adjustments are not required to obtain my desired series for NNP and NI because whatever institutional depreciation series is included in GNP must be deducted to obtain these measures. I have introduced them only to maintain consistency among the three series.

TO ADJUST PRIVATE NONRESIDENTIAL CONSTRUCTION AT CONSTANT PRICES. The need for the last adjustment is related to my measurement of capital stock and depreciation. In the CSS, OBE has provided sets of investment, capital stock, and depreciation data based on two alternative price indexes. One uses the price indexes ("price series 1") that are used to deflate the fixed investment components of GNP. The other uses an alternative index ("price series 2") for private nonresidential construction. Price series 2 was constructed in an attempt to eliminate an upward bias in the GNP deflator resulting from failure to allow for changes in productivity in on-site construction

work. I have chosen to use data based on the alternative series 2 index in measuring depreciation and capital stock. For consistency, I add to OBE's GNP series in 1958 prices the amount (positive or negative) by which gross investment in private nonresidential structures in 1958 prices is raised when the price series 2 index is used instead of price series 1. The 1929–69 and 1950–69 growth rates of GNP in 1958 prices are raised by 0.02 and 0.03 percentage points, respectively, by the price index substitution. It is convenient to note here the effect of the price index substitution on NNP in 1958 prices. The amounts involved are shown in the second column of Table A-3. The change over time in the size of the adjustment to NNP is smaller than it is for GNP (Table A-2, column 8) because the effect of the price substitution on gross capital formation is partially offset by its effect on depreciation. The growth rate of NNP (and also of NI) is raised by less than 0.01 percentage points in both the

Table A-3. Amounts by Which Substitution of the Alternative OBE Price Index Raised Net National Product in Current and Constant (1958) Prices, 1929, 1940–41, and 1947–69
Billions of dollars

Year	Current prices (1)	Constant prices (2)
1929	0.2	0.0
1940	0.2	0.6
1941	0.2	0.4
1947	0.2	−0.2
1948	0.4	0.3
1949	0.5	0.3
1950	0.4	0.2
1951	0.3	0.1
1952	0.3	0.0
1953	0.3	0.0
1954	0.4	0.1
1955	0.5	0.4
1956	0.5	0.2
1957	0.6	0.4
1958	0.7	0.7
1959	0.9	1.0
1960	0.9	1.2
1961	1.0	1.4
1962	0.9	1.3
1963	0.9	1.4
1964	0.7	1.5
1965	1.0	1.8
1966	1.1	1.9
1967	1.0	1.7
1968	1.1	1.8
1969	1.1	1.8

Source: See text for derivation.

3. See especially U.S. Department of Commerce, Office of Business Economics, *U.S. Income and Output*, A Supplement to the *Survey of Current Business* (1958), pp. 74–76.
4. The series is shown in NIA Table 7.3, line 57.
5. Institutional depreciation is not isolated in OBE's GNP series at *constant* prices. I have estimated the amount to be replaced by applying to depreciation at constant cost 2 the ratio of the historical cost estimate from NIA to the estimate at current cost 2 from CSS.

1929–69 and 1950–69 periods. This illustrates a general principle: a *persistent* bias in a price index for capital goods usually introduces less error into the growth rates of NNP than those of GNP.[6]

The price substitution raises the level of NNP in *current* prices very slightly throughout the period. The difference carries over to NI, and ultimately to the earnings of capital and land in my nonresidential business sector. This results in my assigning slightly more weight to capital and land, and slightly less to labor, in analyzing growth in this sector than I would have done had I not made this price substitution.

6. The reason for presuming an upward bias in the NIA deflator for private nonresidential construction applies also to the NIA deflators for private residential construction (until the most recent years) and to some components of government construction. I have not introduced an adjustment to these components of output. Capital stock series for residential and government capital are not used in the growth analysis so consistency is not a problem.

Net National Product at Market Prices

NNP is equal to GNP less capital consumption. Table A-4 shows the capital consumption estimates I used and my estimates of net national product in current and constant (1958) prices.

OBE has computed alternative estimates of depreciation in current and constant prices based on various assumptions as to the average service lives of capital goods, the distribution of retirements, and the pattern of depreciation. I have chosen the estimates based upon use of Bulletin F lives, the Winfrey distribution of retirements, and the straight-line depreciation pattern.[7] The depreciation estimates cover the same types of assets as

7. Service lives based on Bulletin F of the Bureau of Internal Revenue are supplemented by OBE estimates to fill gaps. Bulletin F service lives are, in general, longer than those permitted in 1973 by the Internal Revenue Service. For dwellings, the average service life used is fifty years. Different service lives are used for each of many components of equipment and nonresidential structures.

Table A-4. Derivation of Net National Product in Current and Constant (1958) Prices, 1929, 1940–41, and 1947–69[a]

Billions of dollars

	Current prices			Constant prices		
Year	GNP (Denison) (1)	Less: Depreciation (2)	Equals: NNP (Denison) (3)	GNP (Denison) (4)	Less: Depreciation (5)	Equals: NNP (Denison) (6)
1929	102.4	9.9	92.4	201.0	24.5	176.6
1940	98.6	9.3	89.3	224.5	24.1	200.5
1941	124.1	10.3	113.8	262.4	24.6	237.8
1947	230.6	17.3	213.3	307.9	25.4	282.4
1948	259.8	20.3	239.4	325.9	27.5	298.3
1949	256.4	22.0	234.4	323.5	29.5	294.0
1950	283.5	24.3	259.2	353.1	31.5	321.6
1951	325.3	27.9	297.4	379.2	33.4	345.8
1952	343.6	29.9	313.6	392.2	34.9	357.3
1953	361.9	31.4	330.5	409.0	36.1	372.9
1954	362.4	32.4	330.0	403.7	37.4	366.3
1955	396.1	34.5	361.6	435.6	38.9	396.7
1956	420.7	38.2	382.5	447.2	40.6	406.5
1957	441.6	41.6	400.0	452.7	42.2	410.4
1958	446.2	43.4	402.7	446.1	43.4	402.7
1959	484.8	45.5	439.3	477.4	44.5	432.8
1960	505.2	47.1	458.0	489.7	45.9	443.8
1961	521.2	48.6	472.6	499.1	47.3	451.9
1962	560.3	50.5	509.8	530.6	48.7	481.9
1963	591.2	52.6	538.6	552.6	50.4	502.2
1964	634.3	55.4	578.9	583.9	52.4	531.5
1965	688.6	58.6	630.0	622.6	54.8	567.8
1966	751.5	63.1	688.4	661.2	57.7	603.4
1967	795.3	68.7	726.6	677.8	60.8	617.0
1968	867.7	74.7	793.0	711.2	63.9	647.3
1969	934.1	82.8	851.3	730.4	67.2	663.2

Sources: Columns 1 and 4, Table A-2; other columns, see text for derivation. Detail may not add to totals because of rounding.
a. Alaska and Hawaii are included beginning with 1960.

the fixed private domestic investment components of GNP. The initial valuations of assets at historical cost (current cost when acquired by the business sector) are also the same as in GNP (after my adjustment of the GNP entry for institutional depreciation). The price indexes used to convert historical cost data to current cost and to constant cost are the same as those used to deflate the corresponding components of gross private domestic investment in the GNP after my adjustment of private nonresidential construction. The depreciation estimates are those labeled in the CSS "current cost 2" and "constant cost 2." The estimates are considered to cover the small item of accidental damage to fixed business capital.

National Income at Factor Cost in Current Prices

Table A-5 shows the derivation of my estimates of NI at current prices from the NI estimates pub-

lished by OBE in the NIA. It is necessary only to change the OBE national income series by the difference between capital consumption allowances in the NIA (after the slight adjustment for institutional depreciation) and my estimates of depreciation.

Table A-5 also reconciles my estimates of NI and NNP.

Adjustment for Alaska and Hawaii

Information provided by the Office of Business Economics indicates that $1,475 million was added to national income in 1960 when Alaska and Hawaii were brought into the national accounts. National income in 1960 excluding Alaska and Hawaii, shown in Table A-1, was obtained by subtracting this amount from the 1960 NI including these states. The same adjustment was used in Table A-1 for GNP and NNP in current prices because the reconciliation items between GNP and NNP were not changed when these states were

Table A-5. Derivation of National Income in Current Prices and Reconciliation with Net National Product, 1929, 1940–41, and 1947–67[a]

Billions of dollars

Year	NI (NIA) (1)	Plus: Capital consumption allowances (NIA) (2)	Plus: Adjustment to institutional depreciation (Denison) (3)	Less: Depreciation (Denison) (4)	Equals: NI (Denison) (5)	Plus: Indirect business tax and nontax liability (NIA) (6)	Plus: Business transfer payments (NIA) (7)	Less: Subsidies less current surplus of government enterprises (NIA) (8)	Equals: NNP (Denison) (9)
1929	86.8	7.9	0.0	9.9	84.7	7.0	0.6	−0.1	92.4
1940	81.1	7.5	0.0	9.3	79.3	10.0	0.4	0.4	89.3
1941	104.2	8.2	0.0	10.3	102.1	11.3	0.5	0.1	113.8
1947	199.0	12.2	0.2	17.3	194.1	18.4	0.6	−0.2	213.3
1948	224.2	14.5	0.2	20.3	218.5	20.1	0.7	−0.1	239.4
1949	217.5	16.6	0.2	22.0	212.3	21.3	0.8	−0.1	234.4
1950	241.1	18.3	0.2	24.3	235.3	23.3	0.8	0.2	259.2
1951	278.0	21.2	0.3	27.9	271.6	25.2	0.9	0.2	297.4
1952	291.4	23.2	0.2	29.9	284.9	27.6	1.0	−0.1	313.6
1953	304.7	25.7	0.3	31.4	299.3	29.6	1.2	−0.4	330.5
1954	303.1	28.2	0.3	32.4	299.3	29.4	1.1	−0.2	330.0
1955	331.0	31.5	0.2	34.5	328.2	32.1	1.2	−0.1	361.6
1956	350.8	34.1	0.3	38.2	347.0	34.9	1.4	0.8	382.5
1957	366.1	37.1	0.4	41.6	362.0	37.3	1.5	0.9	400.0
1958	367.8	38.9	0.4	43.4	363.6	38.5	1.6	0.9	402.7
1959	400.0	41.4	0.3	45.5	396.3	41.5	1.7	0.1	439.3
1960	414.5	43.4	0.4	47.1	411.2	45.2	1.9	0.2	458.0
1961	427.3	45.2	0.4	48.6	424.4	47.7	2.0	1.4	472.6
1962	457.7	50.0	0.5	50.5	457.6	51.5	2.1	1.4	509.8
1963	481.9	52.6	0.4	52.6	482.4	54.7	2.3	0.8	538.6
1964	518.1	56.1	0.5	55.4	519.3	58.4	2.5	1.3	578.9
1965	564.3	59.8	0.6	58.6	566.1	62.5	2.7	1.3	630.0
1966	620.6	63.9	0.6	63.1	622.0	65.7	3.0	2.3	688.4
1967	653.6	68.9	0.7	68.7	654.5	70.4	3.1	1.4	726.6

Sources: Columns 1, 2, 6, 7, and 8, Office of Business Economics, national income accounts; column 3, Table A-2, column 3; column 4, Table A-4, column 2. Detail may not add to totals because of rounding

a. Alaska and Hawaii are included beginning with 1960.

added. The percentage reduction from the 1960 figure including Alaska and Hawaii to secure figures excluding these states is the same for each of the three constant-price series as in the corresponding current-price series.

National Income at Constant Prices

OBE has not compiled NI in constant (1958) prices, the series I use to measure output. It was necessary to develop such a series by reweighting NNP data.

NI and NNP measure exactly the same bundle of goods and services. An index of the quantity of any individual type of expenditure is necessarily the same whether one is measuring NI or NNP. However, the 1958 prices of most goods and services are different at factor cost and at market price. Hence, the weights used to combine expenditures for different types of goods and services are not the same. Indexes of NI and NNP in 1958 prices must therefore differ unless there

is no correlation between movements of the component quantity indexes and ratios of factor cost to market price.

An accurate series for NI in constant (1958) prices could be readily constructed from NNP quantity series if expenditures at factor cost in 1958 were available for detailed expenditure categories. The 1958 expenditure for each component at factor cost would simply be multiplied by a quantity index computed from the corresponding NNP series. The components would then be summed to obtain NI in 1958 prices each year. Unfortunately, detailed 1958 factor cost values are not available and their estimation would require a greater statistical effort, based on use of input-output analysis, than could be undertaken for the present study. A summary procedure designed to take account of only the main differences between NNP and NI weights has therefore been adopted.

Table A-6 shows a special breakdown of NNP

Table A-6. Selected Components of Net National Product in Constant (1958) Prices and Adjustments, 1929, 1940–41, and 1947–67[a]

Billions of dollars

Year	NNP (1)	Direct purchases of factor services (2)	Value-added portion of space rental value of nonfarm dwellings (3)	Other expenditures (4)	Other expenditures less certain excises			
					Total (5)	Lightly taxed services (6)	Other measured expenditures (7)	Statistical discrepancy[b] (8)
1929	176.6	21.5	10.2	144.9	143.1	22.9	121.5	−1.3
1940	200.5	30.1	10.5	159.8	155.6	20.8	137.0	−2.3
1941	237.8	35.6	11.2	191.0	186.4	21.1	166.1	−0.8
1947	282.4	37.1	14.7	230.6	224.5	25.3	200.4	−1.2
1948	298.3	37.7	15.4	245.2	239.2	25.8	211.0	2.4
1949	294.0	39.4	16.8	237.8	231.7	26.0	206.1	−0.4
1950	321.6	41.1	17.8	262.7	256.3	27.4	230.7	−1.8
1951	345.8	48.9	19.4	277.5	270.8	27.5	247.1	−3.8
1952	357.3	51.9	21.0	284.4	277.6	28.3	251.7	−2.4
1953	372.9	52.1	22.5	298.3	291.1	28.8	265.7	−3.3
1954	366.3	51.6	24.1	290.6	283.6	30.5	256.1	−3.0
1955	396.7	52.6	25.5	318.6	311.3	31.2	282.4	−2.3
1956	406.5	53.9	26.8	325.8	318.2	32.5	284.5	1.2
1957	410.4	55.0	28.4	327.1	319.3	33.7	285.5	0.0
1958	402.7	55.6	29.9	317.2	309.2	35.4	275.3	−1.6
1959	432.8	56.5	31.0	345.3	337.0	36.6	299.5	0.8
1960	443.8	58.2	33.4	352.2	343.6	38.0	304.6	1.0
1961	451.9	60.3	34.9	356.7	347.9	39.7	307.6	0.7
1962	481.9	63.1	37.1	381.7	372.7	41.1	332.0	−0.5
1963	502.2	64.4	39.6	398.2	388.9	43.2	345.4	0.3
1964	531.5	66.7	42.5	422.2	412.6	45.7	365.7	1.2
1965	567.8	68.9	45.8	453.1	443.1	48.5	391.7	2.9
1966	603.4	73.2	48.1	482.1	471.6	50.3	420.4	0.9
1967	617.0	77.4	50.8	488.8	478.1	53.0	424.5	0.6

Sources: Column 1, Table A-4, column 6; column 2, Office of Business Economics, national income accounts, Table 1.8; column 8, Table A-2; other columns, see text for derivation.

a. Alaska and Hawaii are included beginning with 1960.

b. Sign reversed.

in constant prices that is used in Table A-7 to derive NI at constant prices. The procedure involved the following steps.

STEP ONE. Almost one-seventh of 1958 NNP consisted of the direct purchase of labor services by general government, households, nonprofit institutions, foreign governments, and international organizations. These expenditures are the same at factor cost and at market price and have the same absolute dollar value in NI as in NNP. Net receipts of property income from abroad (a component of net exports) are also the same in NI as in NNP. The sum of these components, "direct purchases of factor services," is shown in Table A-6, column 2, and transferred to Table A-7, column 2, as a component of NI.[8]

STEP TWO. Personal consumption expenditures for space rental value of nonfarm dwellings may

8. The series is the same as OBE's estimates of GNP in constant prices originating outside the business sector of the economy.

be regarded, for the present purpose, as consisting of two components: the gross value added by the dwellings themselves, and purchases from other industries (chiefly maintenance expenditures). Special attention is given here to gross value added (called "nonlabor GNP" in Appendix D) because of the importance of property taxes on dwellings. The series in 1958 market prices is shown in Table A-6, column 3. Its derivation is described on page 178. The corresponding value at factor cost in 1958 is the market price value less property taxes on these dwellings. The market price series shown in Table A-6, column 3, was used to extrapolate the 1958 factor cost value in order to obtain the factor cost series at constant prices which is shown in Table A-7, column 3.

STEP THREE. The remainder of net national product at constant prices ("other expenditures") is shown in Table A-6, column 4. It consists of net private domestic investment plus the components of consumer purchases, government pur-

Table A-7. Derivation of National Income in Constant (1958) Prices, 1929, 1940–41, and 1947–67[a]
Billions of Dollars

		National income in 1958 prices						
Year	NI current prices (1)	Direct purchases of factor services (2)	Value-added portion of space rental value of nonfarm dwellings (3)	Other expenditures (4)	Lightly taxed services (5)	Other measured expenditures (6)	Statistical discrepancy[b] (7)	Total national income (8)
1929	...	21.5	8.2	...	22.0	111.1	−1.3	161.4
1940	...	30.1	8.4	...	20.0	125.2	−2.3	181.5
1941	...	35.6	8.9	...	20.3	151.8	−0.8	215.8
1947	...	37.1	11.8	...	24.3	183.2	−1.2	255.2
1948	...	37.7	12.3	...	24.7	192.9	2.4	270.1
1949	...	39.4	13.4	...	25.0	188.4	−0.4	265.8
1950	...	41.1	14.3	...	26.3	210.9	−1.8	290.8
1951	...	48.9	15.5	...	26.4	225.9	−3.8	312.9
1952	...	51.9	16.8	...	27.1	230.1	−2.4	323.5
1953	...	52.1	18.0	...	27.6	242.9	−3.3	337.3
1954	...	51.6	19.3	...	29.3	234.1	−3.0	331.3
1955	...	52.6	20.4	...	29.9	258.1	−2.3	358.8
1956	...	53.9	21.5	...	31.2	260.1	1.2	367.8
1957	...	55.0	22.7	...	32.4	261.0	0.0	371.1
1958	363.6	55.6	23.9	284.1	34.0	251.7	−1.6	363.6
1959	...	56.5	24.8	...	35.2	273.8	0.8	391.1
1960	...	58.2	26.7	...	36.5	278.5	1.0	400.8
1961	...	60.3	27.9	...	38.1	281.2	0.7	408.1
1962	...	63.1	29.7	...	39.5	303.5	−0.5	435.3
1963	...	64.4	31.7	...	41.5	315.7	0.3	453.6
1964	...	66.7	34.0	...	43.9	334.3	1.2	480.1
1965	...	68.9	36.6	...	46.6	358.1	2.9	513.0
1966	...	73.2	38.5	...	48.3	384.3	0.9	545.2
1967	...	77.4	40.7	...	50.9	388.1	0.6	557.6

Sources: Column 1, Table A-5; columns 2 and 7, Table A-6; columns 3, 4, 5, and 6, see text for derivation; column 8, sum of columns 2, 3, 5, 6, and 7.
a. Alaska and Hawaii are included beginning with 1960.
b. Sign reversed.

chases, and net exports that were not eliminated by deduction of columns 2 and 3 plus the NIA statistical discrepancy (with its sign reversed) which is viewed here as representing unallocated expenditures. The corresponding factor cost value in 1958 ($284.1 billion), obtained by subtraction of columns 2 and 3 from column 1, is shown in Table A-7, column 4.

Three important types of consumer expenditure included in these aggregates are subject to heavy specific excise taxation and therefore receive much less weight in NI than in NNP. These are alcoholic beverages, gasoline and oil, and tobacco products. I have removed these three types of expenditure from column 4 of Table A-6; calculated the value of each of the three in 1958 after the specific excises included in it are eliminated; extrapolated its reduced 1958 value by the index of expenditures at 1958 market prices; and added the three resulting series back to the other components of column 4 of Table A-6. The series obtained is shown in column 5. The three types of consumer expenditure were not completely reduced to a factor cost valuation by this procedure; only the special excises to which they are subject were eliminated.[9]

STEP FOUR. The 1958 factor cost value shown in Table A-7, column 4 ($284.1 billion), still falls short of the value of the same commodities in Table A-6, column 5 ($309.2 billion), by $25.0 billion, or 8.1 percent. The composition of this $25.0 billion is shown in Table A-8. Examination of this table, and of more detailed data, did not reveal sizable taxes or other items that strongly affect one category or a small group of categories of final expenditures included in Table A-6, column 5. Therefore, further ad hoc adjustment for particular taxes or subsidies could not bring the movement of this series appreciably closer to the one that would be obtained by use of factor cost weights.

There is, however, a group of personal consumption expenditures for services whose 1958 prices contained a much smaller percentage of indirect business taxes, on the average, than other products. Provision of these services was largely exempt from sales taxes and excises. Those provided commercially were sold mainly by establishments which themselves used relatively little capi-

9. The taxes eliminated from the consumer expenditure series in 1958 are: alcoholic beverages, $2,886 million; gasoline and oil, $2,746 million; and tobacco products, $2,378 million.

Table A-8. Difference between Values of "Other Expenditures" Shown in Table A-6, Column 5, and Table A-7, Column 4, by Components, 1958
Billions of dollars

Indirect business tax and nontax accruals			**24.5**
Property taxes		7.8[a]	
Sales, excise, and customs taxes		12.2[b]	
State general sales	3.5		
Local sales	1.1		
Excises on gas and oil, alcoholic beverages, tobacco	2.7[b]		
Other federal excises	4.0		
Customs duties	0.8		
Motor vehicle licenses (business use)		0.8	
Other state and local indirect business taxes		2.9	
Nontaxes (business)		1.1	
Less tax refunds, federal		0.2	
Other additions:			
Business transfer payments			1.6
Current surplus of state and local government enterprises			1.8
Subtractions:			
Federal subsidies less current surplus of federal government enterprises			2.7
Total difference			**25.0**

Sources: Office of Business Economics, published and unpublished estimates. Detail may not add to totals because of rounding.

a. Excludes $6.0 billion of property taxes on nonfarm dwellings.

b. Excludes $8.0 billion of excises on gas and oil, alcoholic beverages, and tobacco that are included directly in personal consumption expenditures for these products.

tal subject to property taxation and which had a high ratio of "value added" to sales so that their prices included relatively little for indirect taxes included in purchases from other enterprises. Table A-6, column 6, shows consumer purchases of this group of "lightly taxed services." It consists mainly of purchases by individuals of personal, professional, and financial services together with purchases (other than purchases of labor) by nonprofit institutions and depreciation on their property.[10]

These lightly taxed services should receive

10. To be precise, it includes personal consumption expenditures for services classified in the NIA major groups: "clothing, accessories and jewelry"; "medical care expenses"; "personal business"; "recreation"; "private education and research"; "religious and welfare activities"; and "foreign travel and other, net," except that it excludes the minor group, "admissions to specified spectator amusements," and purchases of labor services by nonprofit institutions.

The estimate is obtained by deducting from the sum of Table A-2, column 7, and NIA Table 2.6, lines 44 and 53, the sum of NIA Table 2.6, line 61, and NIA Table 1.8, line 6.

more weight in NI "other," than in NNP "other." Raising their weight can scarcely affect the results from 1941 forward because expenditures for them move in similar fashion to "remaining expenditures," but it does raise the 1929 and 1940 figures relative to the later years. To effectuate this reweighting, I use the following procedure to complete the estimate of NI in 1958 prices:

1. I estimate that in 1958 the value at factor cost of "lightly taxed services" was 96 percent of their value at market prices. The 1958 value is moved by the index of expenditures at constant market prices shown in Table A-6, column 6. The resulting series is shown in Table A-7, column 5.

2. The 1958 value at factor cost of the remaining measured expenditures is obtained in Table A-7 by deducting columns 5 and 7 from column 4. The 1958 value is moved by expenditures for the same components valued at constant market prices less the three major specific excises (Table A-6, column 7). The resulting series is shown in Table A-7, column 6.

3. The statistical discrepancy with sign reversed, viewed here as representing unallocated expenditures, is simply carried over from Table A-6, column 8, to Table A-7, column 7.

NI in 1958 prices, shown in Table A-7, column 8, is the sum of the five component series.

Its acceptance requires the assumption that differences between NNP and NI price weights in 1958 are not correlated with differences in quantity indexes *within* the "lightly taxed services" group or, after elimination of the three excises from the NNP weights, *within* the "other measured expenditures" group.

The procedure adopted to secure the series for NI at constant (1958) prices is further clarified in Table A-9. This table shows 1958 NNP and NI allocated among the familiar broad categories of expenditures, with further detail corresponding to that used in reweighting from market price to factor cost. My NI series is the same as that obtained by extrapolating the 1958 NI figure for each detailed component by the NNP series for that component. The percentage distributions and ratios indicate the components whose weights have been raised or lowered.

Comparison of Series

Table A-10 shows, in index form, the official OBE series for GNP in 1958 prices and my series for GNP, NNP, and NI. All series were linked at 1960 to eliminate the incomparability caused by bringing Alaska and Hawaii into the coverage of the data.

Table A-9. Composition of Net National Product and National Income, 1958

Components	Millions of dollars		Percentage of total		Ratio of NI to NNP (5)
	NNP (1)	NI (2)	NNP (3)	NI (4)	
Total	402,724	363,642	100.00	100.00	0.903
Personal consumption expenditures	290,456	257,362	72.12	70.77	0.886
Labor services	11,441	11,441	2.84	3.15	1.000
Space rent, nonfarm dwellings (value added only)	29,917	23,927	7.43	6.58	0.800
Alcoholic beverages	9,750	6,274	2.42	1.73	0.643
Tobacco products	5,982	3,295	1.49	0.91	0.551
Gas and oil	10,951	7,499	2.72	2.06	0.685
Lightly taxed services	35,387	33,972	8.79	9.34	0.960
All other	187,028	170,954	46.44	47.01	0.914
Net private domestic investment	17,456	15,956	4.33	4.39	0.914
Net exports of goods and services	2,206	2,191	0.55	0.60	0.993
Net factor incomes	2,030	2,030	0.50	0.56	1.000
Other	176	161	0.04	0.04	0.914
Government purchases of goods and services	94,158	89,685	23.38	24.66	0.952
Purchases of labor services	42,115	42,115	10.46	11.58	1.000
All other	52,043	47,570	12.92	13.08	0.914
Statistical discrepancy[a]	−1,552	−1,552	−0.39	−0.43	1.000

Sources: Column 1, Office of Business Economics, national income accounts, and Table A-4; column 2, derived from Table A-7 by allocating "other measured expenditures," Table A-7, column 6, among detailed components in proportion to values included in Table A-6, column 7.

a. Sign reversed.

My series for GNP (Table A-10, column 2) differs irregularly from that of OBE (column 1), mainly because of the treatment of the statistical discrepancy. My GNP and NNP series differ because of depreciation. My indexes for NNP and NI are very similar; the biggest difference in any postwar year is 0.26 percent in 1952. The national income index is higher in the prewar years, but even then the biggest difference, in 1929, is 1.22 percent. From 1929 to 1969 NNP increased by 274.4 percent and national income by 270.1 percent. The main reason for this difference is that alcoholic beverages, absent in 1929 because of Prohibition, receive less weight in the NI series.

Table A-10. Indexes of GNP, NNP, and NI in Constant (1958) Prices, 1929, 1940–41, and 1947–69[a]

1958 = 100

Year	GNP reported in NIA (1)	Denison		
		GNP (2)	NNP (3)	NI (4)
1929	45.51	45.06	43.85	44.39
1940	50.79	50.33	49.78	49.92
1941	58.95	58.81	59.05	59.35
1947	69.28	69.01	70.14	70.18
1948	72.36	73.04	74.09	74.28
1949	72.45	72.52	73.01	73.09
1950	79.43	79.16	79.88	79.97
1951	85.71	84.99	85.87	86.05
1952	88.32	87.90	88.73	88.96
1953	92.28	91.68	92.59	92.75
1954	90.98	90.49	90.97	91.10
1955	97.91	97.64	98.52	98.67
1956	99.72	100.23	100.95	101.15
1957	101.15	101.46	101.92	102.04
1958	100.00	100.00	100.00	100.00
1959	106.39	107.00	107.48	107.54
1960	108.70	109.44	109.85	109.83
1961	110.82	111.55	111.85	111.83
1962	118.09	118.58	119.28	119.28
1963	122.81	123.50	124.30	124.28
1964	129.52	130.49	131.56	131.56
1965	137.70	139.15	140.54	140.57
1966	146.69	147.76	149.36	149.40
1967	150.50	151.48	152.74	152.78
1968	157.50	158.94	160.23	160.32
1969	161.53	163.23	164.16	164.30

Sources: Calculated from unrounded data underlying Tables A-1 and A-2.

a. Series excluding and including Alaska and Hawaii were linked at 1960.

-»X«-

National Income Estimates for Additional Years

-»X«-

In Figure 2-1 estimates of national income in 1958 prices are plotted for a number of years which are not included in Table 2-2 nor described in Appendix A. These estimates are given below. Alaska and Hawaii are excluded except in 1970 and 1971. Work relief is included. The estimates were obtained by procedures that were generally similar to those followed for other years, but less detail was used (especially for the years 1925 through 1928).

	National income (billions of 1958 dollars)
1925	142.2
1926	150.6
1927	150.5
1928	151.4
1930	146.4
1931	131.0
1932	110.1
1933	107.4
1934	119.4
1935	134.4
1936	152.1
1937	163.0
1938	152.8
1939	165.5
1942	249.4
1943	288.1
1944	304.4
1945	297.1
1946	260.5
1970	592.9
1971	608.1

APPENDIX C

⟫⟩✕⟨⟪

Estimates
of Employment

⟫⟩✕⟨⟪

This appendix presents and describes the estimates of total employment used in this study. It also presents and describes a four-way classification of total employment that is central to the analysis of total labor input and of gains from improved allocation of resources. The estimates are shown in Table C-1.

Total Employment

The employment series presented in Table C-1 were specially prepared for this study. They result from an attempt to develop series that both (1) correspond to a count of persons, as distinguished from jobs, and can be used together with data for characteristics of persons to measure total labor input, and (2) are statistically consistent with the measure of real national income used to measure output.

Total employment is *defined* as the total number of *individuals* employed in the U.S. economy. The definition is the same as the Current Population Survey (CPS) definition of civilian employment and the armed forces except that (1) persons aged 14 (rather than 16) years of age and over are covered, and (2), as in national income data, employed persons in the institutional population and U.S. residents employed abroad as civilians by the U.S. government and U.S. firms are covered.[1] (Both series include military personnel stationed abroad.)

1. The Current Population Survey is conducted monthly by the U.S. Bureau of the Census. Employment estimates based upon it are prepared at the present time by the U.S.

Although, with the exceptions noted, employment is defined as a count of persons corresponding to the latest CPS definitions, the index of employment is not measured by use of CPS employment statistics.

There are two principal reasons for this. First, the CPS series, based on a sample of households, does not provide a very precise time series. It has been subject to sufficient sampling error, particularly when the sample was smaller than it is now, to impair its use for measurement of short-term employment changes. Also, and more important, the series has undergone a number of changes: in sample, in sampling procedures, in procedures for "blowing up" the sample to secure universe totals, in the definition of employment, and in the wording of questions asked respondents. A few revisions in past data have been made by the Bureau of Labor Statistics (BLS) and the Bureau of the Census, which previously issued the series, to improve comparability over time, and I have introduced an additional adjustment to take account of the definitional changes made in 1967 (and described on pages 167–68). But adjustments have not been made for most changes, and the basis for some adjustments that have been made is inadequate. Employment estimates based on comprehensive establishment reports, published both by the Bureau of Labor Statistics and the Office of Business Economics (OBE), provide a more accurate measure of employment changes, particularly over short time spans.

Second, the CPS series is statistically independent of the national income series. Even if it were more accurate than employment estimates consistent with the output measure, its use would be undesirable because it would introduce inconsistencies between the measurement of input and output in this study. Instead of the CPS, my employment index is based primarily on employment data prepared by the Office of Business Economics as part of its statistical program in preparing the national accounts. To the greatest possible extent these employment estimates are developed by OBE from the same sources and by the same procedures as the estimates of employee compensa-

Bureau of Labor Statistics and published monthly in its *Employment and Earnings*. The groups mentioned above in the second exception were included in the data used to establish the *movement* of my series but not in the data used to establish its average level. Because only the index of employment enters into the analysis of growth, the series can be regarded as corresponding to the definition given. However, its *level* is a little too low.

164

Table C-1. Persons Employed, by Type of Worker, 1929, 1940–41, and 1947–69
Thousands

Year	Total (1)	Farm workers (2)	Nonfarm self-employed and unpaid family workers (3)	Workers in general government, households, institutions, and the "rest of the world" (4)	Wage and salary workers in nonfarm business (5)
		Excluding Alaska and Hawaii			
1929	47,535	9,903	5,001	6,416	26,215
1940	51,080	8,908	5,271	10,397	26,504
1941	55,583	8,932	5,323	11,160	30,168
1947	59,361	7,913	6,072	9,516	35,860
1948	60,333	7,833	6,168	9,808	36,524
1949	59,047	7,636	6,154	10,245	35,012
1950	60,756	7,490	6,232	10,754	36,280
1951	64,617	7,018	6,292	12,627	38,680
1952	65,869	6,804	6,368	13,288	39,409
1953	66,721	6,555	6,360	13,360	40,446
1954	64,995	6,486	6,260	13,243	39,006
1955	66,470	6,357	6,306	13,569	40,238
1956	67,940	6,100	6,411	13,945	41,484
1957	68,107	5,792	6,537	14,217	41,561
1958	66,393	5,519	6,524	14,512	39,838
1959	67,793	5,391	6,526	14,733	41,143
1960	68,434	5,162	6,617	15,029	41,626
		Including Alaska and Hawaii			
1960	68,721	5,186	6,641	15,107	41,787
1961	68,693	5,065	6,721	15,574	41,333
1962	70,220	4,876	6,676	16,280	42,388
1963	70,951	4,684	6,609	16,550	43,108
1964	72,379	4,438	6,703	16,988	44,250
1965	74,619	4,276	6,741	17,503	46,099
1966	77,937	3,981	6,699	18,788	48,469
1967	79,479	3,772	6,658	19,604	49,445
1968	81,492	3,690	6,700	20,235	50,867
1969	83,614	3,563	6,852	20,552	52,647

Sources: Column 1, Table C-4, column 9; column 2, Table C-5, column 7; column 3, Table C-6, column 3; column 4, Table C-7, column 9; column 5, column 1 minus columns 2, 3, and 4.

tion and proprietors' income. Their use ensures the greatest possible statistical consistency between the measure of input and the measure of output used in this study. Such consistency is an extremely important, even an overriding, consideration in the choice of employment series. It is the chief reason for selecting the OBE series over the BLS employment series based on establishment reports. Fortunately, in the postwar period differences in movement between the BLS nonagricultural employment series and the comparable portion of the OBE series are minor.[2] Consequently, BLS establishment estimates—which are

2. This is not surprising since the two sets of estimates rest on substantially the same bodies of data reported by establishments.

available in greater industrial detail in some industry divisions, and which are accompanied by comparable data on hours and hourly earnings—can be used for detailed analyses by industry without introducing any appreciable incomparability with the estimates presented in this study for the economy as a whole.

CPS data do enter into the employment estimates in two ways: (1) they were used to measure the number of unpaid family workers, who are excluded from the OBE estimates; and (2) they were used to set the *average level* of civilian employment in order to preserve the average CPS weighting of civilian and military employment and, within the civilian aggregate, of farm and nonfarm employment.

Procedure

The precise procedures used in estimation of the employment series took the following form.

DEVELOPMENT OF CPS-BASED SERIES. A civilian employment series based on CPS data was first developed for the years from 1947 through 1969.

1. The CPS estimates of civilian employment of persons 14 years of age and over were first assembled for the period 1947 through 1966. As shown in Table C-2, they were divided between agriculture and other industries and, within each of these groups, by class of worker: wage and salary, self-employed, and unpaid family. Total employment, agricultural employment, and nonagricultural employment in 1947–65 are given in *Manpower Report of the President, 1966*, Table A-1 (page 153). Class-of-worker detail for the years

1957–65 is from Table A-9 of the same source (page 163). Class-of-worker data for 1950–56 are from OECD, *Manpower Statistics, 1950–1962*.[3] Data for self-employed and for unpaid family workers (total, agriculture, and nonagricultural industries) in 1947–49 were obtained from the *Manpower Report of the President, 1966*, Table A-9 (page 163), and wage and salary workers were obtained as a residual. This procedure corresponds to that followed by the BLS to obtain the class-of-worker data for 1950–56 it reported to OECD. Data for 1966 comparable to those for preceding years are given in *Manpower Report of the President, 1967*, Table A-10 (page 213).

3. Organisation for Economic Co-operation and Development, *Manpower Statistics, 1950–1962* (Paris: OECD, 1963), p. 130.

Table C-2. Civilian Employment Based on the Current Population Survey, Persons 14 Years of Age and Over, 1947–69
Thousands

Year	Total civilian employment (1)	Agriculture				Nonagricultural industries			
		Total (2)	Wage and salary workers (3)	Self-employed workers (4)	Unpaid family workers (5)	Total (6)	Wage and salary workers (7)	Self-employed workers (8)	Unpaid family workers (9)
		Excluding Alaska and Hawaii (old definitions)[a]							
1947	57,812	8,256	1,667	4,973	1,616	49,557	43,085	6,045	427
1948	59,117	7,960	1,733	4,671	1,556	51,156	44,616	6,139	401
1949	58,423	8,017	1,836	4,618	1,563	50,406	43,802	6,208	396
1950	59,748	7,497	1,724	4,346	1,427	52,251	45,778	6,069	404
1951	60,785	7,048	1,640	4,022	1,386	53,737	47,467	5,869	400
1952	61,034	6,792	1,514	3,936	1,342	54,242	48,142	5,670	431
1953	61,945	6,555	1,461	3,821	1,273	55,390	49,173	5,794	423
1954	60,890	6,495	1,444	3,821	1,230	54,395	48,070	5,880	445
1955	62,943	6,718	1,688	3,731	1,299	56,225	49,815	5,886	524
1956	64,708	6,572	1,679	3,570	1,323	58,136	51,618	5,936	581
1957	65,011	6,222	1,687	3,304	1,231	58,789	52,073	6,089	627
1958	63,966	5,844	1,671	3,087	1,086	58,122	51,332	6,185	605
1959	65,581	5,836	1,689	3,027	1,120	59,745	52,850	6,298	597
1960	66,392	5,696	1,839	2,802	1,055	60,697	53,740	6,344	613
		Including Alaska and Hawaii (old definitions)[a]							
1960	66,681	5,723	1,866	2,802	1,055	60,958	53,976	6,367	615
1961	66,796	5,463	1,733	2,744	985	61,333	54,284	6,388	662
1962	67,846	5,190	1,666	2,619	905	62,656	55,762	6,271	623
1963	68,809	4,946	1,676	2,437	834	63,863	57,081	6,195	587
1964	70,357	4,761	1,582	2,366	813	65,596	58,736	6,266	594
1965	72,179	4,585	1,492	2,307	786	67,594	60,765	6,213	616
1966	74,065	4,206	1,369	2,147	690	69,859	63,182	6,101	576
		Including Alaska and Hawaii (new definitions)[a]							
1966	74,127	4,165	1,466	2,023	676	69,961	64,099	5,335	527
1967	75,608	4,078	1,420	2,004	654	71,529	65,745	5,264	520
1968	77,209	4,038	1,393	1,992	652	73,170	67,489	5,182	501
1969	79,221	3,813	1,282	1,905	625	75,408	69,544	5,329	535

Sources: Bureau of Labor Statistics, with the following exceptions: data for 1960 excluding Alaska and Hawaii, Denison, *Why Growth Rates Differ*, Table C-1; columns 3 to 9, 1947–49 and 1966 (new definitions), described in text. Data from various publications occasionally differ by 1,000 because of rounding.
a. See text for explanation of CPS old and new definitions.

Table C-3. Total Employment and Selected Components, Based on the Current Population Survey, Adjusted to 1967–69 Definitions, Persons 14 Years of Age and Over, 1947–69
Thousands

Year	Total employment (1)	Armed forces (2)	Civilian employment (3)	Agricultural employment (4)	Unpaid family workers Total (5)	Unpaid family workers Agriculture (6)	Unpaid family workers Nonagricultural industries (7)
			Excluding Alaska and Hawaii				
1947	59,450	1,590	57,860	8,176	1,941	1,583	391
1948	60,622	1,456	59,166	7,882	1,860	1,524	367
1949	60,088	1,616	58,472	7,939	1,862	1,531	362
1950	61,448	1,650	59,798	7,424	1,740	1,398	370
1951	63,935	3,099	60,836	6,979	1,697	1,358	366
1952	64,679	3,594	61,085	6,726	1,685	1,315	394
1953	65,544	3,547	61,997	6,491	1,612	1,247	387
1954	64,291	3,350	60,941	6,432	1,592	1,205	407
1955	66,045	3,049	62,996	6,653	1,732	1,273	479
1956	67,619	2,857	64,762	6,508	1,809	1,296	532
1957	67,863	2,798	65,065	6,161	1,765	1,206	574
1958	66,657	2,637	64,020	5,787	1,607	1,064	554
1959	68,188	2,552	65,636	5,779	1,633	1,097	546
1960	68,962	2,514	66,448	5,640	1,584	1,034	561
			Including Alaska and Hawaii				
1960	69,251	2,514	66,737	5,667	1,586	1,034	563
1961	69,424	2,572	66,852	5,410	1,565	965	606
1962	70,730	2,827	67,903	5,139	1,452	887	570
1963	71,604	2,737	68,867	4,898	1,350	817	537
1964	73,154	2,738	70,416	4,715	1,337	797	543
1965	74,962	2,723	72,239	4,540	1,332	770	564
1966	77,250	3,123	74,127	4,165	1,203	676	527
1967	79,054	3,446	75,608	4,078	1,174	654	520
1968	80,744	3,535	77,209	4,038	1,153	652	501
1969	82,727	3,506	79,221	3,813	1,160	625	535

Sources: Column 1, sum of columns 2 and 3; column 2, Bureau of Labor Statistics, *Employment and Earnings*, various issues; columns 3 to 7, derived from Table C-2, columns 1, 2, 5 + 9, 5 and 9, respectively, by the procedure described in text. Columns 5 to 7 have not been adjusted to force column 5 to equal the sum of columns 6 and 7. Detail may not add to totals because of rounding.

Alaska and Hawaii are included in data from these sources beginning in 1960. Estimates for 1960 excluding Alaska and Hawaii are from *Why Growth Rates Differ.*[4]

Effective in 1967, several changes in definitions and questions were introduced in CPS data; 14- and 15-year-olds were also eliminated from the regularly published series. The figures for 1967 to 1969 in Table C-2 are the sum of estimates for persons 16 years of age and over and for 14- and 15-year-olds. Data for persons 16 years of age and over for 1967 and 1968 are from U.S. Department of Labor, *Statistics on Manpower: A Supplement to the Manpower Report of the President* (1969), Tables A-1 and A-10 (pages 1 and 11). Data, including class-of-worker detail, for

14- and 15-year-olds were provided by the Bureau of Labor Statistics. (Except for class-of-worker detail, the data are also published in *Statistics on Manpower.*) All 1969 data are from U.S. Bureau of Labor Statistics, *Employment and Earnings,* Vol. 16 (January 1970). Estimates for 1966 based on the same new questions and definitions were then obtained.[5] Data for persons 16 years of age and over are from Robert L. Stein, "New Definitions for Employment and Unemployment."[6] To them were added data for persons 14 and 15

4. Edward F. Denison, assisted by Jean-Pierre Poullier, *Why Growth Rates Differ: Postwar Experience in Nine Western Countries* (Brookings Institution, 1967), Table C-1.

5. The 1966 estimates based on old definitions are derived from one sample (the "CPS sample"), the 1966 estimates based on new definitions are derived from a second sample (the "MLS research sample"), and the 1967 estimates are derived from the two samples combined. No allowance could be made for the effects of differences among the samples.

6. U.S. Bureau of Labor Statistics, *Employment and Earnings and Monthly Report on the Labor Force,* Vol. 13 (February 1967), pp. 3–27.

years of age. These were provided by the Bureau of Labor Statistics, except for class-of-worker detail. For each sex, separately within agricultural and nonagricultural industries, the percentage distribution of 14- and 15-year-olds by class of worker was assumed to be the same in 1966 as in 1967 (both based on the same definitions).

Table C-2 shows the full set of estimates thus compiled.

2. Table C-2 shows one series, for 1947–66, that is based on old definitions, and another, for 1966–69, that is based on new definitions (but with 14- and 15-year-olds included). To eliminate the break in the series, while using levels corresponding to the new definitions, the 1947–65 series for total civilian employment, and for certain components needed subsequently, were multiplied by the ratio of the 1966 estimate for each series based on new definitions to the 1966 estimate based on old definitions. The adjusted series are shown in Table C-3. Military employment, as reported in the CPS, and total employment (the sum of military and adjusted civilian employment) are also shown in order to provide a continuous series for total employment based mainly on CPS household survey data. This series can be used to derive an alternate measure of labor input that is based on such data.

DEVELOPMENT OF OBE-BASED SERIES. A civilian employment series, excluding work relief employment, that is based largely on OBE establishment data was next compiled for 1929, 1940, 1941, and 1947–69 as the sum of three series. The component series and their total are shown in the first four columns of Table C-4. The sources of the three series are as follows.

1. Full-time and part-time employment of wage and salary workers was derived by deducting work relief and military employment from the all-industry aggregates shown in NIA Table 6.3. Data are from the July issues of the *Survey of Current Business,* for 1968, 1969, and 1970,[7] and from the 1966 Supplement, *The National Income and Product Accounts of the United States, 1929–1965: Statistical Tables.*

2. The number of active proprietors of unincorporated enterprises was obtained from the same sources by deducting the all-industry aggregates shown in Table 6.4, number of "full-time equivalent employees," from the all-industry aggregates

shown in Table 6.6, number of "persons engaged in production."

3. The number of unpaid family workers, for which an establishment series is not available, was taken directly from Table C-3, for the years 1947–69.[8] The 1947 figure was extrapolated to earlier years by use of a series prepared by Stanley Lebergott in *Manpower in Economic Growth: The American Record Since 1800* (McGraw-Hill, 1964), page 513.

COMPARISON OF EMPLOYMENT SERIES. The estimates of total civilian employment based on CPS data (Table C-3) are smaller than those based on establishment data (Table C-4). The difference in level is to be expected. Employment in the CPS is a count of persons; each employed person is counted once. With some exceptions, the establishment-based series is a count of jobs: a person who holds two jobs at once, or changes jobs during a pay period, is counted twice.[9] Another reason the

---

7. U.S. Department of Commerce, Office of Business Economics, *Survey of Current Business,* Vol. 48 (July 1968), Vol. 49 (July 1969), and Vol. 50 (July 1970), respectively.

8. If counts of unpaid family workers reported in censuses of farm and nonfarm establishments had been used as the basis for such a series, they would have run at a far higher level than those used here, which are based on the CPS. (See Edward F. Denison, "Comment" on Edward C. Budd, "Factor Shares, 1850–1910," in Conference on Research in Income and Wealth, *Trends in the American Economy in the Nineteenth Century,* Studies in Income and Wealth, Vol. 24 [Princeton University Press for the National Bureau of Economic Research, 1960], pp. 402–03). The reason for the huge discrepancy between counts from the business censuses and counts from household surveys (including the decennial censuses of population) is unknown, and it is therefore impossible to say which level is correct. This was the basis of the original OBE decision to exclude unpaid family workers from its series for "persons engaged in production."

The number of unpaid family workers does not enter into the OBE calculating procedures as such, and there can, therefore, be no series that can be said to be consistent with OBE national income data in a literal sense. Nevertheless, one would ordinarily suppose data from establishment sources to be more consistent with the output measure. However, the discrepancy is far too big (and probably in the wrong direction) to be due to differences in completeness of coverage. It must somehow be due to differences in reporting unpaid family workers. (It seems that, for reasons unknown, proprietors reporting from their business establishments, who are usually the respondents in establishment censuses, are more likely to report unpaid family workers than are family members reporting from their homes, the usual respondents in household surveys—even though, in the case of farms, home and place of business are usually the same.) Under the conditions stated, the criterion of consistency does not seem to indicate use of any particular source. Use of the CPS-based series gives minimum weight to unpaid family workers in the employment aggregate.

From 1950 to 1959 the series exhibits irregular fluctuations that may reflect sampling or reporting errors, but there was no basis for alteration of the series.

9. The chief exceptions are as follows: (a) Persons whose secondary job is as a proprietor (rather a common situation among professional workers) are not double-

Table C-4. Employment Data, Based Primarily on Establishment Reports, and Derivation of Total Employment, 1929, 1940–41, and 1947–69

Thousands

Year	Civilian employment, excluding work relief, based mainly on establishment reports				Ratio of CPS civilian employment to establishment-based civilian employment (5)	Estimated employment			
	Full-time and part-time employment (1)	Active proprietors of unincorporated enterprises (2)	Unpaid family workers (3)	Total (4)		Civilian, except work relief (6)	Work relief (7)	Military (8)	Total (9)
	Excluding Alaska and Hawaii								
1929	37,375	10,320	1,670	49,365	n.a.	47,274	0	261	47,535
1940	37,874	10,150	1,786	49,810	n.a.	47,701	2,830	549	51,080
1941	41,946	10,090	1,948	53,984	n.a.	51,698	2,209	1,676	55,583
1947	48,176	10,199	1,941	60,316	0.9593	57,762	0	1,599	59,361
1948	49,397	10,211	1,860	61,468	0.9625	58,865	0	1,468	60,333
1949	48,027	10,094	1,862	59,983	0.9748	57,443	0	1,604	59,047
1950	49,878	10,056	1,740	61,674	0.9696	59,062	0	1,694	60,756
1951	52,710	9,805	1,697	64,212	0.9474	61,493	0	3,124	64,617
1952	53,530	9,768	1,685	64,983	0.9400	62,231	0	3,638	65,869
1953	54,725	9,633	1,612	65,970	0.9398	63,176	0	3,545	66,721
1954	53,293	9,511	1,592	64,396 *	0.9464	61,669	0	3,326	64,995
1955	55,162	9,357	1,732	66,251	0.9509	63,445	0	3,025	66,470
1956	56,947	9,215	1,809	67,971	0.9528	65,092	0	2,848	67,940
1957	57,362	9,083	1,765	68,210	0.9539	65,321	0	2,786	68,107
1958	56,076	8,898	1,607	66,581	0.9615	63,761	0	2,632	66,393
1959	57,728	8,775	1,633	68,136	0.9633	65,250	0	2,543	67,793
1960	n.a.	n.a.	n.a.	n.a.	n.a.	65,918	0	2,516	68,434
	Including Alaska and Hawaii								
1960	58,814	8,733	1,586	69,133	0.9653	66,205	0	2,516	68,721
1961	58,764	8,689	1,565	69,018	0.9686	66,095	0	2,598	68,693
1962	60,366	8,584	1,452	70,402	0.9645	67,420	0	2,800	70,220
1963	61,453	8,442	1,350	71,245	0.9666	68,228	0	2,723	70,951
1964	62,942	8,461	1,337	72,740	0.9681	69,659	0	2,720	72,379
1965	65,318	8,416	1,332	75,066	0.9623	71,887	0	2,732	74,619
1966	68,570	8,315	1,203	78,088	0.9493	74,781	0	3,156	77,937
1967	70,057	8,191	1,174	79,422	0.9520	76,058	0	3,421	79,479
1968	72,063	8,207	1,153	81,423	0.9482	77,975	0	3,517	81,492
1969	74,276	8,260	1,160	83,696	0.9465	80,151	0	3,463	83,614

Sources: Columns 1, 2, 7, and 8, Office of Business Economics, national income accounts (see Appendix A, note 2); column 3, Table C-3, column 5, except 1929, 1940, and 1941, for which years see text; column 4, sum of columns 1, 2, and 3; column 5, ratio of Table C-3, column 3, to Table C-4, column 4; column 6, column 4 × 0.95765 (the average value of column 5 in 1947–68), except for 1960 excluding Alaska and Hawaii, for which estimate see text; column 9, sum of columns 6, 7, and 8.

n.a. Not available.

CPS series is lower is that it is tied to population totals founded on the Censuses of Population for 1940, 1950, and 1960, which are believed to be understated. The effect of these differences is only partially offset by inclusion in the CPS series—but not the OBE series—of wage and salary work-

counted because they are omitted from the series for active proprietors. (b) Persons are not counted as unpaid family workers if they hold another job; and (c) Private household workers employed by more than one household are counted only once. There are also a few minor components of wage and salary employment in which secondary workers are not counted because the series is based on Census of Population or CPS data.

ers absent from their jobs without pay. There are also many less important differences.[10]

The difference between the levels of the two series is of little concern. But the two series also differ in movement. This forces me to choose between them. Conceptually, I prefer a count of persons, as in the CPS series, to a count of jobs because data used to measure characteristics of

10. For a comprehensive discussion of differences in the levels of the series for nonagricultural wage and salary workers in recent years, see Gloria P. Green, "Comparing Employment Estimates from Household and Payroll Surveys," *Monthly Labor Review*, Vol. 92 (December 1969), pp. 9–14.

employed persons utilized in developing other aspects of labor input refer to persons. The question therefore is: which series measures changes in the number of persons employed better and, more importantly, in a way that is more consistent statistically with the output measure? If the difference in movement between the two series results mainly from the conceptual difference, the CPS series should be used. If the difference is mainly statistical in character, the establishment-based series should be used for consistency with the output measure.

If a suitable measure of the number of multiple jobholders were available annually, the effect of the chief conceptual difference could be tested. But (aside from some early figures that rather clearly are not comparable to later data) only the following scattered data for the number of employed persons with two jobs or more are available; they come from the CPS sample.[11]

	Multiple jobholders	
	Number (thousands)	Percentage of employed persons
Excluding Alaska and Hawaii		
July 1956	3,653	5.5
July 1957	3,570	5.3
July 1958	3,099	4.8
December 1959	2,966	4.5
Including Alaska and Hawaii		
December 1960	3,012	4.6
May 1962	3,342	4.9
May 1963	3,921	5.7
May 1964	3,726	5.2
May 1965	3,756	5.2
May 1966	3,636	4.9
May 1969	4,008	5.2
May 1970	4,048	5.2

It seems clear that data for different years cannot be compared when they refer to different months; the two December figures, for example, are the two smallest in the series. Hence, the multiple jobholder figures could, at most, be used only *within* three short fragments of the period covered in this study: 1956–58, 1959–60, and 1962–69. Even within these periods, the figures reported are erratic. I am unable to discern any

clear trend or consistent cyclical pattern. My conclusion is that data for a single month of the year are too much affected by either sampling error or random fluctuations to be helpful in appraising the reason the two annual employment series differ.[12]

To facilitate closer comparison of the two employment series, the ratio of the CPS-based series to the establishment-based series is shown in Table C-4, column 5. The average ratio for the years 1947 through 1968 is 0.95765. A clear trend in the ratio might indicate a trend in dual jobholding, but no such trend appears. For example, the ratio was lower throughout 1966–69 than in 1947–50, but higher than in 1951–54. Again, a clear cyclical pattern in the ratio might indicate cyclical movements in dual jobholding. The ratio actually did rise in the years in which unemployment increased, indicating a smaller drop or larger increase in the CPS-based than in the establishment-based employment series in these years. This could mean that dual jobholding decreases in recessions. But there is no corresponding pattern of a declining ratio when unemployment was declining. The ratio rose in about half of the years when unemployment declined, and some of the largest increases in the ratio occurred in periods of falling unemployment. A cyclical pattern in dual jobholding may contribute to differences in the movement of the two series but, if so, this influence cannot be isolated. I do not believe it can be the chief cause of changes in the ratio.

Two aspects of the comparison do stand out. One is "runs" in the ratios: a ratio above 0.95765 indicates that, after allowance for the average difference in level, the CPS-based series is above the establishment-based series, and a lower ratio that the CPS-based series is below the establishment-based series. The CPS-based series is higher than the establishment-based series throughout the 1947–50 and 1958–65 periods and lower throughout the 1951–57 and 1966–69 periods. A second aspect is that, within as well as between these periods, the ratios move about in apparently erratic fashion. Changes in employment from one

---

11. Harvey R. Hamel, "Moonlighting—An Economic Phenomenon," reprinted, with detailed statistics added, from *Monthly Labor Review,* Vol. 90 (October 1967), Special Labor Force Report 90, "Multiple Jobholders in May 1970," p. 19. See also Howard V. Hayghe and Kopp Michelotti, "Multiple Jobholders in 1970 and 1971," reprinted, with supplementary tables, from *Monthly Labor Review,* Vol. 94 (October 1971), Special Labor Force Report 139.

12. In a memorandum prepared for the Gordon Committee in 1962, the Bureau of Labor Statistics also concluded that "surveys of dual jobholding ... taken ... since 1943 ... have not been frequent enough to determine whether there is any seasonal, cyclical, or secular trend in the phenomenon. What appears to be an increase since 1950 is probably only the result of a more careful probing for second jobs." President's Committee to Appraise Employment and Unemployment Statistics, *Measuring Employment and Unemployment* (1962), p. 365.

year to the next, and even over several years, are often substantially different in the two series.

Computation of Final Series

In computing the final series for employment I made the judgment that differences in movement between the two civilian employment series result chiefly from statistical inconsistency rather than from differences in definition. This implies that, even though it is desirable to measure employment in terms of persons rather than jobs, the establishment-based series probably provides a more accurate time series for persons employed than the CPS-based series, and certainly one that is more consistent with the output measure. It has therefore been adopted in this study.[13] To incorporate the general level of the CPS series, while retaining the movement of the establishment-based series, the establishment-based estimate for each year was multiplied by the average 1947–68 ratio (0.95765) of the CPS-based to the establishment-based estimate. The resulting series provides the measure of total civilian employment (excluding work relief employment) that is used in this study (Table C-4, column 6).

OBE could not provide 1960 data excluding Alaska and Hawaii. The estimate shown in Table C-4 is based on use of the ratio of 1960 employment excluding Alaska and Hawaii to 1960 employment including these states that is implied by the CPS data shown in Table C-2. This estimate is reexamined later in this appendix.

OBE estimates of military employment and work relief employment (full-time and part-time) were added to the civilian employment series to obtain total employment. The OBE military employment series, which differs only very slightly from the CPS series, was chosen for comparability with the output measure. These data are shown in Table C-4, and the employment aggregate is transferred to Table C-1.

Employment by Type

In Table C-1, columns 2 through 5 divide the total number of persons employed among four groups of workers. The estimates are described in this section.

Farm Employment

The procedure adopted to measure farm employment is similar to that used to obtain total civilian employment: the movement is based chiefly on OBE data, the average level (and therefore the average ratio of farm to total civilian employment) on CPS data. The calculations and estimates are shown in Table C-5.

The series based largely on establishment reports (column 3) is the sum of OBE estimates of full-time and part-time employment and the number of active proprietors of unincorporated enterprises in "farms" (from the same tables and issues of the *Survey of Current Business* as were used in deriving total civilian employment [see page 168]) and the CPS series for unpaid family workers in agriculture (adjusted to the 1966–69 level) from Table C-3. Data from Lebergott, *Manpower in Economic Growth,* were used to extrapolate the unpaid family worker series to 1929, 1940, and 1941.

For comparison with CPS data for agricultural employment, which include the agricultural services industry as well as farms, OBE estimates of full-time and part-time employment and the number of active proprietors in agricultural services were added to the farm estimates (Table C-5, column 5). The series for agricultural services were provided by OBE.

Ratios of the CPS-based estimates to the estimates based largely on OBE data are shown in Table C-5, column 6. The ratios resemble the similar ratios for total civilian employment; they show no particular trend or cyclical pattern, but they do show "runs" of years when the ratio was above or below its average level of 0.9497, as well as apparently random fluctuations. The swings in the ratios are much wider than those in the ratios for all civilian employment.

The final series for farm employment (which excludes agricultural services) was obtained by multiplying the farm employment series based largely on establishment data by the average 1947–68 value of the ratios in column 6. The 1960 estimate excluding Alaska and Hawaii was obtained on the assumption that the ratio of employment excluding these states to employment including them was the same as in the CPS agricultural employment series.

---

13. One set of data that might have been, but was not, used in the reconciliation of establishment and CPS-based employment data concerns persons absent from their jobs without pay. I discuss these data in a final section of this appendix. Their use would very slightly increase the discrepancies between the movements of the establishment and the labor force series.

Table C-5. Derivation of Estimates of Farm Employment, 1929, 1940–41, and 1947–69
Thousands

	Farm employment based largely on establishment reports			Agricultural services: wage and salary workers and proprietors[a] (4)	Agricultural employment based largely on establishment reports (5)	Ratio of CPS agricultural employment to establishment-based agricultural employment (6)	Estimated farm employment (7)
Year	Wage and salary workers and proprietors[a] (1)	Unpaid family workers (2)	Total (3)				
	Excluding Alaska and Hawaii						
1929	8,969	1,458	10,427	138	10,565	n.a.	9,903
1940	7,832	1,548	9,380	151	9,531	n.a.	8,908
1941	7,730	1,675	9,405	151	9,556	n.a.	8,932
1947	6,749	1,583	8,332	195	8,527	0.9588	7,913
1948	6,724	1,524	8,248	210	8,458	0.9319	7,833
1949	6,509	1,531	8,040	202	8,242	0.9632	7,636
1950	6,489	1,398	7,887	204	8,091	0.9176	7,490
1951	6,032	1,358	7,390	225	7,615	0.9165	7,018
1952	5,849	1,315	7,164	241	7,405	0.9083	6,804
1953	5,655	1,247	6,902	240	7,142	0.9088	6,555
1954	5,625	1,205	6,830	245	7,075	0.9091	6,486
1955	5,421	1,273	6,694	245	6,939	0.9588	6,357
1956	5,127	1,296	6,423	245	6,668	0.9760	6,100
1957	4,893	1,206	6,099	246	6,345	0.9710	5,792
1958	4,747	1,064	5,811	243	6,054	0.9559	5,519
1959	4,580	1,097	5,677	238	5,915	0.9770	5,391
1960	n.a.	n.a.	n.a.	n.a.	n.a.	n.a.	5,162
	Including Alaska and Hawaii						
1960	4,427	1,034	5,461	240	5,701	0.9940	5,186
1961	4,368	965	5,333	243	5,576	0.9702	5,065
1962	4,247	887	5,134	249	5,383	0.9547	4,876
1963	4,115	817	4,932	253	5,185	0.9446	4,684
1964	3,876	797	4,673	253	4,926	0.9572	4,438
1965	3,732	770	4,502	261	4,763	0.9532	4,276
1966	3,516	676	4,192	266	4,458	0.9343	3,981
1967	3,318	654	3,972	269	4,241	0.9616	3,772
1968	3,233	652	3,885	277	4,162	0.9702	3,690
1969	3,127	625	3,752	286	4,038	0.9443	3,563

Sources: Columns 1 and 4, Office of Business Economics; column 2, Table C-3, column 5, except 1929, 1940, and 1941, for which estimates see text; column 3, sum of columns 1 and 2; column 5, sum of columns 3 and 4; column 6, ratio of Table C-3, column 4, to Table C-5, column 5; column 7, column 3 × 0.9497 (the average value of column 6 in 1947–68), except for 1960 excluding Alaska and Hawaii, for which estimate see text.

n.a. Not available.

a. This is the sum of average full-time and part-time employment and active proprietors of unincorporated enterprises.

Nonfarm Self-Employed and Unpaid Family Workers

A series based largely on OBE estimates was compiled as the sum of the OBE series for active proprietors of unincorporated enterprises in non-farm industries (computed by deducting proprietors in farms from the all-industry aggregate) and the CPS series for unpaid family workers in nonagricultural industries obtained in Table C-3 by adjusting the figures based on the old definitions to the new definitions. (The 1947 figure for unpaid family workers was extrapolated to 1929, 1940, and 1941 by data from Lebergott.) The series is conceptually similar to a count of per-sons, and therefore comparable to the all-industry employment totals, because the count of proprietors is confined to those devoting the major portion of their time to the business while that of unpaid family workers is based on CPS data. It was used directly to measure this component of employment.[14] The series is shown in Table C-6.

The CPS series was not used to establish the average level of the establishment-based series, as was done in the case of total civilian employment

14. The 1960 figure for proprietors, excluding Alaska and Hawaii, was obtained by applying the ratio of 1960 employment of nonfarm proprietors excluding these states to 1960 employment including them implied by the CPS data in Table C-2.

Table C-6. Estimates of Self-Employed and Unpaid Family Workers in Nonfarm Industries, 1929, 1940–41, and 1947–69

Thousands

Year	Active proprietors of unincorporated enterprises (1)	Unpaid family workers (2)	Total (3)
Excluding Alaska and Hawaii			
1929	4,754	247	5,001
1940	4,997	274	5,271
1941	5,012	311	5,323
1947	5,681	391	6,072
1948	5,801	367	6,168
1949	5,792	362	6,154
1950	5,862	370	6,232
1951	5,926	366	6,292
1952	5,974	394	6,368
1953	5,973	387	6,360
1954	5,853	407	6,260
1955	5,827	479	6,306
1956	5,879	532	6,411
1957	5,963	574	6,537
1958	5,970	554	6,524
1959	5,980	546	6,526
1960	6,056	561	6,617
Including Alaska and Hawaii			
1960	6,078	563	6,641
1961	6,115	606	6,721
1962	6,106	570	6,676
1963	6,072	537	6,609
1964	6,160	543	6,703
1965	6,177	564	6,741
1966	6,172	527	6,699
1967	6,138	520	6,658
1968	6,199	501	6,700
1969	6,317	535	6,852

Sources: Column 1, Office of Business Economics, except for 1960 excluding Alaska and Hawaii, for which estimate see text; column 2, Table C-3, column 7, except 1929, 1940, 1941, for which estimates see text; column 3, sum of columns 1 and 2.

and farm employment, because of uncertainty about the appropriate level. There were two difficulties.

First, and less important, there are some definitional differences between the OBE and CPS class-of-worker data. For example, OBE classifies all persons employed in private households as wage and salary workers whereas some are classified as self-employed in the CPS estimates (65,000 in 1966, by the old definitions; 39,000 plus 14- and 15-year-olds in 1967, by the new definitions). There appear also to be minor differences of a similar type in welfare services (where CPS shows 14,000 in both years), and probably in other groups.

Second, and much more important, is the prob-

lem created by a sharp drop in the CPS series in 1967 when a new question was added to the survey. The 1966 CPS estimate of self-employed workers in nonagricultural industries is 6,101,000. The 1966 figure comparable to the 1967 and later CPS estimates (but including 14- and 15-year-olds like the other 1966 figure) is only 5,335,000.

Up to 1966, the OBE and CPS series for nonagricultural self-employment showed divergencies of movement like those observed in other series, but their levels were similar. The 1966 OBE figure, with proprietors in agricultural services excluded for comparability with the CPS total, is 6,060,000. The CPS figure, adjusted to exclude self-employed persons in the private households industry for comparability with the OBE total, is 6,036,000. This is a trivial difference. But on the basis of the new definitions the CPS figure excluding private households is only about 5,300,000, far below the OBE estimate.

The change in the CPS figure stems mainly from the addition of the new question in 1967, mentioned above. When a person is reported as self-employed, the respondent is asked whether the business is incorporated. If the answer is yes, the individual is tabulated as a wage and salary worker rather than as self-employed. The reduction in the number of self-employed is interpreted by BLS as a correction due to elimination of corporate officers formerly misclassified as self-employed. If it can be assumed that respondents (usually housewives) know whether or not the business is incorporated, this interpretation seems inescapable.

The new series is, however, much below the OBE series, and also seems low in comparison with tax returns. In wholesale and retail trade, for example, returns for 1966 were filed by 1,813,000 sole proprietorships and by 231,000 active partnerships having 524,000 partners.[15] This adds to 2,337,000 firm members. Turnover of firms within the year and inclusion of some proprietors and partners who were either inactive or primarily engaged in another activity could readily explain why the tax figure of 2,337,000 exceeded the 1966 OBE figure of 2,207,000 or the old 1966 CPS figure of 2,145,000. But the amount by which it exceeds the new CPS level, which in 1967 was 1,665,000 persons 16 years of age and over plus less than 100,000 14- and 15-year-olds, seems very

15. U.S. Internal Revenue Service, *Statistics of Income —1966, Business Income Tax Returns* (1969), pp. 12, 164.

large. Hoping to find possible reasons for discrepancies between the estimates, I compared detailed industry breakdowns of the OBE, old CPS, and new CPS estimates but nothing helpful was revealed. Glaringly large differences between the OBE and old CPS estimates by industry are absent. The reduction in the CPS series when the new question was introduced was not concentrated by industry (except that professional services and transportation, communications, and public utilities were little affected). From the information available, it is impossible to judge whether the new CPS or the OBE figures more accurately portray the correct level.

Even if the new CPS level is accepted, there is no satisfactory way to adjust the data prior to 1966 so as to eliminate the large number of corporate officers who, this decision would imply, were misclassified as self-employed. A simple percentage adjustment would not be acceptable in view of the shift toward corporations that has occurred in the composition of the business population by legal form.

Employment in General Government, Households, Institutions, and the "Rest of the World"

Definitions used in this section correspond to those used by the Office of Business Economics in classifying national income by sector and legal form of organization (national income accounts, Table 1.13).

General government employment refers to all government employment except employment in government enterprises. Household employment consists of employment in private households. "Institutions" refer to nonprofit organizations serving individuals. Employment in the "rest of the world," which never exceeds 6,000, consists of American citizens employed in the United States by foreign embassies and international organizations. Together, these sectors cover all employment except that defined as "business."

The average numbers of full-time and part-time employees in these sectors, as estimated by the Office of Business Economics, were obtained from that agency. Except for institutions, the necessary data are published in Table 6.3 of the national income accounts. Unpublished data for institutions were provided by OBE. Summary data of all people employed in the sector are shown in Table C-7.

An adjustment to eliminate secondary employment was needed so that the sectoral series would conform with my total employment series. However, data compiled according to this classification are not available from the CPS. The OBE series, except those for military and work relief employment, were multiplied by the same ratio, 0.95765, that was applied to total civilian employment, except work relief.

The 1960 estimate for general government excluding Alaska and Hawaii is described in the additional comments at the end of this appendix. The 1960 estimate for households and institutions excluding Alaska and Hawaii was obtained by reducing the figure which includes those states by the same percentage as total civilian employment given in Table C-2.

Wage and Salary Workers in Nonfarm Business

Persons employed as wage and salary workers in nonfarm business are obtained by subtraction in Table C-1, column 5.

The movement of this series is extremely close to that of a series for average full-time and part-time employment in nonfarm business obtained directly from OBE data by subtracting farms, general government, households, institutions, and the "rest of the world" from the all-industry total for full-time and part-time employment of wage and salary workers. The ratio of the series shown in Table C-1 to the OBE series is 0.952 in all years except 1941, when it is 0.951, and 1966–69, when it is 0.953. In the postwar period the ratio never changes by more than 0.0003 from one year to the next. Thus the reweighting of other components has not impaired the consistency of movement between employment and employee compensation for this group of workers.

Additional Comments

This section provides supplementary information on two aspects of the employment estimates.

Adjustment for Alaska and Hawaii

As previously noted, CPS data were used to adjust 1960 employment estimates to exclude Alaska and Hawaii. A comparison with the OBE income estimates was made to ensure that the adjustments of the two series were consistent.

When Alaska and Hawaii were brought into the national income series in 1960 the following amounts were added to national income: compen-

Table C-7. Derivation of Estimates of Employment in General Government, Households, Institutions, and the "Rest of the World" Sector, 1929, 1940–41, and 1947–69

Thousands

Year	Full-time and part-time civilian employment in general government, except work relief (1)	Civilians employed by general government, except work relief (2)	Work relief employment (3)	Military employment (4)	Persons employed by general government, total (5)	Full-time and part-time employment in households and institutions (6)	Persons employed by households and institutions (7)	Full-time and part-time employment in the "rest of the world" (8)	Total number of persons employed in the sector (9)
			Excluding Alaska and Hawaii						
1929	2,829	2,709	0	261	2,970	3,598	3,446	0	6,416
1940	3,768	3,608	2,830	549	6,987	3,559	3,408	2	10,397
1941	4,109	3,935	2,209	1,676	7,820	3,485	3,337	3	11,160
1947	4,984	4,773	0	1,599	6,372	3,278	3,139	5	9,516
1948	5,156	4,938	0	1,468	6,406	3,547	3,397	5	9,808
1949	5,340	5,114	0	1,604	6,718	3,678	3,522	5	10,245
1950	5,495	5,262	0	1,694	6,956	3,961	3,793	5	10,754
1951	5,869	5,620	0	3,124	8,744	4,050	3,878	5	12,627
1952	6,069	5,812	0	3,638	9,450	4,001	3,832	6	13,288
1953	6,122	5,863	0	3,545	9,408	4,122	3,947	5	13,360
1954	6,212	5,949	0	3,326	9,275	4,138	3,963	5	13,243
1955	6,450	6,177	0	3,025	9,202	4,555	4,362	5	13,569
1956	6,747	6,461	0	2,848	9,309	4,837	4,632	4	13,945
1957	6,970	6,675	0	2,786	9,461	4,962	4,752	4	14,217
1958	7,200	6,895	0	2,632	9,527	5,201	4,981	4	14,512
1959	7,387	7,074	0	2,543	9,617	5,338	5,112	4	14,733
1960	n.a.	7,336	0	2,516	9,852	n.a.	5,173	4	15,029
			Including Alaska and Hawaii						
1960	7,718	7,391	0	2,516	9,907	5,426	5,196	4	15,107
1961	7,909	7,574	0	2,598	10,172	5,637	5,398	4	15,574
1962	8,267	7,917	0	2,800	10,717	5,805	5,559	4	16,280
1963	8,550	8,188	0	2,723	10,911	5,884	5,635	4	16,550
1964	8,832	8,458	0	2,720	11,178	6,063	5,806	4	16,988
1965	9,262	8,870	0	2,732	11,602	6,158	5,897	4	17,503
1966	10,002	9,578	0	3,156	12,734	6,318	6,050	4	18,788
1967	10,513	10,068	0	3,421	13,489	6,381	6,111	4	19,604
1968	10,936	10,473	0	3,517	13,990	6,517	6,241	4	20,235
1969	11,265	10,788	0	3,463	14,251	6,575	6,297	4	20,552

Sources: Columns 1, 3, 4, 6, and 8, Office of Business Economics, national income accounts, Table 6.3 and unpublished data; columns 2 and 7, columns 1 and 6, respectively, × 0.95765, except for 1960 excluding Alaska and Hawaii, for which estimates see text (multiplication of column 8 by 0.95765 does not change the series); column 5, sum of columns 2, 3, and 4; column 9, sum of columns 5, 7, and 8.

sation of employees in private industries, $967 million; compensation of employees in the "government and government enterprises" industry, $315 million; and proprietors' income, $193 million.[16] I eliminated the total of these components, $1,475 million, to secure 1960 national income comparable to earlier years. This amount is 0.45 percent of total employee compensation and proprietors' income in 1960. The reduction in total employment to eliminate Alaska and Hawaii

16. These data, which are from the Regional Economics Division of OBE, exclude the compensation of federal military and civilian employees in Alaska and Hawaii whose earnings were already included in the national income series. The civilian component alone was $130 million.

(Table C-1) is 0.42 percent. For wage and salary workers alone, the reduction in compensation is 0.44 percent and the reduction in employment is 0.45 percent. The similarity of the income and employment reductions indicates that comparability of the employment and national income series is preserved.

The $315 million added to compensation of employees in the "government and government enterprises" industry in 1960 is 0.75 percent of total compensation in that industry, excluding military personnel. This percentage was used to reduce the civilian general government employment series in Table C-7, column 2, to exclude Alaska and Hawaii in 1960.

Unpaid Absences

One of the differences between CPS and establishment data concerns the treatment of persons who are absent from work. CPS employment data include persons who are "employed but not at work," whether they are paid or not. Establishment data for nonagricultural wage and salary workers include, for the most part, only those who are paid.

Annual averages of nonagricultural wage and salary workers who were absent without pay and are included in CPS employment data in the survey weeks are available for the 1957–69 period. They are shown (with 1967 to 1969 adjusted for comparability with earlier years) in Table C-8, column 1. These persons could have been added to the series for "civilian employment based mainly on establishment reports" in Table C-4, column 4, used to determine the movement of civilian employment on a labor force basis. The addition would have brought the establishment series closer conceptually to the household series. An index of my series for total employment is compared in Table C-8 with an index of an alternative series that would be obtained by adop-

tion of this procedure. The series show minor differences in movement and a tendency for the alternative series to rise a little more at the end of the period, especially from 1967 to 1968. Unpaid absences jumped in 1968, and more than held the gain in 1969 and 1970. Over half of the 1968 jump is ascribable to the numbers reported as absent because of illness, and these numbers also increased further in 1969 and 1970. From 1967 to 1968 the alternative series rises more than the series used—by 122,000. This slightly exceeds the total difference (119,000) between the movements of the two series from 1957 through 1967.

Unpaid absences fluctuate greatly from week to week. Neither the level nor movement of the CPS series for unpaid absences is exactly appropriate for addition to the establishment series because CPS reports refer to survey weeks and the establishment data to payroll periods, which are often longer than a week. Nevertheless, if the CPS indication that illness was greater in 1968–70 than earlier is correct, the alternative series probably portrays the movement of employment on a labor force definition slightly better than the series adopted.

Selection between these two series has no effect on my estimates of total hours worked in the economy as a whole or in the business sector. It affects only their division between employment and average hours worked.[17] Use of the alternative series would, however, require division (by estimation for which data are inadequate) of unpaid absences between the nonfarm business sector and the "general government, households, institutions, and rest of the world" sector. It would also necessitate introduction of an artificial component (essentially, allowance for a statistical discrepancy between employment series) into the breakdown of labor input in the "general government, ..." sector, and would complicate slightly the estimation of changes in hours within the business sector. The difference in movement between the two employment series is too small to warrant such an effort merely to alter marginally the distinction between changes in employment and in average hours. I therefore have not adopted this alternative series.

Table C-8. Effect on Employment Index of Allowance for Unpaid Absences, 1957–69
Indexes, 1957 = 100

| | | Indexes of total employment | |
| | Unpaid absences[a] (thousands) | Series adopted | Alternative series |
Year	(1)	(2)	(3)
1957	1,050	100.0	100.0
1958	1,039	97.5	97.5
1959	1,131	99.5	99.7
1960	1,082	100.5	100.5
1961	1,052	100.4	100.4
1962	1,122	102.7	102.7
1963	1,241	103.7	103.9
1964	1,249	105.8	106.0
1965	1,249	109.1	109.2
1966	1,317	114.0	114.1
1967	1,361[a]	116.2	116.4
1968	1,525[a]	119.2	119.5
1969	1,609[a]	122.3	122.7

Sources: Column 1, Bureau of Labor Statistics; column 2, Table C-1, column 1, series linked at 1960; column 3, see text.

a. The numbers reported in 1967, 1968, and 1969 are 1,454, 1,629, and 1,719, respectively. These were reduced by the ratio of unpaid absences of wage and salary workers in 1966 as reported in the CPS to the number reported in the Monthly Labor Survey (MLS) in 1966, as given in Robert L. Stein, "New Definitions for Employment and Unemployment," *Employment and Earnings and Monthly Report on the Labor Force*, Vol. 13 (February 1967), Table 12. Persons 14 and 15 years old (presumably trivial in number) are excluded in 1967, 1968, and 1969 but included in earlier years.

17. Nonagricultural wage and salary workers not at work do not, of course, work any hours. If I were to adjust my employment series to take account of changes in unpaid absences, I would have to make an offsetting adjustment to my average hours per employed person, which are based on BLS establishment data.

APPENDIX D

-»>«<-

Estimates of National Income by Sector

-»>«<-

This appendix describes the derivation of Tables 3-1 and 3-2. It also provides data on employment and national income per person employed in nonresidential business.

Derivation of Tables 3-1 and 3-2

Table 3-1 presents data for national income by sector in current dollars, and Table 3-2 presents similar data in constant dollars. Revised data for 1968 and 1969 published in the July 1971 *Survey of Current Business* are incorporated in columns 4 and 6. Any revision affecting the series for property income from dwellings (column 5) is absorbed in column 7 ("nonresidential business"), which is obtained by subtraction.

Column 1, Total National Income

Data in current and constant prices are from Table 2-1.

Column 2, Work Relief

Data for the federal government and for state and local governments were provided in current and constant prices by the Office of Business Economics.

Column 3, National Income, Excluding Work Relief

Column 1 minus column 2.

Column 4, General Government (Excluding Work Relief), Households, Institutions, and the "Rest of the World"

CURRENT PRICES. This series represents compensation of employees in "general government," "households and institutions," and the "rest of the world" from the national income accounts,[1] Table 1.13, minus work relief from Table 3-1, column 2.

CONSTANT PRICES. National income and GNP are the same in these sectors. Data for "general government" and "households and institutions," rounded to tenths of a billion dollars, are published in the national income accounts, Table 1.8. The figures were obtained from OBE in millions of dollars to avoid rounding errors when sectors were added. Work relief (Table 3-2, column 2) was deducted. To obtain the figure for foreign governments (which OBE does not calculate separately), compensation of employees in the "rest of the world" sector in 1958 (only $22 million) was extrapolated by employment in the "rest of the world" sector.

1960 EXCLUDING ALASKA AND HAWAII. Current prices: To eliminate Alaska and Hawaii, compensation of civilian employees in "general government" and of employees in "households and institutions" were reduced by the same percentages (0.75 and 0.43) as employment. (See Appendix C, pages 174–75.) Constant prices: The 1960 constant-price figure including Alaska and Hawaii was reduced by the same percentage as the current-price figure.

Column 5, Services of Dwellings

Derivation of series for nonlabor national income originating in the services of dwellings industry required, as intermediate steps, derivation of certain additional series. To assist the explanation, for selected years Table D-1 gives the values of these series. Personal consumption expenditures for the space rental value of dwellings are also provided for comparison. All values are the sum of separate estimates for nonfarm dwellings and for farm dwellings. In the base year 1958, nonfarm dwellings comprised 94 percent and farm dwellings 6 percent of the nonlabor national income aggregate. No adjustment for inclusion of Alaska and Hawaii in 1960 was indicated or made. The data were derived as follows:

---

1. See Appendix A, note 2, for full source reference.

Table D-1. Various Series for the Services of Dwellings Industry, Selected Years, 1929–69
Billions of dollars

Item	1929	1941	1947	1950	1958	1960	1969
Current prices							
1. Nonlabor GNP at factor cost	7.7	5.9	9.1	12.5	25.3	28.6	51.9
2. Depreciation	2.8	2.9	5.3	6.7	10.5	11.7	19.4
3. Nonlabor national income	5.0	3.0	3.8	5.9	14.8	16.9	32.5
4. Nonlabor GNP at market prices	9.6	7.8	11.2	15.4	31.5	36.1	68.5
5. Personal consumption expenditures	11.3	9.9	15.2	20.7	39.9	44.9	81.0
Constant (1958) prices							
6. Nonlabor GNP at market prices	11.7	12.3	15.9	19.3	31.5	35.1	57.2
7. Depreciation	7.2	7.3	7.3	8.1	10.5	11.2	14.1
8. Nonlabor NNP at market prices	4.5	5.0	8.5	11.2	21.0	23.9	43.1
9. Nonlabor national income	3.2	3.6	6.1	8.0	14.8	16.8	30.3
10. Personal consumption expenditures	13.7	15.6	21.4	25.9	40.0	43.6	67.6

Source: See text for derivation.

NONLABOR GNP AT FACTOR COST IN CURRENT PRICES (LINE 1). Data for nonfarm dwellings are totals of the following series: net rental income of all landlords from tenant-occupied nonfarm houses, net rental income from owner-occupied nonfarm houses, mortgage interest paid by all landlords on tenant-occupied nonfarm houses, mortgage interest on owner-occupied nonfarm houses, and capital consumption allowances (as estimated in the national accounts) on all nonfarm houses. Data for farm houses are the sum of the net rental value of all farm dwellings, capital consumption allowances (as implied by the national accounts) on all farm dwellings, and interest on owner-occupied farm homes. The series are from OBE worksheets.

DEPRECIATION IN CURRENT PRICES (LINE 2). The series used for nonfarm and farm dwellings are the same as those used to derive total national income. They are based on a fifty-year average service life, straight-line depreciation, and the Winfrey distribution.

NONLABOR NATIONAL INCOME IN CURRENT PRICES (LINE 3). For the nonfarm and farm components, depreciation in current prices was deducted from nonlabor GNP at factor cost.

NONLABOR GNP AT CURRENT MARKET PRICES (LINE 4). For nonfarm dwellings, the series is the sum of nonlabor GNP at factor cost and taxes on nonfarm dwellings; taxes are from OBE worksheets. For farm dwellings, the series is the sum of nonlabor GNP at factor cost and taxes on owner-occupied farm dwellings.[2]

PERSONAL CONSUMPTION EXPENDITURES AT CUR-RENT PRICES (LINE 5). This is the sum of the space rental values of owner-occupied and tenant-occupied nonfarm dwellings and of farm houses, from the national income accounts, Table 2.5.

NONLABOR GNP AT CONSTANT MARKET PRICES (LINE 6). Nonlabor GNP at current market prices for nonfarm dwellings was deflated by the OBE implicit deflator for the space rental value of nonfarm dwellings, which is the same for owner-occupied and for tenant-occupied dwellings.[3] The farm series was deflated by the implicit deflator for the rental value of farm houses. The deflators are from the national income accounts, Table 8.6.

DEPRECIATION AT CONSTANT PRICES (LINE 7). The depreciation series used for nonfarm and farm dwellings are the same as those used in the derivation of total national income.

NONLABOR NNP AT CONSTANT MARKET PRICES (LINE 8). For the nonfarm and farm components, depreciation in 1958 prices was deducted from nonlabor GNP at constant market prices.

NONLABOR NATIONAL INCOME AT CONSTANT PRICES (LINE 9). Nonlabor national income in current prices in 1958 was extrapolated by nonlabor NNP at 1958 market prices; the calculations were made separately for nonfarm and farm dwellings.

METHODOLOGICAL COMMENTS ON CONSTANT-PRICE ESTIMATES. First, ideally a double-deflation procedure would be followed to obtain GNP at constant market prices instead of the procedure used here, which implies the same price index for purchases from other industries that enter into space rent as for value added. However, purchases from other industries (chiefly maintenance) average only about one-fifth of the gross value of output,

2. Taxes on tenant-occupied farm dwellings are omitted. However, this GNP series is used only to derive national income in 1958 prices, and the omission of these taxes can have only a negligible effect on the estimates for that series.

3. The resulting series for nonfarm dwellings is shown in Table A-6, column 3.

so the error probably is not large. Second, if compensation of employees in the services of dwellings industry were known, a slightly better procedure to secure nonlabor national income in constant prices could be used. Employee compensation would be added to nonlabor GNP at factor cost in current prices and retained until national income at constant prices was derived. This series would then be allocated between labor and nonlabor earnings in proportion to current-dollar earnings. Lack of a series for compensation of employees prevented this procedure. The procedure followed is almost, but not quite, equivalent to doing this. Labor earnings are too small for the difference to be of any importance.

MOVEMENT OF THE CONSTANT-PRICE SERIES. The upward trend in the nonlabor national income in constant 1958 prices originating in the dwellings industry is sharp. This mainly reflects the movement of constant-price GNP, which in turn reflects the very sharp rise in personal consumption expenditures for space rent measured in constant prices (Table D-1, line 10). The rise in real national income is, to be sure, further accentuated in most periods because depreciation in constant prices rises by a smaller percentage than GNP in constant prices. However, the price index for residential construction is generally believed to be biased upward, and substitution of a price series that increased less would probably yield a series for national income in constant prices that would rise even more rapidly than that presented here.

The rise in the constant-price space rent series is so very large as to be suspect. It implies that by 1968 per capita consumption of housing services—exclusive of equipment, furnishings, and utilities—was nearly three times as large as it had been in 1929, more than twice as large as in 1947, and one-third larger than in 1960, only eight years earlier.

One would expect indexes of the gross stock of dwellings and of space rental value, both measured in constant prices, to be fairly similar if data were consistent. The space rental value of nonfarm dwellings (which dominate the total) is deflated by the rent component of the BLS Consumers Price Index. This is an index of rent paid on identical units so, if data are consistent, there should be no change between any two dates in the ratio of rental value to the gross stock of capital and land for nonfarm units occupied at both dates. The overall ratio may appropriately rise if the ratio is higher for new units than for previously existing units, or if the percentage of vacant units declines.

My procedure does not make use of a capital stock series for dwellings, and this is one of its advantages. But it may be noted that the real gross output (space rental value) of dwellings rises more in most periods than a constant-dollar gross capital stock series based on a fifty-year service life, the Winfrey distribution, and the national accounts deflator for residential construction. Indexes of the two in selected years compare as follows for nonfarm and farm units combined (1969 = 100):

	1929	1941	1947	1950	1960	1969
Gross capital stock	52	53	53	58	80	100
Space rent	20	23	32	38	64	100

It is fairly evident that the rise in space rent is too large to be consistent with the rise in gross stock between each of these dates, except perhaps from 1929 to 1941 when the occupancy ratio rose.

A similar comparison of current-price series may be made. These indexes are as follows (1969 = 100):

	1929	1941	1947	1950	1960	1969
Gross capital stock	14	15	27	38	60	100
Space rent	14	12	19	26	55	100

The change in the two series from 1929 to 1969 is similar. Changes are also fairly similar in some subperiods, but in others they are not; however, there is no strong reason to expect the two current-dollar indexes to move alike in the short run.

The comparisons suggest that the reason the constant-dollar space rent series persistently rises more than the capital stock series is the presence of an upward bias in the residential construction cost index used to deflate the capital stock, a downward bias in the rent index used to deflate space rents—or both. That there is an upward bias in the construction cost index is highly probable, and generally accepted. However, I am inclined to suspect that the greater error is in the rental price index. As late as 1968 the price index for nonfarm space rents was only 35 percent above the 1929 index, 68 percent above 1947, and 12 percent above 1960, and its use yields a remarkably large rise in constant-price space rents.

Because the reason for the persistently higher rise in space rental value than in the stock of dwellings when both are measured in constant prices is uncertain, it is difficult to explain why national income in this sector has risen so much, or to project the series into the future. However, this does not restrict one's ability to isolate the contribution of housing to the past increase in measured national income.

Column 6, International Assets

Current prices. The sum of corporate profits and net interest in the "rest of the world" is from the national income accounts, Table 1.13.

Constant prices. This is GNP (which is the same as national income) in 1958 prices originating in the "rest of the world" from the national income accounts, Table 1.8. Labor earnings classified in the "rest of the world" were deducted but are too small to affect the rounded numbers.

Column 7, Nonresidential Business

Table 3-1, column 3 less columns 4, 5, and 6.

Employment and National Income per Person Employed in Nonresidential Business

The constant-price series for national income in nonresidential business, together with the detailed employment data in Table C-1, permit the calculation of total employment and national income per person employed in nonresidential business. Table D-2 provides the data.

Table D-2. Nonresidential Business: Employment and National Income per Person Employed, 1929, 1940–41, and 1947–69

	Employment		National income per person employed, in 1958 prices	
Year	Number (thousands) (1)	Index (1958 = 100) (2)	Dollars (3)	Index (1958 = 100) (4)
Excluding Alaska and Hawaii				
1929	41,119	79.26	3,325	58.84
1940	40,683	78.42	3,641	64.41
1941	44,423	85.62	3,976	70.35
1947	49,845	96.08	4,252	75.24
1948	50,525	97.39	4,471	79.11
1949	48,802	94.07	4,486	79.37
1950	50,002	96.38	4,835	85.55
1951	51,990	100.21	4,908	86.84
1952	52,581	101.35	4,980	88.12
1953	53,361	102.85	5,144	91.02
1954	51,752	99.75	5,179	91.63
1955	52,901	101.97	5,553	98.24
1956	53,995	104.07	5,572	98.59
1957	53,890	103.87	5,608	99.22
1958	51,881	100.00	5,652	100.00
1959	53,060	102.27	6,017	106.46
1960	53,405	102.94	6,080	107.57
Including Alaska and Hawaii				
1960	53,614	102.94	6,077	107.57
1961	53,119	101.99	6,218	110.06
1962	53,940	103.56	6,547	115.89
1963	54,401	104.45	6,776	119.94
1964	55,391	106.35	7,063	125.02
1965	57,116	109.66	7,351	130.11
1966	59,149	113.56	7,546	133.57
1967	59,875	114.96	7,562	133.86
1968	61,257	117.61	7,774	137.60
1969	63,062	121.08	7,740	137.00

Sources: Column 1, Table C-1, sum of columns 2, 3, and 5; columns 2 and 4, computed from column 1 and data underlying column 3; column 3, data underlying Table 3-2, column 7, divided by column 1.

⤳⋙⋘⤝

Total and Average Hours Worked

⤳⋙⋘⤝

To discuss estimates of average and total hours of work, it is necessary to distinguish (1) between employment defined as the number of employed persons and employment defined as the number of jobs filled by employed persons (excluding those absent without pay), (2) between hours worked and hours "paid for," and (3) between establishment reports and household surveys as sources of data.[1]

The *total* number of hours *worked* is conceptually the same no matter how employment is defined. However, *average* hours worked are conceptually longer if employment is measured by persons employed (the definition of employment used in household surveys) than if employment is measured by jobs (the definition of employment used in establishment reports) because there are fewer employed persons than there are jobs. Households report hours worked, whereas establishments report hours paid for that must be adjusted to yield hours worked. Data from household surveys and from establishment reports differ not only conceptually but also statistically.

Like my employment estimates, my estimates of average hours follow the household survey *definitions* of employment and hours but insofar as possible they are derived statistically from

1. In the case of household survey data, it is also necessary to distinguish between persons employed and persons actually "at work" during a week. When I refer to employment from household surveys in this appendix I shall always mean persons employed, and when I refer to "average hours" I shall always mean total hours divided by employment, not by persons at work. Average hours published in the Current Population Surveys (CPS) refer to persons at work and are longer than average hours per person employed.

establishment reports. The Bureau of Labor Statistics is the source of all data for average hours that are used in my estimates for the postwar years.

PART ONE: THE BUSINESS SECTOR

Measurement of labor input in nonresidential business requires estimates of total and average hours worked that refer to persons employed in this sector. These estimates will now be described and presented. The descriptions of the derivation of the estimates refer only to the postwar years. The estimates for 1929, 1940, and 1941 are described in the final section of Appendix G. As noted in Chapter 3 employees of apartment houses are included in labor input so the terms "business" and "nonresidential business" are used interchangeably in describing the labor estimates.

Total Weekly Hours

Total weekly hours worked in the business sector are the sum of estimates for three groups of employed persons. These are persons employed on farms, nonfarm self-employed and unpaid family workers, and wage and salary workers employed in nonfarm business. Total hours for each group are the product of estimates of employment and of average weekly hours. Series developed in Appendix C are used for employment. Establishment data provide the basis of average hours estimates for nonfarm wage and salary workers, who comprise the bulk of business employment, but not for other groups.

Farm and Self-Employed Workers

Farm employment is taken from Table C-1, column 2. The number of nonfarm self-employed and unpaid family workers is taken from Table C-1, column 3. Both series represent my estimates of *persons* employed, measured in accordance with the household survey definition.

Average hours for these groups come from the body of data developed by the Bureau of Labor Statistics (BLS) to measure total man-hours "on an establishment basis." Despite this description, average hours for these components are derived by BLS from household survey data and refer to average hours *worked* (not paid for) per *person* employed (not per job). They are therefore consistent with the definition of my employment series. For farm workers, the BLS series for average hours of all farm workers was used. For nonfarm proprietors and unpaid family workers, the quotient of total weekly hours and total employment for these groups, both as estimated by BLS, was used. These series are shown in Table E-1, columns 5 and 6. Total hours, the product of average hours and my employment estimates, are shown in columns 1 and 2.

Wage and Salary Workers in Nonfarm Business

The starting point for the estimates for wage and salary workers is a series for hours "paid for" per *job*. This series also comes from the body of data developed by BLS to measure total man-

hours on an establishment basis, but in this case actually stems from establishment reports.[2] The series refers to nonfarm wage and salary workers employed in "private industries" (which are defined to include government enterprises). But it does not include industries grouped in the Standard Industrial Classification (SIC) Manual (U.S. Bureau of the Budget, 1967) under numbers 80 (medical and other health services), 82 (educational services), 86 (nonprofit membership organizations), and 88 (private households). The coverage of this series corresponds closely to that

2. BLS, of course, has supplemented reported data with estimates for groups for which data are not available.

Table E-1. Nonresidential Business: Total and Average Hours Worked per Week, 1929, 1940–41, and 1947–69

	Total weekly hours worked (millions)				Weekly hours worked per person employed				Weekly hours worked per job by wage and salary workers in nonfarm business (9)
Year	Farms (1)	Nonfarm self-employed and unpaid family workers (2)	Wage and salary workers in nonfarm business (3)	Total (4)	Farms (5)	Nonfarm self-employed and unpaid family workers (6)	Wage and salary workers in nonfarm business (7)	Total (8)	
			Excluding Alaska and Hawaii						
1929	542.69	270.27	1,222.81	2,035.77	54.8	54.0	46.6	49.51	n.a.
1940	474.98	252.45	1,084.14	1,811.57	53.3	47.9	40.9	44.53	n.a.
1941	470.87	260.88	1,261.65	1,993.40	52.7	49.0	41.8	44.87	n.a.
1947	400.40	291.03	1,456.11	2,147.54	50.6	47.9	40.6	43.08	38.7
1948	394.00	295.94	1,472.03	2,161.97	50.3	48.0	40.3	42.79	38.4
1949	377.22	295.33	1,390.12	2,062.67	49.4	48.0	39.7	42.27	37.8
1950	364.76	299.01	1,452.52	2,116.30	48.7	48.0	40.0	42.32	38.1
1951	345.29	301.95	1,549.93	2,197.17	49.2	48.0	40.1	42.26	38.2
1952	331.36	305.35	1,575.15	2,211.85	48.7	47.9	40.0	42.07	38.1
1953	323.16	305.09	1,603.68	2,231.93	49.3	48.0	39.6	41.83	37.8
1954	313.92	299.98	1,528.29	2,142.19	48.4	47.9	39.2	41.39	37.3
1955	303.23	302.56	1,592.91	2,198.70	47.7	48.0	39.6	41.56	37.7
1956	284.87	313.11	1,630.48	2,228.46	46.7	48.8	39.3	41.27	37.4
1957	264.12	313.19	1,613.73	2,191.04	45.6	47.9	38.8	40.66	37.0
1958	249.46	307.61	1,534.31	2,091.38	45.2	47.1	38.5	40.31	36.7
1959	243.67	306.27	1,604.17	2,154.10	45.2	46.9	39.0	40.60	37.1
1960	234.87	310.73	1,608.24	2,153.84	45.5	47.0	38.6	40.33	36.8
			Including Alaska and Hawaii						
1960	235.96	311.86	1,614.46	2,162.28	45.5	47.0	38.6	40.33	36.8
1961	226.91	311.12	1,591.99	2,130.02	44.8	46.3	38.5	40.10	36.7
1962	221.37	311.10	1,638.19	2,170.66	45.4	46.6	38.6	40.24	36.8
1963	210.78	304.48	1,667.60	2,182.86	45.0	46.1	38.7	40.13	36.8
1964	200.15	310.82	1,709.91	2,220.88	45.1	46.4	38.6	40.09	36.8
1965	195.41	312.58	1,784.96	2,292.95	45.7	46.4	38.7	40.15	36.9
1966	180.74	307.48	1,865.51	2,353.73	45.4	45.9	38.5	39.79	36.7
1967	169.74	301.14	1,876.49	2,347.37	45.0	45.2	38.0	39.20	36.2
1968	165.31	305.99	1,919.05	2,390.35	44.8	45.7	37.7	39.02	36.0
1969	158.91	307.72	1,978.43	2,445.06	44.6	44.9	37.6	38.77	35.8

Sources: Columns 1 to 4 and 9, see text for derivation; columns 5 and 6, Bureau of Labor Statistics; columns 7 and 8, total weekly hours as given in columns 3 and 4 divided by employment from Table C-1, see text for explanation.
    n.a. Not available.

of nonfarm business.[3] Unpublished data required to secure total hours paid for and employment (jobs) with this coverage were provided by BLS. Average hours paid for per job are their quotient.

Estimates from an unpublished study by the Bureau of Labor Statistics that covers the 1952–66 period were used to convert average hours paid for per job to average hours worked per job. BLS first estimated the number of hours paid for but not worked in each industry division in 1966. These estimates were based on a BLS survey of compensation practices in the nonfarm economy in 1966.[4] Estimates of the percentage of the time paid for that was not worked were then developed for wage and salary workers in each industry division for each year from 1952 to 1965, based on extrapolation of the 1966 data. Two types of information were used in the preparation of these estimates: leave practices collected in surveys of metropolitan areas (all areas annually since 1962, seventeen areas annually from 1952 to 1961) and data for job tenure collected for 1951, 1963, and 1966. Job tenure data are needed because the amount of paid leave that is allowed usually is related to length of service. Median age of employees was utilized to interpolate job tenure statistics. Based on such information, annual estimates of the percentage of time paid for that was not worked were derived for each industry division, hours worked were then calculated, and totals for hours worked in the private nonfarm economy were obtained as the sum of the industry estimates.

To use these unpublished BLS data, I started with BLS estimates of hours paid for and hours worked that cover wage and salary workers in private nonfarm industries except private households. SIC industries 80, 82, and 86 were then eliminated.[5] This yielded a series for hours worked

spanning the 1952–66 period with coverage corresponding to the series for hours paid for that I have already discussed.

The percentage of hours paid for that were not worked rose irregularly from 5.00 percent in 1952 to 5.81 percent in 1960 and 6.13 percent in 1966. To complete the series, I assumed that the annual increase in this percentage from 1947 to 1952 was the same (0.10 points) as the average change from 1952 to 1960, and the annual increase from 1966 to 1969 was the same (0.06 points) as the average change from 1960 to 1966. These assumptions permitted a series for average hours worked per job to be completed for the whole 1947–69 period.

This series is shown in Table E-1, column 9. The data imply that, in wage and salary employment in nonfarm business, from 1947 to 1969 average weekly hours worked per job declined by 2.87 hours, or 7.4 percent; average hours paid for declined by 2.29 hours, or 5.7 percent; and average hours paid for but not worked increased by 0.58 hours, or 32 percent.[6]

The unpublished BLS estimates of hours paid for but not worked are approximations, but they are reasonable ones. Their chief limitation probably is the absence of an allowance for irregular fluctuations in paid sick leave that accompany epidemics. Although the unpublished BLS series for 1952–66 is subject to some error and my own extrapolations for 1947–51 and 1967–69 are arbitrary, the resulting series, obtained by adjustment of establishment data for average hours paid for, is superior, in my judgment, to any that can be derived from the only alternative source for average hours worked, CPS data.

To secure total hours worked by wage and salary workers in nonfarm business, average hours worked per job must be multiplied by a count of jobs, not persons. For this multiplication I therefore use my employment series for wage and salary workers in nonfarm business before its reduction to conform to the household survey definition.[7] The product of jobs and average hours

---

3. Business wage and salary workers employed in industries 80, 82, and 86 (in which paid employment is chiefly for nonprofit institutions) are wrongly excluded, and institutional employees working in industries other than these three (in all of which employment is largely in business) are wrongly included. Both groups are small.

4. Data from a 1968 survey later became available but could not be used as directly comparable to the 1966 results because different sampling, benchmarking, and estimating procedures were used.

5. Hours paid for in these industries were provided by BLS. I calculated hours worked. The BLS "790" reports used to estimate hours worked omit these industries, and BLS obtained hours worked by reducing hours paid for by the percentage that was obtained for service industries that are covered in the BLS "790" reports. I followed the same procedure to secure the estimates for these industries that were deducted from the aggregate for hours worked.

6. Estimates presented in Table E-1 are rounded more than those used in this sentence.

7. This series is equal to total civilian employment (excluding work relief) based mainly on establishment reports (Table C-4, column 4) minus civilian employment in general government (Table C-7, column 1), employment in households and institutions (Table C-7, column 6), employment in the "rest of the world" (Table C-7, column 8), employment in farms (Table C-5, column 3), and employment of nonfarm self-employed and unpaid family workers (Table C-6, column 3).

worked per job yields total weekly hours worked by this group, shown in Table E-1, column 3.

Average Hours per Person Employed

To secure weekly hours per *person* employed, conforming to the household survey definition of employment, total hours were divided by my final estimates of employment. The appropriate employment estimates for the three groups are given in Table C-1, columns 2, 3, and 5. Total employment in the business sector is the sum of these three series. For farm workers and the nonfarm self-employed, the series for average hours are the same as the BLS series with which I started. The levels of average hours for nonfarm wage and salary workers and for the business sector as a whole are higher than those of the original BLS series because there are fewer persons employed than there are jobs. Percentage movements of average hours worked in the business sector as a whole are nearly the same as those in a series obtained by dividing BLS estimates of total hours in the three groups combined, based on establishment data, by the corresponding BLS employment series. Slight differences arise mainly from differences in employment weights and levels of average hours for the three groups.

Indexes

The indexes of total and average hours worked in the business sector, shown in Table 4-1, are computed from Table E-1, columns 4 and 8. Data excluding and including Alaska and Hawaii were linked at 1960 in the computation of indexes.

PART TWO: THE WHOLE ECONOMY

Estimates of hours worked outside the business sector are not required to measure labor input, and they affect my analysis of sources of growth only with respect to the detailed breakdown of labor input in general government, households, and institutions. They are used to complete a series for total hours in the whole economy that is used in Tables 2-1 and 2-2.

Hours Worked outside the Nonresidential Business Sector

Estimates of work done outside the business sector in the 1947–69 period were prepared for four employee groups, in each case as the product of an employment series and a series for average hours.

Private Household Workers

Full-time and part-time employment in private households as estimated by the Office of Business Economics (OBE), a component of the series presented in Table C-7, column 6, was multiplied by average hours worked by private household workers, as estimated by BLS for its "establishment" man-hours series. For this category of workers all employment series refer to persons (not jobs) and BLS average hours refer to hours worked (not paid for) per person (not job).

Employees of Nonprofit Institutions

Full-time and part-time employment in nonprofit institutions (Table C-7, column 6, less private household workers) was multiplied by average hours worked per job in SIC industries 80, 82, and 86. The derivation of the latter series in 1952–66 is covered in Part 1 above, as is the corresponding series for hours paid for throughout the period. The 1952–60 movement of the ratio of hours worked to hours paid for was extrapolated back to 1947, and the 1960–66 movement was extrapolated forward to 1969, in order to estimate average hours worked in 1947–51 and 1967–69, respectively.

Civilian Employees of General Government and the "Rest of the World"

BLS provided two sets of data from which average hours for civilian employment in general government were computed. The series are (1) hours worked per person employed (not "at work"), based on household survey data, and (2) hours paid for per job, from its estimates of man-hours based largely on establishment reports. In addition to the usual differences between data based on establishment reports and data based on household surveys, there is a special difference in this group. In both BLS and OBE establishment series, school employees are considered to be employed during school vacation periods even if they are not paid, whereas in the CPS series such persons are not counted as employed (unless they have other jobs). Partly for this reason, government employment is much higher in establishment estimates than in labor force estimates.

The ratio of the first (household survey) series for average hours to the second (establishment) series was computed for each year. The ratio showed a slight downtrend, and also exhibited moderate irregularities. The decision was made to base the level and trend of average hours on the household survey series but to introduce the annual movement of the establishment-based series. The procedure was as follows.

Average hours worked per person employed, from the household survey series, were used directly for 1947 and 1965. The ratio of average hours worked per person to average hours paid for per job in these years (0.9354 in 1947 and 0.9328 in 1965) was interpolated and extrapolated by the straight-line method to secure estimates of the appropriate ratio in the other years of the period. These ratios were multiplied by average hours paid for per job to secure estimates of average hours worked per person employed.[8] These averages were multiplied by my estimates of the number of *persons* employed in general government and in the "rest of the world" (Table C-7, columns 2 and 8) to obtain total hours worked.

Military Employment

BLS multiplies employment in the armed forces by 40 hours a week, a purely conventional figure, to obtain total military hours. The same estimates are used for both of its man-hour series. I have adopted the BLS convention for average hours. My total weekly hours are equal to military employment, from column 4 of Table C-7, multiplied by 40.

Hours Worked in the Whole Economy

My estimates of total weekly hours worked in the entire economy are the sum of the estimates for the business sector and for the four groups just described. They are shown in Table E-2, col-

umn 1. Average weekly hours worked per person employed, computed by use of this series and of my series for total employment (given in Table C-1, column 1), are shown in Table E-2, column 6.

For comparison, I also show in Table E-2 total weekly hours and average weekly hours computed from each of the BLS series for aggregate man-hours. To facilitate comparison of annual changes, I also show the ratio of each BLS series to the estimates developed here.

The definition of the BLS series for total hours worked based on labor force data is very similar to that of my series; it differs only in that hours worked by certain civilians employed abroad, living in institutions, or under 14 years of age are excluded. The actual movements of the two series for total hours nevertheless differ substantially. This is chiefly because of inconsistencies in the estimates of employment; these were discussed in Appendix C. However, as is clear from column 9 of Table E-2, the series for average hours also differ, both irregularly and in amount of decline over the whole postwar period. From 1947 to 1969 my series declines 4.48 hours, while the BLS labor force series declines 4.18 hours, 0.30 hours less.[9]

The BLS series for total hours paid for based largely on establishment reports moves much more closely with my series for total hours worked than does the labor force series. However, as shown by column 5 of Table E-2, minor differences in year-to-year movement are common, and there are also a few fairly substantial differences. These appear in annual changes within the 1947–51 period, in the 1954–55 change, and in the estimate for 1966.

Irregularities in the relationship all stem from differences in the behavior of the estimates of total employment that enter into calculation of the two series; there are no appreciable irregularities in the relationship of average hours, as is clear from column 10 of Table E-2. The reason, of course, is that my reliance upon the average hours data prepared by BLS prevents any inconsistencies in estimation. The ratio of the average hours implied

---

8. The 1965 ratio was reasonably in line with ratios in adjacent years up to 1966. Use of figures based upon labor force data after 1966 was avoided because of changes in CPS questions and procedures.

The Annual and Sick Leave Act of 1951 reduced annual leave accruals for federal employees as of January 6, 1952. It might have been expected to raise abruptly the ratio of hours worked to hours paid for. An abrupt change would have introduced an error into my estimates. However, the relationship between the two BLS series shows no such change; in fact, the ratio drops in 1952. For years surrounding that date, the ratios were: 1950, 0.9325; 1951, 0.9324; 1952, 0.9304; 1953, 0.9347; 1954, 0.9307; the fluctuations seem random. Evidently the 1951 act only gradually affected leave actually taken by employees.

9. The latter decline exceeds by only 0.27 hours the decrease shown by the BLS series for average hours paid for based on establishment data. As BLS staff members have pointed out, if one accepts the establishment series as accurate and makes any considerable allowance for an increase in hours paid for but not worked, it is hard to avoid the conclusion that the decline in average hours worked is understated in the labor force series.

by the BLS series to the average hours implied by my series does, however, gradually increase—from 1947 to 1969 by 1.6 percent. Both this increase and short-term changes in the ratio are a reflection of the specific allowances introduced in my series to remove hours paid for but not worked by civilian wage and salary workers employed in nonfarm industries. The ratio is influenced to only a trivial extent by changes in the relative importance of various groups that receive different weights in the two aggregates for manhours.

Table E-2. Whole Economy: Total and Average Hours Worked per Week, Alternative Series, 1929, 1940–41, and 1947–69

| | Total weekly hours | | | | | Average weekly hours | | | | |
| | Millions of hours | | | Ratio to column 1 of: | | Hours | | | Ratio to column 6 of: | |
Year	Worked, this study (1)	Worked, BLS[a] (2)	Paid for, BLS[b] (3)	Column 2 (4)	Column 3 (5)	Worked, this study (6)	Worked, BLS[a] (7)	Paid for, BLS[b] (8)	Column 7 (9)	Column 8 (10)
			Excluding Alaska and Hawaii							
1929	2,332	n.a.	n.a.	n.a.	n.a.	49.1	n.a.	n.a.	n.a.	n.a.
1940[c]	2,196	n.a.	n.a.	n.a.	n.a.	43.0	n.a.	n.a.	n.a.	n.a.
1941[c]	2,413	n.a.	n.a.	n.a.	n.a.	43.4	n.a.	n.a.	n.a.	n.a.
1947	2,516	2,495	2,623	0.992	1.043	42.4	41.8	42.4	0.986	1.001
1948	2,535	2,523	2,630	0.995	1.037	42.0	41.4	42.1	0.985	1.002
1949	2,447	2,476	2,563	1.012	1.047	41.4	41.0	41.6	0.988	1.003
1950	2,519	2,513	2,616	0.998	1.039	41.5	40.6	41.6	0.980	1.003
1951	2,675	2,621	2,766	0.980	1.034	41.4	40.8	41.6	0.985	1.004
1952	2,714	2,639	2,803	0.972	1.033	41.2	40.6	41.4	0.985	1.005
1953	2,736	2,650	2,823	0.969	1.032	41.0	40.5	41.2	0.988	1.004
1954	2,637	2,553	2,728	0.968	1.035	40.6	39.8	40.8	0.981	1.005
1955	2,704	2,638	2,815	0.976	1.041	40.7	40.0	40.9	0.984	1.006
1956	2,743	2,679	2,864	0.977	1.044	40.4	39.7	40.7	0.984	1.007
1957	2,710	2,653	2,835	0.979	1.046	39.8	39.2	40.1	0.985	1.009
1958	2,616	2,576	2,731	0.985	1.044	39.4	38.8	39.8	0.984	1.010
1959	2,684	2,643	2,813	0.985	1.048	39.6	38.9	40.0	0.982	1.010
1960	2,695	n.a.	n.a.	n.a.	n.a.	39.4	n.a.	n.a.	n.a.	n.a.
			Including Alaska and Hawaii							
1960	2,706	2,677	2,840	0.989	1.050	39.4	38.8	39.8	0.986	1.011
1961	2,686	2,672	2,816	0.995	1.048	39.1	38.6	39.6	0.988	1.012
1962	2,750	2,733	2,883	0.994	1.048	39.2	38.7	39.6	0.988	1.012
1963	2,772	2,758	2,905	0.995	1.048	39.1	38.5	39.5	0.987	1.012
1964	2,819	2,814	2,960	0.998	1.050	38.9	38.5	39.5	0.988	1.013
1965	2,911	2,899	3,056	0.996	1.050	39.0	38.7	39.5	0.992	1.013
1966	3,017	2,985	3,156	0.989	1.046	38.7	38.7	39.3	0.999	1.015
1967	3,041	3,015	3,199	0.991	1.052	38.3	38.2	38.8	0.997	1.015
1968	3,101	3,059	3,266	0.986	1.053	38.1	37.8	38.7	0.994	1.017
1969	3,169	3,115	3,336	0.983	1.053	37.9	37.6	38.5	0.992	1.017

Sources: Columns 1 and 6, see text for derivation; columns 2, 3, 7, and 8, calculated from data furnished by the Bureau of Labor Statistics.
n.a. Not available.
a. Estimates based mainly on Current Population Survey.
b. Estimates based mainly on establishment reports.
c. Includes work relief. Excluding work relief, column 1 is 2,126 in 1940 and 2,359 in 1941; column 6 is 44.1 in 1940 and 44.2 in 1941.

➤➤≻≪≺

The Composition of Man-Hours Worked by Age and Sex

➤➤≻≪≺

This appendix describes the derivation of an index that measures the effect upon labor input in the business sector of changes in the proportions of total hours that are worked by the various age-sex groups. Two types of data were needed: annual distributions of total hours among workers classified by age and sex, and hourly earnings weights with which to combine hours worked by the different age-sex groups. The source of data for both is the Current Population Survey (CPS). First, I describe the derivation of earnings weights, then the derivation of the distributions of hours by age and sex, and, finally, the calculation of quality indexes. As explained elsewhere, the terms "business" and "nonresidential business" are used interchangeably in describing labor input estimates.

PART ONE: THE DERIVATION OF HOURLY EARNINGS WEIGHTS

The desired weights are the relative average hourly earnings, in the business sector, of the different demographic groups. Hourly earnings unfortunately are not collected on a comprehensive basis for age-sex groups, so it was necessary to estimate them. Average annual earnings of year-round full-

time workers in the civilian economy were obtained first, and adjusted to conform as closely as possible to earnings in the business sector. It was then necessary to allow for differences among demographic groups in average hours worked by year-round full-time workers, for earnings of persons who were employed intermittently or part time, and for differences between an individual's age at the date income was earned and the date his age was reported. The earnings weights refer to 1966–67. Differentials among male age groups are based on 1966 data, while differentials between males and females and among female age groups derive mainly from data for 1967. Both the general approach and the dates used were dictated by the availability of data.

Annual Full-Time Earnings

Estimates of the annual earnings of year-round full-time workers were derived first. By sex, the following relevant average annual earnings or income data for such workers with earnings (or with income in the case of lines 6 and 7) were available or could be derived.

1. Mean earnings of males in 1966*	$7,464
2. Mean earnings of males in 1967	7,863
3. Mean earnings of females in 1967	4,333
4. Mean earnings of males excluding government wage and salary workers in 1967	7,840
5. Mean earnings of females excluding government wage and salary workers in 1967	3,988
6. Mean money income of males in 1967*	8,156
7. Mean money income of females in 1967*	4,539

Corresponding data by age were available only for the three items indicated by an asterisk. In the ensuing discussion I shall refer to these data by line number.

These data (by age, where indicated) are published in, or can be derived from data published in, the following sources.

Line 1: U.S. Bureau of the Census, *Current Population Reports,* Series P-60, No. 58, "Year-Round Workers with Low Earnings in 1966" (1969), Table 6.

Lines 2 to 5: *Current Population Reports,* Series P-60, No. 60, "Income in 1967 of Persons in the United States" (1969), Table 9.

Lines 6 and 7: ibid., Table 3.

From these data, mean annual earnings of year-round full-time workers, excluding government wage and salary workers, were estimated by age and sex. These earnings were pitched at the 1967 level for convenience in calculation. However, it is the differentials among groups, not the level, that is of interest. The procedure, which is intricate only because mean earnings of females were not available by age in either year, involved the first five of the following steps.

Step One. Mean earnings of year-round full-time males in each age group in 1966 (corresponding to line 1) were raised by the ratio of line 2 to line 1 to obtain earnings by age pitched at the 1967 level. Together with line 3, this provided comparable earnings data for males by age and for females without an age breakdown. Steps 2 to 5 yield corresponding estimates for females by age.

Step Two. The ratio of 1967 mean income of females in each age group to mean income of all females (line 7) was calculated.

Step Three. The ratio of 1967 mean earnings of males in each age group to 1967 mean income of males in that age group, corresponding to line 6, was calculated, as was the corresponding ratio for all age groups combined.

Step Four. The ratio of mean income of females in each age group to mean income of all females, already calculated in step 2, was multiplied by the ratio of male earnings to male income in the corresponding age group, already calculated in step 3.

Step Five. To obtain estimated average 1967 earnings of females in each age group, the ratio of mean 1967 earnings of all females to the ratio computed for all males in step 3 was multiplied by the ratio computed in step 4 for each female age group.

Step Six. At this point estimated average 1967 earnings of year-round full-time workers were available by age and sex. The estimates are shown in index form in Table F-1, column 1. An adjustment to eliminate government workers was then introduced. Lacking data by age, I multiplied all the male earnings means by the ratio of line 4 to line 2 and all the female earnings means by the ratio of line 5 to line 3. Elimination of government workers appreciably widens the differential between male and female earnings. The estimates are shown in index form in Table F-1, column 2. This step completed the estimation of annual earnings of year-round full-time workers, excluding government workers. Other groups not in the business sector could not be eliminated from the

Table F-1. Indexes of Mean Earnings, Various Concepts, by Sex and Age
Average earnings of males in 35–44 age group = 100

Sex and age group	Year-round full-time workers, annual earnings — All civilians (1)	Year-round full-time workers, annual earnings — Excluding government workers (2)	Year-round full-time workers, hourly earnings, excluding government workers (3)	All full- and part-time workers, hourly earnings, excluding government workers (4)
Males				
14–19	32	32	32	27
20–24	60	60	60	58
25–34	86	86	86	86
35–44	100	100	100	100
45–64	n.a.	n.a.	n.a.	95
45–54	98	98	98	n.a.
55–64	90	90	90	n.a.
65 and over	68	68	68	66
Females				
14–19	42	39	44	37
20–24	45	41	46	45
25–34	51	47	53	52
35–44	51	47	53	51
45–64	n.a.	n.a.	n.a.	52
45–54	51	47	53	n.a.
55–64	50	46	52	n.a.
65 and over	41	38	42	41

Source: See text for derivation.
n.a. Not available.

data (nor could government enterprise workers be reintroduced into the data).[1]

Average Hourly Earnings

Average hours of full-time workers, excluding government workers, in May 1966 were calculated from CPS data as 47.7 for males and 42.5 for females. These data are not available by age, but are not believed to vary much by age.[2] To

1. Private household workers are included in the earnings data to the extent, which is not very great, that they are represented in the totals for year-round full-time workers. This causes the differentials between male and female earnings to be a bit too large for application in the business sector, but the bias from this source is believed to be trivial. A very few unpaid family workers (whose earnings are counted as those of the proprietor) are also included, and also tend to widen slightly the male-female differential.

2. Average hours of *nonagricultural* workers on full-time *schedules* in 1968 are available by sex and age for persons aged 16 years and over in Kathryn D. Hoyle and Paul M. Schwab, "Employment and Unemployment in 1968," reprinted, with detailed statistics added, from U.S. Bureau of Labor Statistics, *Employment and Earnings and Monthly Report on the Labor Force,* Vol. 15 (January 1969). Those for males in the 16–19 age group are 6 percent below the male average. The figure for females aged 65 years and over is 11 percent above the female average. Otherwise, there is little variation by age. Inclusion of agriculture could change these differentials.

obtain estimated average hourly earnings of year-round full-time workers, annual earnings of males in each age bracket were divided by (47.7 × 51 weeks) and those of females by (42.5 × 51 weeks). The choice of number of weeks does not, of course, affect the differentials. These estimates are shown in index form in Table F-1, column 3.

These hourly earnings figures are defective as weights to combine hours worked by different age-sex groups for two principal reasons. First, hourly earnings of year-round workers presumably are higher than those of other workers, and the proportion of hours worked by such workers varies among age-sex groups. The bias is accentuated within the 14–19 age bracket because in this age group both earnings and the proportion of total hours that are worked by year-round full-time workers rise sharply with age. Second, the ages in these data refer to age in the March following the year to which the earnings data refer. This introduces an upward bias in the hourly earnings estimates for the youngest age group. (In other age groups the bias is unimportant.)

The following procedure was introduced to correct for these biases. Total weekly hours worked by all civilians (including government workers) in each age-sex group in 1966 were first divided into two parts: those worked by year-round full-time workers and others. Hours worked in 1966 by year-round full-time workers (including government workers) were calculated as the product of the number of such workers and 47.3 hours in male groups or 42.4 hours in female groups. The hours are May 1966 averages for all full-time civilian workers.[3]

It was then assumed that average hourly earnings for "other" workers were 80 percent of those of year-round full-time workers in the 14–19 age bracket (where hours worked by year-round full-time workers are concentrated at the top of the age bracket, and where the effect of the difference between age when reporting and age when income was earned is greatest) and 90 percent at other ages. A weighted average (using total hours as weights) of the hourly earnings of the two

groups was then computed for each age-sex group.[4] These weighted averages are my final earnings weights.[5] They are shown in index form, with the highest earnings, those of males in the 35–44 age bracket, equal to 100, in Table F-1, column 4. They are also shown, with average earnings for all hours worked by all civilians except government and private household workers equal to 100, in Table F-2, column 1.[6]

4. The average hourly earnings exclude government workers. The weights used to combine hours worked by year-round full-time workers and other workers include hours worked by government workers.

5. Earnings of the 35–44 and 45–64 age groups were calculated separately. In subsequent use these groups were combined. To secure average earnings of the combined age group for each sex, means of the narrower groups were weighted by man-hours worked by civilians excluding government and private household wage and salary workers.

6. To compute the average earnings for all hours worked and the average for each sex, hours worked by civilians except government and private household workers in 1966 (using the old definitions), described in Part 2 of this appendix, were used as weights to combine the various age-sex earnings means.

Table F-2. Nonresidential Business: Indexes of Average Hourly Earnings, and Percentage Distributions of Employment, Hours, and Earnings, by Sex and Age, 1966–67[a]

Sex and age group	Indexes of average hourly earnings (average for all hours worked = 100) (1)	Percentage distribution		
		Employment (2)	Hours worked (3)	Earnings (4)
Males	113[b]	67.6	72.1	81.8
14–19	36	5.8	4.2	1.5
20–24	77	6.7	7.1	5.5
25–34	114	13.8	15.7	17.9
35–64	128	38.3	42.7	54.8
65 and over	88	3.0	2.5	2.2
Females	67[b]	32.4	27.9	18.2
14–19	49	3.2	2.3	1.1
20–24	59	4.3	3.9	2.3
25–34	68	5.5	4.8	3.3
35–64	68	18.3	16.1	11.1
65 and over	54	1.1	0.8	0.4
Total	100[b]	100.0	100.0	100.0

Source: See text for derivation.

a. Employees of government enterprises are unavoidably excluded from the data and employees of nonprofit organizations included. Employment and hours correspond to definitions used until 1966 in the Current Population Survey.

b. These indexes are not used as weights in the computation of quality indexes.

3. The number of such workers in each age-sex group was calculated from data in Forrest A. Bogan and Edward J. O'Boyle, "Work Experience of the Population in 1966," Reprint 2555, with detailed statistics added, from *Monthly Labor Review,* Vol. 91 (January 1968), Special Labor Force Report 91, Table A-1; except for 14- and 15-year-olds, which were taken from *Current Population Reports,* Series P-60, No. 60, "Income in 1967 of Persons in the United States" (1969), Table 3.

Stability of Differentials

These indexes are the final weights. They are used in all years because it was not possible to derive weights for other years that could be confidently regarded as differing significantly from these for reasons other than incomparability of data and procedures. A comparison of differentials of money *income* of *all* civilian year-round full-time workers in 1960 and 1967 can be made, and is presented in Table F-3. The differential that is most important for calculation of quality indexes —that between males and females in the periods of highest earnings—was about the same at the two dates. The relative income positions of older workers and of teenage females was evidently less favorable in 1960 than in 1967; this may suggest that a similar change in relative *earnings* occurred within the *business* sector but this is not at all certain. In any case, the differences are not so big that the quality indexes to be computed would be altered much if these data were used to adjust my 1966–67 earnings weights to secure 1960 estimates.[7]

Victor Fuchs estimated average hourly earnings of *nonagricultural* employed persons in 1959 by a procedure quite different from mine. My 1966–67 indexes, altered by removing my adjustment to eliminate government workers so that they refer to all civilians, are compared with indexes based on his data for nonagricultural workers in Table F-4. The differentials are rather similar except for males aged 14–19 years and 65 years and over. Relative earnings indexes for males in the 14–19 and 65-and-over age groups based on his data are much higher than mine, and those for females in the same age groups slightly higher. His omission of agricultural workers unquestionably explains a great deal of the difference, since farm hours account for a much higher proportion of total hours worked by these age groups than by other ages. My allowance for the change in age from the time earnings are received to the time of

reporting contributes to my obtaining higher indexes for teenagers. The income data in Table F-3 suggest that it is unlikely that much, if any, of the large difference between the indexes for males 65 and over represents a genuine change between 1959 and 1966–67.

Table F-3. Indexes of Mean Annual Income of Year-Round Full-Time Workers, by Sex and Age, 1960 and 1967
Income of males in 35–44 age group = 100

Sex and age group	1960	1967
Males		
14–19	29	30
20–24	58	57
25–34	85	85
35–44	100	100
45–54	97	101
55–64	86	91
65 and over	79	83
Females		
14–19	34	40
20–24	46	43
25–34	51	51
35–44	51	51
45–54	51	53
55–64	50	51
65 and over	43	51

Sources: 1960, unpublished data provided by the U.S. Bureau of the Census, comparable to median income figures published in U.S. Bureau of the Census, *Current Population Reports*, Series P-60, No. 37, "Income of Families and Persons in the United States, 1960" (1962); 1967, ibid., Series P-60, No. 60, "Income in 1967 of Persons in the United States" (1969), Table 3.

Table F-4. Comparison of Indexes of Average Hourly Earnings, by Sex and Age, 1959 and 1966–67
Average earnings of males in 35–64 age group = 100

Sex and age group	Civilians in nonagricultural industries, 1959 (Fuchs)	All civilians, 1966–67 (Denison)
Males		
14–19	46	28
20–24	61	60
25–34	84	89
35–64	100	100
65 and over	93	69
Females		
14–19	44	41
20–24	51	50
25–34	57	58
35–64	58	58
65 and over	49	46

Sources: 1959, Victor R. Fuchs, *Differentials in Hourly Earnings by Region and City Size, 1959*, Occasional Paper 101 (Columbia University Press for the National Bureau of Economic Research, 1967), pp. 39–46; 1966–67, Table F-1, with adjustment to include government wage and salary workers.

7. In the 14–19 age group employed females are older than males and more often are not enrolled in school. This is why female earnings and incomes are persistently higher. It can be estimated from 1969 CPS data that 18- and 19-year-olds not enrolled in school (the group with the highest earnings) accounted for 58 percent of total hours worked by females in the 14–19 age group, but only 45 percent of hours worked by males aged 14–19. Within groups of the same detailed age and school enrollment status, male earnings slightly exceeded female earnings. Vera C. Perrella, "Young Workers and Their Earnings, October 1969," Reprint 2744, with supplementary tables added, from *Monthly Labor Review*, Vol. 94 (July 1971), Special Labor Force Report 132.

The present study distinguishes five age groups in each sex, as compared with three in *Why Growth Rates Differ*.[8] The detail is ample to ensure that all significant changes in age-sex composition are reflected in the quality index.

Table F-2 shows distributions of total employment, total hours, and total earnings. These distributions refer to civilian workers other than government and private household wage and salary workers, coverage which is as close to nonresidential business as I could obtain. The estimates of employment and hours are described in Part 2 below. The earnings distribution was obtained by

8. The weights should be slightly more accurate because mean earnings of year-round full-time workers were available for males and females, and for males by age, whereas the estimates in *Why Growth Rates Differ* (which refer to a broader universe) had to start from *income* data. See Edward F. Denison, assisted by Jean-Pierre Poullier, *Why Growth Rates Differ: Postwar Experience in Nine Western Countries* (Brookings Institution, 1967).

multiplying hours worked in each age-sex cell by average hourly earnings indexes shown in Table F-2, column 1.

PART TWO: THE DISTRIBUTIONS OF HOURS WORKED

Percentage distributions of total hours worked among age-sex groups are shown for all years in Table F-5. The distributions should refer to hours worked by persons employed in the business sector. The closest approximation I could obtain referred to all civilians except nonagricultural wage and salary workers employed in government and private households. Thus the distributions inappropriately exclude employees of government enterprises and include employees of nonprofit organizations. For each sex, most calculations were made for the following age groups: 14–17, 18–19,

Table F-5. Nonresidential Business: Percentage Distributions of Total Hours Worked, by Sex and Age, 1929, 1940–41, and 1947–69[a]

Year	Males (by age group)						Females (by age group)					
	Total	14–19	20–24	25–34	35–64	65 and over	Total	14–19	20–24	25–34	35–64	65 and over
1929	83.48	6.15	10.89	20.63	42.41	3.40	16.52	2.56	3.74	3.99	5.88	0.35
1940	81.67	4.13	9.76	21.21	43.20	3.37	18.33	1.42	3.83	5.29	7.42	0.37
1941	80.82	4.35	10.10	20.55	42.47	3.35	19.18	1.63	4.13	5.23	7.80	0.39
1947	78.01	3.95	8.00	19.13	43.28	3.65	21.99	2.05	3.81	5.16	10.48	0.48
1948	77.75	4.01	8.04	19.06	43.04	3.59	22.25	2.01	3.71	5.25	10.73	0.55
1949	77.16	3.80	7.81	18.94	42.92	3.69	22.84	1.95	3.61	5.35	11.33	0.60
1950	77.06	3.84	7.77	18.94	42.85	3.65	22.94	1.80	3.57	5.34	11.63	0.60
1951	76.31	3.66	6.81	18.79	43.37	3.67	23.69	1.86	3.58	5.58	12.10	0.57
1952	75.57	3.54	5.72	19.05	43.65	3.61	24.43	1.89	3.40	5.73	12.78	0.64
1953	75.71	3.61	5.34	19.22	43.92	3.62	24.29	1.86	3.25	5.45	13.04	0.70
1954	75.88	3.50	5.13	19.13	44.51	3.61	24.12	1.80	3.16	5.37	13.13	0.67
1955	75.44	3.47	5.45	18.97	44.05	3.50	24.56	1.78	3.14	5.32	13.58	0.75
1956	74.86	3.50	5.76	18.32	43.75	3.53	25.14	1.87	3.08	5.27	14.15	0.78
1957	74.46	3.40	5.90	18.03	43.79	3.34	25.54	1.87	3.08	5.19	14.64	0.76
1958	74.33	3.22	5.90	17.64	44.38	3.19	25.67	1.78	3.08	5.08	14.95	0.77
1959	74.38	3.42	6.34	17.36	44.24	3.03	25.62	1.76	3.00	4.88	15.19	0.78
1960	74.18	3.62	6.50	16.92	44.18	2.95	25.82	1.90	3.03	4.71	15.37	0.82
1961	73.93	3.48	6.51	16.69	44.45	2.81	26.07	1.80	3.15	4.75	15.53	0.83
1962	73.73	3.53	6.59	16.40	44.39	2.82	26.27	1.98	3.27	4.62	15.60	0.79
1963	73.68	3.44	6.83	16.12	44.67	2.63	26.32	1.84	3.38	4.54	15.77	0.78
1964	73.35	3.56	7.14	15.99	44.11	2.56	26.65	1.84	3.62	4.49	15.89	0.81
1965	72.85	3.87	7.38	15.74	43.33	2.53	27.15	1.97	3.73	4.62	16.02	0.81
1966[b]	72.08	4.18	7.06	15.71	42.66	2.47	27.92	2.30	3.93	4.75	16.14	0.80
1966[c]	72.04	4.23	7.08	15.69	42.64	2.41	27.96	2.40	4.00	4.71	16.02	0.83
1967	71.63	3.92	7.15	15.86	42.24	2.46	28.37	2.24	4.18	4.95	16.24	0.77
1968	71.29	3.97	6.99	16.22	41.62	2.49	28.71	2.25	4.34	5.11	16.23	0.78
1969	70.35	4.04	7.09	16.32	40.46	2.43	29.65	2.36	4.74	5.30	16.43	0.81

Source: See text for derivation. Detail may not add to totals because of rounding.
a. Distributions are based on hours worked by civilians other than wage and salary workers employed in government or private households.
b. Data comparable to earlier years.
c. Data comparable to later years.

20–24, 25–34, 35–44, 45–54, 55–64, and 65 and over. (Occasionally, different groups were used.) These were later consolidated into the broader groups shown in Table F-5. Because changes introduced in the CPS questionnaire in 1967 affect the data, overlapping series for 1947–66 and 1966–69 were developed. The total man-hours estimates each year are the sum of estimates for persons employed in nonagricultural and in agricultural activities. All data used are annual averages of monthly data unless an exception is noted below. Distortions of the annual averages by disproportionate representation of holidays in the survey weeks are presumed to affect all age-sex groups alike.

Estimates for 1947–66

I first describe the 1947–66 series. References to published annual labor force reports for various years refer to the following sources:[9]

	U.S. Bureau of the Census, Current Population Reports,
Year	*Series P-50*
1947, 1948	No. 13 February 16, 1949
1949	No. 19 March 2, 1950
1950	No. 31 March 9, 1951
1951	No. 40 May 19, 1952
1952	No. 45 July 1953
1953, 1954	No. 59 April 1955
1955	No. 67 March 1956
1956	No. 72 March 1957
1957	No. 85 June 1958
1958	No. 89 June 1959
	U.S. Bureau of Labor Statistics, *Special Labor Force Reports*
1959	No. 4 May 1960
1960	No. 14 April 1961
1961	No. 23 June 1962
1962	No. 31 May 1963
1963	No. 43 June 1964
1964	No. 52 April 1965
1965	No. 69 January 1966

Data for 1966 are from various issues of U.S. Bureau of Labor Statistics, *Employment and Earnings and Monthly Report on the Labor Force; Manpower Report of the President, 1967;* and Paul M. Ryscavage and Hazel W. Willacy, "Employment and Unemployment in 1967," reprinted, with detailed statistics added, from U.S. Bureau of Labor

Statistics, *Employment and Earnings and Monthly Report on the Labor Force,* Vol. 14 (January 1968).

Unpublished data were transcribed from records of the Bureau of Labor Statistics.

Nonagricultural Business, 1947–66

For each age-sex group, the figures for hours worked by all civilians employed in nonagricultural industries were obtained first, as the product of two series:

SERIES 1. The annual average number of persons at work in nonagricultural industries.

SERIES 2. The annual average weekly hours worked by persons at work in nonagricultural industries.

To exclude hours worked by nonagricultural wage and salary workers employed in private households and government, this product was multiplied by the ratio of:

SERIES 3. The number of persons employed in nonagricultural industries excluding government and private household wage and salary workers, to:

SERIES 4. The number of persons employed in nonagricultural industries.

The calculation assumes that in each age-sex group the average weekly hours worked per employed person in nonagricultural industries are the same when government and private household wage and salary workers are excluded as when they are included.[10]

All data needed for the calculation in the later years of the period were available from published and unpublished CPS tabulations. The procedures were somewhat modified in earlier years when information was less complete. These modifications do not, I believe, significantly impair the accuracy of the nonagricultural distributions by sex or, with one possible exception, by age. The possible exception is that in the 1947–55 period it was necessary to assume, for each sex, that average hours worked by each age group moved alike. The distributions initially obtained for nonagricultural and agricultural industries combined in the 1947–52 period were subsequently adjusted to eliminate an incomparability with later years arising from a change in the data used to "blow up" the CPS sample. (The adjustment is described on pages 194–95.) The following description of the four

9. The annual labor force reports were published in the P-50 series of the U.S. Bureau of the Census, *Current Population Reports,* until 1959. Since that date, these reports have been published by the U.S. Bureau of Labor Statistics, appearing from 1959 to 1965 in Special Labor Force Reports and, thereafter, in *Employment and Earnings* and its reprints, which include additional data.

10. A test for May 1966 indicated that this assumption causes a slight overstatement of the percentage of hours I assign to males. The effect on changes over time is unknown.

series needed to obtain nonagricultural hours refers to the estimates prior to this adjustment.

Total nonagricultural employment (series 4 above) is published by age and sex for all years in the annual labor force reports.

Employment data for nonagricultural wage and salary workers employed in private households and in government (needed to obtain series 3 by subtraction from series 4) were obtained by sex and age for years beginning with 1961 from the unpublished Tabulation Table 15 of the Current Population Survey. For earlier years data are published for each sex.[11] But they were not obtained by age, and age distributions had to be estimated.

Distributions by age and sex of persons employed in the private households industry were available for 1959 and 1960 from the annual labor force reports cited above, Table C-10. Within each sex the corresponding age distribution in 1961 for the "industry" was almost identical to that given for wage and salary workers in private households in 1961. In 1959 and 1960, wage and salary workers in private households of each sex were therefore distributed by the industry age distributions.

To obtain age distributions for government wage and salary workers in 1959 and 1960, the following procedure was adopted. Each year from 1959 through 1961, percentage distributions of employment in educational services and in public administration (from the annual labor force reports, Table C-10) were combined by use as weights of OBE data for full-time and part-time employment in public education and in other government civilian employment. A percentage distribution of employment of each sex by age was computed from these data for each year from 1959 through 1961. The percentage in each age group in 1959 and 1960 was multiplied by the ratio of the 1961 percentage to the 1961 percentage of government wage and salary workers in the same age group. The resulting percentage distributions were used to allocate the number of government wage and salary workers of each sex (from the annual labor force reports, Table C-4) by age in 1959 and 1960.

Prior to 1959 the industry distributions by age and sex were not available. For private household and government wage and salary workers,

separately, an age distribution for each sex was obtained each year by the following procedure. Nonagricultural employment in each age bracket was multiplied by the 1959 ratio of employment in the category to total nonagricultural employment in that age bracket. The known total for the sex in the category was distributed among age groups in proportion to these products.

The number of persons at work and average hours worked by persons at work in nonagricultural industries (series 1 and 2 on page 192) were available by age and sex *for the 1959–66 period*—for 1962 through 1966, from unpublished CPS Tabulation Table 31; and for 1959 through 1961, from Table D-7 of the annual labor force reports.[12]

The calculation of total man-hours worked by civilians in nonagricultural industries by sex and age (series 1 × series 2) was done in two stages *for the 1947–58 period*. Totals for each sex were first calculated, and these totals were then distributed by age.

I first describe the derivation of the aggregates *for each sex*. Persons at work (series 1) were available by sex from 1947 through 1954, but for 1955–58 only the totals for the two sexes combined were obtained. The 1954 and 1959 ratios of persons at work to employment were calculated for each sex, and interpolated. The interpolated ratios were multiplied by employment to obtain a preliminary estimate of persons at work for each sex. The preliminary estimates were adjusted proportionately to conform to the known total for the two sexes combined. Average hours worked by persons at work (series 2) were available by sex from 1956 through 1958. In these years, total hours for each sex are the product of persons at work and average hours. In 1947–55, the relevant available information on hours was

---

11. There is an exception. The numbers of government wage and salary workers were not available for 1953 and 1954. They were estimated by straight-line interpolation between the 1952 and 1955 figures.

12. There was a slight problem with the age classification in 1959–61; data are reported for an 18–24 age class as a whole. It was necessary to subdivide this class to permit a transfer of 18- and 19-year-olds to the younger age group. To obtain persons at work of each sex in the detailed age groups in 1959–61, the 1962 ratio of the number at work to the number employed was calculated for the 18–19 and 20–24 age groups, and multiplied by employment in the given year to obtain a preliminary estimate. These were adjusted proportionately to agree with the total number at work in the 18–24 age bracket. Total hours worked by persons aged 18 to 24 were calculated each year as the product of persons at work and average hours. They were allocated between the 18–19 and 20–24 age groups in proportion to aggregates obtained by multiplying persons at work each year by average hours in 1962; this procedure maintains the 1962 average-hours differential between the two age classes.

the average hours of both sexes combined and, by sex, the average numbers of persons at work thirty-five hours or more (full time) and less than thirty-five hours (part time).[13] For each sex, a preliminary estimate of total hours was obtained for each year by multiplying persons at work full time by average full-time hours for the sex in 1956; multiplying persons at work part time by average part-time hours in 1956; and summing the two products. These preliminary estimates for the two sexes were adjusted proportionately to agree with a control total for both sexes combined, obtained by multiplying persons at work by average hours.

The second stage was to allocate *among age groups* nonagricultural hours worked by each sex in 1947–58. The allocations were obtained as follows. In the years 1956–58 average hours worked by persons at work, but not the number of persons at work, were available by age for each sex. Preliminary estimates of total hours worked by each age group were obtained as the product of employment, average hours, and the 1959 ratio for that age group of persons at work to employment. These preliminary estimates for age groups were adjusted proportionately to agree with total hours worked by each sex.[14]

In the years 1947–55, data by age were not available for persons at work, average hours, or full-time or part-time employment. It was necessary to assume that, within each sex, percentage changes in average hours were the same in each age group. To implement this assumption, total hours worked in each age-sex group in 1956 were extrapolated backward by nonagricultural employment in that age-sex group to obtain preliminary estimates of total hours worked. The estimates for each sex were then adjusted proportionately to agree with total nonagricultural hours worked by the sex. The greatest age detail possible was used in the calculation.

Agriculture, 1947–66

In the years 1962–66 total hours worked by agricultural workers in each age-sex group are the product of (1) annual averages of the number of persons at work in agriculture and (2) the average weekly hours worked by persons at work in agriculture. Data are from the unpublished Tabulation Table 31 of the Current Population Survey.

In 1947–61 the information used was confined to persons at work and average hours for all civilians employed in agriculture, and agricultural employment classified by sex and age. Data are from the annual labor force reports. In these years total hours worked by agricultural workers were computed as the product of the annual averages of persons at work and average hours in agriculture. A preliminary total hours figure was obtained for each age-sex group by extrapolating man-hours worked in 1962 backward by employment in the age-sex group. To obtain final figures for total hours in each cell, these preliminary numbers were multiplied by the ratio of total man-hours in agriculture to the sum of the preliminary figures for age-sex groups. The effect of the procedure is to retain 1962 percentage differentials among age-sex groups in average hours per person employed in agriculture.[15] The distributions change only because of changes in employment. The estimates imply that males accounted for 88.6 percent of total hours worked in 1947 and 87.1 percent in 1962.

Adjustment of 1947–52 Data

CPS sample data are controlled to independent estimates of the size of the civilian population in each age-sex group. Through 1952 the independent estimates were extrapolations from the 1940 Census of Population. Starting with the 1953 "revised" CPS estimates, extrapolations from the 1950 Census of Population were substituted. Substitution of these new controls did not affect data for any characteristics of age-sex groups within the population but did change the weights with which groups are combined. The difference in population weights was sufficient to create a discontinuity between the 1952 and 1953 age-sex distributions. A comparison of civilian employment for March 1953 based on new and old weights is provided in U.S. Bureau of the Census, *Current Population Reports,* Series P-57, No. 129, "The Monthly Report on the Labor Force, March

13. For the year 1955, data by sex for persons at work full time and part time were available for only nine months. These were used to allocate twelve-month data for the combined sexes.

14. As in 1959–61, it was necessary to divide total hours worked by an 18–24 age group between 18–19 and 20–24 age groups. Hours worked by each subgroup in 1959 were extrapolated backward by nonagricultural employment to obtain preliminary totals. These were adjusted proportionately to agree with the totals for the 18–24 age group.

15. Beginning with 1955, a division of persons at work in agriculture between full-time and part-time workers was obtained by sex for the month of May. These data are too erratic to be used in these calculations.

1953" (1953), page 5. The difference between the two sets of weights reflects biases that developed between 1940 and 1950 in the original estimates of the population classified by age and sex.

To eliminate the discontinuity, I computed percentage distributions of March 1953 civilian employment by sex and age, based on old and new weights, and the ratio of the latter percentage to the former percentage for each age-sex group. My original figure for the percentage of man-hours contributed by each age-sex group in each of the years 1950 through 1952 was multiplied by the March 1953 ratio for that group. The size of this adjustment for each age-sex group was reduced by one-tenth in 1949, two-tenths in 1948, and three-tenths in 1947. My final distributions of hours worked in 1947–52, shown in Table F-5, are percentage distributions of these adjusted data. This adjustment procedure is not ideal because the development of biases in Census population estimates probably was more closely related to age cohorts than to fixed age groups. But it suffices to eliminate any discontinuity and any appreciable bias in the series as a result of the change in the Census Bureau's control data.

Estimates for 1966–69

In 1967 a number of changes in definitions and questions which impair comparability with earlier years were introduced in the household survey. In addition, 14- and 15-year-olds were eliminated from the regularly published CPS series.

I have included estimates of man-hours for 14- and 15-year-olds in my 1967–69 data. In other respects estimates for 1967–69 were obtained in the same way as those for 1962–66. For persons aged 16 and over all data needed were available from published or unpublished CPS tabulations. Annual data are published in Ryscavage and Willacy, "Employment and Unemployment in 1967," and Hoyle and Schwab, "Employment and Unemployment in 1968," and in *Employment and Earnings,* Vol. 16 (February 1970), Table A-2. Unpublished data were transcribed from the BLS records. Hours worked in 1966 by 14- and 15-year-olds of each sex employed in nonagricultural industries, other than government and private household workers, were extrapolated forward by nonagricultural employment of 14- and 15-year-olds of that sex, and total hours worked in 1966 by 14- and 15-year-olds in agriculture were extrapolated forward by agricultural employment of

14- and 15-year-olds of that sex. Hours worked by 14- and 15-year-olds comprise only a small part of total hours worked by the 14–19 age group: in 1968, 10.9 percent for males and 3.5 percent for females.

Because of changes in questions and definitions, the data for earlier years are not comparable to those for 1967 to 1969 and an adjusted 1966 distribution was attempted to provide an overlap. This was done by adjusting the original distribution for 1966 in two ways: (1) The calculations for 1966 comparable to earlier years had been made with use of a 14–17 age group. The calculations were repeated with separate 14–15 and 16–17 age groups, and the results of this more detailed calculation substituted in the distributions. (2) For each age-sex group (including the 14–15 group), the original estimate of man-hours worked by civilians employed in nonagricultural industries, other than government and private household wage and salary workers, was multiplied by the ratio of nonagricultural employment obtained in the MLS to nonagricultural employment obtained in the CPS.[16] Similarly, for each age-sex group the original estimate of man-hours worked in agriculture was multiplied by the ratio of agricultural employment obtained in the MLS to agricultural employment obtained in the CPS. No allowance for the effects of a change in the reporting of hours could be made because MLS data for hours were not obtained by age and sex. Neither could any adjustment be made for differences between the 1966 MLS research sample and the 1967 CPS sample, which was a combination of the 1966 CPS and MLS samples. Consequently, the movement from 1966 to 1967 of the quality index is subject to greater than ordinary error.

Estimates Prior to 1947

For the years prior to 1947, it was necessary to turn to different sources. The derivation of the estimates for 1929, 1940, and 1941 is described in Appendix G (pages 216–17).

PART THREE: CALCULATION OF THE INDEX

To compute the labor input index for changes in age-sex composition of hours worked (Table 4-1,

16. The MLS research sample used the schedule adopted subsequently, the CPS sample the schedule used in earlier years. See pages 167–68 and 202–03 for explanation.

column 4), the percentages of man-hours worked by each age-sex group, shown in Table F-5, were multiplied by the weights shown in Table F-2, column 1. The products were then added, and their sum divided by the sum of the percentages (not always 100.00 because of rounding). The resulting series for 1929–66 and 1966–69 were linked and converted to index form.

My use of this index in the measurement of *annual* changes in labor input during the postwar period may be questioned. Are annual changes in the percentage distributions of total hours upon which the index is based too much affected by random errors to warrant this use? Would it be better to introduce some device to smooth the index? These questions are reasonable in view of sampling error in the CPS survey, occasional changes in questions and procedures, and my rejection of use of the CPS to measure annual changes in employment and average hours when an alternative source was available. To help the reader judge, the age-sex distributions are presented in full ten-group detail in Table F-5.

Inspection of this table was reassuring to the writer. Percentages for the detailed groups have a strong tendency to move consistently over periods of several years. There is a general absence of irregular fluctuations of sufficient size to affect the index appreciably other than movements that are rather clearly to be explained by fluctuations in the strength of the labor market. The regularity of behavior probably can be ascribed largely to the CPS practice of using independent estimates of the distribution of the population by age and sex as controls when the household sample is "blown up." This prevents fluctuations in the numbers of persons in different age-sex groups represented in the sample from affecting the distributions. My judgment is that this index, though not highly accurate on an annual basis, is usable. By this statement I mean that it measures year-to-year changes as accurately as many other economic series that are used on an annual basis. It may be noted, however, that important changes in CPS procedures make the statistical basis for the changes from 1952 to 1953 and from 1966 to 1967 the least satisfactory of the annual changes.

Employment and Hours in the Business Sector Classified by Sex and Full-Time or Part-Time Status of Workers

➤➤➤✦❮❮❮

Estimates of employment, average hours, and total hours worked by each of three groups of persons employed in the business sector were presented in Tables C-1 and E-1. These groups are: (1) wage and salary workers employed in nonfarm business; (2) nonfarm self-employed and unpaid family workers; and (3) farm workers. In Tables G-1, G-2, and G-3, employment and total hours worked in each of these three groups are further divided among full-time male workers, part-time male workers, full-time female workers, and part-time female workers.[1] Also shown are the average weekly hours worked by employed persons in each of these detailed groups, calculated from total hours and employment. The data are intended to represent averages of all weeks in the

1. Because of differences in procedures, the percentage division between males and females of total hours worked in the business sector that is implied by these tables differs slightly from that shown in Table F-5.

year. Because of a major change in reporting and processing of the basic data, it is necessary to provide series that overlap at 1966. An overlap at 1960 of estimates including and excluding Alaska and Hawaii is also required. Use of the series requires linking at 1960 and at 1966, although for most series differences between overlapping estimates are minor.

Employment, full-time employment, and part-time employment all include both persons at work and persons with a job but not at work. Full-time workers at work in any week consist of persons who worked 35 hours or more and persons who usually work 35 hours or more but worked 1–34 hours that week for noneconomic reasons. Full-time workers not at work consist of persons with a job but not at work who usually work 35 hours or more but worked 0 hours for noneconomic reasons. In the absence of actual data corresponding to this latter classification, the proportion of employed persons working 0 hours who are full-time workers is assumed to be the same in each subgroup of the labor force as the proportion of persons at work who are full-time workers.

All employed persons who are not full-time workers are classified as part-time workers. They are a heterogeneous group. Most wished to work only part time. Some wished to work full time but could find only part-time jobs. Some held what were usually full-time jobs but worked less than 35 hours in a particular week for "economic reasons": lack of demand, materials shortages, or breakdowns of equipment. Some worked only part of a week because they were starting or ending a job.[2]

Control Totals and General Description of Postwar Estimates

To arrive at the postwar estimates provided in Tables G-1, G-2, and G-3, the employment and hours aggregates which Tables C-1 and E-1 provide for each of the three broad class-of-worker groups in the business sector were allocated among the four detailed types of workers (by sex and

2. This description must be modified for application to unpaid family workers. By convention, unpaid family workers are not counted as employed unless they work at least 15 hours in a week. Consequently, there is no category of persons with a job but not at work. This omission raises the average hours of both full-time and part-time workers in this category. The omission of persons working 1 to 15 hours further raises the average hours of part-time workers.

Table G-1. Wage and Salary Workers in Nonfarm Business: Employment and Hours by Sex and Full-Time or Part-Time Status, 1929, 1940–41, and 1947–69[a]

	Employment (thousands)				Total weekly hours (millions)				Average weekly hours			
	Males		Females		Males		Females		Males		Females	
Year	Full-time (1)	Part-time (2)	Full-time (3)	Part-time (4)	Full-time (5)	Part-time (6)	Full-time (7)	Part-time (8)	Full-time (9)	Part-time (10)	Full-time (11)	Part-time (12)
					Excluding Alaska and Hawaii							
1929	19,821	1,073	4,787	534	975.61	17.72	217.93	11.55	49.2	16.5	45.5	21.6
1940	18,554	1,466	5,363	1,121	817.20	24.21	218.47	24.26	44.0	16.5	40.7	21.6
1941	21,627	1,171	6,240	1,130	961.32	19.34	256.54	24.45	44.4	16.5	41.1	21.6
1947	24,497	1,326	8,498	1,539	1,060.61	21.90	340.30	33.30	43.3	16.5	40.0	21.6
1948	24,490	1,722	8,527	1,785	1,060.19	31.29	341.58	38.97	43.3	18.2	40.1	21.8
1949	22,514	2,403	8,261	1,834	970.61	48.55	330.10	40.86	43.1	20.2	40.0	22.3
1950	23,322	2,415	8,598	1,945	1,014.57	48.10	346.63	43.22	43.5	19.9	40.3	22.2
1951	25,031	2,168	9,360	2,121	1,087.39	40.96	375.01	46.57	43.4	18.9	40.1	22.0
1952	25,679	1,656	10,042	2,032	1,102.24	28.78	399.92	44.21	42.9	17.4	39.8	21.8
1953	26,465	1,674	10,371	1,936	1,123.51	28.39	409.35	42.43	42.5	17.0	39.5	21.9
1954	24,762	2,324	9,605	2,315	1,057.48	38.40	382.33	50.08	42.7	16.5	39.8	21.6
1955	25,903	2,063	10,174	2,098	1,110.73	35.81	406.86	39.51	42.9	17.4	40.0	18.8
1956	26,398	2,248	10,482	2,356	1,127.09	43.05	417.04	43.30	42.7	19.2	39.8	18.4
1957	26,244	2,231	10,559	2,527	1,109.42	41.43	414.58	48.30	42.3	18.6	39.3	19.1
1958	24,540	2,642	10,005	2,651	1,035.50	53.07	395.58	50.16	42.2	20.1	39.5	18.9
1959	25,793	2,356	10,409	2,585	1,102.21	39.57	412.39	50.00	42.7	16.8	39.6	19.3
1960	25,798	2,510	10,647	2,671	1,098.36	45.70	414.87	49.31	42.6	18.2	39.0	18.5
					Including Alaska and Hawaii							
1960	25,898	2,520	10,688	2,681	1,102.60	45.87	416.48	49.51	42.6	18.2	39.0	18.5
1961	25,338	2,638	10,505	2,852	1,081.59	47.41	409.74	53.25	42.7	18.0	39.0	18.7
1962	26,111	2,538	10,820	2,919	1,120.76	42.00	421.60	53.83	42.9	16.5	39.0	18.4
1963	26,600	2,477	10,971	3,060	1,144.98	41.27	426.37	54.98	43.0	16.7	38.9	18.0
1964	27,124	2,589	11,462	3,075	1,172.69	39.06	439.69	58.47	43.2	15.1	38.4	19.0
1965	28,134	2,617	11,986	3,362	1,215.83	42.90	463.64	62.59	43.2	16.4	38.7	18.6
1966[b]	29,307	2,716	12,909	3,537	1,257.11	45.16	496.43	66.81	42.9	16.6	38.5	18.9
1966[c]	29,250	2,844	12,849	3,526	1,256.50	47.92	495.10	65.99	43.0	16.8	38.5	18.7
1967	29,541	2,906	13,154	3,844	1,255.64	48.77	500.41	71.67	42.5	16.8	38.0	18.6
1968	30,153	2,943	13,603	4,168	1,277.03	49.72	515.49	76.81	42.4	16.9	37.9	18.4
1969	30,567	3,193	14,351	4,536	1,295.33	54.79	544.70	83.61	42.4	17.2	38.0	18.4

Source: See text for derivation.
a. See Tables C-1 and E-1 for totals.
b. Comparable to earlier years.
c. Comparable to later years.

full-time or part-time status) in proportion to independently derived estimates of employment and total hours for each of the four types. In other words, the data from Tables C-1 and E-1 were used as control totals to which the more detailed, independently derived estimates were adjusted. The control totals, it will be recalled, are intended to represent averages of all the fifty-two weeks in the year.

The independently derived estimates used for the allocations were based on Current Population Survey (CPS) data for civilians 14 years of age and over. Their scope is not exactly the same as that of the control data that were allocated. First, the data used to allocate employment and hours of farm workers inappropriately include, and those for the two nonfarm groups exclude, the agricultural services industry. Second, the data used to allocate wage and salary workers employed in nonfarm business refer instead to nonagricultural wage and salary workers other than those employed by government and private households. In none of the three groups is the number of workers inappropriately included or excluded a very large proportion of the total.[3]

3. Persons wrongly classified in each group were the following percentages of the control employment totals for each group in 1966, as given in Table C-1. Persons in agricultural services inappropriately included in farm employment were about 6.7 percent of farm employment. Agricultural service workers inappropriately excluded from the nonfarm self-employed and unpaid family workers group were about 1.7 percent of that group. Workers in nonprofit institutions inappropriately included in the total for wage and salary workers in nonfarm business were about 7.8 percent of the total for wage and salary workers in nonfarm

Table G-2. Nonfarm Self-Employed and Unpaid Family Workers: Employment and Hours by Sex and Full-Time or Part-Time Status, 1929, 1940–41, and 1947–69[a]

Year	Employment (thousands)				Total weekly hours (millions)				Average weekly hours			
	Males		Females		Males		Females		Males		Females	
	Full-time (1)	Part-time (2)	Full-time (3)	Part-time (4)	Full-time (5)	Part-time (6)	Full-time (7)	Part-time (8)	Full-time (9)	Part-time (10)	Full-time (11)	Part-time (12)
	Excluding Alaska and Hawaii											
1929	3,517	280	820	384	209.25	4.84	48.79	7.39	59.5	17.3	59.5	19.2
1940	3,621	381	843	426	192.78	6.59	44.89	8.19	53.2	17.3	53.3	19.2
1941	3,724	296	887	416	200.09	5.12	47.67	8.00	53.7	17.3	53.7	19.2
1947	4,341	345	943	443	227.18	5.97	49.36	8.52	52.3	17.3	52.3	19.2
1948	4,395	345	973	455	230.37	5.92	50.96	8.69	52.4	17.2	52.4	19.1
1949	4,337	342	1,007	468	227.70	5.92	52.86	8.85	52.5	17.3	52.5	18.9
1950	4,429	353	988	462	232.30	6.14	51.78	8.79	52.4	17.4	52.4	19.0
1951	4,427	347	1,033	485	232.46	5.98	54.24	9.27	52.5	17.2	52.5	19.1
1952	4,491	358	1,030	489	235.60	6.21	54.08	9.46	52.5	17.3	52.5	19.3
1953	4,509	352	1,016	483	236.42	6.04	53.27	9.36	52.4	17.2	52.4	19.4
1954	4,427	428	932	473	234.26	7.24	49.99	8.49	52.9	16.9	53.6	17.9
1955	4,440	349	1,021	496	233.04	6.02	53.60	9.90	52.5	17.2	52.5	20.0
1956	4,509	347	1,066	489	240.17	6.16	57.28	9.50	53.3	17.8	53.7	19.4
1957	4,402	511	1,112	512	236.34	8.61	58.08	10.16	53.7	16.8	52.2	19.8
1958	4,330	546	1,119	529	231.49	9.08	57.58	9.46	53.5	16.6	51.5	17.9
1959	4,328	504	1,102	592	230.21	8.26	56.23	11.57	53.2	16.4	51.0	19.5
1960	4,342	508	1,110	657	232.25	8.82	58.07	11.59	53.5	17.4	52.3	17.6
	Including Alaska and Hawaii											
1960	4,358	510	1,114	659	233.10	8.85	58.28	11.63	53.5	17.4	52.3	17.6
1961	4,329	521	1,140	731	230.21	9.34	58.82	12.75	53.2	17.9	51.6	17.4
1962	4,302	518	1,181	675	230.03	8.89	60.14	12.04	53.5	17.2	50.9	17.8
1963	4,191	581	1,142	695	225.16	10.29	55.95	13.08	53.7	17.7	49.0	18.8
1964	4,298	532	1,138	735	230.27	9.10	57.14	14.31	53.6	17.1	50.2	19.5
1965	4,273	535	1,184	749	230.87	8.49	60.59	12.63	54.0	15.9	51.2	16.9
1966[b]	4,162	553	1,286	698	222.95	8.61	64.21	11.71	53.6	15.6	49.9	16.8
1966[c]	4,073	594	1,227	805	221.12	9.54	62.37	14.45	54.3	16.1	50.8	18.0
1967	4,049	596	1,202	811	215.61	9.51	61.70	14.32	53.3	16.0	51.3	17.7
1968	4,111	605	1,200	784	219.77	9.95	62.73	13.54	53.5	16.4	52.3	17.3
1969	4,145	653	1,232	822	220.07	10.88	62.70	14.07	53.1	16.7	50.9	17.1

Source: See text for derivation.
a. See Tables C-1 and E-1 for totals.
b. Comparable to earlier years.
c. Comparable to later years.

The estimates presented in Tables G-1, G-2, and G-3, in my opinion, fairly accurately reflect the trends of average full-time hours in the various groups during the postwar period. Less confidence can be placed in the occasional irregular movements in the annual series for full-time hours, especially noticeable in two or three years in the series for the small group of full-time female farm workers, or the larger and more pervasive irregularities in the distribution of employment and hours between full-time and part-time workers and in the average hours of part-time workers.

business, and those in government enterprises and agricultural services inappropriately excluded were about 3.0 percent. These percentages are a little overstated because the numerators for the computations represent a count of jobs and the denominators a count of persons.

Such irregular changes may stem from sampling fluctuations and changes in procedures in the CPS, differences in the characteristics of the weeks covered by the CPS in different years, and the necessity of using estimates to fill gaps in data tabulated by CPS. Use of control totals and, where possible, introduction of adjustments to eliminate sources of incomparability only imperfectly compensate for these defects in the source material. However, seemingly random fluctuations may really reflect changes in the intensity of demand for labor. By the definitions adopted, if a worker's hours drop below 35 because of a shortage of work (economic reasons), he ceases to be a full-time worker and becomes a part-time worker. In recession years there is a tendency for the proportion of full-time workers in the non-

Table G-3. Farm Workers: Employment and Hours by Sex and Full-Time or Part-Time Status, 1929, 1940–41, and 1947–69[a]

	Employment (thousands)				Total weekly hours (millions)				Average weekly hours			
	Males		Females		Males		Females		Males		Females	
Year	Full-time (1)	Part-time (2)	Full-time (3)	Part-time (4)	Full-time (5)	Part-time (6)	Full-time (7)	Part-time (8)	Full-time (9)	Part-time (10)	Full-time (11)	Part-time (12)
					Excluding Alaska and Hawaii							
1929	8,243	339	838	483	484.69	5.24	42.24	10.52	58.8	15.5	50.4	21.8
1940	7,645	248	607	408	433.23	3.69	29.50	8.56	56.7	14.9	48.6	21.0
1941	7,384	304	789	455	418.45	4.53	38.35	9.54	56.7	14.9	48.6	21.0
1947	6,060	604	599	650	347.97	9.11	29.50	13.82	57.4	15.1	49.2	21.3
1948	5,914	608	603	708	340.00	9.23	29.73	15.04	57.5	15.2	49.3	21.2
1949	5,739	583	619	695	323.89	8.31	30.31	14.71	56.4	14.3	49.0	21.2
1950	5,604	669	513	704	314.97	10.10	24.85	14.84	56.2	15.1	48.4	21.1
1951	5,211	563	549	695	295.64	8.16	26.79	14.70	56.7	14.5	48.8	21.2
1952	5,130	509	528	637	285.02	7.50	25.12	13.72	55.6	14.7	47.6	21.5
1953	4,965	529	515	546	278.79	7.82	24.83	11.72	56.2	14.8	48.2	21.5
1954	4,799	621	535	531	267.88	8.88	25.82	11.34	55.8	14.3	48.3	21.4
1955	4,551	632	690	484	252.64	10.27	30.46	9.86	55.5	16.3	44.1	20.4
1956	4,196	692	591	621	233.04	11.27	28.26	12.30	55.5	16.3	47.8	19.8
1957	3,955	735	536	566	216.29	12.44	23.71	11.68	54.7	16.9	44.2	20.6
1958	3,723	811	450	535	204.99	12.82	20.86	10.79	55.1	15.8	46.4	20.2
1959	3,646	740	442	563	199.03	12.21	20.90	11.53	54.6	16.5	47.3	20.5
1960	3,502	717	429	514	192.49	11.51	20.71	10.16	55.0	16.1	48.3	19.8
					Including Alaska and Hawaii							
1960	3,519	720	430	517	193.38	11.57	20.80	10.21	55.0	16.1	48.4	19.7
1961	3,399	781	422	463	184.41	13.51	20.13	8.86	54.3	17.3	47.7	19.1
1962	3,231	777	434	434	180.43	12.28	20.06	8.60	55.8	15.8	46.2	19.8
1963	3,031	777	413	463	169.37	12.62	19.96	8.83	55.9	16.2	48.3	19.1
1964	2,876	745	395	422	161.56	11.41	18.96	8.22	56.2	15.3	48.0	19.5
1965	2,768	710	418	380	156.79	11.65	19.64	7.33	56.6	16.4	47.0	19.3
1966[b]	2,586	663	380	352	145.02	10.77	18.09	6.86	56.1	16.2	47.6	19.5
1966[c]	2,587	662	371	361	144.10	11.70	17.73	7.21	55.7	17.7	47.8	20.0
1967	2,430	678	324	340	135.55	11.93	15.46	6.80	55.8	17.6	47.7	20.0
1968	2,385	668	326	311	132.33	11.08	15.56	6.34	55.5	16.6	47.7	20.4
1969	2,268	656	319	320	125.92	10.95	15.56	6.48	55.5	16.7	48.8	20.2

Source: See text for derivation.
a. See Tables C-1 and E-1 for totals.
b. Comparable to earlier years.
c. Comparable to later years.

farm wage and salary group to fall and the proportion of part-time workers to increase. It is likely that substantial numbers whose hours are at the bottom of the distribution of full-time workers prior to recession slip into the top of the distribution for part-time workers when work becomes scarce. This tends to lift the average hours of both groups in comparison with what they would be if such a shift did not take place.

I now describe the derivation from CPS data of the independently derived estimates that were used to allocate the control totals.

The calculations from the CPS data were made, for each sex, in full class-of-worker detail for the whole group of employed civilians covered by the CPS, including groups for whom the final esti-mates were not used. The full detail used in most years included the following for each sex:

Agriculture:
   Wage and salary workers
   Self-employed workers
   Unpaid family workers
Nonagricultural industries:
   Wage and salary workers:
      Private household workers
      Government workers
      Other
   Self-employed workers
   Unpaid family workers

For the earlier years, somewhat less detail was used, as explained below.

The data used to distribute the control totals of employment and hours for the three groups previously specified were, respectively: (1) for wage and salary workers in nonfarm business, "other" wage and salary workers in nonagricultural industries; (2) for nonfarm self-employed and unpaid family workers, the sum of self-employed workers and unpaid family workers in nonagricultural industries; and (3) for farm workers, the sum of all the subgroups in agriculture. Inclusion in the compilations of unneeded detail and unneeded groups was necessary to improve the estimates that were used. It also makes possible a comparison (provided later in this appendix) of the course of part-time employment in the business sector with that in the whole civilian economy.

CPS-Based Estimates for 1966–69

Averages of the twelve weeks covered by the CPS household surveys each year were used to derive the CPS-based estimates for the 1966–69 period.

The basic Bureau of Labor Statistics (BLS) tabulations for 1967 to 1969 from the CPS cover persons 16 years of age and over. Estimates for this group and the 14–15 age group were prepared separately, and added.

All data required for the 16-and-over age group were available for 1968 and 1969 for each detailed class-of-worker group, by sex, from published or unpublished BLS tables. Thus total employment and the number employed on full-time schedules (my full-time employment) are reported in *Employment and Earnings and Monthly Report on the Labor Force,* Table A-18, and the unpublished Tabulation Table 11, respectively. The number of persons at work, the number of persons at work on full-time schedules, and the average weekly hours worked by each of these categories are provided by the Bureau of Labor Statistics CPS Tabulation Tables 32 and 38. The products of numbers at work and the corresponding average hours provided total weekly hours for all workers and for full-time workers. Part-time employment and total weekly hours worked by part-time workers were obtained by subtracting data for full-time workers from data for all workers.

The 1967 estimates for the 16-and-over age group are similar with the following exception. It was necessary to compute twelve-week averages for numbers employed on full-time schedules, by sex and class of worker, from the CPS monthly data, using BLS procedures. For the first half of

the year BLS tabulated these monthly data by use of a computer program that differed from that which it used subsequently. They yielded twelve-week averages for the detailed groups which, when combined, differed a little from published BLS totals for all workers in nonagricultural industries and in all industries combined; the detail was adjusted to agree with published aggregates. The 1967 estimates do not appear to be significantly impaired by the difference in tabulation procedure.

Estimates for persons 14 and 15 years old were added to these 1967–69 data; their inclusion reduces average hours of full-time and part-time workers combined, and raises the proportions of part-time workers, by appreciable amounts. Twelve-week averages for all employment components needed were calculated from *Employment and Earnings and Monthly Report on the Labor Force,* Table A-26, until June 1968, and thereafter from Table A-28. The distributions of employment of 14- and 15-year-olds between full time and part time, and average hours worked, are estimates.[4] In this age group there are relatively few full-time workers, average hours for all workers are very low, and only about three-fifths of civilian employment is in the business sector.

---

4. For each detailed sex and class-of-worker group, the number of full-time workers was assumed to be the same as in 1966, or the same proportion of employment as in 1966, whichever was smaller. In each such group, average hours of full-time workers and part-time workers, separately, were assumed to be the same as in 1966.

The number of full-time workers at work in 1966, obtained by subtracting CPS data for the numbers at work 16 years of age and over from the numbers 14 years of age and over, was used to measure full-time employment in each category. (In these data, government and "other" nonfarm wage and salary workers are combined; allocations between the two groups, for males and females, were based on the numbers of 14- and 15-year-olds at work 35 hours or more.)

Total weekly hours of 14- and 15-year-olds in 1966 were first calculated for all categories by subtracting hours worked by persons 16 years of age and older (calculated as persons at work × average hours) from hours worked by persons 14 years of age and over (similarly calculated). Percentage errors in the residuals for 14- and 15-year-olds are large. (This is partly because average hours were rounded to the nearest tenth of an hour and total hours worked by 14- and 15-year-olds are a small fraction of the total, and partly because BLS used blow-up procedures in the tabulations for persons 14 and over that differed slightly from those in the tabulations for persons 16 and over.) The sums of residuals for subgroups sometimes differ widely from those calculated directly for larger groups, and implied average hours are in some cases absurd. The residuals had therefore to be substantially adjusted. It was also necessary to estimate the average hours of full-time workers; in each detailed category they were assumed to be 80 percent of the average hours of full-time workers 16 years of age and over, or 36 hours, whichever was larger.

Although percentage errors in the detailed hours estimates for this age group separately may be sizable, any error introduced into estimates of total and average hours worked by persons 14 years of age and over in the business sector is of no importance.

The estimates for 1966 that underlie the data shown as comparable to later years were particularly difficult to prepare. Estimates from CPS data comparable to earlier years were made first. The procedure differed in principle from that used in 1968 in only one respect: the basic tabulations refer to persons 14 years of age or older, so no addition for persons 14 and 15 years of age was needed. However, some of the detailed data were missing and had to be calculated or estimated as follows:

1. Although the 1966 numbers employed on full-time schedules, by sex and class of worker, were not directly available from BLS for each detailed group, they could be calculated by multiplying employment by the ratio of persons at work on full-time schedules to the total number of persons at work.

2. The 1966 tabulations of the numbers of persons at work on full-time schedules, by sex, combined government and "other" nonfarm wage and salary workers. Separate estimates were needed. Persons at work on full-time schedules are the sum of (a) persons at work 35 hours or more and (b) persons who usually work full time but worked part time for noneconomic reasons. Component (a) was available, by sex, for the two categories separately. Component (b) for each sex was estimated for the two categories separately by applying to (a) in 1966 the 1967 ratio of (b) to (a), and adjusting the resulting estimates proportionately to agree with the 1966 value of (b) for the two groups combined.

3. Average hours worked by persons at work on full-time schedules were not available. Total hours worked by such persons were estimated, by sex and class of worker, by deducting from total hours worked by all persons estimates of hours worked by persons not on full-time schedules. These estimates were the product of reported part-time employment in 1966 and average part-time hours in 1967.[5] Any error in the assumption that

part-time hours were the same in 1966 as in 1967 would scarcely affect the average hours estimates for full-time workers.

The set of 1966 estimates thus obtained conforms to definitions followed by CPS in 1966 and preceding years. They were not comparable to 1967 and later data because of changes in survey questions and procedures. To arrive at the estimates shown as comparable to 1967–69, adjustments were introduced for two of these changes. These adjustments were based on a comparison of 1966 CPS data with 1966 data from the MLS, the research sample which utilized the questions and procedures followed in later years.[6]

First, introduction of additional questions concerning hours reduced the numbers reported as on full-time schedules. Comparisons are available only for agriculture and nonagricultural industries as a whole. The data, which refer to persons 16 years of age or older, are as follows (with numbers of persons in thousands):

	CPS	MLS
Total employment		
Agriculture	3,979	3,904
Nonagriculture	68,916	69,035
Persons "at work"		
Agriculture	3,847	3,768
Nonagriculture	65,456	65,499
Persons "at work" on full-time schedules		
Agriculture	2,947	2,882
Nonagriculture	56,348	55,991
Percentage of persons "at work" who were on full-time schedules		
Agriculture	76.6051	76.4862
Nonagriculture	86.0853	85.4837

The percentage of persons at work who were on full-time schedules was decreased by 0.1189 percentage points in agriculture and by 0.6016 percentage points in nonagricultural industries. Because persons with a job but not at work are distributed like persons at work, the same percentages may be used for employment. I have therefore adjusted the initial estimates by transferring 0.1189 percent of the persons employed in agriculture and 0.6016 percent of the persons employed in nonagricultural industries from the

---

5. Direct estimates of part-time hours based on 1966 hours data were also prepared by use of the numbers and average hours of persons at work 1–34 hours, and the numbers included in this aggregate who were at work part time for economic reasons, all of which were available by sex and class of worker, and the use for all sex and class-of-

worker groups of a uniform average for the hours worked by persons at work part time for economic reasons. For "other" nonagricultural wage and salary workers the two procedures yielded almost identical results, but use of 1967 averages appeared to yield slightly better estimates for the smaller groups.

6. See pp. 167–68, and 194–95.

full-time to the part-time category. The numbers so transferred were distributed among detailed sex and class-of-worker categories in proportion to the initial estimates of full-time employment. No change in the average hours of persons employed full time or part time in any detailed category of employment was made. Average hours of full-time and part-time workers combined in each category were reduced as a result of the reduction in the weight of full-time workers.

Second, an adjustment of the data for nonfarm self-employed was introduced. A change in question resulted in the transfer of 1.091 percent of all persons employed in nonagricultural industries from the category of self-employed workers to "other wage and salary workers." This number was transferred between these two categories. The number transferred was divided between males and females in proportion to the number of self-employed. Those reclassified were reported by BLS to be mainly corporate officers, whose distribution between full-time and part-time status was not necessarily similar to the remainder of either the self-employed group from which they were transferred (and of which they represented a large fraction) or the wage-salary group to which they were transferred. Detailed 1966 data for the nonfarm self-employed were discarded. The percentage divisions between full-time workers and part-time workers of the adjusted numbers of nonfarm self-employed of each sex, and the average hours of full-time workers and part-time workers of each sex, were assumed to be the same in 1966 as in 1967. The adjustments in the total hours worked by full-time and part-time self-employed of each sex were offset by opposite adjustments to the total hours worked by "other" nonfarm wage and salary workers.

Specific adjustments for other changes in the CPS procedures were not attempted.[7] However, the adjustment of the CPS data to the independent control totals for the three major components of business employment and hours eliminates discontinuities resulting from changes in questions and procedures that affect all subgroups within these groups alike. The effects of these other changes do not appear to be greatly concentrated on any particular subgroup.

CPS-Based Estimates for 1954–66

Below are described the procedures followed in deriving the preliminary CPS-based estimates for 1954–66. However, it should first be pointed out that the series for the whole period 1929 through 1966 was developed independently of the 1966–69 series. The *levels* of the series for average full-time and part-time hours, and for distributions by sex and full-time or part-time status, are less accurate than those for 1967–69, and where interest is in levels the later data are to be preferred. For this period, major emphasis was placed on securing consistency over time.

General Procedure in 1954–66

I now describe the general procedure followed for the years from 1954 through 1966.[8] Departures from this general procedure were introduced in one or more of the years from 1954 through 1959, and these are noted below.

The estimates for 1954–66 are based on different procedures than those for the later period, mainly because detailed annual data for full-time workers who were not working 35 hours or more were not obtained. They make use of data or estimates for both the average of the twelve weeks during the year that were covered by the CPS and the May week covered by the CPS. The May week is always free of holidays and is more free of other irregular disturbances than is the sample week for most other months. For this reason BLS has frequently used May figures when it wished to provide comparable hours data over a period of years for persons at work full time or 35 hours or more. More data have been tabulated, and published, for the May week than for the average of the twelve weeks in which surveys were made each year. May data are incorporated into the estimating procedure where twelve-week averages are not available or where introduction of May data is thought to produce more consistent series during this time span than the twelve-week averages.

The following May data were obtained, from the Bureau of Labor Statistics CPS Tabulation Table 30, for each sex in each class-of-worker

---

7. It may be noted, however, that the two adjustments introduced had the effect of reducing average hours of all persons at work in all industries, and in nonagricultural industries, by 0.2 hours. This is consistent with the differences between the MLS research sample and the CPS sample; the former yielded average hours for persons at work that were lower than averages from the CPS sample by 0.2 hours in each case. This is the only available comparison of hours from the two samples.

8. The same CPS estimates for 1960 were used for the 1960 estimates including and excluding Alaska and Hawaii. The two estimates for 1960 shown in Tables G-1, G-2, and G-3 differ only because of differences in the control totals.

group in agricultural and in nonagricultural industries.

a. The number of persons at work.

b. The number at work 1–34 hours.

c. The number at work 35 hours or more.

d. The average hours worked by persons at work.

The following May data were calculated for each component.

e. Total weekly hours worked by persons at work, calculated as $a \times d$.

f. Average hours worked by persons at work 1–34 hours, calculated from distributions of persons at work by number of hours worked that were obtained from BLS. The class intervals used in the distributions are fairly detailed (1–14; 15–21; 22–29; 30–34).

g. Total weekly hours worked by persons at work 1–34 hours, calculated as $b \times f$.

h. Total weekly hours worked by persons at work 35 hours or more, calculated as $e - g$.

i. Average hours worked by persons at work 35 hours or more, calculated as $h \div c$.

Averages for the twelve weeks during the year that were covered by the CPS were obtained from BLS (published data from sources listed on page 192 or CPS Tabulation Table 30) for the following items.

j. The number of persons employed. Employment includes persons at work and persons with a job but not at work.

k. The number of persons at work. (For years prior to 1962, annual averages were not available from BLS by sex and class of worker. They were calculated by averaging monthly data obtained from BLS.)

l. The average hours worked by persons at work. (For years prior to 1962, annual averages were calculated from BLS monthly data; average hours each month were weighted by the number at work.)

Twelve-week averages were computed or estimated for the following series.

m. Total weekly hours worked by persons at work, computed as $k \times l$.

n. The number of persons at work 35 hours or more. Reported data were used for each class of worker for the two sexes combined. The total for each class of worker was allocated between males and females in proportion to "preliminary" estimates. The latter were equal to $k \times c/a$.

o. The number of persons at work 1–34 hours, computed as $k - n$.

p. Total weekly hours worked by persons at work

1–34 hours. This aggregate was initially calculated for each detailed group as $o \times f$ (the twelve-week average number × May average hours). For nonagricultural industries, the figures so calculated were adjusted proportionately (and very slightly) so as to make their total agree with the product of the twelve-week average number of all nonagricultural workers at work 1–34 hours and their twelve-week average hours, both of which are reported.

q. The number of persons at work 1–34 hours who usually work 35 hours or more but worked less for noneconomic reasons. Reported data were used for the following groupings: total agriculture; nonagricultural wage and salary workers in private households; government and "other" nonagricultural wage and salary workers; nonagricultural self-employed and unpaid family workers (combined); total males in nonagricultural industries and total females in nonagricultural industries. Additional breakdowns were estimated by the following procedures. The figure for agriculture was divided among class-of-worker and sex subgroups in proportion to the numbers of persons at work 35 hours or more (*n*). The reported figures for each of the three class-of-worker groupings in nonagricultural industries were first allocated among subgroups and by sex in proportion to the numbers of persons at work 35 hours or more (*n*). These estimates were then further adjusted to conform to the totals for the number of each sex in nonagricultural industries.

r. Total hours worked by persons at work 1–34 hours who usually work 35 hours or more but worked less for noneconomic reasons. Average hours for such persons were obtained only for nonagricultural industries as a whole. They are longer for persons in this category than for persons who worked 1–34 hours for other reasons. For each subgroup, *r* was calculated as *q* times the average hours of all persons in nonagricultural industries who are in this category (that is, the same average hours figure was used for all subgroups).

From these estimates the desired figures for each sex within each class-of-worker group in agricultural and nonagricultural industries were secured as follows.

s. The total number of full-time workers employed is computed as $j \times \dfrac{n + q}{k}$.

t. The total number of part-time workers employed is equal to $j - s$.

u. The total hours worked by part-time workers is equal to $p - r$.

v. The total hours worked by full-time workers is equal to $m - u$.

Exceptions to General Procedure

There are several exceptions to the preceding citations of the data obtained from the Bureau of Labor Statistics that apply to one or more of the years, 1954 through 1959.[9] I now indicate these exceptions and show how missing data were estimated. Some of these explanations also apply to years before 1954; these are also covered in this section.

1. The detailed data for the number of persons at work in January and February of 1959, and the division of persons at work and their hours between government and "other" wage and salary workers in January through May of 1959, were partially estimated by the author.[10]

2. Slight adjustment of reported data was re-

9. In addition, the 1966 figures for the division by sex of farm workers between full-time and part-time status that were obtained by the procedure just described were adjusted by the transfer of 38,000 females from the full-time to the part-time category and 38,000 males from part time to full time. Possibly because the relationship between May and annual ratios was out of line in 1966, the original estimates for females implied that the percentage of part-time workers was much below other years and also much below the 1966 percentage obtained by the procedures followed for later years. The male percentage was out of line (by a much smaller amount) in the opposite direction. Because 1966 was an overlap year, failure to introduce such an adjustment would have distorted the relationship between estimates for the whole 1966–69 period and those for the whole previous period. Average hours of all farm workers of each sex were not changed. It was assumed for each sex that the percentage differential between average full-time and average part-time hours was the same in 1966 as in 1965.

10. Tabulated data were available from unpublished Tabulation Table 30 in the same form as in later periods but could not be used without adjustment because of obvious errors in the tabulations. In January and February the detailed data for persons at work by sex and class of worker are not consistent with published data for broader groupings and for the total labor force. Also, in each of the first five months of 1959 the unpublished data for "government" and "other" nonfarm wage and salary workers at work are inconsistent with published employment data; a comparison indicated that large numbers of "other" nonfarm wage and salary workers had been erroneously tabulated as government wage and salary workers. (After February, the figures for these two categories combined appeared to be correct.) This misclassification affected average hours as well as the number of persons at work. For use in the present study, the erroneous monthly figures were deleted and replaced by estimates based on use of less detailed published estimates for persons at work; published employment data; and, to subdivide government and "other" wage and salary workers, 1960 relationships between the first five months and the last seven months of the year for persons at work, employment, and average hours.

quired to obtain CPS employment estimates (item *j*) by class of worker prior to 1957. The following description applies to the estimates for the entire 1947–56 period.

Until January 1957 the Bureau of the Census had included in the category of "employed persons" who were working 0 hours ("with a job but not at work") two groups of workers who were not so counted thereafter: those on temporary layoff and those waiting to start new wage and salary jobs within thirty days. The *Manpower Report of the President, 1966,* Table A-1, provides CPS employment figures for agriculture and nonagricultural industries, by sex, adjusted to accord with the new definitions. However, the adjusted figures are not provided in the full detail required.

The change in definition scarcely affected the numbers of self-employed and unpaid family workers; the figures originally reported for these groups were therefore retained in the present study. The entire difference between the *Manpower Report*'s figures and the original figures was subtracted— separately for each sex in agricultural and in nonagricultural employment—from the figures for wage and salary workers originally appearing in *Current Population Reports* (see page 192).

For agriculture this provided all the detail needed. However, the revision in employment of nonfarm wage and salary workers, by sex, had to be further allocated among three components: private household, government, and "other" wage and salary workers. It was obvious from the nature of the change that the chief effect was on the "other" group. Table P of the 1957 *Current Population Reports* indicates that the change in definitions that year reduced employment in "public administration" by only 0.2 percent.[11] On this evidence, in the present study the figures in the *Current Population Reports* for males and females employed in government, 1947 through 1956, were reduced by 0.2 percent. The figures for male and female private household workers were also reduced by 0.2 percent. The category, "other wage and salary workers," is a residual. Since few private household and government workers are affected by the change in definition, the effect on the "other" group of any error in estimating their number is slight.

For the years 1953 and 1954, the *Current Population Reports* combine employment of govern-

11. See U.S. Bureau of the Census, *Current Population Reports,* Series P-50, No. 85, "Annual Report on the Labor Force, 1957" (1958).

ment and "other" nonagricultural wage and salary workers.[12] The numbers of male and female government workers in these years were estimated by straight-line interpolation between the corrected 1952 and 1955 figures. Figures for "other" wage and salary workers, by sex, were obtained as residuals.

3. For the years 1954 through 1958, all tabulations for persons at work and their average hours combine government and "other" nonagricultural wage and salary workers. All calculations were, therefore, first carried out for the two groups combined, resulting in estimates of full-time employment, part-time employment, full-time hours, and part-time hours for the combined groups. A division was obtained by the following procedure. By sex, employment each year in each of the two groups was initially divided between full-time and part-time employment by use of 1959 proportions; these figures were then adjusted to conform with the totals for the combined groups. The numbers of full-time and part-time employed persons in each group were initially multiplied by 1959 average hours; the resulting figures for total hours of full-time workers and of part-time workers in each group were then adjusted to conform with the total hours of full-time workers and of part-time workers in the two groups combined.

4. For the years 1955 through 1957, the annual average number of persons at work 35 hours or more (item n) in agriculture was not available by class of worker (or by sex). For each sex and class-of-worker group, the ratio of this figure to the "preliminary" estimate, $k \times c/a$, was initially assumed to be the same as in 1958; the figures resulting from this assumption were then adjusted to conform with known totals for all agricultural workers combined. For 1954, the procedure was similar except that an intermediate control adjustment could be introduced. Annual average numbers of persons at work 35 hours or more in agriculture were available by sex (though not by class of worker). By sex, figures for each class of worker based on preliminary estimates ($k \times c/a$) and 1958 ratios were adjusted to conform with the reported numbers of males and females at work 35 hours or more in agriculture.

For the years 1954–57, the available data for the annual average numbers of persons at work 35 hours or more (item n) in nonagricultural industries combined private household workers with the remaining nonagricultural wage and salary worker groups, and combined the self-employed with unpaid family workers. For the combined groups, the procedures were similar to those applied, with full detail, in later years. To obtain further breakdowns, the procedure used to divide agricultural workers by class of worker in the period 1955–57 was adopted.[13]

5. In 1955–57 the annual average number of private household workers who usually work full time but worked 1–34 hours for noneconomic reasons (item q) was not available; it was assumed to be the same percentage of the number of private household workers at work as in 1958.

6. For the year 1955 only:

a. The breakdown by sex of the annual average number of persons at work 35 hours or more in nonagricultural industries was lacking. The figure for each sex was initially assumed to bear the same ratio to preliminary estimates, computed as $k \times c/a$, as it did in 1956, and then adjusted to make the sum of the estimates for the two sexes conform to their combined number.

b. The average hours worked by persons at work 1–34 hours in nonagricultural industries were available for only the last eight months of the year. To obtain an annual average, the ratio of the twelve-month average to the average for these eight months was assumed to be the same as in 1956.

c. The number of persons who usually work full time but worked 1–34 hours for noneconomic reasons was lacking for January, March, and April. To obtain a twelve-month average for each group, the average for the other nine months in 1955 was multiplied by the ratio of the twelve-month average in 1956 to the average for the same nine months in 1956.

d. In nonagricultural industries, the ratio of the annual average to an eight-month average for hours worked by persons at work 1–34 hours who usually work full time but worked part time for noneconomic reasons, and the ratio of the annual average to a nine-month average for their number, were both assumed to be the same in 1955 as in 1956.

---

12. In general, the employment and other data used for 1953 are those revised by the Bureau of the Census for comparability with later years. However, revised figures for male and female private household workers were not released by the Census Bureau and the unrevised figures are used in the present study.

13. This procedure still left government and "other" wage and salary workers combined. The division was described in item 3 above.

7. For the year 1954 only:

a. The tabulated distribution by hours worked of female private household workers at work in May differed far too much from other years to be credible. The data were rejected and the total number at work in May was distributed among hours classes in proportion to the May 1955 distribution.

b. The annual average for total weekly hours worked by persons at work 1–34 hours in nonagricultural industries was assumed (in the absence of reported data for average hours) to bear the same ratio to the preliminary figure $o \times f$ as in 1955.

c. Data for the annual average numbers of persons who usually work full time but worked 1–34 hours for noneconomic reasons, and the average hours of such persons in nonagricultural industries, were wholly lacking. The number of agricultural workers in this category was assumed to bear the same ratio to the number of persons at work 35 hours or more as in 1955. A preliminary estimate for nonagricultural workers was made in the same way, but this estimate was adjusted to offset the unusually large effect of holidays in 1954 (resulting from the occurrence of major legal holidays in three of the twelve survey weeks) which, in the twelve-week averages, moved large numbers of persons at work from the group working 35 hours or more to the group working 15–34 hours. In order to do this, synthetic holiday-free averages of the numbers of persons at work 15–34 hours were computed for 1954 and 1955 based on the weeks in the seven survey months that did not contain holidays in either year.[14] The ratio of (1) the *difference* between the actual and synthetic 1955 averages for persons at work 15–34 hours to (2) the 1955 number of all those at work was applied to the 1954 number of all those at work, yielding a figure for what the *difference* between the actual and synthetic 1954 averages for persons at work 15–34 hours would have been if nothing had varied between the two years except the numbers of persons at work. This difference between the two 1954 averages at the 1955 ratio was subtracted from the difference between the synthetic and actual 1954 averages; and the figure thus obtained was added to the preliminary estimate of non-

agricultural workers who usually work full time but who for noneconomic reasons worked only 1–34 hours per week. Preliminary estimates for each class of worker, by sex, based on 1955 ratios of persons of this status to persons at work 35 hours or more were adjusted to add up to the final estimate for nonagricultural workers.[15] Average hours of persons at work 1–34 hours for noneconomic reasons were assumed to be the same as in 1955.

CPS-Based Estimates for 1947–53

For the years 1947 through 1953, the published CPS reports provide May and twelve-week average data for average hours worked in agricultural and in nonagricultural industries, but do not provide average hours by sex or class of worker. They provide employment, numbers of persons at work, and distributions of the numbers of persons at work by hours worked (but with only three class intervals) for persons in agricultural and nonagricultural industries, separately, by sex. Only employment is available by class of worker. (It is cross-classified by sex.)[16] Data for the number and average hours of persons who usually work full time but worked part time for noneconomic reasons are lacking, although some related information is available.

The derivation of the CPS-based estimates for agricultural and nonagricultural industries in the 1947–53 period will now be described. Before these estimates were adjusted to the control totals, an adjustment to reduce slightly the proportion of females was made in the 1947–52 period; the purpose was to correct for the discontinuity introduced in the CPS data when 1950 Census re-

---

14. For each half of each year, figures for the survey weeks that did not contain holidays in either year were added up and converted to a six-month basis. The sums of figures for the two halves of each year were divided by twelve.

15. In order to take account of the fact that full-time self-employed and unpaid family workers work more hours per week than other full-time workers in nonagricultural industries and hence are less likely to drop below 35 hours when there is a holiday, smaller amounts, relative to their size, were added to the preliminary estimates for these two classes of workers than to the estimates for other workers. A figure was derived for male self-employed workers that yields approximately the same number of average hours per person employed part time as in 1955; figures for female self-employed and male and female unpaid family workers are assumed to be in the same proportion to preliminary estimates as this figure for male self-employed workers. Preliminary estimates for other nonagricultural workers were adjusted to add up to the difference between the final estimate of nonagricultural workers and the final estimates of self-employed and unpaid family workers.

16. The employment data used in the estimates are those, already described, which allow for the changes in definitions of employment introduced in the CPS in 1957. See item 2, pages 205–06.

sults were incorporated. All figures for female employment and hours were reduced by a uniform percentage each year. The percentages were based on the adjustments derived in calculating the distribution of total hours worked in the business sector by age and sex. (See Appendix F, pages 194–95.) The following descriptions refer to the estimates prior to this adjustment.

Estimates for Agricultural Workers

Estimates by class of worker within agriculture (which are not needed for the final estimates) were not attempted for 1947–53; estimates were prepared only for males and females. Employment data were described on page 205. The Current Population Survey provided twelve-week averages for the numbers of males and females at work in agriculture, and for the numbers of males and females at work 35 hours or more; for the numbers of males and females at work 1–14 hours and at work 15–34 hours; and for the average hours worked per week by both sexes combined. The product of persons at work and average hours provided total hours worked in agriculture.

Estimates were required of total hours worked per week by males and females at work 35 hours or more, and by those at work 1–34 hours (obtained by adding estimates for those at work 1–14 hours and those at work 15–34 hours); and, by sex, for the numbers who usually worked full time but who for noneconomic reasons worked only 1–34 hours per week and the hours they worked.

Estimates of total hours (twelve-week averages) worked by males and females at work 1–14 hours and at work 15–34 hours were obtained by multiplying published figures for persons at work by "midpoints" for these classes derived for 1954.[17]

Total hours worked by persons at work 35 hours or more (both sexes combined) were obtained by subtraction. Total hours worked by males and females at work 35 hours or more were estimated in a way that preserves the 1954 percentage differential between male and female average hours in the 35-or-more hours class. (Each year the number of persons of each sex at work 35 hours or more was multiplied by 1954 average hours for the corresponding group. These products

were adjusted proportionally to add up to the total for the two sexes combined.)

The ratios of the numbers of workers who usually work full time but who for noneconomic reasons worked only 1–34 hours per week to the numbers at work 35 hours or more were assumed to be the same as in 1955.

The formulas appearing on pages 204–05 were used to derive estimates of male and female full-time and part-time workers and their total weekly hours (s, t, u, and v) from these data and estimates.

Estimates for Nonagricultural Workers

Series were first developed for the years 1947 through 1953 that were not quite comparable to later years. Some 1955 ratios were used in the process of estimation of these years. These series were then adjusted to correspond to the 1955 estimates previously developed.[18]

Preliminary estimates of the numbers of full-time and part-time workers in nonagricultural industries and the hours they worked per week were first derived, by sex but not by class of worker, in the same way as were the final CPS-based estimates of the numbers of agricultural workers and the hours they worked.

Comparability from year to year of the twelve-week averages for nonagricultural workers so obtained was greatly impaired by the uneven incidence of holidays in this period, which caused large irregular movements in the twelve-week average numbers of persons at work 15–34 hours. Holidays throw large numbers of full-time workers into this category. From 1955 on this problem was handled by classifying as full-time workers those who usually work full time but worked part time for noneconomic reasons, including holidays.[19] For 1947–53 such data were not available and a direct adjustment was required. Weeks affected by holidays are indicated in the CPS reports.

To make an adjustment, "synthetic" annual averages of the numbers of persons at work 1–34 hours were first computed, based on published figures for the survey weeks in the nine months that did not contain holidays from 1947 to 1953

---

17. The latter were so set that when the 0–14 and 15–34 groups were combined, they yielded the same averages for those at work 1–34 hours in 1954 as were actually obtained in that year. Distributions of part-time workers in the month of May among four hours categories (1–14, 15–21, 22–29, 30–34) obtained from Tabulation Table 6 were used in setting the midpoints for the two classes separately.

18. The year 1954 was not used to link the estimates, nor in general for ratios, because in 1954 many relationships were abnormal because of the recession and an extraordinary incidence of holidays, and also because 1954 data are particularly incomplete.

19. The irregularity in the incidence of holidays was also smaller in these later years, probably because of the shift in the weeks surveyed. A special adjustment was introduced in 1954, as already described (item 7c, page 207).

or in 1955. (All of the holiday-affected months are in the second half of the year. For each year, the figures for the three months of the second half of the year that do not have holidays in any of the years were added and multiplied by two. The resulting product was added to the figures for the first six months and the sum was divided by twelve.) No survey weeks in 1947 or 1952 contained holidays. The difference (which is small) between twelve-week averages containing no holidays and the "synthetic" nine-week averages was computed for these years and estimated for intervening years by straight-line interpolation. (The difference in 1952 was used for 1953.) The figures so obtained were subtracted from the actual differences between the synthetic and actual twelve-week averages in the years with holidays in one or more survey weeks. The procedure yielded approximations of the differences between the two averages caused by the occurrence of holidays as distinguished from other seasonal differences arising from omission of certain months from the synthetic averages. Comparable estimates were made for 1955, since they were needed at a later stage.[20]

The preliminary estimates of the numbers of full-time and part-time nonagricultural workers at work were adjusted by transferring from part-time to full-time status the estimated "excess" numbers of persons at work 15–34 hours in the twelve-week averages due to the occurrence of holidays. Adjustments of the hours data were also required. To preliminary estimates of *total* hours worked by full-time and part-time workers combined were added the product of 8 hours and the excess numbers of persons at work 15–34 hours because of holidays. The preliminary numbers of total weekly hours worked by part-time workers were reduced by the product of the number working 15–34 hours because of holidays and the average hours worked per week by persons at work 15–34 hours. The adjusted numbers of part-time workers at work were multiplied by the ratios of the num-

bers of persons employed to the numbers of persons at work in order to derive estimates of part-time employment. Adjusted estimates of full-time employment and of total weekly hours worked by full-time workers were obtained by subtracting the adjusted estimates for part-time workers from the adjusted estimates for all nonagricultural workers.

The resulting estimates were further adjusted to make them accord with those for later years. To do this, 1955 estimates were derived according to the procedures just described. The ratios of the estimates actually used for 1955 to these estimates were applied to the estimates for 1947 through 1953.

The estimates thus obtained for all males and females in nonagricultural employment had still to be allocated by class of worker. The only usable information by class of worker available for 1947–53 is employment.

Self-employed and (separately) unpaid family workers of each sex in 1947–53 were divided between full-time and part-time employment in the same proportions as in 1955. Each year's employment in a category (e.g., male part-time unpaid family workers) was multiplied by 1955 average hours to secure an estimate of total hours. Average hours shown in Table G-2 nevertheless fluctuate because of adjustment to the control totals and changes in the mix of self-employed and family workers.

For private household workers, BLS data provide average hours worked per week by both sexes combined. (See Appendix E, page 184.) Average hours in 1955 based on CPS were extrapolated to 1947–53 by this BLS series. Average hours were multiplied by employment to obtain total hours of both sexes combined. Preliminary hours estimates for each sex were calculated by the same procedure; 1955 average hours of each sex were extrapolated by average hours of the combined sexes, and multiplied by employment of that sex. Because of changing proportions of males and females, the preliminary estimates for the two sexes do not add exactly to the estimates for the combined sexes.[21] Total hours of males and females were adjusted proportionately to add up to the controls for the two sexes combined. Average hours of private household workers of each sex were declining sharply in this period. The decline was assumed to result from changes in the proportions of full-time and part-time workers rather than in

20. Data for persons at work 15–34 hours in 1955 are available only for males and females combined, and the breakdown by sex had to be estimated for that year. An estimate of the twelve-week average number of males at work 15–34 hours in 1955 data who were in that class as a result of the occurrence of legal holidays in three of the twelve survey weeks was made by computing the ratio of the difference between the two averages for both sexes combined in 1955 to the corresponding 1954 difference (obtained as described in item 7c, page 207), and multiplying it by the difference (due to holidays) between the two averages for males in 1954. A similar procedure was followed for females.

21. However, there are few males, and any error in the procedure scarcely affects my final estimates.

the average hours of either group separately. Average hours worked by full-time and part-time workers of each sex were therefore assumed to be the same as in 1955. The proportions of full-time and part-time workers were varied to produce the average hours already calculated for each sex.

Estimates of employment and total hours worked by government and "other" wage and salary workers combined, classified by sex and full-time or part-time status, were obtained by subtracting estimates for self-employed, unpaid family, and private household workers from estimates for all nonagricultural workers. These figures were divided between government and "other" wage and salary workers by the same procedures as were followed for the years 1954 through 1958 (see item 3, page 206).

Postwar Proportions of Part-Time Workers

Changes in the importance of part-time employment in the American economy are of widespread interest. The growth of part-time jobs has been one of the more striking labor force developments in the postwar period. There has been a notable rise in the numbers of persons—chiefly of women and of young people of both sexes whose principal activity is attending school—seeking and finding part-time nonfarm work. In addition, there has been a growing awareness that series for average hours of work are much affected by changes in the prevalence of part-time work and do not accurately portray either the level or the movement of the hours of the full-time workers who comprise the bulk of the labor force. Until very recently, the statistical system of the federal government has not provided information in a form that enables the course of part-time employment or of average hours of full-time workers to be traced.

Tabulations from the CPS are now being made available by BLS on a full-year basis and provide data that permit this gap to be substantially eliminated so far as the present and the future are concerned.[22] The gaps in the historical record have remained, however. I believe the series presented in this appendix for the average hours of persons employed full time, though less precise than I should like, are sufficiently good to indicate the course of full-time hours among six large groups

22. However, published data for full-time employment are presented in inadequate detail, and average hours per full-time worker employed (as distinguished from average hours per full-time worker at work) are not shown at all.

of workers. They reveal that over the postwar period there has been much less reduction in the full-time hours of each sex, and particularly of males, than in the average hours of all workers. Average weekly hours in 1969 and in 1947 in the components of the business sector compare as follows after adjustment of 1947 hours, where necessary, for differences between the overlapping 1966 estimates:

| | Average weekly hours | | |
	1947	*1969*	*Change*
Nonfarm wage and salary workers			
All workers	40.6	37.6	−3.0
Full-time males	43.4	42.4	−1.0
Full-time females	40.0	38.0	−2.0
Nonfarm self-employed and unpaid family workers			
All workers	47.9	44.9	−3.0
Full-time males	53.0	53.1	0.1
Full-time females	53.2	50.9	−2.3
Farm workers			
All workers	50.6	44.6	−6.0
Full-time males	57.0	55.5	−1.5
Full-time females	49.4	48.8	−0.6

The estimates provided in this appendix are much less satisfactory for tracing and analyzing the growth of part-time employment. There are two reasons for this.

First, a really satisfactory analysis requires segregation of four groups of part-time workers:
1. Persons desiring and holding part-time jobs.
2. Persons desiring a full-time job but able to find only a part-time job.
3. Persons desiring full-time work and holding what is ordinarily a full-time job, but who worked only part time in a particular week "for economic reasons."
4. Persons, particularly those starting and ending a full-time job within a week, who are classified as part-time workers by convention.

My estimates of part-time employment do not distinguish among these groups. There is no doubt that the large increase in part-time employment during the postwar period stems mainly, if not entirely, from the first group—those who want part-time work—while short-term fluctuations are dominated by the other groups; but this generalization is not very helpful if one is interested in detailed or precise analysis.

Second, the percentages of workers who are employed part time that can be calculated from columns 2 and 4 in Tables G-1, G-2, and G-3 are much more sensitive to errors of estimate than the average hours series and can be used only as rough indicators of changes in the importance of part-time employment.

Despite these limitations, it is probably useful for other research workers to have the employment estimates presented here in full detail, because it is not likely that better estimates for this period will become available. In addition, it appears useful to present estimates, which can be derived as a by-product, for all civilian employment.

This is done in Table G-4. To allow comparisons, the first three columns show, for both sexes combined and each sex separately, part-time employment as a percentage of total employment; these are computed directly from Tables G-1, G-2, and G-3. The next three columns show similar data derived from the CPS, before the adjustment to control totals; they differ only because of

a different weighting of the three broad groups of persons covered. Columns 7, 8, and 9 show comparable percentages with civilian government employees and private household workers included. Inclusion of these groups causes the female percentage to rise more sharply, mainly because of the increase in baby-sitters who are included in the private household component. Finally, because there is particular interest in this category, I show in column 10 the percentages for all females employed in nonagricultural industries. Comparison of the last two columns of the table indicates that inclusion of agriculture appreciably dampens the rise in the part-time percentages for all females in civilian employment.

All the percentages show wide swings in the early years of the period that are only partially

Table G-4. Part-Time Employment as a Percentage of Total Employment, Various Aggregates, by Sex, 1929, 1940–41, and 1947–69

Year	Business sector						All civilian employment, unadjusted estimates			
	Final estimates			Unadjusted estimates						
	Both sexes (1)	Male (2)	Female (3)	Both sexes (4)	Male (5)	Female (6)	Both sexes (7)	Male (8)	Female (9)	Female nonfarm (10)
	Excluding Alaska and Hawaii									
1929	7.5	5.1	17.9	n.a.	n.a.	n.a.	n.a	n.a	n.a.	n.a.
1940	10.0	6.6	22.3	n.a.	n.a	n.a.	n.a	n.a	n.a	n.a.
1941	8.5	5.1	20.2	n.a.	n.a	n.a.	n.a.	n.a.	n.a.	n.a.
1947	9.8	6.1	20.8	9.9	6.1	20.9	10.1	6.1	20.3	17.5
1948	11.1	7.1	22.6	11.1	7.1	22.6	11.4	7.0	22.4	19.7
1949	13.0	9.3	23.3	13.0	9.3	23.3	13.4	9.1	23.9	21.3
1950	13.1	9.3	23.6	13.1	9.3	23.4	13.5	9.2	23.9	21.4
1951	12.3	8.2	23.2	12.3	8.2	23.1	12.9	8.1	23.9	21.6
1952	10.8	6.7	21.4	10.8	6.7	21.3	11.3	6.6	22.2	20.1
1953	10.3	6.6	19.9	10.3	6.6	19.9	11.0	6.5	20.9	19.1
1954	12.9	9.0	23.1	12.9	9.0	23.0	13.6	8.8	24.3	22.7
1955	11.6	8.0	20.6	11.6	8.0	20.6	12.5	7.9	22.3	21.0
1956	12.5	8.6	22.2	12.6	8.6	22.3	13.4	8.5	23.7	21.8
1957	13.1	9.1	22.8	13.2	9.2	22.9	14.0	9.0	24.5	22.9
1958	14.9	10.9	24.3	14.9	10.9	24.3	15.6	10.7	25.7	24.2
1959	13.8	9.6	23.8	13.9	9.7	24.0	14.8	9.6	25.5	23.9
1960	14.2	10.0	24.0	14.2	10.0	24.1	15.2	9.9	26.0	24.6
	Including Alaska and Hawaii									
1960	14.2	10.0	24.0	14.2	10.0	24.1	15.2	9.9	26.0	24.6
1961	15.0	10.6	25.1	15.1	10.7	25.1	16.1	10.6	27.0	25.8
1962	14.6	10.2	24.5	14.6	10.2	24.5	15.7	10.1	26.7	25.8
1963	14.8	10.2	25.2	14.8	10.2	25.2	15.8	10.1	27.0	26.0
1964	14.6	10.1	24.6	14.6	10.1	24.5	15.8	10.1	26.9	26.0
1965	14.6	9.9	24.8	14.6	9.9	24.8	15.5	9.8	26.3	25.5
1966[a]	14.4	9.8	23.9	14.4	9.8	23.9	15.6	9.7	26.1	25.5
1966[b]	14.9	10.2	24.5	14.8	10.2	24.3	16.2	10.3	26.8	26.1
1967	15.3	10.4	25.4	15.2	10.4	25.1	16.5	10.4	27.2	26.6
1968	15.5	10.3	25.8	15.4	10.3	25.6	16.6	10.3	27.6	27.0
1969	16.1	10.9	26.3	16.0	10.8	26.1	17.1	10.8	27.8	27.3

Sources: Columns 1, 2, and 3, computed from Tables G-1, G-2, and G-3; other columns, see text for derivation.
n.a. Not available.
a. Comparable to earlier years.
b. Comparable to later years.

explicable by the business cycle. These swings are clearly implied by the CPS data used. I am not able to judge whether they reflect actual changes in the economy or vagaries of the data. Their presence makes it very difficult to establish the magnitude of the increase in part-time employment over the whole postwar period.

Estimates for 1929, 1940, and 1941

My 1929, 1940, and 1941 estimates are described in this section for the tables presented in this appendix and also for the closely related Tables E-1, E-2, and F-5. Table E-1 shows total and average hours worked in the business sector divided among farm workers, nonfarm wage and salary workers, and nonfarm self-employed and unpaid family workers. Table E-2 shows total and average hours in the whole economy. Table F-5 shows distributions of total hours worked in the business sector among age-sex groups. All of the estimates rely upon the employment data already described in Appendix C and summarized in Table C-1.

Farm Employment by Sex and Full-Time Status, 1940 and 1941 (Table G-3)

Agricultural employment, based on CPS data as they stood in 1951, was obtained, by sex, for 1940, 1941, 1947, and 1950 from U.S. Bureau of the Census Series P-50, Nos. 2, 13, and 31.[23] From the same reports the percentage of persons at work who worked 35 hours or more was calculated for the two sexes combined in all four years, and by sex in 1947 and 1950.[24] Preliminary estimates of these percentages by sex were made for 1940 by assuming the difference from the 1950 percentage for each sex to be the same as the difference in the percentage between the 1940 and 1950 decennial census weeks.[25] A preliminary percentage for each sex in 1941 was estimated by straight-line interpolation between the preliminary 1940 and the 1947 percentages. For both sexes combined and for each sex separately, employ-

ment was then multiplied by these percentages to obtain estimates of the numbers employed 35 hours or more when persons with a job but not at work are distributed like persons at work; the estimates by sex in 1940 and 1941 were preliminary. The implied numbers of persons of each sex employed less than 35 hours in 1940 and 1941 were then proportionately adjusted to agree with the total for the two sexes combined, and the percentages working 35 hours or more were recalculated. Finally, the 1947 CPS employment figures by sex were adjusted (as was done elsewhere) to introduce consistency between CPS data before and after adjustment to the 1950 Census.[26]

Employment figures for each sex in 1947 from Table G-3 were extrapolated to 1940 and 1941 by these CPS employment series, and the numbers for each sex were adjusted proportionally to agree with total farm employment as shown in Table C-1. The percentage of farm workers of each sex who were full-time workers in 1947 was calculated from Table G-3. This percentage exceeds the percentage of persons at work who worked 35 hours or more (because of full-time workers at work less than 35 hours for noneconomic reasons), and the excess in 1947 was calculated for each sex. For each sex, the implied ratio (approximately 0.10 in each case) of full-time workers who worked less than 35 hours to the number who worked 35 hours or more (when those who were not at work are distributed like those at work) was calculated for 1947, and assumed to be the same in 1940 and 1941. The percentage of each sex who worked 35 hours or more in these years, based on CPS data, was raised by these ratios to obtain the percentage who worked full time. These percentages were multiplied by employment to obtain full-time employment. The resulting numbers of full-time and part-time workers of each sex in 1940 and 1941 are shown in Table G-3.

Farm Hours, Total and by Sex and Full-Time Status, 1929, 1940, and 1941 (Tables E-1 and G-3)

Total hours worked by each of the four farm groups distinguished in Table G-3 were next estimated for 1940 and 1941. Initial calculations were made by assuming that average hours for each group were the same as in 1947, and initial estimates of total hours were obtained by addition. These estimates were then compared with the De-

23. *Current Population Reports*, Series P-50, No. 2, "Labor Force, Employment, and Unemployment in the United States, 1940 to 1946" (n.d., about 1948); No. 13, "Annual Report on the Labor Force, 1948" (1949); No. 31, "Annual Report on the Labor Force, 1950" (1951).

24. Adjustments were made to the 1950 percentages to allow for the Labor Day holiday.

25. Data for the census weeks are from U.S. Bureau of the Census, *Sixteenth Census of the United States, 1940: Population: The Labor Force (Sample Statistics): Industrial Characteristics* (1943), Table 13; and from U.S. Bureau of the Census, *U.S. Census of Population, 1950*, Vol. 4, Special Report P-E No. 1D, *Industrial Characteristics* (1955), **Table 10.**

26. See pp. 194–95.

partment of Agriculture series for man-hours of labor used for all farm work. This series is not actual hours but "man-equivalent" hours, described as the total hours that would be required by average adult males to produce farm output. The series for total weekly hours compare as follows in four years:[27]

	Department of Agriculture	Initial estimates	Ratio
1940	393.69	481.28	0.8180
1941	385.50	477.12	0.8080
1947	330.69	400.40	0.8259
1948	323.71	394.00	0.8216

The ratio averaged 1.31 percent less in 1940–41 than in 1947–48. I reduced my initial estimates of total and average hours of each group in 1940 and 1941 by 1.31 percent, so that the percentage change in total hours from the 1940–41 average to the 1947–48 average is the same in my series as in the Department of Agriculture series. These estimates for 1940 and 1941 are entered in Tables G-3 and E-1.

The 1940–41 movement of my series for total farm hours is, of course, appreciably different from that of the Department of Agriculture series, but the movements would be identical if my estimates for female and part-time male hours (which are mostly performed by boys) were given only half the weight of full-time male hours. A series so weighted, to be sure, falls more than the Department of Agriculture series from 1940 to 1947: 15.8 percent as against 14.2 percent. But for estimates as difficult as farm hours, this is rather close agreement.

The 1929 employment estimates in Table G-3 will be described subsequently; I use them here to develop the corresponding hours estimates. If (based on estimates from Table G-3) average hours of each of the four groups had been the same in 1929 as in 1940–41, total hours in 1929 would have been 110.65 percent of their 1940–41 average. If female and part-time male hours were given only half weight, the percentage would change only slightly, to 110.23. The estimate of the Department of Agriculture for adult male man-hours of labor "required" in 1929 is 114.31 percent of its 1940–41 average. For each of the four groups distinguished in Table G-3, average

hours were assumed to be 3.7 percent higher in 1929 than in 1940–41, the percentage by which 114.31 exceeds 110.23. Total hours for each group are the product of employment and average hours.

*Nonfarm Business Employment,
by Class of Worker, Sex,
and Full-Time Status,
1940 and 1941 (Tables G-1 and G-2)*

CPS data, as they stood in 1951, were obtained for the numbers of nonagricultural self-employed workers and unpaid family workers of each sex in 1940, 1941, and 1947.[28] The 1947 estimates were adjusted to conform with the subsequent CPS adjustment to the 1950 Census benchmark. These series were used to extrapolate my 1947 estimate of employment in this category for each sex (from Table G-2) to 1940 and 1941. The figures obtained for the two sexes were adjusted proportionately to agree with total employment in this category as shown in Table C-1. This provided my final estimates of employment by sex.

CPS data, as they stood in 1951, were obtained for the numbers of nonagricultural wage and salary workers of each sex in 1940, 1941, 1947, and 1950. From the 1940 and 1950 Censuses of Population, the ratio to "the total number of employed nonagricultural wage and salary workers" of "the number remaining after deduction of the main nonbusiness categories" was computed for each sex.[29] The 1940 and 1950 ratios were interpolated to obtain estimated 1941 and 1947 ratios. CPS employment of each sex was multiplied each year by the ratio so obtained to secure estimates, by sex, corresponding roughly to business employment on a CPS basis. The 1947 estimates were, as usual, adjusted to conform with the adjustment to the 1950 Census benchmark. My 1947 estimate for each sex of nonfarm business wage and salary employment (from Table G-1) was extrapolated to 1940 and 1941 by the resulting series for that sex. The figures so obtained for the two sexes were adjusted proportionately to agree with total

27. The source for the USDA figures is U.S. Department of Agriculture, *Agricultural Statistics, 1967* (1967), p. 580; the annual totals are divided by fifty-two. The figures for the initial estimates for 1947 and 1948 are from Table G-3; those for 1940 and 1941 are calculated by use of 1947 average hours for each of the four groups distinguished in Table G-3.

28. See page 212, note 23, for sources.
29. Data are from U.S. Bureau of the Census, *Sixteenth Census of the United States, 1940, Population*, Vol. 3, *The Labor Force: Occupation, Industry, Employment, and Income*, Pt. 1, *United States Summary* (1943), Table 78; and from *U.S. Census of Population, 1950*, Vol. 4, *Industrial Characteristics* Table 8. The nonbusiness categories deducted included all government workers, except those in postal service, and private wage and salary workers in the following industries: private households; educational services; and welfare, religious, and nonprofit membership organizations.

employment in this category as shown in Table C-1. This provided my final estimates by sex. My estimates show a much faster rise in the female proportion of business wage and salary employment than occurred in the female proportion of total wage and salary employment from 1940–41 to 1947. The decline in domestic service employment provides much of the explanation.

There remained the problem of separating full-time and part-time workers in Tables G-1 and G-2. CPS data show that the percentage of all nonagricultural civilian employed persons at work who worked 35 hours or more was 84.97 in 1940, 87.16 in 1941, and 87.31 in 1947.[30] The 1947 percentages by sex were 90.87 for males and 79.03 for females. If these percentages had been the same in 1941, the percentages for the two sexes combined would have been about 87.52, close to the actual percentage of 87.16. This suggests that, by sex, part-time employment was about as prevalent in 1941 as in 1947. In view of the impossibility of eliminating nonbusiness workers from these data, or allowing for differences by class of worker, I simply allocate 1941 nonfarm business employment for each sex within each of the two class-of-worker categories between full-time and part-time employment in the same proportions as in 1947.

If the part-time percentage in each category were the same in 1940 as in 1941 and 1947, the percentages of all workers in the nonfarm business sector who worked full time would have been 91.43 in 1940 as compared with 91.51 in 1941, a rise of only 0.08 percentage points. The CPS data already cited indicate that the rise should be 2.19 percentage points, provided that there was no change in the proportion usually working full time who worked one to thirty-four hours for noneconomic reasons, and that the change was the same in nonfarm business as in the whole nonfarm economy. I assume this to be the case. A reduction of this magnitude in the number working part time for economic reasons is entirely plausible in this period of sharp employment expansion. The initial estimates of full-time employment in each category were reduced proportionally so as to obtain this result.

The 1940 and 1941 estimates by sex and full-time or part-time status are shown in Tables G-1 and G-2.

30. Comparability of these years appears not to have been impaired by holidays.

Business Employment by Type, Sex, and Full-Time Status, 1929
(Tables G-1, G-2, and G-3)

The 1929 employment breakdowns were obtained in the following steps:

STEP ONE. The Census Bureau has estimated, by sex, the numbers of persons 14 and over employed and unemployed in the 1930 and 1940 decennial census weeks that conform to 1940 labor force definitions.[31] I assumed that the difference between the sex composition of employment in 1940 and 1929 was similar to that between the sex composition of employment (excluding emergency workers) in the 1940 census week and the sex composition of the sum of employment and one-third of unemployed persons in the 1930 census week. These two aggregates were compiled by sex from the Census Bureau's adjusted data.[32]

STEP TWO. Employed persons (excluding emergency workers) in 1940 and gainful workers 14 and over in 1930, as initially reported in the decennial census tabulations, were divided, by sex, among three groups: (a) the industry, "agriculture"; (b) a nonbusiness group consisting of one industry, government except postal service, and the following occupations: clergymen; college presidents, professors, and instructors; social, welfare, and religious workers; teachers, not elsewhere classified (n.e.c.); librarians; housekeepers and servants, private family; and laundresses, private family; (c) all other workers, consisting chiefly of persons employed in nonagricultural business.[33]

STEP THREE. The employment aggregate for

31. U.S. Bureau of the Census, *Sixteenth Census of the United States, 1940, Population: Estimates of Labor Force, Employment, and Unemployment in the United States, 1940 and 1930* (1944), Tables 2 and 3.
32. Persons 10 to 13 years of age, who are excluded from all CPS and decennial census data after 1930, are omitted whenever use is made of the 1930 Census.
33. The 1940 data are from *Sixteenth Census of the United States, 1940*, Vol. 3, *The Labor Force: Occupation, Industry, Employment, and Income*, Tables 58 and 74. Data for both sexes combined in 1930, adjusted to the 1940 industry and occupation classifications, are from Alba M. Edwards, *Comparative Occupation Statistics for the United States, 1870 to 1940*, in U.S. Bureau of the Census, *Sixteenth Census of the United States, 1940, Population* (1943), Tables I, 2, and 7. Edwards provides "adjusted" data for 1930 only for both sexes combined. These were allocated among males and females in proportion to the "unadjusted" estimates provided by Edwards; however, the adjustments were slight in all categories isolated. To check the agricultural allocation, the calculations were repeated with use of occupational detail; the result was the same.

each sex at each date obtained in step 1 was divided among these three groups in proportion to the estimates obtained in step 2.

STEP FOUR. My 1940 estimate of total employment in nonfarm business for each sex (Tables G-1 and G-2) was extrapolated to 1929 by the series for nonfarm business employment (group c) of that sex obtained in step 3. The estimates for males and females were adjusted proportionally to agree with my estimate of total 1929 nonfarm business employment (Table C-1). To obtain the class-of-worker breakdown, the percentage division between males and females of nonfarm self-employed and unpaid family workers was assumed to be the same in 1929 as in 1940. The 1929 numbers of wage and salary workers in nonfarm business, by sex, were obtained by subtraction.

The procedure for farm workers differed only in that the absolute, instead of the percentage, change between 1929 and 1940 in agricultural employment (group a) that was obtained in step 3 was used to obtain the preliminary 1929 farm employment estimate for each sex that was then adjusted to conform with the aggregate in Table C-1. (The reason is that the 1940 decennial Census estimate of female agricultural employment is only half as big as my estimate, which reflects the CPS level for that year, whereas the estimates for males are of similar size.)

STEP FIVE. Almost no information is available to estimate part-time employment in 1929.[34] In all of the categories distinguished in Tables G-1, G-2, and G-3, I assume the percentage of persons working part time for economic reasons to be the same in 1929 as in 1941.[35] In all but one I also assume the percentage working part time for noneconomic reasons, and consequently the total part-time percentage, to be the same. The exception is female wage and salary employment, where the percentage of voluntary part-time employment in 1929 is guessed to have been much lower than in 1941 because of the change in labor force participation rates. The total female labor force in the 1940 census week would have been 10.26 per-

cent smaller than it was if female labor force participation rates, by age, had been the same as in the 1930 census week.[36] Postwar experience suggests that changes in voluntary part-time employment and changes in labor force participation rates are related. I estimate—very roughly indeed—that around 35 percent of changes in female employment that result from changes in female participation rates consist of voluntary part-time employment. On the assumptions that this was the case in 1929–41, that the 1929–41 change in participation rates was 12/10 of the 1930–40 change, that the percentage of part-time employment in farming did not change, and that the change in nonfarm business employment was the same as in all nonfarm employment, I calculate the percentage of part-time employment among female nonfarm business wage and salary workers at 10.03 in 1929 compared with 15.33 in 1941 (and 24.02 in 1969).

Total and Average Hours in Nonfarm Business, by Sex, Class of Worker, and Full-Time Status, 1929, 1940, and 1941 (Tables G-1 and G-2)

Kendrick's well-known study, *Productivity Trends in the United States,* is the standard source for aggregate estimates of man-hours in the period prior to 1947.[37] His series for total private nonfarm man-hours was used by the Bureau of Labor Statistics to extrapolate both its "establishment" and "labor force" series back of 1947, so all three series have identical movements in the 1929–47 period.[38] In a new study Kendrick has broken out households and institutions to obtain a series for hours worked in what he calls the "private domestic nonfarm business economy."[39] Its coverage is identical to the sum of my series for "wage and salary workers in nonfarm business" and "nonfarm self-employed and unpaid family workers."

For the movement of employment, Kendrick relied, as I do, upon the OBE employment data

34. I disregard data from censuses of establishments because they do not conform at all well to CPS data during postwar periods when both are available.

35. Although unemployment was much higher in 1941, this was a year of very sharp business expansion. Neither comparisons with 1947 nor general patterns of hours changes suggests that part-time employment for economic reasons was particularly large.

36. Computed by use of data from *Sixteenth Census of the United States, 1940, Population: Estimates of Labor Force, Employment, and Unemployment in the United States, 1940 and 1930* (1944), Table 1, p. 1.

37. John W. Kendrick, assisted by Maude R. Pech, *Productivity Trends in the United States* (Princeton University Press for the National Bureau of Economic Research, 1961).

38. For farm hours, Kendrick relied upon the Department of Agriculture series to which I have already referred.

39. John W. Kendrick, assisted by Maude R. Pech, *Postwar Productivity Trends in the United States, 1947–1969* (Columbia University Press for the National Bureau of Economic Research, 1973).

(which for this period are my own estimates), supplemented by estimates for unpaid family workers. Hence, statistical consistency beween his employment series and mine is nearly complete.[40] His hours estimates were developed, by industry, by use of a great deal of detailed information for average hours. I have extrapolated my 1947 estimate of total hours worked in the nonfarm business sector to the prewar years by the index of his series.[41]

Total hours worked in nonfarm business in 1929, 1940, and 1941 were allocated among the eight groups of workers distinguished in Tables G-1 and G-2 by making two assumptions: first, that average hours worked by each of the four groups of part-time workers were the same in each of these years as in 1947; and second, that the ratio of average hours worked in each of the prewar years to average hours worked in 1947 was the same for each of the four groups of full-time workers.[42]

Total Hours, Business Sector and Whole Economy, 1929, 1940, and 1941 (Tables E-1 and E-2)

Total weekly hours worked by nonfarm groups in the business sector in 1929, 1940, and 1941, shown in Table E-1, columns 2 and 3, are obtained by addition from Tables G-1 and G-2. Total hours in nonresidential business, shown in Table E-1, column 4, are the sum of columns 1, 2, and 3.

Total weekly hours for the whole economy that are shown for these years in Table E-2 are the sum of total hours worked in the business sector and the following four components: *households and institutions,* obtained by extrapolating my 1947 estimate for employees of private house-

holds and nonprofit institutions by Kendrick's series for this group;[43] *work relief,* based on Kendrick's method of obtaining annual hours by multiplying the OBE estimates of full-time equivalent employment by 2,040 hours, and then dividing by 52;[44] *civilian general government and rest of the world, excluding work relief,* obtained by extrapolating my 1947 estimates by Kendrick's series for general government, less work relief;[45] and *military,* obtained as the product of military employment (from Table C-7) and 40 hours. Average weekly hours in the whole economy are the quotient of total hours and total employment (from Table C-1, column 1).

Age-Sex Composition of Total Hours Worked in Nonresidential Business, 1929, 1940, and 1941 (Table F-5)

Total hours worked in the business sector by each sex were obtained by adding the components of Tables G-1, G-2, and G-3. The percentage division between male and female hours in 1947 implied by these tables differs very slightly from that shown in Table F-5, and the prewar percentages so obtained were adjusted for consistency with the 1947 estimate to obtain the total percentages for each sex shown in Table F-5.

The percentages for each sex were then allocated among age groups in the following steps.

STEP ONE. Estimates of total employment by sex and age, based on decennial census data as adjusted by the Bureau of the Census, were prepared for 1950, 1940, and 1929. For 1950, census data for employed persons were used as reported. For 1940, census-adjusted data for employed persons, excluding emergency workers, were used. For 1929, census-adjusted data as of the 1930 census week for employed persons 14 and over plus one-third of unemployed persons 14 and over were used.[46]

---

40. Kendrick used a different method to estimate the number of unpaid family workers prior to 1940.

41. There are small differences in movement between Kendrick's series for "persons engaged" and mine for "persons employed" in this sector. Indexes (1947 = 100) compare as follows:

	1929	1940	1941	1947
Persons engaged (Kendrick)	75.2	76.1	85.1	100.0
Persons employed (Denison)	74.4	75.8	84.6	100.0

I assume that the discrepancies stem chiefly from differences in definition (which affect the weights for different components as well as their movements) rather than from statistical inconsistencies, so that extrapolation of my total hours by his is preferable to extrapolation of my average hours by his.

42. Kendrick, for the most part, based the movement of nonfarm proprietors' hours on that of wage and salary workers (in the same industry). Hence, even if the 1929

hours that this procedure yields for full-time self-employed and unpaid family workers, which are quite long, are overstated, it does not follow that hours of wage and salary workers are understated. Changes in average hours of full-time proprietors and unpaid family workers, it will be recalled, do not affect my total labor input series very much.

43. Kendrick, *Postwar Productivity Trends,* p. 226.

44. Kendrick, *Productivity Trends in the United States,* pp. 616, 620.

45. The series prior to deduction of work relief is from ibid., pp. 312–13.

46. The 1930 and 1940 data are from *Sixteenth Census of the United States, 1940, Population: Estimates of Labor Force, Employment, and Unemployment in the United States, 1940 and 1930* (1944), Tables 2 and 3. This source

STEP TWO. For each age-sex group, reported decennial Census data for the total numbers of gainful workers (1930), employed persons except emergency workers (1940), or employed persons (1950) and the corresponding numbers remaining after deducting groups primarily outside the business sector were obtained.[47] The groups outside the business sector were the same as those listed in step 2 (on page 214), except for exclusion of "religious workers." The ratio of employment in the nonbusiness group to the total was computed for each age-sex group.[48]

STEP THREE. The employment estimates obtained for each age-sex group in step 1 were multiplied by the ratios obtained in step 2 to secure approximations to the distribution of business employment by sex and age in 1929, 1940,

and 1950. (The 1930 ratios were used for 1929.)

STEP FOUR. The percentage of business hours worked by each age-sex group in 1950 (Table F-5) was extrapolated to 1929 and 1940 by the business employment series obtained in step 3; the percentages for the age groups within each sex were then adjusted proportionally to agree with the total percentage for the sex that had been established previously. The procedure assumes that the ratio of average hours in 1929 and 1940 to average hours in 1950 was the same for each age group within a sex.

STEP FIVE. The 1941 age distribution for each sex was estimated in two steps. The 1940 percentages for two broad age groups (14–24, and 25 and over) were extrapolated to 1941 by CPS civilian employment estimates, and adjusted proportionally to agree with the total percentages for each sex.[49] The more detailed percentages were obtained by straight-line interpolation between the 1940 and 1947 percentages, with proportional adjustment to the 1941 total for the broader age groups. Despite the large increase in the armed forces from 1940 to 1941, the percentage of hours worked by males in the 14–24 age bracket rises. This reflects the behavior of the CPS civilian employment data, which rise by a greater-than-average amount in this age group despite an actual decline in the male civilian labor force aged 14–24.

combines the 25–34 and 35–44 age groups. The combined group was divided, by sex, in proportion to the numbers of employed persons (1940) or gainful workers (1930) in these age groups as reported in the unadjusted Census tabulations.

47. The 1930 Census data are from Alba M. Edwards, *General Report on Occupations,* in U.S. Bureau of the Census, *Fifteenth Census of the United States, 1930, Population,* Vol. 5 (1933), Table 6, pp. 118 ff.; Table 10, pp. 352 ff.; and Table 2, pp. 572 ff. The 1940 Census data are from *Sixteenth Census of the United States, 1940,* Vol. 3, *The Labor Force: Occupation, Industry, Employment, and Income,* Tables 65, 80. The 1950 Census data are from U.S. Bureau of the Census, *U.S. Census of Population, 1950;* Vol. 2, *Characteristics of the Population,* Pt. 1, *United States Summary* (1953), Tables 127, 132.

48. The percentage of employed females aged 14 to 19 who worked in private households was much bigger in 1940 than in either 1930 or 1950. This contributes to my low estimate of the percentage of business hours that were worked by this age-sex group in 1940.

49. Employment data are from *Current Population Reports,* Series P-50, No. 2, "Labor Force, Employment, and Unemployment in the United States, 1940 to 1946."

APPENDIX H

—»»X««—

Efficiency Indexes for Changes in Hours

—»»X««—

Table 4-1 presents indexes of the efficiency of an hour's work as affected by changes in hours due to "intragroup changes" and to "specified intergroup shifts." The method of computation, including the linking of year-to-year changes to secure continuous indexes, is described in Chapter 4.

Only four points of detail remain to be mentioned:

1. All necessary data for employment and hours were secured from Tables G-1, G-2, and G-3.

2. When calculations of year-to-year changes in the indexes were made that involved 1960 or 1966, the first set of estimates shown in Tables G-1, G-2, and G-3 was used for comparison with the preceding year, the second for comparison with the following year.

3. To facilitate computation of the efficiency offset to changes in hours of full-time nonfarm wage and salary workers, hours in each year were initially expressed as efficiency equivalents to an hour of work in 1960, based on the curve described in Chapter 4, page 39.[1] These efficiency equivalents are shown in Table H-1 for the entire postwar range of hours and for the 1929, 1940, and 1941 levels of hours. The percentage change in efficiency equivalents expressed in 1960 hours was then used in each pair of years to determine

the percentage change in efficiency equivalents expressed in hours of the period.

4. The 1929–40 and 1941–47 periods were spanned by calculating the indexes as if annual changes in the employment and hours data had been continuous during the intervening years.

Table H-1. 1960 Efficiency Equivalents to Average Weekly Hours of Nonfarm Wage and Salary Workers Used in Construction of "Intragroup" Efficiency Indexes

Males		Females	
Average weekly hours	Efficiency equivalents	Average weekly hours	Efficiency equivalents
Postwar values		Postwar values	
...	...	37.9	38.18
...	...	38.0	38.26
...	...	38.1	38.34
...	...	38.2	38.42
...	...	38.3	38.49
...	...	38.4	38.57
...	...	38.5	38.64
42.3	42.41	38.6	38.71
42.4	42.49	38.7	38.79
42.5	42.56	38.8	38.86
42.6	42.63	38.9	38.93
42.7[a]	42.70	39.0[a]	39.00
42.8	42.77	39.1	39.07
42.9	42.84	39.2	39.14
43.0	42.91	39.3	39.21
43.1	42.97	39.4	39.27
43.2	43.04	39.5	39.34
43.3	43.11	39.6	39.41
43.4	43.17	39.7	39.47
43.5	43.24	39.8	39.54
43.6	43.30	39.9	39.60
...	...	40.0	39.66
...	...	40.1	39.73
...	...	40.2	39.79
...	...	40.3	39.85
Prewar values		Prewar values	
44.1	43.61	40.7	40.08
44.5	43.84	41.1	40.31
49.3	45.72	45.5	41.99

Source: See Chapter 4, pp. 38–41.
a. 1960 level.

---

[1] In these computations, the average weekly hours of full-time males shown in Table G-1 for 1929–65 were uniformly raised by 0.1 hours to adjust the series to the 1966–69 level.

APPENDIX I

➤➤×⫷⫷

The Labor Input Index for Education

➤➤×⫷⫷

This lengthy appendix furnishes a full description of the derivation of the education component of my index of labor input in the business sector which is shown in Table 4-1, column 7. The summary in Chapter 4 will help the reader to follow this detailed description. Part 1 below discusses the weights used to combine individuals with different amounts of education, as measured by the highest school grade completed. Part 2 describes the distributions of persons employed in the business sector by highest grade of school completed; the calculation of indexes from these distributions and the weights; and the adjustment of the indexes to allow for changes in days of school per year.

PART ONE: THE DERIVATION OF WEIGHTS

Construction of an index to measure changes in the average quality of labor that have resulted from changes in amount of education requires weights to combine individuals with different amounts of education. The average earnings of persons at different education levels are not satisfactory weights because groups of individuals with different amounts of education also differ with respect to other characteristics that influence earnings but which are not affected by a change in the amount of education received. It is the effect of education alone on earnings that must be measured. The weights should represent percentage differentials in the average full-time equivalent earnings of groups of employed persons who dif-

fer with respect to the amount of their education, and to the length of their work experience as a consequence of differences in length of education, but who are otherwise similar. They should refer only to persons employed in the business sector.

Earnings in Business Standardized by Sex, Age, Color, Farm-Nonfarm Attachment, and Region

The objective of this section is to measure the relative earnings of men at each of nine levels of education when relative earnings (a) refer only to men employed in the business sector, (b) refer to full-time equivalent earnings of employed men, and (c) are free from the effects of differences among the nine education groups in their composition with respect to age, color, attachment to the farm or nonfarm labor force, and geographic region. Differences among education groups in remaining characteristics, particularly natural ability and socioeconomic status, will be considered in the following section (pages 228–40).

Data from the 1960 decennial Census, published in *Occupation by Earnings and Education*, provide most of the material for the analysis.[1] This report covers all males who were 25 through 64 years old and in the experienced civilian labor force at the census date (April 1, 1960) and who, in addition, had earnings in 1959. The experienced civilian labor force on the census date consisted of civilians who were employed at that date and the "experienced unemployed." Data from this report exclude persons who were in the labor force during part or all of 1959 but not on April 1, 1960, and all who did not work for pay at any time in 1959 whether this was because they were out of the labor force, unemployed, or employed only as unpaid family workers.

A man's reported earnings, by census definition, include both wages and salaries (including commissions and tips) and "profits or fees from working in his own business, professional practice, partnership, or farm." Supplements to wages and salaries are not included. Neither are earnings in kind.

The report provides the number of men with the stated characteristics as of April 1, 1960, and their mean earnings in 1959. These data are provided for males cross-classified by color, age, region, occupation, and years of school completed.

1. U.S. Bureau of the Census, *U.S. Census of Population, 1960: Occupation by Earnings and Education*, Final Report PC(2)-7B (1963).

Six educational levels are distinguished in all tables, and I initially prepare estimates only in this detail.

The occupation of employed persons refers to the principal current job, and that of the experienced unemployed to the last job held. Because the availability of numbers and mean earnings permit aggregate earnings for any cell to be obtained by multiplication, it is possible to compute numbers and aggregate earnings, and hence mean earnings, for any combination of cells.

The data are based on a 5 percent sample of the population enumerated in the 1960 Census. Data are not provided for any cell containing fewer than 500 persons on a blown-up basis—that is, fewer than twenty-five persons in the sample.

Step One: Earnings by Education Level for Thirty-Two Groups of Men

I begin by computing from *Occupation by Earnings and Education* the mean earnings of persons at each of six education levels for each of thirty-two groups of men. The thirty-two groups result from a cross-classification by age (four ten-year age groups), color (two categories: white and nonwhite), region (two regions: the South, and the North and West combined, which I shall hereafter refer to as the North), and farm or nonfarm attachment.

The "farm" figures actually refer to persons in two farm occupations: "farmers and farm managers" and "farm laborers and foremen." Persons in all other occupations are in my nonfarm data. However, the difference between persons in the two farm occupations and persons in the farm industry is altogether insignificant in these data, which are confined to males in the 25–64 age group excluding unpaid family workers.

Step Two: Elimination of Men in Nonbusiness Occupations

Men in the nonfarm categories include civilians in the household, institutional, and general government sectors as well as persons employed in business. Private household workers included are trivial in number and can be ignored. An adjustment of the mean earnings figures to eliminate the effect of including persons employed in institutions and general government is, however, necessary.

The 1960 Census report isolates eight occupations or occupational groups whose members are almost all employed outside the business sector and whom I therefore wish to eliminate:

Clergymen
College presidents and deans
College professors and instructors
Teachers[2]
Inspectors, public administration
Officials and administrators (n.e.c.), public administration
Firemen, fire protection
Policemen and detectives

Data are available in this occupational detail for the United States, but not by region. For each age-education group, national mean earnings were first computed for white males employed in all nonfarm occupations and for those employed in nonfarm "primarily business occupations," defined as all occupations except the eight listed. The ratio of the mean earnings in nonfarm primarily business occupations to the mean in all nonfarm occupations was then computed for each category. These ratios are shown in the top half of Table I-1. Elimination of these occupations altered the mean earnings for no age-education category referring to education classes below 4 years of high school by more than three dollars, or 0.05 percent. Even for high school graduates and persons with 1 to 3 years of college differences are small.

For college graduates (including those with additional education), however, the means for the primarily business occupations are considerably higher than those for all occupations: 5.4 percent higher in the 25–34 age group and more than 8 percent in the other age groups. Since persons in six of the eight excluded occupations are heavily concentrated among college graduates, it is hardly surprising that it is at this education level that elimination of these occupations has the greatest effect. However, it is also true that it is at the college graduate level that the differences between earnings in the primarily business occupations and the eight occupations is greatest. This results mainly from low earnings of clergymen and teachers, in comparison with college graduates of the same age in the primarily business occupations.

The mean earnings of whites in nonfarm industries in each age-education category in both the North and South that were obtained in step 1

---

2. This category includes teachers in elementary schools and secondary schools, and a small miscellaneous group covering teachers not included in other occupations listed above or in "musicians and music teachers."

Table I-1. White and Nonwhite Males in Nonfarm Industries: Ratios of Mean Earnings in Primarily Business Occupations to Mean Earnings in All Occupations, by Age and Years of School Completed, 1959[a]

Color and years of school completed	Age group			
	25–34	*35–44*	*45–54*	*55–64*
White				
Elementary				
0–7	1.0000	0.9998	1.0000	0.9998
8	0.9996	1.0002	0.9998	0.9998
High school				
1–3	0.9998	1.0005	1.0003	1.0005
4	1.0013	1.0026	1.0023	1.0020
College				
1–3	1.0058	1.0055	1.0088	1.0080
4 or more	1.0542	1.0824	1.0852	1.0855
Nonwhite				
Elementary				
0–7	1.0000	1.0000	1.0000	1.0000
8	1.0000	0.9980	1.0000	1.0112
High school				
1–3	1.0000	0.9977	1.0035	1.0036
4	0.9957	0.9986	0.9952	0.9859
College				
1–3	0.9882	0.9998	1.0146	0.9824
4 or more	1.0363	1.0740	1.0460	0.9857

Source: See text for derivation.
a. Persons with no money earnings in 1959 are excluded.

were multiplied by the national ratios for the same age-education category, as shown in Table I-1, to obtain the estimated mean earnings of white males in nonfarm business in each region.[3] The resulting estimates, which refer to nonfarm whites in the business sector, are shown in Table I-2.

The same procedure was adopted for nonwhites in nonfarm occupations, but a slight difficulty was encountered. Only 2 percent were in nonbusiness occupations and half of these were in five "cells": policemen with 4 years of high school in the 25–34 and 35–44 age brackets, and teachers with 4 or more years of college in the 25–34, 35–44, and 45–54 age brackets. The re-

3. The procedure requires two assumptions. First, the ratio of earnings in the nonfarm primarily business occupations to earnings in all nonfarm occupations is the same in each region as in the United States for each age-education category. Second, in each age-education group the mean earnings of men in primarily business occupations who are employed in general government and nonprofit institutions are the same as those of persons in the same age-education group who are employed in business. The nonbusiness occupations include all occupations which both employ a considerable number of males and are believed to have earnings affected by nonpecuniary attractions or a desire for service, so errors in this second assumption are not likely to introduce much error in earnings differentials.

maining 1 percent were scattered among cells with fewer than 500 men so that data were not reported in full detail. To eliminate them, estimates based on data for less detailed categories were used. Ratios like those for whites were then computed (Table I-1) and multiplied by the original nonfarm mean earnings data for nonwhites to secure mean earnings in the business sector (Table I-2).

The farm groups include so few persons employed outside the business sector that no adjustment to average farm earnings was required before their entry in Table I-2.

My use of Table I-2 is confined to comparisons of the mean earnings of men at different education levels within the same homogeneous group —that is to say, with horizontal comparisons as the table is arranged. Greatest interest attaches to nonfarm whites, particularly those in the North, because they receive by far the greatest weight in my final results. Vertical comparisons will not be made, so any incomparabilities between mean earnings of various groups (for example, farm and nonfarm groups) are not a source of concern.

Step Three: Weighted Average of the Thirty-Two Groups

For each of the thirty-two detailed groups shown in Table I-2 the mean earnings of men at each education level were expressed as a percentage of the mean earnings of men with 8 years of elementary education. A weighted average of the thirty-two sets of percentages (or indexes) was then computed. The weights are the importance of each group in total labor input, as measured by earnings, in 1959. The total weights for farm workers (3.667 percent) and nonfarm workers (96.333 percent) were based on allocations by sex of the sum of compensation of employees in the business sector (from the national income accounts) and my estimates of the labor earnings of proprietors in these activities (see Appendix J). Within these groups, the weights were based on the total earnings of men in the primarily business occupations, computed in the derivation of Table I-2. Estimated earnings of men under 25 years of age in April 1960 were added to the weight of the 25–34 age groups and earnings of men 65 years of age or over were added to the weight of the 55–64 age groups. The full set of weights is shown in Table I-3. Nonfarm whites receive 91.5 percent of the total weight—those in

Table I-2. Mean 1959 Annual Money Earnings of Males in the Experienced Business Labor Force in April 1960, by Age, Farm or Nonfarm Attachment, Color, Region, and Years of School Completed[a]
Data in dollars

Age group	Work attachment	Color	Region	Years of school completed					
				Elementary		High school		College	
				0–7	*8*	*1–3*	*4*	*1–3*	*4 or more*
25–34	Nonfarm	White	North	4,135	4,694	5,227	5,704	6,134	7,600
25–34	Nonfarm	White	South	3,328	3,959	4,549	5,168	5,717	7,371
25–34	Nonfarm	Nonwhite	North	3,349	3,595	3,785	4,172	4,388	5,401
25–34	Nonfarm	Nonwhite	South	2,190	2,528	2,606	2,859	3,244	4,063
25–34	Farm	White	North	2,100	3,007	3,618	3,883	4,510	5,346
25–34	Farm	White	South	1,596	2,171	3,026	3,828	5,906	8,047
25–34	Farm	Nonwhite	North	1,772	1,838	...	...	...	...
25–34	Farm	Nonwhite	South	1,041	1,183	1,214	1,308	...	...
35–44	Nonfarm	White	North	4,716	5,228	5,905	6,755	8,244	12,083
35–44	Nonfarm	White	South	3,739	4,523	5,241	6,248	7,704	11,668
35–44	Nonfarm	Nonwhite	North	3,766	4,006	4,326	4,810	5,040	7,650
35–44	Nonfarm	Nonwhite	South	2,433	2,827	2,868	3,305	3,731	5,597
35–44	Farm	White	North	2,602	3,422	4,048	4,382	5,630	6,587
35–44	Farm	White	South	1,880	2,629	3,607	4,381	6,620	9,890
35–44	Farm	Nonwhite	North	1,911	2,103	...	5,573	...	...
35–44	Farm	Nonwhite	South	1,089	1,301	1,452	...	...	...
45–54	Nonfarm	White	North	4,764	5,364	6,165	7,054	8,988	15,103
45–54	Nonfarm	White	South	3,758	4,603	5,336	6,640	8,779	13,728
45–54	Nonfarm	Nonwhite	North	3,756	3,978	4,184	4,565	5,234	7,658
45–54	Nonfarm	Nonwhite	South	2,392	2,844	2,949	3,257	3,538	5,839
45–54	Farm	White	North	2,862	3,329	3,800	4,159	5,118	7,177
45–54	Farm	White	South	1,899	2,842	3,509	4,470	6,648	...
45–54	Farm	Nonwhite	North	2,176	...	...	...	...	...
45–54	Farm	Nonwhite	South	1,042	1,220	1,323	...	...	...
55–64	Nonfarm	White	North	4,671	5,297	6,253	7,191	9,089	14,917
55–64	Nonfarm	White	South	3,143	4,013	4,748	6,080	7,967	13,199
55–64	Nonfarm	Nonwhite	North	3,618	3,851	4,057	4,208	4,705	6,470
55–64	Nonfarm	Nonwhite	South	2,239	2,620	2,704	2,853	3,178	4,976
55–64	Farm	White	North	2,657	3,034	3,509	3,890	4,462	5,159
55–64	Farm	White	South	1,751	2,503	3,135	3,942	5,844	...
55–64	Farm	Nonwhite	North	2,163	...	...	...	...	...
55–64	Farm	Nonwhite	South	927	1,154	1,178	...	...	...

Sources: Derived from data in U.S. Bureau of the Census, *U.S. Census of Population, 1960: Occupation by Earnings and Education* (1963), and Table I-1.
... Not applicable because there are less than 500 people in this category. See text for explanation.
a. Persons with no money earnings in 1959 are excluded.

Table I-3. Weights Used for Labor Force Groups to Derive Index of Earnings in the Nonresidential Business Sector by Years of Education
Total weight of 100,000

Work attachment	Color	Region	Age group				Total
			25–34	*35–44*	*45–54*	*55–64*	
Nonfarm	White	North	19,635	20,077	17,319	14,189	71,220
Nonfarm	White	South	6,254	6,054	4,882	3,128	20,318
Nonfarm	Nonwhite	North	1,095	730	647	488	2,960
Nonfarm	Nonwhite	South	624	515	414	282	1,835
Farm	White	North	627	688	660	640	2,615
Farm	White	South	197	173	281	238	889
Farm	Nonwhite	North	4	7	7	10	28
Farm	Nonwhite	South	36	32	36	31	135
Total			28,472	28,276	24,246	19,006	100,000

Source: See text for derivation.

the North, 71.2 percent, and those in the South, 20.3 percent. Hence, of the total of thirty-two indexes, the eight for nonfarm whites wholly dominate the combined index. This would also be the case if any reasonable alternative set of weights, such as employment, were used.[4]

The weighted index so obtained is shown in Table I-4, column 1. This index needs adjustment to eliminate a defect in the mean earnings data from which it is derived. For use in this adjustment, which is described in step 4, similar weighted indexes (which are not shown) were computed for each separate age group.

Step Four: Adjustment
to a Full-Time Equivalent Basis

Mean earnings in Table I-2 were calculated by dividing the total earnings in 1959 of men who were in the experienced civilian labor force on April 1, 1960, and who had earnings in 1959 by the number of such men. The next step was to adjust the estimates to a full-year and full-time equivalent basis. In the calculation of mean earnings, men who did not work throughout 1959 because they were out of the labor force or unemployed for part of the year should be counted as only a fraction of a person, corresponding to the fraction of the year worked. Also, men working only part time for part or all of the year should

be reduced to full-time equivalence. In general (though not without exceptions in particular groups), labor force participation rates rise with level of education (suggesting participation is more regular), unemployment rates fall, and percentages working part time fall. Hence, the earnings differentials by level of education reflected in column 1 of Table I-4 tend to be larger than they would be if they referred to full-time equivalent earnings.

My adjustment is based on 1967 income data. A Current Population Survey report covering all men with income in 1967 provides mean income for men cross-classified by age (the four age groups shown in Table I-2) and years of education, and similar data confined to men who were year-round full-time workers.[5] For each age group, an index of mean income of all men with income was constructed (mean income of men with 8 years of education = 100). A similar index was constructed for year-round full-time workers. The ratio at each education level of the index for year-round full-time workers to the index for all men with income was multiplied by the index of earnings for the age group which underlies column 1 of Table I-4. The resulting indexes for the age groups are shown in Table I-4, columns 3 to 6. The four indexes for the age groups were combined by use of the age weights

4. Table I-2 contains some blank cells. To compute the index, earnings were imputed. All the blanks occur in distributions with trivial weight so the imputations have almost no effect on the weighted index.

5. U.S. Bureau of the Census, *Current Population Reports*, Series P-60, No. 60, "Income in 1967 of Persons in the United States" (1969), Table 4.

Table I-4. Indexes of Standardized Mean Earnings by Years of School Completed, Males, 1959[a]
Mean earnings of men with 8 years of elementary education = 100

Years of school completed	Experienced business labor force: all age groups (1)	Full-time equivalent business employment				
		All age groups (2)	25–34 (3)	35–44 (4)	45–54 (5)	55–64 (6)
None	n.a.	71.6	70.4	67.0	67.7	85.2
Elementary, 1–4	n.a.	86.5	87.1	86.7	81.1	92.1
Elementary, 5–7	n.a.	95.5	92.6	97.5	96.2	96.1
Total, 0–7	87.2	92.4	90.5	93.7	91.9	93.9
Elementary, 8	100.0	100.0	100.0	100.0	100.0	100.0
High school, 1–3	114.2	112.6	109.0	115.3	113.1	113.1
High school, 4	130.6	127.3	119.9	131.2	129.0	130.2
College, 1–3	158.0	153.9	133.7	158.7	165.5	161.9
College, 4	n.a.	201.3	164.2	204.6	220.5	227.4
College, 5 or more	n.a.	264.2	175.8	270.2	323.3	312.3
Total, college 4 or more	236.0	227.5	168.4	232.0	265.8	260.6

Source: See text for derivation.
n.a. Not available.
a. Indexes in columns 1 and 2 are standardized for age. All columns are standardized for farm-nonfarm attachment, color, and region.

shown in Table I-3 to obtain Table I-4, column 2. The reduction in differentials between education groups introduced in moving from column 1 to column 2 is generous because the 1967 data on which the correction is based include men who were not in the labor force in the March following the year to which the income data refer and men with income but no earnings, whereas the 1959 data do not. Inability to standardize the 1967 data by region, color, and farm or nonfarm attachment has also probably led to overcorrection. On the other hand, the proper correction for 1959 may be larger than that for 1967 because the labor market was looser in 1959. In any case, the effect of any errors in the correction ratios on the differentials among education groups can hardly be very large relative to the differentials themselves.

Step Five: Subdivision of College Graduates

The group with the highest level of education, which covers all college graduates, requires subdivision. With the exceptions of data by color and of regional data for the nonbusiness occupations, all of the data used to derive Table I-2 are also available from the 1960 Census volume, *Occupation by Earnings and Education,* both for men who had completed 4 years of college and men who had completed 5 or more years of college. These tabulations were used to derive separate

indexes for the two groups of college graduates by use of the following procedure.

National data (numbers, mean earnings, and total earnings) were computed, by age, for men with 4 or more years of college, 4 years of college, and 5 or more years of college, covering, respectively, men in all nonfarm occupations, in nonbusiness occupations, and in primarily business nonfarm occupations. The mean earnings obtained are shown in Table I-5, rows 1, 2, and 3. It will be noted that the differentials between the mean earnings of men with 4 years of college and those with 5 or more years of college are much greater in nonfarm business than in nonfarm occupations as a whole.[6]

Regional data at each detailed education level were then computed, by age, for men in nonfarm occupations. The numbers and total earnings in each region in each age-education category were then allocated between business and nonbusiness occupations in the same proportions as the national data, and means were computed for the nonbusiness occupations. These means covered both white and nonwhite men, but there are too few nonwhite college graduates in the nonbusiness

6. Men with 5 or more years of college are a much larger proportion of all college graduates in the nonbusiness occupations than in business. They consist mainly of teachers (at all levels) and clergymen and have much lower earnings than those in the business occupations, among whom doctors, dentists, and lawyers have a heavy weight.

Table I-5. Mean 1959 Annual Money Earnings of Males, Nonfarm Experienced Civilian Labor Force, April 1960: Detail for Selected Groups of College Graduates[a]
Data in dollars

Labor force group	Years of college completed	Age group			
		25–34	35–44	45–54	55–64
1. Experienced nonfarm civilian labor force, U.S.	4 or more	7,069	10,891	13,389	13,212
	4	6,999	11,009	11,714	12,198
	5 or more	7,163	11,850	15,060	14,371
2. Nonbusiness nonfarm occupations, U.S.	4 or more	5,125	6,936	7,543	7,335
	4	4,717	6,083	6,535	6,481
	5 or more	5,345	7,147	7,810	7,579
3. Primarily business nonfarm occupations, U.S.	4 or more	7,462	11,616	14,578	14,428
	4	7,262	10,255	12,108	12,638
	5 or more	7,787	13,494	17,701	17,088
4. Business, nonfarm white North	4 or more	7,600	12,083	15,103	14,917
	4	7,442	10,776	12,619	12,988
	5 or more	7,841	13,866	18,210	17,953
5. Business, nonfarm white South	4 or more	7,371	11,668	13,728	13,199
	4	7,094	9,970	11,125	11,591
	5 or more	7,910	14,153	17,153	15,560

Source: See text for derivation.
a. Persons with no money earnings in 1959 were excluded.

occupations to affect the differential between mean earnings of men with 4 years and those with 5 or more years perceptibly. In each age-region category, the ratio of mean earnings of whites to the mean earnings of whites and non-whites combined was assumed to be the same for men with 4 and for men with 5 or more years of college as for the two categories combined. The resulting regional estimates for whites in nonfarm business occupations are shown in Table I-5, rows 4 and 5. They are comparable to the similar data for all college graduates and men at other educational levels shown for the nonfarm white groups in Table I-2.[7]

Nonwhite and white farm college graduates could not be divided between those with 4 years of college and those with 5 or more years, but they receive little weight in the calculation of the combined index.[8] It was assumed that in each of the nonwhite and farm groups the ratio of earnings at 4 years, and at 5 or more years, of college education to earnings at 4 or more years of college education was the same as the corresponding ratio for nonfarm whites in the same age group and region.

Correction ratios required to move the indexes to a full-time equivalent employment basis were assumed to be the same, by age, for the two detailed education groups as for all college graduates.

*Step Six: Subdivision of the Group
with 0–7 Years of Education*

The lowest level of education distinguished thus far covers all men with less than 8 years of education. Separate indexes for men with no education, 1–4 years of elementary education, and

5–7 years of elementary education were next derived. *Occupation by Earnings and Education* provides no data in this detail.

From the 1 in 1,000 census sample, Victor Fuchs obtained data permitting the number, mean 1959 earnings, and total 1959 earnings of men with 0–4, 5–7, and 0–7 years of education who were employed in nonagricultural industries on April 1, 1960, and had earnings in 1959 to be calculated for each age group.[9] I used census income estimates to subdivide Fuchs's 0–4 years of education group between a group with no education (which is small) and one with 1–4 years.[10]

The following calculations were then made for men *in each age group:*

a. The ratio of mean earnings in each detailed education group to mean earnings in the 0–7 group as a whole was calculated from the data just described.

b. Mean earnings of all men in nonagricultural occupations with 0–7 years of education, based on *Occupation by Earnings and Education,* were multiplied by these ratios to obtain mean earnings of all men in nonagricultural occupations by detailed education groups.

c. The effect (which is large) of different color-region mixes within the three detailed education groups on the nonfarm earnings differentials among the three groups was eliminated. From Table 8 of the Census report, *Educational Attainment,* a cross-classification by color, region, and education (as well as age) of the number of men in the experienced civilian labor force in nonfarm occupations was obtained. I then calculated the hypothetical mean earnings that nonagricultural men in each detailed education group would have received if *within each color-region category* earnings of each detailed education group had been the same as those of the 0–7 education group as a whole. The mean earnings of all nonagricultural men in each detailed education group calculated in step (b) above were then adjusted by adding to them the excess (or subtracting the deficiency) of mean earnings in the 0–7 group over the hypothetical mean earnings for the

7. The reader may be surprised that earnings of white men in business occupations with 5 or more years of college are shown to be a little higher in the South than in the North in the 25–34 and the 35–44 age groups. The 1960 Census data for whites and nonwhites, combined, in all occupations themselves show a differential in favor of the South in the 35–44 age group. They show a slight differential in favor of the North in the 25–34 age group, but it is reversed by the adjustment to conform with the average level for white college graduates.

8. Data for the farm occupations are reported in *Occupation by Earnings and Education,* and were eliminated to derive nonfarm aggregates. However, they could not be used to develop farm differentials not only because most cells are empty but also because the very few persons with 5 or more years of college in the farm occupations are mainly government employees. Though classified as "farmers and farm managers," they are not in the business sector. (U.S. Bureau of the Census, *U.S. Census of Population, 1960: Occupations by Earnings and Education,* Final Report, PC[2]-7B [1963].)

9. Victor R. Fuchs, *Differentials in Hourly Earnings by Region and City Size, 1959,* Occasional Paper 101 (Columbia University Press for the National Bureau of Economic Research, 1967), Tables A-2 and A-3. The published tables combine the groups with 5–7 and 8 years of education. Unpublished data generously made available by Fuchs enabled me to separate them.

10. The income estimates are published in U.S. Bureau of the Census, *U.S. Census of Population, 1960: Educational Attainment,* Final Report PC(2)-5B (1963), Table 1.

detailed education groups described in the preceding sentence. In every age group the 5–7 years of education group was much more concentrated among region and color categories in which earnings are high than was the 1–4 group, and the no-education group was a little more favorably distributed than was the 1–4 category; hence, the effect of this step was to reduce sharply the unstandardized earnings differential between the 1–4 and 5–7 years of education groups and to increase slightly the differential between the no-education and 1–4 groups.

d. The ratio of earnings, as adjusted in step (c), in each detailed education group to earnings in the 0–7 group was multiplied by the index of earnings for the 0–7 group, as shown for the various age groups in columns 3, 4, 5, and 6 of Table I-4, to secure the indexes shown in these columns for the detailed education groups.[11]

The indexes for the various age groups were then weighted, using the weights for the age groups as a whole shown in Table I-3, to secure combined indexes for the detailed education groups; these are shown in Table I-4, column 2.

The index for the small group with no education is, by the method of estimation, less reliable than the indexes for other education groups.[12] The results imply a large earnings differential between men with no education and those with 1–4 years of education. This is at least plausible because of the importance of literacy. Nearly three-fourths of the men with no education and less than one-fourth of the men with 1–4 years of education were illiterate.[13] In any case, any error in the allocation between the no-education and

the 1–4 years of education groups can introduce only a trifling error in the quality indexes based upon them.

Effects of Limitations of the Data

The first phase of the derivation of the education weights has now been completed. Before turning to the second phase, when effects of academic aptitude and socioeconomic status will be considered, some limitations imposed by the data used to secure the standardized estimates already developed will be examined.

The definition of "earnings" in data from *Occupation by Earnings and Education* differs from the definition of labor earnings used elsewhere in this study, and desired. In the case of wage and salary workers, supplements to wages and salaries and earnings in kind are omitted. In the case of proprietors, earnings in kind are omitted while earnings from the proprietor's equity in his enterprise are included (but with no precise definition). There are also, of course, reporting errors. Within each of the thirty-two labor force groups distinguished, it is assumed that the ratio of reported earnings to earnings correctly measured by the desired definition is the same at each education level. Limited examination of the data, particularly of the effects of different mixes of proprietors and wage and salary workers at different education levels, did not suggest the likelihood of any appreciable error in the weighted index as a consequence of errors in this assumption nor any way of improving the index by modifying the assumption.

Education as well as earnings may be misreported. The postenumeration "1960 Content Evaluation Study" suggests that as many as one-ninth of the men reported as having 1–3 years of college may actually have had only 4 years of high school. Hence, mean earnings for men with 1–3 years of college are likely to be understated relative to earnings of other education groups. Some of those with less than 8 years of elementary education were evidently reported as having 8 years, presumably leading to understatement of differentials in this range.[14] The net effect of misreporting over the whole education range appears likely to be toward understating differentials, but only trivially. No adjustment was attempted.

11. It may be noted that the procedure followed assumes the ratio of standardized earnings differentials in the detailed education groups to those in the broad group to be the same for farm as for nonfarm workers. Farm differentials did, of course, enter into the calculation of the differential between the 0–7 education group as a whole and other groups.

12. The problem lay mainly in the necessity of allocating earnings between the 0 and the 1–4 years of education groups by use of census income data. If the index at 0 years is too low, that at 1–4 years is too high—but by a much smaller amount because the number in the 1–4 group is far larger.

13. About half of the 1–4 group had 4 years of education; at the 4-year level, illiteracy of men is only about 5 percent. The estimates are derived from John K. Folger and Charles B. Nam, *Education of the American Population*, 1960 Census Monograph (U.S. Bureau of the Census, 1967), p. 125; and U.S. Bureau of the Census, *U.S. Census of Population, 1960: Detailed Characteristics, United States Summary*, Final Report PC(1)-1D (1963), pp. 1–404.

14. Folger and Nam, *Education of the American Population*, p. 213.

The classifications used for standardization are less detailed than perfection would require. Use of finer age brackets would widen the earnings differentials among education groups because age is negatively associated with education and, on balance, positively associated with full-time equivalent earnings. Use of more geographic detail, in contrast, would narrow earnings differentials because education and earnings tend to be positively correlated geographically. Use of more detail by color or ethnic group would probably narrow differentials very slightly.[15] Cross-classification by region limits any bias from this source.

Comment on the Farm-Nonfarm Breakdown

The farm-nonfarm breakdown (which is at once occupational and industrial) calls for special comment. It differs from the other characteristics examined in that use of more industrial or occupational detail would not be appropriate. Education affects earnings both by improving an individual's ability to perform in a particular type of work and by enlarging the range of occupations in which he is able to perform at all effectively. Both are properly counted as results of education that we do not wish to remove. There is no reason to standardize the earnings data by industry or occupation, which would eliminate the second effect.[16] The reason for separating farming is a special one: farm earnings are depressed because of overallocation of labor to this industry and underutilization of labor employed in it. Because farming also happens to be an industry in which the education level is low, earnings differentials by education would be larger if farm workers were not treated separately; they would reflect

correlation between education and misallocation as well as educational differences, and *most* of the correlation clearly is not the result of education. A secondary reason to treat farm workers separately is that farm and nonfarm earnings as measured and reported in these data may not be comparable.

The separate treatment of farm and nonfarm men indirectly removes part of another type of intercorrelation in addition to that between education and misallocation. Parents' socioeconomic status is often regarded as an earnings determinant separate from formal education because it is related to home training and perhaps to advantageous family connections; parents' occupation is an indicator of socioeconomic status, and when it is so used, the distinction between farm and nonfarm occupations shows up as an important occupational break.

Thus an analysis of data from the Wolfle-Smith survey, which I shall describe later in another context, showed that among a group of Northern men about 35 years old the median earnings of high school graduates whose fathers were farmers were distinctly below those of men whose fathers were in any of the five other occupation groups distinguished. The proportion of farmers' sons who attended college was also lower. When earnings of all high school graduates were standardized for fathers' occupation by use of the fathers' occupation weights for men with 1–3 years of college, 10.2 percent of the differential in weighted median earnings between men with 4 years of high school and 1–3 years of college disappeared. When earnings were standardized for fathers' occupation by using the fathers' occupation weights of college graduates, 6.5 percent of the earnings differential between high school and college graduates disappeared.[17] When the calculations were repeated with farmers' sons completely omitted from the sample, standardization eliminated only 6.2 percent of the differential between high school graduates and men with 1–3 years of college, and 4.1 percent of the differential between earnings of high school grad-

15. Folger and Nam provide education data by age and ethnic group in *Education of the American Population* (p. 151). The data do not suggest the possibility of much net bias once the white-nonwhite division is made.

16. The distinction between the two effects is actually artificial, because the work done by persons classified as within an occupation, as usually measured, varies greatly. If one accepts the usual definitions, he finds a rather interesting situation. Within occupations, earnings differentials by education are so close to those for all occupations combined that (provided cells with very few cases are omitted) weighting together separate indexes for the occupations could not greatly reduce differentials. Yet educational distributions differ so much among occupations that one could obtain most of the all-occupation differential among education groups by assigning each man the mean earnings of his occupation. (See Folger and Nam, *Education of the American Population*, pp. 177–78, and their sources; also, Anne Mayhew, "Education, Occupation, and Earnings," *Industrial and Labor Relations Review*, Vol. 24 [January 1971], pp. 216–25.)

17. See Edward F. Denison "Appendix," in Organisation for Economic Co-operation and Development, Study Group in the Economics of Education, *The Residual Factor and Economic Growth* (Paris: OECD, 1964), pp. 94–95. Median earnings of high school graduates in the sample by fathers' occupation were: professional and semiprofessional, $5,200; owners and managers, $5,000; sales and clerical, $5,183; service, $4,611; labor, $4,863; farm, $4,176.

uates and college graduates.[18] Thus much of the effect of standardization is ascribable to the low earnings of farmers' sons. To the considerable extent that sons' occupation is associated with fathers' occupation, the farm-nonfarm breakdown used in deriving the education index in Table I-4, column 2, introduces a partial correction for socioeconomic status.

Elimination of Part of the Gain from Increased Mobility

The standardization procedure adopted partially removes one type of intercorrelation that ought not to be eliminated. Education helps individuals to become better informed about the range of job opportunities available to them, and very likely also to be more willing to make geographic moves when these are advantageous. Thus it leads individuals to move from jobs where their earnings and their contributions to the value of the national income are low to those where earnings are higher. Among these job changes are moves from South to North and from farm to nonfarm work.[19] The standardization procedure adopted eliminates these effects of education, which should be retained, and makes the differentials by level of education too narrow.

Quality of Education

Differences in the quality of education provided by schools could bias earnings differentials. Differentials will be too big if, *within* the thirty-two labor force groups isolated, men with more education received better training in lower level schools than men who ended their education at that lower level and if, *in addition,* earnings of men at the lower level are favorably affected by receipt of high-quality education.[20] Classification

18. In actual dollars, the 4.1 percent figure is nearly double the 6.2 percent figure ($80 as against $43). The total differential in earnings between college graduates and high school graduates was three times as large as that between high school graduates and men with 1–3 years of college.

The farmers' sons may have been drawn from lower strata with respect to rank in class and IQ than the other occupations; if so, the percentages computed with farmers' sons included are too high to measure socioeconomic status alone. They may also be too high because of relative understatement of farm earnings. Hence, they may be regarded as maximum estimates.

19. Quantification appears impossible. See Folger and Nam, *Education of the American Population,* pp. 178–86.

20. The mere presence among men at the *same* education level of earnings differentials that are related to differences in quality of education does not bias the indexes.

by age, color, region, and farm-nonfarm attachment eliminates the grosser differences in quality of education. Some overstatement of differentials from this source probably is present, but it is surely trivial except, perhaps, as it is related to socioeconomic status, which will be considered separately.

Adjustments for Ability and Socioeconomic Status

Data from the 1960 Census can carry us no further than the earnings index shown in Table I-4, column 2, but this is quite a long way. They have permitted construction of an index of earnings by level of education that is largely free of the effects of most other variables that are correlated with both education and earnings but are not consequences of education. This section considers those which remain.

My objective in developing weights, I repeat, is to restrict differences in earnings among education groups to the differences that result from amounts of education. The only remaining attributes of individuals for which adjustment is required are attributes that, *within* the thirty-two labor force groups previously distinguished, have all three of the following characteristics: (1) they are distributed differently among men with different amounts of education; (2) they are not themselves the result of differences in amounts of education; and (3) they are correlated with earnings among men at a given level of education. Only academic aptitude and socioeconomic status of parents qualify as important possibilities.

By academic aptitude I mean ability to perform well in school and interest in doing so—characteristics that may affect both continuation in school and earnings at a given level of education. Rank in class and scores on IQ or similar tests are suitable indicators. Although types of ability that are not related to school retention may greatly influence earnings differences among individuals at a given education level, they do not contribute to differences between the average earnings of men at different education levels except as a consequence of additional education itself.

Socioeconomic status of parents requires consideration because of the possible presence of all three of the following correlations: (1) status with amount of education; (2) status with individual attributes (for example, good speech or family connections, important in securing an initial job) that are separable from education; and (3) these attributes with earnings.

There is ample evidence that persons with high academic aptitude or a background of high socioeconomic status do receive more education, on the average, than persons with less aptitude or a lower background and that, among persons with the same amount of education, persons with high academic aptitude or socioeconomic background receive higher earnings than persons with lower aptitude or background. Some of the earnings differential between men in different education groups would therefore be present even if there were no difference in their education. The problem is to estimate the amount.

Research by a number of individuals has led to an apparent consensus that academic aptitude and status account for only a small fraction of the earnings differentials between high school and college graduates, the differential which has been studied most.[21] This is also my conclusion. However, these characteristics account for a bigger fraction of earnings differentials between other education groups. Throughout the distribution the fraction is too big to ignore, and I shall attempt specific adjustments.

R_1 and R_2 Ratios

In examining the earnings differential between men at any two levels of education, it is necessary to distinguish two questions to which the answers need not be the same. How much more would men at the lower education level earn, on the average, if they were distributed like men at the higher level with respect to academic aptitude and/or socioeconomic status? How much less would men at the upper education level earn, on the average, if they were distributed like men at the lower level with respect to aptitude and/or socioeconomic status?

The answer to the first question is the amount that must be eliminated from the earnings of men at the higher level to estimate what these men would have earned if they had not received the additional education. The earnings differential between the two education groups which remains

after this deduction is appropriate for construction of an input index if it can be assumed that the average aptitude or status of men at the upper education level has not deteriorated over time as a result of increasing the proportion of people receiving additional education. This appears to be the case with respect to education groups above the high school graduate level.[22] Hence, it is this question that I shall seek to answer for comparisons among high school graduates and all the higher education levels.

Maintenance of the level of aptitude at the upper levels could have been achieved only by draining lower levels of much of their better talent. I shall assume that there has been no change in aptitude at the high school graduate level, and that the average aptitude of men at all lower education levels has deteriorated over time. In comparisons among lower education levels, I shall therefore seek to eliminate from the earnings differential the amount given by the answer to the second question stated above. This procedure implies that the upward shift of men from one education level to the next higher level corresponds to men with ability of the lower education level. However, in this range the choice between the two procedures has little effect on the results.

It is sometimes convenient to express the amounts eliminated by these procedures as ratios to the unadjusted earnings differentials, as Burton A. Weisbrod and Peter Karpoff do in a study to which I shall refer shortly. If these ratios can be estimated the earnings differentials can be readily adjusted. With the Weisbrod-Karpoff notation adapted to make it general:

Y'_{uu} is the actual mean earnings of men at the upper education level.

Y'_{ll} is the actual mean earnings of men at the lower education level.

Y'_{lu} is the mean earnings of men at the lower education level who were similar to men at the upper level with respect to nonschooling variables (aptitude and/or socioeconomic status).

---

21. Several investigators are mentioned later in this appendix. Among others, Zvi Griliches should be cited: "Notes on the Role of Education in Production Functions and Growth Accounting," in W. Lee Hansen (ed.) Conference on Research in Income and Wealth, *Education, Income, and Human Capital,* Studies in Income and Wealth, Vol. 35 (Columbia University Press for the National Bureau of Economic Research, 1970), pp. 71–115.

22. For example, Taubman and Wales find that the average ability level of high school graduates entering college was higher in the late 1950s and early 1960s than in the 1920s and 1930s. Paul Taubman and Terence Wales, "Net Returns to Education," in National Bureau of Economic Research, *Economics—A Half Century of Research 1920–1970: 50th Annual Report* (NBER, 1970), p. 66. See also Griliches, in *Education, Income, and Human Capital,* p. 102, note 33.

Y'_{ul} is the mean earnings of men at the upper education level who were similar to men at the lower level with respect to nonschooling variables.

The first subscript refers to the education level at which earnings are measured, the second to the nonschooling characteristics of the men.

The ratio we need for every pair of adjacent education groups at the high school graduate level and above is:

$$R_1 = \frac{Y'_{lu} - Y'_{ll}}{Y'_{uu} - Y'_{ll}}.$$

The second ratio, needed for lower pairs of adjacent education groups, is:

$$R_2 = \frac{Y'_{uu} - Y'_{ul}}{Y'_{uu} - Y'_{ll}}.$$

The second ratio is of some interest even for the upper education groups because it can be stated rather confidently that R_1 will always be smaller than R_2 when the nonschooling variable is aptitude unless both ratios are zero. One reason is that dollar earnings rise more with academic aptitude at higher than at lower education levels (so the numerator of R_2 exceeds that of R_1) even if *percentage* differentials among groups classified by ability are the same at both education levels. In addition, it appears (from data that will be introduced) that in the upper portion of the educational distribution, percentage differentials are bigger at upper than at lower education levels. Thus R_2 sets an upper limit to the value of R_1.

Among the numerous studies that provide some evidence on the question at hand, four are most useful in arriving at quantitative results, the first two for differentials above the high school level, the others mainly for differentials at lower levels.

The Weisbrod-Karpoff AT&T Study

Weisbrod and Karpoff use data that are seemingly unrelated to the question under discussion but which these authors are able to bring to bear upon it by introduction of an ingenious and plausible assumption.[23] They secured 1956 earnings and a variety of other data for a sample of about 7,000 male college graduate employees of the American Telephone and Telegraph Company

23. Burton A. Weisbrod and Peter Karpoff, "Monetary Returns to College Education, Student Ability, and College Quality," *Review of Economics and Statistics*, Vol. 50 (November 1968), pp. 491–97.

(AT&T). The sample includes men with more than 4 years of college, but the authors believe few were in this category. They computed mean earnings for sixteen groups of men who were cross-classified by the quality of the college they attended and their rank in their college class. The data have the rare merit of covering the whole age range (except those with less than three or more than fifty years of service with the company). Their means, happily, have been standardized by age. They are reproduced in Table I-6.

Weisbrod and Karpoff introduce the plausible assumption that in nonschooling variables (they refer to ability and motivation) men who graduated from colleges of average quality and ranked in the lowest third of their classes are similar to high school graduates who did not attend college. Earnings of this group averaged 91.0 percent of the average for all the AT&T college graduates. If this assumption is accepted, if AT&T earnings differentials are the same as those in the business sector as a whole, and if the average earnings of high school and college graduates in the business sector are known, R_2 can be computed for the differential between high school and college graduates.

Column 2 of Table I-4 indicates that men with 4 years of college earn 158.1 percent as much as men with 4 years of high school, after standardization for other variables. If Y'_{ll} is expressed as 100, Y'_{uu} is therefore 158.1. Y'_{ul} is 91.0 percent of 158.1, or 143.9. Substitution of these values in the formula yields 0.244 as the value of R_2 between men with 4 years of high school and those

Table I-6. College Graduates Employed by the American Telephone and Telegraph Company: Earnings Index Values by College Quality and Class Rank

Mean earnings of sample = 100[a]

	College quality			
Rank in college class	Best (1)	Above average (2)	Average (3)	Below average (4)
1. Top 10 percent	118.7	111.6	103.0	102.8
2. Rest of highest third	113.0	103.9	99.4	97.6
3. Middle third	103.5	99.1	94.4	93.7
4. Lowest third	96.9	95.0	91.0	90.1

Source: Burton A. Weisbrod and Peter Karpoff, "Monetary Returns to College Education, Student Ability, and College Quality," *Review of Economics and Statistics*, Vol. 50 (November 1968), p. 493.

a. An index value of 100 represents earnings equal to the mean earnings of the entire sample, after adjustment to the age distribution for all U.S. male college graduates.

with 4 years of college.[24] Weisbrod and Karpoff note that if high school graduates were assumed (with almost equal plausibility) to be similar to men in the lowest third of graduating classes of below-average colleges, R_2 would not change much.

The same data can be used to estimate R_1 between men in the business sector with 4 years of college and those with 5 or more years of college. This requires selection of a category of men in the AT&T data who are similar in nonschooling characteristics to those in the primarily business occupations who have 5 or more years of college. It will be recalled that the latter exclude teachers, ministers, and the other occupations itemized earlier. In 1960, 30 percent of the group were physicians and surgeons, dentists, or lawyers and judges; 15 percent were engineers or natural scientists; 25 percent were in other professional occupations; 15 percent were managers, officials, and proprietors, except farm; and 15 percent were in all other occupations combined.[25] That it is a select group can be inferred both from the usual education of men in the occupations it includes and from general observation. We need, therefore, to consider only the upper left corner of Table I-6 (columns 1 and 2, rows 1 and 2) in seeking comparable groups of college graduates.

Among the AT&T employees, men who ranked in the top 10 percent of the graduating classes of the best colleges earned 118.7 percent as much as all the college graduates, and men in the rest of the top third 113.0 percent; the figure for the top third as a whole is therefore 114.7. The percentage for men in the top 10 percent of above-average colleges is 111.6. It is likely that, at the time of their college graduation, the nonschooling characteristics of men in primarily business occupations with 5 or more years of college were within the range of the two latter groups (the upper third from the best colleges and the upper tenth from above-average colleges). I shall use 113 (which happens also to correspond to earnings of the 11th to 33rd percentiles, counted from the top, in the best colleges). This figure may be generous for two reasons. Inclusion in the AT&T data of men with more than 4 years of college may result in overstatement. If such men, though few, are concentrated among the top groups from the best and above-average colleges, part of the 13 percent differential in the AT&T data is due to more education rather than to nonschooling attributes. Also, the Weisbrod-Karpoff procedure and my extension of it to this level ignore the probability that some of the earnings difference among the AT&T groups reflects better education obtained in the higher quality colleges rather than differences in academic aptitude of the graduates. This also applies to the differential between high school and college graduates.

Standardized earnings of men with 5 or more years of college are 131.2 percent of the earnings of men with 4 years of college (Table I-4, column 2). If we set Y'_{ll} equal to 100, Y'_{uu} is therefore equal to 131.2. Y'_{ul}, by the assumption just made, is 113.0. The desired ratio, R_1, is 0.42 $(13.0 \div 31.2)$.[26]

The Weisbrod-Karpoff data and methodology, as extended, have provided an estimate of 0.42 for the desired ratio, R_1, for the differential between men with 4 years and men with 5 or more years of college. This means that 42 percent of the unadjusted differential in earnings is due to

24. Weisbrod and Karpoff themselves use (although they present a number of alternatives) the 1959 earnings of men in the occupation "managers, officials, and proprietors, except farm" for Y'_{ll} and Y'_{uu}. Their values for these terms are, respectively, $8,742 and $13,400, and that for Y'_{ul} is therefore $12,194. Thus they obtain R_2 equals 0.26. Their figure for college graduates refers to earnings of men with 4 or more years of college rather than with 4 years of college, but there is little difference in this occupation. They do not standardize the difference between Y'_{ll} and Y'_{uu} by age; this appears to be an oversight inasmuch as the difference between Y'_{uu} and Y'_{ul} is age standardized. Had they done so, their R_2 and mine, already very close, would have been almost identical.

This correspondence is actually somewhat reassuring. The procedure adopted requires the assumption that indexes covering all college graduates in the business sector, and standardized by color, farm-nonfarm attachment, and region, as well as by age, would be similar to those for AT&T employees, standardized by age, which are shown in Table I-6. Weisbrod and Karpoff believe men in the AT&T sample are most like men in the "managers, officials, and proprietors, except farm" occupation group and that a large proportion actually are in this occupation. If the high school–college (4 years) percentage earnings differential in this occupation, standardized by age, were much different from the differential in the whole business sector, fully standardized, it might suggest that differentials among groups of college graduates employed by AT&T would also be narrower or wider.

25. Computed from *Occupation by Earnings and Education* (cited above), with "occupation not reported" excluded. Data refer to men 25 to 64 years of age.

26. In this case, the ratio as such is not actually needed because the ingredients required for my estimate are those which entered into its calculation. I estimate that, in the business sector, men with 5 or more years of college would have earned 13.0 percent more than men with 4 years of college even without additional education; that they actually earned 31.2 percent more; and that the additional education therefore raised their average earnings by 16.1 percent, calculated as $(131.2/113.0) - 1$.

characteristics other than education itself. They have also provided an estimate that the desired ratio, R_1, for the differential between men with 4 years of high school and men with 4 years of college is below 0.24, because that is the value of R_2, which is larger. Because quality of college attended is related to socioeconomic status, these ratios should be regarded as covering at least part of this characteristic as well as academic aptitude.

The Wolfle-Smith Survey

A survey by Dael Wolfle and Joseph G. Smith secured annual 1953 "salaries" of a group of men who graduated from high school in the 1930s.[27] The sample consists of (1) 967 men who graduated in 1935 from 200 of the 304 Illinois high schools outside the Chicago area and whose scores on IQ tests were in the top 60 percent of all high school graduates or, if this information was not available, ranked in the upper 60 percent of their graduating class; (2) 980 men who graduated in 1938 from Minnesota high schools and who ranked either in the upper half of all high school students in the American Council on Education Psychological Examination or in the upper 60 percent of their class in class standing; (3) an additional 167 Minnesota graduates of 1938, selected without regard to ACE score or class standing; and (4) 639 men who graduated from Roch-

ester, New York, high schools from 1933 to 1938 and were in the upper 20 percent of their class with respect to either class standing or IQ test score.[28] Information on class standing and subsequent education was obtained for the whole sample. The salary data refer to men who were, on the average, about 17½ years out of high school, and therefore about 35 years old—just at the breaking point between my 25–34 and 35–44 age classes.

I have analyzed these data before but was handicapped because only medians were available for salaries and the entire lower 60 percent in class standing were combined in a single group.[29] Tabulations obtained from Wolfle by Taubman and Wales, which they generously made available to me, provide means and a full distribution by class standing. With some consolidation of education groups, they are presented in Table I-7.

To analyze these data, I initially assume that *within* each education–rank-in-class cell the sample is representative and subject only to sampling error, and I make some mechanical calculations before considering their applicability to the present problem.

Inspection of the table indicates that the pattern of means is erratic, and the sample in many cells, mostly in the five lowest rank-in-class deciles, is very small. Starting from the tenth (high-

27. The original report is "The Occupational Value of Education for Superior High-School Graduates," *Journal of Higher Education*, Vol. 27 (April 1956), pp. 201–12, 232.

28. Edward F. Denison, "Appendix," in *The Residual Factor and Economic Growth*, pp. 86–100, amended by use of data obtained from Taubman and Wales.

29. Ibid.

Table I-7. Mean Earnings and Numbers of Men in the Wolfle-Smith Sample, Classified by Rank in High School Class and Education

Earnings in dollars

Decile rank in high school class	High school		College, no degree		College, one degree		College, two or more degrees	
	Earnings (1)	Number (2)	Earnings (3)	Number (4)	Earnings (5)	Number (6)	Earnings (7)	Number (8)
1 (lowest)	4,346	34	4,750	16	8,056	9	10,250	1
2	5,603	39	6,289	13	7,692	13	8,400	5
3	5,897	34	8,656	24	6,187	20	5,500	3
4	5,072	45	5,894	33	6,667	24	5,300	5
5	4,956	97	6,546	60	5,987	40	7,844	16
6	5,458	100	6,330	75	8,970	58	7,030	25
7	5,468	93	5,823	75	6,386	93	6,691	34
8	4,960	112	6,477	109	8,079	139	7,278	62
9	5,322	136	6,042	125	8,045	201	8,487	120
10 (highest)	5,472	117	6,189	106	8,571	234	9,607	218
Consolidated								
1–5	5,124	249	6,526	146	6,563	106	7,358	30
6–7	5,462	193	6,077	150	7,379	151	6,835	59

Source: Unpublished data provided by Paul Taubman and Terence Wales. The "high school" education category is a consolidation of three groups in their table and the "college, no degree" category a consolidation of two.

est) decile, I have consolidated deciles until there are at least 100 men in all cells except those referring to men with two or more college degrees. This required consolidating the sixth and seventh deciles, and all of the first five deciles. The latter consolidation would lead me to attribute too little of the education-earnings differential to ability if earnings at the high school level actually rise with academic aptitude within these five rank-in-class deciles. But the unconsolidated earnings data show no such tendency.[30] Even with this consolidation, the pattern of means by rank in class is somewhat jumpy, but further consolidation would destroy all possibility of analysis.

The sample is, of course, heavily overweighted with men at the upper end of the rank-in-class distribution. To remedy this, I first estimated the percentage of male high school graduates in each decile. (This is necessary because boys rank lower than girls.) My estimates of the percentage of boys who are in each decile, starting with the lowest, are: 14.73; 12.19; 11.20; 10.94; 10.41; 9.53; 8.74; 8.05; 7.46; 6.75.[31] I then distributed 10,000 men among the deciles by these percentages. The number in each decile was allocated among the four education groups in proportion to the numbers in the Wolfle-Smith sample for that decile. This provided an estimated distribution of men at each level of education by rank in class. The distributions rose consistently toward higher class rank as level of education increased. Data for the first five deciles, and for the sixth and seventh deciles, were then consolidated to correspond to the consolidated earnings data.

From these distributions and the Wolfle-Smith mean earnings, means were calculated for each rank-in-class distribution at each level of education, sixteen means in all. They are shown in Table I-8. Thus the first number in column 1 shows that a group of high school graduates dis-

30. Similarly, an analysis by Rogers, summarized in Table I-11, suggests little or no variation in earnings of men with 4 years of high school when they are classified by IQ score.

31. Data for whites classifying males, females, and both sexes combined by average high school grade were used to obtain the percentages of males and females in each of six spans of the distribution. Graphic interpolation of the percentages of males in each part was used to derive distributions by deciles. The data refer to high school graduates who were seniors in October 1965, but the male-female differences in grades and class rank are long-standing. Data are unpublished detail provided by the Bureau of the Census from tabulations summarized in U.S. Bureau of the Census, *Current Population Reports,* Series P-20, No. 185, "Factors Related to High School Graduation and College Attendance: 1967" (1969).

Table I-8. Standardized Mean Earnings Calculated from Wolfle-Smith Data
Dollars

Men distributed by rank in class like:	Earnings level used for each class rank			
	High school graduates (1)	College, no degree (2)	College, one degree (3)	College, two or more degrees (4)
1. High school graduates	5,187	6,422	6,893	7,384
2. College, no degree	5,204	6,390	7,022	7,413
3. College, one degree	5,230	6,345	7,249	7,582
4. College, two or more degrees	5,282	6,277	7,602	7,932

Source: See text.

tributed by rank in class as high school graduates actually were distributed earned an average of $5,187. The rest of the first *column* (rows 2, 3, and 4) shows that a group distributed like men who attended college but did not receive a degree earned $5,204; a group distributed like men with one college degree, $5,230; and a group distributed like men with two or more degrees, $5,282. The top *row* shows that a group of men distributed by rank in class like high school graduates earned an average of $5,187 if they graduated from high school; $6,422 if they attended college but received no degree; $6,893 if they earned one degree; and $7,384 if they received two or more degrees.

The Wolfle-Smith data are not confined to men in business occupations. Inclusion of teachers, ministers, and the like, greatly reduces mean earnings of men with graduate education. It may also narrow rank-in-class differentials in this group. Fortunately, the differentials for men with two or more college degrees enter only into a calculation of the R_2 ratio between men with 4 years of college and those with 5 or more years of college, and this ratio is not needed.

The main impressions conveyed by the columns of Table I-8 are that (1) altering the weight assigned to different class-rank groups to correspond to the distributions of men at different education levels changes mean earnings only slightly when either high school or "college, no degree" earnings are used; (2) the effect is much greater when either "college, one degree" or "college, two or more degrees" earnings are used; but that (3) throughout the table vertical differences are much smaller than horizontal differences (particularly when one allows for the depressing effect upon the level of earnings throughout the fourth column of the inclusion of nonbusiness occupations). The table thus indicates that amount of education itself is much more important than rank in high school class in explaining differences among mean earnings of the various education groups.

In the Wolfle-Smith data, the earnings of men in the "college, no degree" category are, to a slight extent, inversely related to rank in high school class. Consequently, at this level earnings decline instead of increase as the rank-in-class distribution is adjusted upward to correspond to rising education levels. This peculiarity is presumably a vagary of the data, and I therefore make no direct use of the column for this group. This decision does not imply that the data are worthless. Rather, it indicates that the relation between rank in class and earnings is so slight that it is easily effaced or overborne by sampling error or slight biases in the survey data. The same comment might be made about the column for high school graduates. Changes in the column for this group, though in the expected direction, are even smaller than those for men with "college, no degree." One might reasonably suppose from these data that at neither of these levels are there any earnings differentials by rank in class. Although I shall actually accept the high school differentials as shown in the first column of Table I-8, it would make but little difference to my results if I assumed no differentials at all.

Percentage differentials between earnings of education groups rise with age, very sharply in the younger age groups. There probably are two distinct reasons for this. First, a high school graduate, for example, has four fewer years of education than a college graduate, but he typically has four more years of full-time work experience. At age 25, he has about seven years as against three, more than twice as much. By age 35, the Wolfle-Smith age group, he still has about 30 percent more experience. (Because of World War II, the difference in civilian work experience in this sample probably was even greater.) By age 55, he has only 12 percent more. The importance of a difference of four years in experience surely declines as experience rises, and it becomes a less important offset to additional education. Second, the value of additional education and, probably, of aptitude rise as experience accumulates. The Wolfle-Smith data refer to men of a below-average age, at which the earnings differential between high school and college graduates of the same age (35) is appreciably smaller than that between high school and college graduates with the same experience (but who are 4 years apart in age). R_1 will be higher for this group than for older groups if the percentage division of observed education-earnings differentials between education and aptitude is the same at all experience levels when men are classified by experience as distinguished from age.

The Wolfle-Smith men correspond most closely to my white nonfarm North category. In Table I-9 I compare earnings differentials by level of education from the Wolfle-Smith sample (row 1) with differentials for my white nonfarm North men in the 25–34 and 35–44 age groups (rows

Table I-9. Indexes of Mean Earnings by Level of Education and Adjustment of Wolfle-Smith Index
Mean earnings of men with 4 years of high school = 100

	High school, 4 years (1)	College, 1–3 years (2)	College, 4 years (3)	College, 5 or more years (4)
1. Wolfle-Smith men, all occupations	100.0	123.2	139.8	152.9
Census 1959 earnings, all occupations, North white nonfarm:				
2. Age 25–34	100.0	107.1	126.2	126.9
3. Age 35–44	100.0	121.7	154.0	178.3
Census 1959 earnings, business occupations, North white nonfarm:				
4. Age 25–34	100.0	107.5	130.5	137.5
5. Age 35–44	100.0	122.0	159.5	205.3
6. Ratio of row 4 to row 2	1.000	1.004	1.034	1.084
7. Ratio of row 5 to row 3	1.000	1.002	1.036	1.151
8. Average of columns 6 and 7	1.000	1.003	1.035	1.118
9. Wolfle-Smith indexes adjusted to business occupation basis: row 1 × row 8	100.0	123.6	144.7	170.9

Sources: Row 1, computed from Table I-8; rows 2 through 5, computed from Table I-2 and similar data before elimination of nonbusiness occupations, and the further division of college graduates, described in a previous section.

2 and 3). (For comparability, the latter data are before adjustment to full-time equivalence and include men in the nonbusiness occupations.) The Wolfle-Smith differentials among the three categories other than the "some college" group are intermediate between the census-based differentials for the 25–34 and 35–44 age groups; this is as expected because they were about 35 years old. Wolfle-Smith "some college" earnings are too high (relative to those of both high school and college graduates) to fall within this range. The fourth and fifth rows of the table show the census-based means after the primarily business occupations are excluded. Row 6 shows the ratios of the indexes for the business sector to the all-occupation index for the 25–34 age group, row 7 shows similar ratios for the 35–44 age group, and row 8 the average of rows 6 and 7. This average ratio is multiplied by the Wolfle-Smith indexes in row 1 to adjust them to a business sector basis.

This row can be combined with the data in Table I-8 to compute the desired ratios if one additional assumption is made: percentage differentials among entries in the columns of Table I-8 would be the same if the data referred to men in the business sector instead of all men. I tentatively make this assumption and compute the ratios; they are shown in Table I-10. To avoid use of the peculiar earnings data for the "some college" group, I assume percentage differentials among the entries in column 2 of Table I-8 to be the same as in column 1, which uses earnings of high school graduates. To avoid the problem completely, I also compare men with 4 years of high school directly with men with 4 years of college.

I have indicated that ratios for the Wolfle-Smith men are likely to be higher than those appropriate for all men because of the youthfulness of the men sampled. A bias in the sample selection, already described, may operate in the other direction: men in the lower deciles in class rank must have had IQ scores above the average for men in that decile. If, within education classes, men with higher IQs earn more than men with lower IQs in the same class rank decile, then the rise in earnings with class rank is understated and so are the ratios. This observation affects mainly the R_1 ratios between high school and higher education groups. Also, rank in class is only one measure of scholastic aptitude; IQ is another. Standardization by both rank in class and IQ would presumably yield higher ratios than standardization by rank in class alone (if the sample were big enough to yield reliable results with such detail). These qualifications are, however, minor. The main conclusion from the Wolfle-Smith data is that earnings differentials by ability among high school graduates exist but are too small to provide an R_1 of substantial size between high school graduates and those with higher education.[32]

This conclusion is not challenged by any data I have seen and is supported by a number of bits and pieces of information. Information from Project Talent is particularly interesting because the data are both new and good. Hause reports:

Initial calculations with the Project Talent high school graduates who had no additional formal training suggest that differential measured aptitude has a small but positive effect on earnings five years after graduation. Some people had conjectured that higher-aptitude individuals might well have obtained significantly higher incomes even without college education. The conjecture, if it had been correct, would have implied an understatement of the opportunity costs of acquiring more education.[33]

32. Taubman and Wales analyze part of the same sample by use of regression rather than standardization techniques. They obtain what amounts to an R_1 ratio of "less than 4 per cent" based on use of IQ to measure ability, with evidently nothing to be added for rank in class. ("Net Returns to Education," in National Bureau of Economic Research, *Economics—A Half Century of Research 1920–1970*, p. 66.)

33. John C. Hause, "Aptitude, Education, and Earnings Differentials," in National Bureau of Economic Research, *Economics—A Half Century of Research 1920–1970*, p. 73.

Table I-10. Ability Ratios, Based on Rank in High School Class, and Component Values, Derived from Wolfle-Smith Data

Lower education level	Higher education level	R_1	R_2	Y'_{ll}	Y'_{uu}	Y'_{lu}	Y'_{ul}
High school, 4 years	College, 1–3 years	0.013	0.017	100.0	123.6	100.3	(123.2)
College, 1–3 years	College, 4 years	0.036	0.213	123.6	144.7	(124.2)	140.2
College, 4 years	College, 5 or more years	0.267	0.286	144.7	170.9	151.7	163.4
High school, 4 years	College, 4 years	0.018	0.159	100.0	144.7	100.8	137.6

Sources: Y'_{ll} and Y'_{uu}, Table I-9, row 9; Y'_{lu} and Y'_{ul}, computed by multiplying these values by appropriate ratios computed from Table I-8. Figures in parentheses were based on use of ratios from the first (high school) column of that table instead of the second. R_1 and R_2 are computed from the following columns by use of the formulas provided on p. 230.

Reference may also be made to my analysis of the Cutright data later in this appendix.

I have already referred to the Wolfle-Smith data classified by fathers' occupation, which may be viewed as a measure of socioeconomic status.[34] My analysis of these data (after farmers' sons were eliminated because my data are standardized by farm-nonfarm attachment, and based on weighted medians) produced R_1 ratios for socioeconomic status of 0.062 between high school graduates and men with 1–3 years of college, and 0.047 between high school graduates and college graduates including those with more than one degree. Men in the nonbusiness occupations are included in this calculation. Table I-5 suggests that at the relevant age, 35, men in nonfarm business occupations with 4 years of college earn about as much as men in all nonfarm occupations with 4 or more years of college. (In the 25–34 age class they earn 2.7 percent more, in the 35–44 age class 5.8 percent less.) Hence, the ratio between men in the business sector who are high school graduates and men with 4 years of college is likely to approximate 0.047. My standardization of earnings by farm-nonfarm attachment may not warrant complete omission of farmers' sons, in which case the ratios are a bit too low. On the other hand, there is undoubtedly some duplication between the ratios for socioeconomic status and academic aptitude.

Selection of R_1 Ratios above the High School Level

For the upper education levels, data already reviewed permit selection of reasonable R_1 ratios for ability and socioeconomic status in the business sector. Between high school graduates and men with 1–3 years of college I use the sum of the rank-in-class ratio (0.017) from Table I-10 and the fathers' occupation ratio (0.062), which is also based on Wolfle-Smith data, for a total ratio of 0.079. The rank-in-class ratio may be a bit low as a full measure of the effects of academic aptitude. But in view of the probability that the fathers' occupation ratio picks up some aptitude differences, I do not regard the combined ratio as likely to be too small. Between high school graduates and men with 4 years of college I use the same procedure, combining the rank-in-class ratio of 0.018 and the fathers' occupation ratio

of 0.047 to obtain 0.063. The Weisbrod-Karpoff and Wolfle-Smith data can be compared with respect to the R_2 ratios at this level. The Wolfle-Smith R_2 ratio for rank in class is 0.159, and the R_2 ratio based on fathers' occupation (excluding farmers' sons) is 0.144. If there were no duplication (which there almost surely is), the two ratios together would yield 0.303. The Weisbrod-Karpoff data provided an R_2 ratio of 0.244, 19 percent smaller. This ratio picks up part of the socioeconomic factor through college selection but probably not all of it. However, an upward bias results from effects upon earnings of differences in the quality of college attended. The agreement is reasonably good; reducing the Wolfle-Smith R_1 ratio by 19 percent, from 0.063 to 0.051, would have only a trivial effect on my education differentials.

Gary S. Becker, in his admirable book, *Human Capital*, also analyzed the ratios appropriate for adjustment of differentials between high school and college graduates. The information he provides (some of which overlaps mine) is generally consistent with my estimates.[35]

Application of the two ratios already selected to my standardized index in Table I-4, column 2, yields an implied R_1 of 0.064 for the differential between men with 1–3 years of college and those with 4 years.

Between men in the business sector with 4 years of college and those with 5 or more years, analysis of the Wolfle-Smith data yielded an R_1 ratio of 0.267 and an R_2 ratio of 0.286. These refer only to rank in class; similar ratios for fathers' occupation are not available. The Weisbrod-Karpoff data yielded an R_1 of 0.42, which again may be assumed to include socioeconomic status only incompletely, but to be inflated by effects of quality of college attended and inclusion in the sample of some men with more than 4 years of college. I shall adopt 0.42 as the value of R_1 at this level.

Analysis of Connecticut Men by Rogers

The first set of evidence relating to ratios at lower education levels comes from a study by Daniel C. Rogers. Rogers analyzed a sample of 364 males who were in eighth or ninth grade in Connecticut schools in 1935, for whom annual

---

34. These data are based on Minnesota and Rochester men only.

35. *Human Capital: A Theoretical and Empirical Analysis, with Special Reference to Education* (Columbia University Press for the National Bureau of Economic Research, 1964), pp. 79–88.

earnings in 1950, 1955, 1960, and 1965 were obtained, and for whom a great deal of other information was available.[36] He estimated the lifetime earnings, measured in 1957–59 prices, of these men. At the same level of education, differentials in average annual earnings (my interest) may be expected to be similar to those in lifetime earnings.[37]

Rogers's sample is much too small to permit use of standardization techniques. He used multiple correlation analysis to relate earnings to a large number of variables, including education and IQ. For men at each education level, Rogers presented the estimates of lifetime earnings of men at each of four IQ levels that were implied by his preferred formula when a number of other variables were held constant. The IQ levels are 100 (the national mean for the whole population), 86 (the national mean less one standard deviation), 106.69 (the mean for his sample), and 121 (the sample mean plus one standard deviation).

In Table I-11 I compare the mean earnings at different IQ levels. The comparison is in index form, with the mean earnings of men with IQs of 100 equal to 100. The levels of education range from 8 years of elementary school through 4 years of college.[38] The table shows a clear pattern: the lower the education, the less earnings differentials vary by IQ level. Indeed, the table shows no differential at all at 8 years of education. However, this is unlikely, and in his text Rogers expresses belief that ability affects earnings at all education levels. In fact, we may be observing no more than an extrapolation downward of the fact, already noted, that ability differentials are smaller at the high school than at the college level. However, Rogers's results support the belief that at the high school graduate level the variation of earnings with ability is small, and they probably provide some evidence that variation does not increase again at lower levels. At the high school level, according to the Rogers analysis, men at the high IQ level of 121 earn

Table I-11. Indexes of Lifetime (1936–85) Earnings, in 1957–59 Prices, of Men Born about 1922, by IQ Level at Various Education Levels, Estimated from Regression
Earnings of men with IQ of 100 = 100

Years of school completed	IQ level			
	86	100	106.69	121
Elementary				
8	100.0	100.0	100.0	100.0
High school				
1–3	98.5	100.0	100.9	102.4
4	98.0	100.0	101.9	103.4
College				
1–3	96.4	100.0	101.8	105.6
4	94.8	100.0	102.7	108.6

Source: Computed from Daniel C. Rogers, "Private Rates of Return to Education in the United States: A Case Study," *Yale Economic Essays,* Vol. 9 (Spring 1969), Table 8, p. 114.

only 1.5 percent more than those at 106.69. These IQs correspond roughly to the actual average IQs of college and high school graduates in the 1950s.[39] Other variables used by Rogers may "steal" some of the IQ effect, but the latter is apparently not very powerful at the high school level and below.[40]

The Rogers analysis is based on a very small sample. Nevertheless, it suggests that when one deals with a geographically homogeneous group variations of earnings with IQ are small below the high school level.

Before I turn to the next study, it is necessary to note that the reductions in crude earnings differentials up to the high school graduate level that were introduced by standardizing for farm-nonfarm attachment, color, and region, and adjusting to a full-time equivalent employment basis, are large (except for the comparison involving those with no education). The first column of the following text table shows the percentage increase in male earnings between adjacent education levels when earnings are standardized only by age. The second column shows percentage increases derived in the present study after full

36. Daniel C. Rogers, "Private Rates of Return to Education in the United States: A Case Study," *Yale Economic Essays,* Vol. 9 (Spring 1969), pp. 89–134.
37. The situation is, of course, entirely different with respect to comparisons of men with different amounts of education because those with more education start work later.
38. Rogers also gives estimates for men with graduate work; these appear to be distorted for my purpose by inclusion of men in nonbusiness occupations. The index for men with 4 or more years of college is the same as that for men with 4 years of college.

39. Gary Becker gives 106.8 and 120.5 as the average IQs of high school and college graduates in the 1950s. See *Human Capital,* p. 80.
40. Rogers also compares lifetime earnings of men with different amounts of education and the same IQ. It appears to me likely that the other variables, such as private versus public education, absorb education effects much more than they do IQ effects.

standardization and the full-time equivalent (f.t.e.) adjustment.[41]

Years of education	*Age standard-ization only*	*Full standard-ization and f.t.e. adjustment*
None to elementary, 1–4	19.6	20.8
Elementary, 1–4 to 5–7	36.1	10.4
Elementary, 5–7 to 8	20.5	4.7
Elementary 8 to high school, 1–3	16.0	12.6
High school, 1–3 to 4	16.4	13.1

Cutright's Data for Earnings of Veterans

By matching military records with social security data Phillips Cutright secured education, score on Armed Forces Qualification Test (AFQT), color, and estimated 1964 earnings for a large sample of male veterans who had earnings at any time in the 1962–64 period. Table I-12 cross-classifies the data for white males in three education groups by five AFQT score intervals.[42] These data allow a rough comparison between variations in earnings with aptitude at 8–9 and 10–11 years of education levels and variations at the high school graduate level. They can serve this limited purpose even though these earnings presumably vary more with AFQT score than would my standardized earnings, provided the differences are fairly similar at the three education levels. (The reasons these earnings for veterans vary more than would standardized earnings are that both AFQT score and earnings vary with region and with farm-nonfarm attachment, and that these earnings are not adjusted to a full-year or full-time equivalent basis.)

The bottom third of Table I-12 shows the mean earnings of each group of men as a percentage of the earnings of men with the same amount of education who were in the 30–49 AFQT score range.[43] The usual wiggles are present in the fig-

41. The first column, computed from *Why Growth Rates Differ*, p. 374, includes nonbusiness occupations, but this has little effect at the education levels shown. Percentages in the second column are computed from Table I-4, column 2.

42. Cutright also gives data for men with "0 to 7" years of education (as well as for those with "13 or more"), but that range is too wide to permit their use here. (Phillips Cutright, "Achievement, Mobility, and the Draft: Their Impact on the Earnings of Men," Staff Paper 14, U.S. Department of Health, Education, and Welfare, Office of Research and Statistics, DHEW Publication [SSA] 73-11854 [1973; processed].)

43. This interval was used as a base because the smallest sample size (1,079) is bigger than the smallest sample size in any other interval.

Table I-12. Number and Mean 1964 Earnings of White Male Veterans with Earnings in 1962–64, Classified by AFQT Score and Years of Education[a]

Years of education	AFQT interval					
	0–9	*10–29*	*30–49*	*50–79*	*80–99*	*Total[b]*
	Number in sample					
8–9	670	1,875	1,079	638	138	4,404
10–11	165	1,153	1,200	1,312	539	4,375
12	64	749	1,652	3,456	2,906	8,831
	Mean earnings (dollars)					
8–9	4,365	4,838	5,302	5,653	6,034	5,035
10–11	4,947	5,101	5,546	5,593	6,960	5,597
12	4,813	5,470	5,995	6,224	7,025	6,371
	Earnings as a percentage of the earnings of men in the 30–49 AFQT interval					
8–9	82	91	100	107	114	95
10–11	89	92	100	101	125	101
12	80	91	100	104	117	106

Source: Phillips Cutright, "Achievement, Mobility, and the Draft: Their Impact on the Earnings of Men," Staff Paper 14, U.S. Department of Health, Education, and Welfare, Social Security Administration, Office of Research and Statistics, DHEW Publication (SSA) 73-11854 (1973; processed), Table I-12, p. 37.
a. Nonwhites other than Negro are included.
b. Totals include a small number of men for whom AFQT score is unknown.

ures but variations in earnings with AFQT score in the 8–9 and 10–11 years of education groups do not appear to differ systematically from those in the 12 years of education group. In every AFQT interval the percentage for men with 12 years of education either falls between or is close to the percentages for the 8–9 and 10–11 years of education levels.

It might be preferable to divide men in each education group among quartiles (or quintiles, and so on) based on AFQT scores within the group, and to compare variations among quartiles. An approximation to this procedure based on an unpublished tabulation from the Cutright data did not change the conclusion that the percentage variation in earnings among men classified by AFQT score is fairly similar at the three education levels.

The evidence from other studies shows that earnings differentials by aptitude are small among high school graduates. The Cutright data suggest differentials at lower education levels are similar to differentials among high school graduates.

I digress from consideration of differentials at the lower levels to observe that data from the Cutright sample for men with 13 or more years of education, not shown here, support the conclusion already reached that the numerator of the R_1 ratio for academic aptitude between high school graduates and men with college education is small. It must first be noted that AFQT scores are raised by education as well as by aptitude; consequently, distributions by AFQT score must differ more between education groups than do distributions by measures of academic aptitude. Also, earnings variations by AFQT score in these data exceed those in standardized full-time equivalent earnings for reasons already stated. Both biases lead to overstatement when the data are used to compute the numerator of an R_1 ratio. Nevertheless, when veterans with 13 or more years of education are assigned the earnings of high school graduates in the same AFQT score interval (based on the intervals shown in Table I-12), the resulting mean earnings exceed the actual earnings of high school graduates by only 5.2 percent. The use of even this overstated figure would provide a small R_1 ratio between the high school graduate level and any combination of higher education levels likely to match the composition of the 13 or more years of education group.

Aptitude and Education at Lower Education Levels

Available information is ample to show that academic aptitude and amount of education are positively correlated throughout the educational distribution. Thus Benson obtained the subsequent education of 1,680 children of both sexes who, in April 1923, took the Haggerty Intelligence Examination: Delta 2, while they were in grade 6A in Minneapolis elementary schools.[44] This group was about 48 years old in 1959, the year upon which my earnings differentials are based. Percentage divisions by test score of those at five levels of education were as follows:[45]

	Test score		
Education	*60–99*	*100–129*	*130–199*
Entered sixth grade, but not high school	65.6	33.3	1.1
Entered high school, but did not graduate	30.2	60.3	9.5
Graduated from high school, but did not enter college	10.3	65.2	24.5
Entered college, but received no degree	5.9	64.3	29.8
Received bachelor's degree, but did no graduate work	2.0	42.4	55.6

44. Viola E. Benson, "The Intelligence and Later Scholastic Success of Sixth-Grade Pupils," *School and Society,* Vol. 55 (Feb. 7, 1942), pp. 163–67. I am indebted to a citation by Gary Becker for this reference.

45. Among those who entered sixth grade, but not high school and had a test score of 60–99 is included one person (0.4 percent) with a test score below 60.

Several other studies have been summarized by Taubman and Wales.[46]

The education levels at which important changes in academic aptitude occur may, of course, vary greatly among age groups. For persons of the age group finishing high school in 1960, Folger and Nam point to the senior year in high school as a particularly important dividing line, probably as a result both of compulsory education and of school policy in granting diplomas. Data they cite permit a calculation (for both sexes combined) that about 64 percent of those who graduated from high school (who completed 12 *or more* years of education) and only 13 percent of those who did not were in the top half of the IQ distribution. Within the latter group the percentage was 37 for those who entered but did not complete the senior year of high school and 4 for all those who dropped out earlier.[47] Men 25–64 in 1959 were all educated before this date, most of them long before, when more were dropping out at lower education levels.

Some adjustment for differences in aptitude is required throughout the educational distribution. But the indications from the Rogers data, and from the combination of the Cutright and Wolfle-Smith data, that earnings vary only a little with aptitude at the lower education levels suggest the required adjustment is not very big.

Selection of R_2 Ratios below the High School Graduate Level

The evidence cited is suggestive, but insufficient to permit calculation of R_2 ratios below the high school level without introducing a more exact relationship. I base the calculation on what amounts to a projection downward from the high school–college differential.

From the Wolfle-Smith data, I calculated that high school graduates distributed by rank in class like college graduates earn 0.83 percent more than actual high school graduates.[48] I have also calculated from the same data that high school graduates distributed by fathers' occupation like college graduates earn 1.84 percent more than actual high school graduates when farmers' sons

46. Paul Taubman and Terence Wales, *Mental Ability and Higher Educational Attainment in the 20th Century,* National Bureau of Economic Research Occasional Paper 118 (Carnegie Commission on Higher Education and NBER, 1972).

47. Folger and Nam, *Education of the American Population,* Table II-8, p. 46.

48. The estimates from Table I-8 are $5,230 and $5,187.

are omitted.[49] Adding the two percentages, I estimate that high school graduates distributed by aptitude and socioeconomic status like college graduates earn 2.67 percent more than high school graduates.

I now assume that (after standardization for other variables) percentage earnings differentials by aptitude and socioeconomic status together are the same at lower education levels as at the high school graduate level, and that the differentials in ability and socioeconomic status between groups differing in education by 4 years are the same as those between high school and college graduates. Consequently, I assume that actual high school graduates earn 2.67 percent more than high school graduates having the nonschool characteristics of men with 8 years of elementary school, that actual elementary school graduates earn 2.67 percent more than elementary school graduates having the nonschool characteristics of men with 4 years of elementary school, and that men with 4 years of elementary school earn 2.67 percent more than men with 4 years of school having the

nonschool characteristics of men with no education. To apply this assumption to my grouped education classes, I interpolate by average years of school in each group.[50] The resulting percentage differences between adjacent education groups up to the high school graduate level are shown in column 6 of Table I-13. The implied R_2 ratios, shown in column 2 of Table I-13, range from 0.095 to 0.258; the variation stems from differences in the differentials prior to allowance for ability and socioeconomic status.

The Final Education Weights

The ratios and other estimates provided in the preceding sections allow calculation of final education weights. The calculations to remove the effects of academic aptitude and socioeconomic status from the standardized earnings index pre-

49. This calculation is similar to the one reported earlier except that earnings of high school graduates are used in place of earnings of college graduates.

50. Estimates of the mean of years of school completed in the six lowest education classes based on 1960 decennial Census data for all men 25–64 are, respectively, 0, 2.97, 6.22, 8, 9.98, and 12. Figure I-1 shows in addition 1–3 and 4 years of college groups, for which means are 13.83 and 16 years. The "5 or more" years of college group, for which data are not available, is plotted at 18 years.

Table I-13. Derivation of Education Weights

Years of school completed	Standardized earnings index (earnings at 8 years of education = 100) (1)	R_2 or R_1 (2)	Increase in index from preceding level, in points		Percentage increase in standardized earnings from preceding level			Education weights, 100 = weight of persons with:	
			Total from column 1 (3)	Not due to education (4)	Total (5)	Not due to education (6)	Due to education (7)	No education (8)	8 years of education (9)
1. None	71.6	...	...	...	...	...	...	100.00	75
2. Elementary, 1–4	86.5	0.095	14.9	1.42	20.81	1.98	18.46	118.46	89
3. Elementary, 5–7	95.5	0.204	9.0	1.84	10.40	2.13	8.10	128.06	97
4. Elementary, 8	100.0	0.258	4.5	1.16	4.71	1.21	3.46	132.49	100
5. High school, 1–3	112.6	0.099	12.6	1.25	12.60	1.25	11.21	147.34	111
6. High school, 4	127.3	0.107	14.7	1.58	13.06	1.40	11.50	164.28	124
7. College, 1–3	153.9	0.079	26.6	2.10	20.90	1.65	18.94	195.39	147
8. College, 4	201.3	0.064	47.4	3.03	30.80	1.97	28.27	250.63	189
9. College, 5 or more	264.2	0.420	62.9	26.42	31.25	13.12	16.03	290.81	219

Sources: Column 1, Table I-4, column 2.
Column 2, rows 2 to 6 are estimates of R_2, calculated as column 4 ÷ column 3; rows 7 to 9 are estimates of R_1, see text, p. 236, for method of estimation.
Column 3, calculated from column 1.
Column 4, rows 2 to 6 are calculated from column 1 in the next row above and column 6; rows 7 to 9 are the product of columns 2 and 3.
Column 5, column 3 as a percentage of column 1 in the next row above.
Column 6, rows 2 to 6, see text, pp. 239–40, rows 7 to 9, column 4 as percentage of column 1 in next row above.
Column 7 equals (column 5 + 100) ÷ (column 6 + 100) minus one, expressed as a percentage.
Column 8, computed from column 7.
Column 9, computed from column 8.

viously calculated are shown and described in detail in Table I-13 and its description of sources. The final weights are shown in column 9 of that table.

The differences between the index values at different education levels are estimates of the effect of additional education on male earnings, computed on a full-time equivalent basis, in the business sector. The quality of education received by men at each level implied in the index is the quality that men employed in 1959 had actually received.

The Pattern of Differentials

Figure I-1 compares the final education weights with the standardized earnings differentials secured before the allowances for academic aptitude and socioeconomic status were introduced and thus shows the effect of the allowances for academic aptitude and socioeconomic status. Data for each education group are plotted at a point corresponding to the estimated average number of years of education held by members of the group.

Both lines reveal the tendency for *absolute* increments in earnings per year of additional education to rise as education level rises. However, the increment between "None" and "Elementary, 1–4" is larger than that at succeeding levels, and the increment from "College, 4" to "College, 5" is rather small. The increment between "Elementary, 5–7" and "Elementary, 8" which also appears rather small, may be understated a little as a result of erroneous classification of some persons who were educated in Southern elementary schools with a seven-year curriculum. The tendency for some of these individuals to be misreported as having 8 years of school is present both in the data from which the weights are derived and in the distributions of persons by level of education to which the weights are applied, so this misreporting does not bias appreciably the time series indexes for the education component of labor input which is calculated from them.

Increases in both weights and standardized earnings appear at every education level distinguished; there is no hint of a stairstep pattern in which rises occur only or predominantly at levels corresponding to completion of elementary, secondary, or college education. This important characteristic—continuity of increases—is also present in the earnings of the individual groups of men that are shown in Table I-2 and in the earnings or income of a host of occupational or industrial groups for which the Census Bureau reports earn-

Figure I-1. Nonresidential Business: Standardized Earnings of Males and Education Weights, by Level of Education

Percentage of 8-year earnings or weights

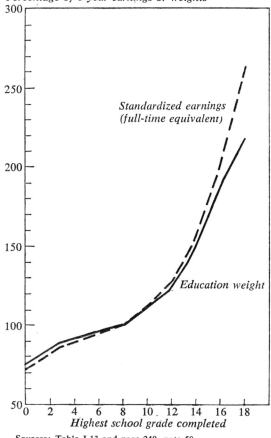

Standardized earnings (full-time equivalent)

Education weight

Highest school grade completed

Sources: Table I-13 and page 240, note 50.

ings by amount of education. Two implications of this pattern are of interest.

First, it is not the case, as some education planning studies imply, that study terminated before a "certificate" or "degree" is granted is wasted even from the narrow standpoint of the effect on earnings. It is not legitimate to evaluate the efficiency of an educational system by comparing the number entering the system and the total expenditures made for their education with the number who complete the system (that is, excluding dropouts).

Second, the absence of the stairstep pattern conflicts with the belief that earnings rise with education not because education adds to the worth of workers and because of the associated characteristics dealt with here, but only because of the "sheepskin effect" (that employers use certificates or degrees merely to sort out individuals who had enough ability and perseverance to receive a sheepskin). No doubt there is some sheepskin effect in the initial hiring of inexperienced workers; but evidence of a continuing effect on earnings data for adults does not appear in data derived from the decennial census.

Education Weights for Females

The rapid movement of females in and out of employment and the great prevalence of part-time employment would make it impossible to duplicate for females the calculations made for males even if the same data were available. Actually, similar data are not available, mainly because statistical agencies and investigators have not found it worthwhile to make tabulations for females in view of the difficulties in using them. I shall use the male weights for females in the absence of any persuasive evidence that would indicate use of different weights.[51] Thus I assume that percentage differences among education groups in full-time equivalent earnings of females are the same, after elimination of the effect of intercorrelations, as for males; this implies that absolute differences in earnings are much smaller.

Comparison with Why Growth Rates Differ

The weights obtained here are compared in Table I-14 with those derived in a previous study. In that study the nonbusiness occupations were not excluded. National mean earnings were calculated for men in each of four age groups; in-

51. Crude data suggest no important difference. See *Why Growth Rates Differ*, p. 85, note 17.

dexes of earnings were calculated for each age group, with earnings of men with 8 years of education equal to 100; the indexes for the four age groups were averaged; and the differential in the resulting index between men with 8 years of education and those at every other level was reduced by two-fifths to allow for the correlation of all noneducational earnings determinants (except age and sex) with education. The new weights are based on explicit examination of all such determinants.

The new weights imply smaller differentials between some education levels, larger differentials between others. The earnings differentials among men with 8 or less years of education have been reduced; the previous procedure did not allow sufficiently for the effects of region, race, and farm-nonfarm attachment upon the national averages of earnings. Differentials above the elementary level have been increased. This is partly because the two-fifths adjustment was overgenerous. At the highest levels the main factor was the elimination of nonbusiness occupations.

Use of Constant Weights

The education weights developed for 1959 were used throughout the period covered by this study because it was not possible to develop similar estimates for other dates that could be adopted with any assurance that any differences which might appear would represent anything more than errors of estimate.[52] Even decennial census data for 1969 will, at best, allow estimation only to the stage reached in Table I-4. Much cruder comparisons suggest that percentage earnings differentials have not narrowed over time; those between high school and college graduates may have widened since 1959 but this is uncertain.

PART TWO: EDUCATION DISTRIBUTIONS AND INDEXES

The series for the education component of labor input in the business sector was computed in several steps. The first three sections of Part 2 describe the calculation of separate indexes for males and females based on changes in the distributions of employed persons by highest school grade completed. These indexes were next adjusted to allow for changes in the school term and

52. My previous estimates for 1949 and 1959 were almost identical throughout the distribution (*Why Growth Rates Differ*, p. 374).

Table I-14. Comparison of Education Weights with Weights Derived in *Why Growth Rates Differ*
Weight of persons with 8 years of education = 100

Years of school completed	New weights	Why Growth Rates Differ weights
None	75	71
Elementary, 1–4	89	77
Elementary, 5–7	97	90
Elementary, 8	100	100
High school, 1–3	111	110
High school, 4	124	121
College, 1–3	147	139
College, 4	189	170
College, 5 or more	219	195

Sources: Table I-13, column 9, and *Why Growth Rates Differ*, p. 374.

in absenteeism. Finally, the male and female indexes were combined. All data cited in the descriptions that follow were available by sex unless otherwise indicated.

Distributions of Full-Time Equivalent Business Employment, by Years of Education and by Sex, Postwar Survey Dates

For each sex, indexes were first constructed for the dates up to 1970 on which information concerning the distribution of the civilian labor force by years of education were available from the Current Population Survey (the household surveys). These dates are October of 1948 and 1952 and March of 1957, 1959, 1962, 1964, 1965, 1966, 1967, 1968, 1969, and 1970.[53]

Construction of indexes for the survey dates required distributions of persons employed in the business sector by years of school completed, with full-time and part-time workers appropriately weighted. Table I-15 gives these distributions.

A general description of their derivation is as follows. From distributions of total civilian employment, the principal groups of government, household, and institutional workers were eliminated to obtain distributions for a universe approximating business employment. Workers in this universe were divided between agricultural and nonagricultural workers. Each distribution was converted to a full-time equivalent basis. The farm and nonfarm distributions were then combined by use of weights, based on establishment data as derived elsewhere in this study, for part-time employment and for full-time employment in farm and nonfarm business.[54] A detailed description of the estimates will now be provided.

Data Available from Surveys, 1959–70

Beginning with March 1959, the following data were available, separately for each sex, from the survey reports and were used to obtain the desired distributions. The data are confined to persons 18 years of age or older.

1. The number of employed persons in the civilian labor force, classified by years of school completed. Nine educational levels are distinguished.[55]

2. Persons employed in agricultural industries and in nonagricultural industries, classified by years of school completed.[56]

---

53. Data are from U.S. Bureau of the Census, *Current Population Reports,* the P-50 Series: No. 14, "School Enrollment and Educational Attainment of Workers in the United States: October 1948" (1949); No. 49, "Educational Attainment and Literacy of Workers: October 1952" (1953); No. 78, "Educational Attainment of Workers: March 1957" (1957); and from U.S. Bureau of Labor Statistics, Special Labor Force Reports (which are reprints from the *Monthly Labor Review* with detailed statistics added): No. 1, Arnold Katz, "Educational Attainment of Workers, 1959," Reprint 2333, from Vol. 83 (February 1960), pp. 113–22; No. 30, Denis F. Johnston, "Educational Attainment of Workers, March 1962," Reprint 2416, from Vol. 86 (May 1963), pp. 504–15; No. 53, Denis F. Johnston, "Educational Attainment of Workers, March 1964," Reprint 2463 from Vol. 88 (May 1965), pp. 517–27; No. 65, Denis F. Johnston and Harvey R. Hamel, "Educational Attainment of Workers in March 1965," Reprint 2488, from Vol. 89 (March 1966), pp. 250–57; No. 83, Harvey R. Hamel, "Educational Attainment of Workers, March 1966," Reprint 2528 from Vol. 90 (June 1967), pp. 39–47; No. 92, Harvey R. Hamel, "Educational Attainment of Workers, March 1967," Reprint 2559 from Vol. 91 (February 1968), pp. 26–34; No. 103, Elizabeth Waldman, "Educational Attainment of Workers, March 1968," Reprint 2600 from Vol. 92 (February 1969), pp. 14–22; No. 125, William Deutermann, "Educational Attainment of Workers, March 1969 and 1970," Reprint 2696 from Vol. 93 (October 1970), pp. 9–16; and from unpublished tabulations from the 1968, 1969, and 1970 surveys.

54. Use of full-time equivalent employment largely eliminates the effect on the labor input series of any correlation between education and hours. However, when the education index derived from these distributions is combined with the other labor series to obtain total labor input, it *is* necessary to ignore any correlation that may possibly exist between level of education and average hours worked *within* each of the six categories of *full-time* business workers who are distinguished in Appendix G (full-time workers of each sex who are farm workers, nonfarm wage and salary workers, and nonfarm self-employed and unpaid family workers).

55. In the report for March 1959 (Special Labor Force Report 1) 1.62 percent of employed males and 1.47 percent of employed females are shown with "school years not reported." For each sex, I allocated those in each occupation by education level like those in the same sex-occupation group who reported years of school. Reports for later dates eliminated this category by allocating nonrespondents "according to the pattern for individuals reporting this item."

56. In these tabulations for March of 1968, 1969, and 1970, the educational distribution is curtailed. All persons of each sex with 0 through 7 years of schooling are combined, as are all persons of each sex with 4 or more years of college. However, it was possible to make good estimates of persons employed in agriculture in each of the five education categories consolidated into these two. The survey reports for the three dates give the numbers employed in the two farm occupations, "farmers and farm managers" and "farm laborers and foremen," in full education detail. The March 1967 ratio of employment in agriculture to employment in the two farm occupations was computed for each of the three lowest and two highest education categories, and then applied to the corresponding numbers in the two farm occupations at the later dates. The resulting figures were adjusted to add up to the totals reported for the lowest and highest education groups shown.

Estimates of persons employed in nonagricultural industries in the detailed education categories were obtained by subtraction of the numbers in agriculture from the reported total numbers of employed civilians in each of these categories.

Table I-15. Percentage Distributions of Persons 18 Years of Age and Over Employed in the Business Sector, by Sex and Years of School Completed, Full-Time Equivalent Basis, Survey Dates 1948–70

Years of school completed	Oct. 1948 (1)	Oct. 1952 (2)	Mar. 1957 (3)	Mar. 1959 (4)	Mar. 1962 (5)	Mar. 1964 (6)	Mar. 1965 (7)	Mar. 1966 (8)	Mar. 1967 (9)	Mar. 1968 (10)	Mar. 1969 (11)	Mar. 1970 (12)
Males Total	100.00	100.00	100.00	100.00	100.00	100.00	100.00	100.00	100.00	100.00	100.00	100.00
No school years completed	8.76	8.34	6.88	0.98	0.93	0.67	0.58	0.61	0.57	0.47	0.46	0.46
Elementary, 1–4				4.78	4.09	3.56	3.61	3.25	3.00	2.80	2.74	2.46
Elementary, 5–7	14.64	13.46	11.94	10.77	9.97	8.90	8.50	8.35	8.10	7.58	7.27	7.07
Elementary, 8	21.04	20.21	17.84	16.45	14.68	14.13	13.49	13.05	12.36	11.77	11.21	10.82
High school, 1–3	20.17	19.11	19.81	20.35	19.90	19.78	19.54	19.62	19.10	18.96	18.48	17.91
High school, 4	23.10	24.29	27.14	28.34	29.96	32.50	33.57	34.08	34.33	35.32	36.17	36.77
College, 1–3	6.58	7.70	7.98	8.99	10.25	10.23	10.13	10.08	11.29	11.67	11.94	12.67
College, 4	5.71	6.88	8.40	5.74	6.42	6.25	6.56	6.91	7.12	6.94	7.06	7.27
College, 5 or more				3.58	3.78	3.97	4.00	4.05	4.14	4.49	4.66	4.62
Females Total	100.00	100.00	100.00	100.00	100.00	100.00	100.00	100.00	100.00	100.00	100.00	100.00
No school years completed	4.37	4.16	3.10	0.50	0.40	0.34	0.30	0.30	0.30	0.32	0.23	0.21
Elementary, 1–4				1.92	1.86	1.67	1.58	1.24	1.37	1.11	1.25	1.00
Elementary, 5–7	9.88	8.64	7.84	7.17	6.33	5.93	5.67	5.65	5.34	5.06	4.89	4.19
Elementary, 8	18.15	16.25	14.36	13.37	11.90	11.72	11.26	9.97	9.55	9.04	8.33	8.14
High school, 1–3	18.77	19.64	19.96	19.92	19.45	19.58	19.31	19.21	19.55	18.75	18.41	18.16
High school, 4	37.33	38.40	41.93	43.85	44.15	46.02	46.67	48.13	47.90	49.24	50.23	50.60
College, 1–3	7.51	8.31	8.48	9.20	10.78	10.14	10.18	10.59	11.41	11.77	11.80	12.70
College, 4	3.98	4.62	4.34	3.07	3.81	3.42	3.62	3.40	3.30	3.35	3.35	3.49
College, 5 or more				1.01	1.33	1.20	1.44	1.49	1.29	1.35	1.49	1.52

Source: See text for derivation. Detail may not add to totals because of rounding.

3. The number of employed persons included in item 1 who were in each occupation group, and a percentage distribution of each occupation group by level of education. In the survey reports twenty-five occupation groups are distinguished for males and seventeen for females.[57]

4. A division of persons at each level of education who were employed in nonagricultural industries between persons who worked either 0 hours or 35 hours or more in the survey week and persons who worked 1–34 hours.[58] This division corresponds to my distinction between full-time workers and part-time workers, except that a few persons employed 0 hours are actually part-time workers; I ignore this minor difference in using the data.

In addition to these data, cross-classifications of the total civilian labor force (not employed persons) 18 years of age and over by sex, age, and education level are provided in the surveys. Percentage distributions of employed persons of each sex in each industry group by education level are provided in March 1968 and thereafter; these distributions were used for certain checks but did not enter directly into the estimates.

Estimating Procedures

The procedures used to derive the desired employment distributions at the survey dates will now be described. The description under *A* below applies precisely only to survey dates beginning with March 1959 because some data that are reported in this period had to be estimated at earlier dates; these variations are discussed in *C*. The description in *B* applies to all of the survey dates.

57. For males I count private household workers, who, though not shown separately, can be isolated by deducting data for females from data for both sexes combined.

58. Data for March 1968, 1969, and 1970 are condensed in the same way as data for all persons employed in agricultural and nonagricultural industries: the three lowest and the two highest education groups are combined. The March 1967 ratio of full-time to total employment in nonagricultural industries was computed for each of the three lowest and two highest education categories and applied to the corresponding estimates of persons employed in nonagricultural industries at the later dates. The resulting figures were adjusted to add up to the totals reported for the combined education groups.

A. ELIMINATION OF NONBUSINESS EMPLOYMENT. The first problem was to adjust the distributions of employed persons in the civilian labor force classified by years of education (item 1 above) to conform as closely as possible to distributions of persons employed in the business sector. The CPS cross-classification by sex, occupation, and education (item 3 above) was most helpful, but had to be supplemented by other data.

1. Private household workers, who are outside the business sector, were first eliminated from the distributions by years of education for each survey date.

2. The remaining persons of each sex employed in civilian industries at each survey date were divided into four categories. The total numbers in each (not the distributions by education) were obtained by the following procedures:

a. Government wage and salary workers. The data were obtained from CPS reports. (A small deduction for persons 14 to 17 years of age was made.)

b. Persons employed in "educational services, private." These numbers are estimates. The percentages of civilians of the two sexes combined employed in industries other than agriculture, forestry, and fisheries in March 1950 and in March 1960 who were employed in this industry were calculated from U.S. Bureau of the Census, *U.S. Census of Population, 1950: Occupation by Industry,* Special Report P-E No. 1C (1954), Table 2; and *U.S. Census of Population, 1960: Detailed Characteristics, United States Summary,* Final Report PC(1)-1D(1963), Table 209. The March 1950 and March 1960 percentages for both sexes combined were interpolated and extrapolated by the ratio (based on annual data) of the number of "persons engaged in production" in the "educational services" industry to the number in all industries except agriculture, forestry and fisheries, and military employment; these data are from NIA Table 6.6 The number of persons of both sexes combined employed in "educational services, private" at each survey date was estimated by multiplying the resulting percentage for that date by employment in non-agricultural industries from item 2 (page 243, above). The figure thus obtained at each survey date was divided by sex in proportion to numbers obtained by interpolating and extrapolating the 1960 figure for persons of each sex in the industry (based on the census division by sex) by total nonagricultural employment of persons 18 years of age and over for that sex.

c. Persons employed in "welfare, religious, and [other] nonprofit membership organizations." The numbers in this industry were estimated in the same way as the numbers in "educational services, private." NIA data for the "nonprofit membership organizations" industry were used in the interpolation and extrapolation.

d. All other employed civilians. The numbers were obtained by subtracting the first three groups from the totals excluding private household workers.

3. Persons of each sex in each of these four categories in March 1960, as reported in the decennial Census, were classified by occupation, using a classification corresponding to that available in the periodic CPS reports on education. A thirteen-way occupational classification (exclusive of private household workers) was used.[59]

Data are from *U.S. Census of Population, 1960: Detailed Characteristics.* Those for government wage and salary workers are from Table 206. Those for "educational services, private" and "welfare, religious, and nonprofit membership organizations" are from Table 209. Those for the "other" group were obtained by deducting these three groups, private household workers, and persons not reporting occupation, industry, or both, from the totals for all employed civilians. The procedure was repeated for 1950 by use of data from U.S. Bureau of the Census, *U.S. Census of Population, 1950;* Vol. 2, *Characteristics of the Population,* Pt. 1, *United States Summary* (1953), Table 128; and *U.S. Census of Population, 1950: Occupation by Industry,* Table 2 (cited in full above).

4. Persons of each sex in each of the four categories distinguished in step 2 at each survey date after 1960 were distributed by occupation in proportion to the occupational distribution of the group in March 1960. Interpolated distributions were used for survey dates between 1950 and 1960. For October 1948 the 1950 distribution was used. This procedure provided preliminary estimates of the numbers in each category in each

---

59. For females, the number is reduced to eleven, but this does not appreciably reduce the accuracy of the education distribution for the business sector.

Additional occupational detail available from the surveys (chiefly within the "craftsmen, foremen, and kindred workers" and "operatives and kindred workers" groups) either could not be matched with the 1960 Census data or would not improve the desired estimates. The latter is the case if the occupations that are combined are similarly distributed among the four categories listed in item 2 or if the occupations are similarly distributed by education.

occupation. The preliminary numbers in each occupation in the first three categories (government, private education, and nonprofit organization workers), all of which are outside the business sector, were then consolidated, leaving a two-way division of employment in each occupation. The actual numbers of each sex in each occupation, as reported in the survey, were then divided between the remaining two categories in proportion to the preliminary numbers in each category. This provided final estimates, by sex, of the number in each occupation who were in each category. Table I-16 shows the estimates for March 1962. It will be noted that, for each sex, many occupations fall almost entirely in one category or the other. (For simplicity, a few numbers of trivial size were set at zero.) This greatly reduces the possibility of error resulting from the assumption in step 5 that the educational distribution of persons of each sex in any given occupation is the same for persons in each of the two categories. The main exceptions are: other professional, technical, and kindred workers; salaried managers, officials, and proprietors except farm; clerical and kindred workers; male craftsmen, foremen, and kindred workers; other service workers; and male laborers except farm and mine.

5. Persons of each sex in each occupation

group in each of the two categories at each survey date were next distributed by years of education. The percentage distribution by education level for the entire occupation of each sex, as reported in the surveys, was used for each of the two categories. The data for the occupations were then added to secure a distribution by years of education of all persons in each of the two categories. Trivial discrepancies, due to rounding of the percentages, between the sum of the two numbers for persons at each education level and the reported numbers for all persons in civilian employment (except private household workers) were eliminated. For each survey date, the figures thus obtained for the "other" group provide, by sex, final distributions by years of education of persons in civilian employment other than government wage and salary workers, persons employed in private education and in nonprofit membership organizations, and private household workers. This is the closest I can come to persons employed in the business sector. The chief misclassifications are the exclusion of persons employed by the Post Office and the inclusion of persons employed in nonprofit hospitals.

B. WEIGHTING OF EMPLOYMENT CATEGORIES. The remaining adjustments were introduced to improve the weighting of persons employed in

Table I-16. Distribution of Civilian Employment by Sex, Group, and Occupation, March 1962
Thousands

	Males		Females	
Occupation	*Household, government, education, and nonprofit*	*Other*	*Household, government, education, and nonprofit*	*Other*
All occupations	6,243	36,089	6,547	15,060
Total, excluding private household	6,183	36,089	4,687	15,060
Teachers, except college	583	0	1,321	0
Other professional, technical, and kindred workers	1,473	3,056	829	900
Farmers and farm managers	1	2,506	1[a]	539[a]
Farm laborers and foremen	11	1,032	[a]	[a]
Salaried managers, officials and proprietors, except farm	525	2,885	156	481
Self-employed managers, officials and proprietors, except farm	5	2,997	8	500
Clerical and kindred workers	918	2,179	1,501	5,352
Sales workers	16	2,314	12	1,542
Craftsmen, foremen, and kindred workers	745	7,221	15	237
Operatives and kindred workers	439	7,729	64	3,027
Protective service	514	179	[b]	[b]
Other service workers, except private household	572	1,522	773[b]	2,385[b]
Laborers, except farm and mine	381	2,469	7	97

Source: See text.
a. Female "farm laborers and foremen" are combined with "farmers and farm managers."
b. Female "protective service" workers are combined with "other service workers."

agriculture and in nonagricultural industries and of full-time and part-time workers. The weighting structure is governed by decisions made and procedures followed in estimating other aspects of labor input. Besides the decision to weight the sexes by their earnings, the following considerations are pertinent. Within each sex, full-time workers with similar characteristics, including education, who are employed in agriculture, as nonfarm self-employed or unpaid family workers, or as nonfarm wage and salary workers, and who work the average hours of their group, are counted as the same amount of labor despite differences among these categories in average hours worked. An hour's work by part-time workers with similar characteristics, including education, is regarded as the same amount of work regardless of the group by which it is worked. Total hours worked, adjusted for labor characteristics such as education, are used to combine full-time workers and part-time workers. To conform with this general treatment as closely as the data allow, the following procedures were used.

1. For each survey date "employed civilians of each sex other than government wage and salary workers, persons employed in private education and in nonprofit membership organizations, and private household workers" who were at each level of education were divided between persons employed in agriculture and persons employed in nonagricultural industries. Data for persons employed in agriculture, who are almost all in the business sector, were taken directly from the survey reports. Persons employed in nonagricultural industries, other than the excluded groups, were obtained by subtraction. The percentage distribution by years of education of persons of each sex in this nonagricultural group was then used to distribute persons of that sex in nonfarm business, despite minor differences in coverage.

2. The nonagricultural distributions by years of education were next adjusted by reducing the weight of part-time workers. At each survey date persons of each sex employed in nonagricultural industries who were at each education level were divided between full-time workers and part-time workers by use of data reported in the surveys. Part-time workers of each sex were multiplied by the ratio of average part-time hours to average full-time hours for all persons of that sex employed in nonfarm business in that year; the ratios were computed from data presented in Tables G-1 and G-2. In 1962, the ratio for males was

0.38, that for females 0.46.[60] The reduced number of part-time workers was added to the number of full-time workers to obtain full-time equivalent employment at each education level. The ratio of full-time equivalent employment to total employment for each sex-education category was computed. This ratio was multiplied by the number of nonagricultural workers other than the excluded groups in the corresponding sex-education category to obtain estimated full-time equivalent employment by sex and education level. For each sex, the percentage distribution by years of education of persons in this group was used to represent the percentage distribution of full-time equivalent employment of persons employed in nonagricultural business.

3. The surveys do not divide agricultural employment, classified by level of education, between full-time and part-time workers. In the absence of such information, the agricultural distributions were adjusted by multiplying the number in each sex-education category by the nonagricultural ratio of full-time equivalent employment to total employment in that category. It was, of course, recognized that the nonagricultural ratios may be inappropriate for agriculture. But if no adjustment were made, a slight bias might creep into the education quality indexes as the distribution of employment shifted from agricultural to nonagricultural employment. The adjustment eliminates this possibility.

4. For each sex, the adjusted percentage distributions by years of education of agricultural and nonagricultural employment in the business sector were now weighted together to obtain a combined distribution for the business sector. Weights for farm and nonfarm employment were based on annual data, provided in Tables G-1, G-2, and G-3, for the year in which the survey occurred. They were computed as follows. The total weight of 100 percent was first allocated between full-time workers and part-time workers in proportion to the total hours worked by each in the business sector. The weight assigned to full-time workers was allocated between farm and nonfarm in proportion to full-time employment. The weight assigned to part-time employees was allocated between farm and nonfarm in proportion to total hours worked by part-time workers. The total farm weight is the sum of the weights

60. The ratios vary but little. For 1969 and 1970, 1968 ratios were used.

for full-time and part-time farm workers. Because the surveys classify agricultural services in agriculture, whereas my farm data do not, the farm weight was raised by the ratio of employment in agriculture to employment in farms.[61] In March 1962, the agricultural distribution received 10.58 percent of the weight in the combined male distribution. For females, agriculture received 4.80 percent of the weight.

C. ESTIMATES OF DATA NOT REPORTED IN 1948–57. Some modifications of the procedures described in *A,* above, were required for the survey dates, October 1948, October 1952, and March 1957, because the available tabulations were different or less complete than those for later dates.

1. The education reports for these dates include a category "school years not reported." Persons in this category were distributed by educational level like persons of the same sex in the same occupation who reported this information. (This was also done in March 1959, when such a category last appears.)

2. The education reports for these dates do not separate persons employed in agriculture. The agricultural distributions can, however, be approximated quite well. The survey reports provide data for "farmers and farm managers" and "farm laborers and foremen." In March 1959, the number of males employed in agriculture exceeds the number in these two occupations by only 156,000, or 3.9 percent; for females, the corresponding numbers are 32,000, and 5.0 percent. The March 1959 ratio of agricultural employment to employment in the two farm occupations was computed, by sex, for each education category. At the earlier dates, the numbers in the two farm occupations in each sex-education category were multiplied by these 1959 ratios to obtain estimated agricultural employment. The resulting distributions were adjusted to agree with the actual numbers of each sex aged 18 years and over employed in agricultural industries, as reported in the CPS reports for these dates.

3. The occupational classification in these education reports was less detailed than in later years. In the calculations for all three dates it was necessary to combine "teachers, except college" with "other professional, technical and kindred workers"; and "protective service" with "other service workers, except private household." For October

1948 and 1952 it was necessary, in addition, to combine self-employed with salaried managers, officials, and proprietors except farm. For October 1948, clerical and kindred workers were combined with sales workers. In each of these cases, base data for combined groups were obtained by merging the separate groups at the earliest date for which separate estimates had been made. In the October 1948 report, private household workers are combined with other service workers. The proportion of each sex-education category of service workers who were private household workers was assumed to be the same as in October 1952.

4. These three education reports do not separate full-time and part-time nonagricultural workers. At each of these survey dates, the percentage of nonagricultural workers of each sex at each education level who worked part time was estimated to be the sum of two percentages:

a. The percentage who worked part time for noneconomic reasons in March 1959, the earliest date for which such information is available.

b. The percentage who worked part time for economic reasons in March 1964. The reason that the March 1959 percentages were not used for this category is that March 1959 fell in a recession period, when these percentages are high, whereas the three dates for which estimates were needed fell in prosperous periods. The March 1964 percentage for all males was 2.6, which compares with 3.7 in March 1959. For females, the percentages were 4.2 and 5.1. Most of the difference between these dates (and most of the variation among all the dates for which such information is available) occurs in the percentages who *usually* work part time for economic reasons. This group has a particularly low average level of education.

5. The reports for these dates combined persons having no years of school with persons completing 1–4 years of school. They also combined persons having 4 years of college with persons having 5 or more years of college. All of the calculations for these dates were carried through using these less detailed education groups.

6. The education report for October 1948 excludes persons 65 years of age and over. This age group represented 5.9 percent of employed males 18 years of age and over, and 3.0 percent of females. Data for this age group were estimated and added to the reported data for persons 18–64 years of age.

61. The ratio of columns $(1+4)$ to column 1, in Table C-5, was used for each sex.

a. The number of persons of each sex aged 65 and over employed in October 1948 was obtained from the 1948 CPS report.[62]

b. The number of each sex in each occupation in October 1948 was estimated in three steps. First, the number of each sex who were either 14–17 or over 64 years of age in each occupation was obtained by subtracting the number of those aged 18–64 (from the education report) from the number aged 14 years and over (from the CPS report). Second, the figure so derived for each sex and occupation was divided between the 14–17 and 64-and-over age groups in proportion to the numbers of the two age groups reported in the 1950 decennial Census for the sex and occupation. Third, for each sex the numbers thus allocated to persons over 64 were adjusted proportionally to agree with the actual number employed in October 1948.

c. To estimate the distribution by years of education of employed persons 65 and over of each sex in October 1948, use was made of three percentage distributions by years of education for this age group: of civilian employment and of the civilian labor force in March 1950 (as reported in U.S. Bureau of the Census, *U.S. Census of Population, 1950: Education,* Special Report P-E No. 5B [1953], Table 9, page 5B-74) and of the civilian labor force in October 1952 (as reported in the education report for that date). The percentage of employed persons 65 and over of each sex who were at each education level in October 1948 was estimated to be equal to the corresponding March 1950 percentage plus eighteen-thirtieths of the algebraic excess of the March 1950 percentage of the labor force over the October 1952 percentage of the labor force. (October 1948 and March 1950 are eighteen months apart; March 1950 and October 1952 are thirty months apart.) The numbers of males and females over 64 employed in October 1948 were distributed among education groups by these percentages.

d. Finally, the estimated occupation and education distributions of employed persons of each sex aged 65 and over were cross-classified. The percentages in each occupational group at the various education levels were initially assumed to be the same as for this age group in March 1950 (as reported in *Education,* Table 11, pages

5B-89, 5B-93). The figures yielded by this procedure for all the occupation groups at each level of schooling were then adjusted to add up to the previously estimated totals for each education level (described in 6c above).

7. The education classes used in the October 1948 education report differ from those in later reports in that persons with 7 years of elementary school are combined with persons with 8 years instead of those with 5 or 6 years. The distributions for persons 18–64 years of age, including those for each occupation, had to be adjusted to conform to the desired classification.[63] The 5–6 and 7–8 year education categories were first combined, and then redivided into 5–7 and 8 year classes. In October 1952, approximately 41.2 percent of employed males and 39.0 percent of employed females 18–64 years of age who had 5–8 years of elementary education had 5–7 years.[64] Based on a rough allowance for the earlier education of persons employed in October 1948, the percentages at that date were estimated at 41.7 for males and 39.3 for females. Multiplication by the numbers 18–64 years of age having 5–8 years of education in October 1948 yielded estimates of the numbers with 5–7 years. The numbers with 8 years were obtained by subtraction. A similar division was required for each occupation group. In October 1952 the percentages of the 5–8 years of education groups who had 5–7 years varied greatly among occupations.[65] It was initially assumed for each sex-occupation group 18–64 years of age that in October 1948 the percentage of the 5–8 years of education class that had 5–7 years of education was equal to the corresponding October 1952 percentage for persons 18 and over plus 0.9 percentage points in the case of male groups and 0.5 points in the case of females. (The latter numbers are the difference between the all-occupation estimates for persons 18–64 in October 1948 and persons 18 and over in October 1952.) When the occupations were added, the figures for males agreed with the totals previously estimated. A small proportional adjustment of the female estimates was made to secure conformity.

---

62. U.S. Bureau of the Census, *Current Population Reports,* Series P-50, No. 13, "Annual Report on the Labor Force, 1948" (1949).

63. The estimates, previously described, for persons 65 and over corresponded to the desired classification.

64. For employed persons 18 and over, the percentages were 40.8 and 38.8. For the civilian labor force the percentages for persons 18–64 were 0.4 and 0.2 percentage points higher than those for persons 18 and over and the same difference was assumed for employed persons.

65. The differences appeared reasonable. The less educated an occupation, the higher was the percentage.

Postwar Quality Indexes for Each Sex, Based on Years of School Completed

A "quality index" based on years of education was next computed for each sex at each of the twelve survey dates by applying the weights shown in Table I-13, column 9, to the distributions shown in Table I-15. The resulting indexes for full-time equivalent business employment are shown in column 4 of Table I-17.[66] As the indexes are shown, 100 is equal to the weight assigned to persons with 8 years of education. My interest is in changes over time in these indexes,

66. The education distribution at the three earliest survey dates is less detailed than at later dates (Table I-15). The March 1959 weight implied for combined groups was used for combined groups at the earlier dates.

not their level, but it is convenient to retain them in this form for the present.

The next requirement was to use these indexes to estimate annual averages of similar indexes for each year in the postwar period. Because they refer to employed persons, a procedure that allows for the effect of changes in unemployment on the indexes was required.

Relationships at Survey Dates

The method adopted required calculation of two additional sets of indexes for the survey dates. The weights for the business sector were applied to educational distributions of the civilian labor force 18 years of age and over, and of employed civilians in this age group. The resulting indexes

Table I-17. Civilians 18 Years of Age and Over: Unemployment Rates and Education Quality Indexes, Based on Years of Education, by Sex, Survey Dates 1948–70
Weight of persons with 8 years of education = 100

Sex and date	Percent unemployed[a] (1)	Civilian labor force (2)	Civilian employment (3)	Business FTE[b] employment (4)	Percent by which column 3 exceeds column 2 (5)	Ratio of column 4 to column 3 (6)
Males						
October 1948	2.40	n.a.[c]	116.04	114.98	n.a.[c]	0.9909
October 1952	1.48	118.26	118.41	116.95	0.13	0.9877
March 1957	4.07	120.73	121.25	119.61	0.43	0.9865
March 1959	6.27	122.44	123.23	121.54	0.65	0.9863
March 1962	5.95	124.74	125.50	123.43	0.61	0.9835
March 1964	5.20	126.04	126.69	124.25	0.52	0.9807
March 1965	4.42	126.55	127.08	124.77	0.42	0.9818
March 1966	3.44	127.18	127.60	125.28	0.33	0.9818
March 1967	3.09	128.13	128.55	126.19	0.33	0.9816
March 1968	2.96	129.02	129.38	126.92	0.28	0.9810
March 1969	2.59	129.78	130.09	127.52	0.24	0.9802
March 1970	3.74	130.55	130.93	128.13	0.29	0.9786
Females						
October 1948	3.02	n.a.[c]	119.11	117.49	n.a.[c]	0.9864
October 1952	2.70	120.85	120.93	118.90	0.07	0.9832
March 1957	4.10	122.39	122.77	119.76	0.31	0.9755
March 1959	6.01	122.96	123.56	120.42	0.49	0.9746
March 1962	5.96	125.23	125.79	122.28	0.45	0.9721
March 1964	5.78	125.66	126.17	121.99	0.41	0.9669
March 1965	5.32	126.33	126.81	122.62	0.38	0.9670
March 1966	4.10	126.80	127.12	123.06	0.25	0.9681
March 1967	4.54	127.13	127.50	123.09	0.29	0.9654
March 1968	4.23	128.07	128.43	123.65	0.28	0.9628
March 1969	3.98	128.43	128.78	124.04	0.27	0.9632
March 1970	4.90	129.20	129.59	124.74	0.30	0.9626

Sources: Column 1, computed from *Current Population Reports*; other columns, see text for derivation.
n.a. Not available.
a. Based on definitions in effect at each survey date.
b. FTE, full-time equivalent.
c. For October 1948, column 2 is estimated at 115.79 for males and 118.95 for females, and column 5 at 0.22 for males and 0.14 for females. See p. 251 for explanation.

appear in columns 2 and 3 of Table I-17.[67] In addition, the table shows the percentage of the civilian labor force of each sex, 18 and over, that was unemployed at each survey date (column 1).[68]

Because the unemployed are less educated than the employed, the education index for the civilian employed (column 3) is always higher than the corresponding index for the civilian labor force (column 2). Because changes in unemployment are concentrated among the less educated, the percentage by which the index for the employed of either sex exceeds that for the labor force (column 5) is largest when the unemployment rate for that sex is highest. The relationships are, in fact, close.

For males, a relationship calculated from data for the eleven dates at which both indexes are available states that the percentage by which the education quality index for the employed exceeds the index for the labor force is equal to −0.039 percent + (0.1079 × the percentage of males unemployed). A similar relationship calculated for females states that the percentage by which the index for the employed exceeds that for the labor force is equal to −0.190 + (0.1083 × the percentage of females unemployed). The actual index for employed males at the eleven dates never differs from the value that would be estimated from the formula by more than a trivial 0.07 percent and only in March 1967 by more than 0.03 percent. The largest difference between the actual and "estimated" values of the index for employed females is 0.06 percent.

Within the observed ranges of unemployment rates (1.48 to 6.27 for males, 2.70 to 6.01 for females) and the time span covered, one index can evidently be estimated from the other with little error.[69]

I first use these relationships to estimate the October 1948 indexes for the civilian labor force, which could not be calculated directly because the survey for that date reported information only for employed persons. The estimates are shown in Table I-17, note c.

Annual Estimates

The indexes were next estimated on an annual basis; Table I-18 shows the estimates obtained.

1. Annual education quality indexes for the civilian labor force of each sex (column 1) were obtained by straight-line interpolation between the indexes at the survey dates. These indexes change gradually and smoothly, and there should be little error in this procedure. The movement from October 1948 to October 1952 was extrapolated back to January 1947.

2. Annual education quality indexes for employed civilians of each sex (column 3) were estimated from the indexes for the labor force and the percentages of the labor force 18 and over that were unemployed (column 2) by use of the relationships just described. These unemployment rates are adjusted to current definitions.

3. The business sector indexes are lower than those for civilian employment because persons in the business sector are less educated than those outside it. (A little of the true difference is offset by my omission of a full-time equivalent employment adjustment in the civilian employment estimates.) The ratios of the indexes for the business sector (computed from distributions of full-time equivalent employment) to the indexes for civilian employment are shown for survey dates in Table I-17, column 6.[70] Annual estimates of the ratios were obtained by straight-line interpolation between the ratios at the survey dates. The ratios exhibit a general downdrift throughout the postwar period.

---

67. Use of the business sector weights based on full-time equivalent earnings might not be appropriate if interest were in indexes for these groups as such. My interest is in using the indexes to aid in interpolation of the business sector indexes.

68. Neither the indexes nor the unemployment rates in Table I-17 have been adjusted for changes that have been made since 1948 in definitions of the labor force and employment. They are based on the definitions in effect at the survey date to which they refer.

69. The female relationship could not be extended to much lower unemployment rates. By definition, the two indexes would be the same if unemployment were zero, and it is unlikely that the labor force index would ever be higher than the employment index. If the female relationship were extended, it would imply that the indexes would be the same when female unemployment was 1.75 percent; it could not be used with lower unemployment rates because it would

yield a lower index for the employed than for the labor force. The probable explanation is that female unemployment persistently contains a large component of women just entering or reentering the labor force whose education is not below average.

70. The ratios for the survey dates show some irregularity. In particular, the March 1962 index for females in the business sector (and perhaps that for males as well) is surprisingly high compared to the preceding and following survey dates, whereas the movement of the index for all civilian employment is smoother. Careful comparison of the 1959, 1962, and 1964 survey data for all employed females, and for full-time equivalent female employment in the business sector, show that the elimination of private household workers, the elimination of other nonbusiness workers, and the full-time equivalent adjustment all contribute to the difference in movement.

Table I-18. Derivation of Education Quality Indexes for the Business Sector, Based on Years of Education, by Sex, Annually, 1929, 1940–41, and 1947–69

Sex and year	Index for civilian labor force[a] (1)	Percent of civilian labor force unemployed[b] (2)	Index for civilian employment[a] (3)	Estimated ratio of index for FTE[c] business employment to index for civilian employment (4)	Index for FTE[c] business employment[a] (5)
Males					
1929	108.39	n.a.	108.64	n.a.	107.48
1940	112.44	n.a.[d]	113.65	0.9893	112.43
1941	112.88	n.a.[d]	113.82	0.9894	112.61
1947	115.00	3.80	115.43	0.9920	114.51
1948	115.61	3.43	115.99	0.9912	114.97
1949	116.22	5.72	116.89	0.9904	115.77
1950	116.84	4.91	117.41	0.9896	116.19
1951	117.46	2.67	117.75	0.9888	116.43
1952	118.08	2.56	118.36	0.9880	116.94
1953	118.66	2.60	118.95	0.9875	117.46
1954	119.22	5.13	119.83	0.9872	118.30
1955	119.78	3.96	120.24	0.9870	118.68
1956	120.34	3.59	120.76	0.9867	119.15
1957	120.98	3.86	121.44	0.9865	119.80
1958	121.84	6.56	122.66	0.9864	120.99
1959	122.66	4.99	123.27	0.9860	121.54
1960	123.43	5.06	124.06	0.9851	122.21
1961	124.20	6.11	124.97	0.9842	123.00
1962	124.93	4.92	125.54	0.9831	123.42
1963	125.58	4.86	126.19	0.9816	123.87
1964	126.18	4.22	126.70	0.9811	124.31
1965	126.73	3.57	127.17	0.9818	124.86
1966	127.46	2.84	127.80	0.9817	125.46
1967	128.39	2.68	128.71	0.9814	126.32
1968	129.24	2.48	129.54	0.9808	127.05
1969	130.00	2.39	130.28	0.9797	127.64
Females					
1929	112.26	n.a.	112.45	n.a.	110.96
1940	116.46	n.a.[d]	117.35	0.9868	115.80
1941	116.79	n.a.[d]	117.50	0.9867	115.94
1947	118.34	3.48	118.56	0.9874	117.07
1948	118.81	3.91	119.09	0.9866	117.49
1949	119.28	5.67	119.79	0.9858	118.09
1950	119.76	5.41	120.23	0.9850	118.43
1951	120.24	4.18	120.56	0.9842	118.66
1952	120.71	3.42	120.93	0.9834	118.92
1953	121.10	3.08	121.27	0.9820	119.09
1954	121.45	5.82	121.98	0.9802	119.56
1955	121.79	4.63	122.17	0.9785	119.54
1956	122.14	4.54	122.51	0.9767	119.66
1957	122.47	4.42	122.82	0.9754	119.80
1958	122.76	6.49	123.39	0.9749	120.29
1959	123.19	5.57	123.70	0.9744	120.53
1960	123.94	5.53	124.45	0.9735	121.15
1961	124.70	6.83	125.39	0.9727	121.97
1962	125.28	5.86	125.84	0.9713	122.23
1963	125.51	5.98	126.08	0.9687	122.13
1964	125.86	5.73	126.40	0.9670	122.23
1965	126.46	5.10	126.92	0.9673	122.77
1966	126.90	4.37	127.26	0.9672	123.09
1967	127.42	4.79	127.84	0.9646	123.31
1968	128.16	4.33	128.52	0.9630	123.76
1969	128.66	4.22	129.00	0.9630	124.23

Sources: 1929–41, all columns, see text; 1947–69, column 1, straight-line interpolation of Table I-17, column 2, with October 1948 to October 1952 change extrapolated to January 1947; column 2, computed from *Manpower Report of the President, 1970*, Tables A-3 and A-8; column 3, for males, column 1 was raised by a percentage which is equal to −0.039 plus (column 2 × 0.1079), and for females, column 1 was raised by a per-

4. These ratios were multiplied by the annual indexes for the civilian employed to obtain indexes for full-time equivalent employment in the business sector. They are shown in column 5 of Table I-18.

Prewar Quality Indexes for Each Sex, Based on Years of School Completed

Estimates for the prewar years are less satisfactory. The only directly relevant education data are from the 1940 decennial Census.

Estimates for 1940 and 1941

Education indexes for March 1940 and April 1950 based on decennial Census data were first computed for three distributions by level of education for each sex. Persons 14 (rather than 18) years of age or older are included. The three distributions cover:

1. The civilian labor force (including public emergency workers in 1940).

2. Civilian employment (excluding public emergency workers in 1940).

3. Civilian employment (excluding public emergency workers in 1940) minus persons employed in seven nonbusiness occupations for which approximately comparable data were available at both dates. These occupations are: college presidents, professors, and instructors; social and welfare workers, except group; teachers, n.e.c. (not elsewhere classified); private household workers; clergymen; firemen, fire protection; and policemen and police detectives. The last three occupations enumerated, which contained few females, could be eliminated only from the male distributions.

April 1950 Census distributions, by sex, for the civilian labor force and civilian employment were obtained from *U.S. Census of Population, 1950: Education*, Table 9 (page 5B-74), by adding data for the age groups.

To secure April 1950 education distributions for persons employed in the seven nonbusiness occupations, the ratio of persons of each sex employed in these occupations to persons employed in all occupations was assumed to be the same at each education level as the corresponding ratio for the experienced labor force. Distributions for the experienced labor force were obtained from the 1950 Census report, *Occupational Characteristics*.[71] This report combines persons with 0–7 years of education. Employed persons in the selected occupations who had 0–7 years of education were allocated among more detailed education classes in proportion to the distribution of "private household workers," obtained from *Education*, Table 11.

In the 1950 Census, education is overstated relative to the 1940 Census, at least for the older age groups.[72] A conservative adjustment for comparability was based on two assumptions. First, that the percentage of any age cohort in the whole population who graduated from college, or who graduated from high school (including in each case those with additional education), should not exceed the higher of the corresponding percentages for that age cohort obtained from the 1940 and 1960 Censuses.[73] Second, that within an age group the overstatement was the same for any labor force, or employed group, as it was for all persons. The 1950 adjustments (in percentages of total labor force or employment) were:

Education bracket	Males	Females
None to high school, 3 years	+0.77	+0.51
High school, 4 years, to college, 3 years	−0.57	−0.35
College, 4 years or more	−0.20	−0.16

The percentages differ by sex because of the difference in age distributions. The adjusted percentages within these three broad education categories were allocated among detailed categories in proportion to the unadjusted estimates.

March 1940 Census distributions for all employed persons except those employed on public

71. U.S. Bureau of the Census, *U.S. Census of Population, 1950: Occupational Characteristics*, Special Report P-E No. 1B (1956), Table 10.

72. I noted this in *The Sources of Economic Growth*, p. 79, note 11. Folger and Nam, in *Education of the American Population*, pp. 220–24, confirm it, and show that in 1950 education was overstated relative to the 1960 Census as well as to the 1940 Census.

73. Percentages from the three Censuses are given in Folger and Nam, ibid., Table A-11, p. 223. The assumption led to adjustments only in the age brackets from 40 to 74.

centage which is equal to −0.190 plus (column 2 × 0.1083); column 4, straight-line interpolation of Table I-17, column 6, with the October 1948 to October 1952 change extrapolated to January 1947; column 5, the product of columns 3 and 4.
  n.a. Not available.
  a. Weight of persons with 8 years of education = 100.
  b. Percentages for persons 18 years of age and over. Data adjusted to current definitions.
  c. FTE, full-time equivalent.
  d. See Table I-19 for estimates on a different basis.

emergency work are from the 1940 Census, *Occupational Characteristics*, Table 3.[74] Data for "soldiers, sailors, marines, and coast guards," obtained from the same table, were deducted to obtain an approximation to civilian employment. Data for persons employed in the selected nonbusiness occupations are from the same table.

To obtain 1940 distributions for the civilian labor force, it was necessary to add three other groups to the distributions of civilian employment. The table already cited provides education data for the largest of them, "experienced workers seeking work." But education data are not provided for "new workers" and persons employed on public emergency work, who together represented about 6.3 percent of the male labor force and 5.8 percent of the female labor force. They were distributed among education categories in the same proportions as the "experienced unemployed" of the same sex.[75]

To compute quality indexes, it was necessary (because of lack of more detailed data on a comparable basis) to combine the "no education" with the "1–4 years of elementary education" class; the "5–7" with the "8" years of elementary education class; and the "4 years of college" with the "5 or more years of college" class.[76]

The March 1940 indexes expressed as percentages of the April 1950 indexes are as follows:

	Males	*Females*
Civilian labor force	96.22	97.25
Civilian employment, except public emergency work	96.72	97.58
Civilian employment, excluding nonbusiness occupations	96.69	97.75

The percentages for full-time equivalent business employment are assumed to be the same as those for employment excluding the nonbusiness occupations.

The percentage of the civilian labor force unemployed at relevant dates was next compiled for each sex. The unemployment rate from the 1950 Census was calculated and a comparable rate for 1950 as a whole was estimated by use of the CPS ratios. The unemployment rate (counting emergency workers as unemployed) from the 1940 Census was calculated, and comparable rates for 1940 and 1941 as a whole were estimated. Table I-19 shows these unemployment rates and their derivation.

Education quality indexes, comparable to those shown in columns 1, 3, and 5 of Table I-18, were then estimated for the month of April 1950, using the same method as for the annual estimates.[77] The percentages shown in the preceding text table were then applied to obtain comparable estimates for March 1940. The estimates of the quality indexes are:

	Males		*Females*	
	March 1940	*April 1950*	*March 1940*	*April 1950*
Civilian labor force	112.31	116.72	116.37	119.66
Civilian employment, except public emergency work	113.60	117.45	117.19	120.10
Full-time equivalent business employment	112.39	116.24	115.66	118.32

Annual averages for 1940 and 1941 of the quality index for the civilian labor force were next estimated by straight-line interpolation between the March 1940 and April 1950 indexes (and extrapolation to January and February 1940). To estimate the percentage by which the index for civilian employment was higher than that for the civilian labor force in these two years, proportional interpolation was used, based on use as interpolator of the unemployment percentages shown in rows 8 to 11 of Table I-19. For example, in 1941, 60 percent of the difference between the March 1940 and April 1950 unemployment rates for males had been eliminated. It was estimated that 60 percent of the difference between the two dates in the percentage by which the employment index exceeds the labor force

74. U.S. Bureau of the Census, *Sixteenth Census of the United States, 1940: Population; The Labor Force (Sample Statistics): Occupational Characteristics* (1943), Table 3.

75. An alternative procedure for distribution of the unemployed (including emergency workers) is available. Educational distributions of persons "seeking work and on emergency work" who were 18–64 years of age and either native white or Negro were published in U.S. Bureau of the Census, *Population, Education: Educational Attainment by Economic Characteristics and Marital Status* (1947), based upon tabulations from the *Sixteenth Census of the United States, 1940*. The numbers covered are larger than those for "experienced, seeking work," but I suspected that distributions excluding all young and old workers, the foreign born, and nonwhites other than Negroes would probably be less representative of all unemployed and emergency workers than would distributions of all "experienced, seeking work."

76. Weights for the consolidated classes were based on the detailed data for 1950, except that for the college graduate group combined weights in 1959 were used.

77. April 1950 unemployment percentages comparable to those shown in Table I-18 are needed for these calculations. They were estimated to be 6.13 for males and 5.18 for females by assuming the ratio of the April to the annual unemployment rate for persons of each sex 18 and over to be the same in the revised as in the originally published CPS data.

**Table I-19. Percentage of Civilian Labor Force
14 Years of Age and Over That Was Unemployed
or Employed on Public Emergency Work,
Selected Dates, 1940, 1941, and 1950**

Source and date	Males	Females
Based on decennial censuses		
1. March 1940	14.89	13.30
2. April 1950	4.95	4.66
Based on CPS		
3. March 1940	15.85	13.87
4. Annual average 1940	14.30	15.47
5. Annual average 1941	9.50	11.20
6. April 1950	5.96	5.17
7. Annual average 1950	4.85	5.29
Estimates consistent with decennial censuses		
8. March 1940	14.89	13.30
9. Annual average 1940	13.43	14.83
10. Annual average 1941	8.92	10.74
11. April 1950	4.95	4.66
12. Annual average 1950	4.03	4.77

Sources: Rows 1 and 8, U.S. Bureau of the Census, *Sixteenth Census of the United States, 1940: Population*, Vol. 3, *The Labor Force: Occupation, Industry, Employment, and Income*, Pt. 1, *United States Summary* (1943), pp. 18, 82; rows 2 and 11, U.S. Bureau of the Census, *U.S. Census of Population, 1950*, Vol. 2, *Characteristics of the Population*, Pt. 1, *United States Summary* (1953), p. 1–247; rows 3, 4, and 5, U.S. Bureau of the Census, *Current Population Reports*, Series P-50, No. 2, "Labor Force, Employment and Unemployment in the United States, 1940 to 1946," pp. 11–12; rows 6 and 7, U.S. Bureau of the Census, *Current Population Reports*, Series P-50, No. 31, "Annual Report on the Labor Force, 1950" (1951), p. 15; rows 9 and 10, the product of (the ratio of row 1 to row 3) and rows 4 and 5; row 12, the product of (the ratio of row 2 to row 6) and row 7.

index had also been eliminated.[78] Finally, the ratios of the indexes for full-time equivalent business employment to the indexes for civilian employment in March 1940 and April 1950 were interpolated by the straight-line method to obtain 1940 and 1941 ratios. These were multiplied by the civilian employment indexes to obtain indexes for full-time equivalent business employment. The resulting annual indexes for all the series are shown in Table I-18.

Estimates for 1929

The 1940 decennial Census cross-classifies all males 20 years of age and over in the population by age (five-year age brackets) and highest school grade completed.[79] In preparing the education estimates for *The Sources of Economic Growth*, I used the "cohort method" to estimate similar

78. The female relationship had to be extrapolated to obtain a 1940 estimate because the unemployment percentage for the year 1940 was higher than that for March, according to the CPS estimates.
79. U.S. Bureau of the Census, *Sixteenth Census of the United States, 1940: Population*, Vol. 4, *Characteristics by Age, Marital Status, Relationship, Education, and Citizenship*, Pt. 1, *United States Summary* (1943). Table 18, p. 78.

distributions for 1930.[80] For cohorts whose education had been completed by 1930 and who were still alive in substantial numbers in 1940, the 1940 percentage distribution by level of education was used for 1930. For example, the distribution of men 40–44 in 1944 was used for men 30–34 in 1930. For other cohorts, the distribution was estimated.

The numbers in the civilian labor force in each age group in 1930 and 1940 were distributed by education level like all men in the age group.[81] The age groups were then combined to obtain distributions for the 1930 and 1940 Census dates. Education quality indexes were computed from these distributions; the percentage increase in the index from 1930 to 1940 was 3.34 percent.[82]

The cohort method yields unbiased estimates of the change in education from 1930 to 1940 only if errors in the reporting of the highest grade of school completed, as given in the 1940 Census, are not correlated with age and if during adult life there is no increase in highest grade completed. In using these estimates in *The Sources of Economic Growth*, I concluded that there was a bias. One indication was that the proportions in the younger age groups reporting graduation from high school and college in the 1940 Census are consistent with available information about actual graduations, but in the older age groups these proportions exceed the actual proportions graduating at the time persons of their age were completing school. A second indication was that the proportion of each cohort reported as high school graduates or above was higher in the 1950 Census than in the 1940 Census—by about 3 percentage points in each cohort up to the group 55–59 years old in 1950. A possible interpretation lay in "self-promotion" in reporting—a tendency for increasing proportions of a cohort to exaggerate educational attainment as it grows older. To test the possible bias, a 1940 distribution was constructed by application of the cohort method to 1950

80. The estimates made then were compiled for males 25 and over. I have added estimates for the 20–24 age group.
81. Less detailed age distributions were used at this step. Labor force data are from U.S. Bureau of the Census, *Sixteenth Census of the United States, 1940, Population: Estimates of Labor Force, Employment, and Unemployment in the United States, 1940 and 1930* (1944), pp. 2–3.
82. The levels of the indexes, expressed with earnings of men with 8 years of education equal to 100, are slightly understated because men in the labor force tend to have more education than those of the same age not in the labor force. The percentage of understatement is assumed to be the same at both dates.

Census data. The rise from 1940 to 1950 in the education quality indexes for all males 25 and over computed from the Census data for those years was substantially larger than that in indexes computed from the 1950 Census data and the 1940 cohort estimate (4.44 percent as against 3.63 percent). The difference was presumed at that time to represent a bias in the cohort method. In that study I assumed the size of the bias in the cohort method to be the same (0.81 percentage points) from 1930 to 1940, and over earlier decades, as from 1940 to 1950.[83]

Appearance of the 1960 Census data put a very different light on the matter. As already indicated, comparison of the three censuses showed that educational attainment was overstated in the 1950 Census relative to both the 1940 and 1960 Censuses. It became clear that most of the difference between the two estimates of the 1940–50 change was due to overstatement of the change computed directly from the Census data rather than from understatement in the series obtained by use of the cohort method. This was confirmed by a 1950–60 calculation. A 1950 education distribution based on application of the cohort method to 1960 Census data was constructed. Contrary to 1940–50 experience, an index based on the cohort estimate for 1950 rose more than one based on direct use of the census distributions—by 0.55 percentage points. In a later study, I therefore concluded that, although use of the cohort method apparently does lead to a downward bias over time in the education quality index, this bias is very much smaller than initially supposed. By averaging the 1940–50 and 1950–60 differences between cohort estimates and census data, I estimated it at 0.13 percentage points per decade.[84] (This assumes the 1940 and 1960 Censuses to be comparable.) I therefore raise to 3.47 percent the initial cohort estimate that the educational quality of the male labor force rose 3.34 percent from 1930 to 1940. The 1920–30 percentage increase was previously estimated to be 78 percent as large as the 1930–40 increase.[85] Applying this relationship and interpolating, I estimate that the quality index for the male labor force in 1940, 112.44, was 3.74 percent above 1929. The in-

dex for 1929 is therefore 108.39 (Table I-18, column 1).

The Bureau of Labor Statistics estimates the unemployment rate for the civilian labor force 14 and over (both sexes combined) at 3.15 percent in 1929 and 14.59 in 1940.[86] In 1940 the comparable unemployment rate for males alone was 14.30, and the education quality index for civilian employment was 1.08 percent above that for the civilian labor force.[87] I assume that the male unemployment rate in 1929 was 3.00 percent, which is 21 percent of the 1940 rate; and that the percentage by which the education index for male civilian employment exceeded that for the civilian labor force was 21 percent as large as in 1940. Finally, I assume the percentage change from 1929 to 1940 in the index for full-time equivalent business employment to be the same as for all civilian employment. The resulting 1929 estimates are shown in Table I-18.

The procedure adopted to secure 1929 indexes for males employed in the business sector is reasonably satisfactory because the percentages of all men who are in the labor force and the percentages of employed men who work in the business sector are both high, and the educational distributions of men employed in the business sector are not very different from those for all employed men.

None of these conditions hold for females, so that reliable 1929 estimates for females cannot be obtained; it is fortunate that the weight of females in labor input in the business sector is small in the 1929–40 period. To obtain the 1929 estimates for females shown in Table I-18, the percentage change from 1929 to 1940 in the quality index for the civilian labor force was assumed to be the same for females as for males. The female unemployment rate was estimated to be 23 percent as high in 1929 as in 1940, and the percentage difference between the education indexes for the civilian employed and the civilian labor force was assumed also to be 23 percent as large as in 1940.[88] Finally, the percentage change in the index for full-time equivalent business employment was assumed to be the same as that in the index for all civilian employment.

83. *The Sources of Economic Growth*, pp. 70–71 and p. 79, note 11.

84. Edward F. Denison, "Measuring the Contribution of Education (and the Residual) to Economic Growth," in Organisation for Economic Co-operation and Development, Study group in the Economics of Education, *The Residual Factor and Economic Growth* (Paris: OECD), p. 29.

85. Ibid., p. 28, Table 4, column 1.

86. Computed from U.S. Bureau of the Census, *Historical Statistics of the United States: Colonial Times to 1957* (1960), p. 70.

87. Tables I-18 and I-19.

88. The female unemployment rate was 15.47 in 1940 (as compared with 14.59 for both sexes) and estimated at 3.60 percent in 1929 (as compared with 3.15 for both sexes).

Allowance for Changes in School Term and in Absenteeism

The indexes in Table I-18 count individuals who completed any given school grade as having received the same amount of education at all dates. An adjustment is next introduced to allow for the fact that persons who had completed the same school grade had received more education in later years than at earlier dates as a result of a longer school term and a reduction in absenteeism. Pupils enrolled in elementary and secondary schools in the 1870s, when many persons still employed in 1929 attended school, spent an average of 79 days a year in school according to data from the U.S. Office of Education. The average reached 100 days by 1902, 120 days by 1915, 140 days by 1928, and 160 days by 1960.

The length of the school term in large cities has not increased since at least 1900, and probably for a much longer period.[89] But in the late nineteenth century the average length of the school term was much shorter in towns and rural areas than in large cities. Gradually the school terms in smaller places and rural schools rose toward big-city standards. Simultaneously, the proportion of all students who attended urban schools rose because of population movements. In consequence, the average length of the school term (based on enrollment weights) increased greatly in the country as a whole. It was 131 days in the 1870s, 145 days in 1902, 159 in 1915, 172 in 1928, and 178 in 1960. Still more important in most periods was the reduction in absenteeism. This can be seen in the following table, which shows percentage increases in the average number of days attended per enrolled pupil and in the two reasons it increased: changes in the average length of the school term and changes in the ratio of the days attended per enrolled pupil to the length of the school term.

	Percentage increase in:		
Period	Days attended per enrolled pupil	Length of school term	Ratio of days attended to school term
1870–1890	10.1	1.9	8.0
1890–1910	30.9	16.9	12.0
1910–1930	26.5	9.7	15.4
1930–1950	10.4	3.0	7.2
1950–1968	3.4	0.5	2.8

As persons educated at later dates replaced those educated at earlier dates, the amount of schooling held by the average employed person

89. Denison, "Measuring the Contribution of Education," p. 31.

with, say, 8 years of education increased. I now describe the procedure adopted to adjust the indexes to allow for this fact.

1. The distributions of full-time equivalent business employment by highest school grade completed shown in Table I-15, and the products of these distributions and the education weights which yielded the indexes shown in Table I-17, column 4, were divided into two parts. An adjustment for changes in days per year was made only in the second part of the distribution.

The first part, to which no adjustment was made, had two quite different components. One was persons with no school years completed, who are unaffected by changes in school attendance. The other consisted of the three highest education groups, those with 1 or more years of college. Even in the late nineteenth century persons who attended college typically had attended urban or equivalent private schools regularly; if they had not, they were required to secure additional education in academies, often attached to the colleges, to attain appropriate qualifications before being admitted to the college level. The best assumption for persons in the three highest education categories—those with college attendance—is that they had received the same amount of education at all dates.

The second part of the distribution, to which an adjustment was made, consists of persons with 1–12 years of school completed. To determine its importance in the total, the percentage of the total weight in the education quality indexes for full-time equivalent business employment that stemmed from this group was first calculated for each survey date. For males, the percentage was 80.7 in October 1948; it declined to 66.6 by March 1970. The corresponding percentages for females were 83.3 and 77.0. The percentages at survey dates were interpolated to secure postwar annual averages, and comparable prewar percentages were estimated. The annual indexes shown in Table I-18, column 5, were multiplied by these percentages to obtain the weight of the 1–12 year education group in these indexes each year.

2. Persons within the second group who *regularly* attended big-city schools attended school about the same number of days per year regardless of the date at which they were educated, and are regarded as having received the same amount of education at all dates. The general assumption behind the adjustment procedure adopted is that the ratio of the amount of education received by persons who attended other schools where the

school term was shorter, or who attended school less regularly, to that received by persons regularly attending big-city schools at the same grade level and age (the two can be taken as approximately interchangeable) was the same as the ratio of the days of school attended during the year. The remaining steps reflect my attempt to implement this assumption statistically.

3. Estimates were made of the average number of days of schooling, per year of public elementary and secondary school enrollment, that had been received by persons in every five-year cohort represented in the labor force at any time from 1920 to 1970. The approximations were based on U.S. Office of Education data for "average number of days attended per enrolled pupil."[90] These estimates were then used to calculate (as of selected dates) the average number of days represented by a year of education held by those members of the labor force of each sex who (a) were 18 years of age and over and (b) had 1–12 years of education. For the postwar calculations, this portion of the labor force of each sex was cross-classified by age and years of education.[91] The total number of years of education held by persons in each age group was then calculated. The years of education held by each age group were multiplied by the average number of days per year of school for that age group. Total days for all age groups combined were divided by total years to obtain the average number of days per year for all age groups combined. Estimates, necessarily less exact, were also prepared for prewar decennial census years by using the same source materials as were used to estimate the indexes shown in Table I-18.

Growth rates of the mean number of days represented by a year of education held by labor force members with 1–12 years of education between the dates for which estimates were prepared are shown in the first two columns of Table I-20.

Table I-20. Civilian Labor Force, Aged 18 and Over, with 1–12 Years of Education: Growth Rates of Average Days of Education per Year, and Effect on Growth Rates of Education Quality Indexes for This Group, by Sex, 1920–70

Growth rates in percentage points

Period	Growth rate of days attended per year of education		Addition to growth rate of quality index for group with 1–12 years of education	
	Males (1)	Females (2)	Males (3)	Females (4)
1920–30	0.99	1.01	0.27	0.29
1930–40	1.20	1.21	0.32	0.35
1940–50	0.89	0.67	0.24	0.19
1950–55	0.70	0.51	0.19	0.15
1955–60	0.84	0.63	0.23	0.18
1960–65	0.76	0.73	0.21	0.21
1965–70	0.63	0.63	0.17	0.18

Source: See text for derivation.

Subsequently, the growth rates were assumed uniform within these periods.[92] Also, the rates were assumed to be the same for full-time equivalent employment in the business sector as for the civilian labor force.

4. For selected postwar survey dates, the mean education quality index based on highest grade completed and the mean number of years of education held were calculated from the full-time equivalent business employment distributions for persons in the 1–12 year education span. Within this education span, the 1948–70 growth rate of the index for males was 41 percent as large as the growth rate of the mean number of years of education, and for females it was 44 percent as large.[93] Thus, within the 1–12 years of education span, a 1 percent yearly increase in average years of education was associated with a 0.41 percent increase in the quality index for males, and with a 0.44 percent increase for females.

5. If average days attended had been the same at all grade levels at each date, the assumption stated in item 2 could be statistically implemented by letting any percentage change in the number of days of education per year of school have the same effect on the index (within the 1–12 years of education span) as an equal percentage change in the average number of years of school. How-

90. The U.S. Office of Education data for school years ending 1870 through 1956 are from U.S. Bureau of the Census, *Historical Statistics of the United States: Colonial Times to 1957* (1960), p. 207. Data for later years are from various issues of U.S. Bureau of the Census, *Statistical Abstract of the United States*. For each age cohort, a five-year average of these data was used. For persons aged 60–64 years in 1970, this average was centered in the 1917–18 school year; for those 65–69, in the 1912–13 school year, and so on. This approximation appeared quite adequate for the purpose to which the data were put.

91. The postwar age distributions of the labor force were annual averages from the CPS surveys. Percentage distributions by education level of each age group are from the CPS education surveys; when necessary, the distributions were interpolated to approximate the appropriate year.

92. Annual estimates were not attempted because age distributions are not available with class intervals that hold the cohorts constant.

93. These ratios were a bit bigger after 1964 than earlier but not sufficiently so as to suggest subdividing the postwar period.

ever, the effect on the index should be smaller if, as seems probable, the increase in average days was less at the higher than at the lower grade levels. This is so because the spread in earnings weights is larger at the higher levels. In addition, the increase in the U.S. Office of Education series may slightly exceed the average rise in days of education of persons at given grade levels.[94] Because of these considerations, the ratios described in item 4 were reduced by one-third for use with changes in average days. The size of the reduction is based solely on judgment but believed to be ample. I thus let the growth rate in the average days of school attended by persons with 1–12 years of education, as estimated, raise the index within this education range by 27 percent of that rate for males and 29 percent for females.

6. The growth rates of average days of education per year (Table I-20, columns 1 and 2) were multiplied by the percentages just provided to obtain the appropriate additions to the growth rates of the quality indexes for persons with 1–12 years of school to allow for changes in school days per year; these additions are shown at the right of Table I-20. The growth rates were then converted to annual indexes. To conform with the year upon which earnings weights used to combine persons having 1–12 years of education with other persons are based, 1959 was taken as 100. For each sex, the index for each year was multiplied by the weight (described in item 1) of the 1–12 years of education groups in the indexes shown in column 5 of Table I-18. The product was added to the weight of the other education groups to obtain final indexes for each sex expressed with the average weight of persons with 8 years of education in 1959 equal to 100.

94. There are three possible reasons: (1) The data refer to days attended per pupil enrolled rather than per pupil in average daily class membership, which would be preferable. The ratio of average daily membership to reported enrollment may have increased—but the opposite is also possible since the ratio of dropouts to enrollment must have declined as the education of pupils was extended. (2) The indexes to be adjusted are calculated from distributions based on highest school grade completed as reported to the Census Bureau rather than on years of school attended. In practice, there is probably little difference at the 1–12 year levels, but some persons with scant attendance may have reported on the basis of promotion to a recognized grade, or of the "reader" last finished. In such cases the data classified by highest school grade completed already allow for cases of absenteeism much above what was average in the school attended, though not for changes in the school term. (3) The increase in the proportion of secondary pupils would have raised the average number of days attended by all pupils even without a change in any separate grade because absenteeism is normally greater in elementary than in secondary schools.

Computation of Final Indexes

These indexes for each sex were converted to time series indexes with 1958 equal to 100. They are shown in Table I-21, columns 3 and 4.[95]

The final step was to combine the indexes for males and females. Percentage changes in the two indexes from year to year (or growth rates in 1929–40 and 1941–47) were weighted by total earnings of males and females in the business sector at each date.[96] The weighted percentage changes were linked to obtain the final index shown in column 5 of Table I-21.

95. For comparison, indexes based directly on Table I-18, without allowance for changes in days of education per year, are shown in columns 1 and 2.

96. The procedure was the same as that described in Chapter 4 for the computation of the index for the efficiency of an hour's work due to intragroup changes in hours.

Table I-21. Indexes of the Effect of Amount of Education on Labor Input in the Business Sector, 1929, 1940–41, and 1947–69
1958 = 100

Year	Before allowance for changes in days per year of school		Final indexes		
	Males (1)	Females (2)	Males (3)	Females (4)	Both sexes (5)
1929	88.83	92.24	83.18	86.79	83.71
1940	92.93	96.27	89.85	93.70	90.42
1941	93.07	96.38	90.17	93.96	90.73
1947	94.64	97.32	92.84	95.82	93.30
1948	95.02	97.67	93.40	96.33	93.85
1949	95.69	98.17	94.25	96.98	94.67
1950	96.03	98.45	94.78	97.42	95.20
1951	96.23	98.64	95.13	97.73	95.54
1952	96.65	98.86	95.70	98.07	96.08
1953	97.08	99.00	96.27	98.33	96.60
1954	97.78	99.39	97.12	98.83	97.39
1955	98.09	99.38	97.57	98.94	97.80
1956	98.48	99.48	98.14	99.18	98.31
1957	99.02	99.59	98.85	99.46	98.95
1958	100.00	100.00	100.00	100.00	100.00
1959	100.45	100.20	100.63	100.35	100.58
1960	101.01	100.71	101.34	101.02	101.29
1961	101.66	101.40	102.16	101.86	102.11
1962	102.01	101.61	102.66	102.26	102.59
1963	102.38	101.53	103.18	102.34	103.04
1964	102.74	101.61	103.70	102.60	103.51
1965	103.20	102.06	104.32	103.22	104.14
1966	103.69	102.33	104.93	103.63	104.71
1967	104.41	102.51	105.75	103.95	105.44
1968	105.01	102.88	106.47	104.48	106.12
1969	105.50	103.28	107.08	105.01	106.71

Sources: Columns 1 and 2, computed from Table I-18, column 5; columns 3 to 5, see text for derivation.

※※※

Weights for Inputs in Nonresidential Business

※※※

This appendix presents and describes an allocation of earnings in the business sector, except earnings of dwellings and their sites, among four types of resources (or inputs), and the derivation from these earnings allocations of the weights used to combine various inputs in the construction of a series for total factor input. The inputs distinguished are labor, nonresidential structures and equipment, inventories, and nonresidential land. I first give a summary description of the procedures, then a detailed description of the data, and finally some comments on the procedures.

Summary Description

Allocations of earnings were first made for each year (except 1969, which was not used); a percentage distribution is shown in Table J-1. These were then adjusted for use as weights.

Allocations of Annual Earnings

To obtain annual earnings allocations by type of input, national income originating in the business sector *excluding earnings of dwellings and their sites* is divided into the four parts described below, each of which is separately allocated among inputs. The total earnings of each type of input is the sum of the allocations to it from these four types of income.

1. *Total compensation of employees.* This is allocated entirely to labor.

2. *National income originating in nonfarm corporations other than compensation of employees of these corporations.* This income is divided among the three types of tangible assets (nonresidential structures and equipment, inventories, and nonresidential land) in proportion to the values of these assets owned by nonfarm corporations, measured in current prices. The procedure assumes that the ratio of earnings to asset values is the same for each type of asset; this is an approximation to implementation of the assumption that in nonfarm corporations the rate of return is the same for each type of asset.

3. *The earnings of the labor provided by farm proprietors and unpaid family workers together with earnings from all nonresidential property used on farms, regardless of its ownership.* The series consists of national income (except earnings

Table J-1. Nonresidential Business: Percentage Distribution of Earnings in the Sector, by Type of Input, 1929, 1940–41, and 1947–68

Year	Total (1)	Labor (2)	Nonresidential structures and equipment (3)	Inventories (4)	Land (5)
Excluding Alaska and Hawaii					
1929	100.00	79.38	10.80	4.46	5.36
1940	100.00	81.19	10.51	4.27	4.03
1941	100.00	77.18	12.55	5.44	4.83
1947	100.00	80.44	10.19	4.90	4.47
1948	100.00	77.71	11.69	5.65	4.95
1949	100.00	79.46	11.33	4.95	4.26
1950	100.00	77.58	12.70	5.26	4.46
1951	100.00	77.51	12.40	5.52	4.57
1952	100.00	80.09	11.00	4.89	4.02
1953	100.00	81.34	10.67	4.41	3.58
1954	100.00	81.59	10.77	4.20	3.44
1955	100.00	79.02	12.56	4.66	3.76
1956	100.00	81.08	11.39	4.14	3.39
1957	100.00	82.07	10.91	3.85	3.17
1958	100.00	83.18	10.20	3.52	3.10
1959	100.00	81.04	11.69	3.92	3.35
1960	100.00	82.17	10.88	3.66	3.29
Including Alaska and Hawaii					
1960	100.00	82.22	10.85	3.65	3.28
1961	100.00	82.26	10.75	3.60	3.39
1962	100.00	80.87	11.55	3.87	3.71
1963	100.00	80.47	11.74	3.94	3.85
1964	100.00	79.80	12.19	4.06	3.95
1965	100.00	78.33	12.94	4.33	4.40
1966	100.00	78.14	12.94	4.42	4.50
1967	100.00	79.83	12.00	4.07	4.10
1968	100.00	79.94	12.06	3.96	4.04

Source: See text for derivation.

of dwellings) originating in the "farms" industry minus compensation of employees in the industry plus property income paid to nonfarm landlords.

To allocate this aggregate, a calculation was first made of the amounts each resource would earn if the average earnings of proprietors and unpaid family workers from their labor were the same as the average compensation of employees in the business sector and if the ratio of the earnings of each type of tangible asset to its value were the same on farms as in nonfarm corporations. (The ratio is, of course, the same for each type of asset.) Actual earnings were allocated among the four types of input in proportion to these imputed values.

The actual earnings to be allocated among the four types of input are always smaller than the sum of the imputed earnings figures; with the exception of a few early postwar years, they are less than half as big. The procedure adopted reduces the initially imputed earnings of labor and each type of tangible asset by the same percentage. It yields the same ratio of earnings to asset value within farming for each type of tangible asset.

4. *The earnings of the labor provided by nonfarm proprietors and unpaid family workers together with the earnings (except earnings of dwellings) of nonfarm business property not owned by corporations.* The series consists of all nonfarm proprietors' income, net interest paid by all private noncorporate nonfarm business except dwellings, and rental income of persons that is not derived from farm or residential property.

The allocation procedure is similar to that adopted for series 3 above. Actual earnings were allocated among the four inputs in proportion to imputed earnings. For labor, the imputed earnings are the product of the number of nonfarm proprietors and unpaid family workers and the average compensation of employees in the business sector. For each type of tangible asset, the imputation is the product of the nonfarm corporate ratio of earnings to asset values and the value of nonfarm business property not owned by corporations.

In contrast to farm earnings, actual earnings in this nonfarm noncorporate area do not differ greatly from the sum of the imputed earnings series. Actual earnings usually (after 1949, always) are smaller than imputed earnings, but the shortfall is not great.

The series for the labor share shown in Table J-1 may be compared with the percentage of na-

tional income originating in nonfinancial corporations that consists of employee compensation.[1] In all postwar years the former is higher by 1.42 to 2.27 percentage points; this narrow range indicates the similarity of movement of the two series. In 1929 it is higher by 1.38 points.[2]

Derivation of Weights

For use as weights, some adjustment of the annual shares is desirable, particularly of the division between labor and property earnings.

For the weight of labor, I seek the labor share of the total earnings of labor, land, and capital. I have actually measured the labor share of national income, which also includes "pure" profit. Since profit presumably is positive except in depressed years, the share of labor presumably is understated and the property shares overstated in most of the years shown in Table J-1 (although not in the 1930s, which are not shown).[3] I make no adjustment for this probability. I do, however, attempt to smooth out fluctuations in the labor share that result from fluctuations in profits in the course of the business cycle, as well as from the effects of wartime controls on prices and wages. The objective is to approximate the shares that would have prevailed in normal circumstances with the rate of utilization of resources at about the postwar average. This adjustment was made in the following steps.

STEP ONE. To secure comparability for later steps, the labor share in years prior to 1960 was raised by 0.05 percentage points, the difference between the 1960 share excluding Alaska and Hawaii and the share including them.[4]

STEP TWO. The actual labor shares in the recession years 1949, 1954, 1958, and 1961 were replaced with the average of the percentages for the preceding and following years, and the abnormally low 1969 share by the share in 1968. Also, the percentages (most of which are not shown in Table J-1, column 2) for all years in the period from 1930 through 1947 were discarded and replaced with percentages interpolated between 1929 and 1948. Thus the period of the depressed

---

1. The series for nonfinancial corporations is the national income accounts (NIA) series plus NIA capital consumption less my estimates of depreciation.
2. It is higher by 3.27 points in both 1940 and 1941. As indicated later, the labor share for these years does not enter into my final weights.
3. Other possible biases are discussed in a later section.
4. The difference stems from partial coverage of these states in the national income estimates prior to 1960; it is not related to true shares in them.

1930s, when the actual labor share was large, and the period of wartime controls and shortages, when share relationships were distorted, were rejected. The interpolated percentages for 1940 and 1941, it may be noted, fall between the actual percentages for 1940 and 1941. I have observed in previous work that trend ratios representing compositional aspects of national income and product, such as industry shares of national income, or particular types of personal consumption expenditures as a percentage of total consumption, typically fall between actual 1940 and 1941 ratios, and I therefore regard this relationship as reasonable.

STEP THREE. A five-year moving average of these adjusted labor shares was substituted for the annual shares. This further smoothed out random and cyclical fluctuations.[5]

STEP FOUR. These figures were raised by a uniform 0.26 percentage points. This made the average level for 1948–68 the same as that for the actual original data in Table J-1 (except for the Alaska-Hawaii adjustment).

STEP FIVE. The estimates prior to 1960 were reduced by 0.05 points to restore the Alaska-Hawaii exclusion.

In the postwar period these final labor weights, shown in Table J-2, differ but little from the annual shares shown in Table J-1, and their substitution modifies the analysis of growth sources to only a trivial extent. Also, given the average postwar level of the labor share and its basic stability, my estimates of sources of growth are not at all sensitive to the particular pattern of small postwar movements in the labor weight that is shown.[6] In the 1929–47 period, on the other hand, the weights differ substantially from "actual" shares in the depression and war years, and the substitution has a significant effect.

5. The figures for 1929 and 1969 (actually 1968) were repeated to obtain averages at the ends of the period.

6. This is fortunate because it is necessary to caution that inferences about changes in trends in the labor share should not be drawn from the series for the labor weight. I was reluctant to depart far from the unadjusted earnings in deriving my basic weights. Discarding a few extreme years and applying a moving average smooths out short-term fluctuations but does not produce a precise cyclically adjusted series. The labor share, appropriately adjusted for changes in utilization, probably was higher in the latter years of the period than in the earlier period as this series shows, but it is unlikely that it moved up and then slightly down, a movement that reflects the series of low-utilization years in the middle of the period. In Appendix O, I assume in a rather similar case that the uptrend was continuous throughout the postwar period.

Table J-2. Nonresidential Business: Weights Used for Inputs in the Sector

Period ending[a]	Total (1)	Labor (2)	Nonresidential structures and equipment (3)	Inventories (4)	Land (5)
1940	100.00	79.15	11.29	4.62	4.94
1941	100.00	78.63	11.85	4.97	4.55
1947	100.00	78.32	11.61	5.30	4.77
1948	100.00	78.03	11.48	5.54	4.95
1949	100.00	77.95	11.86	5.45	4.74
1950	100.00	78.14	12.22	5.20	4.44
1951	100.00	78.73	11.89	5.10	4.28
1952	100.00	79.35	11.40	5.07	4.18
1953	100.00	79.75	11.38	4.88	3.99
1954	100.00	80.25	11.42	4.59	3.74
1955	100.00	80.80	11.36	4.32	3.52
1956	100.00	81.03	11.39	4.18	3.40
1957	100.00	81.12	11.42	4.10	3.36
1958	100.00	81.52	11.22	3.92	3.34
1959	100.00	81.88	11.08	3.77	3.27
1960	100.00	81.80	11.17	3.75	3.28
1961	100.00	81.61	11.18	3.75	3.46
1962	100.00	81.37	11.27	3.77	3.59
1963	100.00	80.86	11.54	3.86	3.74
1964	100.00	80.12	11.98	4.00	3.90
1965	100.00	79.67	12.20	4.08	4.05
1966	100.00	79.52	12.18	4.11	4.19
1967	100.00	79.48	12.17	4.15	4.20
1968	100.00	79.66	12.17	4.06	4.11
1969	100.00	80.00	12.04	3.90	4.06

Source: See text for derivation.

a. Entries for 1940 refer to the 1929–40 period and those for 1947 to the 1941–47 period. All others refer to the two-year period ending in the year shown.

The weight not assigned to labor each year was allocated among the three types of tangible assets in proportion to the original estimates of the earnings of the three types shown in Table J-1. Percentages for years in the 1930–39 and 1942–46 periods are interpolations.

The resulting estimate for each year is an approximation to what shares would have been, in the absence of special controls, if the rate of utilization of employed resources had been anticipated and if the postwar average represents a reasonable approximation of long-term anticipations. The smoothing and interpolating prevents certain anomalous results. For example, given the actual capital stock in 1929 and 1941, use of unadjusted annual shares as weights would imply that additions to the stock made in 1937 contributed more to the 1929–41 growth rate than additions made in 1938, when profits were smaller because of the severe recession.

The weights assigned to changes in each type of input between each pair of adjacent years are the averages of the adjusted shares in the two years.[7] These estimates are shown in Table J-2. For the 1929–40 and 1941–47 periods, they are the averages of the annual percentages so computed for the intervening years.

This completes the summary description of procedures. I next provide a detailed description

7. The adjusted labor share for each year may be found in Table Q-6, column 20.

of the data used to derive the original share estimates shown in Table J-1.

The Division of National Income by Groups

As noted earlier, national income originating in the business sector, except earnings of dwellings, was divided into four components before it was allocated by type of earnings. Total national income in the sector is from Table 3-1. The four component series are shown in Table J-3. They were obtained by the following procedures.

Table J-3. Nonresidential Business: National Income Originating in the Sector, and Distribution among Type of Incomes, 1929, 1940–41, and 1947–69
Billions of dollars

| | | | Income except compensation of employees | | |
Year	Total (1)	Compensation of employees (2)	Originating in nonfarm corporations (3)	Earnings of farm proprietors and property used on farms (4)	Earnings of nonfarm proprietors and noncorporate nonfarm property (5)
			Excluding Alaska and Hawaii		
1929	71.7	43.9	10.4	7.2	10.2
1940	66.0	41.9	9.2	5.2	9.6
1941	86.8	52.8	14.5	7.4	12.1
1947	167.6	107.0	21.7	16.6	22.3
1948	190.4	118.1	28.2	19.0	25.0
1949	180.6	115.6	25.8	14.1	24.9
1950	200.9	127.2	31.8	15.3	26.6
1951	229.2	146.4	36.0	17.9	28.9
1952	237.1	156.9	33.3	17.0	29.9
1953	248.5	169.4	33.7	14.8	30.6
1954	245.6	167.4	33.1	14.3	30.8
1955	270.9	181.2	42.9	13.1	33.7
1956	285.9	196.6	40.9	13.1	35.3
1957	296.7	206.3	40.2	12.9	37.2
1958	293.2	204.2	36.2	15.2	37.6
1959	322.4	222.5	46.3	13.1	40.4
1960	330.0	232.5	44.7	13.7	39.2
			Including Alaska and Hawaii		
1960	331.2	233.5	44.7	13.7	39.3
1961	338.7	237.7	45.2	14.7	41.0
1962	365.3	253.9	52.8	15.2	43.3
1963	383.7	266.9	56.7	15.4	44.8
1964	411.8	285.4	63.8	14.9	47.8
1965	449.9	307.5	74.0	18.1	50.2
1966	493.6	338.7	81.5	19.8	53.7
1967	512.7	359.3	78.1	18.8	56.6
1968[a]	556.7	394.1	84.5	19.1	59.0
1969[a]	594.7	433.2	79.2	21.5	60.8

Source: See text for derivation. Detail may not add to totals because of rounding.
a. Adjustments to revisions in NIA are approximate (see pp. 7–8 above).

1. *Compensation of employees in business.* Data are from National Income Accounts (NIA) Table 1.13.[8]

2. *National income originating in nonfarm corporations other than compensation of employees.* This series is equal to the following items:

a. National income originating in corporate business, including mutual financial institutions, from NIA Table 1.13.

b. Minus compensation of employees in corporate business, including mutual financial institutions, from NIA Table 1.13.

c. Minus corporate profits and corporate net interest in the farm industry; these are unpublished estimates provided by OBE.

d. Plus corporate capital consumption allowances, from NIA Table 6.18.

e. Minus corporate depreciation (nonresidential and residential) as estimated in this study. Depreciation of corporate nonresidential property is a component (provided by OBE from its capital stock study) of the total depreciation of nonresidential property that was used to obtain my estimates of national income; it is based on use of straight-line depreciation, Bulletin F service lives, and the Winfrey distribution, and valued at current cost 2. Depreciation on corporate residential property (my concept) was estimated by multiplying OBE's unpublished estimates of capital consumption allowances on corporate nonfarm residential property by the ratio of the estimates (provided by OBE from its capital stock study) of depreciation on all private nonfarm residential structures used in this study to OBE's estimates of capital consumption allowances on all private nonfarm residential structures.

The resulting series erroneously includes any net earnings (computed by use of the depreciation concepts used in this study) of nonfarm corporations from their ownership of farm or residential property. The amount of such earnings is clearly small.

3. *The earnings of the labor provided by farm proprietors and unpaid family workers together with earnings from all nonresidential property used on farms, regardless of ownership.* This series is equal to the following items:

a. National income originating in farming, from NIA Table 1.17.

b. Minus compensation of employees in farming, from NIA Table 6.1.

8. See Appendix A, note 2, for full citation.

c. Plus gross rents paid to nonfarm landlords (excluding operating expenses), from NIA Table 1.17.

d. Plus government payments to nonfarm landlords (excluding operating expenses), from U.S. Department of Agriculture, Economic Research Service, *Farm Income Situation,* FIS-214 (July 1969), Table 14H, page 57, and FIS-216 (July 1970), Table 14H, page 57.

e. Minus the net rental value of farm dwellings and interest on owner-occupied farm dwellings, as included in the national accounts series; these unpublished series, obtained from OBE, are the same as those cited in Appendix D (page 177).

f. Plus NIA estimates of capital consumption allowances on nonresidential farm property, obtained by deducting from farm capital consumption allowances given in NIA Table 1.17, the NIA estimates of capital consumption allowances on farm dwellings; the latter series, obtained from OBE, is the same as the one cited in Appendix D.

g. Minus depreciation on farm equipment and nonresidential structures; this is the same series, obtained from the OBE capital stock study, that was used in the derivation of total national income (page 10).

4. *The earnings of the labor provided by nonfarm proprietors and unpaid family workers together with the earnings (except earnings of dwellings) of nonfarm business property not owned by corporations.* This series is equal to national income originating in the nonresidential business sector minus the above three series.

Asset Values

The estimated values of tangible assets used in the derivation of the income share estimates are shown in Table J-4. The net asset values in current prices for structures and equipment and for inventories are based on the body of data that also provided capital formation in current and constant prices for my measure of output, capital stock data for my measure of capital input, and (in the case of structures and equipment) depreciation in current and constant prices for my measure of national income. The estimates for land were based on other sources. Vacant lots were excluded because they have no current earnings from production but derive their value from the expectation of future use. I now describe the sources of the asset values used.

Table J-4. Nonresidential Business: Estimated Value of Tangible Assets Owned by the Sector, Excluding Dwellings and Sites, 1929, 1940–41, and 1947–69[a]

Billions of dollars

Year	Nonfarm corporate				Nonfarm noncorporate				Farm			
	Total (1)	Nonresidential structures and equipment (2)	Inventories (3)	Land (4)	Total (5)	Nonresidential structures and equipment (6)	Inventories (7)	Land (8)	Total (9)	Nonresidential structures and equipment (10)	Inventories (11)	Land (12)
1929	119.2	74.3	24.7	20.2	22.7	9.6	6.7	6.5	51.6	8.4	9.6	33.7
1940	97.9	62.0	22.1	13.9	18.1	8.6	4.4	5.1	36.6	6.7	8.1	21.8
1941	108.6	67.8	25.4	15.3	19.9	9.8	5.1	5.1	39.5	7.4	9.6	22.5
1947	171.2	106.3	42.2	22.6	35.8	19.2	9.4	7.1	81.3	14.0	20.7	46.7
1948	196.7	121.0	49.0	26.7	42.2	23.0	11.4	7.9	88.4	17.0	22.7	48.8
1949	210.4	131.4	50.2	28.9	45.1	25.1	11.9	8.2	93.3	19.8	21.8	51.8
1950	225.4	143.3	51.8	30.4	48.1	27.2	12.3	8.6	95.5	22.6	22.8	50.1
1951	255.6	159.3	62.3	34.0	53.5	30.0	13.9	9.6	110.8	25.9	26.7	58.2
1952	279.7	173.3	69.7	36.7	56.8	32.0	14.6	10.2	118.8	28.4	26.1	64.3
1953	291.5	183.8	70.6	37.0	58.3	33.4	14.6	10.3	117.7	29.7	22.4	65.6
1954	300.9	193.0	70.4	37.4	60.2	35.0	14.7	10.6	116.5	30.7	20.9	65.0
1955	319.6	206.6	72.8	40.2	64.0	37.6	14.9	11.4	119.7	31.9	19.9	67.9
1956	352.3	228.0	80.0	44.2	70.2	42.1	15.6	12.5	124.6	33.5	19.1	72.0
1957	382.2	250.2	85.3	46.7	75.5	46.2	16.2	13.1	133.4	34.9	20.4	78.1
1958	397.4	264.5	85.7	47.2	78.3	48.5	16.5	13.2	143.5	36.2	24.3	83.0
1959	411.2	273.9	87.3	50.0	81.4	50.1	17.0	14.3	152.7	37.6	25.0	90.2
1960	428.4	284.1	91.4	53.0	84.7	51.5	17.5	15.7	157.0	38.2	23.2	95.5
1961	443.5	294.0	93.6	56.0	87.8	52.6	17.8	17.4	160.4	38.4	24.4	97.6
1962	460.8	304.9	96.8	59.1	91.9	53.8	18.2	19.8	167.6	38.6	25.9	103.1
1963	481.7	317.9	101.7	62.0	96.4	55.3	18.5	22.6	173.9	39.3	26.1	108.6
1964	506.7	334.0	107.5	65.2	101.7	57.4	18.8	25.5	180.8	40.3	24.7	115.8
1965	542.4	357.3	115.6	69.5	110.2	61.0	19.6	29.5	190.7	41.8	25.5	123.4
1966	594.4	389.9	129.3	75.3	121.6	66.4	20.6	34.6	205.6	44.2	28.1	133.3
1967	650.1	427.4	142.4	80.3	133.0	72.7	21.3	39.0	217.3	47.0	28.7	141.6
1968	708.4	469.5	152.1	86.7	146.2	80.1	22.1	44.1	230.0	49.9	29.6	150.6
1969	782.0	522.0	164.3	95.7	163.9	89.5	23.4	51.0	243.5	52.6	32.5	158.4

Source: See text for derivation.

a. Classified by ownership except that property used on farms is classified as "farm" regardless of ownership. Data are averages of values at the beginning and end of the year.

Farm Assets

The value of farm equipment and nonresidential structures is the OBE capital stock study estimate of net value based on Bulletin F service lives, straight-line depreciation, the Winfrey distribution, and current cost 2.[9] The value of farm inventories is the sum of the Department of Agriculture estimates of the values of livestock and of "crops stored on and off farms."[10] The value of

nonresidential farm land represents the Department of Agriculture estimate of the value of farm land minus a small allowance for farm dwelling sites. This allowance was computed as 25 percent of the department's estimates of the value of farm dwellings (structures only).[11]

9. Values on December 31 of the preceding and current years were averaged.

10. Values on January 1 of the current and following years were averaged. Data are from U.S. Department of Agriculture (USDA), Economic Research Service (ERS), *The Balance Sheet of the Farming Sector, 1970*, Agriculture Information Bulletin 350 (January 1971), pp. 28–29, with the following exceptions. Data for January 1 of 1941 and 1942 are from USDA, ERS, *The Balance Sheet of Agricul-*

ture, 1966, Agriculture Information Bulletin 314 (September 1966), Table 23, p. 26. Livestock data for January 1 of 1929 and 1930 are from USDA, *Agricultural Statistics, 1952* (1952), p. 625; and crop estimates for these dates are from Raymond W. Goldsmith, *A Study of Saving in the United States* (Princeton University Press, 1955), Vol. 1, Table A-31, col. 3, p. 795.

11. Data referring to March were used as representative of the year. They were provided for all years by the Department of Agriculture. They are consistent with more summary data published for selected years in *The Balance Sheet of the Farming Sector, 1970*.

Corporate and Noncorporate Nonfarm Assets

The Office of Business Economics provided, from its capital stock study, series for the value of the net stock of private nonresidential nonfarm structures and equipment (structures and equipment separately) based on Bulletin F service lives, straight-line depreciation, the Winfrey distribution, and the current cost 2 price series; the series were provided separately for corporate and noncorporate property. OBE provided, in addition, special estimates of the value of the net stock of institutional structures; these were eliminated from the value of private noncorporate structures.[12]

OBE also furnished estimates of the current value of corporate and of noncorporate nonfarm inventories, based on the inventory investigation undertaken as part of its national accounts estimates. Because detailed data on OBE's worksheets are not summarized in the form desired, a special study by OBE was required to secure these series. A division of nonfarm inventories valued in 1958 prices between corporations and noncorporate enterprises was developed for all years by use of the full industry detail used to obtain the NIA estimates of the change in nonfarm inventories. From this detail, total holdings of durables and nondurables in 1958 prices were then computed for each legal form of organization. Durable and nondurable stocks in 1958 values under each legal form of organization were multiplied by indexes which expressed the relationship of average prices in each year to average prices in the year 1958. Durables and nondurables were added to secure total stocks in current prices for each legal form of organization. Prior to the beginning of 1947 a different procedure was adopted at this stage because price indexes for conversion to current values were not available. It was necessary to use book values instead of current values to compute implicit deflators, and to link the resulting series to the current value series at 1947. This procedure should not introduce large errors into the estimates for 1929, 1940, and 1941 because LIFO accounting was not widely used prior to 1947.

The estimates of inventories, structures, and equipment were provided for the end of each year of the period; I used an average of data for the beginning and end of each year.

Estimates of the value of nonfarm nonresidential business land were prepared by multiplying the value of nonfarm nonresidential structures by estimated ratios of the value of land to the value of structures. These ratios, shown in Table J-5, column 4, do not correspond to the usual breakdown of the value of commercial and industrial property between site value and structure value. Some of the land included, such as private forests and underground mineral resources, has little counterpart in structures. Even within the "commercial and industrial" category, shifts in the composition of property between and within the "commercial" and "industrial" categories cause the ratios to change.

Ratios based on three sources are shown in the first three columns of Table J-5.[13] For 1956 and 1966 (and hence for the level of the series) I use ratios (column 1) based on estimates by Allen D. Manvel. Manvel's estimates (in the form used in Table J-5) are based on application of assessment ratios (the ratio of sales price to assessed value) to assessed values of locally assessed property and adjustments to include state-assessed property and separately assessed mineral rights. Separate assessment ratios for land and structures in 1966 were based mostly on data for twelve major areas and for California; changes from 1956 to 1966 were based mainly on California and FHA data.

Ratios for 1947 through 1958, shown in column 2, were available from Raymond W. Goldsmith's study of postwar national wealth. The 1956 ratio is very close to Manvel's. I have raised Goldsmith's ratios for these years by 0.007 to conform to the 1956 ratio.[14] The 1959–65 ratios are interpolated values, and the 1966 ratio was held constant in later years.

Column 3 shows ratios for the prewar years and 1947 based on Goldsmith's earlier study of saving. The ratio drops sharply from 1929 to 1940–41 and drops again to 1947. However, the 1947 ratio is far below that based on the postwar

---

12. This was an important step in the derivation of the estimates. The bulk of the noncorporate nonfarm nonmanufacturing structures component of the OBE capital stock estimates was eliminated by this deduction.

13. The description of sources to Table J-5 provides full citations of sources and an exact description of the ways I utilized the data they contain. I have used the wording of the authors in citing lines from their tables. This wording is insufficient to indicate the coverage of the series and the reader is referred to the original sources for further explanation.

14. The Goldsmith ratio drops in 1957 and 1958, and its use for these years might be questioned in view of the sharp rise from 1956 to 1966 shown by Manvel. However, the drop in the Goldsmith ratio stemmed from the short-term movement of his price series for mineral and forest properties. In addition, it is unlikely that the sharp rise in site values began until the 1958 recession was over.

series. In the absence of a more satisfactory method of adjustment, I have raised the 1929 ratio of column 3 by one-half of the difference between columns 3 and 4 in 1947. The ratios for 1940 and 1941 were then obtained by proportional interpolation.

Table J-5. Ratios of the Value of Land[a] to the Value of Structures, Nonfarm Nonresidential Business Property, 1929, 1940–41, and 1947–69

Year	Manvel[b] (1)	Goldsmith, National Wealth[b] (2)	Goldsmith, Study of Saving[c] (3)	Ratios used in this study (4)
1929	...	...	0.452	0.509
1940	...	...	0.344	0.439
1941	...	...	0.335	0.433
1947	...	0.395	0.288	0.402
1948	...	0.422	...	0.429
1949	...	0.433	...	0.440
1950	...	0.430	...	0.437
1951	...	0.439	...	0.446
1952	...	0.436	...	0.443
1953	...	0.417	...	0.424
1954	...	0.406	...	0.413
1955	...	0.411	...	0.418
1956	0.419	0.412	...	0.419
1957	...	0.399	...	0.406
1958	...	0.383	...	0.390
1959	...	...	...	0.402
1960	...	...	...	0.415
1961	...	...	...	0.427
1962	...	...	...	0.440
1963	...	...	...	0.452
1964	...	...	...	0.464
1965	...	...	...	0.477
1966	0.489	...	...	0.489
1967	...	...	...	0.489
1968	...	...	...	0.489
1969	...	...	...	0.489

Sources of land and structures values underlying the ratios:

Column 1: Data are from Allen D. Manvel, "Trends in the Value of Real Estate and Land, 1956 to 1966," in *Three Land Research Studies*, Research Report 12, Prepared for the consideration of the National Commission on Urban Problems (U.S. Government Printing Office, 1968), pp. 1–17.

Land value is the sum of (a) the market value of locally assessed "commercial and industrial" property from Table 1, row E, column 7, and (b) an allowance for state-assessed property and mineral rights computed as 5 percent of the total value of all taxable locally assessed land from Table 1, row E, column 1, minus the allocation to land. Structures value is the sum of (a) the market value of taxable locally assessed "commercial and industrial" structural value from Table 1, row F, column 7, and (b) an allowance for state-assessed property and mineral rights computed as 7 percent of the total market value of taxable locally assessed real estate from Table 1, row C, column 1, minus the allocation to land. The 5 and 7 percent figures are from Manvel.

Column 2: Data are from Raymond W. Goldsmith, *The National Wealth of the United States in the Postwar Period* (Princeton University Press for the National Bureau of Economic Research, 1962).

Ratios were computed from Goldsmith's year-end values; those shown are averages of ratios for the previous and current year ends. Land value is the sum of "business land" from Table B-124, column 6; "subsoil assets" from Table B-133, column 1; and "private nonfarm forest land" from Table B-132, column 1. Structures value is the sum

The ratios shown in Table J-5, column 4, were multiplied by the value of structures in this sector (already described) to obtain the value of land each year.

Percentages computed from Goldsmith's study of postwar national wealth were used to divide this total land value between corporate and noncorporate holdings in the years 1947–58.[15] Changes in the percentages in other years were based on changes in holdings of structures.[16]

Imputed Labor Earnings

Data used for the numbers of nonfarm and farm proprietors and unpaid family workers and the average compensation of employees in the business sector were obtained from the following sources.

1. The number of nonfarm proprietors and unpaid family workers is from Table C-1, column 3.

2. The number of farm proprietors and unpaid family workers is equal to farm employment from Table C-1 minus the number of farm wage and

15. Year-end ratios of noncorporate to total values were computed from the following aggregates compiled from Goldsmith's data. Noncorporate: Table B-59, column 5, plus Table A-42, column 2, plus Table A-43, column 2. Total: Table B-124, column 6, plus Table B-133, column 1, plus Table B-132, column 1. Ratios at the end of the preceding and current years were averaged.

16. The 1947 corporate and noncorporate land values were extrapolated backward, and the 1958 values were extrapolated forward, by corporate and noncorporate structure values; the results were adjusted proportionately to agree with the total value of corporate and noncorporate land established by use of the ratios of land to structure values.

of (a) "business structures" from Table B-123, column 1, and "underground mining construction" from Table B-126, columns 6 and 9.

Column 3: Data are from Raymond W. Goldsmith, *A Study of Saving in the United States* (Princeton University Press, 1955), Vol. 2, and Raymond W. Goldsmith, Dorothy S. Brady, and Horst Mendershausen, ibid. (Princeton University Press, 1956), Vol. 3.

Ratios were computed from Goldsmith's year-end values; those shown are averages of ratios for the previous and current year ends. Data are from Volume 3, Table W-1, except for "vacant lots." Land value is the sum of "private nonfarm nonresidential" from column 22 and "forests" from column 23 minus "institutional land" computed as one-third of column 8 and "vacant lots," interpolated from Volume 2, Table B-51, column 3. Structures value is the sum of "private nonfarm nonresidential" from Table W-1, column 5, and "mining (underground)" from column 6.

Column 4: 1956 and 1966, column 1; 1947–55 and 1957–58, column 2 plus 0.007 to conform to 1956 estimate; 1959–65, straight-line interpolation of 1958 and 1966 ratios; 1967–69, assumed to be the same as 1966; 1929, column 3 plus 0.057, which is half the difference between columns 3 and 4 in 1947; 1940–41, proportional interpolation (using column 3) between 1929 and 1947 ratios.

a. Excludes vacant lots. Includes subsoil resources and forests.

b. Data are shown for all years available.

c. Data are shown only for years used in estimation of column 4.

salary workers, estimated at the same percentage of farm employment that the number of farm wage and salary workers reported in NIA Table 6.3 represents of farm employment based on establishment sources as given in Table C-5, column 3.

3. The number of wage and salary workers in the business sector is the sum of nonfarm wage and salary employment from Table C-1, column 5, and farm wage and salary employment as estimated in item 2.

4. Compensation of employees in the business sector is from NIA Table 1.13.

5. Average compensation of employees in the business sector is item 4 divided by item 3.

Comments on the Allocations

The exact estimates obtained in Table J-1 for the division of income (prior to the adjustments introduced in Table J-2 for use of the data as weights) result from acceptance of certain conventions and procedures. I note and comment upon the more important of them. In some cases I indicate the effect that alternative procedures would have had in 1956, a year about midway through the postwar period and as representative as any other. My review suggests to me that I am more likely to underweight labor and overweight property inputs than the reverse. In addition to the points discussed here, the reader is reminded of the earlier mention of the inclusion of "pure" profit in property earnings, which tends to have this effect.

The Treatment of Taxes
in National Income at Factor Cost

To secure income shares, I have accepted the OBE measure of national income at factor cost, except for my revaluation of depreciation. To compile this series, OBE was required to make decisions with respect to the treatment of all types of taxes. My use of these data implies that the following statement is correct.

Given the quantity of each type of input actually used in the nonresidential business sector and its distribution among farms, nonfarm corporations, and other business:

1. The personal income tax and other personal taxes do not alter the percentage distribution among inputs of earnings measured inclusive of such taxes;

2. indirect business taxes do not alter the per-

centage distribution of earnings measured exclusive of such taxes;

3. the corporation income tax does not alter the distribution of earnings measured before deduction of these taxes from corporate profits; and

4. payroll taxes, whether nominally levied on employers or employees, do not alter the distribution of earnings when these taxes are included in employee compensation.

The statement is not, of course, exactly correct but I believe it to be substantially so. Errors are likely to be offsetting. A change in the classification of two items most likely to be questioned would affect the estimates in opposite directions. First, it is arguable that the property tax (or, alternatively, the portion levied on land) should be eliminated from indirect business taxes and counted instead as a return to property. If this change were made for the entire tax and my estimates recomputed, the labor share in 1956 would be lowered by 1.48 percentage points.[17] Second, it is arguable that the corporate income tax on firms in regulated industries should be treated as an indirect business tax instead of a tax on profits. If this change were made and my estimates recomputed, the labor share in 1956 would be raised by 1.13 percentage points.[18]

There are, of course, dissenting views with respect to the classification of many taxes. The one whose acceptance would most affect the estimates is that the corporate income tax not only in regulated industries but in its entirety is shifted "in the short run"—that is, taking as given the quantities of each type of input actually used by corporations—and that it should therefore be classified as an indirect tax. In 1956, this treatment would raise the labor share by 8.84 percentage points and reduce the nonlabor shares by nearly half. I myself share what I take to be the majority view of economists that outside the regulated in-

17. The calculation is based on use of $6,344 million as the total property tax on nonresidential property, of which $3,912 million was assigned to nonfarm corporate property, $1,454 million to nonfarm noncorporate property, and $978 million to farm property. (The total property tax was $11,453 million, of which $4,909 million is allocable to nonfarm dwellings and $200 million to farm dwellings, leaving $6,344 million. The farm figure of $978 million is the Department of Agriculture estimate for farm property less farm dwellings. The remainder was allocated between nonfarm corporate and nonfarm noncorporate in proportion to my estimates of the values of structures and land.)

18. The calculation is based on use of $3,159 million, all allocable to nonfarm corporations, for the value of this tax. (It is the value of the tax in the transportation, communications, and public utilities industries from NIA Table 6.14.)

dustries, at least, no large fraction of this tax is shifted. But it is possible that *some* amount of shifting takes place, resulting in understatement of my labor share.

Other Items Affecting National Income

My national income and property income estimates are based on the use of depreciation estimates calculated by use of Bulletin F service lives for structures and equipment and of straight-line depreciation. Use of shorter service lives would raise the labor earnings share a little; use of longer service lives would lower it. Adoption of the widely used double-declining balance formula to compute depreciation would raise the labor share. Estimates by Young suggest that in 1956 substitution of double-declining balance depreciation and 85 percent of Bulletin F lives for straight-line depreciation and Bulletin F lives would raise the labor share of national income in nonfinancial corporations by 1.0 percentage point.[19] The effect on the labor share of business national income would be about the same.

In national income measurement, consumer interest received by business lenders offsets interest paid by the firms lending to consumers. This is correct insofar as consumer interest really *is* "interest" matched by interest paid by these firms or returns to their owners, but questionable to the extent that it represents a service charge that covers salaries, rent, and other expenses of the lender. If half, for example, of consumer interest were classified as a service charge, this would lower the labor share in 1956 by about 0.7 percentage points.

The Allocation of Proprietors' Income

As explained earlier, I have allocated the earnings of farm proprietors and property income earned from farm property, together, between labor and property earnings in proportion to initial imputations of the amounts that (a) farm proprietors and unpaid family workers would earn from labor if their average compensation were the same as that of paid employees in the business sector and that (b) farm property would earn if the ratio of its earnings to the value of tangible assets were the same as in nonfarm corporations. The allocation procedure for nonfarm noncorporate earnings is similar. The farm earnings to be

allocated fall far short of the sum of (a) and (b). Nonfarm earnings fall moderately short in most years.

The initial imputations to labor and property in 1956 totaled $34.5 billion in farms and $37.3 billion in the noncorporate nonfarm sector. The amounts to be allocated were $13.1 billion and $35.3 billion, respectively.

The totals allocated in 1956 and the allocations are shown, in billions of dollars, in the first three rows of the following table.

	Farm	Noncorporate nonfarm
1. Earnings allocated	13.1	35.3
2. Labor	7.6	27.6
3. Property	5.5	7.7
4. Proprietors' property earnings	3.1	4.4
5. Other property earnings	2.4	3.3

The labor earnings in row 2 refer entirely to earnings of proprietors and unpaid family workers. But the earnings of nonresidential property in row 3 cover both the earnings of proprietors from their equity in the property they use (shown in row 4) and explicit property income components; the latter (shown in row 5) include earnings originating in business entities other than proprietorships and partnerships as well as in proprietorships and partnerships.[20]

Elimination of other property earnings indicates that in 1956 I allocated about 29 percent of farm proprietors' income (excluding earnings of farm dwellings) and about 14 percent of nonfarm proprietors' income to property income.

My general assumption that, with farm and nonfarm enterprises treated separately, unpaid labor and noncorporate nonfarm business property earn less, by the same percentage, than do paid labor and corporate property is dictated by the absence of any good reason to distinguish between the two.[21] The exact procedures could, however, have been varied; most, though not all, alternatives would yield a higher labor share.

---

19. Allan H. Young, "Alternative Estimates of Corporate Depreciation and Profits: Part II," *Survey of Current Business,* Vol. 48 (May 1968), Table 6, pp. 26–27.

20. "Other property earnings, farm" consist of net interest originating in the "farms" industry; rents paid to nonfarm landlords (excluding operating expenses); government payments to nonfarm landlords (excluding operating expenses); and profit of farm corporations.

"Other property earnings, noncorporate nonfarm" consist of rental income of persons from nonresidential nonfarm property; nonresidential interest paid by all types of nonfarm business except corporations and mutual financial institutions; and patronage dividends of cooperatives.

21. I see no good reason to impute earnings to either labor or property at the rate earned elsewhere and thus assign the entire shortfall to the other share, although such procedures have sometimes been adopted.

Thus hours of both farm and nonfarm proprietors and family workers are much longer than those of paid employees. If I had initially imputed the same hourly earnings instead of the same annual earnings to unpaid as to paid labor, more of the total would therefore have been allocated to labor. I believe the annual wage provides a better indication of the opportunity cost of not working in paid employment but some attention might have been paid to hours.

In making the initial imputations to unpaid labor, I made no adjustment for differences between the quality of paid and unpaid labor. A calculation, necessarily crude, attempted for 1966 yielded estimates that the average labor input provided by nonfarm proprietors and unpaid family workers was 4 percent bigger per person employed than that provided by business wage and salary workers, while that of farm proprietors and unpaid family workers was 15 percent smaller. This calculation took account of sex, years of education, and full-time or part-time status, but ignored differences among the three groups in the average hours of full-time workers.[22] If in 1956 the initial imputation to unpaid nonfarm labor had been raised 4 percent and that to farm workers lowered by 15 percent, to adjust for quality differences, my labor share in the nonresidential business sector would be lowered, but by only 0.10 percentage points.[23] If differences in full-time hours were considered to represent proportional differences in labor input, the 1966 calculation would yield estimates that the average labor input per worker provided by nonfarm proprietors and unpaid family workers was 32 percent bigger than that of business wage and salary workers,

and that of farm proprietors and unpaid family workers 13 percent bigger. Use of these percentages to adjust the initial labor imputations in 1956 would raise my labor share in the nonresidential business sector by 0.68 percentage points. However, as already indicated, I believe but little emphasis should be placed on the differences in full-time hours.

Total earnings of agricultural proprietors from all sources (farm and nonfarm) are apparently smaller (in 1967, by 5 percent) than total self-employment income from agriculture (including such income that is received by persons who are not agricultural proprietors); allowance for the difference would raise my labor share slightly.[24] The labor share would also be raised if an imputation were made for farm and nonfarm unpaid family workers at work less than fifteen hours a week, or if the numbers of farm and nonfarm unpaid family workers were based on establishment rather than household survey data. (See page 168, note 8.) It would be lowered if the number of nonfarm proprietors were pitched at the level indicated by the most recent household survey data. (See pages 173–74.)

My initial imputation of property earnings was obtained by multiplying the value of tangible farm and nonfarm corporate assets by the ratio of earnings to asset values in nonfarm corporations. It is sometimes suggested that the corporate income tax should be deducted from corporate earnings before the corporate ratio is calculated for application to noncorporate assets because this represents the opportunity cost to noncorporate investors. In 1956, adoption of this procedure would raise my labor share in the nonresidential business sector by 2.0 percentage points. It would transfer from property earnings to labor earnings $2.2 billion in farming and $3.6 billion in nonfarming. After deduction of explicit property earnings, only $0.9 billion in farming and $0.8 billion in nonfarming would be left for the return to proprietors from their equity. These amounts seem so small as to be unreasonable.[25]

22. "Full" earnings differentials, standardized by age, were used for education in this calculation, not the reduced differentials obtained after eliminating the effects of aptitude and other earnings determinants that are correlated with education.

23. The 15 percent used as the farm differential is a little bigger than that implied for the average year in Appendix N, but the difference scarcely affects the 0.10 point result.

Proprietors and unpaid family workers are sometimes assigned the same labor earnings as wage and salary workers in their industry, implying greater similarity between employees and proprietors in the same industry than in all industries combined. This procedure would yield a lower labor share because employee earnings in the professional service industries, retail trade, and farming are low. But it has no justification. Characteristics of wage and salary workers in these industries in which proprietors are concentrated are those generally associated with low earnings, but this is not at all the case with respect to proprietors in the same industries.

24. Calculations for 1967 are from U.S. Bureau of the Census, *Current Population Reports*, Series P-60, No. 60, "Income in 1967 of Persons in the United States" (1969), Tables 9 and 16.

25. If one accepted the rationale of the method, he would apply it better if he could divide the value of noncorporate farm and nonfarm assets separately between proprietors' equity in their ownership and the share of others; use actual earnings as shown in row 5 of the text table on page 269 for the earnings of the latter; and then apply the after-tax assumption only to allocate proprietors' income

They are sufficient reason to reject the procedure.[26]

The initial imputation to property is affected by errors in the percentage distribution of the value of tangible assets among the three sectors distinguished, though not in absolute values.[27] Since the estimates are based only on tangible assets, the procedure assumes that net holdings of non-income-yielding financial assets required for the conduct of business are distributed like tangible assets, but the possible error in the allocation deriving from this assumption appears to be trivial.

My estimates imply that in 1956 the ratio of property earnings to the value of tangible assets for nonresidential farm property was only 38 percent of the corresponding ratio for nonfarm corporations, and the ratio for nonresidential noncorporate nonfarm property was 95 percent of the nonfarm corporation ratio. The corresponding percentages in 1966 were 43 and 86. Some corroboration of the approximate level of the 1966 farm percentage of 43, and hence for the general procedure as applied to farms, is obtained from a comparison of farm and nonfarm corporations in 1966. The ratio of earnings to tangible asset value for farm corporations was 41 percent of the corresponding ratio for nonfarm corporations. In this calculation, earnings were based on use of tax depreciation and tangible asset values were book values as reported to the Internal Revenue Service.

The method of allocating proprietors' income now adopted replaces the method used in my previous studies. In them, I assumed the ratio of labor earnings in sole proprietorships and partnerships (farm and nonfarm) to national income originating in sole proprietorships and partnerships to be the same as the ratio of the compensation of employees of nonfinancial corporations to national income originating in nonfinancial corporations.[28] Abandonment of this method reflects the development of additional and improved information on asset values that permits use of a better method. My intent previously, as now, was to assume that labor not paid an explicit wage and noncorporate tangible assets earned less than paid labor and corporate assets by the same percentage. I was, of course, aware that the assumption of the same labor share implements this assumption accurately only if corporations, and proprietorships and partnerships, use labor and self-owned tangible assets in the same proportions. This turns out not to be the case.[29]

The Allocation of Property Earnings by Type of Asset

The property earnings of an enterprise can be observed (if one abstracts from the difficulties associated with noncorporate firms) but its earnings from each separate type of asset cannot. However, if it acts in such a way as to minimize costs, it will earn the same rate of return on each. This is the general assumption of my method for allocating earnings by type of asset. However, the method can implement the assumption only approximately.

First, I did not apply the assumption to individual enterprises. After eliminating dwellings and their sites, and vacant lots, I applied it to three groups of enterprises: nonfarm corporations, farms, and all noncorporate nonfarm business property. Within each of these groups, I must assume there is no correlation between rates of return earned by individual enterprises and the composition of their asset holdings.

Second, I implement the assumption that rates

---

between labor and property. I have been unable to derive the required allocation of asset values, but I am fairly sure this method would yield estimates more similar to mine than to those obtained by application of the after-tax assumption in the way illustrated in this paragraph.

26. In addition, I have considerable difficulty with the assumption that equilibrium would equalize the noncorporate rate of return and the corporate after-tax rate of return, while still allowing corporate and noncorporate firms to coexist. It ignores the personal income tax, and may also imply that corporate and noncorporate firms can charge different prices.

27. Because the distribution of tangible assets by type varies in the three sectors, it is also slightly affected by the accuracy of the statistical assumption, mentioned in the following section, that the same rate of return on different types of tangible assets implies the same ratio of earnings to asset values.

28. See *Why Growth Rates Differ*, p. 37.

29. In 1956, the old procedure would assign as labor earnings $8.6 billion to farm proprietors and $19.5 billion to nonfarm proprietors; these compare with my present estimates of $7.6 billion and $27.6 billion, respectively. The $15.8 billion that the old procedure would leave for the earnings of all nonfarm noncorporate property (which compares with my present estimate of $7.7 billion) is untenably high. It would imply that the ratio of earnings to the value of tangible assets was almost twice as large for noncorporate nonfarm property as for corporate nonfarm property with corporate profits measured before tax.

Not all of the error is due to a smaller labor component of input in the corporate sector than in proprietorships and partnerships as a whole. Part is due to the fact that the return to labor and property in farming, in which the labor proportion is low, was much below the return in the nonfarm noncorporate sector, in which the labor proportion is high. Separate treatment of the farm and nonfarm components clearly is appropriate.

of return from production on different assets are the same by assuming the ratio of net earnings to net asset values to be the same. This is a reasonable approximation, but it is not exact for two reasons. One is that the values of nonresidential land used by business may be elevated by the expectation of its transfer to a more remunerative use in the future than in the present, which would cause the ratio of current earnings to asset value to be lower for land than for reproducible assets used by the same enterprise. This possibility refers chiefly to farm land. (Residential and vacant land, it will be recalled, are excluded.) Suppose that in 1956 as much as one-fifth of farm land value were eliminated on these grounds before making the calculation.[30] The land share in the nonresidential business sector would be reduced by only 0.18 percentage points in 1956. The method of allocating earnings in agriculture would place most of the offset, 0.14 points, in the share of labor; the share of structures and equipment and that of inventories would each be raised by 0.02 percentage points. The other reason is that in the case of depreciable assets the ratio of current net earnings to net asset value varies with the amount of service life that has been exhausted and only by chance is exactly the same as the rate of return. I have discussed this point elsewhere.[31]

---

30. This would seem to be an overly generous reduction even in later years, when farm land values had risen further. Schultze concluded that the sharp rise in farm land values is fully explained by the rise in the earnings of farm land in farm use, without taking account of nonfarm demand for land on the fringes of urban areas. See Charles L. Schultze, *The Distribution of Farm Subsidies: Who Gets the Benefits?* (Brookings Institution, 1971), pp. 33–36, 50–51. For a discussion of the effect of prospective urban use on farm land values, see also Grace Milgram, *U.S. Land Prices— Directions and Dynamics,* Research Report 13, Prepared for the Consideration of the National Commission on Urban Problems (U.S. Government Printing Office, 1968).

31. See *Why Growth Rates Differ,* p. 143, and *The Sources of Economic Growth,* pp. 28, 33, 112–13, Appendix D.

⇉⟩⟨⟨

Relationship of Business Capital Input to Government Capital and Valuation of Used Capital Goods

⇉⟩⟨⟨

This appendix deals with two topics: the distinction between business capital and government capital in the capital stock series used in Chapter 5 to measure capital input, and the valuation of used structures and equipment sold by government to business.

Distinction between Business and Government Capital

The coverage of the series for capital stock (inventories and fixed capital) in the business sector that are presented in Table 5-2 is confined to privately owned assets. The distinction between business and government capital requires some explanation and comment.

1. All capital owned and used by general government is correctly omitted from the capital stock of the nonresidential business sector.[1]

1. See *Why Growth Rates Differ*, pp. 135–37, for a short discussion of the relationship between certain government services, including those requiring use of general government capital, and output per unit of input in business.

2. Privately owned capital goods leased to general government or government enterprises are correctly included. Their earnings are part of the earnings of private business capital, and their rent is part of the output of private business.

3. Capital owned and used by government enterprises is omitted even though government enterprises are classified in the business sector. A series for such capital is not available, but this is not the only reason. Although its omission is not wholly satisfactory, its inclusion would be even less so.

The difficulty with inclusion stems from the omission from national income in current prices (in both the series of the Office of Business Economics and my series) of property income (net profit before deduction of interest cost) earned by such enterprises.[2] Because of this omission, government enterprise capital carries zero weight in my weighting structure for the calculation of total input. Given these weights, its inclusion in the capital stock would have the effect of incorrectly assigning some of the weight properly belonging to private capital to government enterprise capital. Inclusion of government capital as a separate input with zero weight would, of course, change nothing.

Unfortunately, my omission of government enterprise capital is not satisfactory either because changes in the capital input of government enterprises may affect output. Although the base year *level* of national income in constant (1958) prices, like the current-price series, omits any earnings of government enterprise capital, if the movement of output is affected by changes in the stock of government enterprise capital the data will reflect it. This is because the same techniques of deflation are used for government enterprise production as for private business production.[3]

Consistent and correct treatment in national income measurement would require inclusion of the earnings of government enterprise capital in the national income. The value of this capital would then be counted in the business capital stock. Because the earnings and value of such capital are small relative to the earnings and value

2. OBE's reason, apparently, is reluctance to publish estimates of such earnings because this would require not only estimation of depreciation on government enterprise capital but also, and more difficult, distinguishing net earnings from losses that are intentionally incurred as a result of government policy and are in essence subsidies.
3. Most of the output is actually intermediate and consequently does not require explicit deflation. Final product is deflated by price indexes.

of private capital, their exclusion can cause but little error in the analysis of inputs in the business sector as a whole. Because suitable capital stock series for government enterprises are not available, the direction of any bias resulting from their omission is not known.

4. Government-owned capital goods made available to private business without charge, almost entirely for use in the production of commodities for sale to the government, are omitted. These government-owned, privately operated assets consist of Atomic Energy Commission plants and capital assets provided by the Department of Defense to contractors. Their exclusion is deliberate. Estimates that would permit inclusion of such capital, if it were desirable, are available from OBE.

The appropriate treatment of this capital depends upon the final contract prices (after renegotiation) that the federal government ultimately pays to contractors using these assets.

If the contract price does not provide government contractors with a return upon assets provided free by the government for use in filling contracts, then neither the value of output (national income) in current prices nor the return to capital includes any contribution from such assets. By the method of deflation, what is true of output in current prices is also true of output in constant prices. Under these conditions, this kind of capital is indistinguishable from other general government capital and is correctly omitted from capital input.

Inclusion of these assets in the capital stock with full weight based on their values would be appropriate only if contract prices were no lower than they would be if government contractors were required to provide their own capital goods at their own expense—or, more precisely, if they earned as much on government assets as business generally earns on its own assets. In that case, output and capital earnings would include a contribution from these assets similar to that from private capital. That this is so seems to me implausible. In general, the capital is placed in industries where all contractors obtain it free so that no return would result if contracts were competitive. If (more typically) contracts are placed at cost plus a fixed fee, nonexistent capital costs would have to be included in "cost" for such a return to be earned.

Changes that would be introduced in my estimates if these assets were included with full weight can be approximated because OBE has estimated their value. Their gross stock value in constant prices was trivial in 1929 and 1940, shot up sharply during World War II, and declined from the end of the war until about 1950. Thereafter, it remained stable, but declined relative to private capital. If it were added to the value of the gross stock of private fixed capital shown in Table 5-2, the series would be raised by approximately the percentages shown for selected years in column 1 of Table K-1. This would considerably change the movement of the structures and equipment index within the 1940–50 period. From 1950 to 1968 it would reduce the average growth rate of structures and equipment input by about

Table K-1. Percentage Increases in Business Gross Stock of Nonresidential Structures and Equipment Valued in 1958 Dollars if Two Alternative Procedures Were Adopted, Selected Years, 1929–68[a]

Year	Addition of government-owned, privately operated capital (1)	Substitution of cost to government for sales price in valuing used assets sold by government to business[b] (2)
1929	0.3	1.1
1940	0.1	1.5
1941	1.0	1.4
1947	10.0	3.6
1950	5.9	5.0
1955	4.6	4.2
1960	3.8	3.0
1965	3.2	1.9
1968	2.8	1.2

Source: Robert C. Wasson, John C. Musgrave, and Claudia Harkins, "Alternative Estimates of Fixed Business Capital in the United States, 1925–1968," *Survey of Current Business*, Vol. 50 (April 1970), pp. 18–36. Data are based on use of the OBE "series 2" price deflator, and are averages of values at the beginning and end of each year.

Column 1: Government-owned, privately operated stock from Table 7 as a percentage of the difference between all privately owned stock from Table 1 and institutional, social, and recreational stock from Table 2.

Column 2: Difference between privately owned stock from Table 4 and privately owned stock from Table 1 as a percentage of the difference between all privately owned stock from Table 1 and institutional, social, and recreational stock from Table 2.

a. Values of business gross stock of nonresidential structures and equipment, valued in 1958 dollars, appear in Table 5-2, column 3. Percentages presented here are not strictly comparable with data shown in Table 5-2, however, because percentages in this table are based on use of 85 percent of Bulletin F service lives whereas data in Table 5-2 are based on use of 100 percent of Bulletin F service lives. Also, the deletion for nonprofit organization capital is slightly different.

b. These increases are slightly understated as a result of the valuation of business sector sales of used equipment to foreigners (which are eliminated from the stock) at original cost in the standard series and at sales price in the alternative series.

0.17 percentage points. The growth rate of total input and the contribution of capital to growth in the business sector would each be reduced by less than 0.02 percentage points in this period.

Given the complexities of pricing and re-negotiating government contracts, the possibility that contractors secure the equivalent of *some* return on assets provided by the government cannot be disregarded. If they do, inclusion of these assets with a reduced weight would be justified. My presumption is that if any weight at all is warranted, the fraction is small in relation to the value of the assets and the error in the capital input series is small relative to the changes that would be introduced by including their full value in the business stock. I do not believe any error deriving from their complete omission can significantly impair the index for structures and equipment input.

Valuation of Used Assets Sold by Government to Private Business

The federal government regularly sells surplus structures and equipment to business. Quantities are ordinarily small but were large from 1945 through 1948. Capital goods sold in that period had originally been acquired by the government for defense production or for use by the armed forces in World War II. Purchases of used assets by business from government were entered into both of the capital stock series for nonresidential structures and equipment shown in Table 5-2 at their purchase prices (adjusted by the difference between capital goods prices in the year acquired and 1958). The net stock series so constructed is correct if the prices paid by business were such that the expected return to business from the purchase of these assets was the same as that expected from the alternative open to firms—purchase of capital assets newly produced at the time the government assets were sold. Because surplus is generally sold on a competitive basis and the government seeks the highest available sales price, it would seem plausible at first sight that the stated condition is a tolerable approximation to the truth. Those most familiar with the situation believe, however, that business purchases of important classes of assets were at bargain prices. Large quantities of equipment were thrown on the market immediately after World War II under the equivalent of forced sale conditions. Government-owned manufacturing plants which had been used

by defense contractors in wartime were sometimes subsequently sold to the same firm; because of their location and installation, such plants had greater value to the purchasing firm than to potential competitive bidders, and sales price was usually negotiated. It is likely that assets acquired from the government are undervalued in the net stock series relative to those acquired new at the same time. They are undervalued more in the gross stock series because they were entered into this series, too, at their sales price. A more appropriate gross stock valuation, it would seem, would be obtained if the sales price had been raised by the ratio of gross value to net value for assets of their type, age, and condition.

Capital goods purchased new and those purchased used at the same time should be combined in the gross stock series by use of their marginal products (or ability to contribute to business production) as weights.[4] Although use of sales prices probably causes assets acquired by business from government to be underweighted by reference to this criterion, I find it impossible to venture a guess as to the amount by which they are underweighted. Moreover, their weight in the capital stock series used is not available, so that the effect of adjusting their prices by any given percentage cannot be tested easily or with precision.

OBE *has* prepared an alternative gross stock series in which used assets sold by government to business are valued at their original cost to the government (adjusted to 1958 prices). These original cost values range from less than the sales price in the case of pipelines and not much more than sales price in the case of manufacturing facilities for standard commodities in peacetime demand, such as synthetic rubber, to many times the sales price for certain types of equipment.[5] In the immediate postwar period sales price for structures may have averaged about 40 percent, and that of equipment 10 or 15 percent, of orig-

4. I regard all capital obtained by business in a given year as of the same "vintage."
5. OBE estimates of the sales value, adjusted to 1958 prices, of sales to business (including items later resold abroad) indicate the composition of these sales by broad categories. In the four-year period, 1945–48, sales totaled $4.8 billion (at constant price 2). Structures were $2.0 billion, of which $1.8 billion were manufacturing structures and $0.2 billion pipelines. Equipment was $2.8 billion, including $1.2 billion of ships and boats; $0.5 billion of trucks, buses, and truck trailers; $0.4 billion of metal-working machinery; $0.2 billion of aircraft; and $0.1 billion each of construction machinery, special industry machinery, tractors, and general industry machinery. No other category amounted to as much as $50 million.

inal cost to the government, but these are rough estimates.

While sales price is too small, it is obvious that original cost to the government greatly exceeds the value of the goods to their business buyers at the time they were purchased, relative to newly produced goods then available. They were produced at an earlier time, and hence were less technologically advanced. They were purchased by the government for particular uses that sometimes were quite different from those to which business applied them in supplying peacetime markets. Munitions plants and landing craft, for example, were highly specific to wartime demand patterns and military requirements and could be disposed of only at very low prices for this reason. The cost of much equipment was raised by special features required for wartime use by government but not necessary for peacetime use by business. Some items, notably vessels, were produced under crash conditions with specifications that sacrificed economy in operation to quick mass production. Some of the capital goods purchased required expensive change and modification for business use. Probably but little of what was sold (most metal-working machinery is an exception) corresponded exactly to what business would have selected if ordering new capital goods. Ground transportation equipment and construction equipment used by the armed forces was badly maintained after fighting stopped and in poor condition when sold. The government did not provide guarantees like those ordinarily furnished by business firms that sell new capital goods, nor similar provisions for servicing. It was sometimes difficult for purchasers even to be sure just what they were obtaining.

The approximate percentages by which the gross stock series used in my calculation would be raised if original cost to the government were substituted for sales price in valuing these assets is shown for selected years in Table K-1, column 2.[6] Half of these amounts would seem to

me to provide an outer limit (*not* an estimate) of the amounts by which the capital input series might be in error as a result of undervaluation of used assets acquired by business from the government. It would imply valuation of structures at something like 70 percent, and equipment at perhaps 55 or 60 percent, of the original cost to the government adjusted for changes in capital goods prices. If my estimates of the stock of business nonresidential structures and equipment were raised by half of the percentages shown in Table K-1, the growth rate of this input would change by the amounts shown in the first column of the following table, and the growth rate of total input in the business sector (excluding dwellings) and the contribution of structures and equipment to this growth rate would both change by the amounts shown in the second column.

Period	Change in growth rate of structures and equipment	Change in growth rate of total input
1929–68	0.00	0.00
1929–50	0.09	0.01
1929–40	0.02	0.00
1940–41	−0.05	−0.01
1941–47	0.18	0.02
1947–50	0.23	0.03
1950–68	−0.10	−0.01
1950–55	−0.08	−0.01
1955–60	−0.12	−0.01
1960–65	−0.11	−0.01
1965–68	−0.12	−0.01

It is within the period from 1941 through 1950 that the index of structures and equipment input is most subject to error from undervaluation of these assets. Possible error is largest in comparisons involving the years 1947 to 1949. The increase in structures and equipment input since 1950 could be overstated by as much as 0.10 percent a year, on the average, and the growth rate of total input in the business sector and the contribution of capital to that growth rate by as much as 0.01 percentage points a year. Undervaluation of these assets could not have been a source of erratic error in year-to-year changes after 1950.

6. An additional difference is actually involved in these percentages; business sales to foreigners are valued at sales price in the series I use and at original cost in the alternative series. The two differences cannot readily be disentangled for the following reason. Large amounts of government surplus were sold to foreigners. In the capital stock study calculations, part of these sales (notably the large aircraft component) was handled as both entering the business stock as sales by government to business (that is, to dealers) and leaving the stock as sales by business to foreigners. The way assets that have been used by business since they were new, and are then sold abroad, are valued has little effect on the capital stock index.

Addendum

The author cautions that he has no special knowledge of government contracting nor of surplus disposal and claims no more for judgments expressed on these matters than that they seem reasonable to him. Government-owned, privately operated capital and/or the valuation of used assets have been discussed by OBE staff members in the *Survey of Current Business*[7] and by Gordon and Jaszi in the *American Economic Review*.[8] I have benefited greatly from discussion of these (and other) aspects of capital stock measurement with Robert C. Wasson, but he bears no responsibility at all for judgments expressed here.

7. See especially Donald G. Wooden and Robert C. Wasson, "Manufacturing Investment Since 1929 in Relation to Employment, Output, and Income," *Survey of Current Business*, Vol. 36 (November 1956), pp. 8–20; Lawrence Grose, Irving Rottenberg, and Robert C. Wasson, "New Estimates of Fixed Business Capital in the United States, 1925–65," *Survey of Current Business*, Vol. 46 (December 1966), pp. 34–40; and Robert C. Wasson, John C. Musgrave, and Claudia Harkins, "Alternative Estimates of Fixed Business Capital in the United States, 1925–1968," *Survey of Current Business*, Vol. 50 (April 1970), pp. 18–36.

8. Robert J. Gordon, "$45 Billion of U.S. Private Investment Has Been Mislaid," *American Economic Review*, Vol. 59 (June 1969), pp. 221–38; George Jaszi, "Comment," and Robert J. Gordon, "Reply," *American Economic Review*, Vol. 60 (December 1970), pp. 934–39 and 940–45, respectively.

APPENDIX L

⇢⋙✕⋘

Alternative Computations of Total Factor Input in Nonresidential Business

⇢⋙✕⋘

This appendix examines only the question of whether my division of changes in output between changes in total factor input and changes in output per unit of input is sensitive to the particular way that I have used my adjusted estimates of income shares to construct an index of total input. It is not concerned with the accuracy, or relevance, of the estimates of the adjusted shares themselves nor with the implications of the alternative procedures examined here for the allocation of the contribution of total input among the individual inputs.

My index of total factor input in the business sector, excluding dwellings, is repeated in Table L-1, column 1. As explained in Chapter 5, this index was computed by linking annual percentage changes. The annual percentage changes were obtained by weighting the percentage change in each input by its average share of earnings (adjusted to eliminate cyclical fluctuations) in the two-year period.[1] Two purposes are served by altering the weights for each annual change. First, the procedure takes account of any developments other than changes in factor proportions that may

1. Longer periods are used in 1929–40 and 1941–47.

have altered the relative marginal products of the factors from time to time. Second (given the conditions other than factor proportions prevailing in the two-year period), the relative marginal products of the factors are based on factor proportions actually prevailing, on the average, in the two-year period examined. Thus there is no need

Table L-1. Nonresidential Business: Indexes of Total Factor Input Calculated by Alternative Procedures,[a] 1929, 1940–41, and 1947–69

1958 = 100

	Chain indexes of percentage changes using total share weights		Constant marginal product weights based on marginal products in:		
Year	Weights changed annually (1)	Constant (1929–69 average) weights (2)	1929 (3)	1958 (4)	1969 (5)
1929	72.12	72.06	72.22	72.36	73.00
1940	73.79	73.72	73.94	74.20	74.88
1941	80.06	80.03	80.30	80.68	81.31
1947	89.12	89.14	89.61	90.10	90.62
1948	90.54	90.56	90.92	91.39	91.86
1949	88.40	88.35	88.51	88.85	89.30
1950	91.17	91.12	91.27	91.65	92.06
1951	95.52	95.45	95.63	96.00	96.31
1952	97.91	97.81	97.98	98.30	98.55
1953	99.98	99.88	100.04	100.37	100.57
1954	97.67	97.59	97.64	97.85	98.04
1955	100.67	100.57	100.62	100.88	101.02
1956	102.51	102.40	102.45	102.65	102.73
1957	102.59	102.51	102.54	102.66	102.69
1958	100.00	100.00	100.00	100.00	100.00
1959	103.17	103.11	103.11	103.17	103.13
1960	103.99	103.96	103.98	103.98	103.90
1961	103.98	103.99	104.05	103.98	103.85
1962	106.07	106.07	106.15	106.07	105.89
1963	107.64	107.66	107.80	107.65	107.41
1964	109.80	109.82	110.02	109.83	109.51
1965	113.35	113.35	113.63	113.40	113.00
1966	117.31	117.32	117.73	117.41	116.88
1967	119.20	119.20	119.80	119.33	118.68
1968	122.37	122.36	123.09	122.56	121.80
1969	125.48	125.45	126.33	125.74	124.87

Addendum: shares of total earnings used in calculations[a]

Labor	b	79.54	79.59	81.84	80.18
Structures and equipment	b	11.54	10.69	11.01	11.94
Inventory	b	4.58	4.41	3.80	3.82
Land	b	4.35	5.31	3.35	4.06

Sources: Column 1, Table 5-4, column 7; other columns, see text for derivation.

a. See text for explanation.

b. Shares used each period are shown in Table J-2.

278

for any special assumption as to what would happen to relative marginal products if factor proportions were to change appreciably (as they did over the forty-year period as a whole) but no change in relative marginal products were to occur for other reasons.

One alternative would be to change the procedure only by substituting the average shares during the whole 1929–69 period for the two-year average shares in the computation of annual percentage changes in the composite index. This would be consistent with the assumption of unit elasticity of substitution among the four factors (the Cobb-Douglas assumption extended to four factors) and the additional assumption that nothing except changes in factor proportions (for example, non-neutral "technological change") altered relative marginal products of the factors at any time during this forty-year period.

The combination of these two assumptions would produce constant shares. Because this is inconsistent with my estimates, which show moderate changes in shares, the procedure would be superior only if the changes in shares that I find did not really occur and are mere errors of estimate. A series constructed by this procedure is shown in the second column of Table L-1. It turns out to be scarcely distinguishable from my preferred series. This is not very surprising since the actual variation in my weights is quite modest. It is reassuring because it indicates that errors in my estimates of fluctuations in the shares could introduce but little error in the index. It also has a practical implication for projections to future periods for which "actual" shares are not available so my method cannot be used; it suggests that substitution of this alternative procedure will scarcely affect the results.

It is also possible to compute indexes incorporating a very different assumption, namely, that the relative marginal products of the factors were wholly unaffected by changes in factor proportions. This implies that the elasticity of substitution is infinite. To incorporate this assumption easily, it is necessary to retain the assumption of the preceding variant that nothing other than factor proportions altered relative marginal products. An index incorporating the assumption that relative marginal products at all other dates were the same as in 1929 is shown in column 3 of Table L-1. It was constructed by converting each of the four input indexes from 1958 = 100 to 1929 = 100, multiplying each index by the 1929

share of the input in total earnings, and adding the four products. To allow comparison with the other series, the resulting index was shifted to 1958 = 100. Columns 4 and 5 of the table show indexes similarly constructed but using marginal products in 1958 or 1969, respectively, in place of 1929 marginal products. To construct these series, shares in 1958 or 1969 were used to combine indexes expressed with 1958 or 1969 as 100.[2]

It is remarkable how little the index in column 2 is altered by so drastic a change in the assumption as to substitutability of the factors, or even—as indicated by comparison of columns 3 to 5—by changing the year used to measure marginal products.

If the assumption of these last three indexes were correct, then the share of any factor whose quantity increased over time by more than the average amount would rise. The following table shows my estimate of the shares in 1929 and 1968, and the shares that would be predicted for 1968 if the relative marginal products of the four inputs were the same in 1968 as in 1929 (the assumption of the index in column 3 of Table L-1).[3]

	Estimated		*Predicted by assumption of third series,*
	1929	*1968*	*1968*
Labor	79.59	79.82	76.82
Structures and equipment	10.69	12.14	13.51
Inventories	4.41	3.98	6.55
Land	5.31	4.06	3.12

The Cobb-Douglas prediction that 1968 shares would be the same as the 1929 shares would come much closer to the estimated 1968 shares than the prediction based on this extreme assumption of infinite elasticity of substitution among the factors.

The latter assumption contradicts the principle

---

2. Total shares in the three years used are shown in the addendum to Table L-1. They are the adjusted annual estimates which were averaged with those for adjacent years to obtain the weights shown in Table J-2. These total shares should not be confused with earnings per unit of each of the four inputs, which are the real weights used in the three indexes. The latter differ among the indexes much more than do the total share weights, and not necessarily in the same direction. It is the expression of the individual input indexes with alternative base years (1929, 1958, 1969) as 100 that produces the major differences among the composite indexes with respect to weighting of the component indexes.

3. This is a percentage distribution of the products obtained by multiplying the 1929 share of each input by the 1968 index for that input expressed with 1929 equal to 100.

of diminishing returns and is not recommended by any economist I know; the point of calculating indexes based upon it is to show that use of a more reasonable intermediate assumption (elasticity of substitution greater than one) could not yield an index of total factor input much different from that obtained on the assumption of unit elasticity—or from that which I obtain.

The consequences of introducing an assumption at the opposite extreme—that elasticity of substitution among the factors is zero—cannot be calculated in any interesting fashion because it implies constant factor proportions, and if these actually existed there would be no problem of weighting. The assumption bars the possibility that different inputs can increase at different rates—or, if we observe that they in fact do so, it requires us to believe that only increases in other factors that are no greater than that in the factor increasing least add anything to output; the excess is merely wasted. If land is counted as a separate input in this formulation there could be

no change in total input. If land and the two types of capital input are considered a single input, then the growth of total factor input after 1947 would be the same as that in labor input under this assumption.

There is, of course, no similar anomaly in an assumption that elasticities of substitution are less than one but greater than zero. It is fair to infer from the effects of moving to an assumption of elasticity greater than one (in moving from column 2 to column 3, 4, or 5 of Table L-1) that moving to elasticity somewhat less than one would have similarly small effects. Indeed, Richard Nelson has shown by use of illustrative numbers that a measure of total input is not sensitive to even large changes in either direction in assumptions with respect to elasticity of substitution.[4]

4. Richard R. Nelson, *Aggregate Production Functions and Medium-Range Growth Projections,* Rand RM-3912-PR (Santa Monica, Calif.: RAND Corporation, December 1962); and Nelson, "The CES Production Function and Economic Growth Projections," *Review of Economics and Statistics,* Vol. 47 (August 1965), pp. 326–28.

Comparison
of Output per
Man-Hour Series

➤➤✕◀◀

Table M-1. Comparison of Indexes of GNP per Man-Hour in the Private Economy (BLS) and National Income per Man-Hour in Nonresidential Business (Denison), 1929, 1940–41, and 1947–69
1958 = 100

Year	Output per man-hour, total private economy, BLS		Output per man-hour, nonresidential business, Denison (3)	Ratio of output per man-hour, Denison, to:	
	Establishment basis (1)	Labor force basis (2)		Output per man-hour on establishment basis, BLS (4)	Output per man-hour on labor force basis, BLS (5)
1929	48.3	47.7	47.9	0.9919	1.0046
1940	58.4	57.6	58.3	0.9982	1.0116
1941	62.0	61.3	63.2	1.0188	1.0313
1947	69.1	68.3	70.4	1.0182	1.0305
1948	72.1	70.6	74.5	1.0329	1.0552
1949	74.3	72.3	75.7	1.0181	1.0465
1950	80.5	79.0	81.5	1.0127	1.0317
1951	82.9	82.6	82.8	0.9996	1.0028
1952	84.5	85.0	84.4	0.9997	0.9934
1953	88.0	88.9	87.7	0.9971	0.9864
1954	90.1	91.3	89.2	0.9906	0.9768
1955	94.1	95.3	95.3	1.0128	1.0002
1956	94.3	95.2	96.3	1.0214	1.0119
1957	97.1	97.8	98.4	1.0131	1.0059
1958	100.0	100.0	100.0	1.0000	1.0000
1959	103.6	104.0	105.7	1.0203	1.0162
1960	105.2	105.1	107.5	1.0219	1.0227
1961	108.8	107.9	110.6	1.0168	1.0250
1962	114.0	113.7	116.1	1.0180	1.0210
1963	118.1	117.4	120.5	1.0200	1.0263
1964	122.7	121.7	125.7	1.0240	1.0326
1965	126.9	125.8	130.6	1.0299	1.0389
1966	132.0	131.5	135.3	1.0253	1.0290
1967	134.7	134.4	137.6	1.0221	1.0241
1968	138.5	139.4	142.3	1.0266	1.0202
1969	139.1	140.7	142.5	1.0241	1.0127

Sources: Columns 1 and 2, U.S. Bureau of Labor Statistics; column 3, estimates by Edward F. Denison; column 4, column 3 ÷ column 1; column 5, column 3 ÷ column 2.

A by-product of my analysis is a series for output per man-hour in the nonresidential business sector. For general-purpose use, it provides an alternative to the Bureau of Labor Statistics (BLS) indexes of output per man-hour in the private economy. The two BLS series are compared with mine in Table M-1.

The general trend of the three series is so similar that one's perception of the long-term rate of increase in output per man-hour is scarcely affected by the choice of series. However, there are some fairly pronounced differences in short-term movement. A reconciliation of the numerators, the measures of output, of my series and the BLS series is provided in Table M-2 for the postwar years. A reconciliation of the denominators, man-hours, of my series and the more widely used of the BLS series—that based on establishment data—is provided in Table M-3.[1]

My series for output per man-hour differs in several respects from the BLS establishment series, and BLS might wish to consider whether adoption of at least some of my procedures would increase the accuracy or usefulness of its own series.

1. Three steps have been taken to increase statistical consistency between the output and man-hours estimates. Output is measured "from the income side" (by subtracting the deflated sta-

1. All of the reconciliation items have been discussed and described elsewhere in this study.

tistical discrepancy). The man-hour series is tied to the OBE employment series which is consistent with the employee compensation estimates entering into the output measure so derived. The introduction of Alaska and Hawaii into the estimates in 1960 is handled by linking, which avoids slight understatement of the 1959–60 increase in output per man-hour resulting from a larger addition to man-hours than to output.

Table M-2. Reconciliation of Private GNP with National Income Originating in Nonresidential Business, 1947–69
Billions of 1958 dollars

Year	Private GNP, OBE (1)	Statistical discrepancy (2)	Private GNP from "income side" (col. 1 − col. 2) (3)	Substitution of price deflator 2 for private nonresidential structures (4)	Private GNP from "income side" adjusted for prices (col. 3 + col. 4) (5)	GNP originating in households, institutions, and "rest of the world"[a] (6)	Nonlabor GNP originating in dwellings (7)	GNP originating in nonresidential business (col. 5 − col. 6 − col. 7) (8)	Adjustments to arrive at national income (9)	National income originating in nonresidential business, Denison (col. 8 − col. 9) (10)
				Excluding Alaska and Hawaii						
1947	281.4	1.2	280.2	−1.1	279.1	9.2	15.9	254.1	42.1	212.0
1948	295.0	−2.4	297.4	−0.6	296.9	9.6	16.6	270.6	44.7	225.9
1949	294.1	0.4	293.7	−0.5	293.2	10.0	18.2	265.1	46.1	218.9
1950	324.2	1.8	322.4	−0.6	321.8	10.6	19.3	291.9	50.2	241.8
1951	344.6	3.8	340.8	−0.7	340.0	10.7	20.9	308.4	53.3	255.2
1952	353.2	2.4	350.8	−0.8	350.0	10.7	22.5	316.8	54.9	261.9
1953	371.1	3.3	367.8	−0.8	367.0	11.1	24.0	331.8	57.3	274.5
1954	366.2	3.0	363.2	−0.6	362.6	11.6	25.6	325.4	57.4	268.0
1955	397.2	2.3	394.9	−0.4	394.5	12.7	27.1	354.7	60.9	293.7
1956	404.8	−1.2	406.0	−0.5	405.5	13.5	28.4	363.6	62.7	300.9
1957	410.5	0.0	410.5	−0.3	410.2	14.0	29.9	366.3	64.1	302.2
1958	405.2	1.6	403.6	0.0	403.6	14.4	31.5	357.7	64.5	293.2
1959	433.4	−0.8	434.2	0.3	434.5	15.0	32.6	387.0	67.7	319.3
1960[b]	...	...	...	...	...	...	...	...	...	324.7
				Including Alaska and Hawaii						
1960	444.0	−1.0	445.0	0.6	445.6	15.6	35.1	395.0	69.2	325.8
1961	452.3	−0.7	453.0	0.8	453.9	16.5	36.6	400.8	70.5	330.3
1962	482.9	0.5	482.4	0.8	483.3	17.5	38.8	427.0	73.8	353.1
1963	503.2	−0.3	503.5	0.9	504.4	17.9	41.2	445.2	76.6	368.6
1964	532.0	−1.2	533.2	1.1	534.3	18.9	44.2	471.2	79.9	391.2
1965	567.0	−2.9	569.9	1.4	571.3	19.6	47.4	504.3	84.5	419.8
1966	603.5	−0.9	604.4	1.6	606.0	20.1	49.8	536.1	89.8	446.4
1967	617.5	−0.6	618.1	1.5	619.5	21.4	52.5	545.7	92.9	452.8
1968	647.0	−2.3	649.3	1.6	650.9	22.2	54.6	574.1	97.9	476.2
1969	664.0	−3.3	667.7	1.6	669.3	22.4	57.2	589.8	101.7	488.1

Sources: U.S. Office of Business Economics and estimates by Edward F. Denison.
a. Includes institutional depreciation.
b. Not used by U.S. Bureau of Labor Statistics.

2. The scope of my series is narrower. BLS omits general government from its series because output is measured by labor input. My series excludes, in addition, households, institutions, foreign governments, and international organizations, whose output is also measured by labor input. Also omitted are two important components of output for which there are no corresponding man-hour inputs: net property income from abroad, and the earnings of dwellings.

3. Estimates of hours paid for but not worked are deducted from man-hours.

4. Output is measured by national income (net national product at factor cost) rather than by gross national product.

In addition, I have substituted OBE nonresidential construction estimates based on use of OBE price deflator 2 for those based on deflator 1. However, this has little effect on the index of GNP and even less on that of national income.

Table M-3. Reconciliation of Total Weekly Hours Paid for in the Private Economy (BLS, Establishment Basis) with Total Weekly Hours Worked in Nonresidential Business (Denison), 1947–69
Hundreds of thousands of hours

Year	Total weekly hours paid for:					Total weekly hours paid for but not worked (6)	Business sector, total weekly hours worked, Denison (col. 5 − col. 6) (7)
	Private economy, BLS (1)	Households and institutions (2)	Business sector (col. 1 − col. 2) (3)	Business sector, statistical difference between Denison and BLS (4)	Business sector, Denison (col. 3 + col. 4) (5)		
	Excluding Alaska and Hawaii						
1947	23,635	1,450	22,185	− 21	22,164	689	21,475
1948	23,721	1,442	22,279	50	22,329	709	21,620
1949	22,925	1,444	21,481	−170	21,311	684	20,627
1950	23,377	1,562	21,816	79	21,894	731	21,163
1951	24,133	1,592	22,540	227	22,768	796	21,972
1952	24,263	1,581	22,682	264	22,946	828	22,118
1953	24,467	1,625	22,842	343	23,185	866	22,319
1954	23,571	1,613	21,958	316	22,274	852	21,422
1955	24,489	1,752	22,738	141	22,878	891	21,987
1956	24,913	1,810	23,103	114	23,217	932	22,285
1957	24,546	1,821	22,725	141	22,866	956	21,910
1958	23,506	1,858	21,648	199	21,847	933	20,914
1959	24,273	1,906	22,367	137	22,504	963	21,541
1960ᵃ	...	...	...	...	...	...	21,538
	Including Alaska and Hawaii						
1960	24,474	1,962	22,512	102	22,615	992	21,623
1961	24,099	1,991	22,108	186	22,294	994	21,300
1962	24,574	2,043	22,531	199	22,730	1,024	21,707
1963	24,713	2,092	22,621	253	22,874	1,046	21,829
1964	25,148	2,122	23,026	265	23,291	1,083	22,209
1965	25,920	2,146	23,774	288	24,062	1,132	22,929
1966	26,534	2,170	24,364	389	24,753	1,216	23,537
1967	26,602	2,250	24,353	361	24,714	1,240	23,474
1968	27,103	2,229	24,874	310	25,185	1,281	23,903
1969	27,689	2,429	25,261	521	25,782	1,332	24,451

Sources: U.S. Bureau of Labor Statistics and estimates by Edward F. Denison.
a. Not used by U.S. Bureau of Labor Statistics.

⭆⭆⭆⭆⭆

Nonresidential Business: Gains from the Reallocation of Resources

⭆⭆⭆⭆⭆

This appendix describes the derivation of Table 6-1, columns 2 and 3.

The Shift of Resources from Farming

Throughout the period covered by this study the fraction of the economy's employed labor that was devoted to farming was much larger than the fraction that would have maximized national income.

The main reason is embedded in history. One need not ask whether the allocation of labor to farming was always too large for maximum output. It suffices to observe that the proportion and even the absolute number of the nation's workers that would optimally have been allocated to farming have been persistently declining since long before 1929, and the actual movement of labor has not kept pace. The decline in the optimal number of workers was the result of differences between farm and nonfarm products with respect to trends in demand, in technology, and in the substitution of capital for labor. In addition, the production of agricultural products themselves was increasingly obtained by use of nonfarm intermediate products, such as commercial fertilizer, produced with nonfarm labor. The movement of labor from farming to other activities that was needed to keep pace with changing labor requirements encountered substantial obstacles: it entailed not only the change in occupation and industry that accompanies most shifts in demand patterns, but also geographic relocation and even a change in the farm workers' way of life. Because proprietors and family workers provided most farm labor, declining demand for labor did not promptly force a corresponding curtailment of employment or average hours as in the case of industries, such as coal mining, that relied on hired labor. The decline in farm employment continually lagged far behind the decline in requirements. Much of the transfer of labor was achieved only with the passing of generations—as farmers' sons did not replace their fathers on the farm. During the decade of the 1930s, moreover, the movement away from farming was greatly checked—and for a time even reversed—by the absence of nonfarm jobs. A massive reduction of farm employment has nevertheless occurred.

Much of the surplus labor in farming has been inefficiently used on small farms with little output, and these farms have been the source of most of the decline in farm employment. At any point in time total farm output would have been but little smaller if such farms, accounting for a large fraction of farm employment, had simply vanished. If the land had been transferred to the remaining farms, the output loss would have been even less. The labor used on these farms could have added substantially to nonfarm output if it had been transferred to nonfarm work. Much farm labor, of course, has been used on farms of reasonably large size. It was efficiently used in the sense that it could not have been withdrawn from farm work without substantially reducing farm output, but even this labor contributed less to the value of national income than it would have done if employed in nonfarm work because overallocation held down farm earnings and prices relative to those in nonfarm activities.

The cost of overallocation of resources to farming has been declining as the farm sector has shrunk. In the postwar period this is partly because the labor withdrawn from farming has been drawn chiefly from small inefficient units, and its elimination has contributed to an exceptionally large rise in output per unit of input in farming as a whole; stated differently, the percentage of *farm* labor that has been misallocated has declined. But the more important point is that farm resources that were misallocated would have been a sharply declining percentage of *total* resources, and the cost of misallocation as a percentage of total national income would have declined, even if the percentage of farm resources that were misallocated had not changed. This contributed substantially to the rise in output per unit of input in the nonresidential business sector as a whole.

The Farm Shares of Output and Labor

Table N-1 shows changes in the importance of farming in the total output of the nonresidential business sector and the total labor used by the sector.

The percentage of sector national income that originated in farming, expressed in 1958 prices and in current prices, is shown in columns 1 and 2.[1] Farm national income in 1958 prices dropped from 11.4 percent of the nonresidential business total in 1929 to 7.6 percent in 1947 and 4.2 percent in 1969. Over the postwar period, the drop in the farm percentage was equal to 3.4 percent of total income in the sector.

Columns 3 to 5 show alternative measures of the percentage of labor in the sector that was used in farming. Column 3 shows simple percentages of total employment. Percentages in column 4 are computed from data that are moved as far toward my labor input measure as can readily be done on an annual basis. They are consistent with the way labor input was measured (in Chapter 4) with respect to the treatment of employment, hours of work, and sex composition.[2] However, farm-non-

Table N-1. Farm Percentages of Output, Employment, and Labor Input in the Nonresidential Business Sector, 1929, 1940–41, and 1947–69

Year	National income measured in: Constant 1958 prices (1)	Current prices (2)	Employment Full-time and part-time (3)	Full-time equiv-alent weighted by sex[a] (4)	Labor input (5)
1929	11.41	11.84	24.08	25.01	22.74
1940	11.07	9.49	21.90	23.78	21.54
1941	10.14	10.01	20.11	21.28	19.21
1947	7.55	11.56	15.88	16.37	14.69
1948	7.79	11.56	15.50	15.97	14.33
1949	7.63	9.35	15.65	16.28	14.61
1950	7.20	9.00	14.98	15.52	13.92
1951	6.35	9.04	13.50	13.95	12.49
1952	6.34	8.31	12.94	13.46	12.04
1953	6.38	7.01	12.28	12.81	11.45
1954	6.60	6.80	12.53	13.10	11.71
1955	6.16	5.73	12.02	12.38	11.05
1956	5.95	5.42	11.30	11.37	10.15
1957	5.69	5.20	10.75	10.89	9.71
1958	6.08	6.08	10.64	10.75	9.58
1959	5.64	4.90	10.16	10.28	9.16
1960	5.74	4.97	9.67	9.82	8.75
1961	5.78	5.18	9.54	9.74	8.68
1962	5.38	4.95	9.04	9.15	8.14
1963	5.29	4.76	8.61	8.62	7.66
1964	4.91	4.30	8.01	8.03	7.13
1965	4.95	4.65	7.49	7.55	6.71
1966	4.32	4.59	6.73	6.82	6.05
1967	4.57	4.22	6.30	6.39	5.67
1968	4.35	4.03	6.02	6.12	5.42
1969	4.20	4.08	5.65	5.74	5.09

Sources: Columns 1, 2, 4, and 5, see text for derivation: column 3, computed from Table C-1, column 2 ÷ columns (2 + 3 + 5).

a. Percentages for years prior to 1966 were adjusted slightly for statistical consistency with percentages for later years.

---

1. Net rents paid to nonfarm landlords are included in farm national income. The farm national income series in current dollars is the sum of series 3 and series 3b, described on page 264. The series in 1958 prices was obtained by extrapolating 1958 farm national income in current prices by a series for farm net national product in 1958 prices. Farm net national product in 1958 prices is equal to "gross farm product" in 1958 prices plus "gross rents paid to nonfarm landlords, excluding operating expenses" in 1958 prices (both series from the national income accounts, Table 1.18) minus nonlabor GNP originating in farm dwellings in 1958 market prices (described on page 178) minus depreciation on farm nonresidential structures and equipment at constant cost 2, a component of my series for total business depreciation (from the OBE capital stock study).

2. Each year, total hours worked in the sector by persons of each sex were first divided between those worked by full-time and by part-time workers. Hours of full-time workers were allocated among farm workers, nonfarm self-employed and unpaid family workers, and nonfarm wage and salary workers in proportion to full-time employment in order to accord with the convention that differences in hours among these groups do not represent differences in labor input. Hours worked by part-time workers were added

farm differences in education are not taken into account in this measure. (Neither, unimportantly, are differences in age *within* full-time and part-time categories for each sex.) No attempt to measure the education differential annually was made, but column 5 provides percentages based on a series in which the level of labor input in farming (as measured in column 4) was reduced 12 percent, relative to nonfarm labor, every year to

---

to each group which yielded an allocation of labor input for each sex. (Data used in these calculations are from Tables G-1, G-2, and G-3.) The two sexes were combined by use of the weights in total labor input that are implied by age-sex weighting of the annual distributions shown in Table F-5.

allow for lower educational attainment of farm workers.[3] This series will be used to measure the farm percentage of total labor input. It dropped from 22.7 percent in 1929 to 14.7 in 1947 and 5.1 in 1969. Thus the percentage of the labor used in the business sector that was devoted to farming dropped by an amount equal to 9.6 percent of the total from 1947 to 1969. This is 2.8 times as large as the drop in the farm percentage of the sector's national income in constant prices.

Measurement of Productivity Gain from Resource Reallocation

I now seek to measure the changes in output per unit of input in the nonresidential business sector that resulted from the reduction in the proportion of resources (chiefly labor) employed in the sector that was devoted to farming. The gain results from the fact that labor transferred contributes more to the value of output in its new use than in its old use. Some investigators divide the gain into two parts: that corresponding to the increase in output per worker (or other input measure) in farming as surplus labor is withdrawn, and that corresponding to the difference between farm and nonfarm industries in output per worker. They call the former part a gain from reduction in underemployment of farm labor, the latter part a gain from reallocation of resources. My estimates of the gains from reallocation of resources include both parts.

The method adopted is, with small modifications, the same as I used in *Why Growth Rates Differ*, Chapter 16. It uses the farm percentages of constant-dollar national income and of labor input shown in Table N-1, columns 1 and 5. A calculation is made for each year of the percentage by which national income in constant prices (and consequently output per unit of input) originating in the nonresidential business sector would have been raised if labor input in the sector had been distributed between farm and nonfarm use in the following year's proportion. Two estimates are required. First, it is estimated that if labor input used in farming in any year had been smaller by 1 percent, farm output would have been smaller by 0.33 percent. This estimate, which is explained

in *Why Growth Rates Differ* (see pages 212–14), derives from a minimal downward adjustment (to allow for the fact that most land and capital remained in farming) of results obtained on the assumptions that workers left farming in inverse proportion to their income and that their net output in farming was proportional to their income.[4] I consider the estimate that the percentage reduction in farm output would have been one-third as large as that in farm labor likely to be generous. Use of a lower fraction would yield a larger, but not greatly larger, estimate of the gain from reallocation. The second estimate is that if labor input in nonfarm nonresidential business had been larger by 1 percent, nonfarm output would have been larger by 0.80 percent. This is approximately the average labor share over the whole period, so no allowance is made for any increase due to a shift in capital and land.[5] In fact, there was but little shift in the farm share of the other inputs, except for inventories.[6]

The procedure may be illustrated by the calculation shown at the top of the next page which yields my estimate that the shift of resources from farm to nonfarm use raised sector national income by 0.31 percent from 1963 to 1964.

Similar calculations were made for each pair of years, and the percentage changes were linked to secure the continuous index shown in Table N-2, column 1, and in Table 6-1, column 2.

I have referred to this index as a measure of the output gain from "reallocation of resources." Because output and its farm and nonfarm shares were measured in 1958 prices, the gains are not identical to the gains from "reduction of misallocation of resources" if, as seems reasonable, output and misallocation at each date are appraised by use of current prices and earnings of that date. The calculations pick up the effect of the difference between current and 1958 farm-nonfarm price ratios as well as the effect of improved re-

---

3. Application of education weights to distributions of full-time equivalent employment in farm and nonfarm business in March 1964 yields an education index for the farm distribution nearly 12 percent lower than that for the nonfarm index. The distributions are described in Appendix I, page 247.

4. For convenience, I write as if changes in the labor percentages resulted from the actual movement of workers from farm to nonfarm jobs. Much of the change, of course, resulted from nonreplacement in farming of workers leaving the farm labor force, and some from the failure of farming to share in the growth of total business employment.

5. In *Why Growth Rates Differ* percentages for employment rather than for labor input were used in the calculations, and a lower percentage, 0.75, was used for the gain in output to allow for the lower quality of farm labor. That procedure would yield estimates of gains from the shift of resources from farming a little larger than those obtained here.

6. Estimates for nonlabor inputs are shown in Table N-3.

	Farm (1)	Nonfarm (2)	Non-residential business sector (columns 1 + 2)
1. Percentage of national income in 1958 prices: 1963	5.29	94.71	100.00
2. Percentage of labor input: 1963	7.66	92.34	100.00
3. Percentage of labor input: 1964	7.13	92.87	100.00
4. Change: row 3 − row 2	−0.53	0.53	0.00
5. Percentage change in 1963 labor input if distribution had been that of 1964: row 4 ÷ row 2	−6.92	0.57	...
6. Assumed ratio of percentage change in output to percentage change in labor input (see text)	0.33	0.80	...
7. Percentage change in 1963 farm or nonfarm national income with 1964 labor distribution (row 5 × row 6)	−2.28	0.46	...
8. Percentage change in 1963 national income in sector (row 1 × row 7)	−0.12	0.43	0.31

source allocation as judged from current-price data. Both effects contribute to the change in total output per unit of input, and are correctly counted as contributing to it, but merging them raises a question of interpretation. The index was therefore also computed with farm and nonfarm shares of current-dollar national income substituted for the constant-dollar shares. This series, which is shown in column 2 of Table N-2, can be regarded as a measure of the gains from improved resource allocation based on relative prices of each period and the ratio of this index to the index computed by use of constant-price data (shown in column 3) as a measure of the price effect. The price effect is so trivial that I have thought it unnecessary to carry the distinction into Chapter 6.

Alternative Series

An alternative index of the gain from reallocation of resources from farming was also calculated. Its construction required that the index of

total input in the nonresidential business sector be divided between inputs used in farming and in nonfarm activities; this, in turn, required a division of the series for each of the four inputs.

The estimated percentages of each input, and of total input, used in farming are shown in Table N-3. The labor percentage has already been described. The two types of capital input in the nonresidential business sector were derived from value data in 1958 prices, and the farm component of each is available separately.[7] In consequence, farm percentages for the capital inputs can be readily computed. For nonresidential structures and equipment, separate percentages were

7. The farm component of structures and equipment rests, ultimately, on an allocation from gross investment to farm investment, so the farm-nonfarm breakdown of the stock is less reliable than the total. In contrast, the total stock of inventories is obtained by adding farm and nonfarm components.

Table N-2. Nonresidential Business: Indexes of Gains from Reallocation of Resources from Farming, 1929, 1940–41, and 1947–69
1958 = 100

Year	Gain in constant-dollar national income (1)	Gain based on current-dollar national income (2)	Price effect (3)
1929	91.18	91.26	99.90
1940	92.00	92.08	99.92
1941	93.58	93.74	99.82
1947	96.61	96.79	99.81
1948	96.85	96.99	99.86
1949	96.67	96.84	99.82
1950	97.13	97.26	99.86
1951	98.09	98.14	99.94
1952	98.39	98.41	99.99
1953	98.79	98.76	100.03
1954	98.62	98.59	100.02
1955	99.05	99.02	100.03
1956	99.63	99.62	100.01
1957	99.92	99.91	100.00
1958	100.00	100.00	100.00
1959	100.26	100.26	100.00
1960	100.52	100.53	99.99
1961	100.56	100.58	99.98
1962	100.89	100.92	99.97
1963	101.18	101.23	99.96
1964	101.50	101.56	99.94
1965	101.75	101.83	99.93
1966	102.14	102.22	99.92
1967	102.36	102.44	99.92
1968	102.50	102.58	99.92
1969	102.69	102.78	99.91

Source: See text for derivation.

Table N-3. Nonresidential Business: Farm Share of Inputs, Output per Unit of Input in Farm and Nonfarm Industries, and Alternative Index of Gains from Reallocation of Labor from Farming, 1929, 1940–41, and 1947–69

| | Farm percentages of inputs | | | | Output per unit of input in nonresidential business | | | Alternative index of gains from reallocation of labor from farming | |
| | | | | | | | | | |
Year	Labor (1)	Nonresidential structures and equipment (2)	Inventories (3)	Total[a] (4)	Total (5)	Farm (6)	Nonfarm (7)	Unadjusted (8)	Adjusted for irregular fluctuations (9)
1929	22.74	8.86	25.58	22.14	64.66	60.05	69.75	92.70	92.60
1940	21.54	8.82	28.07	21.05	68.45	64.90	73.10	93.64	94.25
1941	19.21	8.85	26.63	19.18	75.23	71.66	79.31	94.86	94.86
1947	14.69	9.42	23.07	15.67	81.11	70.40	84.32	96.20	96.63
1948	14.33	9.64	22.22	15.34	85.09	77.88	87.88	96.83	96.50
1949	14.61	9.98	22.26	15.48	84.45	75.00	87.52	96.50	96.53
1950	13.92	10.32	21.72	14.87	90.44	78.86	93.48	96.75	96.48
1951	12.49	10.56	20.57	13.73	91.10	75.92	93.76	97.16	97.36
1952	12.04	10.68	20.08	13.32	91.22	78.22	93.46	97.60	97.70
1953	11.45	10.76	19.84	12.76	93.63	84.32	95.28	98.28	98.12
1954	11.71	10.82	19.98	12.89	93.58	86.39	95.14	98.37	98.25
1955	11.05	10.78	20.03	12.28	99.51	89.95	100.94	98.59	98.39
1956	10.15	10.62	19.05	11.49	100.10	93.41	100.85	99.26	99.14
1957	9.71	10.38	18.59	11.05	100.45	93.21	100.99	99.47	99.57
1958	9.58	10.27	19.15	10.94	100.00	100.00	100.00	100.00	100.00
1959	9.16	10.20	19.22	10.54	105.53	101.70	105.55	99.98	99.96
1960	8.75	10.03	18.70	10.22	106.48	107.77	106.00	100.45	100.31
1961	8.68	9.81	18.50	10.18	107.95	110.51	107.36	100.55	100.43
1962	8.14	9.63	18.33	9.75	113.15	112.56	112.47	100.60	100.58
1963	7.66	9.46	18.07	9.41	116.38	117.87	115.37	100.88	100.77
1964	7.13	9.28	17.41	8.99	121.09	119.09	119.96	100.94	100.96
1965	6.71	9.04	16.70	8.66	125.88	129.77	124.20	101.35	101.13
1966	6.05	8.80	15.78	8.10	129.31	124.38	127.64	101.30	101.45
1967	5.67	8.58	14.97	7.72	129.10	137.79	126.58	101.99	101.82
1968	5.42	8.38	14.60	7.43	132.27	139.46	129.57	102.07	101.91
1969	5.09	8.16	14.20	7.10	132.21	140.89	129.27	102.25	102.18

Source: See text for derivation.
a. Includes land input with farm percentage estimated at 37.045 in all years.

first computed for gross stock and net stock; these were weighted (3 and 1) to correspond to the procedure adopted to obtain the index for this type of input. The percentage of structures and equipment input used in farming rose until the mid-1950s; only in recent years has it been below 1929. The inventory percentage has declined substantially since 1940, though less than that for labor. My index of land input was measured without a farm-nonfarm break. The farm percentage of land input has probably declined, but only slightly. Farm land averaged 37 percent of the total nonresidential business land weight in my weighting structure (from 1929 to 1969), and no major error can be introduced in the following

calculation if this percentage of total land is assigned to farming every year.

It is now possible to estimate the percentage of total input in the nonresidential business sector that was used in farming each year. The calculation is illustrated below with data for 1962. The weight of each of the four inputs in total input in the sector is shown in the first column.[8] The second column shows the farm share of each input. The third column, the product of the first two, shows the farm share of each input expressed as a percentage of total input in the sector;

8. The weight is the adjusted share of earnings that was averaged with the share for the following year to secure the weights shown in Table J-2.

their sum (9.75, based on unrounded detail) represents total input in farming expressed as a percentage of total input in the nonresidential business sector. The corresponding percentages for all years are shown in Table N-3, column 4.

	Weight of each input in total non-residential business sector	*Input in farming as percentage of:*	
		Individual inputs	*Total input*
Labor	81.24	8.14	6.61
Nonresidential structures and equipment	11.33	9.63	1.09
Inventories	3.79	18.33	0.69
Land	3.64	37.04	1.35
Total factor input	100.00	...	9.75

The alternative index based on these estimates is conceptually straightforward. It rests on the single proposition that, if resources had been allocated between farm and nonfarm use in such a way as to maximize national income in the nonresidential business sector, measured in 1958 prices, output (in 1958 prices) per unit of input in the sector as a whole would have been the same each year as it actually was in the nonfarm portion of the sector (aside from any gain from economies of scale, which is classified elsewhere). This proposition implies as a corollary, because it is based on 1958 prices, that the index of output per unit of input in farming would have been the same as that in nonfarm industries in the sector if there had been no misallocation, and hence if there had been no change in the percentage by which overallocation reduced the level of productivity within farming.

The value that national income in the sector would have taken each year if the specified condition had been met is obtained by multiplying nonfarm national income in the sector (in 1958 prices) by the ratio of total input in the sector to total nonfarm input. The ratio of actual national income in the sector to this hypothetical figure is then calculated. The index of this ratio, shown with 1958 equal to 100, is shown in Table N-3, column 8.[9]

9. The same index could be obtained by dividing the index of output per unit of input in the nonresidential business sector by the index of output per unit of input in the nonfarm portion of the sector. These indexes, along with that for farms, are also shown in Table N-3. The farm and nonfarm input indexes required for the calculations were derived by multiplying the index of total input (Table 5-4,

Because this index reflects irregular fluctuations in farm output, it must be divided by the index for that growth determinant (Table 6-1, column 4) to obtain the desired measure of changes in output per unit of input in the nonresidential business sector resulting from reallocation of resources from farming. The resulting series is shown in Table N-3, column 9.

The growth rate of this alternative series from 1950 to 1969 is 0.30, almost the same as that of the series I use, which is 0.29. From 1929 or 1947 to 1969, the alternate series grows less than the series I use, but the differences are small so the choice between the series is not very important for analysis of long-term trends. However, annual movements in the alternate series are more erratic than, and sometimes appreciably different from, those in the series adopted. The alternative series has the virtue of conceptual simplicity, but the statistical results are overly sensitive to errors in both the level and movement of the estimated percentages of input that are used in farming. The sensitivity arises from the fact that the movement of the index rests on an estimate of differences between years in the *total* cost (to output measured in 1958 prices) of overallocation to farming and hence, in effect, is an estimate of small residuals from large aggregates. The series actually adopted rests on an estimate of the *change* in the cost of misallocation each year resulting from the change in allocation that year.

Comparisons of output per unit of input in the sector and its farm and nonfarm components (Table N-3, columns 5, 6, and 7) bring out the long-term relationships among them. Productivity rose much more in the sector as a whole than in nonfarm industries despite the small weight of farming in total output. Growth rates from 1929 to 1969 were 1.80 percent for the sector, 1.55 for nonfarm industries, and 2.15 for farms.

The Reduction in the Importance of Nonfarm Self-Employment

The self-employed population includes a core of professionals with high incomes, proprietors of sizable business establishments with paid employees and of successful smaller establishments, and some workers in skilled trades who do well

column 7) by the farm and nonfarm percentages of input (Table N-3, column 4, and 100 minus that column) and expressing the products as indexes with 1958 equal to 100.

enough operating on their own. These groups are in no sense misallocated. *Changes* in the importance of self-employment, however, refer largely to what I have called elsewhere a "fringe" group of persons who operate small enterprises in retail trade or service industries, who contribute little to output in their nonpaid status, but who are competent to hold wage and salary jobs. Much of the evidence for this generalization comes from international comparisons presented in *Why Growth Rates Differ,* Chapter 16. Reduction in the relative size of this fringe group has contributed to the increase in productivity.

Self-employed persons and unpaid family workers represented 15.15 percent of nonfarm business employment in 1929, 14.12 percent in 1951, and 11.46 percent in 1969, when employment is measured on a full-time equivalent basis and weighted by sex. Percentages for other years appear in Table N-4.[10] There had been a temporary fillip in the percentage immediately after World War II as many individuals, some aided by GI benefits, entered business for themselves. Most of these enterprises were very short-lived; their life spans terminated as soon as their owners had lost their equity.

I estimate the contribution made to output per unit of input by the shift of nonfarm self-employed and unpaid family workers to wage and salary employment in the same way as I did in *Why Growth Rates Differ* (except that a more refined employment figure is used) and quote the relevant paragraphs from page 216:

The gains from reducing the importance of nonfarm proprietors and family workers within the nonfarm employment total must now be estimated. The contraction must have been concentrated among members of the fringe group, and especially those with the lowest earnings. Hence, the increment to wage and salary employment required to make up for the work formerly performed by self-employed and family workers could hardly be large. Not only did those leaving self-employment have a low value of output per person but also the work they formerly did could often be absorbed by those remaining. I shall assume that an increase in wage and salary employment one-fourth as large as the decline in self-employment was required. More precisely, I shall suppose that the transfer of four workers from the status of nonfarm proprietors and family workers was equivalent to a net addition of three workers to nonfarm employment. This assumption refers only to labor. I make no allowance for any possible saving in the use of capital or land corresponding to this shift.

10. The construction of these estimates was described on page 285, note 2.

The following illustration describes one situation in which the one-fourth reduction would be appropriate. Assume that the unincorporated firms that disappeared are drawn from the lower portion of a distribution, by volume of business, of firms without paid employees; that firms of this type could readily handle more volume without increasing employment; and that the volume, per person engaged, of such firms was half that of firms in the same business with paid employees. Let half the business formerly handled by the disappearing firms go to other firms without paid employees which would be able to absorb it without adding to employment. Let the other half go to firms with paid employees, which would need to add only one employee to handle the volume formerly handled by two self-employed and family workers in the discontinued firms. Under these circumstances, the business handled by the discontinued firms would be taken care of by the addition of one paid employee to replace four self-employed and family helpers in the discontinued firms.

An estimate of the percentage gain each year was made on this assumption, and the annual figures were linked. The calculation of the percentage gain from 1951 to 1952 illustrates the procedure. Self-employed and unpaid family workers comprised 14.12 percent in 1951 and 14.01 percent in 1952 of sex-weighted full-time equivalent nonfarm business employment. The decline of 0.11 percentage points was multiplied by 0.75 to obtain 0.082 percent as the addition to effectively used labor input in nonfarm business. The estimated gain in output per unit of input in the nonresidential business sector is the product of this 0.082; the 1951–52 labor share, which was 0.7935; and the 1951 ratio of nonfarm to total national income in the sector (in 1958 prices), which was 0.9365. The resulting estimate is 0.06 percent.

Table N-4. Self-Employed and Unpaid Family Workers as a Percentage of Nonfarm Nonresidential Business Employment, 1929, 1940–41, and 1947–69[a]

Year	Percentage	Year	Percentage
1929	15.15	1957	13.62
1940	16.09	1958	14.10
1941	14.50	1959	13.66
		1960	13.64
1947	14.40	1961	13.87
1948	14.45		
1949	15.10	1962	13.52
1950	14.87	1963	13.14
1951	14.12	1964	13.09
		1965	12.56
1952	14.01	1966	11.91
1953	13.69		
1954	14.11	1967	11.69
1955	13.75	1968	11.57
1956	13.63	1969	11.46

Source: See text for derivation.

a. Employment measured on a full-time equivalent basis and weighted by sex. Percentages for years prior to 1966 were adjusted slightly for statistical consistency with percentages for later years.

APPENDIX O

➤➤❯❮❮❮

Irregular Fluctuations

➤➤❯❮❮❮

This appendix describes the series, shown in Table 6-1, for the effects upon output per unit of input in the nonresidential business sector of irregular fluctuations in three determinants, and discusses a fourth whose effects could not be measured.

PART ONE: IRREGULAR FLUCTUATIONS IN FARM OUTPUT

Irregular fluctuations in farm output (see Table 6-1, column 4) are mainly attributable to changes in weather, pest infestation, and other natural conditions, although production controls also have some influence. Their effect upon the value (in 1958 prices) of national income in the nonresidential business sector is estimated to be equal, in absolute amount, to the excess (which may be positive or negative) of actual nonresidential farm GNP over an estimated "normal" nonresidential farm GNP (both measured in 1958 prices).[1]

To measure "normal" nonresidential farm GNP each year, a five-year moving average of actual nonresidential farm GNP, centered in that year, was ordinarily used.[2] The excess was subtracted each year from national income in the

1. Nonresidential farm GNP in 1958 prices is almost identical when valued at market price and at factor cost. Depreciation is unaffected by irregular fluctuations in output, so variations in gross output affect net output equally.

2. The five-year moving average declined from 1948 to 1949 and from 1967 to 1968, an unreasonable result for a measure of normal farm GNP. These abnormal declines were eliminated by substituting the mean of the 1948 and 1949 moving averages in both of these years, and the mean of the 1967 and 1968 moving averages in both of those years.

nonresidential business sector to obtain an adjusted series representing the value of the latter series under normal farm conditions. The ratio of actual to adjusted national income in the sector was computed. The index of this ratio (1958 = 100), which is shown in Table 6-1, column 4, measures the effect of irregular fluctuations in farm output upon the index of output per unit of input in the nonresidential business sector.

The figures for actual nonresidential farm GNP were derived by subtracting residential from total farm GNP in 1958 prices. The latter series is from the national income accounts, Table 1.18.[3] Nonlabor GNP at market prices originating in farm homes, measured in 1958 prices, is the series described on page 178.[4]

PART TWO: WORK STOPPAGES DUE TO LABOR DISPUTES

This section describes the index of the effects of work stoppages due to labor disputes upon output per unit of input in the nonresidential business sector (Table 6-1, column 5). It should be recalled at the outset that labor input excludes time lost from work as a direct or indirect result of strikes, whether by persons on strike, nonstrikers laid off by struck firms, or persons in other firms who are laid off because of materials shortages, interruption of transport, or reduction of sales. Thus labor disputes reduce input as well as output. But the percentage reduction in total input is ordinarily smaller than that in output, so that strikes tend to reduce output per unit of input.

3. A reminder of the sources of national income accounts: Data for 1929–63 are published in U.S. Department of Commerce, Office of Business Economics, *The National Income and Product Accounts of the United States, 1929–1965: Statistical Tables,* A Supplement to the *Survey of Current Business* (1966). Data for 1964 are published in the July 1968 issue of the *Survey of Current Business,* for 1965 in the July 1969 issue, for 1966–69 in the July 1970 issue. Revisions for 1968–69 published in the July 1971 issue are incorporated where changes are significant (see pp. 7–8). Unpublished detail for all years was provided by the Office of Business Economics.

To compute five-year averages for 1929 and 1969, estimates for 1927, 1928, and 1971 were needed. Gross farm product measured in 1958 dollars in 1929 was extrapolated to 1927 and 1928 by the same series measured in 1954 dollars, as estimated by the Office of Business Economics (national income accounts, Table 1.16). Gross farm product in 1971 was estimated from the trend in prior years.

4. Some years needed for the five-year averages were not available. The ratio of nonresidential farm GNP to total farm GNP was assumed to be the same in 1927–31 as in 1929, in 1938–39 as in 1940, in 1942–43 as in 1941, and in 1970–71 as in 1969.

Firms Involved in Work Stoppages

One set of reasons for this pertains to firms experiencing work stoppages. Although the capital and land ordinarily used by strikers and others who are laid off are left idle, the nonlabor input indexes, as measured, do not decline. In addition, the disruption of activities resulting from the strike is likely to impair the productivity of persons who remain at work. A rough index of the impact of developments *within* struck firms upon my index of output per unit of input was constructed by the following procedure.

The Bureau of Labor Statistics (BLS) reports the time lost because of labor disputes by all persons (not only strikers) who are employed in establishments (not firms) that are involved in labor disputes. Man-years worked in the nonresidential business sector were expressed as a percentage of the sum of man-years worked and of man-years not worked in establishments involved in labor disputes[5] because of disputes. Table O-1, column 1, shows these percentages. The amount by which the percentage fell short of 100 each year was computed. Three-tenths of this amount was used as an estimate of the adverse impact of labor disputes upon output per unit of total input. Of the three-tenths, two-tenths correspond approximately to the weight of nonlabor inputs, and offset the inclusion in total input of idle capital and land ordinarily used by persons on strike or laid off in struck establishments. The remaining one-tenth is a conservative allowance for the continuance of depreciation during disputes (which reduces net output), for the possible impairment of productivity of persons who remain at work

5. Man-years worked is my total employment in the business sector, from Table C-1, columns 2, 3, and 5. Man-years not worked is the product of two BLS series: (1) man-days idle during the year because of labor disputes expressed as a percentage of estimated total private nonagricultural wage and salary working time (U.S. Bureau of Labor Statistics, *Analysis of Work Stoppages, 1969,* Bulletin 1687 [1971], Table A-1, p. 11), and (2) private nonagricultural wage and salary employment, establishment basis (U.S. Bureau of Labor Statistics, *Employment and Earnings,* Vol. 17 [January 1971], Table B-1, p. 51). The First BLS series is available only since 1950. Percentages published for years prior to 1950 excluded government and agricultural workers from estimates of total working time but included them in estimates of man-days idle. Percentages for 1950 are available on both bases (Howard N. Fullerton, " 'Total Economy' Measure of Strike Idleness," *Monthly Labor Review,* Vol. 91 [October 1968], pp. 54–56). The published percentages for years prior to 1950 were adjusted downward by applying to them the ratio of the 1950 percentage on the new basis to the 1950 percentage on the old basis.

Table O-1. Nonresidential Business: Estimated Effect of Work Stoppages Resulting from Labor Disputes upon Output per Unit of Input in the Sector, 1929, 1940–41, and 1947–69

Year	Man-years worked as a percentage of the sum of man-years worked and man-years not worked because of work stoppages (1)	Indexes of effect of work stoppages upon output per unit of input (1958 = 100) (2)
1929	99.96	100.04
1940	99.94	100.04
1941	99.79	99.99
1947	99.72	99.97
1948	99.74	99.98
1949	99.58	99.93
1950	99.69	99.96
1951	99.83	100.01
1952	99.54	99.89[a]
1953	99.79	99.99
1954	99.84	100.01
1955	99.78	99.99
1956	99.76	99.98
1957	99.88	100.02
1958	99.82	100.00
1959	99.48	99.85[a]
1960	99.86	100.01
1961	99.90	100.02
1962	99.86	100.01
1963	99.89	100.02
1964	99.84	100.01
1965	99.84	100.01
1966	99.84	100.01
1967	99.73	99.97
1968	99.71	99.97
1969	99.74	99.98

Source: See text for derivation.
a. Includes special adjustment described in text.

for struck firms, and for the possible idling of nonlabor inputs ordinarily used by nonstrikers who are laid off in establishments that are not struck though owned by struck firms.

An adjusted input index incorporating this estimate was computed. In 1958, when 99.82 percent of available time was worked, output per unit of input is estimated to be 99.946 percent of what it would have been in the absence of labor disputes, calculated as $100 - 0.3(100 - 99.82)$. In 1961, when 99.90 percent of available time was worked, output per unit of input is estimated to be 99.97 percent of what it would have been in the absence of labor disputes. Expressed with 1958 equal to 100, the index for 1961 is therefore 100.02, calculated as $99.97 \div 99.946$. Calculations for other years are similar. Fluctuations in this index are small; the extreme range is 0.14 percent. However, I have yet to consider the effect of strikes upon output per unit of input in firms that are not struck.

Firms Not Involved in Work Stoppages

Output per unit of input may also be reduced in nonstruck firms whose operations are curtailed or disrupted by strikes in other firms. As in the firms directly involved, workers may be laid off, leaving the nonlabor inputs they use idle, and the efficiency of labor remaining at work may be impaired. Unfortunately, no systematic information is available concerning the effects of strikes on the employment, or other aspects of the operations, of other firms. However, only very major strikes in key industries are likely to have secondary effects sufficient to affect the movement of annual data for output per unit of input in the sector as a whole.

The major strikes occurring in the four years in which time lost from labor disputes was largest (1949, 1950, 1952, and 1959) were examined by reviewing descriptions of their effects as given at the time, chiefly as reported in the *Survey of Current Business*.[6] (The BLS quarterly series for output per man-hour in private nonagricultural industries was also examined in periods before, during, and after such strikes to see whether their effects could be discerned, but this approach did not prove fruitful. The quarterly series displays frequent erratic movements, and there is no tendency for even the biggest strikes to show up in the index in any systematic way.) The examination led to ad hoc adjustments to the index already calculated only for the years 1952 and 1959.

The Coal and Steel Strikes, 1949

In October 1949, 800,00 coal and steel workers were on strike. (The coal strike began September 19, the steel strike October 1.) Coal and steel production recovered rapidly in November. The descriptive material indicates that these strikes had no appreciable effect upon other industries except perhaps freight transport. No special adjustment was made.

The Chrysler and Coal Strikes, 1950

There were two major strikes in early 1950. A ninety-nine-day Chrysler strike of 90,000 workers, ending May 4, seems to have had little net secondary effect; total auto production and sales were high throughout the period so activities of auto suppliers and dealers as a group could not have been greatly affected. The only appreciable secondary effect of a coal strike in February (ending the first week in March) was a brief contraction of steel production. This may have adversely affected productivity for a short period but any effect on the annual index of output per unit of input was trivial. No special adjustment was made.[7]

The Steel Strike, 1952

A strike of 560,000 steel workers from June 2 to late July 1952 had wider effects. To maintain defense production, the National Production Authority banned steel shipments to manufacturers of the less essential products. Secondary effects were unimportant in June, as steel inventories were drawn down, but in July, or in some cases even later, operations of steel-using and steel-transporting industries were affected. Automobiles were affected most. Manufacturers of machinery and freight cars, steel fabricators generally, and highway and commercial construction are also mentioned, but in most cases the effects on their output were moderate. Production in all these industries recovered rapidly during August and by the end of that month was near normal. Compared to the second quarter average, passenger car output was at 40 percent in July, 60 in August, and 110 in September. I estimate that 12 million man-days (an average of 400,000 workers for six weeks) were lost in other industries because of the steel strike. The special secondary effect of the steel strike upon output per unit of input is assumed to have been equal to that which would have been exerted by an extra 12 million man-days lost in struck establishments, and the index previously computed for 1952 was adjusted accordingly. This changed the index (1958 = 100) from 99.92 to 99.89.

The Steel Strike, 1959

A very long steel strike, running for 116 days from July 15 to November 7, 1959, directly in-

---

6. Also examined were a 1956 steel strike which was too short (thirty-four days) to have had much secondary effect and a 1963 dock strike that affected foreign trade significantly, but not production.

7. In the second quarter of 1950 there were several fairly important strikes but they were not of a type likely to have especially large secondary effects.

volved 500,000 workers.[8] Bituminous and iron ore mining and freight transportation were curtailed promptly. About 125,000 workers were laid off in these industries for a period that approximately coincided with the duration of the strike. Steel inventories were large when the strike started, and the problem for steel users was further mitigated because the strike coincided with the model changeover period of the auto industry. Effects on steel-using industries were consequently minor until mid-October. They then became important. The auto industry was affected most. Auto assemblies, building up from the model changeover, reached a peak of 134,000 the week of October 17. Thereafter, the steel shortage forced a cutback. Assemblies dropped to 65,000 in the first week of November and to a total of about 260,000 for the whole month. Finished steel products remained in short and unbalanced supply in December, and the effects of the strike were not fully dissipated until the end of the year. I allowed for the special secondary effects of this strike by adding 22.5 million man-days to time lost from strikes in making the 1959 calculation (12.5 million in mining and transportation, and 10 million in steel-using industries). This lowered the 1959 index (1958 = 100) from 99.90 to 99.85.

PART THREE: INTENSITY WITH WHICH EMPLOYED RESOURCES ARE USED RESULTING FROM VARIATIONS IN THE INTENSITY OF DEMAND

Total factor input measures the labor, capital, and land that are present in business establishments and available for use. It is not affected by short-term fluctuations in the intensity with which these "employed" inputs are used. The effects of such fluctuations in intensity of use upon output consequently appear in the series for output per unit of input (Table 6-1, column 1). The main reason for fluctuations is that intensity of demand varies from time to time. The effect upon output per unit of input of variations in intensity of demand, shown in Table 6-1, column 5, is estimated in this section.

General Approaches

Any analysis of growth requires that the effects upon productivity of fluctuations in intensity of utilization resulting from swings in demand be

8. There was also a copper strike in this period.

separated from the effects of longer-term determinants of productivity change. Three approaches have been used.

First, analysis may be confined to a comparison of selected years which appear from general considerations to be comparable with respect to intensity of utilization, and which are also far enough apart in time so that small errors in the assumption of comparability affect growth rates between those dates to only a minor extent. Selection of such years is difficult. The procedure was nevertheless adopted in *The Sources of Economic Growth,* but it cannot be used in a study which seeks to analyze annual data covering years which are obviously not comparable.

Second, one may fit a trend to a productivity series from which the effects of other measurable determinants have been eliminated and regard deviations from trend as due to changes in intensity of utilization. Dorothy Walters used this method ingeniously for Canada (*Canadian Growth Revisited, 1950–67,* Staff Study 28 [Economic Council of Canada, 1970], pp. 62–64). Its major disadvantage is that it almost bars investigation of the question: Has the contribution of the "semiresidual" changed over time? Use of a single trend for the whole period *assumes* the answer to be no, but changes in trend are hard to identify in a series not already cyclically adjusted. For the United States, I believe the method I adopt is more reliable.

The third approach is to estimate directly the effect upon output per unit of input of differences in the intensity of utilization. I used this approach in *Why Growth Rates Differ,* and do so again in the present study. However, the method of estimation used previously was not satisfactory and would be even less so if applied to a continuous series of annual data. (Only three separated years were used in the previous study.) The previous procedure, which relied upon the unemployment rate as an indicator of intensity of utilization, has been replaced by a method which I regard as greatly superior.

Reasons for Fluctuations

Business responds to changes in the strength of demand for its products by changing its production and inputs, but output per unit of input is also affected because changes in output and input are not proportional. This is partly because fluctuations in demand, and hence in output, are not foreseen accurately enough nor far enough in advance to adjust inputs to what they would be if production requirements were known for distant future periods. Decisions affecting the inputs present on any given day must be made at times ranging from the start of that day, in the case of some types of casual labor, to many years earlier, in the case of some capital goods. Fluctuations in output per unit of input also result from the presence of overhead costs. It is almost impossible to vary some inputs at all in the short run; others can be varied, but less than output; and still others could be varied as much as output, but the process of doing so would itself entail costs so substantial as to make the process uneconomic. Even if a firm knew many years in advance what its production would be in September 1969, it could not plan September inputs to accord with September production if September production were out of line with production in other periods. Most fluctuations in individual firms and establishments are random and offsetting and scarcely affect aggregate series, but general changes in the strength of aggregate demand have a great effect.

A brief examination of the reasons that individual inputs, as measured, do not vary like production is useful in order to indicate both the nature of the problem and the complexity of the relationship whose effects must be measured.

Labor. My measure of labor input takes full account of short-term changes in total hours worked as well as in the composition by sex, age, and education of those who work them. However, a great deal of labor is of an overhead character, remaining at work in slack periods. There is a substantial element of "indivisibilities" in labor. Although it may be possible quickly to add or lay off a proportion of the production workers in large departments of manufacturing establishments or to vary their working hours as the need for their services changes, it usually is not possible, so long as operations continue at all, to vary the numbers or hours of executive or supervisory personnel (including self-employed persons) or of large numbers of other workers, ranging from the corporation president's secretary to locomotive engineers on scheduled trains and clerks in any but the largest stores. Moreover, firms do not adjust changes in labor finely to changes in production even to the extent that the presence of indivisibilities allows. To find, hire, and train workers is expensive. If it is expected in periods of slack that more workers will be needed again in the future, it may be deemed cheaper to retain present employees than to seek new ones when they are

needed again. To dismiss employees is also expensive because of merit rating provisions in unemployment compensation tax laws, and sometimes of provisions for dismissal pay. It is, moreover, unpleasant. In periods of unexpected expansion of demand it may be impossible to add personnel quickly. Even if this is possible, it may be deemed desirable to wait to see whether the expansion is more than ephemeral; in the meantime, the pace of work tends to quicken, and to exceed that likely to be sustainable over an extended period.

Fixed Capital. The input of fixed capital is measured by the capital stock. The stock at any time reflects the expectations existing at some series of past dates concerning present and future needs. The stock of capital is not reduced when production falls or the rate of its increase slackens, and even the increase in the stock of fixed capital can be checked only with a considerable lag because of the time involved in ordering, manufacturing, and installing equipment, and in building structures.

The contribution of fixed capital to current net output is its contribution to current gross output less depreciation on existing assets. Depreciation is related—entirely as measured in this study, and largely in fact—to the passage of time and not to the intensity of use. Consequently, variations in the contribution of fixed capital to net output that are associated with changes in the intensity of its use are the same as those in its contribution to gross output in absolute amount, but even larger in percentage terms.

Inventories. Inventory input is also measured by the stock. The stock can and does vary with the level of activity because firms adjust their holdings to their requirements, but there is no presumption that adjustments are proportional. Moreover, the first response of stocks to an unexpected change in business activity is usually perverse. Trade stocks and manufacturers' inventories of finished goods pile up when sales decline, and are drawn down when sales increase. Only with a lag, if at all, are firms able to bring inventories to desired levels.

Land. Land input, too, is measured by the stock. The series actually adopted does not vary at all.

IT IS OBVIOUS that changes in the intensity of utilization of inputs can importantly affect the annual series for output per unit of input. It is also obvious that the relationships are complex. It can be stated in very general terms that productivity is likely to be high when demand is strong and has recently strengthened, especially if the strengthening was unanticipated and/or not expected to continue, and to be low when the opposite conditions prevail, but timing and magnitudes are unpredictable. It is also clear that there is no way to measure directly the intensity of use of the several inputs. Under these circumstances the only solution available is to find another series that moves like the intensity of utilization, and from which its effect on output per unit of input can be inferred.

In *Why Growth Rates Differ,* I used the unemployment rate for this purpose because it was the only series for which a relationship had been estimated. Its adoption assumed that the intensity of use of employed inputs could be inferred from the percentage of people in the labor force who were wholly unemployed. I was dissatisfied at the time with the choice of unemployment as the indicator of the intensity with which employed resources are used, and am now convinced that it is almost useless. Employment or total hours worked, or the changes in them, might as I then suggested be somewhat more pertinent indicators of the utilization of the labor component of total input because they are not affected by extraneous changes in the size of the labor force. A high rate of utilization is in fact often accompanied by a large increase in hours worked because both accompany a rapid expansion of output. But the causal relationship is perverse, and this is particularly serious because of the phenomenon of labor hoarding. The more that business retains unneeded labor when business slackens, the larger is the increase (or the smaller the decrease) in hours worked but the lower is the intensity of utilization of labor. The converse is the case when output is expanding. In addition, hours worked, like other series mentioned, give no direct indication of changes in inputs other than labor.

Relationship of Utilization to Productivity and the Nonlabor Share

In undertaking the present study I asked myself the following question: Is there not some series which is affected by changes in the intensity of utilization of inputs in much the same way and at the same time as output per unit of input?

Clearly, there is: profits have the desired characteristic.

The series I actually use as an indicator is the ratio of nonlabor earnings in corporations to corporate national income, with depreciation computed on a consistent basis at current prices.[9] Data for corporations are used, rather than those for the entire nonresidential business sector, because they provide a more accurate annual series. Nonlabor earnings, which include corporate net interest, are used in preference to profits alone in order to avoid problems related to changes in methods of financing, in market interest rates, and in the distribution of corporate portfolios between stocks and bonds, all of which affect the division between profits and net interest.

When overhead labor costs are spread over a smaller number of units of output because demand falls or is unexpectedly low, or because labor is hoarded, the ratio of nonlabor earnings to national income in corporations is reduced just as is productivity. Because depreciation is measured as a function of time rather than of volume, depreciation cost per unit of output varies inversely with utilization of fixed capital; short-term reductions in the rate of utilization of fixed capital adversely affect both the ratio of nonlabor earnings to national income and output per unit of input. Costs ascribable to inventories and land, and the costs of fixed capital input that correspond to its net earnings weight, also are relatively fixed in the short run. These costs are included in nonlabor earnings along with "pure" profit, but because they are relatively fixed in the short run, variations in utilization of these assets cause fluctuations in the ratio of nonlabor earnings (inclusive of these costs) to national income that are much like those which would be observed in a purer measure of profit.

Having concluded on a priori grounds that short-term changes in the utilization of employed resources would affect the nonlabor share and output per unit of input in much the same way, the next step was to test whether the data supported the expectation. The preliminary test was

9. As elsewhere in this study, depreciation is computed by use of the straight-line formula, Bulletin F service lives, the Winfrey distribution, and price series 2 for valuation of depreciation on nonresidential structures. Data are directly from the OBE capital stock study except that estimation of depreciation on corporate-owned dwellings required introduction of the assumption that the ratio of depreciation in current prices to depreciation at original cost is the same for corporate-owned as for all nonfarm dwellings.

to correlate changes in output per unit of input with changes in the nonlabor share during the postwar period.

The nonlabor share of corporate national income is shown in Table O-2, column 1. For output per unit of input in the nonresidential business sector I use in this analysis a series from which the effects of shifts from agriculture and from nonfarm self-employment, and of irregular fluctuations in farm output, have been eliminated; for

Table O-2. Nonresidential Business: Derivation of Preliminary Index of Effects of Fluctuations in Pressure of Demand upon Output per Unit of Input, 1947–69 and Selected Prewar Years

								Preliminary series	
	Nonlabor earnings as percentage of corporate national income		*Adjusted output per unit of input*		*Effect of intensity of utilization upon output per unit of input*		*Index of effect of fluctuations in pressure of demand upon output per unit of input (1958 = 100)*	*Index of adjusted output per unit of input after elimination of effects of work stoppages (1958 = 100), with fluctuations in pressure of demand:*	
Year	*Percent, (X) (1)*	*Deviation from trend (percentage points) (2)*	*Index (1958 = 100) (Y) (3)*	*Deviation from trend as percent of trend value (4)*	*Ratio to trend value (I) (5)*	*Index (1958 = 100) (6)*	*(7)*	*Not removed (8)*	*Removed (Z) (9)*
			Postwar years						
1947	21.026	−1.215	84.47	−0.373	0.9860	102.11	102.14	84.49	82.72
1948	23.785	1.644	87.72	1.535	1.0193	105.56	105.59	87.74	83.09
1949	22.631	0.591	87.86	−0.184	1.0069	104.28	104.35	87.93	84.26
1950	24.495	2.555	93.24	3.947	1.0301	106.69	106.73	93.27	87.39
1951	23.975	2.135	93.07	1.834	1.0251	106.17	106.16	93.07	87.66
1952	21.344	−0.396	92.75	−0.405	0.9954	103.09	103.20	92.85	89.97
1953	20.136	−1.504	94.41	−0.507	0.9827	101.77	101.78	94.42	92.77
1954	20.083	−1.456	94.78	−1.972	0.9832	101.83	101.82	94.77	93.08
1955	22.888	1.449	100.06	1.566	1.0170	105.32	105.33	100.07	95.00
1956	20.571	−0.768	100.07	−0.313	0.9911	102.65	102.66	100.09	97.49
1957	19.496	−1.743	100.36	−1.887	0.9800	101.49	101.47	100.34	98.89
1958	18.124	−3.014	100.00	−4.056	0.9656	100.00	100.00	100.00	100.00
1959	20.523	−0.515	104.96	−1.169	0.9940	102.95	103.10	105.12	101.96
1960	19.168	−1.770	105.50	−2.506	0.9796	101.46	101.44	105.49	103.99
1961	19.117	−1.721	107.09	−2.883	0.9802	101.51	101.49	107.06	105.49
1962	20.466	−0.272	111.75	−0.537	0.9968	103.24	103.22	111.74	108.25
1963	20.816	0.178	114.26	−0.191	1.0021	103.78	103.76	114.24	110.10
1964	21.624	1.087	118.63	1.696	1.0127	104.88	104.87	118.62	113.11
1965	22.914	2.477	122.35	2.937	1.0292	106.59	106.58	122.34	114.79
1966	22.883	2.546	125.20	3.376	1.0300	106.67	106.67	125.19	117.37
1967	21.139	0.903	124.19	0.630	1.0105	104.66	104.68	124.22	118.66
1968	20.809	0.673	127.00	0.996	1.0078	104.38	104.41	127.04	121.67
1969	18.169	−1.867	126.74	−1.085	0.9785	101.34	101.36	126.77	125.06
			Prewar years						
1929	23.315	1.074	71.23	. . .	1.0126	104.87	104.83	71.20	67.92
1940	21.954	−0.287	75.68	. . .	0.9967	103.22	103.18	75.65	73.31
1941	25.857	3.616	80.56	. . .	1.0429	108.01	108.02	80.57	74.59

Sources: In column 1, corporate national income is the sum of corporate national income and corporate capital consumption allowances as reported in the national income accounts (NIA), Table 1.13, row 3, and Table 6.18, row 1, *minus* corporate depreciation valued in current prices (using price deflator 2 for structures) and based on use of Bulletin F service lives, straight-line depreciation, and the Winfrey distribution; the depreciation series is from the OBE capital stock study, except that depreciation on corporate-owned dwellings is partly estimated; nonlabor earnings are corporate national income less compensation of corporate employees from NIA, Table 1.13, row 4; revised NIA data published in the July 1971 (Vol. 51) *Survey of Current Business* are used.

Column 2 is derived from column 1 and trend values computed in postwar years as 22.34094 minus 0.10021t, t_1 = 1947; the 1947 trend value (22.241) was used for prewar years.

Column 3 is derived from Table 6-1, column 1 divided by columns 2, 3, and 4.

Column 4 is the percentage by which column 3 exceeds its postwar trend value; the log of the trend value equals 4.42133 plus 0.01877t, t_1 = 1947; not computed for prewar years.

Column 5 is computed as: log of column 5 equals 0.01162 (column 2).

Column 6 is an index (1958 = 100) of column 5.

Column 7 is Table O-2, column 6, divided by Table 6-1, column 5.

Column 8 is Table O-2, column 3, divided by Table 6-1, column 5.

Column 9 is column 8 divided by column 7.

brevity, I shall call it "adjusted output per unit of input." It is shown in Table O-2, column 3. With one exception, the effects of all the determinants of productivity which I attempt to estimate on an annual basis have been thus eliminated except those (economies of scale, and "advances in knowledge and n.e.c.") whose estimation itself requires use of the effects of changes in intensity of utilization. The exception is the series, just derived, for the effects of work stoppages on output per unit of input. The reason for this exception is that work stoppages may be expected to affect both the nonlabor share and productivity in much the same way as do variations in demand pressure. I shall use the nonlabor share to estimate the combined effects of these two determinants, and then subdivide them. I believe the "adjusted productivity" series used here to be both statistically and conceptually superior to any productivity series previously available for analysis of the effects of changes in utilization.

The preliminary test was a simple correlation between $\dot{Y}$, the percentage change from the previous year in adjusted output per unit of input, and ΔX, the change from the previous year in the nonlabor share of corporate national income, measured in percentage points. The line of relationship, based on use of annual data from 1948 (the first year for which the changes were available) through 1969, is:

(1) $\dot{Y} = 2.0322 + 1.1511\ \Delta X.$

The test showed that the two variables were rather closely correlated, with $r = 0.903$ and $\bar{r}^2$ (r^2 reduced for degrees of freedom) $= 0.806$.

For comparison, I successively substituted as the independent variable in the correlation the unemployment rate, the change from the previous year in the unemployment rate (measured in percentage points), and the percentage change from the previous year in total hours worked in the business sector by nonfarm wage and salary workers.[10]

Values of r and $\bar{r}^2$ from these three correlations compare as follows with those based on the change in the nonlabor share:

Independent variable	r	$\bar{r}^2$
Change in the nonlabor share of corporate national income	0.903	0.806
Percentage of civilian labor force unemployed	0.157	−0.024
Change in the percentage of civilian labor force unemployed	0.458	0.171
Percentage change in nonfarm business wage and salary worker hours	0.486	0.198

As indicated by the values of $\bar{r}^2$, none "explains" even one-fourth as much of the variation in annual productivity change. The unemployment rate has no explanatory value.

Because annual data may obscure changes within the year, at least the latter two of these measures would probably perform better if accurate monthly or quarterly data could be obtained for adjusted output per unit of input and used in the regressions with lags introduced. A great merit of the use of income shares is that intensity of utilization affects income shares and productivity simultaneously so that use of annual data involves little or no loss.

Correspondence between the Nonlabor Share and Productivity Not Helped by Wage-Price Movements

Annual changes in the corporate nonlabor share are mainly a function of changes in the intensity of utilization, but they are also affected by the size of differentials between changes in the price of corporate value added and changes in corporate money wage rates.

Suppose that particularly large annual productivity increases occurring for any reason at all had a systematic tendency to cause the excess of the annual increase in wage rates over the annual increase in prices to be particularly small (which would tend to cause the nonlabor share to rise). Such a relationship would contribute to the positive relationship between changes in productivity and in the nonlabor share that I ascribe to the influence on both of intensity of utilization.

Estimates from an OBE study of nonfinancial corporations, which are shown in Table O-3, permit the hypothesis that such a tendency is present to be tested and rejected.[11] For the years 1949

---

10. Values for the first and third of these series are shown in Table O-5, columns 2 and 3. The second series is derived from the first. The way that the adjusted series for output per unit of input is constructed indicated that nonfarm business wage and salary worker hours would be the most appropriate hours series.

11. Wage-price differentials in all corporations (to which the nonlabor shares I use refer) could scarcely differ much from those in nonfinancial corporations. The price and wage data do not conform exactly to the definitions of output and a unit of labor that are appropriate for use with my output per unit of input, but they are near enough for this test.

Table O-3. Nonfinancial Corporations: Annual Changes in Selected Variables, 1949–70

| | Percentage change from preceding year in: | | | Change in compensation per hour minus change in price per unit $\dot{c} - \dot{p}$ (4) |
| | Compensation per man-hour, $\dot{c}$ (1) | Price per unit of gross product originating, $\dot{p}$ (2) | Constant-dollar GNP originating per man-hour worked, $\dot{o}$ (3) | |
Year				
1949	3.8	1.5	2.6	2.3
1950	5.5	1.1	6.6	4.4
1951	8.1	5.3	1.8	2.8
1952	5.9	2.6	0.6	3.3
1953	6.1	0.8	3.2	5.3
1954	3.8	1.4	2.8	2.4
1955	3.7	1.6	5.1	2.1
1956	6.2	3.9	−0.3	2.3
1957	6.3	3.3	2.6	3.0
1958	3.9	2.1	1.0	1.8
1959	4.2	1.1	5.0	3.1
1960	4.0	1.1	1.7	2.9
1961	2.8	0.7	3.0	2.1
1962	4.1	0.5	4.5	3.6
1963	3.6	0.5	3.9	3.1
1964	3.1	1.1	3.1	2.0
1965	3.4	0.5	3.8	2.9
1966	5.0	1.7	2.3	3.3
1967	5.3	2.9	1.1	2.4
1968	7.5	2.5	4.3	5.0
1969	6.7	3.0	1.1	3.7
1970	6.5	4.2	1.1	2.3

Sources: Columns 1–3, unpublished estimates of the Office of Business Economics, subsequently published with modifications in John A. Gorman, "Nonfinancial Corporations: New Measures of Output and Input," *Survey of Current Business*, Vol. 52 (March 1972), pp. 21–28; column 4, column 1 − column 2.

through 1970, this study provides the percentage change from the preceding year in compensation of corporate employees per man-hour worked, which I designate $\dot{c}$; in the price of corporate GNP, which I designate $\dot{p}$; and in corporate output (constant-dollar GNP) per hour worked in corporations, which I designate $\dot{o}$.

The amount by which the percentage change in corporate compensation per hour worked exceeded that in the price of corporate GNP, $\dot{c} - \dot{p}$, was related to the percentage change in each of two productivity measures.[12] One is the OBE estimate of output per man-hour in corporations, $\dot{o}$. The other is my series for adjusted output per

12. The calculations are based on annual changes for 1948–49 through 1968–69, all the years for which the three series are available.

unit of input in the nonresidential business sector, previously designated $\dot{Y}$. The results were as follows:

	Line of relationship	r	$\bar{r}^2$
(2)	$\dot{c} - \dot{p} = 2.465 + 0.201\,\dot{o}$	0.361	0.084
(3)	$\dot{c} - \dot{p} = 2.851 + 0.105\,\dot{Y}$	0.236	0.006

The values of $\bar{r}^2$ fail to confirm the presence of any appreciable relationship between wage-price differentials and either measure of productivity change. The value of this measure is approximately zero when my series for adjusted productivity is used, as it is in equation (1), the relationship being tested. Moreover, the coefficients for the productivity variables not only are small and statistically nonsignificant but also have the wrong sign. If their values were significant, their positive sign would indicate that it is when productivity rises most that wage rates rise most relative to prices. This would introduce positive correlation between changes in productivity and in the labor share, and negative correlation between changes in productivity and in the nonlabor share —the opposite of the observed relationship. These results permit rejection of the hypothesis that wage-price movements contribute to the correlation between changes in the corporate nonlabor share and in adjusted output per unit of input.

They do not imply that *irregular* changes in wage and price relationships can be ignored. The presence of such movements prevents the relationship between changes in the nonlabor share and in productivity from being even closer than it is, and they must be considered again when the nonlabor share is used to estimate annual values of an index for the effects of intensity of utilization on productivity.

Estimation of the Index

The exact method by which the nonlabor share was used to estimate the effect upon output per unit of input of fluctuations in the intensity of use of employed resources due to changes in the intensity of demand is now described. The first five steps (for which the calculations are shown in detail in Table O-2) lead to a preliminary index which takes no account of irregular wage-price movements. The sixth step (for which calculations are detailed in Table O-4) introduces a rather minor adjustment to correct for their influence.

Step One

Trends were fitted to the 1947–69 data for the nonlabor share, *X,* and for adjusted output per unit of input, *Y.* With $t = 1$ set at 1947, the computed trend value of the corporate nonlabor share, *Xc,* is

$$(4) \qquad Xc = 22.34094 - 0.10021t,$$

and the computed trend value of adjusted output per unit of input, *Yc,* is

$$(5) \qquad \log Yc = 4.42133 + 0.01877t.$$

Step Two

The number of percentage points by which the nonlabor share deviated from its 1947–69 trend value, $X - Xc$, and the percentage by which adjusted output per unit of input departed from its trend value, $100\left(\dfrac{Y}{Yc} - 1\right)$, were computed. These deviations are shown in Table O-2, columns 2 and 4. That they have a general tendency to vary together is apparent.

Step Three

The ratio of the actual adjusted productivity index to its trend value, $\dfrac{Y}{Yc}$, was correlated with the deviation (in percentage points) of the nonlabor share from its trend value, $X - Xc$. If the value of $\dfrac{Y}{Yc}$ that is computed from the regression is designated I, then

$$(6) \qquad \log I = 0.01162(X - Xc).$$

The relationship implies that a deviation of 1 percentage point in the nonlabor share (which is about 4.7 percent of its average value) is associated with a deviation of about 1.18 percent in adjusted output per unit of input.[13] The value of r is 0.949 and that of $\bar{r}^2$ is 0.896.

Step Four

The relationship obtained in step 3 is used to estimate the effect upon adjusted output per

13. The Durbin-Watson statistic is 1.89, close to the value of 2 which indicates a random distribution of residuals over time. Hence, it appears that this relationship has not changed despite different growth rates for the different types of input. This is to be expected. The weights used to combine labor (the more variable input) with capital and land (the less variable inputs) to calculate total input have changed but little, and even if they had changed considerably this would not cause the coefficient of $(X - Xc)$ to change because these weights correspond to relative business costs in current prices for the factors.

unit of input of variations in the intensity of utilization. Values of I calculated from equation (6) are shown in column 5 of Table O-2. In column 6, the ratios are converted to an index with 1958 = 100. This index provides a preliminary measure of the estimated effect of variations in the intensity of utilization of employed resources upon the index of output per unit of input.

Step Five

This index is divided by the index of the effects of work stoppages to obtain a preliminary series for the desired measure of the effects of fluctuations in the pressure of demand upon output per unit of input. This wording implies that all fluctuations in intensity of utilization that are not due to labor disputes derive from demand fluctuations; I believe this is substantially the case. The series is shown in Table O-2, column 7. It is also plotted (expressed with its average postwar value as 100) as the dotted line in Figure O-1, where it may be compared with the index finally obtained after the refinement to be introduced at step 6 has been incorporated.

Table O-2 also shows, in column 8, the index of adjusted productivity after eliminating the effects of labor disputes and, in column 9, a preliminary index, obtained by use of column 7, for productivity with the effects of fluctuations in the pressure of demand also removed.

Step Six

The sixth and final step is to adjust the preliminary indexes shown in Table O-2, columns 7 and 9, in order to remove the effects of erratic fluctuations in wage-price movements upon the nonlabor share, and hence upon the utilization series. It has only a modest effect upon the preliminary estimates already derived.

The procedure adopted thus far could yield entirely accurate estimates of year-to-year changes only if, at all times when intensity of utilization is changing in a particular way, changes in the differential between the price of corporate net value added at factor cost and the compensation of corporate employees per unit of labor input, as I define labor input, occur in a uniform way. An unusual movement in the relationship between prices and wages could alter the pattern of change in the nonlabor share as utilization changes, and hence the preliminary utilization series. If prices for net output of nonfinancial corporations valued

Figure O-1. Nonresidential Business: Indexes of Effect of Fluctuations in Pressure of Demand upon Output per Unit of Input, 1947–69

Index (postwar average = 100)

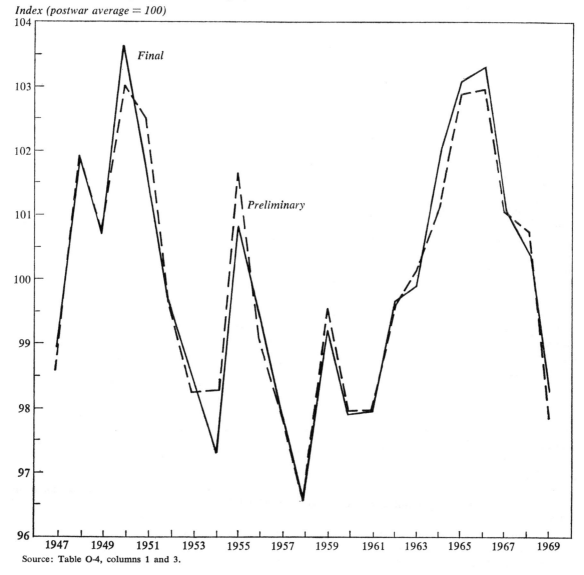

Source: Table O-4, columns 1 and 3.

at factor cost, and compensation per unit of labor input used by such corporations, had been available, the nonlabor share could have been adjusted to eliminate the effects of irregular wage-price movements before it was used in equations (4) and (6) and this difficulty avoided. Such data are not available and the requisite series for compensation of corporate employees per unit of labor input cannot be derived from available data.

The OBE data for the price per unit of GNP originating in nonfinancial corporations and cor-

porate compensation per man-hour can, however, be used as substitute indicators to improve the annual estimates by a less direct procedure. There can be little question that the spread between the change in the price of GNP and the change in compensation per man-hour in nonfinancial corporations, previously designated $\dot{c} - \dot{p}$, ordinarily is especially large or small in the same years that the spread between the change in the price of net national product at factor cost (NI) and the change in compensation per unit of labor input in nonresidential business is especially large or small.[14] This relationship is assumed to be present, and used to adjust the preliminary estimates even though erratic differences between the series are likely to occur in individual years.[15] A two-stage procedure is adopted. The first ignores, and the second corrects for, an important restriction upon the use of the OBE data: it cannot be assumed that the *amplitude* of fluctuations in the differentials between hourly compensation and GNP price in nonfinancial corporations obtained from OBE is the same as that in differentials between compensation per unit of labor input and price of NI in nonresidential business.

It was found in equation (3) that there is no correlation between $\dot{c} - \dot{p}$ and the change in adjusted productivity, $\dot{Y}$, before the effect of intensity of utilization is eliminated.[16] I now designate as $\dot{Z}$ the annual percentage change in column 9 of Table O-2, the preliminary series for adjusted productivity after the effects of changes in intensity of utilization are eliminated by use of the preliminary series shown in column 7. If there is significant correlation between $\dot{Z}$ and $\dot{c} - \dot{p}$ it must have been introduced by the preliminary utilization adjustment, and this is possible only insofar as irregular wage-price movements affected the behavior of the labor share.

Such a relationship is in fact present. The regression line is

$$(7) \qquad \dot{Z} = 0.31024 + 0.54614(\dot{c} - \dot{p}).$$

The fit, though only fair, is statistically significant. The value of r is 0.593, when a value greater than 0.439 indicates significance at the 95 percent probability level, and $\bar{r}^2$ is 0.317. This relationship can be used to remove the effects of unusual wage-price changes upon the preliminary utilization index.

In the first stage, computed values of $\dot{Z}$ were obtained for the change between each pair of years by applying equation (7) to $\dot{c} - \dot{p}$ (shown in Table O-3). These values were linked to obtain a continuous index (1958 = 100) that is similar in concept (but with a defect yet to be removed) to that shown in Table O-2, column 9, for adjusted productivity with the effects of changes in intensity of utilization eliminated.[17] The index for the effect of fluctuations in the pressure of demand (comparable to column 7 of Table O-2) that is implied by this series was then calculated. The ratio of the value of this index to its postwar average is shown in Table O-4, column 2. Comparable values for the original index, which did not take wage-price movements into account, are shown in column 1.

Because it allows for irregular wage-price movements, column 2 presumably displays a better ordering of the years and the relationships among them with respect to intensity of utilization due to fluctuations in demand. But the procedure by which this was accomplished incorrectly changed —in fact, widened—the amplitude of the fluctuations in the index. The best estimate of the *amount* by which output per unit of input fluctuates with changes in the nonlabor share is that obtained from equation (6), and it should be retained.[18] The second stage corrects for this defect. The deviations from the postwar average shown in Table O-4, column 2, were simply squeezed enough to obtain the same standard deviation as that in the original series that was obtained before allowance for wage-price changes.[19] The resulting estimates are shown in Table O-4, column 3. Expressed with 1958 = 100, this series is shown in column 4; it is my final index of the effects of fluctuations in intensity of demand upon output per unit of in-

---

14. Both output series are measured "from the income side" so the statistical discrepancy does not introduce an incomparability between them.

15. An indirect indication that the assumption is probably correct is that when corporate GNP per man-hour shows an especially big or small change, my series for adjusted productivity in the nonresidential business sector usually but not always shows a similar change.

16. This result is unchanged if, for precise comparability with equation (7) below, Y is first adjusted to remove the effects of work stoppages, and equation (3) is then recomputed with $\dot{Y}$ as the dependent and $\dot{c} - \dot{p}$ as the independent variable.

17. A 1947–48 link cannot be obtained because $\dot{c} - \dot{p}$ is not available. The 1947–48 movement shown by the original index was therefore retained.

18. It was obvious that the introduction of equation (7) into the estimate was likely to change the amplitude of fluctuations if only because $\dot{c}$ and $\dot{p}$ are not the wage and price measures we really want. Indeed, we can be certain that the movement of $\dot{c}$, which is obtained by dividing total compensation of employees by total hours worked, differs systematically over the cycle from total compensation per unit of labor input because total labor input is more stable than total man-hours; as was discovered in the development of the labor input series, persons receiving the least weight in labor input are those most likely to be unemployed or employed part time in periods of slack demand. A difference in the opposite direction between $\dot{p}$ and the price of net value added at factor cost is probable though not established.

19. The exact procedure was to calculate annually the square of the deviation of each series from its postwar mean; compute the ratio (0.731) of the sum of the squares of the deviations in the first series to that in the second; multiply the annual squared deviation in the second series by this ratio; and compute the square root of the product.

Table O-4. Nonresidential Business: Derivation of Final Index of Effects of Fluctuations in Pressure of Demand upon Output per Unit of Input, 1947–69 and Selected Prewar Years

| | Ratio of index of effects of fluctuations in pressure of demand to its 1947–69 average | | | Final indexes (1958 = 100) | | |
| | | | | Effect of fluctuations in pressure of demand upon output per unit of input | Adjusted output per unit of input after elimination of effects of work stoppages and fluctuations in pressure of demand | Percentage change from previous year in column 5 |
Year	Preliminary index (1)	Intermediate index (2)	Final index (3)	(4)	(5)	(6)
			Postwar years			
1947	0.9859	0.9882	0.9895	102.45	82.48	n.a.
1948	1.0192	1.0215	1.0191	105.51	83.15	0.82
1949	1.0072	1.0079	1.0070	104.26	84.33	1.42
1950	1.0302	1.0409	1.0364	107.30	86.92	3.07
1951	1.0247	1.0199	1.0177	105.36	88.33	1.62
1952	0.9962	0.9965	0.9969	103.21	89.96	1.85
1953	0.9824	0.9818	0.9838	101.86	92.69	3.03
1954	0.9828	0.9698	0.9732	100.75	94.06	1.48
1955	1.0167	1.0093	1.0083	104.39	95.86	1.91
1956	0.9909	0.9940	0.9946	102.98	97.20	1.39
1957	0.9794	0.9774	0.9799	101.45	98.91	1.76
1958	0.9652	0.9616	0.9659	100.00	100.00	1.11
1959	0.9952	0.9910	0.9920	102.70	102.35	2.35
1960	0.9792	0.9760	0.9787	101.32	104.11	1.72
1961	0.9796	0.9763	0.9789	101.35	105.63	1.46
1962	0.9964	0.9963	0.9967	103.19	108.28	2.51
1963	1.0015	0.9986	0.9988	103.40	110.48	2.03
1964	1.0123	1.0225	1.0201	105.61	112.32	1.67
1965	1.0288	1.0350	1.0312	106.76	114.60	2.03
1966	1.0296	1.0372	1.0331	106.96	117.05	2.14
1967	1.0105	1.0128	1.0113	104.71	118.64	1.36
1968	1.0078	1.0052	1.0046	104.01	122.14	2.96
1969	0.9784	0.9802	0.9824	101.71	124.64	2.04
			Prewar years			
1929	1.0119	n.a.	1.0119	104.76	67.96	n.a.
1940	0.9959	n.a.	0.9959	103.11	73.37	n.a.
1941	1.0426	n.a.	1.0426	107.95	74.64	1.73

Sources: Column 1, computed from Table O-2, column 7; column 2, computed for postwar years from intermediate index of effects of fluctuations in pressure of demand, obtained by dividing Table O-2, column 3, by Table 6-1, column 5, and by the index derived from equation (7) (no index available for prewar years because of lack of wage-price data); column 3, computed for postwar years from column 2 adjusted to obtain the same standard deviation as column 1 (as explained in text) and for prewar years, same as column 1; column 4, column 3 recomputed with 1958 = 100; column 5, Table O-2, column 8, divided by Table O-4, column 4; column 6, computed from column 5.

n.a. Not available.

put. The final index of adjusted productivity, with the effects of changes in utilization eliminated by use of this series, is shown in column 5.

Because this explanation of procedures in the sixth step is a bit complex, an illustration of its effect on the analysis of year-to-year changes may be helpful. Adjusted productivity, with the effects of labor disputes removed, decreased by 0.77 percent from 1966 to 1967. Based on use of the observed decline in the nonlabor share alone, it was estimated (in Table O-2) that changes in the intensity of demand pressure reduced adjusted pro-

ductivity by 1.87 percent while all other determinants raised it by 1.10 percent. However, the percentage change in corporate wages from 1966 to 1967 exceeded that in corporate prices by only 2.4 percentage points, much less than the average difference of 3.04 points. If wage-price changes had been normal the nonlabor share would have fallen more than it did from 1966 to 1967, and I would have estimated a greater drop in intensity of utilization. The procedure just described provides an estimate of the amount: the corrected estimate (from Table O-4) is that the reduction in demand intensity reduced adjusted productivity by 2.10 percent and all other determinants raised it by 1.36 percent. In most years the correction was much smaller.

In Figure O-1 the final index of the effect of fluctuations in the pressure of demand is charted. It is apparent that this final adjustment had only a minor effect upon the series, but the estimates for a few years were, I believe, improved.

Comments on the Procedure

I now pause for five observations upon the procedure just described.

1. For comparison with the relationship that is crucial in the procedure, equation (6), the deviations of adjusted output per unit of input from its trend were correlated with deviations from trend of the unemployment rate (measured in percentage points), with deviations from trend of man-hours worked by nonfarm wage and salary workers in the business sector, and with the percentage change from the preceding year in this man-hour series.[20] In addition, a multiple correlation was calculated in which both the deviation from trend of the unemployment rate and the percentage change from the previous year in total hours worked in the business sector by nonfarm wage and salary workers were used as independent variables. This relationship introduces both a measure of the general looseness or tightness of the labor market and a measure of the change in labor on hand in the sector, and seems about as sensible as any formulation that relies on labor force data. The values of r and $\bar{r}^2$ obtained by use of the alternative independent variables are as follows:

	r	$\bar{r}^2$
Corporate nonlabor share (deviation from 1947–69 trend)	0.949	0.896
Unemployment rate (deviation from 1947–69 trend)	0.441	0.156
Nonfarm business wage-salary hours (deviation from 1947–69 trend)	0.416	0.133
Percentage change in nonfarm business wage-salary hours	0.670	0.421
Unemployment rate and percentage change in nonfarm business wage-salary hours	0.681	0.407

The unemployment rate and deviations of hours worked by nonfarm business wage and

20. The trend was removed from the first two series to avoid biasing comparisons in favor of the relationship based on the nonlabor share. Because the third series is not available for 1947, the regression was based on 1948–69 data, as was the multiple regression described in the following sentence.

salary workers from their trend have almost no explanatory value. The percentage change in hours worked performs better but (as indicated by $\bar{r}^2$) has less than half the explanatory value of the nonlabor share. Inclusion of the unemployment rate, in addition, turns out not to improve its predictive power significantly; the value of $\bar{r}^2$ is actually reduced a bit. Although my strong preference for the corporate nonlabor share as an indicator of intensity of utilization of employed resources is based on a priori considerations, it is again supported by the data.

2. Although it was necessary to compute trends to derive the relationship with the nonlabor share obtained in step 3, the relationship itself is used without change throughout the period to estimate the effects of intensity of utilization upon productivity each year. The procedure in no way imposes a constant trend upon the series obtained for output per unit of input after the effects of changes in utilization are eliminated, or prevents a change in trend, if it exists, from appearing in that series. Neither are the effects of any other determinants upon the movement of the series smoothed or eliminated by this procedure. This statement is not compromised by the method adopted at step 6 to eliminate the effects of irregular wage-price changes upon the nonlabor share and hence upon the preliminary estimate of intensity of utilization.

There can, of course, be no ironclad guarantee against the possibility that some unsuspected, unidentified influence other than utilization or wage-price movements might have altered the underlying trends of both the nonlabor share and adjusted productivity at the same time and in the same direction; if this happened, it could obscure a change in trend in the series obtained for productivity after elimination of the effects of changes in utilization. But I am aware of no such possible influence.

3. In the calculations, I have used deviations of the nonlabor share from its linear trend, rather than from its mean value or a trend computed in some other way. It is fairly clear that the correct trend value was lower in the last several years of the period than in the first several years, and hence that use of the mean value would be incorrect. But the necessity of selecting a particular formula to express the downward trend is probably the weakest link in the procedure because the downward trend may not have been gradual. The most plausible alternative assumption is that it was stronger in the first half of the period than in the second half, or possibly even confined to

the first half. If so, I may have underestimated intensity of utilization in the middle years. But any alternative to selection of a simple linear trend would be at least equally arbitrary.

4. The minor correction for wage-price movements introduced at step 6 probably improved the series as a whole. Nevertheless, because the price and wage series used differ in definition from those which would be appropriate, it is quite possible that the adjustment worsened the estimates for some individual years. It would be unwise to draw from the estimates any conclusions that would be reversed if the preliminary series were substituted for the final series. The differences are so small that this particular caution limits use of the estimates for only a few comparisons.

5. Although the procedure based on use of the nonlabor share is the best I can devise, I am under no illusions that the resulting estimates are wholly free from error. The only remaining check that can be made is a detailed examination of the estimates themselves to see whether they appear to be generally reasonable. I shall first consider the utilization estimates themselves and then, in less detail, the series for productivity with the effect of utilization eliminated.

Examination of Demand Pressure Indexes for Individual Postwar Years

The estimates for individual postwar years of the effect of the intensity of the pressure of demand upon output per unit of input are next examined. Are they reasonable on the basis of general knowledge about these years? In Table O-5 the years are ranked by the size of the estimated effect upon output per unit of input of variations in the pressure of demand upon employed resources. The ratio of the estimate for each year to the average value in the postwar years is shown in column 1. Thus, an entry above one indicates that employed resources were used with more than average intensity, an entry of less than one the converse.

The most important type of information, other than the income shares themselves, that is relevant to an examination concerns the dates of business cycles. There have been five recessions since 1945. Based on annual data, the troughs were in 1949, 1954, 1958, 1961, and 1970, and the peaks occurred in the immediately preceding years. Monthly peaks and troughs up to 1969, as dated by the National Bureau of Economic Research (except for the 1969 date), were as follows:[21]

Trough	*Peak*
October 1945	November 1948
October 1949	July 1953
August 1954	July 1957
April 1958	May 1960
February 1961	Summer 1969

Peaks are dated by reference to series that are not adjusted for trend. When a downturn is preceded by a period of only slight advance, as is usually but not always the case, these peaks occur later than they would if allowance were made for normal growth. Similarly, the troughs sometimes occur earlier than they would if such an allowance were made.

For the reader's convenience, the unemployment rate and the percentage change from the preceding year in total man-hours worked by nonfarm wage and salary workers are also shown in Table O-5 as indications of the market for labor, the biggest input. The unemployment rate, however, has almost no relevance for examination of productivity: it was rejected as an indicator both on a priori grounds and because, empirically, it is barely related to productivity change.[22] The change in hours worked has somewhat more pertinence but must be used with great caution because it can be raised either by strong demand or by labor hoarding, reasons that have opposite implications for productivity. A general characterization of each year is also provided. Finally, I show what the estimate in Table O-5, column 1, would have been if I had omitted the final step in the estimation procedure, the adjustment to eliminate the effect of the differential movement of wages and prices.[23]

For convenient discussion, I have divided the

21. "Summer 1969" is debatable. In 1969 output and labor force data diverged widely. Although the NBER has tentatively set November as the peak month, the choice appears to have been dominated by series reflecting labor market conditions. My interest is in output which (as explained later) appears to have peaked by summer. Ilse Mintz found that the "deflated growth cycle" turned down earlier, in March, and the undeflated one in June. See "Dating U.S. Growth Cycles," in National Bureau of Economic Research, *52nd Annual Report, September 1972: Innovations in Economic Research* (New York: NBER, 1972), pp. 28–29.

22. It is also obvious from the most casual inspection of Table O-5 that use of the unemployment rate as an indicator would yield a very different ranking of the years with respect to intensity of utilization and one which, I am convinced, would be grossly in error.

23. The final estimate differs from the preliminary estimate by as much as 0.5 percent in five of the twenty-three years; it is higher in 1950 and 1964 and lower in 1951, 1954, and 1955.

postwar years into three groups in Table O-5, using 1.5 percent above and 1.5 percent below the postwar average as the boundaries.

Low-Utilization Years. The group at the bottom of the table contains seven years in which, it is estimated, low intensity of utilization of employed resources resulting from weak demand pressure reduced output per unit of input most: by 1.6 to 3.4 percent in comparison with an average postwar year. Three years were annual recession troughs. Four were years in which recession began; in each case, the peak had been reached by about mid-year. Contractions are the normal examples of periods when intensity of utilization is low so that all seven would be expected to fall in this group. All seven of these years (and no others) would also have been in this group if I had not introduced the adjustment for wage-price movements, and only for 1954 would the value of the intensity index have been noticeably different.

The year 1969 is a particularly interesting case and calls for additional comment. Interpretation of the 1969 economic situation was controversial at the time. There were many signs of sluggishness in demand all year, and especially in the second half. Retail sales were nearly flat all year despite rising prices. Industrial production dipped in August and moved down steadily after September. Real GNP, which is available only quarterly, rose by much less than its trend rate in each of the first three quarters and declined in the fourth; the pattern was consistent with a peak in any of the summer months. In contrast, the year-to-year increase in man-hours worked was large, employment rose until the very end of the year, and unemployment failed to move up. The available evidence suggested weak demand for products—given the sharp rise in prices which was concurrently under way—accompanied by a tight labor market.[24] Those who accepted the data explained the situation as one in which employers, conditioned by a business expansion of unprecedented length and anticipating an early recovery, were hoarding labor on an extraordinary scale. This interpretation was consistent with the surprising decline that was being reported in output per man-hour. Other observers, unpersuaded that labor hoarding could explain so large a difference between output and labor data, suspected one or the other to be in error. The behavior of income shares, which leads to my estimate of utilization, is consistent with the former interpretation of the year.[25] The strength of employment in the face of weakening demand was the main *cause* of low utilization of employed resources in 1969, not an indication that at prevailing prices the pressure of demand for products was strong. The capital stock was also increasing rapidly in that year.

High-Utilization Years. Grouped at the upper end of Table O-5 are six years in which output per unit of input is estimated to have been raised 1.8 to 3.6 percent above average by intense utilization of employed resources resulting from demand pressure. Actually, the six might be subdivided between a "very high" subgroup (3.1 to 3.6 percent) and a "high" subgroup (1.8 to 2.0 percent). Four (1950, 1951, 1965, and 1966) of the six years, including the three in the highest category, are "war boom" years: years in which a sudden and largely unanticipated rise in defense spending occurred as a result of war. The Korean hostilities started in mid-1950, at a time when output already was rising very sharply from the 1949 recession low. Accentuated by the entry of China into the war and by waves of buying by consumers who recalled World War II shortages, the boom continued through 1951. In 1965 the escalation of U.S. involvement in Vietnam transformed the strong but fairly orderly expansion then under way to one of excess demand, and this situation prevailed through 1966. A fifth year, 1964, was one of strong expansion, but on general grounds might have been expected to appear a little lower in the ranking of years (as, indeed, it would if the preliminary index had been adopted).

The remaining year in this group, 1948, requires comment because it is the only year preceding a recession trough in which intensity of utilization is not estimated to be decidedly *below* average. However, it differs from the others in two basic respects. First, the cyclical peak was not reached until November, whereas in other such years the peak was reached in July or earlier (with the possible exception of 1969). Second, the downturn was not preceded by a slow expansion. Real GNP rose by more than its trend rate in each of the four quarters of 1948, and without

---

24. The Bureau of Labor Statistics series for "percent of labor force time lost," which turned up early in 1969, is an exception to the latter statement.

25. It would not have done so on the basis of profits estimates for 1969 that were available at the time. Profits in 1969 were seriously overstated until the corporate income tax returns provided benchmark data. The overestimate of profits may have contributed to confusion at the time as to the actual situation.

Table O-5. Nonresidential Business: Postwar Years Ranked by Effect on Output per Unit of Input of Fluctuations in Pressure of Demand, with Selected Characteristics, 1947–69

Year	Ratio of index of demand pressure effect to its mean (1)	Unemployment rate (2)	Percentage change from preceding year in total hours worked in business by nonfarm wage and salary workers (3)	Characterization (4)	Ratio of preliminary demand pressure index to its mean (5)
High utilization					
1950	1.036	5.3	4.489	War boom	1.030
1966	1.033	3.8	4.513	War boom	1.030
1965	1.031	4.5	4.389	War boom	1.029
1964	1.020	5.2	2.537	Expansion	1.012
1948	1.019	3.8	1.093	Cyclical peak	1.019
1951	1.018	3.3	6.706	War boom	1.025
Medium utilization					
1967	1.011	3.8	0.589	Expansion	1.010
1955	1.008	4.4	4.228	Expansion	1.017
1949	1.007	5.9	−5.564	Trough	1.007
1968	1.005	3.6	2.268	Expansion	1.008
1963	0.999	5.7	1.795	Expansion	1.002
1952	0.997	3.0	1.627	Expansion	0.996
1962	0.997	5.5	2.902	Expansion	0.996
1956	0.995	4.1	2.359	Expansion	0.991
1959	0.992	5.5	4.553	Expansion	0.995
1947	0.990	3.9	n.a.	Expansion	0.986
Low utilization					
1953	0.984	2.9	1.811	2nd half recession	0.982
1969	0.982	3.5	3.094	2nd half recession	0.978
1957	0.980	4.3	−1.027	2nd half recession	0.979
1961	0.979	6.7	−1.392	Trough	0.980
1960	0.979	5.5	0.254	2nd half recession	0.979
1954	0.973	5.5	−4.701	Trough	0.983
1958	0.966	6.8	−4.922	Trough	0.965

Sources: Columns 1 and 5, Table O-4, columns 3 and 1; column 2, percentage of civilian labor force unemployed, as reported by U.S. Bureau of Labor Statistics; column 3, computed from Table E-1, column 3; column 4, see text.

n.a. Not available.

diminution of the size of quarterly gains except that the third quarter was especially strong. Thus 1948 did not include more than one month in which the lag of cuts in hours worked behind cuts in output could enter the picture. It is therefore to be expected that intensity of utilization was very much higher in 1948 than in 1953, 1957, 1960, or 1969, though perhaps not quite so high as my estimate implies.

Medium-Utilization Years. The middle group in Table O-5 contains ten years in which the pressure of demand on employed resources is estimated to have been such as to affect output per unit of input by amounts ranging from 1.0 percent below to 1.1 percent above the postwar average. Nine of these ten were years of business expansion that did not include business cycle turning points, neither peaks nor troughs, and were not "war boom" years. All such years except 1964 fall in this middle group. Although the ranking of these nine years within the middle group could

not have been predicted, all would have been expected to fall within the middle range, as they do.

Appearance of the tenth year, 1949, in this middle group with a ratio above average is the greatest surprise in the entire ranking of all the twenty-three years. All other trough years appear within the low-utilization group. The utilization ratio for 1949 exceeds those for 1954, 1958, and 1961 by 3.4, 4.1, and 2.8 percent, respectively. There are, however, reasons that the intensity of utilization may in fact have been much higher in 1949. The main reason is that intensity of utilization was much higher in the preceding year, 1948, than it was in the years preceding the later recession years.[26] To be sure, the immediate pre-trough years in later cycles were themselves affected by part years of recession, but the 1948 ratio was also much above (2.2, 2.4, and 2.7 percent) even

26. This statement assumes, of course, that the 1948 ratio, which has already been discussed, is itself approximately correct.

the ratios for those years (1952, 1956, and 1959) two years ahead of the later trough years (1954, 1958, and 1961). It can be inferred that even if the rate of utilization had dropped as much in the 1949 recession as in those of 1954 and 1961, it would have remained far above the rates in these other recession years.

Although the differences among the months in which turning points occurred obscure comparisons, my estimates probably also imply a drop in the intensity ratio during the 1949 recession that was smaller than average from peak to trough. If this is so, an unusually fast or drastic reduction in hours worked as demand for products slackened is probably implied. This possibility is not inconsistent with the man-hours data. The year-to-year decline in hours was greater in 1949 than in any other postwar year (though smaller than the two-year decline from 1956 to 1958 at the time of the deeper 1958 recession). The real evidence to support this conjecture, however, is the development that underlies my estimate: the fact that profits declined strikingly less in 1949 than in any subsequent recession period. Unusual wage-price movements do not obscure this comparison much because 1949 was in no way exceptional. The OBE estimates for nonfinancial corporations show the difference between the percentage change in wages and the percentage change in prices from the preceding year to have been as follows in recession years (Table O-3, column 4):

1949	2.3
1954	2.4
1958	1.8
1961	2.1
1970	2.3

It may also be noted that the 1949 ratio would be the same if the wage-price adjustment had not been introduced in the utilization estimate.

In summary, the method yields generally plausible results for the ranking of the years. The estimates for two or three of the years to which I have devoted most attention are surprises but they are tenable. There is no evidence sufficient to warrant altering them.

Productivity with Effects of Fluctuations in Demand Eliminated

Figure O-2 compares the series for output per unit of input in the nonresidential business sector, adjusted to eliminate the effects of reallocation of resources, of irregular fluctuations in farm output, and of work stoppages, before and after the estimated effects of variations in the pressure of demand upon employed resources are also removed. Because the base year, 1958, is the year of least intensive use of resources, the adjusted index is the lower of the two in all other years.

It is evident from the figure that eliminating the effects of fluctuations in the pressure of demand removes most of the irregularity in the series of output per unit of input. Table O-4, column 6, shows that appreciable variations in year-to-year changes nevertheless remain in the series from which the effects of such fluctuations are eliminated, perhaps larger than one might suspect from the figure. They are largest during the first eight years of the period. Variations in this series may in part reflect imperfections in the adjustment for fluctuations in the pressure of demand as well as in the other series entering into its construction, but there is no reason to expect irregularities to be absent from such a series even if it were perfectly accurate. Moreover, variations in the calendar (discussed in Part 4 of this appendix) alone would ensure their presence.

This series permits one final check to be made upon the *amplitude* of the swings in the series for the effect of demand pressure upon productivity. If it is correctly estimated, percentage changes in the final productivity index should not be correlated with those in the demand-intensity index: the coefficient for the latter in a regression should not differ significantly from zero. This expectation is satisfied; the coefficient is 0.06, very close to zero. The value of $\bar{r}^2$ is −0.008.

The Prewar Years

Estimates are also required for 1929, 1940, and 1941. A brief reminder of the characteristics of those years is in order.

The year 1929 was the last year of the generally prosperous, but noninflationary, 1920s. The BLS estimates that unemployment averaged a very low 3.2 percent. The preceding year, 1928, had been rather a poor one for output. From 1927 to 1928 real GNP had risen only 0.7 percent despite the depressing effect on output in the earlier year of the six-month Ford shutdown for conversion to the Model A. The retardation was made up in 1929, when real GNP rose by a strong 6.7 percent from 1928. The NBER dates a cyclical trough in November 1927, the last month of the

**Figure O-2. Nonresidential Business: Indexes of Adjusted Output per Unit of Input[a]
Including and Excluding the Effect of Fluctuations in Intensity of Pressure of Demand, 1947–69**

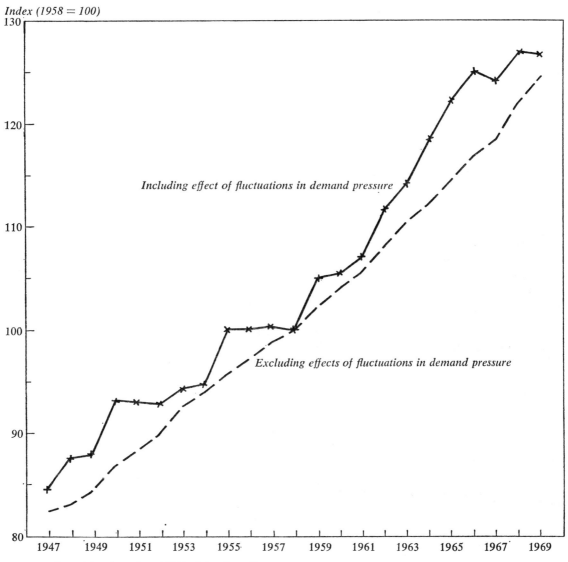

Index (1958 = 100)

Including effect of fluctuations in demand pressure

Excluding effects of fluctuations in demand pressure

Sources: Table O-2, column 8, and Table O-4, column 5.
a. Excludes the effects of reallocation of resources, irregularities in farm output, and work stoppages.

Ford shutdown, and a peak in August 1929. Thus most of 1929 was characterized by strong advance from the retarded output level of the preceding year, but the last four months followed the peak. Businessmen did not then know, of course, that the greatest depression in U.S. history had begun.

Following the tumultuous decline in output to its 1932–33 lows, a partial recovery to 1937, and the deep recession of 1938, output again began a strong recovery. After the outbreak of war in Europe in 1939 the expansion was reinforced by foreign orders for munitions, and in 1940 and especially 1941 by the United States preparedness program. The actual entry of the United States into the war came too late to affect 1941 figures appreciably. Real GNP rose by 8.6 percent in 1939 and by 8.5 percent in 1940, two of the largest advances on record. They were followed by a further increase of 16.1 percent in 1941, the largest single-year advance since 1891 when annual estimates first became available. Man-hours worked by nonfarm wage and salary workers in the business sector jumped 16.4 percent in 1941; in contrast, the largest increase in any postwar year was 6.7 percent (in 1951). Unemployment (including persons on work relief) had reached 24.9 percent in 1933. It was still very high, 14.6 percent, in 1940 and even in 1941 averaged 9.9 percent.

The nonlabor shares of corporate national income not only in these years but also, to provide perspective, in all years from 1925 to 1946 are given in Table O-6. They are comparable to the later data provided in Table O-2, column 1, but estimates for the years prior to 1929 are less reliable than the others.[27]

Estimates that do not incorporate the revaluation of depreciation are available back to 1922.[28] According to these estimates, the 1929 nonlabor share is the second highest, after 1926, of the eight years in the entire 1922–29 period. It appears that this would also be the case if estimates with depreciation revalued were available prior to 1925.[29] The level of the 1940 nonlabor share was much above any that had been previously attained since 1929, including the 1936–37 peak years. The 1941 nonlabor share was the highest in the entire 1922–69 period with the exception of the World War II years from 1942 through 1944.

The procedure used to obtain the preliminary

27. The 1929–46 estimates were obtained in the same way and from the same sources as those for later years (see source to Table O-2, column 1). So also were the 1925–28 estimates of capital consumption in current prices. Corporate compensation of employees and corporate nonlabor earnings on a national accounts basis (that is, based mainly on use of tax data for capital consumption) in 1925–28 were computed from the data in Harlow D. Osborne and Joseph B. Epstein, "Corporate Profits Since World War II," *Survey of Current Business*, Vol. 36 (January 1956), p. 20; and comparable 1929 data were obtained from U.S. Department of Commerce, Office of Business Economics, *National Income, 1954 Edition*, A Supplement to the *Survey of Current Business* (1954), Table 12. The levels of these 1925–29 series were adjusted (slightly) to conform with the revised 1929 levels currently reported in the NIA. Corporate capital consumption allowances as reported in the NIA for 1929 were extrapolated to 1925–28 by corporate depreciation as reported in U.S. Internal Revenue Bureau, *Statistics of Income* (for years 1925 through 1929).

28. Osborne and Epstein, "Corporate Profits Since World War II," p. 20.

29. Neither depreciation data from the capital stock study nor depreciation reported on corporate tax returns are available prior to 1925. However, it is clear that revaluation of depreciation would lower the nonlabor share in these earlier years relative to 1929.

Table O-6. Nonlabor Earnings as a Percentage of Corporate National Income, 1925–46

Year	Percent	Year	Percent
1925	19.600[a]	1936	18.404
1926	23.500[a]	1937	17.820
1927	20.100[a]	1938	14.547
1928	21.500[a]	1939	17.010
1929	23.315	1940	21.954
1930	19.364	1941	25.857
1931	10.525	1942	27.004
1932	−0.736	1943	26.901
1933	−2.446	1944	25.951
1934	10.379	1945	23.016
1935	14.651	1946	18.704

Sources: 1929–46, same as Table O-2, column 1; 1925–28, see note 27, below.

a. Estimates for these years are rounded to a tenth of a point but are actually subject to a much larger rounding error because in the principal source from which they are derived data were rounded to the nearest whole percentage point.

index of intensity of utilization in the postwar years can be applied to 1929, 1940, and 1941, but one modification is required. There is no reason to extend backward in time the downward trend ascribed, for reasons other than intensity of utilization, to the nonlabor share in the postwar period. There may even be some question as to whether the downward "postwar trend" was not a movement back toward a stable long-term level that offset a temporary upward "trend" from 1929 to 1947. The behavior of the ratio of fixed business capital to potential output or labor input might be a possible reason for such a reversal.

The 1947 trend value of the nonlabor share that was derived earlier was 22.241 percent. The constant underlying the calculation of this level is consistent with a utilization rate pitched at the average postwar level. A comparable value for 1929 needs to be estimated.

The actual nonlabor share in 1929 was 23.315. This rather clearly was above the value that would correspond to the average postwar utilization rate. One way to judge the amount is to examine a series of years within which 1929 lies. The nonlabor shares in years following 1929, unfortunately, were too radically reduced by the depression to be of any use for this purpose. The average value in the four years ending with 1929 was 22.1, just a shade below the 1947 trend value. That period included two good years (1926 and 1929), one (1927) that was affected by the Ford shutdown and includes the trough of a very mild recession, and one (1928) which is classified as an expansion but in which output scarcely increased.[30] The average intensity of utilization in this four-year period can reasonably be supposed to have been the same as, or perhaps a shade below, that in the postwar period. If so, the value of the non-labor share at the same intensity of utilization was about the same in 1929 as in 1947.

Another approach is to judge the intensity of utilization due to variations in demand pressure directly, and to work backward to obtain a "trend" value for the nonlabor share. The general characteristics of 1929 were such as to suggest to me that intensity of utilization due to pressure of demand on employed resources might place it between the "high" and "medium" utilization groups as they are arranged in Table O-5. Suppose that if 1929 were in that table it would appear with a value of 1.0114. Working backward (and taking into account the trivial effects of the labor disputes index but omitting the wage-price adjustment for lack of data) it can be computed that the deviation from trend in the 1929 nonlabor share that would be consistent with this estimate is 1.039. This would make the 1929 "trend" value for the nonlabor share that is consistent with the average postwar intensity of demand 22.276, just above the value of 22.241 for 1947.

Such considerations lead me to accept as reasonable a judgment that there was no appreciable trend in the nonlabor share from 1929 to 1947. The 1947 trend value can then be used as the trend value for the earlier years to approximate the preliminary index for the effect of fluctuations in pressure of demand in 1929, 1940, and 1941. The results of doing so are shown in the lower portion of Table O-2. They are then used without further adjustment to secure the final estimates in Table O-4 because the wage-price refinement cannot be introduced. If these years were inserted in Table O-5, 1929 with a ratio of 1.012 would appear at the top of the "medium-utilization" group of years and 1940 with a ratio of 0.996 in the middle of the group. The year 1941 with a ratio of 1.043 would stand well above any postwar year. This seems a reasonable result because the rate of economic expansion in 1941 was far bigger than in any other year and accelerating rapidly, and output was far above any previous year.

A year-to-year change in adjusted output per unit of input, with the effects of strikes removed, is available only from 1940 to 1941 in the period prior to 1947. Without allowance for the change in utilization the percentage increase was 6.50 percent, far above any postwar year. After eliminating this effect the change is 1.73 percent, not far from the average rate (1.58) from 1940 to 1948. Evidently, the method of adjustment by use of the nonlabor share handles reasonably well even as large a change in economic conditions as occurred from 1940 to 1941.

PART FOUR: VARIATIONS IN THE CALENDAR

The year varies from fifty-two weeks plus one Sunday to fifty-two weeks plus two weekdays. The amount of production that takes place in the nonresidential business sector on different days of the week is not known, but for illustration let us assume that output is the same on all weekdays, and one-fourth as large on Saturdays and one-tenth as large on Sundays as it is on weekdays. Assume also that holidays reduce work time by the equivalent of one workweek each year. A minimum year would then consist of the production equivalent of 272.95 weekdays.[31] A maximum year would consist of the equivalent of 274.85 workdays or 0.7 percent more. When a maximum year like 1968 follows a minimum year like 1967, output, if it were accurately measured, would rise by this amount due solely to the calendar. Output per unit of input would be affected by the same amount because my measure of total factor input takes no account of the length of the year. (Labor input is based on weekly averages and other inputs on average stocks.) Table O-7 shows, in column 1, an illustrative index of the effect of the calendar upon actual output per unit of input in the sector, based upon the assumed weights for the days of the week. If output were measured accurately so that it properly took account of the length of the year, output per unit of input could be adjusted by use of such an index.

The actual situation is much less satisfactory. The calendar affects output as measured, but in a way that cannot be ascertained because of the reporting of employee compensation. Output, it

30. The reader will notice that I have omitted 1925, the first year for which an estimate based on the same procedure is available. I can justify its exclusion only by the observation that, based on the estimates available to me which may be inaccurate for the earlier years, the share seems to have moved at a lower level in 1922–25 than in 1926–29.

31. The calculation for fifty-two weeks is the sum of 255 weekdays, one-fourth of fifty-one Saturdays, and one-tenth of fifty-one Sundays, a total of 272.85. The extra Sunday brings the total to 272.95.

Table O-7. Nonresidential Business: Relation of Output to the Calendar, 1929, 1940–41, and 1947–69

Year	Illustrative index of effects of variations in the calendar upon true output (1958 = 100)[a] (1)	Perpetual calendar number (2)
1929	100.00	3
1940	100.37	9
1941	100.00	4
1947	100.00	4
1948	100.37	12
1949	99.73	7
1950	99.67	1
1951	100.00	2
1952	100.37	10
1953	100.00	5
1954	100.00	6
1955	99.73	7
1956	100.04	8
1957	100.00	3
1958	100.00	4
1959	100.00	5
1960	100.09	13
1961	99.67	1
1962	100.00	2
1963	100.00	3
1964	100.37	11
1965	100.00	6
1966	99.73	7
1967	99.67	1
1968	100.37	9
1969	100.00	4

Sources: Column 1, computed by weighting Saturdays one-fourth and Sundays one-tenth of weekdays, see text for explanation; column 2, Robert E. Johnson, *Calendars for the Years 1776 to 2027* (New York: Western Electric Co., 1952).

a. This index is not used in the general analysis of growth because it does not conform to the effects of the calendar upon output as actually measured; see text.

will be recalled, is measured, before deflation, from the "income side."[32] To evaluate the effect of the calendar, total income in the sector can be regarded as equal to (1) corporate profits and interest before deduction of depreciation *minus* (2) corporate depreciation *plus* (3) proprietors' income and noncorporate property income before deduction of depreciation *minus* (4) noncorporate depreciation *plus* (5) compensation of employees.

Item 1 appears to reflect fully and correctly the length of the year, at least for large corporations.[33] Receipts pick up extra days in the year

32. The situation is no clearer when output is measured from the "expenditures side." The effect of the calendar on expenditure components cannot be established.

33. Corporations reporting on other than a calendar year basis make it necessary to qualify this statement slightly.

and so do expenses including payrolls, which are so accrued that they increase when extra days are worked. Item 2, corporate depreciation, is wholly unaffected by the length of the year not only in corporate accounts but also in my estimates. Consequently item 1 minus item 2, which is corporate nonresidential nonlabor income, reflects variations in the length of the year to a degree that is even exaggerated, but by an ascertainable amount, when expressed in terms of percentage changes. Direct information about item 3 is lacking, but the best guess is that it is similar to item 1. Item 4, noncorporate depreciation, is measured in the same way as corporate depreciation in construction of the estimates. Given appropriate weights for the days of the week, such as were assumed earlier and used to construct Table O-7, one could readily estimate the effect of fluctuations in the calendar upon the first four components. But the measurement of employee compensation, which comprises most of the national income, makes such an estimate for the total impossible to construct.

Annual wages and salaries are based chiefly on the four quarterly reports required of employers by the state unemployment compensation systems; annual supplements to wages and salaries are almost entirely based on the same or similar reports, or else tied statistically to wages and salaries. Employers do not report payrolls on an accrual basis. They report wages paid during the quarter. The pay period varies from employer to employer both in length and in ending day or date. One week is the most common payroll period but the week may end on any day of the week.[34] The four quarterly reports by an employer on a weekly pay period will usually cover fifty-two weeks but sometimes fifty-three. Diversity of practice among employers helps to smooth out year-to-year fluctuations in total payrolls but concentrations of extra pay periods in particular years are undoubtedly present. Years in which reported payrolls are highest are only haphazardly related to those in which the index shown in Table O-7 is highest. For example, if Friday were the most common payday, then payrolls would be elevated most by irregularities in the calendar in years with an extra Friday (1948, 1954, 1960, 1965). But there is no information on the distribution of actual paydays or pay periods. Under these condi-

34. See U.S. Department of Labor, Manpower Administration, *Employment and Wages: Fourth Quarter 1968 and Annual Summary* (1971), p. 96.

tions it is impossible to ascertain the actual effect of the calendar on measured output per unit of input but there is no doubt that it has an effect that may appreciably affect year-to-year changes.

The best comparisons are between years in which the calendar is identical; they are impaired only if the distribution of payroll periods and days itself changes. Such years bear the same number in the last column of Table O-7. There are few identical years to provide such comparisons. Growth rates of the semiresidual between such years are shown with asterisks in Table 6-2.

The calendar may affect not only output per unit of input, the semiresidual, and the residual but also the index computed in Part 3 of this appendix for the effect of fluctuations in the intensity of the pressure of demand upon output per unit of input. That index, it will be recalled, is based on use of the nonlabor share of corporate national income, and corporate national income is obtained as the sum of labor and nonlabor earnings. If the second of two years that are identical except for effects of the calendar has more weekday-equivalent workdays than the first, but the same number of paydays, then nonlabor earnings and the nonlabor share will be higher in the second year and the intensity of utilization index will rise. If the second of the two years has the same number of workdays as the first, but more paydays, then the nonlabor share will be lower in the second year and the intensity of utilization index will decline. It is apparent that the calendar may introduce year-to-year changes in this index that are in the same or the opposite direction from those introduced into the index for total output per unit of input.

APPENDIX P

->>X<<-

Economies of Scale

->>X<<-

The estimation of the size of gains from economies of scale and the development of an index based on that estimation are described in Chapter 6. Further explanation of the procedure is given in this appendix.

PART ONE: ESTIMATION OF THE SIZE OF GAINS

The correlation analysis of postwar data undertaken for the purpose of estimating the *size* of gains from economies of scale is discussed in Chapter 6. Tables P-1 and P-2 provide additional detail.

The first two columns of Table P-1 show the indexes of M and Y from which growth rates for these variables, $\dot{M}$ and $\dot{Y}$, were computed. The third series used, $O + S$, is shown in Table 6-1, column 7 (the semiresidual).

Table P-2 shows the values for the variables in the first and second equations described in Chapter 6 that were obtained by use of growth rates over periods of different lengths. Values of the *t*-statistics and $\bar{r}^2$ are also shown, as are the Durbin-Watson statistics.

The values of the *t*-statistics and $\bar{r}^2$ are used only to compare the results of employing periods of different lengths to estimate terms in the same formula. They confirm the judgment that a period of three years is too short, but they suggest no great difference in reliability among the other periods. Their absolute values do not have the usual meaning as measures of significance because the number of independent observations is exaggerated. Thus, nineteen observations were used to estimate the equations from the four-year growth

Table P-1. Nonresidential Business: Indexes Used in Analysis of Economies of Scale, 1929, 1940–41, and 1947–69

1958 = 100

Year	Series used in correlation analysis[a]		Income series used to estimate economies-of-scale index (3)	Index of gains from economies of scale (4)
	Total factor input and gains from reallocation of resources (M) (1)	Constant-price national income with effects of irregular factors on output per unit of input eliminated (Y) (2)		
1929	65.40[b]	44.45[b]	42.66	89.35
1940	67.18[b]	49.29[b]	50.74	91.39
1941	74.76[b]	55.80[b]	52.81	91.88
1947	85.96	70.89	67.58	94.93
1948	87.52	72.78	69.85	95.35
1949	85.00	71.68	71.69	95.67
1950	88.19	76.65	73.58	96.00
1951	93.70	82.76	77.47	96.67
1952	96.39	86.71	82.41	97.47
1953	99.00	91.77	86.78	98.14
1954	96.32	90.60	90.25	98.65
1955	99.92	95.78	92.20	98.93
1956	102.41	99.54	95.01	99.33
1957	102.79	101.67	97.89	99.72
1958	100.00	100.00	100.00	100.00
1959	103.70	106.14	102.18	100.28
1960	104.81	109.12	104.72	100.61
1961	104.71	110.60	107.87	101.01
1962	107.37	116.27	111.35	101.43
1963	109.52	121.00	115.41	101.91
1964	112.10	125.91	120.10	102.45
1965	116.36	133.35	126.09	103.12
1966	121.32	142.01	133.91	103.95
1967	123.71	146.76	140.50	104.62
1968	127.26	155.42	146.99	105.25
1969	130.80	163.02	154.92	105.99

Sources: Column 1, Table 5-4, column 7, multiplied by Table 6-1, columns 2 and 3; column 2, Table 5-4, column 1, divided by Table 6-1, columns 4, 5, and 6; columns 3 and 4, see text of Chapter 6 and Appendix P.

a. The index of $O + S$ appears in Table 6-1, column 7.

b. Prewar years were not used in correlation analysis.

rates, and the measures were computed as if there were nineteen independent observations. But there are only five and one-half nonoverlapping four-year periods from 1947 to 1969. To recompute measures of significance as if there were only five- and one-half observations would be to reduce them far too much; the probability that correlation would appear by chance in five and one-half

Table P-2. Equations Relating to Economies of Scale

	Coefficients		t-statistics			
Length of time span	a	b	a	b	$\bar{r}^2$	Durbin-Watson
	First equation: $\dot{O} + \dot{S} = a + b\dot{M}$					
Three-year	1.7076	0.1056	22.47	3.20	0.33	1.16
Four-year	1.5839	0.1635	21.45	4.88	0.56	1.16
Five-year	1.5987	0.1589	22.59	4.74	0.56	1.52
Six-year	1.6540	0.1331	28.54	4.62	0.56	1.46
Seven-year	1.6315	0.1450	32.14	5.44	0.66	1.77
	Second equation: $\dot{O} + \dot{S} = a + b\dot{Y}$					
Three-year	1.4929	0.1077	13.77	4.13	0.46	1.21
Four-year	1.3200	0.1496	13.48	6.26	0.68	1.09
Five-year	1.3403	0.1459	13.86	6.03	0.68	1.47
Six-year	1.4320	0.1237	16.85	5.66	0.66	1.52
Seven-year	1.4052	0.1308	18.74	6.60	0.74	1.79

Sources: Computed from indexes appearing in Table 6-1, column 7, and Table P-1, columns 1 and 2.

observations is much higher than that it would appear by chance in the nineteen observations used. But how much of a reduction would be appropriate is unclear.[1]

As indicated in Chapter 6, there is no reason to suppose that the size of additional gains from economies of scale is not the same for changes in input and for components of output per unit of input (except economies of scale themselves). But it may be noted that if the size of gains were not the same the near consistency of the coefficients obtained from the two equations for periods of four to seven years in length shown by Table 6-3, columns 3 and 4, would be improbable. This is because the economy-of-scale effects measured in the first equation refer only to inputs and changes in two types of resource allocation, while those measured in the second equation refer in addition to all other determinants of output per unit of input (except the irregular factors whose effects were eliminated).

PART TWO: ESTIMATION OF THE INDEX OF GAINS FROM ECONOMIES OF SCALE

As explained in Chapter 6, the index of the gains from economies of scale (Table P-1, column 4) was derived by use of a series (shown in column 3) that was intended to reflect the changes in the size of markets to which the organization of business may reasonably be expected to have adapted.

1. The problem appears to be the same as that encountered when year-to-year changes in quarterly series are correlated.

The starting point for the series used in the postwar period to measure the size of markets appropriately was the index of national income in the nonresidential business sector with the effects of irregular factors upon output per unit of input removed. Index values for the trough recession years—1949, 1954, 1958, and 1961—were discarded and replaced by interpolated values.[2] The percentage change from the prior year was then calculated for each year.[3] For each year-to-year percentage change, the average of that percentage and the similar percentage for the previous year was then substituted. This introduced a small degree of smoothing without altering the general pattern of alternation of periods of fast and slow growth, and without using for any date index values for a future date. These percentages were then linked to obtain a continuous index, which was used as the measure of output pertinent to calculation of economies of scale. The series is rather free of irregular movements.

The percentage change in this index each year (already calculated) was multiplied by 0.1304 (see page 75) to obtain the contribution of economies of scale to that year's change in output. These annual estimates were then linked to obtain the index for the effects of economies of scale shown in Table P-1, column 4, for the 1947–69 period.

The 1929 index was estimated on the assump-

2. The same percentage change (that required to secure the correct 1948–50 movement) was used from 1948 to 1949 and from 1949 to 1950 in order to obtain the interpolated value for 1949. A similar procedure was used for the other interpolations.
3. The 1941–47 growth rate was used for the 1947–48 change.

Figure P-1. Nonresidential Business: Indexes of Total Sector National Income, Actual and Adjusted, 1929, 1940–41, and 1947–69

Based on data in 1958 dollars

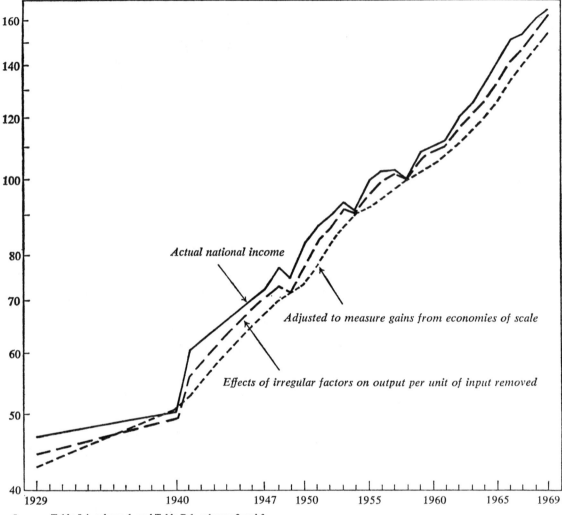

Index (1958 = 100)

Actual national income

Adjusted to measure gains from economies of scale

Effects of irregular factors on output per unit of input removed

Sources: Table 5-4, column 1, and Table P-1, columns 2 and 3.
Note. The years 1930–39 and 1942–46 are not plotted.

tion that the pertinent change in output from 1929 to 1948 is adequately measured by the growth rate of national income with the effects of irregular factors on output per unit of input removed; substitution of another postwar year for 1948 would scarcely change the figure. Index values for 1940 and 1941 were more difficult to estimate. Extreme depression during the preceding decade and the rapid changes under way in these years, which were briefly discussed on pages 309–10, make it difficult to judge an appropriate output level. The 1940 estimate assumes the appropriate growth rate of output from 1929 to 1940 to be equal to the weighted average of the 1929–40 growth rate of national income adjusted to exclude the effects of irregular factors on output per unit of input (weighted one) and the higher 1929–41 growth rate of that series (weighted

Table P-3. Distribution of Differences between Two Estimates of the Growth Rate of the Index of Gains from Economies of Scale Associated with Growth of the National Market

Number of periods[a]

Difference between growth rates (percentage points)	Time span				
	Four years	Five years	Six years	Seven years	Total, four to seven years
0.00	1	1	0	2	4
0.01	1	5	3	4	13
0.02	4	2	2	2	10
0.03	3	0	1	1	5
0.04	0	3	3	1	7
0.05	1	1	0	0	2
0.06	2	0	1	0	3
0.07	0	0	0	0	0
0.08	0	0	0	0	0
0.09	1	0	0	0	1
Total	13	12	10	10	45

Source: See text for derivation and explanation.

a. Periods beginning or ending in 1949, 1954, 1958, and 1961 are excluded.

unit of input removed, and with the raw series for national income.[4]

Postwar business fluctuations have been of moderate amplitude. It has seemed to me that over any postwar period of at least four years' duration the change in the index of national income with the effects of irregular factors removed would itself provide a reasonable measure of output changes for use in estimating economies of scale. Periods beginning or ending with 1949, 1954, 1958, and 1961, the trough years of recessions, are exceptions to this statement. In any other period, the growth rate of that output series could be multiplied by 0.1304 to obtain an estimated growth rate for the economies of scale series during that period.[5] Growth rates obtained in that way were compared with the growth rate of the series actually adopted in all such periods of four to seven years duration. Differences are summarized in Table P-3; they are small.

4. Differences among the general levels of the series on the figure reflect only the fact that the base year, 1958, was the trough of a deep recession. Movements only are of interest.

5. Indexes computed from growth rates for a variety of such periods could be linked to obtain an annual series (omitting the recession years). In fact, a variety of such series can be constructed; results depend upon which exact periods are used and in which order. Combinations tested yielded closely similar results but one or more erratic changes in year-to-year movements appear in most such series; the procedure actually adopted appeared slightly superior.

two). The 1940–48 growth rate was then used as the percentage change from 1940 to 1941.

In Figure P-1 the national income index used to calculate the annual economies of scale series is compared with the index of national income with the effects of irregular factors on output per

APPENDIX Q

-»»«««-

Derivation of Potential National Income

-»»«««-

This appendix amplifies and supplements the description and discussion of potential national income which is presented in Chapter 7. Part One describes the estimates of the difference between labor input under actual conditions and under the 4 percent variant of potential conditions, and the effect of this difference upon the national income gap, as shown in Table 7-1, column 4.

Part Two describes the derivation of the 3.5 percent and 4.5 percent variants of potential national income.

Part Three discusses the ways short-term and irregular fluctuations are reflected in my potential output series and in certain trend-based series, and suggests ways my data can be used to derive trend-based or smoothed series.

PART ONE: THE 4 PERCENT UNEMPLOYMENT VARIANT

Table 7-1, in columns 2, 3, and 4, summarizes the adjustments made to actual national income to obtain the 4 percent unemployment variant of potential national income. Derivations of columns 2 and 3 are fully described in Chapter 7. This appendix furnishes a more detailed description of Table 7-1, column 4, than the chapter provides.

The first broad requirement was to estimate the difference between actual and potential hours worked for each age-sex group in the population. These differences result from the effect of fluctuations in the intensity of demand upon (1) the average hours worked by employed persons; (2) the distribution of the labor force between employed and unemployed persons; and (3) the size of the labor force itself. The first three sections of Part 1 (A, B, and C) describe these estimates; section D then describes how the estimates of the difference between potential and actual national income due to labor input were made; and the last section (E) comments further on the estimates for the years of peak unemployment.

A. Adjustments of Hours Worked by Employed Workers

Table G-1 cross-classified wage and salary workers employed in nonfarm business by sex and by full-time or part-time status, and provided estimates of total and average hours worked by each of the four employee groups. In this section, employment totals are not changed for males or females, but their distributions between full-time and part-time workers and the average hours worked by each group are adjusted to convert them to a potential basis.

Part-Time Employment

Demand pressures can be expected to affect the prevalence of part-time employment in only one category: those who work part time for "economic reasons." Economic reasons include slack work, inability to find a full-time job, job changing, and materials shortages. Persons in this category consist of two groups: those who usually work full time on their present jobs but work only part time in a particular week because full-time work is not available, and those who would like to have a full-time job but can find only a part-time job and consequently usually work part time.

STEP ONE. A continuous series from 1955 to 1969 was first derived for the numbers of non-agricultural wage and salary workers of each sex who were employed part time for economic reasons. The Current Population Survey (CPS) provides (1) the number of civilian nonagricultural wage and salary workers who worked part time for economic reasons, classified by their usual status as full-time workers or part-time workers; and (2) similar data for all civilian nonagricultural workers combined, with a cross-classification by sex in addition.[1] The second series was used to divide the first series by sex, on the assumption that *within* both the usual full-time and the usual part-time categories, the percentage of males was the same in the first series as in the second.[2] This CPS-based series was then adjusted to conform to the total employment series used in this study.[3] The usual full-time and usual part-time series were then combined to obtain for each sex a single series measuring the number of nonagricultural wage and salary workers who worked part time for economic reasons. The effect of adding Alaska and Hawaii in 1960 was then estimated.[4]

STEP TWO. For each sex, the ratio of the number of nonagricultural wage and salary workers who worked part time for economic reasons (just described) to the number of full-time wage and salary workers in nonfarm business was calculated

for each year.[5] The latter series is from Table G-1. (For continuity the pre-1966 data were adjusted to the level of the new definitions by use of the 1966 relationship between the series.)

It was next estimated that under potential conditions this ratio would have been 0.0322 for males and 0.0668 for females. These ratios were obtained by computing lines of relationship, based on 1955–69 data, between the actual ratios and the percentage of the civilian labor force (aged 16 and over) that was unemployed, and then computing the ratio that the line of relationship showed to be associated with a 4 percent unemployment rate.[6]

The *difference* between the actual number of persons of each sex who were employed part time for economic reasons each year and the number who would have been in this category if the ratio had been at the potential level was calculated for the years from 1955 to 1969. The numbers so obtained (Table Q-1) were then transferred between full-time and part-time status to obtain the potential series. No change was made in the number of persons working part time for noneconomic reasons, which is much the larger component of part-time employment.

STEP THREE. Prior to 1955 the numbers of persons employed part time for economic reasons had to be estimated because they were not reported. Except in 1940 and 1941, the number of each sex who were in this category was estimated from the unemployment rate and full-time employment by use of the ratios provided at the observed unemployment rate by 1955–69 regression lines (those used to obtain the potential ratios at 4 percent unemployment). Thereafter the procedure was the same as in 1955–69.

Use of the regression lines was not satisfactory for 1940 and 1941, when unemployment was much higher than at any time during the period from which the regression was calculated. Instead, for each sex, the ratio of total potential part-time employment to total employment was calculated for 1929 and 1947 and interpolated to obtain ratios applicable to 1940 and 1941. The differ-

1. Data for 1960 through 1969 appear in *Manpower Report of the President, 1971*, Table A-24; for 1957 through 1959, in the 1970 *Manpower Report*, Table A-25. Figures for 1956 were calculated by applying 1956 percentage distributions from U.S. Bureau of the Census, *Current Population Reports*, Series P-50, No. 72, "Annual Report on the Labor Force, 1956" (1957), Tables 18 and 21, to absolute numbers from the unpublished Bureau of Labor Statistics Tabulation Table 6. Data for nine months of 1955 were drawn from Tables 17, 18, and 20 of *Current Population Reports*, Series P-50, No. 67, "Annual Report on the Labor Force, 1955" (1956), and BLS Tabulation Table 6. Because of lack of data for January, March, and April, annual averages in 1955 for each series were derived by applying the ratio of the twelve-month average to the nine-month average in 1956 to the nine-month average in 1955.

2. As in other CPS series, in 1967 14- and 15-year-olds were eliminated, new definitions were adopted, and the sample was changed. Estimates for 1966 were available on both old and new bases, but the reasons for differences could not be isolated. Additions were made to the 1967-69 CPS data, for comparability with earlier years, on the assumption that the 1966 differences were due to the age change. The 1966 number of 14- and 15-year-old nonagricultural wage and salary workers of each sex who worked part time for economic reasons was extrapolated to 1967-69 by total nonagricultural wage and salary employment of 14- and 15-year-olds of that sex. (These employment series are described in Appendix G.)

3. Each series for nonagricultural wage and salary workers working part time for economic reasons was multiplied by the ratio of the figure used in this study for total civilian nonagricultural wage and salary employment (Table C-1, columns 4 and 5, less Table C-7, column 4) to the CPS figure for total civilian nonagricultural wage and salary employment (Table C-2, column 7, with figures prior to 1966 adjusted to the level of the new definitions by multiplying them by the ratio of the 1966 figure based on new definitions to the 1966 figure based on old definitions).

4. The ratio of the number of persons working part time for economic reasons to the number working full time was assumed to be unchanged by the addition of these states to the data.

5. The industrial scope of the numerator is greater than that of the denominator (chiefly, by inclusion of general government), but it appears from the limited information available that the numerator includes very few workers in activities excluded from the denominator.

6. The unemployment rate for both sexes combined was used in the regression for each sex. Although a slightly better fit can be obtained for males by using the unemployment rate for males, use of the female unemployment rate for females provides a much worse fit.

ences between actual and potential part-time employment thus obtained seemed plausible.

Table Q-1 shows the numbers of persons employed on a part-time basis for economic reasons who were transferred to full-time status in order to shift the distributions between full-time and part-time employment in Table G-1 to a potential basis.

Average Hours of Full-Time and Part-Time Workers

The average hours worked by the four wage and salary worker groups in nonfarm business (full-time and part-time workers of each sex) are influenced by the strength of demand for output because it affects the strength of demand for labor. But the timing and magnitude of the relationships are difficult to establish. Changes in the demand for labor and the demand for products need not be simultaneous. Moreover, employers may respond to a perceived change in labor requirements

by changing employment, average hours, or both. They tend to change average hours first and to change employment only if the change in requirements persists, but lags may vary and there need be no persistent or consistent relationship. Furthermore, although a weakening in the demand for labor may be expected to shorten average hours of workers who were employed full time *before* the weakening in demand, there is an offsetting effect on the movement of average full-time hours: some of the full-time workers with the shortest usual hours drop below thirty-five a week and thus out of the full-time category. Their transfer to the part-time category tends to lengthen average hours of full-time workers, and of part-time workers as well since they enter the top of the part-time distribution.

The net influence of demand changes on the movement of the actual hours series for the separate groups is small both in absolute terms and in relation to the influence of other determinants of hours. That the size of the required adjustment is small is fortunate because the influence of other determinants makes it difficult to calculate accurately.

In the postwar years the adjustment of actual average hours of each group to obtain potential average hours was based on formulas that make joint use of two cyclical indicators: the unemployment rate and the index of fluctuations in intensity of utilization of resources in use that is due to strength of demand.

Definitions of the variables that appear in the formulas follow:[7]

P = potential average hours
A = actual average hours
U = the percentage of the civilian labor force 16 years of age and over who were unemployed (as reported by the Bureau of Labor Statistics) minus 4.0
I = 103.9 minus the demand intensity index (1958 = 100) as given in Table 6-1, column 6

The formulas for the four groups follow. To illustrate how they work in practice, I have also entered the values of the terms in 1958, a year in which both cyclical indicators were exceptionally depressed and the differences between actual and potential hours were the greatest of the postwar era. In that year the value of U was 2.8 and that of I was 3.9.

Table Q-1. Nonfarm Business: Numbers of Part-Time Wage and Salary Workers Transferred to Full-Time Status to Derive Potential National Income, 1929, 1940–41, and 1947–69
Thousands

Year	Males	Females	Total
Excluding Alaska and Hawaii			
1929	−156	−51	−207
1940	388	231	619
1941	−71	100	29
1947	−24	−12	−36
1948	−48	−23	−71
1949	421	208	629
1950	298	148	446
1951	−173	−87	−260
1952	−253	−133	−386
1953	−287	−151	−438
1954	366	191	557
1955	83	44	127
1956	195	89	284
1957	315	131	446
1958	849	396	1,245
1959	374	236	610
1960	503	275	778
Including Alaska and Hawaii			
1960	505	276	781
1961	630	363	993
1962	327	201	528
1963	257	178	435
1964	151	111	262
1965	−9	29	20
1966	−133	−114	−247
1967	−34	−28	−62
1968	−177	−80	−257
1969	−147	−107	−254

Source: See text for derivation.

7. The value of 4.0 used in the definition of U and that of 103.9 (rounded from 103.86) used in the definition of I are those consistent with potential conditions at 4 percent unemployment, as explained in Chapter 7.

(1) Males employed full time:
$$P = A - 0.001 - 0.00224\,U + 0.12617\,I$$
1958: $42.74 = 42.26 - 0.001 - 0.006 \qquad + 0.492$

(2) Females employed full time:
$$P = A - 0.004 - 0.06052\,U + 0.03102\,I$$
1958: $39.57 = 39.62 - 0.004 - 0.169 \qquad + 0.121$

(3) Males employed part time:
$$P = A + 0.226 - 0.35305\,U - 0.00929\,I$$
1958: $19.55 = 20.35 + 0.226 - 0.989 \qquad - 0.036$

(4) Females employed part time:
$$P = A - 0.190 + 0.24977\,U + 0.09151\,I$$
1958: $19.61 = 18.74 - 0.190 + 0.699 \qquad + 0.357$

Formulas (1) and (2), referring to full-time workers, are the important ones; the first is by far the most important because full-time males comprise the great bulk of labor input. The formula for males indicates that the combination of high unemployment and low intensity of utilization is associated with a shortfall of actual hours below potential hours, but that the effect is not great. Even in so depressed a year as 1958 average hours of full-time male workers are estimated to have dipped only 0.48 hours (or 1.12 percent) below their potential level. The formula for full-time females yields estimates for potential hours that are only trivially different from average hours. (This difference is sometimes, as in 1958, in the opposite direction from that for males.) There are two obvious reasons for differing cyclical behavior of full-time hours for males and females. Female employment is concentrated in industrial and occupational groups that are less sensitive to short-term fluctuations in demand, and a higher proportion of females working full time than of males drop below thirty-five hours when demand is slack (because normal full-time hours of females are much shorter than those of males).

Formulas (3) and (4) for males and females working part time are wholly unreliable but fortunately have little effect on the potential national income estimates as these groups contribute little labor input. Because the formulas imply that in recessions actual hours of part-time males rise above potential hours while those of females fall below, the adjustments for the two groups are offsetting.[8]

All four formulas were obtained by correlating the deviations of actual hours from their trend values, used as the dependent variable, with U

and I.[9] Calculations were based on the 1947–69 period. The problem in deriving the formulas was to estimate trend values; this required more artistry than mathematics because graphs and careful analysis of the data made it very clear that even on a potential basis hours did not change at a constant rate over the whole period. The trend values I describe below (and which are shown for full-time workers in Table Q-2) were used only in calculation of the formulas; they were not used as estimates of potential hours.

To analyze average hours of males on full time, three periods were distinguished *within* which, it was estimated, the trend value of hours did not change but *between* which the trend value declined. Values of 43.25 in 1947–50, 42.96 in 1953–65, and 42.41 in 1967–69 were used. The levels were based on examination of actual hours and the cyclical position in the years covered by the period. Trend values for 1951 and 1952 were obtained by straight-line interpolation; the trend value for 1966 was estimated on the assumption that actual hours exceeded trend hours slightly more in 1966 than in 1965.

To analyze average hours of males on full time, workers, the postwar period was also divided into three parts, but the method was rather different because females' hours showed a more persistent downtrend. The average value of actual hours in 1947–51 (40.17) and in 1967–69 (37.97) were used as the trend values in each year of the two periods, respectively. For 1953–65 a time trend was fitted to the actual data and in each year the trend value from this calculation was used. Trend values in 1952 and 1966 were obtained by straight-line interpolation.

For males and females working part time, calculated time trends for the whole 1947–69 period were used. This procedure was not used because it was satisfactory but because the data are so irregular as to prevent introduction of a series based on inspection and judgment.

To appraise potential hours in the prewar years, it was recalled that the Fair Labor Standards Act required payment of time and one-half after forty hours (as it did in the postwar years) after October 24, 1940. Earlier in 1940 the standard was

---

8. Consideration was given to adoption of the assumption for the part-time groups that potential hours are equal to average hours, but there seemed to be a slight advantage in including adjustments based on the same variables as those used for full-time hours.

9. Before the analysis was begun, total employment and total hours for each employee group in years prior to 1966, as shown in Table G-1, were adjusted by the ratio of the values of the 1966 new-definition series to the 1966 old-definition series, and average hours recomputed, in order to obtain continuous series.

Table Q-2. Nonfarm Business: Average Weekly Hours of Full-Time Wage and Salary Workers, by Sex and on a Trend, Potential, and Actual Basis, 1929, 1940–41, and 1947–69

Year	Males			Females		
	Trend (1)	Potential (2)	Actual[a] (3)	Trend (4)	Potential (5)	Actual[a] (6)
1929	...	49.18	49.29	...	45.63	45.61
1940	...	44.17	44.11	...	40.82[b]	40.82
1941	...	44.02	44.51	...	40.71	41.19
1947	43.25	43.54	43.36	40.17	40.17	40.12
1948	43.25	43.15	43.35	40.17	40.10	40.14
1949	43.25	43.11	43.17	40.17	39.91	40.04
1950	43.25	43.16	43.57	40.17	40.21	40.39
1951	43.15	43.33	43.51	40.17	40.15	40.15
1952	43.06	43.07	42.99	40.08	39.98	39.90
1953	42.96	42.76	42.51	40.00	39.67	39.55
1954	42.96	43.16	42.77	39.89	39.89	39.89
1955	42.96	42.87	42.94	39.78	40.03	40.07
1956	42.96	42.87	42.76	39.67	39.89	39.87
1957	42.96	42.63	42.33	39.55	39.39	39.34
1958	42.96	42.74	42.26	39.44	39.57	39.62
1959	42.96	42.93	42.80	39.33	39.64	39.70
1960	42.96	42.95	42.64	39.22	39.02	39.04
1961	42.96	43.06	42.75	39.11	38.99	39.08
1962	42.96	43.06	42.99	39.00	38.96	39.04
1963	42.96	43.16	43.11	38.89	38.85	38.94
1964	42.96	43.08	43.30	38.78	38.31	38.44
1965	42.96	42.94	43.28	38.67	38.64	38.76
1966	42.63	42.59	42.96	38.32	38.45	38.53
1967	42.41	42.40	42.50	37.97	38.02	38.04
1968	42.41	42.34	42.35	37.97	37.92	37.90
1969	42.41	42.64	42.38	37.97	38.05	37.96

Sources: Columns 1 and 4, see text; columns 2 and 5, estimated from columns 3 and 6 by use of formulas (1) and (2) on page 321; columns 3 and 6, calculated from data underlying Table G-1.
a. Numbers prior to 1966 differ from those in Table G-1 because they have been linked for continuity.
b. Estimated to be equal to actual hours.

forty-two hours. In 1929 there was no such law. No close relationship between "legal" and potential hours can be assumed, but in view of all the legal and economic changes which took place it seemed highly probable that (1) the great bulk of the large decline in potential hours of full-time workers that occurred from 1929 to 1947–51 had taken place by 1940; (2) potential hours should be a little higher in 1941 than in 1947–51; and (3) potential hours should probably be a little lower in 1941 than in 1940 and surely not higher.

For full-time males and females, potential hours in 1929, 1940, and 1941 were first estimated by use of the postwar formulas. Five of the six estimates so obtained were reasonable, and were adopted. The sixth, the 1940 estimate obtained for females (40.23), was too low in relation to the 1941 and probably also to the postwar estimates, and the value of actual hours (40.82) was used instead. The postwar formulas for part-time workers yield implausible estimates of potential hours in the prewar years, and actual hours were used without adjustment.

Table Q-2 shows average potential and actual hours for the two full-time groups as well as the estimated trend values that were used in the derivation of the formulas. The potential series are by no means "smooth" series like the trend values nor are they meant to be. They are intended to differ from the actual series only by the elimination of the systematic relationship of actual hours to demand pressure, and thus to retain all other sources of irregularity and temporary trend reversals in the actual series.

The differences between total actual and potential hours of employed workers that are implied by the differences between the actual and potential distributions of workers between full- and part-time status, and by the differences between actual and potential average hours in each

Table Q-3. Nonfarm Business: Potential Less Actual Total Weekly Hours of Wage and Salary Workers, by Components, 1929, 1940–41, and 1947–69[a]

Millions of hours

Year	Employed workers			Shift from unemployment to employment			Labor force response to demand for labor			All components		
	Males (1)	Females (2)	Total (3)	Males (4)	Females (5)	Total (6)	Males (7)	Females (8)	Total (9)	Males (10)	Females (11)	Total (12)
1929	−7.3	−1.2	−8.5	−17.4	−4.4	−21.8	−4.8	−6.0	−10.8	−29.5	−11.6	−41.1
1940	11.8	4.5	16.3	181.0	53.1	234.1	26.6	36.4	63.0	219.4	94.0	313.4
1941	−12.6	−1.1	−13.7	96.7	30.4	127.1	8.5	11.7	20.2	92.6	41.0	133.6
1947	4.1	0.0	4.2	−4.6	−1.6	−6.3	−1.2	−2.2	−3.3	−1.7	−3.8	−5.4
1948	−5.6	−1.4	−7.1	−6.4	−2.7	−9.0	−1.7	−3.2	−4.9	−13.7	−7.3	−21.0
1949	7.2	3.1	10.2	32.5	12.7	45.3	8.9	17.0	25.9	48.6	32.8	81.4
1950	−3.0	0.8	−2.2	20.8	8.8	29.6	5.7	11.1	16.8	23.4	20.7	44.1
1951	−7.4	−2.6	−10.0	−13.7	−7.3	−21.1	−4.4	−8.6	−12.9	−25.5	−18.6	−44.0
1952	−3.2	−2.5	−5.7	−19.0	−9.7	−28.7	−6.2	−12.0	−18.1	−28.4	−24.2	−52.6
1953	0.4	−2.0	−1.6	−21.8	−10.5	−32.3	−7.0	−13.8	−20.8	−28.5	−26.3	−54.8
1954	18.7	4.6	23.2	23.8	10.7	34.4	5.9	11.7	17.7	48.4	27.0	75.3
1955	0.4	0.3	0.7	3.8	1.8	5.7	0.8	1.7	2.5	5.1	3.8	8.8
1956	7.9	2.0	9.9	−0.4	−0.2	−0.6	−0.3	−0.5	−0.8	7.3	1.3	8.6
1957	15.4	3.4	18.9	2.1	1.0	3.1	0.4	0.8	1.2	18.0	5.2	23.2
1958	29.3	9.7	39.0	48.9	21.9	70.8	12.4	24.5	36.9	90.6	56.1	146.8
1959	12.5	5.0	17.4	24.2	11.6	35.8	6.4	12.4	18.8	43.0	29.0	72.0
1960	19.8	6.4	26.2	25.8	12.3	38.1	7.0	13.0	20.0	52.6	31.7	84.2
1961	21.9	8.2	30.2	47.4	22.9	70.3	12.7	23.5	36.2	82.0	54.7	136.6
1962	9.8	3.9	13.7	25.9	13.2	39.1	7.1	13.1	20.3	42.9	30.3	73.1
1963	7.2	3.6	10.8	28.3	14.8	43.1	7.8	14.0	21.8	43.4	32.3	75.6
1964	−2.2	0.6	−1.6	19.4	10.8	30.2	5.6	9.6	15.2	22.8	21.0	43.8
1965	−9.6	−1.9	−11.4	7.4	4.2	11.6	2.2	3.6	5.8	0.0	6.0	5.9
1966	−13.2	−5.2	−18.4	−6.3	−4.0	−10.3	−2.2	−3.6	−5.8	−21.7	−12.8	−34.5
1967	−3.1	−2.1	−5.2	−3.0	−2.0	−5.0	−1.2	−1.9	−3.0	−7.3	−5.9	−13.2
1968	−3.7	−2.5	−6.2	−8.0	−5.2	−13.2	−2.7	−4.3	−7.0	−14.4	−12.0	−26.4
1969	5.6	−1.3	4.2	−9.7	−6.4	−16.1	−3.1	−5.0	−8.1	−7.2	−12.7	−19.9

Source: See text for derivation. Detail may not add to totals because of rounding.

a. Includes Alaska and Hawaii beginning in 1960.

category, are shown, by sex, in the first three columns of Table Q-3. At a later stage in the calculations distributions by age of the series shown for each sex were needed. Percentage distributions by age of the total hours worked by workers of that sex employed in nonagricultural industries, excluding government and private household workers, were applied to obtain this distribution. These estimates had been developed in securing the age-sex distribution of hours worked.

B. Transfers between Unemployed and Employed Groups

If unemployment had amounted to 4 percent of the civilian labor force, aged 16 and over, each year, employment would have differed from its actual amount because of a switch between employment and unemployment. The difference between actual and potential hours worked that

corresponds to this employment difference was estimated for each age-sex group.

The first requirement was an unemployment series, by sex and age, that corresponds to current CPS definitions. Its construction required adjustment of published CPS data prior to 1967 to take account of the definitional changes in unemployment which BLS introduced in 1967 as well as of delays in adjusting to census benchmarks. George L. Perry had constructed such a series back to 1947, using adjustment procedures similar to those I used to adjust CPS data for employed workers, and made his unpublished data available to me.[10] Perry's age classification includes a 25–64 age group. To obtain the additional detail used elsewhere in this study, Perry's estimate for the 25–64 age group of each sex was allocated

10. Perry describes them in "Labor Force Structure, Potential Output, and Productivity," in *Brookings Papers on Economic Activity* (3:1971), pp. 561–62.

between 25–34 and 35–64 age groups in proportion to unemployment as reported by the CPS.[11]

A series for the total civilian labor force, aged 16 and over, that is statistically consistent with the civilian employment series used in this study was next constructed for 1947–69. It is equal to my total civilian employment (Table C-4, column 6) plus the Perry unemployment series minus the CPS series for the number of 14- and 15-year-olds employed.[12]

Given the size of the labor force, the change in actual employment that must be introduced to adjust to a potential basis is simply 4 percent of this civilian labor force series minus the Perry unemployment series.[13] The persons transferred between employment and unemployment had next to be allocated among age-sex groups. At any date the percentage distribution by age-sex groups of employed persons differs from that of unemployed persons. In recent years the distributions have diverged much more than formerly as teenagers have come to represent an extraordinary proportion of the unemployed. Their 30 percent

11. These groups are combined in Robert L. Stein, "New Definitions for Employment and Unemployment," *Employment and Earnings and Monthly Report on the Labor Force*, Vol. 13 (February 1967), pp. 3–27, which is the principal published source for data required to adjust earlier years to new concepts.
12. The series is almost identical with Perry's labor force ("Labor Force Structure," p. 563) minus the CPS series for the armed forces, which he includes.
13. No transfer of 14- and 15-year-olds was made because the labor input that would be represented by such a transfer is of no importance at all.

share of 1968 unemployment compares with 16 percent of 1948 unemployment, and with only 8 percent of 1968 employment.[14] The age-sex distribution of persons who move between employment and unemployment when the strength of demand changes probably lies somewhere between the distributions of the employed and unemployed. To obtain estimates for the postwar period I have applied the simple average of the distributions of employed and unemployed to the persons transferred.[15]

To show the implications of the procedure, Table Q-4 gives the distributions of civilian employment and unemployment and the distribu-

14. The increase over time has resulted mainly from students seeking after-school or vacation work. The economy was able to provide an enormous increase in the number of part-time and summer jobs for students even though two occupations that formerly provided many such jobs (pinsetting in bowling alleys and caddying) almost disappeared and even though adult females were also seeking and finding a hugely increased number of part-time jobs. But the increase in such jobs fell short of the increase in the number of students seeking them.
15. This procedure was adopted after a different and initially attractive method of allocating the persons transferred had been tested and rejected. Perry had computed "trend" unemployment series for each age-sex group. Use of the difference between his actual and trend unemployment estimates by age and sex to allocate persons transferred was tried. The difficulties were that the sum of the differences between actual and trend values for the age-sex groups was sometimes (and especially in the late 1960s) far away from the total numbers to be transferred; that in some years the signs were wrong for some age-sex groups; and that the percentages obtained for an age-sex group in any year did not necessarily fall between its percentages of employment and unemployment. These results, of course, imply no criticism of Perry's trend estimates for the uses to which he put them (see page 327).

Table Q-4. Distributions of Civilian Employment, Unemployment, and Persons Transferred between Employment and Unemployment, by Sex and Age, 1948, 1958, and 1968[a]

Sex and age	Employment			Unemployment			Persons transferred		
	1948	1958	1968	1948	1958	1968	1948	1958	1968
Male, total	71.52	67.31	63.38	65.87	65.72	50.35	68.71	66.51	56.87
16–19	4.02	3.19	4.29	11.18	8.95	15.13	7.60	6.07	9.71
20–24	7.46	5.22	6.34	13.61	10.08	9.16	10.54	7.65	7.75
25–34	17.21	15.53	13.71	11.86	14.41	7.28	14.54	14.97	10.50
35–64	38.89	39.78	36.29	25.10	29.31	16.62	32.00	34.54	26.46
65 and over	3.95	3.58	2.76	4.12	2.98	2.17	4.04	3.28	2.46
Female, total	28.48	32.69	36.62	34.13	34.28	49.65	31.29	33.49	43.13
16–19	2.88	2.49	3.33	5.18	4.97	14.67	4.03	3.73	9.00
20–24	4.43	3.61	5.20	6.55	5.22	10.12	5.49	4.42	7.66
25–34	6.45	6.16	6.40	8.80	7.33	8.45	7.62	6.74	7.42
35–64	13.86	19.18	20.41	13.10	16.14	15.45	13.48	17.66	17.93
65 and over	0.86	1.25	1.28	0.50	0.62	0.96	0.68	0.94	1.12
Total, both sexes	100.00	100.00	100.00	100.00	100.00	100.00	100.00	100.00	100.00

Source: See text for derivation.
a. Excludes persons under 16 years of age.

tions (their averages) that I have applied to persons transferred between employment and unemployment for three years. Two are high-employment years near the beginning and end of the postwar period; in these particular years, of course, few persons were transferred so the distribution is actually of little importance. The third, 1958, is a year of high unemployment in which a large number were transferred from unemployment to secure potential employment.

Estimates of unemployment and the numbers to be transferred were also required for 1929, 1940, and 1941. In this period they refer to the labor force, aged 14 and over. For total unemployment I use the estimates currently published by the Bureau of Labor Statistics minus 0.1616 percent of the civilian labor force.[16]

Unemployment in 1940 and 1941 was distributed by sex and two age classes (14–24 and 25 and over) in proportion to the CPS monthly averages for those years.[17] The 1940 total for each of these four broad groups was then allocated among more detailed age groups (14–19, 20–24, 25–44, 45–64, and 65 and over) in proportion to comparable March 1940 unemployment data.[18] The similar detailed allocation for 1941 was based on proportional interpolation (using unemployment as the interpolator) between percentages for March 1940 and the fourth quarter of 1941.[19] Unemployment in 1929 was allocated by detailed age-sex groups in proportion to a distribution obtained by multiplying the final estimate of 1940 annual average unemployment in each group by the ratio of unemployment from the 1930 Census to unemployment from the 1940 Census, adjusted for comparability.[20]

The total number to be transferred between employment and unemployment in all three years, and the 1929 distribution by sex and age, were obtained by the procedures followed in the postwar years.[21] A different approach was used to obtain age-sex distributions of the number transferred in 1940 and 1941, when the numbers unemployed (including public emergency workers) were large. In these years the distribution of potential unemployment (4 percent of the civilian labor force) was estimated by reference to the distribution of actual unemployment after it had fallen to about the potential unemployment level. The number in each age-sex group to be transferred was then obtained by subtracting potential unemployment from actual unemployment. The reference period chosen to estimate the distribution of potential unemployment was March 1942 through February 1943. The ratio of unemployment to civilian labor force for each age-sex group in this period was multiplied by the labor force in that age-sex group in 1940 and 1941. The resulting distributions were then used to allocate potential unemployment in 1940 and 1941 by age and sex.[22] This completes the description of the estimates, by age and sex, of the numbers to be transferred between employment and unemployment to obtain potential employment.[23]

---

16. BLS estimates for these years and 1947 were taken from *Employment and Earnings*, Vol. 18 (December 1971), p. 27. This 1947 estimate (which is based on old definitions) exceeds the sum of the 1947 Perry estimate and the CPS estimate for 14- and 15-year-olds by 97,000, or by 0.1616 percent of the civilian labor force as estimated in the present study.

17. U.S. Bureau of the Census, *Current Population Reports*, Series P-50, No. 2, "Labor Force, Employment, and Unemployment in the United States, 1940 to 1946," pp. 47–48.

18. Ibid., p. 4.

19. Monthly averages for the fourth quarter of 1941 were calculated from ibid., p. 48. The interpolation method may be illustrated for males aged 14 to 24. CPS unemployment for this group is 2,020,000 in March 1940, 1,220,000 in 1941 (monthly average), and 613,000 in the fourth quarter of 1941. In March 1940, 44.1 percent of the group were aged 14 to 19, but in the fourth quarter of 1941 the percentage had risen to 53.3. The 1941 percentage is estimated at 49.3, obtained as

$$53.3 - (53.3 - 44.1)\frac{1,220,000 - 613,000}{2,020,000 - 613,000}.$$

On a CPS basis, unemployment of males aged 14 to 19 is estimated at 49.3 percent of 1,220,000, or 601,000. After adjustment of all age-sex groups to my estimate of total unemployment, the final figure for males aged 14 to 19 is 592,000.

20. Data are from U.S. Bureau of the Census, *Sixteenth Census of the United States, 1940, Population: Estimates of Labor Force, Employment, and Unemployment in the United States, 1940 and 1930* (1944), Tables 2 and 3, pp. 2 and 3.

21. For 1929, the adjusted 1930 Census distribution (ibid., Table 3, p. 3) of employment was used.

22. Data used in these calculations are from U.S. Bureau of the Census, *Current Population Reports*, Series P-50, No. 2, "Labor Force, Employment, and Unemployment in the United States, 1940 to 1946," except that in 1940 and 1941 distributions of the labor force of each sex were available only by broad age groups. The numbers in broad age groups of each sex in 1940 were distributed among detailed age groups in proportion to the March 1940 labor force distribution, except that the share of the 14–24 age group of each sex that was allocated to the 14–19 group was increased to allow for the jump in its participation during summer months. The 1941 labor force of each sex in broad age groups was allocated to detailed age groups by use of 1940 proportions.

23. The age distribution obtained for the prewar years included a 25–44 age group. For each sex, it was divided between 25–34 and 35–44 age groups in proportion to employment, as reported in the decennial Census of Population (the 1930 Census for 1929, the 1940 Census for 1940 and 1941).

Table Q-5, columns 4 and 5, shows the total number of each sex transferred.

To estimate the potential hours of persons transferred between employment and unemployment, in each age-sex group the average potential hours of persons who were transferred were assumed to be the same as the average potential hours of employed nonfarm business wage and salary workers. The latter estimates had not previously been calculated by age, but (as a step in obtaining the age-sex distribution of hours in the business sector) estimates by sex and age had been made of the employment of, and total hours worked by, nonfarm workers excluding government and private household workers. The levels were based on CPS rather than establishment data, inappropriate for the present purpose because they

included nonfarm proprietors and family workers, were based on CPS rather than establishment data, and referred to actual rather than potential hours. An adjustment of employment and total hours was therefore made each year to correct the levels. For each sex, employment in each age group was multiplied by the ratio of employment of nonfarm business wage and salary workers (the sum of full-time workers and part-time workers of that sex in Table G-1) to total employment of that sex in the series for which the age distribution was available. Similarly, for each sex the total hours in each group were multiplied by the ratio of potential hours of employed nonfarm business wage and salary workers (the sum of actual hours of full-time and part-time workers of that sex in Table G-1 and the adjustment to po-

Table Q-5. Potential Less Actual Labor Force and Employment, 1929, 1940–41, and 1947–69[a]
Thousands

| | | | | Potential employment less actual employment | | | | | | |
| | Potential labor force less actual labor force | | | Transfers from unemployment | | Adjustment from labor force | | Total adjustment | | |
Year	Total (1)	Male (2)	Female (3)	Male (4)	Female (5)	Male (6)	Female (7)	Male (8)	Female (9)	Total (10)
1929	−271	−123	−148	−374	−105	−118	−142	−492	−247	−739
1940[b]	1,751	752	999	4,390	1,411	722	959	5,112	2,370	7,482
1941[b]	563	241	322	2,365	816	231	309	2,596	1,125	3,721
1947	−93	−33	−60	−111	−44	−32	−57	−143	−101	−244
1948	−139	−49	−90	−156	−72	−47	−86	−203	−158	−361
1949	736	257	479	799	342	247	459	1,046	801	1,847
1950	476	165	311	510	236	158	299	668	535	1,203
1951	−370	−127	−243	−338	−200	−122	−233	−460	−433	−893
1952	−520	−178	−342	−469	−264	−171	−329	−640	−593	−1,233
1953	−599	−206	−393	−541	−285	−197	−378	−738	−663	−1,401
1954	507	174	333	583	290	167	320	750	610	1,360
1955	73	25	48	95	49	24	46	119	95	214
1956	−23	−8	−15	−9	−5	−7	−14	−16	−19	−35
1957	36	12	24	53	28	12	23	65	51	116
1958	1,089	376	713	1,205	607	361	684	1,566	1,291	2,857
1959	553	193	360	599	323	186	345	785	668	1,453
1960	594	210	384	636	347	201	369	837	716	1,553
1961	1,088	387	702	1,168	651	371	674	1,539	1,325	2,864
1962	611	219	392	644	377	210	376	854	753	1,607
1963	666	242	424	705	428	233	407	938	835	1,773
1964	468	173	296	488	315	166	284	654	599	1,253
1965	179	67	112	186	124	64	108	250	232	482
1966	−180	−68	−112	−160	−119	−65	−107	−225	−226	−451
1967	−96	−37	−59	−78	−58	−35	−57	−113	−115	−228
1968	−223	−85	−138	−206	−157	−82	−132	−288	−289	−577
1969	−255	−98	−157	−249	−195	−94	−150	−343	−345	−688

Source: See text for derivation.
a. Includes Alaska and Hawaii beginning in 1960.
b. Employment data refer to differences from actual figures which exclude persons on work relief.

tential hours in Table Q-3, column 1 or 2) to total hours of that sex in the age distribution.[24] Total potential hours were then divided by employment to obtain average potential hours for each age-sex group. In the prewar years this calculation could be made by sex, but not by age, and 1947 age differentials in average potential hours were retained for each sex.[25]

Table Q-3, columns 4, 5, and 6, shows, by sex, the total hours that correspond to persons transferred between unemployment and employment.

C. Adjustment of the Labor Force

George Perry's analysis of the response of the labor force to changes in the demand for labor is uniquely appropriate for use in this study because it rests upon labor force data that are statistically consistent with my employment series and the movements in the actual labor force that it implies.[26]

Perry estimates that, at any point in time during the postwar period, each reduction of one percentage point in the unemployment rate would have increased the labor force in each age-sex group by the following percentage of the total population in that age-sex group.[27]

Age group	Males	Females
16–19	1.2961	0.9871
20–24	0.9373	0.4991
25–64	0.0106	0.4780
65 and over	0.4393	0.0821

These estimates were obtained by correlation

24. The calculation was also made for *actual* hours worked by wage and salary workers in nonfarm business in order to permit calculation of an age distribution of the total hours worked by nonfarm business wage and salary workers of each sex. For the prewar years, it was also necessary to obtain employment estimates by age. The procedure duplicated that used in securing distributions for the business sector as a whole except that farm occupations were deleted from the "primarily business" occupations. (See pp. 216–17.)

25. The youngest age group in the calculations was 14–19, whereas there are no 14- and 15-year-olds in the employees transferred between unemployment and employment in the postwar period. In 1966 the average hours of nonagricultural workers at work in the 16–19 age group are 10 percent higher than those in the 14–19 age group for both males and females. Average hours of the 14–19 age group were raised 10 percent each year for application to 16- to 19-year-olds in the postwar years.

26. I believe that the labor force series used is also statistically superior to that usually used in such analyses. The labor force response to changes in unemployment appears more clearly in these data, especially in the 1949 recession.

27. Data are from George L. Perry, "Labor Force Structure, Potential Output, and Productivity," in *Brookings Papers on Economic Activity* (3:1971), Table A-2, p. 564.

of labor force participation rates with the unemployment rate and time. He found that use of lagged relationships with unemployment did not improve fits so that a simultaneous relationship could appropriately be used.

Perry used these percentages to adjust actual labor force participation rates, and then the labor force itself, to a potential basis. The size of his adjustment each year is based solely upon the difference between the actual unemployment rate and the potential unemployment rate, and the adjustment is added to or subtracted from the actual labor force to obtain the potential labor force.[28]

The unemployment rates Perry used to derive his adjustment factors differed a little from unemployment expressed as a percentage of the civilian labor force. The armed forces were necessarily included in employment, and to secure a better measure of labor market tightness for this purpose he used a weighted unemployment rate in which earnings weights were attached to different age-sex groups. However, he calculated the difference between the actual and potential labor force each year in such a way that "potential" refers to the situation in which 4 percent of the civilian labor force aged 16 and over is unemployed. I have therefore used his estimates of the difference between actual and potential labor force without adjustment.

Labor force response to unemployment is almost entirely confined to secondary workers; it is negligible among males 25 to 64 years of age. In the high unemployment year 1958, the addition to the actual labor force required to obtain the potential labor force, according to the Perry estimates I adopt, was 1,089,000, and they were distributed as follows (in thousands of persons):[29]

Age group	Males	Females
16–19	158	118
20–24	129	69
25–64	11	508
65 and over	79	17

Perry's estimates start with 1947. I have used his coefficients to obtain estimates for 1929, 1940, and 1941 as well. However, the postwar estimate that one point in the unemployment rate changes the number of females 25 to 64 years of age in the labor force by almost 0.48 percent of the

28. Perry's procedures are described in ibid., pp. 538–40.

29. For my estimates, the number of each sex in the 25–64 age group was allocated between 25–34 and 35–64 age groups in proportion to civilian employment.

whole population in that age-sex group was cut to 0.32 percent in 1940 and 1941 and to 0.27 percent in 1929. The reduction is roughly proportional to that, dated from the middle of the postwar period, of female participation in the labor force. It seemed unreasonable to suppose that the labor force response was as large, relative to the population, in these earlier years as it became when it was much more common for women in this age bracket to work. The unemployment gap used to estimate the potential labor force in 1940 and 1941 counted persons employed on public emergency work as employed.[30]

Additions and subtractions to the labor force are shown, by sex, in Table Q-5, columns 1, 2, and 3.

To maintain the conditions stipulated for potential output, the adjustment to employment is only 96 percent of the labor force adjustment. Because almost none of the labor force adjustment is made in the highly weighted male groups 25 to 64 years of age, it scarcely matters how the other 4 percent are allocated by age and sex. I have simply reduced the figure for each age-sex group by 4 percent. Table Q-5, columns 6 and 7, shows the adjustments to employment by sex.

Persons in each age-sex group who were added to or subtracted from employment as a result of the labor force adjustment were assigned the same average potential hours as were those transferred between employment and unemployment.[31] Table Q-3, columns 7, 8, and 9, shows the total hours added or subtracted.

THE DIFFERENCES between actual and potential hours were next summed, by sex and age; the totals are shown, by sex, in Table Q-3, columns 10 to 12. The differences in each age-sex group were then added to actual hours worked by nonfarm wage and salary workers employed in the business sector to obtain the total potential hours of each age-sex group.

D. Adjustment of Labor Input and National Income

These distributions of actual and potential hours are the starting point for estimates of the difference between potential and actual national income that is due to labor input.

Total hours by age and sex, on both actual and potential bases, were weighted by the earnings weights in Table F-2. The results were used for two purposes. First, the male and female proportions of the age-sex weighted aggregates of actual hours were used to allocate between males and females the total compensation of nonfarm business wage and salary workers, which had been obtained in the process of estimating income share weights. (This division is needed later to combine the adjustments to labor input of males and females.) The estimates are shown in the first three columns of Table Q-6.[32] Second, the ratio of age-weighted potential hours to age-weighted actual hours was computed for nonfarm business wage and salary workers of each sex. These ratios are shown in columns 4 and 5 of the table. Ratios of potential labor input to actual labor input would be the same for these workers if only employment, average hours worked, and the age-sex distribution of hours worked affected labor input.

My estimates of labor input also include an efficiency offset to changes in full-time hours. Efficiency unit equivalents of actual hours worked in the business sector by each sex had been computed previously, but not for nonfarm wage and salary workers separately; this was now done. The calculation was then redone with potential hours substituted for actual hours. The ratio of the efficiency equivalent per hour under potential conditions to the efficiency equivalent under actual conditions was computed. Columns 6 and 7 of Table Q-6 provide these ratios. The ratio exceeds 1 when actual hours of full-time nonfarm business wage and salary workers are longer than their potential hours, and it is less than 1 when potential hours are longer.[33]

Multiplication of the compensation of nonfarm wage and salary workers by these two ratios

---

30. Counting them as unemployed in this calculation would yield potential labor force participation rates in 1940 that are unreasonably high on the basis of information about the period. (Depression experience has been carefully analyzed by Clarence D. Long in *The Labor Force under Changing Income and Employment* [Princeton University Press for the National Bureau of Economic Research, 1958], Chap. 10.) It would also yield an improbable movement of the potential labor force from 1940 to 1941.

31. Since the change referred to persons 16 and over in all years, the 10 percent increase in average hours of the 14–19 age group for application to the 16–19 age group was made in all years.

32. All numbers shown in Table Q-6 have been rounded from those actually used in the calculations.

33. The original indexes were based on hours data rounded to one-tenth of an hour, and differences between actual and potential hours were also rounded to one-tenth of an hour in these calculations. Consequently, a ratio of 1.000 appears unless the difference between potential and actual hours in Table Q-2 exceeds 0.05.

provides, in columns 8 and 9, their compensation adjusted to potential conditions, except that education remains to be considered.

My measure of labor input includes an index for education. The index is positively related to the level of unemployment because fluctuations in unemployment tend to be concentrated among the less educated workers. For each sex, it was therefore necessary to compute the ratio of the education index at potential employment to the index at actual employment. This computation was relatively simple because the effects of unemployment had been specifically introduced in obtaining the index for each sex under actual employment conditions. An index for each sex had first been constructed for the civilian labor force, based on years of education. (No effect of fluctuations in the size of the labor force on the indexes was found or introduced, so possible differences between actual and potential education indexes arising from labor force variations could be disregarded.) An index for the employed civilian labor force of each sex had next been computed from the labor force education index and the unemployment rate by use of a formula. For the present calculation, the same formula was applied to obtain the index at potential employment by substituting the potential unemployment rate for the actual rate. The ratio of the index at potential employment to the index at actual employment was the desired ratio for each sex.[34] However, it refers to all business employment rather than to nonfarm wage and salary workers alone. The ratios are shown in Table Q-6, columns 12 and 13.

All data and formulas needed for computation of these ratios are provided by Table I-18 with the exception of potential unemployment rates for males aged 18 and over and for females aged 18 and over that are consistent with a rate of 4 percent for the civilian labor force of persons 16 years and over. Such rates were first computed for persons aged 16 and over of each sex. They are the ratios of (unemployment plus persons transferred from employment to unemployment to secure potential employment) to (employment plus unemployment).[35] To obtain estimates for persons 18 and over of each sex, the percentage for persons aged 16 and over was reduced by the amount by which the BLS actual unemployment percentage for persons 16 years and over of that sex exceeded the percentage for persons aged 18 and over.[36] (Data for persons aged 16 and over were calculated from *Manpower Report of the President, 1970*, page 215. Data for persons aged 18 and over, calculated from the same source, are shown in Table I-18.)

The ratios for the education indexes shown in columns 12 and 13 of Table Q-6 refer to all nonresidential business sector employment so they were multiplied by total labor earnings in the sector (columns 10 and 11).[37] However, in accordance with the general procedure, the differences (column 14 for males and 15 for females) between these products (columns 10 × 12 or 11 × 13) and actual labor earnings (column 10 or 11) were attributed to nonfarm wage and salary workers.

The differences between potential and actual compensation for nonfarm business wage and salary workers of each sex are brought together in columns 16 and 17, and for the two sexes combined in column 18. Column 18 was then computed as a percentage (shown in column 19) of total labor earnings in the nonresidential business sector.[38] This percentage was multiplied by the

34. No systematic effect of fluctuations in unemployment was introduced into the estimates of the ratio of the education index for full-time business employment to that for civilian employment nor in the subsequent adjustment for changes in "days of education," and no such effects can be discerned.

35. This calculation was based on the Denison-Perry estimates described in section B above; there was no reason to suppose that the percentage for each sex when the combined percentage was 4 percent would be different for the BLS series.

36. Ratios so obtained for 1940 and 1941 were unsatisfactory, and ratios interpolated between 1929 and 1947 were substituted.

37. Total labor earnings in the nonresidential business sector had been obtained in the process of estimating income shares in the sector. They were allocated between males and females in proportion to total labor input of the two sexes as estimated in the age-sex calculations for the sector.

38. This percentage may be thought of as the product of (1) the percentage by which the potential labor input of nonfarm wage and salary workers in the business sector exceeds their actual labor input, which can be computed as 100 (column 18 ÷ column 1), and (2) the ratio of the compensation of nonfarm wage and salary workers in the business sector to total labor earnings in that sector, which can be computed as column 1 ÷ (columns 10 + 11).

Despite the complex calculations underlying the first percentage, it bears a fairly stable relationship to the percentage difference between actual and potential hours worked by nonfarm business wage and salary workers. The percentage adjustment to labor input for this group is usually 78 to 85 percent as large as the percentage adjustment to hours. Except for 1948, all years in which the ratio lies outside this range are years in which both percentages are very small (1947, 1956, 1965, and 1967).

Table Q-6. Derivation of the Excess of Potential over Actual National Income That Is Due to Labor Input, 1929,
Values in billions of dollars

	Nonfarm business wage and salary workers									All non-	
	Compensation			Ratio of potential to actual				Potential compensation, not adjusted for education		Labor earnings	
				Age-weighted hours		Intragroup hours efficiency index					
Year	Total (1)	Male (2)	Female (3)	Male (4)	Female (5)	Male (6)	Female (7)	Male (8)	Female (9)	Male (10)	Female (11)
1929	42.6	37.7	4.9	0.973	0.950	1.001	1.000	36.7	4.7	51.1	5.8
1940	40.9	35.1	5.8	1.228	1.371	0.999	1.000	43.1	7.9	47.4	6.1
1941	51.6	44.4	7.2	1.083	1.139	1.005	1.005	48.3	8.3	59.0	8.1
1947	104.3	87.2	17.0	0.999	0.990	0.998	1.000	87.0	16.9	116.2	18.7
1948	115.1	96.1	19.0	0.984	0.981	1.002	1.000	94.7	18.7	127.1	20.8
1949	112.9	93.6	19.3	1.042	1.088	1.001	1.001	97.6	21.0	122.7	20.8
1950	124.5	103.0	21.5	1.019	1.052	1.003	1.002	105.2	22.7	133.2	22.7
1951	143.6	118.5	25.1	0.980	0.956	1.002	1.000	116.2	24.0	150.9	26.7
1952	154.2	126.2	28.0	0.978	0.946	0.999	0.999	123.3	26.4	160.5	29.4
1953	166.8	136.7	30.1	0.979	0.942	0.999	0.999	133.6	28.4	171.0	31.1
1954	165.0	135.1	29.9	1.041	1.062	0.997	1.000	140.2	31.8	169.8	30.6
1955	178.8	146.7	32.1	1.004	1.008	1.001	1.000	147.4	32.4	180.7	33.4
1956	194.2	159.0	35.3	1.006	1.003	0.999	1.000	159.8	35.4	194.7	37.2
1957	203.8	166.1	37.7	1.015	1.011	0.998	1.000	168.4	38.1	203.8	39.7
1958	201.6	163.9	37.8	1.077	1.124	0.997	1.000	175.9	42.5	204.0	39.9
1959	219.9	178.9	41.0	1.034	1.062	0.999	1.001	184.9	43.5	218.5	42.8
1960	230.7	187.6	43.1	1.042	1.067	0.998	1.000	195.2	46.0	227.2	45.1
1961	234.9	190.7	44.2	1.066	1.116	0.998	1.001	202.8	49.4	232.1	46.5
1962	251.1	204.0	47.1	1.033	1.062	0.999	1.001	210.6	50.1	245.7	49.7
1963	264.0	214.7	49.3	1.032	1.066	1.000	1.001	221.7	52.5	256.7	52.1
1964	282.6	229.2	53.4	1.016	1.041	1.001	1.000	233.1	55.6	272.3	56.4
1965	304.7	246.1	58.6	0.999	1.011	1.002	1.000	246.3	59.3	290.5	61.9
1966	335.8	269.7	66.1	0.984	0.978	1.003	1.001	266.2	64.6	315.7	70.0
1967	356.5	285.2	71.2	0.995	0.990	1.001	1.000	284.0	70.5	333.8	75.6
1968	390.8	311.6	79.2	0.990	0.980	1.000	1.000	308.6	77.7	362.2	83.4
1969	429.2	339.1	90.1	0.996	0.981	0.998	1.000	337.1	88.3	392.7	94.7

Sources: Columns 1 to 7, see text for derivation; column 8, the product of columns 2, 4, and 6; column 9, the product of columns 3, 5, and 7; columns 10 to 13, see text for derivation; column 14, column 10 × column 12, minus column 10; column 15, column 11 × column 13, minus column 11; column 16, column 8 minus column 2, plus column 14; column 17, column 9 minus column 3, plus column 15; column 18, the sum of columns 16 and 17; column

labor weight in the sector (column 20) to obtain the percentage by which total factor input in the sector under potential conditions exceeded actual input. This percentage was multiplied by national income in 1958 prices in the sector, adjusted to allow for the difference between potential and actual utilization of resources in use (column 21), to obtain the addition to national income in 1958 prices that would have been provided under potential productivity conditions by the additional labor input that would have been supplied under potential conditions. This series is shown in Table Q-6, column 22, and transferred to Table 7-1, column 4.

E. Comment on Years of Peak Unemployment

In a footnote to Chapter 7 I cautioned that, in Table 7-3, potential national income per person employed may be understated and potential employment overstated in the peak unemployment years of some or all of the postwar recessions (1949, 1954, 1958, and 1961). This caution is based solely upon the behavior of the series.

Potential national income per person employed rises from the previous year by an unusually small amount in each of these four years and by an unusually large amount in each of the following

1940–41, and 1947–69[a]

residential business employment				Nonfarm business wage and salary workers, potential less actual compensation			Column 18 as a percentage of column 10 plus column 11 (19)	Labor weight, nonresidential business (20)	Nonresidential business national income in 1958 prices, adjusted to potential utilization (21)	Excess of potential over actual national income due to labor input (22)	Year
Education index, ratio of potential to actual		Adjustment of potential earnings for education									
Male (12)	Female (13)	Male (14)	Female (15)	Male (16)	Female (17)	Total (18)					
1.002	1.000	0.1	0.0	−0.9	−0.2	−1.1	−2.006	0.796	135.5	−2.2	1929
0.993	0.995	−0.3	0.0	7.6	2.1	9.7	18.192	0.787	149.2	21.4	1940
0.995	0.996	−0.3	0.0	3.6	1.0	4.6	6.936	0.786	169.9	9.3	1941
1.000	1.000	0.0	0.0	−0.2	−0.2	−0.4	−0.283	0.781	214.9	−0.5	1947
1.000	1.001	0.0	0.0	−1.3	−0.3	−1.7	−1.137	0.780	222.4	−2.0	1948
0.998	0.998	−0.3	0.0	3.8	1.7	5.4	3.796	0.779	218.1	6.5	1949
0.998	0.999	−0.2	0.0	2.1	1.1	3.2	2.070	0.784	234.0	3.8	1950
1.000	1.001	0.1	0.0	−2.2	−1.1	−3.2	−1.824	0.791	251.6	−3.6	1951
1.001	1.002	0.1	0.0	−2.8	−1.5	−4.2	−2.236	0.796	263.5	−4.7	1952
1.001	1.002	0.2	0.0	−2.9	−1.7	−4.6	−2.290	0.799	279.9	−5.1	1953
0.998	0.998	−0.3	0.0	4.8	1.8	6.6	3.307	0.806	276.5	7.4	1954
1.000	1.000	−0.1	0.0	0.6	0.3	0.9	0.402	0.810	292.2	1.0	1955
1.000	1.000	0.0	0.0	0.8	0.1	1.0	0.414	0.810	303.5	1.0	1956
1.000	1.000	−0.1	0.0	2.1	0.4	2.5	1.047	0.812	309.4	2.6	1957
0.997	0.997	−0.7	−0.1	11.4	4.6	15.9	6.535	0.818	304.5	16.3	1958
0.998	0.999	−0.4	−0.1	5.7	2.5	8.2	3.123	0.819	322.9	8.3	1959
0.998	0.999	−0.4	−0.1	7.1	2.8	9.9	3.636	0.817	334.0	9.9	1960
0.997	0.997	−0.7	−0.1	11.4	5.0	16.5	5.913	0.815	338.5	16.3	1961
0.998	0.999	−0.4	−0.1	6.1	2.9	9.0	3.063	0.812	355.6	8.8	1962
0.998	0.998	−0.5	−0.1	6.5	3.2	9.7	3.126	0.805	370.4	9.3	1963
0.999	0.999	−0.4	−0.1	3.6	2.2	5.8	1.758	0.798	384.7	5.4	1964
0.999	1.000	−0.2	0.0	0.0	0.6	0.7	0.196	0.796	408.4	0.6	1965
1.000	1.001	0.0	0.0	−3.4	−1.4	−4.8	−1.252	0.795	433.5	−4.3	1966
1.000	1.000	0.1	0.0	−1.2	−0.7	−1.9	−0.462	0.795	449.1	−1.7	1967
1.000	1.000	0.1	0.0	−2.8	−1.5	−4.3	−0.973	0.798	475.5	−3.7	1968
1.000	1.001	0.2	0.1	−1.8	−1.7	−3.5	−0.715	0.802	498.4	−2.9	1969

19, column 18 ÷ (column 10 plus column 11) × 100; column 20, annual data that were averaged to obtain the "labor" column in Table J-2; column 21. Table 3-2, column 7, plus Table 7-1, column 2; column 22, the product of columns 19, 20, and 21. Detail may not add to totals because of rounding.
a. Includes Alaska and Hawaii beginning in 1960.

years. The series is not smooth in other periods so such movements do not, in themselves, necessarily indicate procedural errors; the pattern, in fact, is probably due in part to happenstance. Calendar effects almost certainly contribute to the 1948–49 and 1960–61 movements, and both the weather and work stoppages to the 1948–49 movement. Moreover, perusal of all of the series in Table 7-3 provides no clear indication that estimates for 1949 are out of line with adjacent years.

The clearer indication of possible error is that the increase in potential employment is particularly large in 1954, 1958, and 1961, and improb-

ably small in 1955, 1959, and 1962, suggesting an overestimate of potential employment in 1954, 1958, and 1961. The average increase in total potential national income, in contrast, is about the same in 1954, 1958, and 1961 as in 1955, 1959, and 1962; this is so both in the whole economy and in the nonresidential business sector. The pattern suggests the possibility of an overly large adjustment for labor force response to unemployment in the peak unemployment years. This adjustment affects potential employment much more than potential national income and therefore cuts potential national income per person employed in the peak unemployment years. However, output per person employed would increase less in the peak unemployment years than in the following years even if no adjustment at all were made for labor force response, so this cannot be the whole explanation of its behavior.

If the gap between actual and potential labor force actually is overestimated in peak unemployment years, this must be due to something special about these years. It would not imply that the gap is systematically overestimated in all years because the method of estimation would bar such a possibility. It might suggest a curvilinear relationship between unemployment and labor force shortage or surplus, or a lagged response of the labor force when unemployment first becomes high.

PART TWO: THE 3.5 PERCENT AND 4.5 PERCENT UNEMPLOYMENT VARIANTS

The adjustments to actual national income introduced to derive the 4 percent variant of potential national income were recalculated to obtain the 3.5 percent and 4.5 percent variants. They are shown in Table Q-7, along with the estimates of potential national income so obtained.

The adjustment for intensity of utilization of employed resources (Table Q-7, columns 2a and 2b) was made each year by the method followed to obtain the adjustment for the 4 percent variant, as described in Chapter 7. Values of 103.60 for the 4.5 percent variant and 104.12 for the 3.5

Table Q-7. Derivation of 3.5 Percent and 4.5 Percent Variants of Potential National Income in Constant Prices, 1929, 1940–41, and 1947–69

Billions of 1958 dollars

		Adjustments for labor input									
	Actual national income	Adjustment for intensity of utilization				Other			Potential national income		
Year	*(1)*	+	*3.5 percent (2a)*	*or*	*4.5 percent (2b)*	+	*Work relief (3)*	+	*3.5 percent (4a)*	*or*	*4.5 percent (4b)*	=	*3.5 percent (5a)*	*or*	*4.5 percent (5b)*
			Excluding Alaska and Hawaii									
1929	161.4		−0.8		−1.5		0.0		−1.2		−3.1		159.4		156.8
1940	181.5		1.5		0.7		−3.5		22.8		19.9		202.3		198.6
1941	215.8		−6.3		−7.1		−2.7		10.7		7.8		217.5		213.8
1947	255.2		3.5		2.4		0.0		1.1		−2.1		259.8		255.5
1948	270.1		−3.0		−4.1		0.0		−0.4		−3.6		266.7		262.4
1949	265.8		−0.3		−1.4		0.0		8.2		4.7		273.7		269.1
1950	290.8		−7.2		−8.3		0.0		5.6		1.9		289.2		284.4
1951	312.9		−3.0		−4.3		0.0		−1.7		−5.6		308.2		303.0
1952	323.5		2.3		1.0		0.0		−2.7		−6.8		323.1		317.7
1953	337.3		6.1		4.7		0.0		−2.9		−7.4		340.5		334.6
1954	331.3		9.0		7.6		0.0		9.7		4.9		350.0		343.8
1955	358.8		−0.8		−2.2		0.0		3.4		−1.5		361.4		355.1
1956	367.8		3.3		1.8		0.0		3.6		−1.6		374.7		368.0
1957	371.1		8.0		6.4		0.0		5.2		−0.1		384.3		377.4
1958	363.6		12.1		10.6		0.0		19.0		13.5		394.7		387.7
1959	391.1		4.4		2.8		0.0		11.1		5.3		406.6		399.2
1960	399.4		9.0		7.3		0.0		12.9		6.9		421.3		413.6
			Including Alaska and Hawaii									
1960	400.8		9.0		7.3		0.0		12.9		6.9		422.7		415.0
1961	408.1		9.0		7.3		0.0		19.4		13.1		436.5		428.5
1962	435.3		3.2		1.4		0.0		2.0		5.6		450.5		442.3
1963	453.6		2.6		0.7		0.0		12.6		6.0		468.8		460.3
1964	480.1		−5.5		−7.4		0.0		8.7		2.0		483.3		474.7
1965	513.0		−10.4		−12.4		0.0		4.1		−2.9		506.7		497.7
1966	545.2		−11.9		−14.0		0.0		−0.7		−8.0		532.6		523.2
1967	557.6		−2.6		−4.8		0.0		2.1		−5.5		557.1		547.3
1968	585.1		0.5		−1.9		0.0		0.3		−7.8		585.9		575.4
1969	599.6		11.6		9.1		0.0		1.4		−7.2		612.6		601.5

Source: See text for derivation.

percent variant were used for the index (1958 = 100) of "intensity of utilization of employed resources resulting from fluctuations in the intensity of demand," in place of the value of 103.86 used for the 4 percent variant. These values were obtained from the same regression line as the 103.86 value.

The adjustment for labor input was reworked in full detail for the 3.5 and 4.5 percent variants only for 1967. It was calculated that in 1967 the ratios of the labor input of nonfarm wage and salary workers in nonresidential business at 3.5 percent unemployment and 4.5 percent unemployment to input at 4 percent unemployment were 1.012190 and 0.987407, respectively. These ratios were applied in all years to the sum of columns 1 and 18 in Table Q-6 to obtain the 3.5 and 4.5 percent unemployment variants of the potential labor input of nonfarm business wage and salary workers. Thereafter, the procedures were the same as those used to obtain the estimates for the 4 percent variant.

PART THREE: SMOOTHED AND TREND-BASED SERIES

Short-term movements of my potential output series, like those of actual output, reflect variations in the calendar, errors in estimates of actual output, and all irregular influences on actual output except those related to short-term changes in the strength of demand. This similarity between the two series is highly desirable whenever emphasis is upon the difference between them.

Irregular Movements in Potential Output

However, any reader who wishes to use potential output to measure year-to-year changes in annual output that result from "persistent" or "underlying" growth factors, terms which I shall not try to define, may find the irregularities in its movement annoying. I myself do not, because I would not interpret potential output this way and I regard measurement of annual changes in the influence of persistent factors as impossible. The following observations are nevertheless offered to more ambitious readers.

The influence upon output per unit of input in nonresidential business of the weather in farming and of labor disputes could easily be eliminated from the "4 percent unemployment" variant of potential output by dividing the potential out-

put of the sector (Table 7-3, column 4) by the indexes for these determinants (Table 6-1, columns 4 and 5) after adjusting their base from 1958 to the postwar average. The influence of calendar effects, errors of estimate, and irregularities in other determinants cannot be directly removed because their size is unknown; one might, however, simply smooth the annual potential output series on the assumption that year-to-year irregularities are due to such influences.

Effect of the Business Cycle upon Capital

Anyone seeking a series reflecting only persistent factors might also wish to remove the effects of the business cycle on capital input. To secure an adjustment to potential output in nonresidential business he would need to cyclically adjust the input series for inventories and for nonresidential structures and equipment (given in Table 5-4, columns 3 and 4); multiply the percentage differences between the actual and adjusted indexes for each of these inputs by the weight of the input in nonresidential business (two-year averages are given in Table J-2, columns 3 and 4); and multiply the products by potential output in nonresidential business (Table 7-3, column 4). He would need also to cyclically adjust output in the dwellings sector (Table 3-2, column 5).

Trend-Based Estimates

The direct estimates of potential output could readily be used to derive a "trend-based" series for the postwar years. The best method of deriving such a series from potential output alone would be to simply smooth the direct estimates, retaining all changes except annual irregularities as well as the general level of the series. (If, instead, computed trends are used, separate trends should be used for at least the four periods distinguished in Chapter 7: 1947–49, 1949–53, 1953–64, and 1964–69.) It is also possible to use such procedures for certain determinants of output only. One such possibility is to retain the movements of the direct estimates of potential output insofar as they correspond to movements of determinants that are directly estimated each year, but to substitute smoothed values for the index of the semiresidual in nonresidential business shown in Table 6-1, column 7. (If, instead, computed trends are used, separate trends should be used for at least the periods distinguished in

Table 6-4.) None of these procedures would yield a potential estimate that is very different from the direct estimate except for elimination of irregularities.

A variation of the procedure last described, which I do not recommend but which may appeal to some readers, produces differences from the direct estimates which are larger but still not very large. This potential output series, shown in Table Q-8, makes no use at all of my estimates of the effect of demand fluctuations upon output per unit of input (or, consequently, of the corporate income shares on which they are based). An index of potential national income in nonresidential business is computed by retaining the direct estimates for the effects of total factor input and the effects upon output per unit of input of resource reallocation, weather in farming, and labor disputes, but substituting for the combined effects of other components of output per unit of input

(Table 6-1, columns 6, 8, and 9) a trend value which is based on a single trend computed for the entire postwar period.[39] Like all other trend-based series that do not result from simple smoothing of direct estimates, construction of this potential output series requires that some base level be set independently. My direct estimate for 1955 is arbitrarily used as such a base because the approximate size of potential output in that year appears to be relatively noncontroversial. Actual output is retained as the potential estimate for sectors other than nonresidential business.[40]

Table Q-8, column 2, shows the percentage by which the estimate obtained by this procedure exceeds my direct estimate each year. Erratic year-to-year fluctuations in this percentage, such as occur from 1952 to 1953, reflect the elimination of all irregular movements in the semiresidual, including those stemming from the calendar or errors in the estimate of actual output. Longer swings in the percentage reflect the elimination of the mid-period dip in the growth rate of the semiresidual. I regard this feature of the partially trend-based series as highly undesirable because my statistical results indicate that such a dip actually occurred and because part of this dip is to

Table Q-8. Partially Trend-Based Series for Potential National Income with Level Determined by 1955 Direct Estimate, 1947–69

Year	Amount in billions of 1958 dollars (1)	Percentage difference from direct estimate (2)
Excluding Alaska and Hawaii		
1947	257.6	0.0
1948	267.0	0.9
1949	274.8	1.2
1950	287.7	0.3
1951	307.3	0.5
1952	322.3	0.6
1953	336.5	−0.3
1954	346.9	0.0
1955	358.3	0.0
1956	372.7	0.4
1957	382.8	0.5
1958	395.5	1.1
1959	406.0	0.7
1960	421.1	0.9
Including Alaska and Hawaii		
1960	422.6	0.9
1961	437.8	1.2
1962	449.7	0.7
1963	467.5	0.6
1964	483.0	0.8
1965	505.8	0.7
1966	530.8	0.5
1967	557.9	1.0
1968	581.5	0.1
1969	607.3	0.0

Sources: Column 1, see text; column 2, computed from column 1 and Table 7-1, column 5.

39. A trivial departure from this procedure was made so as to permit use of the trend values for "adjusted output per unit of input" described in Appendix O, Part 2. Because "adjusted output per unit of input" includes the labor disputes index in addition to the series for which substitution of a trend value is now desired, substitution of its trend value eliminated variations in the labor disputes index, which were then reintroduced.

40. Derivation of this potential output estimate is illustrated by use of data for the year 1961. Actual national income in nonresidential business was $330.3 billion (Table 3-2, column 7). Adjusted output per unit of input was 2.883 percent below its postwar trend value, when the level as well as the slope of the trend line is determined by all postwar years (Table O-2, column 4); hence, it is 97.117 percent of its trend value. Dividing $330.3 billion by 0.97117 yields $340.1 billion when adjusted output per unit of input is raised to this trend level. Multiplication by the labor disputes index of 100.02 (Table 6-1, column 5), which reintroduces the effect of that determinant (see note 39), yields $340.2 billion. The same procedure yields $289.2 billion in the benchmark year 1955, whereas the corresponding direct estimate for actual output adjusted to the potential level of intensity of utilization of employed resources is 1.037 percent higher at $292.2 billion (actual output of $293.7 billion plus the adjustment for intensity of utilization of −$1.5 billion, from Table 7-1, column 2). The initial 1961 trend-based estimate of $340.2 billion is therefore raised by 1.037 percent to $343.7 billion to correspond to the potential level determined for 1955. Addition of $16.3 billion to allow for the difference between actual and potential labor input (Table 7-1, column 4) yields $360.0 billion for potential national income in nonresidential business. Addition of actual national income of $77.8 billion in the three remaining sectors (Table 3-2, columns 4, 5, and 6) yields $437.8 billion for potential national income in the whole economy.

be expected once consideration is given to economies of scale. That the series usually runs above the direct estimates—it is lower in only one year —results simply from the use of 1955 to set its level (combined with the elimination of the mid-period dip in the semiresidual). Use of a different base year (1967, for example) would reverse this relationship.

Despite these objections to the series, it may be noted that it is much closer in movement, and usually in level as well, to my direct estimates than to the national income estimates implied by either GNP series of the Council of Economic Advisers. This is because the series retains the effects of the changes in input growth rates which I found to have taken place (as well as those of movements in the resource reallocation, weather, and labor disputes indexes).

꧁꧂

Supplementary Estimates for Sources of Growth

꧁꧂

Most information required to secure tables in Chapters 8 and 9 that provide sources of growth in accord with the classification generally used in this study is given in earlier chapters. Data to fill the gaps follow in sections 1, 2, and 3 of this appendix. Section 4 then explains the relationship among the various tables which follow this classification. Section 5 provides supplementary information relating to the alternative classification in which the contribution of economies of scale is allocated among other components. The last section, section 6, explains how detailed estimates can be rearranged to approximate the results of altering my assumptions as to the effects of changes in working hours.

1. Potential National Income in Nonresidential Business

Indexes of input and output per unit of input in the nonresidential business sector computed on a potential basis differ from indexes on an actual basis only for labor input components and for the effects of shifts from farming and from nonfarm self-employment.[1] The procedure by which potential national income was derived did not directly provide potential values for these series, except

employment which is shown in Table 7-3, column 5, because the adjustments to components of labor input (other than the effects of intergroup shifts) were related to nonfarm wage and salary workers rather than to all workers in the sector and because adjustments to the intergroup shift labor input index and to the resource allocation indexes were not made separately.

To derive sources of growth of potential national income it was necessary to estimate indexes on a potential basis comparable to those provided on an actual basis in Chapters 4 and 6. This was done only for the six years (1929, 1941, 1948, 1953, 1964, and 1969) that begin or end periods for which sources of growth tables are provided. To avoid changing the base year, it was also done for 1958.[2] The indexes on a potential basis were obtained by simply replacing actual with potential values of the data entering into their construction. All of the potential data needed were available from the preparation of potential national income, which is described in Appendix Q. Indexes on a potential basis which differ from corresponding indexes on an actual basis are provided in Table R-1.

Some of these indexes are partially independent of and therefore not necessarily consistent with the direct estimates of potential national income. Indeed, it is possible to calculate an alternative index of potential national income (though not to establish a level for the series) by combining these indexes with indexes of nonlabor input and output per unit of input, which are the same on a potential as on an actual basis. The growth rates of the direct estimates of potential national income and of this indirectly constructed series compare as follows:

	Direct estimates	Indirect estimates
1929–69	3.33	3.34
1929–48	2.68	2.70
1948–69	3.92	3.92
1929–41	2.50	2.58
1941–48	3.00	2.91
1948–53	4.51	4.45
1953–64	3.20	3.25
1964–69	4.90	4.86

The discrepancies are 0.00 to 0.02 percentage points in the long periods and no more than 0.06 percentage points in the shorter periods except that they were 0.08 or 0.09 in the two periods

---

1. The index of "changes in intensity of utilization of employed resources resulting from fluctuations in intensity of demand" is eliminated in analysis of potential national income.

2. The 1958 estimates, some of which are subject to an unusual degree of uncertainty, do not affect the sources of growth estimates for the selected periods.

Table R-1. Nonresidential Business: Indexes of Labor Input and Gains from Reallocation of Resources on a Potential National Income Basis, Selected Years, 1929–69
1958 = 100

Year	Employment (1)	Average weekly hours (2)	Total weekly hours (3)	Age-sex composition of total hours (4)	Efficiency of an hour's work as affected by changes in hours due to		Amount of education (7)	Gains from reallocation of resources from	
					Intra-group changes (5)	Specified intergroup shifts (6)		Farming (8)	Nonfarm self-employment (9)
1929	73.77	120.81	89.12	100.58	92.94	96.24	84.09	90.58	98.73
1941	87.95	108.05	95.03	100.07	98.68	97.63	90.61	94.13	99.94
1948	91.64	104.38	95.66	100.66	99.26	98.38	94.16	96.46	99.22
1953	94.92	102.47	97.27	101.58	99.96	99.09	97.01	98.26	99.49
1958	100.00	100.00	100.00	100.00	100.00	100.00	100.00	100.00	100.00
1964	103.08	97.77	100.79	99.27	99.75	100.60	103.71	101.25	100.22
1969	113.51	95.08	107.93	97.58	100.30	101.26	107.10	102.31	100.91

Source: See text for derivation.

which began or ended in 1941, a difficult year. They cause an initial discrepancy in most periods between the growth components and the directly measured growth rate. This was eliminated by "forcing" the components so that they would add to the growth rate.

2. Actual National Income in the Whole Economy

The estimates of the sources of growth of total actual national income in the whole economy (Tables 9-4 and 9-9) were obtained by adding the contributions made by each source in the four sectors.

The contributions made by the three special sectors were provided in Tables 3-3, 3-5, and 3-7. Table R-2 provides the similar estimates for the nonresidential business sector. The total contribution of the sector in each period shown in the top row of Table R-2 comes from Table 3-3. It was allocated among the sources in proportion to their contributions to the growth rate of national income originating in nonresidential business (shown in Tables 8-2 and 8-5).

3. Potential National Income in the Whole Economy

Sources of growth of total potential national income in the whole economy, shown in Tables 9-4 and 9-10, like the similar estimates for actual national income, were obtained by adding the contributions made in the four sectors. Table R-3 shows the contributions of each

sector to growth rates of potential national income and the sector growth rates and weights from which they are derived. The table is parallel in all respects to Table 3-3, which provides similar estimates for actual national income.

Potential national income originating in the three special sectors is always the same in dollar amount as actual national income (excluding work relief) so the contributions of these sectors to potential and actual growth rates of total income are very similar. They diverge at all only because the difference between total potential and total actual national income in the initial year of a period causes the same change in dollar amount in national income in a sector to represent a different percentage of all-sector income in the initial year. Rounded to hundredths of a percentage point, most figures for contributions to the growth rate are the same.

Differences of 0.01 percentage points appear for the contributions of general government, households, and institutions in four time periods and for dwellings in two time periods, and change the contribution of some detailed growth sources within the sector correspondingly. Estimates for the special sectors which differ from the corresponding estimates for actual national income are shown in Table R-4 (page 339).

Table R-5 shows the contribution of each source within the nonresidential business sector to the growth rate of total potential national income. The total contribution of the sector, from Table R-3, was allocated in proportion to the contributions of the sources to the growth rate of potential national income originating in the sector.

Table R-2. Nonresidential Business: Sector's Contribution to Growth Rates of Total Actual National Income, by Source, Eight Selected Periods, 1929–69

Contributions to growth rates in percentage points

	1929–69	1929–48	1948–69	1929–41	1941–48	1948–53	1953–64	1964–69
Contribution of sector	**2.68**	**2.26**	**3.07**	**1.81**	**2.98**	**3.29**	**2.64**	**3.68**
Total factor input	**1.17**	**1.02**	**1.31**	**0.74**	**1.49**	**1.67**	**0.70**	**2.23**
Labor	0.88	0.94	0.83	0.75	1.25	1.11	0.33	1.60
Employment	0.71	0.73	0.70	0.44	1.22	0.72	0.20	1.75
Hours	−0.19	−0.20	−0.18	−0.18	−0.24	−0.06	−0.21	−0.24
Average hours	−0.41	−0.51	−0.32	−0.55	−0.44	−0.29	−0.26	−0.45
Efficiency offset	0.13	0.24	0.04	0.32	0.07	0.12	−0.02	0.10
Intergroup shift offset	0.09	0.07	0.10	0.05	0.13	0.11	0.07	0.11
Age-sex composition	−0.05	0.01	−0.10	0.04	−0.04	0.07	−0.09	−0.31
Education	0.41	0.40	0.41	0.45	0.31	0.38	0.43	0.40
Capital	0.29	0.08	0.48	−0.01	0.24	0.56	0.37	0.63
Inventories	0.09	0.05	0.12	0.02	0.12	0.18	0.08	0.18
Nonresidential structures and equipment	0.20	0.03	0.36	−0.03	0.12	0.38	0.29	0.45
Land	0.00	0.00	0.00	0.00	0.00	0.00	0.00	0.00
Output per unit of input	**1.51**	**1.24**	**1.76**	**1.07**	**1.49**	**1.62**	**1.94**	**1.45**
Advances in knowledge and n.e.c.[a]	0.92	0.62	1.19	0.46	0.86	1.34	1.13	1.15
Improved resource allocation	0.29	0.29	0.30	0.22	0.42	0.41	0.24	0.34
Farm	0.25	0.27	0.23	0.19	0.42	0.33	0.21	0.19
Nonfarm self-employment	0.04	0.02	0.07	0.03	0.00	0.08	0.03	0.15
Economies of scale	0.36	0.29	0.42	0.19	0.45	0.48	0.32	0.56
Irregular factors	−0.06	0.04	−0.15	0.20	−0.24	−0.61	0.25	−0.60
Weather in farming	0.00	0.01	−0.01	−0.01	0.04	−0.03	−0.02	0.02
Labor disputes	0.00	0.00	0.00	0.00	0.00	0.00	0.00	−0.01
Intensity of demand	−0.06	0.03	−0.14	0.21	−0.28	−0.58	0.27	−0.61

Source: Derived from Tables 3-3, 4-1, 5-4, 6-1, and J-2.
a. n.e.c. Not elsewhere classified.

4. Relationships among Contributions to Various Output Measures

As explained in Chapter 8, contributions of individual sources to the growth rates of two or more of the four measures of output in nonresidential business that are analyzed in this study often differ a little for reasons that are not really substantive. These reasons are (1) the presence of interaction terms and the forcing of estimates, where necessary, to eliminate discrepancies between totals and the sums of components that arise from rounding and (2) the small difference, already described in this appendix, between the "direct" and "indirect" estimates of the growth rates of potential output. Cases where contributions would otherwise be identical are indicated in Table R-6 by insertion of the

Almost all of the differences between the contributions of the sources to actual and potential national income originate in this sector.

same letter beside a growth source in columns for different output measures. For example, except for these reasons "hours" would contribute the same amount to total actual national income and to actual national income per person employed, "inventories" to total actual national income and to total potential national income, and "advances in knowledge and n.e.c." to all four output measures.

With one slight amendment, Table R-6 also describes the relationships among the sources of growth tables for the whole economy. The amendment is that the contributions of a source to different output measures bearing the same letter may differ not only because of interaction and forcing but also because the contributions of the special sectors to actual and potential national income are not the same. Also, four sources appear in the tables for the whole economy but not in Table R-6. The situation is the same for the "unallocated" line under labor as for hours, for "dwellings" and "international assets" as for in-

Table R-3. Growth Rates of Potential National Income by Sector and Contributions of the Sectors to the Growth Rate of Total Potential National Income, Eight Selected Periods, 1929–69

Period	Whole economy	Government, households, and institutions	Dwellings	International assets	Nonresidential business
Growth rate of sector national income					
Long periods					
1929–69	3.41	3.41	5.76	2.66	3.33
1929–48	2.75	3.22	3.72	−0.93	2.68
1948–69	4.02	3.59	7.64	6.02	3.92
Shorter periods					
1929–41	2.63	3.98	0.95	−3.76	2.50
1941–48	2.96	1.92	8.64	4.11	3.00
1948–53	4.99	6.78	10.62	1.65	4.51
1953–64	3.20	1.89	6.90	10.67	3.20
1964–69	4.85	4.23	6.35	0.62	4.90
Weight for calculation of contributions					
Long periods					
1929–69	1.00	0.1270	0.0349	0.0078	0.8304
1929–48	1.00	0.1323	0.0223	0.0068	0.8386
1948–69	1.00	0.1329	0.0366	0.0055	0.8250
Shorter periods					
1929–41	1.00	0.1368	0.0187	0.0067	0.8378
1941–48	1.00	0.1441	0.0200	0.0042	0.8316
1948–53	1.00	0.1432	0.0273	0.0042	0.8254
1953–64	1.00	0.1415	0.0385	0.0057	0.8142
1964–69	1.00	0.1295	0.0479	0.0075	0.8152
Contribution to growth rate in whole economy					
Long periods					
1929–69	3.41	0.43	0.20	0.02	2.76
1929–48	2.75	0.43	0.08	−0.01	2.25
1948–69	4.02	0.48	0.28	0.03	3.23
Shorter periods					
1929–41	2.63	0.54	0.02	−0.03	2.10
1941–48	2.96	0.28	0.17	0.02	2.49
1948–53	4.99	0.97	0.29	0.01	3.72
1953–64	3.20	0.27	0.27	0.06	2.60
1964–69	4.85	0.55	0.30	0.01	3.99

Sources: Derived from Tables 3-2 and 7-1. Detail may not add to totals because of rounding.

Table R-4. Contributions of Detailed Components in Special Sectors to Growth Rates of Total Potential National Income[a]

Period	General government, households, and institutions sector		Effect of changes in hours		Services of dwellings sector	
	National income	Employment	Total	Efficiency offset	National income	Quantity of housing
1929–48	0.43	0.30	a	a	a	a
1948–69	0.48	a	−0.02	0.03	a	a
1941–48	0.28	0.19	a	a	a	a
1948–53	0.97	a	−0.01	0.02	0.29	0.32
1953–64	a	a	a	a	0.27	0.28

Source: See text for derivation.

a. All estimates for general government, households, and institutions that are not shown are the same as those shown for total actual national income in Tables 3-5 and 3-7. Estimates for international assets are the same as those shown for total actual national income in Table 3-3.

Table R-5. Nonresidential Business: Sector's Contribution to Growth Rates of Total Potential National Income, by Source, Eight Selected Periods, 1929–69

Contributions to growth rates in percentage points

	1929–69	1929–48	1948–69	1929–41	1941–48	1948–53	1953–64	1964–69
Contribution of sector	**2.76**	**2.25**	**3.23**	**2.10**	**2.49**	**3.72**	**2.60**	**3.99**
Total factor input	**1.18**	**1.02**	**1.31**	**1.12**	**0.91**	**1.54**	**0.91**	**1.94**
Labor	0.89	0.94	0.83	1.12	0.67	0.97	0.56	1.30
Employment	0.72	0.75	0.68	0.96	0.41	0.49	0.50	1.30
Hours	−0.19	−0.20	−0.17	−0.21	−0.17	−0.05	−0.21	−0.21
Average hours	−0.40	−0.51	−0.29	−0.62	−0.31	−0.24	−0.29	−0.36
Efficiency offset	0.13	0.23	0.03	0.33	0.06	0.10	−0.01	0.07
Intergroup shift offset	0.08	0.08	0.09	0.08	0.08	0.09	0.09	0.08
Age-sex composition	−0.05	0.00	−0.10	−0.03	0.06	0.13	−0.14	−0.22
Education	0.41	0.39	0.42	0.40	0.37	0.40	0.41	0.43
Capital	0.29	0.08	0.48	0.00	0.24	0.57	0.35	0.64
Inventories	0.09	0.05	0.12	0.03	0.12	0.18	0.07	0.18
Nonresidential structures and equipment	0.20	0.03	0.36	−0.03	0.12	0.39	0.28	0.46
Land	0.00	0.00	0.00	0.00	0.00	0.00	0.00	0.00
Output per unit of input	**1.58**	**1.23**	**1.92**	**0.98**	**1.58**	**2.18**	**1.69**	**2.05**
Advances in knowledge and n.e.c.[a]	0.92	0.62	1.19	0.46	0.86	1.36	1.12	1.17
Improved resource allocation	0.30	0.31	0.31	0.34	0.23	0.36	0.28	0.30
Farm	0.26	0.28	0.24	0.26	0.30	0.32	0.22	0.18
Nonfarm self-employment	0.04	0.03	0.07	0.08	−0.07	0.04	0.06	0.12
Economies of scale	0.36	0.29	0.43	0.19	0.45	0.49	0.31	0.57
Irregular factors	0.00	0.01	−0.01	−0.01	0.04	−0.03	−0.02	0.01
Weather in farming	0.00	0.01	−0.01	−0.01	0.04	−0.03	−0.02	0.02
Labor disputes	0.00	0.00	0.00	0.00	0.00	0.00	0.00	−0.01

Sources: Derived from Tables R-3, R-4, 3-3, 4-1, 5-4, 6-1, and J-2.
a. n.e.c. Not elsewhere classified.

ventories, and for the "dwellings occupancy ratio" as for "advances in knowledge and n.e.c."

5. Potential National Income with Economies of Scale Allocated

Table R-7 shows the distributions of potential national income and potential national income per person potentially employed that are obtained in the economy as a whole in each of the long periods when the contribution of economies of scale is allocated among other determinants, except irregular factors, in proportion to their contributions to the growth rate of total actual national income originating in the nonresidential business sector. The last three columns of Tables 9-5 and 9-8 were computed from Table R-7 (page 342).

6. Effects of Alternative Assumptions about the Effects of Changes in Hours

The effect on output of changes in average hours worked within the nonresidential business sector is divided in the sources of growth tables of Chap-

ters 8 and 9 among three components, corresponding to the three indexes having to do with hours that were developed in Chapter 4. Presentation of this detail, as is noted in Chapters 8 and 9, allows any reader who so wishes to reclassify any of the components from total factor input to output per unit of input. A decision to divide growth sources between total factor input and output per unit of input in a different way would not imply any difference of opinion as to the effect of changes in hours upon output per person employed.

The detail also serves another purpose. It is possible by merely transferring components to approximate the sources of growth estimates that would be obtained if my assumptions as to the effects on output of changes in hours were to be amended in certain extreme ways.[3] To illustrate, I present the results for total potential national income in 1948–69 in Table R-8. Similar pro-

3. The results are approximations because some of the changes in assumptions would also imply changes in the age-sex and education components of labor input. These changes are ignored here.

Table R-6. Nonresidential Business: Relationships among Contributions to Various Output Measures[a]

	Total actual national income	Actual national income per person employed	Total potential national income	Potential national income per person potentially employed
Sector national income	A	B	C	D
Total factor input	A	B	C	D
Labor	A	B	C	D
Employment	A	. . .	C	. . .
Hours	A	A	C	C
Average hours	A	A	C	C
Efficiency offset	A	A	C	C
Intergroup shifts	A	A	C	C
Age-sex composition	A	A	C	C
Education	A	A	C	C
Capital	A	B	A	D
Inventories	A	B	A	D
Nonresidential structures and equipment	A	B	A	D
Land	A	B	A	D
Output per unit of input	A	A	C	C
Advances in knowledge and n.e.c.[b]	A	A	A	A
Improved resource allocation	A	A	C	C
Farm	A	A	C	C
Nonfarm self-employment	A	A	C	C
Economies of scale	A	A	A	A
Irregular factors	A	A	C	C
Weather in farming	A	A	A	A
Labor disputes	A	A	A	A
Intensity of demand	A	A	. . .	. . .

a. See text for explanation.
b. n.e.c. Not elsewhere classified.

cedures can be used for any other period or output measure. The upper half of Table R-8 refers to nonresidential business, and the procedure is most readily followed on that half. The lower half refers to the whole economy.[4]

Under alternative 1 in Table R-8, I present my actual estimates, which stem from my set of assumptions as to the effect on output when average hours change. These assumptions are summarized on pages 105–06.

Alternative 2 assumes that when there is a change in the average weekly hours of any of the six relatively homogeneous groups of full-time workers distinguished in my estimates, the work performed in a week by that group changes by the same percentage (that is, there is no efficiency offset at all). My assumptions as to the consequences of changes in average hours for other reasons are retained. The change introduced in the estimate for labor input by omitting "efficiency offset" is matched by an offsetting change in the contribution of "advances in knowledge and n.e.c."[5]

Changing my assumption to the opposite extreme so as to assume that work performed per week is unchanged when hours of any of the six groups of full-time workers change (that is, the efficiency offset is complete) would alter my estimates only for male and female full-time wage and salary workers.[6] For them the change would

4. Transfers of hours components for the whole economy must be confined to the contributions stemming from nonresidential business, shown in Table 9-3. Contributions stemming from general government, households, and institutions are unchanged by changing the assumptions and account for entries in the lower half of Table R-8 when none appears in the corresponding portion of the upper half.

5. The results of changing my assumption only for nonfarm wage and salary workers are given for total actual national income in nonresidential business in 1929–41 and 1941–48 on page 82. This calculation cannot be made directly from the sources of growth tables, but all necessary data are shown in the detailed tables of the appendixes.

6. My estimates already make this assumption for farm workers and the nonfarm self-employed.

Table R-7. Potential National Income and Potential National Income per Person Potentially Employed: Sources of Growth with Economies of Scale Allocated, Three Long Periods, 1929–69

Contributions to growth rate in percentage points

	Potential national income			Potential national income per person potentially employed		
	1929–69	1929–48	1948–69	1929–69	1929–48	1948–69
Potential national income	**3.41**	**2.75**	**4.02**	**1.95**	**1.42**	**2.44**
Total factor input	**2.00**	**1.65**	**2.31**	**0.57**	**0.35**	**0.78**
Labor	1.46	1.51	1.44	0.36	0.46	0.28
Employment	1.20	1.16	1.26	0.10	0.11	0.10
Hours	−0.25	−0.26	−0.22	−0.25	−0.26	−0.22
Average hours	−0.55	−0.71	−0.39	−0.55	−0.71	−0.39
Efficiency offset	0.21	0.36	0.07	0.21	0.36	0.07
Intergroup shift offset	0.09	0.09	0.10	0.09	0.09	0.10
Age-sex composition	−0.06	0.00	−0.11	−0.06	0.00	−0.11
Education	0.48	0.45	0.48	0.48	0.45	0.48
Unallocated	0.09	0.16	0.03	0.09	0.16	0.03
Capital	0.54	0.14	0.87	0.26	−0.06	0.55
Inventories	0.10	0.06	0.14	0.04	0.01	0.08
Nonresidential structures and equipment	0.23	0.03	0.41	0.08	−0.09	0.23
Dwellings	0.19	0.06	0.29	0.13	0.03	0.22
International assets	0.02	−0.01	0.03	0.01	−0.01	0.02
Land	0.00	0.00	0.00	−0.05	−0.05	−0.05
Output per unit of input	**1.41**	**1.10**	**1.71**	**1.38**	**1.07**	**1.66**
Advances in knowledge and n.e.c.[a]	1.06	0.72	1.37	1.04	0.70	1.33
Improved resource allocation	0.34	0.35	0.36	0.33	0.34	0.35
Farm	0.29	0.32	0.28	0.28	0.31	0.27
Nonfarm self-employment	0.05	0.03	0.08	0.05	0.03	0.08
Dwellings occupancy ratio	0.01	0.02	−0.01	0.01	0.02	−0.01
Irregular factors	0.00	0.01	−0.01	0.00	0.01	−0.01
Weather in farming	0.00	0.01	−0.01	0.00	0.01	−0.01
Labor disputes	0.00	0.00	0.00	0.00	0.00	0.00

Sources: Derived from Tables 8-2, 9-4, and 9-7.
a. n.e.c. Not elsewhere classified.

be larger than and in the opposite direction from the change introduced by alternative 2. The size of the change cannot be calculated from the sources of growth tables, but only from the more detailed underlying data shown in the appendixes, so this alternative is omitted from Table R-8.

Alternative 3, while retaining all my other assumptions, removes my procedure of counting an average week's work by full-time nonfarm wage and salary workers as equivalent to an average week's work by full-time farm workers or nonfarm self-employed workers of the same sex; instead, it counts an hour's work as equivalent. This substitution might be desired as a matter of classification, but it seems absurd as an alternative opinion about the effect on output per worker when the distribution of employment among the three groups changes. It requires not only the assumption that, if full-time wage and salary workers' hours were as long as those of farm

workers or nonfarm self-employed workers (far longer than they actually are), they would accomplish proportionally more in a week, but also the seemingly impossible assumption that a change in the distribution of employment among the three groups does not change their combined average hours. If all this were true, misallocation and gains from reallocation would be much greater than my estimates imply. The change in the contribution of labor input obtained by deleting "intergroup shifts" would be matched by an approximately offsetting change in the contribution of "improved resource allocation."

Alternative 4 simply assumes that when average hours in the business sector as a whole change for any reason at all the work done per week changes proportionately. This is equivalent to combining the changes in my assumptions that are incorporated in alternatives 2 and 3 because I myself assume that a change in average hours

Table R-8. Total Potential National Income: Effect upon Sources of Growth Estimates of Certain Extreme Changes in Assumptions as to the Effects of Hours Changes, 1948–69

	Alternatives				
	1	*2*	*3*	*4*	*5*
	Nonresidential business				
Labor input	1.00	0.96	0.89	0.85	1.21
Hours	−0.21	−0.25	−0.32	−0.36	...
Average hours	−0.36	−0.36	−0.36	−0.36	−0.36
Efficiency offset	0.04	...	0.04	...	0.25
Intergroup shift offset	0.11	0.11	...	...	0.11
Advances in knowledge and n.e.c.[a]	1.45	1.49	1.45	1.49	1.24
Improved resource allocation	0.37	0.37	0.48	0.48	0.37
	Whole economy				
Labor input	1.31	1.28	1.22	1.19	1.48
Hours	−0.19	−0.22	−0.28	−0.31	−0.02
Average hours	−0.34	−0.34	−0.34	−0.34	−0.34
Efficiency offset	0.06	0.03	0.06	0.03	0.23
Intergroup shift offset	0.09	0.09	...	...	0.09
Advances in knowledge and n.e.c.[a]	1.19	1.22	1.19	1.22	1.02
Improved resource allocation	0.31	0.31	0.40	0.40	0.31

Sources: Alternative 1, Tables 8-2 and 9-4; other alternatives, see text for explanation.
a. n.e.c. Not elsewhere classified.

in the sector that results from a change in the importance of part-time or female employment, or in average hours of part-time workers, reduces the amount of work done proportionately. The offsetting changes are those of alternatives 2 and 3.

Alternative 5 simply measures labor input by employment, thus assuming that a change in average hours for any reason (including changes in the part-time and female proportions of employment) is fully offset by a change in work done per hour. This assumption would alter my esti-

mates of the contributions of "intergroup shifts" and of resource reallocation because the proportions of part-time workers and female workers differ among the various labor force groups at a point in time. However, these changes are probably small enough for the effect of this change in assumption to be approximated by placing the entire change in labor input in "efficiency offset" and the offsetting change in "advances in knowledge and n.e.c."

—➤➤✗≪≪—

Comparisons with Previous Estimates of Sources of Growth

—➤➤✗≪≪—

Two of my previous studies contained estimates of sources of growth of actual national income.[1] To permit comparisons, estimates based on the present study were computed for the 1950–62 and 1929–57 periods. They are shown in Table S-1.

Why Growth Rates Differ

Estimates for 1950–62 published in *Why Growth Rates Differ* are compared with those from the present study in Table S-2. The growth rate itself has been revised upward by 0.07 percentage points. Estimates of the contributions made by the great majority of sources in this period are scarcely changed, but revisions are appreciable for three components: nonresidential structures and equipment, "advances in knowledge and n.e.c.," and fluctuations in the intensity of demand.

Labor Input

Estimates for total labor input, employment, hours, and other components as a group are

1. Edward F. Denison, *The Sources of Economic Growth in the United States and the Alternatives Before Us,* Supplementary Paper 13 (rev., Committee for Economic Development, 1962 [reprinted 1973]); and Edward F. Denison, assisted by Jean-Pierre Poullier, *Why Growth Rates Differ: Postwar Experience in Nine Western Countries* (Brookings Institution, 1967).

Table S-1. Sources of Growth of Total Actual National Income, 1950–62 and 1929–57

Contributions to growth rate in percentage points

	1950–62	*1929–57*
National income	**3.39**	**3.02**
Total factor input	**1.85**	**1.68**
Labor	1.11	1.32
Employment	0.89	1.03
Hours	−0.19	−0.23
Average hours	−0.34	−0.58
Efficiency offset	0.05	0.26
Intergroup shift offset	0.10	0.09
Age-sex composition	−0.03	0.01
Education	0.42	0.40
Unallocated	0.02	0.11
Capital	0.74	0.36
Inventories	0.10	0.08
Nonresidential structures and equipment	0.31	0.13
Dwellings	0.28	0.14
International assets	0.05	0.01
Land	0.00	0.00
Output per unit of input	**1.54**	**1.34**
Advances in knowledge and n.e.c.[a]	1.15	0.80
Improved resource allocation	0.32	0.30
Farm	0.27	0.28
Nonfarm self-employment	0.05	0.02
Dwellings occupancy ratio	−0.02	0.01
Economies of scale	0.38	0.33
Irregular factors	−0.29	−0.10
Weather in farming	−0.02	−0.01
Labor disputes	0.00	0.00
Intensity of demand	−0.27	−0.09

Source: Calculated in the same way as Table 9-4, columns 1, 2, and 3.
a. n.e.c. Not elsewhere classified.

scarcely changed.[2] Within the subtotal for other components the positive figure for education is reduced by 0.07 points and the negative figure for age-sex composition by an offsetting 0.07 points, but these changes may simply reflect my decision not to attempt separate estimates for the two components in the general government, households, and institutions sector. As suggested in Chapter 3, the small contribution (0.02 points) of the "unallocated" component appears to be the net of a sizable positive contribution for education and a negative one for age-sex composition.

Capital and Land Input

The only appreciable change among capital and land components is a reduction from 0.43 per-

2. Detailed components of the "hours" estimate are not available on a comparable basis from *Why Growth Rates Differ.*

centage points to 0.31 percentage points in the estimated contribution of nonresidential structures and equipment. This estimate is approximately equal to the product of the growth rate of the stock of nonresidential structures and equipment and its weight in total input in the economy as a whole. Both were revised downward. Revisions of the capital stock data reduced the growth rate of this type of input from 3.74 to 3.26, while additional sectoring of the economy (including the use of constant-price data to combine sectors) and reworking of the share data (particularly a different allocation of proprietors' income as described on page 271) reduced the average weight from 0.112 to 0.093.[3]

Components of Output per Unit of Input

Estimates for improved resource allocation and for economies of scale were barely changed. The change from 0.00 to 0.02 in the figure for the effects of weather in farming stems solely from a decision in the earlier study to include an entry for this item in any country only if it exceeded 0.05 percentage points.[4]

The estimate for the effects on output per unit of input of fluctuations in the intensity of demand has been substantially changed: from −0.04 percentage points to −0.27 percentage points. This is by far the biggest change in any directly estimated component. It resulted from adoption of an estimating procedure that I believe to be vastly better than that used in *Why Growth Rates Differ*, which rested on use of the unemployment rate.

The estimate for "advances in knowledge and n.e.c." was obtained as a residual in both studies. The chief errors in the earlier study (as viewed from the perspective of the present estimates) happened all to be in a direction that led to understatement of the residual. The residual was raised 0.23 percentage points by the new procedure adopted in this study for estimating the effects of fluctuations in the intensity of demand, 0.12 points by the revised data for nonresidential structures and equipment, and 0.07 points by the upward revision of the growth rate itself. The net effect of these changes and slight revisions for the other components was to raise the estimate for "ad-

3. The latter figure is the product of the 82.22 percent share of nonresidential business in total national income in 1958 prices and 11.35 percent share of nonresidential structures and equipment within nonresidential business.
4. *Why Growth Rates Differ*, p. 278.

Table S-2. Present and Previous Estimates of Sources of Growth of Total Actual National Income, 1950–62
Contributions to growth rate in percentage points

	From present study	From Why Growth Rates Differ
National income	3.39	3.32
Total factor input[a]	1.83	1.95
Labor	1.11	1.12
Employment	0.89	0.90
Hours	−0.19	−0.17
Other	0.41	0.39
Age-sex composition	−0.03	−0.10
Education	0.42	0.49
Unallocated	0.02	0.00
Capital and dwellings occupancy ratio	0.72	0.83
Inventories	0.10	0.10
Nonresidential structures and equipment	0.31	0.43
Dwellings and occupancy ratio	0.26	0.25
Dwellings	0.28	n.a.
Occupancy ratio	−0.02	n.a.
International assets	0.05	0.05
Land	0.00	0.00
Output per unit of input[a]	1.56	1.37
Advances in knowledge and n.e.c.[b]	1.15	0.76
Improved resource allocation	0.32	0.29
Farm	0.27	0.25
Nonfarm self-employment	0.05	0.04
Reduction of international trade barriers	0.00	0.00
Economies of scale	0.38	0.36
Irregular factors	−0.29	−0.04
Weather in farming	−0.02	0.00
Labor disputes	0.00	0.00
Intensity of demand	−0.27	−0.04

Sources: Table S-1 and *Why Growth Rates Differ*, p. 298, Table 21-1.
n.a. Not available.
a. For comparability, "dwellings occupancy ratio" is classified in total factor input in this table.
b. n.e.c. Not elsewhere classified.

vances in knowledge and n.e.c." by 0.39 points: from 0.76 percentage points to 1.15.

The estimates shown for the United States in *Why Growth Rates Differ* can legitimately be replaced by the new estimates without changing estimates for other countries, except as noted in the following paragraph. The changes in the U.S. estimates result either from revisions of the underlying source data or from improvements in estimating technique. The former have no implications for the estimates for other countries, and there is no presumption as to the direction in which adoption of the new techniques, if data for their use were available, might change any of the European estimates.[5]

One purpose of the earlier study was to discover whether there was evidence that production technique in other countries was "catching up" to that in the United States. To focus the estimates on this question, I divided the residual into two parts in presenting the European estimates. The contribution of advances in knowledge as such in all countries was assumed to be the same as the 0.76 figure obtained for the residual in the United States. I then subtracted that amount (and, where relevant, the contribution from the change in the age of capital) from the residual to obtain the line "changes in the lag in the application of knowledge, general efficiency, and errors and omissions: other." The revision of the United States estimate implies changing the entry for advances in knowledge from 0.76 to 1.15, and subtracting an offsetting 0.39 points from the "other" line. The conclusion was reached in *Why Growth Rates Differ* that there was no evidence of "catching up" by the European countries, except France and possibly Italy, in 1950–62. The revision of the U.S. data does not change this conclusion except by permitting elimination of the reference to Italy.[6]

The Sources of Economic Growth

Estimates for 1929–57 presented many years ago in *The Sources of Economic Growth* are compared with the present estimates for that period

5. The main changes in procedure were: (1) the segregation of labor in general government, households, and institutions, together with direct estimates of all the labor input components that are specific to labor employed in nonresidential business; and (2) the procedure for estimating the effects of fluctuations in demand pressure. European data required for their adoption were not available to me when *Why Growth Rates Differ* was written, and I believe they are still unavailable. Even if the requisite data existed for use of the procedure for demand pressure, the method would, of course, need to be tested with domestic data before it could be adopted for use in another country.

6. Complete revised sources of growth tables for the United States in the 1950–55 and 1955–62 subperiods shown in *Why Growth Rates Differ* were not computed, but in the new estimates, as in the old, the contribution of advances in knowledge was the same in the two subperiods. The new estimates imply large offsetting revisions for the contributions of changes in the intensity of demand and of employment in the subperiods. The former results from the improved estimating technique, the latter from replacement of Current Population Survey employment data by establishment-based data. My selection of the CPS employment series in the earlier study was a poor choice. I failed to appreciate how much it affected a comparison of 1955 with 1950 and 1962.

Table S-3. Present and Previous Estimates of Sources of Growth of Total Actual National Income, 1929–57
Contributions to growth rate in percentage points

	From present study	From The Sources of Economic Growth
National income	3.02	2.93
Total factor input	1.68	2.00
Labor	1.32	1.57
Employment	1.03	1.00
Hours	−0.23	−0.20
Age-sex composition	0.01	−0.01
Education	0.40	0.67
Increased experience and better utilization of women workers	0.00	0.11
Unallocated	0.11	0.00
Capital	0.36	0.43
Inventories	0.08	0.08
Nonresidential structures and equipment	0.13	0.28[a]
Dwellings	0.14	0.05
International assets	0.01	0.02
Land	0.00	0.00
Output per unit of input	1.34	0.93
Advances in knowledge and n.e.c.[b]	0.80	0.59[c]
Restrictions against optimum use of resources	n.a.	−0.07
Improved resource allocation	0.30	0.07
Farm	0.28	0.07[d]
Nonfarm self-employment	0.02	0.00
Dwellings occupancy ratio	0.01	n.a.
Economies of scale	0.33	0.34
Irregular factors	−0.10	0.00
Weather in farming	−0.01	0.00
Labor disputes	0.00	0.00
Intensity of demand	−0.09	0.00

Sources: Table S-1 and *The Sources of Economic Growth*, p. 266, Table 32.
n.a. Not available.
a. Includes farm dwellings.
b. n.e.c. Not elsewhere classified.
c. Includes "change in lag in application of knowledge," estimated at 0.01.
d. Includes "reduced waste of labor in agriculture" and "industry shift from agriculture."

in Table S-3. When the earlier estimates were made, output was measured in 1954 prices. The shift to 1958 prices affects some components, but an adjustment for this difference has not been attempted.

The growth rate itself has been revised upward by 0.09 percentage points, although the later base year would in itself be expected to lower it. For many individual sources the present estimates are close to the original ones despite complete re-working and many changes in procedure, but a few figures are substantially different. Most of the procedural changes which contribute to these differences were already incorporated in *Why Growth Rates Differ*.

Labor Input

Estimates for employment, hours, and age-sex composition are little changed, but the total labor contribution was cut 0.25 percentage points by elimination of a component and reduction of the education estimate. The original estimate for labor input included 0.11 percentage points as the contribution of "increased experience and better utilization of women workers." This was dropped when better data indicated the correct estimate to be of trivial size.[7] The education estimate was considerably curtailed, even when allowance is made for the "unallocated" component. The change stemmed mainly from a reduction in the allowance for the number of days attended per school year and a reduction in the estimate of bias in Census data.[8]

Capital and Land Input

The revision in the capital contribution was moderate, but the estimate for nonresidential structures and equipment was cut and that for dwellings raised, each by a large amount. The change for the nonresidential component resulted from use of new capital stock data which reduced the input growth rate from 1.84 to 1.39 and reduction of the share weight in total input in the whole economy from 0.150 to 0.0954. The change in the estimate for dwellings resulted from adoption of the technique of measuring dwellings output directly, a procedure which had not been devised when the earlier estimates were made.

7. See *Why Growth Rates Differ*, p. 111, note 4.
8. See *Why Growth Rates Differ*, p. 383, and, on the second point, Appendix I of the present study, pp. 255–56.

Components of Output per Unit of Input

Among the large output per unit of input components, only the estimate for economies of scale is substantially unchanged.

The earlier study assumed that 1929 and 1957, both business cycle peaks with fairly similar unemployment rates, were comparable years so that a cyclical adjustment of productivity could be omitted. The new estimates show a contribution of −0.09 percentage points for the effects of intensity of demand on productivity.

The estimated gain from the reallocation of resources from farming has been raised from 0.07 to 0.28 percentage points. Much of this difference results from the change from 1954 to 1958 as the base year for output measurement. Because 1954 was an exceptionally good year for agriculture, the curtailment of farm employment contributed more to the growth of total output measured in 1958 prices than in 1954 prices.[9] However, the method of estimate has been completely changed. The estimate for the shift from nonfarm self-employment, now estimated at 0.02 percentage points, was omitted in the earlier estimates.

The Sources of Economic Growth included an estimate of −0.07 percentage points for "restrictions against optimum use of resources" which has now been dropped as a separate component.

The residual estimate for advances in knowledge has been raised from 0.59 to 0.80 percentage points. Of the change of 0.21 points, 0.09 stem from the change in the growth rate itself and 0.12 from changes in estimates for other growth sources.

The Sources of Economic Growth contained estimates for 1909–29 as well as for 1929–57. It is obvious that for many components the 1909–29 estimates are not comparable with those developed in the present study for 1929–57 or other periods after 1929.

9. The effect of the 1954 base year was stressed in *The Sources of Economic Growth*, pp. 226–27.

Index